THE

FISHES

OF

MALABAR

THE FISHES OF MALABAR.

BY

FRANCIS DAY, F. L. S., F. Z. S.

GYAN

Published by

Gyan Publishing House
5, Ansari Road
Daryaganj, New Delhi-110002
Phone: 011-47034999, 9811692060
E-mail: books@gyanbooks.com

Distribution Network
gyanbooks.com
India, USA, Canada, UK, Australia, France

ISBN: 978-81-212-8300-7 (PB)
First Published, 1865

2nd Impression 2023

Printed at: Gyan Press, Delhi.

THE FISHES OF MALABAR
Author: FRANCIS DAY

THE

FISHES OF MALABAR.

THE FISHES OF MALABAR.

BY

FRANCIS DAY, F.L.S. F.Z.S.,

SURGEON, MADRAS ARMY,

AUTHOR OF "THE LAND OF THE PERMAULS; OR, COCHIN, ITS PAST AND ITS PRESENT;"

ETC. ETC.

LONDON:

BERNARD QUARITCH, 15 PICCADILLY.

MDCCCLXV.

LIST OF SUBSCRIBERS.

	Copies Coloured.	Plain.
Government of Madras	5	..
,, ,, Bombay	4	..
H. H. the Maharajah of Travancore	1	..
,, ,, ,,	..	4
H. H. the First Prince of Travancore	1	..
H. H. the Rajah of Cochin	6	..
The Commissioner of Mysore	2	..
Medical Department, Bombay	..	7
Board of Trade, London	..	1
Chamber of Commerce, Calcutta	..	1
,, ,, Madras	..	1
Zoological Society of London	1	..
Biblioteca Nacional, Madrid	1	..
Universitäts-Bibliothek, Wien (per Mr. Carl Gerold's Son, Vienna.)	1	..
Free Public Library, Liverpool	1	..
Madava Row, Esq., Dewan of Travancore	..	1
Dr. Johnstone, Secretary to Principal Inspector General, Medical Department, Bombay	1	..
Colonel Playfair, H.M. Consul of Zanzibar	1	..
W. T. Vrolik, Esq., Leyden	1	..
Messrs. Asher and Co., Booksellers, Berlin	1	..
,, Friedlænder and Co., Booksellers, Berlin	..	1
Mr. J. Higginbotham, Bookseller, Madras	..	2
,, Fredk. Müller, Bookseller, Amsterdam	..	1
,, J. G. Robbers, Bookseller, Rotterdam	1	..

ERRATA.

P.					
P. 17, 24	lines from	bottom,	insert	FAM.	PRISTIPOMATIDÆ.
27, 9	„	„	„	„	MULLIDÆ.
29, 17	„	„	„	„	SPARIDÆ.
31, 15	„	„	„	„	SQUAMIPINNES.
38, 17	„	top	„	„	TRIGLIDÆ.
46, 16	„	bottom	„	„	TRACHINIDÆ.
48, 10	„	„	„	„	SCIÆNIDÆ.
108, 7	„	„	„	GENUS	GOBIUS.
208, 6	„	top *for* “COPOËTA” *read* “CAPOËTA.”			

DIRECTIONS TO THE BINDER.

Place plate			page
Place plate	I.	opposite	4
„	II.	„	12
„	III.	„	14
„	IV.	„	26
„	V.	„	66
„	VI.	„	84
„	VII.	„	112
„	VIII.	„	130
„	IX.	„	140
„	X.	„	148
„	XI.	„	154
„	XII.	„	156
„	XIII.	„	184
„	XIV.	„	204
„	XV.	„	206
„	XVI.	„	210
„	XVII.	„	216
„	XVIII.	„	218
„	XIX.	„	238
„	XX.	„	258

PREFACE.

WHILST stationed at Cochin on the Malabar Coast of India, from 1859 to 1864, the annually increasing importance of its fisheries came most prominently to my notice. Desirous of ascertaining what species of fish were most abundant, and which were best adapted for different manufactures, I was induced to make a collection of those procurable from the sea, estuaries, or fresh waters, with notes on their habits and uses, to elucidate which plain and coloured drawings of each species were made as soon as possible after the fish had been captured.

When returning to Europe a note-book and two boxes of specimens were unfortunately mislaid, but one of the latter having been recovered, several species will be found included in this work which are absent from my Catalogue of *The Fishes of Cochin*, published in the Proceedings of "The Zoological Society of London."

The portion of India comprised under the denomination of Malabar, and the fishes of which are included in this work, extends from Mangalore on its western coast, in latitude 15° 25′ N. and longitude 74° 50′ E., to Cape Comorin, in latitude 8° 10′ N. and longitude 77° 30′ E.; whilst inland it reaches to the Western Ghauts.

Having through the kindness of COLONEL SIR HENRY JAMES, R. E. been shown the mode of engraving on copper pursued at the Ordnance Office, I have been induced to personally delineate most of the new species described in this work, as well as some whose existence was previously deemed doubtful.

My thanks are especially due to the following friends. To the REV. HENRY BAKER, Junior, who kindly collected many specimens from the Hill ranges of Travancore, a portion of Malabar which I was unable to personally visit; six species received from him appear to be new and will be severally pointed out in the descriptions. To G. A. BALLARD, ESQ., the Collector of Malabar, for the returns of his collectorate and much useful and interesting information on the present state of the coast fisheries. To J. NEWILL, ESQ., the British Resident of Travancore and Cochin, for the returns from those Native States. To A. C. BRISBANE NEILL, ESQ., retired list Madras Medical

Service, for his valuable assistance in carrying this work through the Press: and to Dr. Bleeker, for having courteously examined various specimens of fish which I forwarded to him, and been so good as to give me his opinion upon them.

The following new species, described in this work, have been placed in the British Museum—*Caranx melanostethos*: *Nandus Malabaricus*: *Mugil poicilus*: *Ophiocephalus diplogramme*: *Mastacemblus Güntheri*: *Hypselobagrus armatus*: *Pseudobagrus chryseus*: *Hara Malabarica*: *Nemacheilus triangularis*: *Platacanthus agrensis*: *Garra Malabarica*: *Puntius melanampyx*: *Puntius Denisonii*: *Puntius parrah*: *Puntius perlee*: *Puntius vittatus*: *Amblypharygnodon Jerdoni*: *Barilius Bakeri*: *Paradanio aurolineatus*, &c. Whilst the East Indian Museum has been furnished with six of the foregoing, and also a specimen of the *Engraulis auratus*, and upwards of one hundred species which were personally collected in Cochin, but of which I possess duplicate specimens.

The vignette represents the present state of the flag-staff tower in Cochin, raised on the ruins of the Portuguese Cathedral of *Santa Cruz*, the memorable spot where the body of the illustrious Don Vasco de Gama, Portuguese Viceroy, High Admiral of the Indies, the discoverer of the Cape route, is believed to have been temporarily interred about December 26th, 1524.

INTRODUCTION.

To study the wants of a people, to inquire into the history, language, habits, and customs of a nation, is generally deemed a duty on the part of its rulers: but hardly any objects of research are more worthy of the attention of a Government than the sources whence the food of the population is derived, or the nature of the articles most adapted for its manufacturing processes, or best fitted in the raw state for its home or foreign trade. In India the details of Native agriculture have been carefully studied, if they have not been improved; the earth has been ransacked for its minerals; the forests have been explored for their timber; the land for its agricultural capabilities, even the atmosphere for its meteorological variations; and in all these matters Government has wisely shown its interest; but the fish with which the fresh waters of Hindustan teem, and which abound in the seas that wash her coasts, have rarely met with attention from those in authority, or even from individuals whose private tastes have led them towards the cultivation of zoological science.

In the British possessions in the East, no branch of natural history has received less assistance than Ichthyology; its utility seems to have been questioned, its scientific value nearly ignored. Searching among the records of past times, we find that so long ago as 1777 the Dutch East India Company directed the Governor of Cochin, then their chief town in India, to send them information on all branches of natural history and the allied sciences; but though rare animals and birds were ordered to be transmitted to Europe in spirit, fish were not specially alluded to. On the capture of Cochin in 1795, the whole of Malabar came under British rule; but so little has since been done in inquiring into its natural riches, that the National Collection in London* appears to have obtained one solitary ichthyological species from the whole of that territory in the course of seventy years, during which period the French and other European collections have received and preserved much of what we have neglected, and observations on the sea fishes of Western India, are to be sought for, not in English works, but in the proceedings of French Societies, and in the splendid "Histoire Naturelle des Poissons" of CUVIER AND VALENCIENNES.

The first, if not the last, direct assistance which the Court of Directors of the English East India Company gave to Ichthyology was by the publication in 1803 of DR. RUSSELL's work, describing 200 ***Fishes from the Coast of Coromandel***, the materials for which were collected by the Author whilst stationed at Vizagapatam—a book which CUVIER observed was the most important up to

* See the Catalogues of the British Museum, viz.: *Chondropterygii*, by DR. GRAY, 1851; *Lophobranchiate Fish*, DR. KAUP, 1856; *Apodal Fish*, DR. KAUP, 1856; and 5 vols. of DR. GÜNTHER's *Catalogues of the Fishes of the British Museum.* The E. I. Museum possesses neither mammal, bird or fish from the whole of Malabar, with the exception of those presented by myself.

that period on the fishes of the Oriental Seas. Since then no individual work on the ichthyology of the Seas of India has been produced, with the exception of one in 1834 by BENNETT, describing thirty fishes of Ceylon. DR. HAMILTON BUCHANAN, published in 1822 *The Fishes of the Ganges*, in which 269 fresh water and estuary species are given: GRAY AND HARDWICKE's magnificent *Illustrations of Indian Zoology*, commenced in 1830, were never completed: even COLONEL SYKES's *Report to the Court of Directors of the East India Company*, accompanied by beautiful drawings of some fish which he had discovered in the Dukhan, was only rescued from oblivion by being published by the Zoological Society of London, and other Societies have saved to the public ichthyological papers by McCLELLAND, CANTOR, AND JERDON. In contrast to this, the Dutch East India Company, alive to the importance of this branch of zoology in the East, is at the present time giving to the world the splendid and scientific *Atlas Ichthyologique*, the fruit of the patient and persevering labours carried on for many years by DR. BLEEKER of the Dutch army.

But setting aside the scientific value of Ichthyology, the question arises whether materials fitted for manufactures and even food most valuable to the inhabitants of India are not lost, owing to a neglect and ignorance of the wealth contained in its waters. It is only of late years, since animal oils have become so dear, partially due to a deficiency of that of the whale, that attention has been directed to the immense shoals of Sardines, *Sardinella Neohowii*, which are found off Malabar and Ceylon. It is probably this fish, of which *Friar* ODORIC, who visited Ceylon about A.D. 1320, observed, that "there are fishes in those seas that come swimming towards the said country in such abundance, that for a great distance into the sea nothing can be seen but the backs of fishes, which, casting themselves on the shore, do suffer men for the space of three daies to come and take as many of them as they please." (*Hakluyt*, ii. p. 57.) NIEUHOFF recorded (Ed. A.D. 1673) that they were abundant, and DUSSUMIER about 1827 observed that they were employed for manuring the rice-fields and cocoa-nut trees, but were too fat to salt well. In fact, it may be safely asserted that owing to ignorance of their existence and uses, Sardines, (*Charlay*, Malayalim), until within the last few years, were mostly captured to manure the trees and land with, or for the purpose of feeding pigs and poultry, the number consumed by the population being trifling in comparison with the amount taken: whilst the *Spratella fimbriata*, also known as a Sardine, (*Cuttay charlay*, Mal.), is much preferred for food, as well as being adapted for salting.

It appears to be but little known that Isinglass not only can be, but is, prepared in large quantities in Malabar, from whence it is exported to Bombay under the name of "Fish sounds," or "Fish maws," and eventually finds its way to China.

Salt fish is also exported in rather considerable quantities—a trade apparently susceptible of great increase, and one which must at a future date become most important to the coffee planters along the Western Ghauts, for this kind of food is in great request amongst the Coolies employed as agricultural labourers, and the carriage which brings down coffee from the interior re-conveys a large amount.

It may, then, with safety be asserted, that amongst the animal products of Malabar its fish are exceedingly valuable, and their capture even now gives employment to large numbers of fishermen along the coast and backwater; whilst further inland the slave castes obtain much nutriment from those which they catch early in the morning and late in the evening, when not employed in agricultural labour. On the Travancore hills the REV. HENRY BAKER states that in some of the deep pools in the rivers, the numbers of large Cyprinidæ are surprising; hundreds on hundreds are killed by striking them at night with knives as they rise to a torch held close to the surface of the water.

Some fish are mostly eaten fresh, some are preferred salted, others are employed in the arts, in manufactures, or in medicine. The roes of the large *Mullets* and of the small *Hemiramphi* are considered great delicacies, either fresh, salted, or dried. The best *Tamarind fish* is prepared from the *Seir fish* and from the *Lates calcarifer,* a rather inferior quality from the *Polynemus,* and the most common from any kind of fish. The process is as follows:—The fish is boiled, then its bones are removed; it is next cut into thick slices, and having been highly spiced, is left to soak for some days, and subsequently packed in jars. It is held in great estimation in the East.

In ancient times the "Meen Kodah" or "Fish Standard" was the symbol of the kings of Pandya, the rulers of Malabar, who up to recent times received tribute from the Rajahs of Travancore. This device may still be traced on many of the copper coins which pass current in the country, whilst the same design it is well known exists upon Buddhist seals. To this day the Rajpoots are said to have a fish carried before their most illustrious chieftains when setting out on important expeditions. Even witchcraft claims its share in the finny tribes, and the fortunate possessor of the tail of a Ray, *Trygon uarnak,* with its spine intact, is believed to be safe from the effects of spells and charms, as well as able to face the "evil eye" with impunity.

Fish are kept as objects of adoration by pious Hindus, being held typical of Vishnu, who in this form is considered to have rescued the Vedas from the waters of the flood.

Catching a fish is asserted to be still one of the ceremonies at the nuptials of Konkanie Brahmans, typical of the fact that they were originally fishermen before the attainment of their present dignity of Brahmans. The adherents to various religious creeds show antipathies to particular tribes; high caste Hindus of course abjure the use of all, and almost as zealously do the Jews and Mahomedans refrain from the Rays, Skates, Eels, and the scaleless families.

No form of animal food is more common in Malabar, for it is palatable to both Europeans and Natives: indeed, without its presence the Native Christians consider their curries to be imperfect. Light and easy of digestion, strengthening and savoury, no wonder that it is so highly esteemed. The flesh of sharks and rays are salted, and find a ready sale in inland places, as they are considered especially desirable for women soon after childbirth. The fins of the sharks are dried, and find their way to China, whilst even the bones of some (the Mass) are boiled down for gelatine.

To the medical profession the subject of the effect of a fish diet upon the health of a large population offers a wide field for investigation. A few species are observed to be highly indigestible, or even poisonous, as the Tetraodons, known as "sea porcupines" to Europeans, but "sea frogs," (*kuddul mahcutchee,* Mal.) to the Natives, and so termed from the noise they make when captured. An Anchovy, ***Engraulis belama,*** C. V., if dressed previous to the removal of its head and viscera, has been frequently observed to occasion death in a few hours, with all the symptoms produced by an irritant poison. In certain seasons of the year, mostly about October, fatal attacks resembling cholera are caused by some species if eaten. The Mackerel and allied families if kept until they are tainted, are also highly irritating, sometimes poisonous; while a constant fish diet is commonly reputed to be one of the causes of the horrible leprosy *Elephantiasis Græcorum,* which is not rare in Malabar, as well as of the inveterate *Scabies* which when checked often results in fatal dropsy. In Bengal, HAMILTON BUCHANAN observes, eating the *Rohita cursis* and drinking copious draughts of milk on the same day, is believed to be one of the causes of *Elephantiasis Arabum.*

Some families, especially the *Siluridæ,* which dwell in estuaries and fresh waters, and are consequently in the vicinity of man, are deemed venomous, being armed with saw-like pectoral spines, with which wounds apparently poisoned are inflicted; they occasion intense irritative pain and occasionally lock-jaw; while so apprehensive are the fishermen of such wounds, that as soon as these fish are captured the dreaded spines are at once broken off: amongst these the Scorpion fish, *Saccobranchus singio,* stands pre-eminent; but according to Cuvier and Valenciennes there are other siluroids nearly as much feared, such as the *Plotosus Arab.* The voracity of the Sharks in Malabar is perhaps less than might be anticipated, but injuries inflicted by the Saw-fish, *Pristis semisagittatus,* are frequent and frightful. Dangerous wounds, apparently so from the manner of their infliction and not from the presence of any poison, are occasioned by the saw-like spine on the tail of some of the Rays, and also from the lateral spine of the Lancet fishes. Even the spinous rays of the Acanthopterygians often set up intense inflammation in persons in a previously bad state of health, or during certain atmospheric conditions, whilst the bite of the *Conger telabon* is considered very dangerous.

Other fish are used in India as medicines, thus the *Tetraodons* are prescribed by the Native doctors in phthisis, *Shark's-liver oil* in night blindness, and the jaw of the *Belone* with its teeth intact is employed as an instrument for acupuncture, its toothed side being placed over the spot and the back of the jaw struck with a piece of wood, so that its numerous sharp teeth penetrate the skin.

The habits of the fish might be very advantageously inquired into, for a constant succession of arrivals and departures occurs all along the coast. The gregarious Sardine, the Indian Mackerel, and several other families are uncertain as to the times of their advent and departure; in some years arriving in millions, in others all but absent, their presence in shoals can never be entirely relied upon. Where the fish go to, and from whence they come, are interesting subjects for inquiry; thus the little *Chætodon prætextatus,* which is usually only about a fortnight in South Malabar, and that merely at the commencement of the S.W. monsoon, seems hardly adapted for making long migrations.

Their colours, wonderful forms, and still more extraordinary habits, such as the saw-like prolongation of the snout in the *Saw-fish,* the curious lateral development of the *Hammer-headed shark,* the elongated lower jaw in the *Hemiramphus,* and the developed pectoral fins in the *Flying-fish,* must attract the attention of the most incurious. The brilliant colouration which obtains in the East can scarcely be believed by those who have not examined fish when alive or just fresh from their native element; the brilliancy of the *Pterois* genus, in fact, is so great, that on showing a specimen just captured to a resident in Cochin, he could not be persuaded but that some of the colouration was artificial.

The migration of fish from tank to tank, and the means at their disposal for that purpose, are also most wonderful. While their gills are kept moist by water retained in hollow receptacles above them, they are able to live, and thus when water fails in one spot to seek a more suitable abode, as will be more especially alluded to in the genera *Anabas, Polyacanthus, Ophiocephalus,* and *Saccobranchus.* Again, the alleged ability of the Anabas scandens (p. 133) to climb palmira trees is believed in by the Natives of South India and Ceylon, in fact the species has once been captured in such a situation by an European gentleman. That fish can live in the mud of ponds from the period of their drying up in one year to the commencement of the rains in the next, is also credited by many excellent observers, but is an opinion personal observation as yet has neither confirmed nor refuted.

Stocking new-made tanks with fish evidently receives the attention of the Natives of India, for whenever one examines the artificial pieces of water, even the moats of fortifications, numerous species of the finny tribes are apparent, in fact it is the rule to stock fresh pieces of water as soon as such are collected. At Coondapoor in North Canara the *Chanos argenteus* exists in some large tanks, where they are said to have been introduced by Hyder Ali, and for some years after the British assumed the district they were under Government protection. But Natives usually stock their new tanks with fish from the nearest pieces of water, irrespective of the size they attain, their flavour, or their adaptability for that purpose.

Dr. McClelland suggested in 1841 (*Asiatic Researches,* xix.) that at the various hill sanitaria it would be practicable and easy to make *rivaria,* which would at all times yield a supply of fish. He proposed damming up a portion of some of the valleys or large water-courses, and thus forming lakes sufficient for the purpose. He at the same time pointed out the benefit that might be derived from care being taken when stocking large tanks, especially near military cantonments or towns in which Europeans resided, to choose only good and eatable fish.

Having personally observed this great requirement to exist on the Neilgherry hills, and proposed to H. E. Sir W. Denison, K.C.B., the Governor of Madras, to attempt to remedy it by trying to introduce the European trout by means of ova transported overland, he has sanctioned the experiment being attempted in January, 1866, and it is to be hoped that it will succeed.

Owing to fish being able to retreat into deep pools or under overhanging banks during the heat of the day, or to ascend to the surface or sun themselves in the shallows when it is cool, they are not so sensible to changes of climate as are mammals and birds. Advantage has been taken of this, and the gold carp of China is now naturalised in most of the countries of Europe, whilst the common carp, a native of the South of Europe, was first brought to England in 1514, and to Denmark in 1560; but Bloch observes that in his time, 1782, owing to the degeneration of the species in the North, due to the coldness of the climate, several vessels were yearly dispatched from Prussia to Stockholm with further supplies of live carp.

Although the transport of good species of fish from England to India could hardly be expected to succeed, that of the ova may more probably be attended with success. Bloch made many experiments on the feasibility of fish being artificially hatched, and also as to whether it were possible to carry ova. He proposed placing them in mud allowing it to dry, and thus conveying it without shaking from one pond to another: his theory was based upon the supposition that as fish appeared in dried-up tanks after they had become filled with rain water, the eggs must have retained vitality in the mud, and that as they became moistened they vivified, and subsequently hatched out. But the fish which appear as the tanks fill with water are full grown, so that they must either ascend from the mud or migrate from other situations. In Europe, ova subsequent to the appearance of the eyes, can be conveyed alive, packed in bottles with wet moss, for two or three days; but whether this would succeed in India has yet to be proved or disproved by actual experiment.*

The most valuable discovery as yet effected respecting the conveyance of fish ova for long distances is that of James A. Youl, Esq., who successfully introduced salmon and trout into Tasmania. I propose giving, from an account which he has kindly furnished to me, a short resumé of his most interesting experiment.

Sir William Denison, K.C.B., then Governor of Tasmania, considering that some of the snow-fed rivers of that Colony, which were almost destitute of fish, would be well adapted for their residence, drew the attention of the Secretary of State for the Colonies to the subject, and he deputed Mr. Boccius, to make the attempt of introducing them. He tried by changing the water three times daily to convey them from Europe to Tasmania, but failed.

In the year 1854, the attention of Mr. Youl was first directed to the subject, and he came to the conclusion that it was not the mature fish, but the ova or small fry alone which could be successfully conveyed through the tropics, and that the aid of iced water would be indispensable. Unfortunately, when commencing his first experiment, no vessel could be procured proceeding

* How to obtain and treat fish ova, and how to hatch and rear the young, are fully detailed in Buckland on "piscaculture" and several other works, so it has been deemed unnecessary to do more than introduce the subject in this place.

direct, to suit the time of year. The ova were therefore shipped to Melbourne, from whence they were to be reshipped to Tasmania. On February 25th, 1860, about thirty-thousand salmon ova were deposited in the ship "Curling," loading at Liverpool, and about to sail for Melbourne. The ova were placed in a swing tray with a small stream of water flowing from a tank on deck through small tin pipes placed inside and around the ice house, which contained upwards of fifteen tons of ice. MR. BLACK, who went out in charge of the experiment, reported that the last of the ova died in lat. 29° 52′ S., and long. 27° 33′ W., 65 days after having been put on board, all the ice having melted and the temperature of the water having suddenly risen to 74°.

The experiment was so far satisfactory, that it proved fish ova could be kept alive by means of ice, whilst passing through the tropics. The result induced the Governments of Tasmania, Victoria, and Southland New Zealand to vote money for a further experiment, which was undertaken by MR. YOUL.

On March 4th, 1862, a vessel named "The beautiful Star," sailed from England conveying a second quantity of ova, which were packed in the following manner. A wooden tank lined with pure tin, and holding two hundred gallons, was built on the deck, and surrounded by a casing of charcoal. Directly underneath it was the ice house, constructed to carry twenty-five tons: at the bottom and nearly extending over the whole of it was placed a flat iron tank capable of containing one hundred gallons, and connected with the upper tank by an iron pipe which passed nearly through the centre of the ice. Other iron pipes conducted the water after it had been cooled, to the vivarium in which were placed the ova. The water which flowed out of the vivarium ran into a receiving tank, from which it was pumped back to the large tank upon deck. Consequently the water flowed owing to its gravity from the large tank on deck, through the iron pipe which went through the ice-house to the second pipe, from whence it went to the vivarium, the pipes being regulated by stop-cocks, attached to flexible gutta-percha piping at their extremities, and from fifty to two thousand gallons could be passed through at discretion during the twenty-four hours. Every fourth day there was a complete change of water. In the vivarium were two sets of trays, with gravel, on which were placed the ova, one in a gimbal frame like that of a ship's compass, the other fitted up in a frame resembling an ordinary swing tray, such as is used on board ship, whilst each had a separate supply of water.

It was in this vessel that the great discovery was made by MR. YOUL, second to nothing yet known on the subject of the transport of fish ova. Having seen in Paris, moss used for packing salmon ova, and in which they travelled short distances with perfect safety after their eyes were developed, he packed some in moss within a wooden box, made of inch pine, and having its sides perforated: this he deposited in the centre of the ice in the hopes that the extreme cold might retard vivification, and the melting ice would permit sufficient water necessary to preserve their vitality. The vessel met with contrary winds and misfortunes, and on May 8th, 1862, the ice was found to be very low, and the little box came to light, but in it were nineteen living ova.

Nine days subsequently in S. lat. 22° 19′ and W. long. 25° 53′, the ice had all melted, and the ova died seventy-four days after leaving London. This time about twenty fry were hatched out, but killed by the excessive pitching and rolling of the ship which caused the water and gravel to be thrown with violence against them.

Since then Salmon and Trout have been safely introduced into Tasmania by conveying the boxes of ova in ice, and it is hoped Trout may be introduced on to the Neilgherries by the same process. The danger will be in crossing the desert: there will also be a difficulty in having a sufficient supply of ice between Suez and Madras.

Fisheries, it is almost needless to observe, give employment to many individuals, either in capturing the spoil, in preparing them for the market, or in their carriage to distant places: as well as to the numerous trades to which they are of a greater or less importance. In the State of Travancore each fisherman had formerly to pay a yearly tax upon the net he used, and those who lived in the town of Cochin, or under Dutch protection, had to bring eight pounds weight of fish daily to the senior official. Whilst in the Portuguese territory, besides their taxes, none of their produce could be taken to market until the clergy were first served with what they required. At the present time there is no tax upon fishermen or on their implements of trade either in the British Territory or in the Native State of Cochin.

The modes of fishing vary with the season of the year, and whether employed in the sea, backwater, rivers or tanks. Wall, cast, stake, and Chinese nets are all used. The last situated on the banks of rivers—as that of Cochin—are about sixteen feet square, suspended by bamboos attached to each corner, and let down like buckets into the water, when, after having remained there a few minutes, they are drawn up again. Besides the foregoing, fishing with a bait is employed, both from the shore and from small canoes. Trolling at the mouths of rivers, chiefly for the *Polynemus tetradactylus* takes place mostly in the cold months. Likewise shooting with a Chittagong bow, or bows and arrows, capturing by means of bamboo labyrinths, and poisoning the water by Nux vomica, Cocculus Indicus, Croton-oil seed, or other deleterious substances are all common; also damming up and lading out streams, purse-nets in small water-courses, especially in rice fields, catching by the hand, or by means of wicker baskets, somewhat resembling the eel-traps of Europe, but which are rapidly pressed down over the fish by the fisherman.*

I now proceed to touch on matters well worthy the attention of those in authority. An accurate survey of the Ichthyology of the Western Coast, and an extensive inquiry into its fisheries and the uses to which the fish are put, appears advisable for the purpose of ascertaining the cause of the remarkable increase in the exports of fish oil, salt fish, and isinglass, which has occurred during the last few years. The following subjects would necessarily have to be considered.

---

* The various modes of fishing are detailed at pp. 488 to 493 of a work published by me, under the title of the *Land of the Permauls, or Cochin its past and its present.*

1. *Are the sea fisheries of Malabar at present being over-fished?*

2. *Are fish which contain but a small quantity of oil, but are well adapted for salting and human food, being boiled down along with the oil Sardines for the little that can be procured from them?*

3. *Has the salt tax any bearing upon the occupation of the fish curers?*

Salting and drying fish is largely carried on in Malabar, as the following returns will demonstrate, but further inquiries are needed for the purpose of ascertaining whether species well adapted for salting are not finding their way into the fish-oil boiling pot, for the preparation of the oil entails but slight labour, little skill, and very small outlay, whilst it is not easily spoiled when obtained; on the other hand the manufacture of salting fish requires a large outlay—the price of salt being so high—whilst the profits are doubtful, owing to the moisture of the Western coast, and the perishable nature of the article, which is increased if the impure black salt is employed in curing it. Large taxes on its sea export, duties in the Native States upon its transit along the backwater—the highway of Malabar—vexatious scrutinies and detentions at the various customs houses, have hitherto proved very detrimental to this trade in the States of Cochin and Travancore.

Before examining into the salt returns a few preliminary remarks are necessary. In British Malabar there are no salt manufactories, and the Natives are permitted to collect the salt earth or impure salt as it exudes from the ground, and employ it for the purpose of curing fish, as no duty is levied upon it, and no fiscal impediment exists in the way of their using it, so that for this purpose it is almost exclusively employed, and manufactured salt used to a very limited extent. But in the Native States it is manufactured by the Native government, and therefore the fish curers must employ either the Native manufactured or Bombay salt.

The selling price of manufactured (*i. e.* English) salt is now the same in the British and Native States. The latter has been induced to raise the price to what obtains in the British territory, whilst these States are no longer treated as foreign countries, as was the case formerly, but (save as regards two or three excepted articles) are placed on a similar footing with British Indian ports.

The *average market price of Bombay or English salt in Malabar,* has been as follows :—

	Rupee.	A.	P.
1858-59 price per maund or $82\frac{1}{4}$ lbs.	1	2	6
1859-60 ,, ,,	1	4	6
1860-61 ,, ,,	1	8	0
1861-62 ,, ,,	1	8	0
1862-63 ,, ,,	1	8	0

The price will thus appear to be about $3\frac{1}{2}$ lbs. for one anna, or an average of one rupee six annas a maund. Variations in the price of salt are greatly affected by transit charges, which imperfect communications and consequently expensive carriage renders very heavy.

In the *Cochin State,* previous to the agreement with the Madras Government, the selling price of *Bombay salt* was as follows, except in the Chittoor district, where it has always been sold at the Madras Government rates :—

				R.	A.	P.
1030 to 1033	Malabar Era price per maund or $82\frac{1}{4}$ lbs.			0	9	2
1034	,,	,,	,,	0	10	3
1035	,,	,,	,,	0	13	9
1036 to 1039	,,	,,	,,	0	12	7

Thus in the ten years ending 1039 M.E. or A.D. 1863-64, the average price has been slightly more than eleven annas per maund, or nearly one-half the average cost of the same article in British territory, as the selling price of salt is now raised to the British rate, it is equivalent to an increase of about 100 per cent.: whether this will affect the salt-fish trade either as to quantity or quality must be soon apparent.

The above return from the Cochin Native State has no reference to home made salt, which for the ten years ending 1863-64, was sold at the rate of 5 Parrahs and $9\frac{1}{2}$ Edungalies a rupee.

In the State of Travancore, the price of black salt is 77 rupees a garce, or about ten annas a maund.

Unless in the case of large fish, or any very particularly and carefully salted, only the Native manufactured salt is usually employed in the Native States and the salt-earth in British territory, the consequence is, that in the latter the article produced is of an inferior description. It may perhaps be a fact that in the British territory, where salt-earth can be obtained duty free, the "Salt monopoly" does not directly affect the salt-fish trade—or rather its *price* irrespective of its *quality*—because under no circumstances could English or Bombay salt be sold so cheaply as salt-earth. But it is open to question as to the quantity of saline matter which would be contained in a given quantity of the two kinds of salt, and whether, if the manufacturer could procure the better commodity at a cheaper rate than at present, he would not cure his fish in a superior manner; in such a case they would keep better, be more wholesome for the consumer, and could be conveyed to much greater distances inland. The opening up of the country by means of rail-roads is widening the field for the sale of salt-fish, whilst the coffee plantations along the hill ranges have given an impetus to the trade, and a better article would certainly be a great boon. It may be objected to this, that the consumer is satisfied with what he at present obtains; but that is not the question, which is, could not a more wholesome commodity be procured as cheaply, and with an enormous gain in the saving of quantities of fish at present wasted? It can hardly be denied that taxes upon salt are directly or indirectly taxes on the longevity of the dwellers in whatever country such taxes obtain.

There are no duties between British-Indian ports, which are only collected upon exports and imports over-sea from and to Great Britain, the Colonies, or foreign parts: consequently no statistics are available of "the inland trade, but there is no doubt it has vastly increased of late "years, and in greater proportion than the sea exports."

DISTRICT OF MALABAR.

Memorandum of Imports and Exports of Salt Fish yearly for the last 10 years.

Year.	Cannanore.		Tellicherry.		Kalai.		Badagara.		Quilandi.		Calicut.		Beypore.		Tanur.		Ponani.		Chowghát.		Cochin.		Total.	
	Value.	Duty.	Value.	Duty.	Value.	Duty.	Value.	Duty.	Value.	Duty.	Value.	Duty.	Value.	Duty.	Value.	Duty.	Value.	Duty.	Value.	Duty.	Value.	Duty.	Value.	Duty.
Import.																								
1854-55	268	1	304	1	..	..	..	..	..	..	160	7	..	..	..	..	113	..	..	..	3,325	10	4,170	19
1855-56	620	22	291	1	..	..	55	3	..	..	264	1	..	..	..	..	70	3	..	..	6,587	185	7,887	215
1856-57	1,354	2	1,211	10	434	..	500	..	..	..	2,453	..	..	..	..	..	..	..	..	..	4,513	109	10,465	121
1857-58	107	..	199	..	210	10	269	2	..	..	393	..	..	..	..	..	110	..	..	..	7,335	126	8,623	138
1858-59	374	1	130	..	..	..	..	..	6	..	582	6	..	..	..	..	143	..	..	..	6,779	64	8,014	71
1859-60	330	..	169	6	..	..	119	14	..	..	897	86	..	..	2	..	10	..	..	..	960	53	2,487	159
1860-61	161	..	150	..	..	..	..	..	..	..	138	13	..	..	..	..	1,359	..	..	..	1,803	180	3,611	193
1861-62	8	..	..	..	..	..	..	..	..	..	36	..	..	..	295	..	1,384	..	..	..	3,709	26	5,432	26
1862-63	346	5	3,245	11	..	..	..	..	88	9	681	..	226	..	..	..	1,210	..	..	..	2,090	29	7,886	54
1863-64	747	3	921	..	..	..	..	..	366	36	498	8	450	..	..	..	1,700	..	..	..	891	4	5,573	51
Total .	4,315	34	6,620	29	644	10	943	19	460	45	6,102	121	676	..	297	..	6,099	3	..	..	37,992	786	64,148	1,047
Export.																								
1854-55	11	..	1,902	9	545	..	..	..	358	..	632	..	..	..	202	..	200	..	..	..	14,443	412	18,293	421
1855-56	96	..	1,581	17	58	..	54	..	162	..	118	..	..	..	..	..	..	..	..	..	25,618	742	27,687	759
1856-57	134	1	5,515	..	5,500	..	158	..	350	..	387	..	..	..	985	..	232	..	..	..	49,126	1,235	62,387	1,236
1857-58	1,764	..	5,630	..	44	..	439	..	120	..	215	..	..	..	347	..	..	..	..	..	33,474	865	42,033	865
1858-59	2,707	..	3,993	..	..	..	51	..	360	10	313	..	..	..	434	..	..	..	..	..	32,012	807	39,870	817
1859-60	1,083	..	5,744	..	3,352	16	68	..	1,742	..	840	..	..	..	12	..	31	..	..	..	32,374	733	45,246	749
1860-61	616	..	10,762	..	4,780	26	95	3	4,750	39	501	1	..	..	951	..	..	..	..	..	46,713	1,174	69,170	1,343
1861-62	4,942	..	11,647	30	3,773	..	2,472	63	2,993	90	1,902	..	..	..	..	..	..	..	..	..	34,411	887	62,140	1,070
1862-63	97	..	7,257	50	1,873	..	964	25	6,692	158	784	20	..	..	10	..	..	..	..	..	28,626	813	46,303	1,066
1863-64	960	..	14,594	64	2,522	..	4,230	122	16,418	491	538	8	..	..	23	..	..	..	..	..	48,060	1,175	87,345	1,860
Total .	12,410	1	68,625	170	22,447	42	8,531	213	33,947	888	6,230	29	..	..	2,964	..	463	..	..	..	3,44,857	8,843	5,00,474	10,186

N.B.—The Values and Duties are computed in Rupees.

G. A. Ballard, *Collector of Malabar.*

The imports of salt-fish into British Malabar are chiefly from Canara, or when duty has been charged from the Persian Gulf and Arabia. The exports are mostly to Tinnevelly and Colombo, the latter being subject to the duty shown.

The Native States of Travancore and Cochin were formerly treated as foreign ports in this trade, but that has now ceased.

"The statements (respecting Malabar) have been revised, so that the quantities exported "from one district port to another, and re-exported from the latter port do not appear twice over "in the tables."

In the Native State of Cochin a considerable trade is carried on in dried and salt fish, but much larger, as the following returns will demonstrate, in the former than in the latter commodity:—

NATIVE STATE OF COCHIN.

Imports and Exports of Salt Fish.

Years of the Malabar Era.	IMPORTS.							EXPORTS.							TOTAL DUTY.		
	Number.	Value.			Duty.			Number.	Value.			Duty.			Rupees.	Annas.	Pies.
		Rs.	A.	P.	Rs.	A.	P.		Rs.	A.	P.	Rs.	A.	P.			
1036	325	48	12	..	1	15	2	..	..	..	..	..	..	..	1	15	2
1037	..	..	..	..	..	..	..	3,750	562	8	..	16	14	..	16	14	11
1038	..	..	..	..	..	..	..	4,800	720	..	..	21	9	7	21	9	7
Total . .	325	48	12	..	1	15	2	8,550	1,282	8	..	38	7	7	40	6	9

NATIVE STATE OF COCHIN.

Imports and Exports of Dried Fish from $\frac{1030}{1854\text{-}55}$ to $\frac{1039}{1863\text{-}64}$ Malabar Era.

Years of the Malabar Era.	IMPORTS FROM TRAVANCORE.							EXPORTS BY SEA.							EXPORTS INTO TRAVANCORE.							Total Duty.		
	Bundles.	Value.			Duty.			Bundles.	Value.			Duty.			Bundles.	Value.			Duty.					
		Rs.	A.	P.	Rs.	A.	P.		Rs.	A.	P.	Rs.	A.	P.		Rs.	A.	P.	Rs.	A.	P.	Rs.	A.	P.
1030	1649¼	1178	0	7	62	9	5	218	155	11	5	9	12	10	837	597	13	9	30	2	5	102	8	8
1031	1438¼	1013	0	7	52	3	11	31	22	2	4	0	10	7	1078¼	772	2	11	41	6	8	94	5	2
1032	1480¼	1057	5	2	54	9	0	..	..				..		853½	609	10	4	31	3	9	85	12	9
1033	1363¼	973	12	0	50	3	7	..	..				..		867	548	3	5	27	15	9	78	3	4
1034	1714	1224	4	6	73	13	7	..	..				..		1012¾	723	3	6	36	8	9	110	6	4
1035	1533	1105	5	4	55	7	6	246	175	15	5	5	4	5	1080	772	2	0	40	4	1	101	0	0
1036	1380¾	986	4	0	50	2	7	76	542	13	9	26	13	8	1093½	781	1	2	40	1	0	117	1	3
1037	693⅝	495	7	2	26	10	11	1898½	1356	1	2	49	9	2	1340½	957	8	3	50	8	6	126	12	7
1038	746½	533	3	5	29	4	11	2344	1674	4	7	77	8	6	210	149	15	11	7	13	7	114	11	0
1039	2005¾	1432	10	10	73	3	11	991	707	13	9	28	3	10	1047	748	0	7	38	0	3	139	8	0
Total	14004½	9099	5	7	528	5	4	5804½	4634	14	5	197	15	0	9419½	6659	13	10	344	0	9	1070	5	1

NATIVE STATE OF TRAVANCORE.

STATEMENT SHOWING THE QUANTITY, TARIFF, VALUE OF, AND THE AMOUNT OF DUTY LEVIED ON SALT FISH IMPORTED INTO AND EXPORTED FROM, DURING THE 10 YEARS ENDING 1039, M.E.
1863-64

SALT FISH IMPORTED.

Year of Malabar Era.	By Sea.			By Land.			Total.		
	Quantity. Cwts.	Tariff Value. G. Rs	Duty. G. Rs.	Quantity. Cwts.	Tariff Value. G. Rs.	Duty. G. Rs.	Quantity. Cwts.	Tariff Value. G. Rs.	Duty. G. Rs.
1030	152¼	160	12	806	848	42	958¼	1,008	54
1031	98	103	8	769¼	809	40	867¼	912	48
1032	121½	127	10	992¼	1,044	52	1,113¾	1,171	62
1033	101¼	106	8	1,071	1,127	56	1,172¼	1,233	64
1034	58¾	61	4	1,365½	1,437	71	1,424¼	1,498	75
1035	221¼	233	18	1,219	1,283	64	1,440¼	1,516	82
1036	137	144	11	2,030½	2,137	106	2,167½	2,281	117
1037	74¾	147	11	2,887¼	3,143	157	2,962	3,290	168
1038	¾	1	0	4,012	4,265	256	4,012¾	4,266	256
1039	200½	394	39	4,194¾	4,492	244	4,395¼	4,886	283

SALT FISH EXPORTED.

Year of Malabar Era.	By Sea.			By Land.			Total.		
	Quantity. Cwts.	Tariff Value. Govt. Rs.	Duty. G. Rs.	Quantity. Cwts.	Tariff Value. G. Rs.	Duty. G. Rs.	Quantity. Cwts.	Tariff Value. Govt. Rs.	Duty. G. Rs.
1030	11,327	11,922	596	15,655	16,479	823	26,982	28,401	1,419
1031	12,030	12,663	633	16,560	17,431	871	28,590	30,094	1,504
1032	20,213	21,276	1,063	22,038¼	23,198	1,159	42,251¼	44,474	2,222
1033	13,672	14,413	720	16,541½	17,342	867	30,213½	31,755	1,587
1034	16,950	17,843	892	18,034	18,983	949	34,984	36,826	1,841
1035	16,903	17,796	889	10,827½	11,397	569	27,730½	29,193	1,458
1036	19,032	20,035	1,001	20,084¾	23,909	1,195	39,116¾	43,944	2,196
1037	22,922¼	45,199	2,260	26,733¼	52,565	2,633	49,655½	97,764	4,893
1038	13,626	26,908	1,617	22,297½	43,706	2,635	35.923½	70,614	4,252
1039	30,068	60,982	3,561	24,098¾	47,357	2,707	54,166¾	108,339	6,268

In examining the returns of the exports and imports of salt fish it is evident how vastly the trade has increased of late years. Thus in British Malabar the value of the exports have averaged upwards of £5000 yearly during the last ten years: for the first half of which period the yearly average was under £4000, and for the last half rather above £6000.

In the *Native State of Cochin* the exports of salt fish are recorded in the numbers exported, but having been only furnished with the returns for three years, they are insufficient for drawing deductions from. In dried fish there is also a difficulty respecting the exports and imports owing to the returns being made in bundles, but it will be perceived that the Cochin State imports more dried fish than it exports; in fact, although it has exported 9,419½ bundles into Travancore, it has imported from thence 14,004⅝, leaving a balance of 4,585⅛ in favour of Travancore: whilst the exports by sea have increased from 249 in the first moiety of that period, to 5555½ in the latter half. In fact, the Native State of Cochin appears to be of little note as an exporting country for salt and dried fish.

In the *Native State of Travancore,* although the imports of salt fish have become five times larger than they were ten years since, the exports show that the quantity cured in that State has largely augmented: thus the imports which averaged a little above 11 cwt. yearly in the first half of the last ten years, rose to very close upon 3000 cwt. yearly in the last half of that period. In the exports the rise has been much greater than in the imports; for the first half of the period under review the average yearly exports were 36,605 cwts. and for the last half 41,318 cwts.; showing an augmented yearly export of about 4,713 cwts. of salt fish, or after deducting from the increased imports, an average yearly increase exported of upwards of 3,600 cwts. of salt fish; consequently the State of Travancore has done much more during the last few years towards increasing the food productiveness of Malabar than the State of Cochin has: this last, as will be presently shown, has done more towards the trade of fish-oil, but it must be left for future years to demonstrate whether the present increase of this fish-oil trade is a healthy or an unhealthy stimulus due to present high prices; for if the latter, the fisheries are being over-worked, and the future loss will be great. The extreme violence of the S.W. monsoon of course protects the fish from the commencement of June until September, but the periods of year at which the various species spawn, more extended observations on their arrival and departure, and a thorough examination into the fish captured as to whether the young are or are not used for salting or fish-oil, are objects which it would be very important to ascertain.

Captain Lloyd, on the Marine Survey of the Coasts of Bengal, Cantor remarks, in the Journal of Asiatic Society of Bengal, Vol. V., "tried salting and drying fish, and the experiment turned out so satisfactory that I feel convinced that the process of curing, salting, and drying fish may be easily accomplished there during the N.E. monsoon." In Malabar, could the fisherman afford the required outlay to salt his spoils, his market would commence in the S.W. monsoon, a period of the year during which he is now unemployed. Whilst conceding that the amount salted is yearly augmenting, it must be admitted that much is wasted owing to an inability to afford the outlay to cure it, whilst the price is higher than there is any occasion for, because what is now wasted and spoiled would find its way to market, and probably would reduce the price to all.

The Indian Mackerel, *Scomber kanagurta,* which averages about seven and a half inches in length, is one of the chief species which is salted, dried in the sun, and exported in bundles of about 1000 each. They abound in shoals from January until May, and the process of curing is as follows:—A coolie makes a cut with a sharp knife along the back bone, from the head to the tail, and then a second along the abdominal surface, exposing the intestines. The fish is then tossed over to a woman, who, having removed the entrails, throws it into a large basket which has a handle on either side, this when half full is carried by two men to the sea shore, where the fish are washed without being removed. Women and children rapidly put some black salt into each cut, and then throw the fish into a boat close behind them on the shore—in which there is brine; in this last place they remain for a few hours, and are subsequently spread out in the sun, dried, and packed in bundles. The various species of *Trichiurus* and the *Chirocentrus dorab* are also extensively salted in the same way, and last, not least, the *Spratella fimbriata.*

The Bombay salt is generally employed in salting large fish: for this purpose the Rays, Skates, and Sharks are made use of, and these last are termed *Pāl sora,* Mal., or milk producer, referring to the powers attributed to its flesh, which when salted is considered especially good for women who have young infants. The large fish are cut up into square pieces for salting, and cured much in the same way as are the smaller fish.

It is evident that along the coasts of Malabar shoals of fish come as regularly as do the crops to the land, but the quantity is much more varied, for it is sometimes abundant, at other times deficient. It is probable that it is not so much a deficiency in fish, or increased enterprize in fishing, which is requisite in Malabar, as a want of economy in dealing with those captured.

Fish-oil is of two sorts, that of the Sharks and Rays which is considered medicinal, and that of the Sardines which is made in quantities and exported very largely to Europe and elsewhere. The following figures will show the exports and imports from the various places in Malabar for the last few years, where the *export duty* was 3 per cent. "ad valorem," the imports 5 per cent. from 1854 to 1858, and 10 per cent. from 1859 to 1864. The values in the following table since 1860 are according to the "market value," before that period according to the "Tariff value." Most of the exports were to London.

From the following official return it will be seen that although the yearly imports and exports of fish-oil from Malabar have shown great variations, that for the last ten years they have rather exceeded the annual value of £7391. Irrespective of the variations due to the absence of fish, the state of the home markets has exercised a considerable effect upon the exports. Examining the return from British Cochin, the chief exporting town in Malabar, it appears that in five years ending 1858-59, 61,078 cwts. were exported; in five years ending 1863-64, 82,799 cwts. were exported. In former times, as for instance thirty years ago, this export was unknown, and in fact, as lately as the five years ending 1845-46, it had only reached 66 cwts. It rose in the next five years to 3,586 cwts. It must therefore be admitted that the trade is a comparatively new one, which has been and is being rapidly developed.

In the Native State of Cochin a considerable amount of fish-oil is prepared, but it mostly finds its way into British Cochin, and thus becomes incorporated into the exports from the district of Malabar. The average export by sea for the last ten years has been about £31, but the land exports which would be into the British territory are not included.

DISTRICT OF MALABAR.

MEMORANDUM OF IMPORTS AND EXPORTS OF FISH OIL YEARLY FOR THE LAST TEN YEARS.

Year.	Cannanore.			Tellicherry.			Calai.			Badagara.		
	Quantity.	Value.	Duty.	Quantity.	Value.	Duty.	Quantity.	Value.	Duty.	Quantity.	Value.	Duty.
	Cwt.	Rs.	Rs.	Cwt.	Rs.	Rs.	Cwt.	Rs.	Rs.	Cwt.	Rs.	Rs.
Import.												
1854-55	..	..	..	1	8	..	..	..	..	..	..	..
1855-56	..	..	..	..	..	..	..	..	..	..	..	..
1856-57	..	..	..	..	..	..	..	..	..	..	..	..
1857-58	..	..	..	425	3282	5	..	..	..	..	..	..
1858-59	9	35	..	..	..	..	..	..	..	..	..	..
1859-60	2	18	2	32	300	..	8	37	..	..	..	..
1860-61	..	..	..	..	..	..	..	..	..	..	..	..
1861-62	1 doz.	24	..	..	..	..	..	..	..	..	..	..
1862-63	..	..	..	9	90	..	..	..	..	..	..	..
1863-64	..	..	..	..	..	..	..	..	..	..	..	..
Total.	1 doz. 11	77	2	467	3680	5	8	37	..	..	..	..
Export.	Doz.											
1854-55	111-2	355	..	54	223	..	..	..	..	..	..	..
1855-56	..	..	..	163	671	..	..	..	..	..	..	..
1856-57	..	..	..	8	33	..	..	..	..	..	..	..
1857-58	..	..	..	..	..	..	..	..	..	..	..	..
1858-59	1	3	..	..	..	..	..	..	..	..	..	..
1859-60	7	30	..	..	..	..	..	..	..	..	..	..
1860-61	..	..	..	..	..	..	..	..	..	..	..	..
1861-62	1	6	..	1	9	..	..	..	..	..	..	..
1862-63	30	314	..	5	30	..	..	..	..	3	35	..
1863-64	..	..	10	..	..	1	..	..	..	3	28	..
Total.	Doz. 111-41	708	10	231	966	1	..	..	..	6	63	..

Year.	Quilandi.			Calicut.			Beypore.			Tanur.		
	Quantity.	Value.	Duty.	Quantity.	Value.	Duty.	Quantity.	Value.	Duty.	Quantity.	Value.	Duty.
	Cwt.	Rs.	Rs.	Cwt.	Rs.	Rs.	Cwt.	Rs.	Rs.	Cwt.	Rs.	Rs.
Import.												
1854-55	..	..	..	..	..	..	..	..	..	..	..	..
1855-56	..	..	..	..	..	..	..	..	..	..	..	..
1856-57	..	..	..	83	776	..	..	..	..	..	..	..
1857-58	..	..	..	405	1744	..	..	..	..	..	..	..
1858-59	..	..	..	..	..	..	..	..	..	..	..	..
1859-60	..	..	..	..	..	..	..	..	..	..	..	..
1860-61	..	..	..	..	..	..	..	..	..	..	..	..
1861-62	..	..	..	256	2562	..	..	..	..	..	..	..
1862-63	..	..	..	..	..	..	..	..	..	..	..	..
1863-64	..	..	..	..	..	..	..	..	..	..	..	..
Total.	..	..	..	744	5082	..	..	..	..	..	..	..
Export.												
1854-55	234	962	..	1328	5462	..	..	..	..	..	..	..
1855-56	..	..	..	..	..	..	..	..	..	..	..	..
1856-57	..	..	..	..	..	..	..	..	..	..	..	..
1857-58	..	..	..	1547	6190	..	..	..	..	..	..	..
1858-59	2	9	..	64	258	4	..	..	..	..	..	..
1859-60	3	10	..	872	3485	1	..	..	..	..	..	..
1860-61	4	20	..	435	2423	43	..	..	..	..	..	..
1861-62	3	15	..	2019	12,740	37	..	..	..	..	..	..
1862-63	8	66	..	103	806	24	..	..	..	..	..	..
1863-64	9	54	..	1179	6511	47	18	111	3	..	..	..
Total.	263	1136	..	7547	37,875	156	18	111	3	..	..	..

Year.	Ponani.			Chowghat.			Cochin.			Total.		
	Quantity.	Value.	Duty.	Quantity.	Value.	Duty.	Quantity.	Value.	Duty.	Quantity.	Value.	Duty.
	Cwt.	Rs.	Rs.	Cwt.	Rs.	Rs.	Cwt.	Rs.	Rs.	Cwt.	Rs.	Rs.
Import.												
1854-55	..	..	..	..	..	..	499	2322	3	500	2330	3
1855-56	..	..	..	..	..	..	..	..	..	..	..	..
1856-57	..	..	..	..	..	..	1498	9720	113	1581	10,496	113
1857-58	..	..	..	..	..	..	7968	59,263	53	8798	64,289	58
1858-59	12	94	5	..	..	..	1374	8702	50	1395	8831	55
1859-60	..	..	..	..	..	..	4417	22,599	..	4459	22,954	2
1860-61	..	..	..	..	..	..	1335	6299	18	1335	6299	18
1861-62	..	..	..	..	..	..	6985	69,856	..	1 doz. 7241	72,442	..
1862-63	..	..	..	..	..	..	65	653	65	74	743	65
1863-64	..	..	..	..	..	..	..	..	..	..	..	..
Total.	12	94	5	..	..	..	24,141	179,414	302	1 doz. 125,38	188,384	314
Export.										Doz		
1854-55	227	936	..	826	3393	..	16,058	66,039	1888	111. 18,729	77,370	1888
1855-56	..	..	..	..	..	..	360	1489	45	523	2160	45
1856-57	..	..	..	476	1904	..	1796	7183	181	2280	9120	181
1857-58	..	..	..	1987	7947	..	17,132	68,499	1660	20,666	82,636	1660
1858-59	..	..	..	41	165	..	25,732	102,924	3020	25,840	103,359	3024
1859-60	..	..	..	..	..	..	33,285	133,143	3692	34,167	136,668	3693
1860-61	..	..	..	..	..	..	18,296	85,519	2440	18,735	87,962	2483
1861-62	..	..	..	86	589	..	9560	61,765	1853	11,670	75,124	1890
1862-63	..	..	..	..	..	..	566	3938	115	715	5189	150
1863-64	..	..	..	460	4607	..	21,092	148,206	4097	22,761	159,517	4147
Total.	227	936	..	3876	18,605	..	143,877	678,705	18,991	Doz. 111. 156,086	739,105	19,161

G. A. Ballard,

Collector of Malabar.

NATIVE STATE OF COCHIN.

Exports and Imports of Fish Oil by Land and by Sea from 1030 to 1039, Malabar Era.
1854-55 1863-64

Years of Malabar Era.	Exports by Sea.								Imports from Travancore.								Imports by Sea.								Total Duty.		
	Quantity.		Value.			Duty.			Quantity.		Value.			Duty.			Quantity.		Value.			Duty.					
	Parahs.	Edingalies.	Rs.	As.	P.	Rs.	As.	P.	Parahs.	Edingalies.	Rs.	As.	P.	Rs.	As.	P.	Parahs.	Edingalies.	Rs.	As.	P.	Rs.	As.	P.			
1030	..	..	..	..		..	..		..	..	..	..		..	..		724	1	517	3	5	26	11	2	26	11	2
1031	..	..	..	..		..	..		..	..	..	..		..	..		60	..	42	13	9	2	9	2	2	9	2
1032	48	..	34	11	5	1	11	9	49	1	34	11	5	1	11	9	1,711	2	1,222	4	6	61	2	1	64	9	7
1033	28	2	20	0	0	1	2	3	56	4	40	0	0	2	4	7	1,100	1	785	12	7	36	12	4	40	3	2
1034	431	7	309	5	8	18	8	4	1,295	1	924	1	2	55	9	3	1,801	2	1,286	9	2	59	13	9	133	15	4
1035	1,125	9	804	3	5	41	14	5	3,377	7	2,412	10	4	125	11	5	1,336	4	9,543	13	9	418	15	10	586	9	8
1036	456	6	326	2	3	17	4	4	1,369	8	978	6	11	51	13	0	2,647	2	1,890	13	9	93	0	0	162	1	4
1037	52	8	37	11	5	1	14	2	52	8	37	11	5	1	14	2	94	8	67	11	5	4	1	1	7	13	5
1038	110	..	55	0	0	2	12	0	219	8	109	2	3	5	7	7	47	3	33	9	2	2	0	6	10	4	1
1039	2,150	1	1,352	12	7	81	12	0	6,450	3	4,607	5	9	245	4	0	11,952	9	8,537	12	6	383	8	11	710	8	11
Total	4,442	..	3,122	14	9	166	15	3	12,871	..	4,144	1	3	489	11	9	33,440	2	23,928	8	11	1,088	10	10	1,745	5	10

The State of Travancore has a much larger sea-board than that of Cochin, but is not so great an exporter of fish-oil, which may be due to the shoals of fish not being so numerous to the south as they are opposite Cochin. Also there have been great changes in the duties and modes of levying them, which may have occasioned more or less discouragement to the trade. At the end of the year 1037 Malabar era (A.D. 1861-62), the 5 per cent. import duty was raised to 6 per cent. and the 8 per cent. duty to 10 per cent.; in the middle of 1039 M. E. (A.D. 1863-64), the old duties were reverted to. The same remarks apply to the exports, the tariff for which was revised in 1036 M.E. (A.D. 1860-61), when the duty on fish-oil was raised to more than three times what it previously was, or from rupees 3, annas 1, and pice 3, to rupees 9, annas 13, and pice 2, per cwt. The duties were also raised from 5 to 6, and from 6 to 8 per cent. but in 1863-64 were again lowered to what they originally were. On referring to the tables, one observes that the export of fish-oil fell off immediately on extra duties being imposed, in fact it totally ceased until the year 1863-64, which was the one in which the old rates of duties were returned to. Referring to the returns of the Cochin State, one does not perceive a total cessation of the export of fish-oil at these periods, although there is certainly a great decrease in the amount exported: the same decrease is also apparent in the exports at these periods from Malabar, without doubt it was partially due to a diminution in the shoals of sardines, but there can be no question that high duties are most detrimental to this species of trade.

NATIVE STATE OF TRAVANCORE.

Exports and Imports of Fish Oil by Land and Sea from $\frac{1030}{1854\text{-}55}$ to $\frac{1039}{1863\text{-}64}$ Malabar Era.

Years of Malabar Era.	Exports.									Imports.								
	By Sea.			By Land.			Total.			By Sea.			By Land.			Total.		
	Quantity. Cwts.	Tariff Value. G. Rs.	Duty. G. Rs.	Quantity. Cwts	Tariff Value. G. Rs.	Duty. G. Rs.	Quantity Cwts.	Tariff Value. G. Rs.	Duty. G. Rs.	Quantity. Cwts.	Tariff Value. G. Rs.	Duty. G. Rs.	Quantity. Cwts.	Tariff Value. G. Rs.	Quantity. Cwts.	Quantity. Cwts.	Tariff Value. G. Rs.	Duty. G. Rs.
1030	$6\frac{9}{16}$	20	1	138	424	21	$144\frac{9}{16}$	444	22	..	..	..	$31\frac{1}{4}$	95	4	$31\frac{1}{4}$	95	4
1031	..	..	..	$17\frac{1}{2}$	54	2	$17\frac{1}{2}$	54	2	..	..	..	..	..	..	..	..	..
1032	$619\frac{3}{4}$	1,768	88	$5\frac{1}{2}$	17	$\frac{7}{8}$	$625\frac{1}{4}$	1,785	$88\frac{7}{8}$	..	..	..	..	..	..	..	..	..
1033	$636\frac{3}{4}$	1,960	98	$170\frac{1}{4}$	524	26	807	2,484	124	..	..	..	..	..	..	..	..	..
1034	$89\frac{5}{8}$	276	13	$206\frac{1}{2}$	635	31	$296\frac{1}{8}$	911	44	..	..	..	$4\frac{1}{2}$	14	..	$4\frac{1}{2}$	14	..
1035	$1,306\frac{1}{4}$	4,023	201	$1,694\frac{1}{2}$	5,217	260	$3,000\frac{3}{4}$	9,240	461	..	..	..	..	..	..	..	..	..
1036	$56\frac{1}{8}$	172	8	476	1,972	98	$532\frac{1}{8}$	2,144	106	..	..	..	$3\frac{1}{4}$	10	..	$3\frac{1}{4}$	10	..
1037	..	..	..	$13\frac{1}{4}$	130	6	$13\frac{1}{4}$	130	6	..	..	..	72	223	11	72	223	11
1038	..	..	..	$\frac{3}{20}$	1	..	$\frac{3}{20}$	1	..	..	..	..	$73\frac{3}{4}$	234	14	$73\frac{3}{4}$	234	14
1039	1,451	14,257	845	1,619	15,906	934	3,070	30,163	1,779	..	..	..	4	12	..	4	12	..

There are several modes in which fish-oils are prepared, as well as several descriptions of fish from which they are manufactured. Some oils are contained in the areolar tissue beneath the skin, or between the folds of the lining membrane of the abdomen, or in the substance of the liver.

From the livers of the Rays, Skates and Sharks is prepared the best fish-liver oil, which is almost invariably extracted by heat. In the Madras Exhibition Report it is stated that the bad taste and smell are due to the employment of the livers of this last family. The gland is removed from the fish and carefully washed, the gall bladder having been rejected, it is then cut into pieces and gently boiled in a large earthen pot for about an hour; if the heat is excessive the quantity of oil obtained is greater, but it has a rank fishy odour, and its colour is heightened. Whilst the boiling is going on, the fluid is kept stirred about with a wooden spoon, and as the oil floats it is skimmed off. The residue is then allowed to settle for two days, when it is again subjected to the same process, with the addition of filtration for the purpose of clearing away impurities.

Fish-liver oil should be of a clear amber colour, and its smell and taste almost the same as that of cod-liver oil. The rancid odour and bad taste which are often present are probably due to great heat in boiling; the admixture of impurities consequent upon proper care not having been taken in the careful preservation of the livers from tainting, or in choosing those most adapted for the purpose. If sulphuric acid be poured on the oil it causes discoloration, the same as in cod-liver oil. Even the most transparent specimen deposits after many filtrations a considerable quantity of white slightly thick grumous matter.

In the Report of the Juries for the Madras Exhibition for 1855 it is stated that the livers are specifically lighter than water, and if when they are cut into any of their substance flows out in a semi-liquid state, they should be rejected. It is found in Newfoundland that in a therapeutic point of view fat livers are not so good for cod-liver oil as lean ones.

Government possesses at Calicut on the Malabar coast a small establishment, for the preparation of fish-liver oil for hospital use, the returns from which, with an account of the mode pursued in preparing the oil, have unfortunately not been received, although applied for. If its rancid fishy taste and high colour could be obviated, it would probably form as good an article for consumptive patients as the cod-liver oil. Information is still needed as to the period of the year when the livers of the Indian fishes possess the most iodine and other medicinal ingredients, and also whether sex has any bearing on the efficacy of the drug.

Common fish-oil, which forms so large an article of export in Malabar, may be said to be manufactured from the Oil Sardine, *Sardinella Neohowii, C. & V.*, for the addition of other fishes must be considered accidental or wasteful, whilst medicinal fish-liver oil is too valuable to be thus disposed of. This fish-oil is prepared either by heat or putrefaction. The first is much the same mode as is employed in obtaining the fish-liver oil, except that large iron cauldrons are used, and that a longer time is required for its preparation. The second plan is mostly carried out in a boat divided into two by a perforated iron compartment, the fish being left to decompose in water on one side, and the oil floats through the partition to the other, where it is skimmed off. The fish-oil is adapted for every use to which animal oils can be put, and its export which a few years since was almost unrecognized, and in fact so lately as 1850-51 only amounted to the value of £1271, has now reached an average in British Malabar of above £7000 yearly value.

Isinglass is obtained in Malabar under the designation of "fish maws" or "fish sounds," and is exported to Bombay, from whence it finds its way to China. It is in fact an unprepared isinglass, and the trade in it appears to be steadily increasing in Malabar, the amount having averaged 239 cwts. yearly during the last ten years. In the first half of this period the average yearly exports were only 121 cwts., in the latter half they rose to 357 cwts. In examining the ports from which the exports were despatched, it is unfortunate that the subject is not mentioned in the returns from the two native States, but it is corroborative of what appears to be the case, that the isinglass-furnishing species are more numerous towards the north than to the south: Tellicherry and Calicut being the chief places of export, whilst the amount from Cochin only just exceeds 11 cwts. yearly.

The Malabar isinglass or "fish maws" appears to be principally prepared from the swimming bladder of a species of *Siluroid*, one of the sub-group *Arii* (p. 175) or Cat-fish, which G. A. BALLARD, ESQ.,—who has been good enough to furnish me with a drawing of it—informs me is termed *Yêta* at Calicut, and grows to two and a half feet in length: it has four cirri reaching almost to the base of the pectoral fin; but without examining a specimen it is impossible to determine the exact species, still all the members of the family are probably employed for this

DISTRICT OF MALABAR.

MEMORANDUM OF EXPORTS OF FISH-MAWS YEARLY FOR THE LAST TEN YEARS.

Year.	CANNANORE.			TELLICHERRY.			KALAI.			BADAGARA.			QUILANDI.			CALICUT.			BEYPORE.			TANUR.			PONANI.			CHOWGHAT.			COCHIN.			TOTAL.		
	Quantity.	Value.	Duty.	Quantity.	Value.	Duty.	Quantity.	Value.	Duty.	Quantity.	Value.	Duty.	Quantity.	Value.	Duty.	Quantity.	Value.	Duty.	Quantity.	Value.	Duty.	Quantity.	Value.	Duty.	Quantity.	Value.	Duty.	Quantity.	Value.	Duty.	Quantity.	Value.	Duty.	Quantity.	Value.	Duty.
	Cwt.			Cwt.																																
1854-55	..	..	..	74	1318	..	..	..	..	3	61	..	2	20	..	34	366	..	..	..	..	1	24	..	..	..	..	14	180	..	5	289	..	133	2258	..
1855-56	1	7	..	55	418	..	..	..	..	..	..	..	..	..	..	47	305	..	..	..	..	1	27	..	..	..	..	7	238	..	12	444	..	123	1439	..
1856-57	..	..	..	46	800	..	..	..	..	8	37	..	..	..	..	37	319	..	..	..	..	14	103	..	9	128	..	5	207	..	7	335	..	126	1919	..
1857-58	..	..	..	35	352	..	..	..	..	..	..	..	..	..	..	61	458	..	..	..	..	14	64	..	1	6	..	2	23	..	7	363	..	120	1266	..
1858-59	..	..	..	55	989	..	..	..	..	..	..	..	..	..	..	44	486	..	..	..	..	..	..	..	1	6	..	1	15	..	5	233	..	106	1729	..
1859-60	..	..	..	137	1255	..	..	..	..	5	25	..	..	..	..	90	454	..	..	..	..	..	..	..	..	..	..	1	70	..	20	772	..	253	2576	..
1860-61	..	..	..	188	3430	..	..	..	..	22	693	..	..	..	..	155	5117	..	..	..	..	20	152	..	..	..	..	18	892	..	18	931	2	421	11,215	2
1861-62	..	..	..	233	3278	..	..	..	..	..	..	..	3	23	..	36	1767	..	..	..	..	..	..	..	26	1294	..	1	19	..	11	638	..	310	7049	..
1862-63	..	..	..	215	10,771	..	..	..	..	25	318	..	..	..	..	103	5172	..	..	..	..	21	996	..	..	..	..	..	..	..	22	1132	..	386	18,389	..
1863-64	..	..	..	220	11,027	..	..	..	..	1	30	..	21	1045	..	146	7292	..	..	..	..	18	884	..	..	..	..	..	..	..	12	580	..	418	20,858	..
Total	1	7	..	1258	33,638	..	..	..	..	64	1164	..	26	1088	..	753	21,756	..	..	..	..	89	2250	..	37	1434	..	49	1644	..	119	5717	2	2396	68,698	2

G. A. BALLARD, *Collector.*

manufacture. "The 'maws' are roughly circular, two or three inches in diameter, and somewhat resembling a bad muffin."

The *Polynemus Indicus* (p. 60) is also another of the isinglass producing fish, and is known under the name of (*Kora,* Mal.) at Calicut. "Its maws are shaped somewhat like the blade of a trowel, and from seven to eight inches in length, by two or three in width: they are not obtained in nearly so large quantities as those of the *Yêta.*"

There are other species of fish, as the *Lates calcarifer; Lobotes surinamensis;* some species of *Sciæna,* &c. from which isinglass could be procured, but perhaps the small quantity which they yield, and the trouble it would entail in procuring and preparing it, render them little used in Malabar for this purpose.

The "fish maws" of Indian commerce are the swimming bladder or sounds extracted from the fish and dried in the sun. McClelland gives the following as the Bengal process:—"The sounds when received fresh are opened and stripped of the vascular covering and internal membrane, washed, and at once made up into any form the manufacturer finds most convenient for packing." If dry before receiving it, it is steeped in water and the same process adopted. For the removal of discoloured parts and softening the more solid without dissolving the thinner, they are steeped a short time in alum water (consisting of alum 1 ounce to 4 or 5 gallons of water), when saturated they are removed, spread on a linen or cotton cloth that has been saturated with the same solution, then rolled up lightly and set aside for twelve hours, this is repeated till they are bleached. It should be observed, bleaching neither improves the quality nor increases the value of the article.

The Indian isinglass is said, (by Dr. Royle on Isinglass, at page 74) to be "essentially good, "and its defects such as are easily susceptible of improvement by increased attention to the pre-"paration, so as to remove the present (1849) objection; and in fact some specimens (from India) "being better prepared than others, proves that there can be no difficulty in preparing them all "equally well." . . . "Its objectionable properties consist of its still retaining something of "the fishy smell as well as being in part insoluble, apparently from some portion of the albuminous "membranes still continuing adherent to the purer gelatinous parts. It is probable that by increased "care in cleaning and drying, by exposure to air, some of these defects may be removed." (p. 37.) Its thickness might be decreased by stripping off more of the outer membranes, and also by beating and pressing between slabs and rollers. Bengal isinglass appears more fibrous, because the middle and not the inner coat is used (but this is not a proof that the inner coat of the Polynemus Indicus is the best), instead of being torn into shreds by the hand it might be rasped or cut, for if in shreds doubts arise as to its genuineness, whilst it cannot be cut in India so evenly as is done in Europe by machinery, therefore sending it home in sheets is the best. It should be prepared when the fish is fresh, and under a light roof, because the action of the sun may melt any oily particles, and diffuse them through the membraneous structure. Oiliness and smell may perhaps be removed by chemical re-agents, as lime and chlorine, but their use (unless very carefully employed) is likely to leave a taint to which purchasers would object.

The first Indian isinglass imported into England about 1840 was only valued at four shillings a pound, and a second specimen at one shilling and eightpence. The samples were of two qualities, the first being the sounds removed from the fish and dried by exposure to the sun: the second the same substance partially prepared by being cut open, the interior membrane taken out, then washed, and subsequently flattened by beating out with pieces of wood.

The fins of some fish—more especially of the Sharks—are dried, exported, and probably eventually find their way to China, where they are largely employed in soups. So large is the consumption that from seven to ten thousand hundredweights are annually exported there from Bombay. FORBES states that they sell in the Celestial Empire at £6. 1*s* per cwt. These fins are assorted into the "white" and the "black," the former being the dorsal fins, which are uniformly light coloured on both sides, and are reputed to yield more gelatine than the other: the "black" fins are the pectoral, ventral, and anal, the upper surfaces of which are grey or darkish, the lower of a light colour; this variety is less esteemed than the white, and consequently realizes a lower price.

The skins of some species, as the *Hypolophus sephen,* are converted into shagreen, as are also those of the sharks, which are employed for sword belts, the coverings of boxes, or for smoothing wood or ivory preparatory to its being polished.

The refuse of fish, as their entrails, scales, heads, and fins, are employed for manuring the cocoa-nut trees, and likewise for feeding fowls, ducks, and pigs. It is stated (*Speid,* "Our last Years in India") that at Rosa, near Aurungabad, the finest grapes are raised by manuring the vines with fish.

The scales of some of the Cyprinidæ are employed in the manufacture of false pearls.

In forming collections of Indian fishes, the difficulty of preserving specimens when obtained is great; for in conveying them from place to place they are often damaged. Personally, I have experienced the same results as are recorded by SIR JOHN RICHARDSON to have occurred to SIR JAMES CLARK ROSS's collection of specimens in spirits, made during the voyage of the Erebus and Terror, in which, "owing to the deterioration of the spirit in jars that were crowded with fish, and the long continued action of the brine, where that liquid was employed, very many specimens entirely perished, or merely fragments of skeletons could be rescued from the mass."

There are two methods of preserving fish for collections—the moist and the dry; and of these an infinite number of variations, a very short synopsis of which is here given.

The dry method consists in simply drying the preserved skins, or in the fish being stuffed, and is well adapted for large museum specimens. In many inland places in India, it is, in fact, the only way in which such could be preserved, for spirit is frequently not to be had, or that which is procurable is bad. The Natives of India in some places, as Madras, are able to stuff fish most beautifully, and specimens preserved in the Museum at Fort St. George are second to none prepared in Europe: but inland the naturalist is thrown on his own resources. There is but little difference between the dried skin and the stuffed fish, excepting that one has glass eyes which the other is without, and the latter is usually mounted, whilst the former is fixed on a board or to cardboard. In skinning fish there are two methods, each of which has its followers: in one mode both sides of the specimen are preserved, which is done, as in birds or mammals, by dividing the skin along the mesial line of the abdomen and removing the whole of the body through the opening, it is the most difficult of execution, and more of the scales are usually rubbed off and more injury done to the specimen than in the second mode, in which nearly the whole of one side of the body and head of the fish is removed, the vertical fins being left intact. The specimen should be laid on a smooth flat moist dish, and if the scales are very deciduous it is advisable to cover the side of the fish next to the dish with a piece of moistened thin paper: of course whichever mode is preferred, it is necessary to preserve and stuff the skin to its natural size, arsenical soap being the best preservative, whilst the fish should be subsequently painted over both externally and internally with spirits of turpentine. The specimen should be dried upon a board, and the fins retained in their proper situation until dry by means of pins. Subsequently the specimens should be varnished, and then each separately fastened on to a piece of cardboard.

There is this disadvantage in dried skins and stuffed specimens, that the shape is usually altered in preserving them, and accidents occur to the specimen, whilst they are not nearly so useful for scientific purposes as specimens in spirits, as they cannot be examined with reference to many important points in their anatomy: but they are easier to carry from place to place, take up less room, and are not so liable to spoil as those in spirit.

The moist method is no doubt superior to the dry, provided the specimens can safely reach a Museum: an incision should be made into the abdomen, penetrating the air bladder; the specimen should then be placed in spirit strong enough to burn when a flame is brought into contact with it. It should be allowed to remain thus some days, when the spirit should be removed, and some about 4 or 5 degrees stronger substituted. Should it be desired to carry the specimens any distance, each should be separately sewn up in some soft calico. It is necessary from time to time to examine the bottles, in order to see if the strength of the spirit is decreasing.

In some specimens received from the Rev. H. Baker, Junior, from Travancore, bichloride of mercury was added to the spirit, but apparently without acting beneficially. A small amount of arsenic would probably prove advantageous in the spirit, but there are of course certain dangers to be guarded against in poisonous fluids.

Catalogues of Indian fishes, as "*Ichthyological Gleanings in Madras,*" in the Madras Journal of Literature and Science, by Dr. Jerdon, and my own paper on *the Fishes of Cochin,* in the Proceedings of the Zoological Society of London, are not referred to unless they contain descriptions of new species. Some of Dr. Jerdon's descriptions in his ***Fresh Water Fishes of Southern India,*** are also omitted, as they appear to be only briefly detailed for collectors on the spot, and will no doubt be more fully described in his forthcoming work on the "Fishes of India." Some of his new species I have considered as identical with specimens in my own collection, as the *Nemacheilus (cobitis) rubripinnis: Puntius parrah (Systomus amphibius): Puntius (systomus) Hamiltonii: Rasbora (Leuciscus) Malabarica.*

Being compelled to return to the East, but unwilling to defer the publication of my researches on the Ichthyology of Western India, a difficulty respecting the classification arose in the preparation of this work, as I determined not to attempt any innovations in the existing nomenclature.

As several systems of Ichthyology are now passing through the press, and each begins at a different point, my descriptions could not be classified in accordance with the views of any individual author, consequently the following have been adopted: — For the *Acanthopterygii* and *Anacanthini* the "*Catalogue of the Fishes of the British Museum,*" by Dr. Günther, a work of most elaborate research, invaluable to travellers, and to those who have neither the time or opportunity, had they the untiring energy, necessary for the examination of the numerous ichthyological works and notes of scientific travellers. For the *Physostomi* and *Plectognathi*, Dr. Bleeker's arrangement in his magnificent "*Atlas ichthyologique*"—so far as it is published—a splendid record of personal industry in the East, unwearied research amongst the finny tribes in Malaysia and elsewhere, and a model of accuracy in the discrimination of families, genera, and species. For the *Lophobranchiæ*, Dr. Kaup's "*British Museum Catalogue*:" and for the *Plagiostomi*, Duméril's "*Ichthyologie générale*" in the "Suites à Buffon." The alterations in the classification have been made as few as possible, commensurate with giving the whole collection in a connected manner. To increase the utility of the work, all fishes recorded by other observers as having been collected in Malabar have been added, which, if not at present in my collection, are denoted by * before them.

In order to avoid employing more synonyms than possible, only those given in the following works and papers have been enumerated, except in the case of those authors who first named the species:—Russell's *Fishes of Coromandel,* 1803; Hamilton Buchanan's *Fishes of the Ganges,* 1822; Gray and Hardwicke, *Illustrations of Indian Zoology,* 1830; Cuvier and Valenciennes, *Histoire Naturelle des Poissons,* 1828-1849; Bennett's *Selections from the most remarkable and interesting of the Fishes of Ceylon,* 1834; McClelland's *Indian Cyprinidæ,* in the XIXth volume of the Asiatic Researches, 1839, and his various papers in the Calcutta Journal of Natural History; Sykes' *Fishes of the Dukhan,* in the second volume of the Transactions of the Zoological Society, 1841; Cantor's *Malayan Fishes,* 1849; Jerdon's *Fresh-water Fishes of Southern India,* in the Madras Journal of Literature and Science, XVth volume, 1848-49; Gray's *Chondropterygii in the British Museum,* 1851; Kaup's *Catalogue of Apodal and Lophobranchiate Fishes in the British Museum,* 1856; Bleeker's *Atlas Ichthyologique,* up to the commencement of Volume V, 1862-1865;

Günther's *Catalogue of the Fishes of the British Museum,* the first five volumes, 1859-1865; Duméril, *Ichthyologie générale,* volume the first, 1865.

Before commencing the individual descriptions, a few explanatory remarks are requisite on the mode adopted in taking measurements, &c.

Roman figures are employed to designate the number of the branchiostegous rays: also the finlets, as in the *Caranx Rottleri,* &c., or elongated free rays, as appendages to the pectoral fins in the *Polynemi;* an exceptional case being in the *Bregmaceros Macclellandi,* in which it is impossible to give the various portions of the fins distinctly without using these figures.

O signifies an adipose fin.

In counting the number of rays, *when two arise from one interneural or interhæmal spine,* as frequently takes place in the last of the dorsal and anal fins, they are reckoned as one, a plan sanctioned by high authorities, but open to objection and not adopted by Dr. Bleeker. In the caudal fin the small outer rays are not included. The horizontal procumbent spine which exists in many genera before the base of the dorsal fin is not included in the formulary, neither is the short vertical bone before the dorsal spine in many of the siluroids.

By *L. l.* is meant the number of pierced scales, extending from the shoulder bones to the base of the caudal fin. By *L. r.* the numbers of rows of scales passing downwards from the back to the lateral line along its whole extent. By *L. tr.* the number of scales in a row passing downwards from the origin of the dorsal fin to the lateral line, and between the lateral line and the abdomen. In speaking of the lateral line of *mullets,* the term is only used for convenience of description, as it is absent.

By the *total length,* is meant that included between the end of the snout and the centre of the termination of the caudal fin, unless otherwise stated, as in the *Fistularia serrata,* in which the two central rays are produced into long filaments.

By the *length of the head,* is commonly meant from the anterior end of the jaws when closed to the posterior extremity of the bony opercle; to this several exceptions exist, as in the *Alutarius lævis,* in which the eye and much of the skull is behind that situation, whilst in the *Hemiramphus* the lower jaw is extended in the form of a beak far beyond the mouth.

By the *length of the snout,* is meant the distance between the anterior margin of the orbit and the centre of the intermaxillaries, unless otherwise stated, as in the Genus *Belone.*

By the *length of the base of a fin,* as the dorsal, is meant the distance between the base of its foremost to that of its hindermost spine or ray, except in those genera which have a procumbent horizontal spine before them, which is not included.

By the *length of a fin* is meant its extreme length even when it is prolonged, thus in the *Polyacanthus cupanus* the pectoral is given to the end of its filament.

By the *height of a fin* is meant the length of its longest spine or ray, unless otherwise expressed.

The *diameter of the eye* is its horizontal, unless its vertical is also given. The comparative size of this organ varies with age, being almost invariably comparatively larger in the immature than in the mature specimen, but even here an exception occurs in the ***Elops apalike.***

By *height of body* is meant its greatest vertical diameter. By *width of body* its greatest thickness.

By *spine* is meant an unarticulated bony or spinous ray. By *ray* those which are articulated, whether branched or single.

The measurements are intended to refer to the adult fish.

In speaking of the *origin* or *commencement of a fin,* the anterior extremity of its base is referred to, unless otherwise specified.

The terms right *(dextral)* and left *(sinistral)* are employed with reference to a flat fish when placed with its tail towards the observer, its dorsal fin upwards and its anal downwards.

The term *Seas of India* has reference to the sea on the Eastern side of the Peninsula of Hindustan, as well as to that on the Western.

CHELTENHAM,
August 27th, 1865.

THE FISHES OF MALABAR.

SUB-CLASS.—TELEOSTEI.

ORDER.—ACANTHOPTERYGII.

Fam. BERYCIDÆ.

GENUS HOLOCENTRUM, *Artedi.*

CORNIGER, *Agassiz.*

Branchiostegals, eight. Form of body oblong, compressed; eyes large, lateral; jaws equal, or lowest slightly the longest; muzzle moderate, nearly horizontal. Two dorsals scarcely united; ventrals with one spine, and seven rays; caudal forked; anal with four spines, the third long and strong. Opercles and suborbitals serrated, opercle with two spines. Villiform teeth in both jaws, vomer, and palatine bones. Scales moderate, ctenoid. Swimming bladder simple, oval. Pyloric appendages many.

* HOLOCENTRUM RUBRUM.

SCIÆNA RUBRA, *Forskål*, Descript. anim. p. 48.

HOLOCENTRUM ORIENTALE, *Cuvier & Valenciennes*, Histoire Naturelle des Poissons, iii. p. 197, vii. p. 497.

HOLOCENTRUM MARGINATUM, *Cuv. & Val.* iii. p. 216.

HOLOCENTRUM RUBRUM, *Günther*, Catalogue of the Fishes in the British Museum, i. p. 35.

B. viii. D. $\frac{11}{12\text{-}13}$. P. 15. V. $\frac{1}{7}$. A. $\frac{4}{9}$. C. 17. L. l. 35. L. tr. $\frac{3}{7}$. Vert. $\frac{11}{16}$. Cæc. pylor. 20.

Length of head $\frac{2}{7}$, of caudal $4\frac{2}{3}$ in total length. Height of body $\frac{2}{7}$, of third anal spine $4\frac{1}{3}$-$\frac{1}{5}$ in total length. Interorbital space $\frac{1}{5}$ of length of head.

Preopercle serrated; interopercle coarsely denticulated; opercle with two strong spines, the upper the largest. Groove for intermaxillary process shorter than the diameter of the eye. Suprascapular and coracoid denticulated.

Teeth—Villiform in jaws, vomer, and palatines.

Fins—Third, fourth, and fifth dorsal spines the longest; the soft rays being a little higher than the spines. The third anal spine longest. Ventral slightly longer than pectoral, and reaches to the anus. Caudal divided into two equal lobes. Scales slightly striated.

Colours—Red, with eight alternate longitudinal bands of red, and gold or silver. Dorsal, purplish with a red base. Caudal, ventral, and pectoral, reddish. Anal, with a purplish mark between the second, third, and fourth rays.

Good eating, said to be obtained in Malabar most abundantly during the N. E. monsoon.

Habitat—Red Sea, seas of India, Malaysia, and China.

Fam. PERCIDÆ.

GENUS LATES, *Cuvier and Valenciennes.*

Branchiostegals, seven: pseudobranchiæ present. Preorbital, and humeral bones strongly serrated, preopercle with strong spines at its angle, and denticulated along its inferior margin, opercle spinate. First dorsal with seven or eight, anal with three spines. Tongue smooth. Teeth villiform, on upper and lower jaws, vomer and palatine bones.

LATES CALCARIFER.

HOLOCENTRUS CALCARIFER, *Bloch*, Ausländische Fische, t. 244.
LATES NOBILIS, *Cuv. & Val.* ii. p. 96, pl. 13; *Cantor*, Catalogue of Malayan Fishes, p. 1.
LATES CALCARIFER, *Günther*, Catal. i. p. 68.
COIUS VACTI, *Hamilton Buchanan*, Fishes of the Ganges, pp. 86, 369, pl. 16. f. 8.
PANDOOMENOO, *Russell*, Fishes of Coromandel, pl. 131.
BEGTI, *Bengallee.* NUDDEE MEEN, *Malayalim.*

B. vii. D. 7-8 | $\frac{1}{11\text{-}12}$. P. 17. V. $\frac{1}{5}$. A. $\frac{3}{8\text{-}9}$. C. 17. L. l. 52. L. tr. $\frac{7}{11}$.

Length of head about $\frac{1}{3}$, of pectoral $\frac{1}{9}$, of caudal $\frac{1}{5}$, of base of dorsal $\frac{1}{3}$, of base of anal $\frac{1}{9}$ of total length. Height of head $\frac{1}{6}$, of body $\frac{2}{9}$ of total length.

Eyes—Diameter $\frac{2}{7}$ length of head, $\frac{3}{4}$ of a diameter apart, $1\frac{3}{4}$ from end of snout.

Preorbital and preopercle finely serrated, the latter with its angle obtuse, having a large tooth directed backwards, and three smaller (but strong) denticulations along its inferior margin. Opercular spine weak. Suprascapular and coracoid bones toothed, about five on the former, from six to ten on the latter.

Teeth—Villiform on upper and lower jaws, vomer, and palatine bones.

Fins—Dorsal spines strong, the first half as high as the second, which is not quite a third as long as the next, which is the highest: from thence they rapidly decrease. Third anal spine more than double the length of second, which is twice that of the first. The first dorsal triangular, second dorsal and anal square. Pectoral small and rounded. Ventral slightly rounded, caudal fan-shaped.

Colours—Generally grey with a dash of green along the back, and silvery on the abdomen: in the monsoon time with a tinge of purple, whilst young specimens are darker than adults.

Very plentiful, grows to five feet in length. Is excellent eating, salts well, and from it some of the best "Tamarind fish" is made. Air bladder thin, a large fish not yielding above one ounce of isinglass. It is known as the "Nair fish" in Malabar, and the "Cock-up" in Calcutta.

Habitat—Seas and estuaries of India and Malaysia.

GENUS SERRANUS, *Cuv. and Val.*

Branchiostegals, seven. Preopercle more or less serrated, with its lower limb entire: opercle with two or three flat spines. Dorsal fin single, with from eight to twelve spines: anal with three. Teeth villiform in jaws, with more or less pointed ones and distinct canines in each intermaxillary, also on vomer and palatine bones. Tongue smooth. Scales small.

SERRANUS SEXFASCIATUS.

SERRANUS SEXFASCIATUS, *Cuv. & Val.* ii. p. 360; *Günther*, Catal. i. p. 108.

B. vii. D. $\frac{11-12}{16}$. P. 18. V. $\frac{1}{5}$. A. $\frac{3}{8}$. C. 17. L. r. about 100.

Length of head $\frac{1}{3}$, of pectoral $\frac{1}{7}$, of caudal $\frac{1}{5}$, of base of dorsal $\frac{2}{5}$, of base of anal $\frac{1}{8}$ of the total length. Height of head $\frac{1}{6}$, of body $\frac{1}{5}$, of hard dorsal $\frac{1}{5}$, of soft dorsal $\frac{1}{8}$, of ventral $\frac{1}{8}$, of anal $\frac{1}{8}$ of the total length.

Eyes—Transversely oval, longest diameter $\frac{1}{4}$ length of head, $\frac{1}{4}$ of a diameter apart, $\frac{1}{4}$ of a diameter from end of snout.

Maxilla extends to beneath the centre of the orbit, preorbital entire: preopercle strongly serrated at the posterior portion of its vertical limb, two strong teeth at its angle, the superior directed backwards, the inferior which is the strongest directly downwards; inferior limb horizontal, entire. Opercle with three spines, the central flat, strong, distinct, the inferior less developed, the superior almost concealed. Sub- and interopercles entire.

Teeth—Villiform in upper and lower jaws, vomer and palate, an external larger band in superior maxilla, and a large canine on either side of each intermaxillary: teeth in centre of lower jaw largest, whilst all are directed more or less backwards.

Fins—First dorsal spine $\frac{3}{10}$ shorter than the second, which is $\frac{1}{10}$ shorter than the third, from thence the rest of the spines and the first thirteen soft rays are about the same height. Anal, first spine half the height of the second, which is stronger than, but of the same length, as the third; and they are $\frac{3}{10}$ shorter than the soft rays. Fins rounded.

Lateral line—In upper fifth of body, and on about the twentieth row of scales.

Colours—Brownish with a dash of pink on the back, and becoming of a pinkish rose colour on the abdomen. Six vertical dark bands, one passing over the head; the second from fourth to sixth spine passes downwards over the pectoral to the base of the ventral; the third from between the eighth and eleventh spines is lost midway between ventral and anal fins; the fourth arising opposite from the third to seventh dorsal rays, passes to base of spines and first soft ray of anal; the fifth arising between the tenth to the fourteenth soft dorsal rays passes down to last four rays of anal; the sixth passes over the tail just before the origin of the caudal fin. A black line passes from the lower margin of the orbit to the angle of the preopercle. Fins stained darker at their margins, and the bands partially continued on to them. Eye rose coloured.

Small in size, nearly eight inches in length, being the largest captured in Cochin. In *Sir Emerson Tennent's* collection of drawings of the "Fishes of Ceylon" is one apparently of this species, with a remark that the specimen was four feet and a half in length.

Habitat—Seas of India, and Malaysia.

SERRANUS BONTOO.

SERRANUS BONTOO, *Cuv. & Val.* ii. p. 334, vi. p. 523; *Cantor*, Catal. p. 11; *Günther*, Catal. i. p. 138.

MADINAWA BONTOO, *Russell*, pl. 128.

B. vii. D. $\frac{11}{16-17}$. P. 19. V. $\frac{1}{5}$. A. $\frac{3}{8}$. C. 17. L. r. about 100.

Length of head $\frac{1}{3}$, of pectoral $\frac{2}{13}$, of caudal $\frac{1}{6}$, of base of dorsal $\frac{4}{9}$, of base of anal $\frac{1}{8}$ of total length. Height of head $\frac{1}{6}$, of body $\frac{1}{3}$, of hard dorsal $\frac{1}{12}$, of soft dorsal $\frac{1}{9}$, of ventral $\frac{1}{7}$, of anal $\frac{1}{7}$ of total length.

Eyes—Diameter $\frac{1}{7}$ of length of head, the two slightly approximate at their upper margins, where they are $\frac{1}{6}$ of the length of the head apart, and the same distance from the end of the snout.

Posterior extremity of maxilla extends to slightly behind the orbit. Preorbital entire. Preopercle finely serrated on the posterior margin of its vertical limb, four large serratures at its angle directed downwards and backwards, inferior limb rather oblique and entire. Opercle with three spines, the upper and lower partially hidden by the scales, the centre one flat and distinct.

Teeth—Villiform in upper and lower jaws, vomer, and palate; a canine on either side of each intermaxillary, teeth in front of upper jaw the strongest, and curved slightly backwards; in the lower jaw the posterior teeth the longest and strongest.

Fins—First dorsal spine rather more than half the height of the second, which is slightly shorter than the third, from thence the rest of the spines are about the same height. Ventral spine weak. Anal, first spine a little more than half the length of the second, which is the strongest but not quite so long as the third, the soft rays twice the length of the third spine. Fins rounded.

Lateral line—In upper fifth of body on the thirteenth row of scales.

Colours—Brownish grey on the back, the intensity of which gradually fades towards the abdomen. When living there are five or six dark vertical bands on the sides, but these fade after death. The whole of the head, body, and fins is covered with round dark brown, or black spots (sometimes absent on the fins), the largest, amounting to blotches, being on the sub- and inter-opercles and jaws. Fins darkish grey; dorsal darkest at its basal half, its margin also stained of a deep colour. Iris with a golden margin.

It does not appear to exceed thirteen inches in length.

Habitat—Seas of India, and Malaysia.

* Serranus flavo-cœruleus.

Serranus flavo-cœruleus, *Cuv. & Val.* ii. p. 297; *Bennett*, Fishes of Ceylon, pl. 19; *Günther*, Catal. i. p. 145.

B. vii. D. $\frac{11}{16\text{-}17}$. P. 18. V. $\frac{1}{5}$. A. $\frac{3}{8}$. C. 15.

Preopercle with flat and strong denticulations at the angle. Opercle with three flat spines, the superior and inferior of which are small, and with difficulty to be distinguished.

Fins—Caudal slightly emarginate, the other fins rounded.

Colours—Deep blue with some paler spots on the sides posterior to the pectorals, which as well as the back become brown after death. All the fins yellow, some black at the extremity of the ventrals.

Habitat—Seas of Ceylon, Malabar, Mozambique, and of the Mauritius.

* Serranus erythrurus.

Serranus erythrurus, *Cuv. & Val.* ii. p. 320.

B. vii. D. $\frac{11}{16}$. P. 17. V. $\frac{1}{5}$. A. $\frac{3}{9}$. C. 17.

Preopercle finely denticulated posteriorly, smooth inferiorly. Fins rounded.

Colours—Back and upper part of head greenish shot with red, the lower portion of the body silvery white. Dorsal greenish, pectorals, ventrals, and anal yellow, caudal red.

Serranus lanceolatus, Plate I. Fig. 1 and 2.

Holocentrus lanceolatus, *Bloch*, t. 242, f. 1. (*young.*)

Serranus lanceolatus, *Cuv. & Val.* ii. p. 316; *Cantor*, Catal. p. 8; *Günther*, Catal. i. p. 107.

PLATE I.

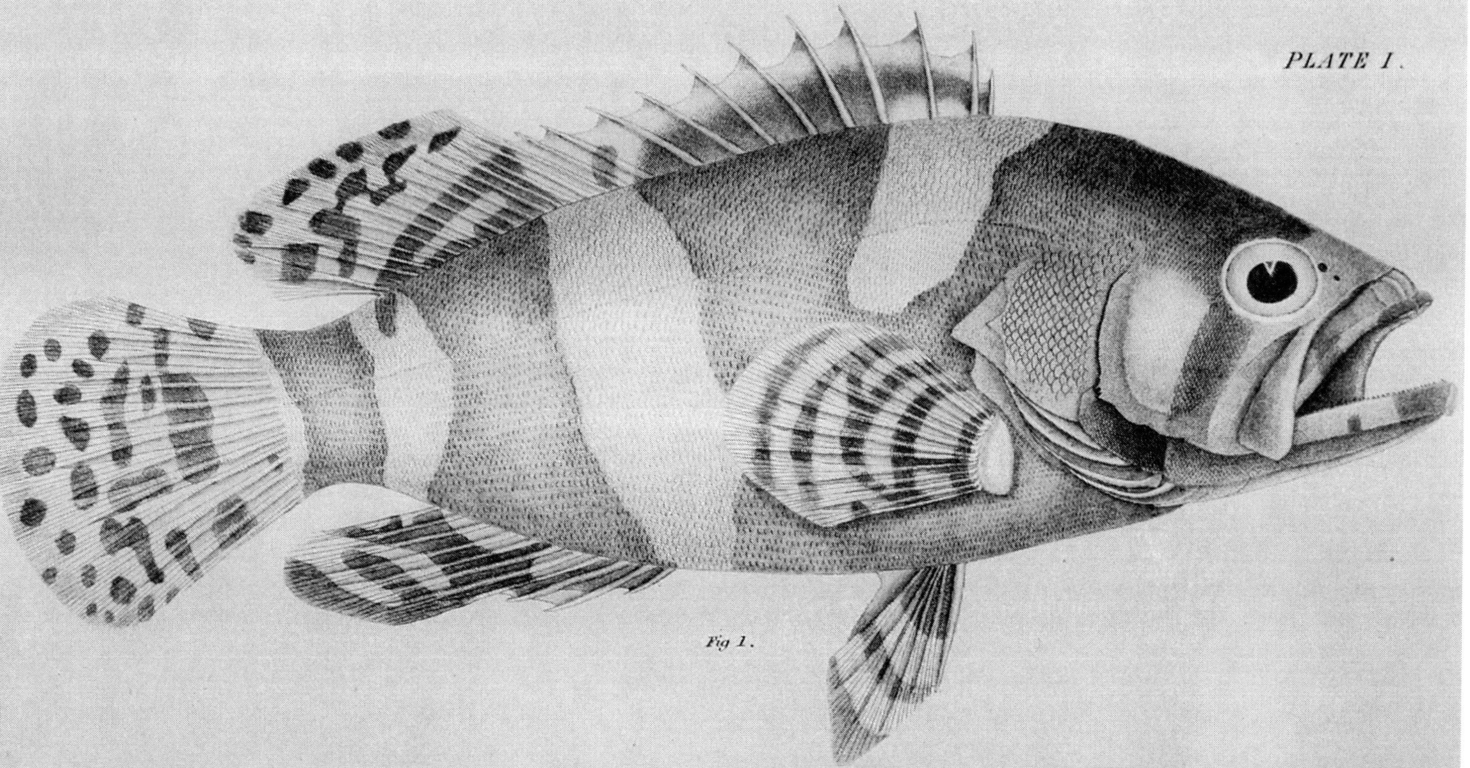

Fig 1.

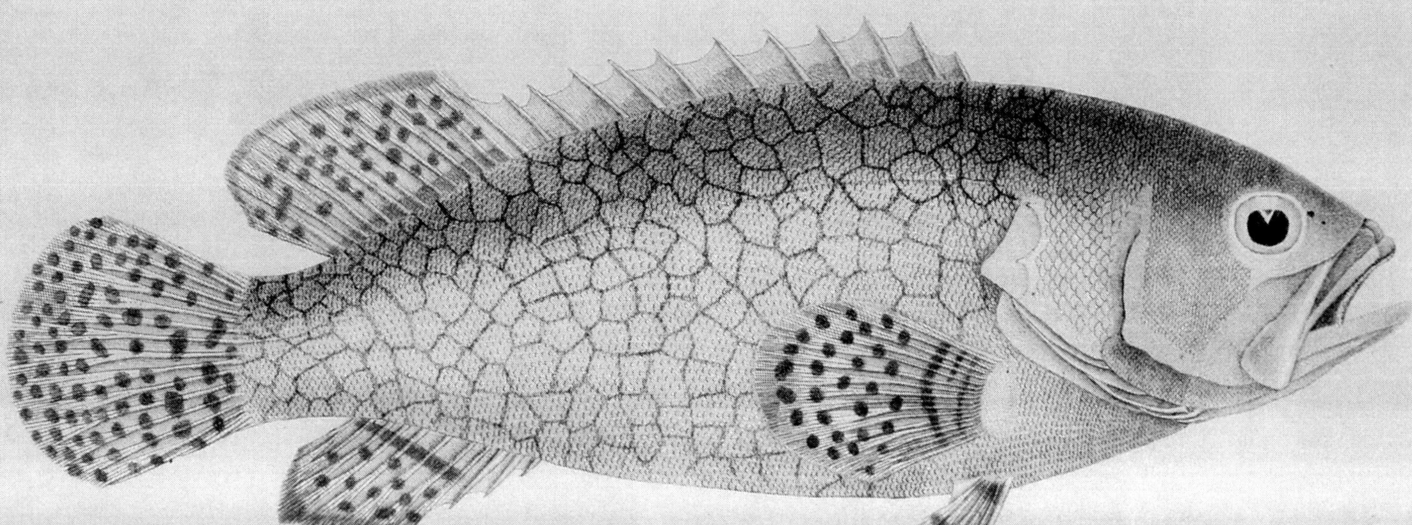

Fig 2.

F. Day, del. et sculp.

1. SERRANUS LANCEOLATUS. (Young.) 2. SERRANUS LANCEOLATUS. (Adult.)

SERRANUS HORRIDUS, *Cuv. & Val.* ii. p. 321; *Cantor*, Catal. p. 9; *Günther*, Catal. i. p. 136.

SUGGALAHTOO BONTOO, *Russell*, pl. 130. (*young.*) KURRUPU, *Mal.*

B. vii. D. $\frac{11}{15\text{-}16}$. P. 19. V. $\frac{1}{5}$. A. $\frac{3}{8}$. C. 17. L. r. 90-105.

Length of head $\frac{2}{7}$, of pectoral $\frac{1}{6}$, of caudal $\frac{1}{5}$, of base of dorsal $\frac{1}{2}$, of base of anal $\frac{1}{8}$ of the total length. Height of head $\frac{1}{5}$, of body $\frac{1}{4}$, of hard dorsal $\frac{1}{17}$, of soft dorsal $\frac{1}{9}$, of ventral $\frac{1}{8}$, of anal $\frac{1}{9}$ of the total length. In young specimens the proportionate height of the dorsal spines (as in some other Serrani) is greater than in the adult.

Eyes—Diameter $\frac{1}{8}$ length of head, $1\frac{1}{2}$ diameters apart, $1\frac{1}{4}$ from end of snout.

The maxilla reaches to beneath the posterior margin of the orbit: sub- and interopercles entire: preopercle with a rounded, finely serrated, posterior vertical margin: the serratures roughest at the angle, horizontal portion entire. Opercle with two spines, the inferior the most distinct. Preorbital entire, as are also the suprascapular, scapular, and coracoid bones.

Teeth—Villiform in jaws, vomer, and palatines: some larger ones in each intermaxillary: an external series of conical ones in the lower jaw: no canines.

Fins—The dorsal spines are not nearly so long as its rays: the first spine is little more than half the height of the second, which is a little more than three-quarters that of the third, from this they are all about equal in height, and nearly half as long as the soft portion of the fin. Ventral spine moderately strong. First spine of anal one-third the height of the second, which is two-thirds that of the third. Fins rounded.

Lateral line—In upper fifth of the body.

Colours—These vary exceedingly with the age of the fish; the very young are of a fine citrine or sulphur ground colour, with irregular black bands and markings, which become more distinct as the size of the fish increases: up to about a foot in length it continues of a bright gamboge, with five vertical blackish blue bands, the first passing from the orbit directly downwards over the preopercle: the second from the crown of the head downwards over the opercle, and slightly impinging on the preopercle joins the first band anteriorly whilst passing backwards over the pectoral fin it joins the third band, which last commences in the space occupied between the third and tenth dorsal spines, passes downwards, becomes narrower and coalesces with the second band in front as already described, and loses itself on the abdomen. The fourth band extends from the fifth to the last soft ray of the dorsal fin, and passes directly downwards to the whole of the base of the anal. The fifth band is situated between the base of the caudal, and the terminations of the dorsal and anal fins. There are some large black blotches on the jaws. The fins are of the same bright yellow ground colour as the body, and have black spots or blotches forming confluent lines near their bases, which in the pectoral are disposed in three or four arched undulating bands.

As the fish becomes upwards of a foot in length the intensity of the dark bands decreases, the vividness of the yellow ground colour of the body lessens, and marbling can be distinctly perceived over the whole of the surface, but the colour of the fins remains the same.

In the adult, hitherto known as the *Serranus horridus* (Plate I. figure 2, reduced from a specimen $22\frac{7}{10}$ inches in length), the back is brownish gradually fading into grey on the abdomen, the whole being marked over with blackish grey lines. The spinous portion of the dorsal brownish yellow, with a dark base: the soft portions of the fins of the same colours as in the young. Iris brown, with a golden rim.

It grows to a large size in Malabar. *Cantor* mentions one captured at Pinang, the weight of which exceeded 130 pounds. It is good eating.

Habitat—The seas of India and Malaysia.

SERRANUS DIACANTHUS.

SERRANUS DIACANTHUS, *Cuv. & Val.* ii. p. 319; *Günther*, Catal. i. p. 110.

KILLI MEEN, *Mal.*

B. vii. D. $\frac{11}{15}$. P. 19. V. $\frac{1}{5}$. A. $\frac{3}{8}$. C. 16-17. L. r. about 90.

Length of head $\frac{1}{3}$, of pectoral $\frac{1}{6}$, of caudal $\frac{1}{5}$, of base of dorsal $\frac{1}{2}$, of base of anal $\frac{1}{7}$ of total length. Height of head $\frac{2}{9}$, of body $\frac{1}{3}$, of hard dorsal $\frac{1}{12}$, of soft dorsal $\frac{1}{8}$, of ventral $\frac{2}{13}$, of anal $\frac{1}{8}$ of total length.

Eyes—Diameter $\frac{1}{5}$ length of head, $1\frac{1}{4}$ diameters apart, $1\frac{1}{2}$ diameters from end of snout.

The maxilla reaches to beneath the posterior margin of the orbit. Preorbital entire: sub- and interopercles entire: preopercle with a roughly serrated posterior vertical margin, the serratures becoming larger at the angle which is cut nearly square, the four lower teeth flat and exceedingly sharp, horizontal portion oblique, entire. Opercle with three spines, the central one of which is the largest, the other two being nearly concealed.

Teeth—Sharp and numerous in upper and lower jaws, vomer, and palate. A large canine on either intermaxillary, teeth in maxilla largest in front and curved backwards; in lower jaw largest behind and also directed backwards.

Fins—First dorsal spine slightly more than half the height of second, which is four-fifths of the height of the third, from thence all are the same. Ventral spine rather weak, not quite half the length of the rays. First anal spine not quite half so long as the second which is rather shorter than the third, which last is the strongest. In young specimens the comparative length of the spine to the rays is more than obtains in the adult. Fins rounded.

Lateral line—In upper fifth of body, on sixteenth row of scales.

Colours—Back brownish, fading into white on the abdomen, whilst the whole of the fish even over its brachiostegal rays is covered with bright orange spots, intermingled on the head and tail with brown ones. Head darkish, one vertical brown band commences at the margin of the first four dorsal spines, passes down them and descends nearly as low as the pectoral fin: a second arises between the seventh and ninth spines and is lost on the abdomen: two more descend from the soft portion of the dorsal fin, and a fifth crosses the tail between the termination of the dorsal fin and the origin of the caudal: whilst a sixth broad one crosses the base of this last fin. Pectoral reddish spotted with yellow: eye dark-brown, its upper part of the deepest tint.

Sometimes the caudal, pectoral, and ventral are unspotted, but marked with darker shades, and the bands are continued on to them. In young specimens the bands are most distinct, when the fish becomes upwards of a foot in length they begin to fade, likewise they always become more or less indistinct after death, and sometimes quite disappear.

The descriptions of the *Serranus suillus, C. & V.* and *S. salmonoides, Lacép.* apparently taken from large specimens, seem hardly to be dissimilar from the *S. diacanthus, C. & V.* excepting that the latter is banded: but as this portion of the colouration usually becomes obsolete in large specimens the distinction between the species appears to be still a desideratum.

Grows to a large size, and is good eating.

Habitat—The seas of India, China, and the Mauritius.

* Serranus formosus.

Rahtee bontoo, *Russell*, pl. 129.

Serranus formosus, *Cuv. & Val.* ii. p. 311; *Günther*, Catal. i. p. 154.

B. vii. D. $\frac{9}{16\text{-}18}$. P. 15. V. $\frac{1}{5}$. A. $\frac{3}{8\text{-}9}$. C. 17. L. r. 75.

Length of head nearly $\frac{1}{3}$ of total length. Eyes, diameter $\frac{2}{13}$ of length of head. Preopercle finely and evenly serrated; subopercle with some serratures: interopercle entire. Three strong spines on the opercle.

Colours—When alive extremely brilliant, but they soon fade after death; snout pale blue, lips and throat spotted with a deeper blue, and fillets of the same colour diverge from the orbit, and cross the yellow opercle, and branchial membrane. Back and sides variegated alternately with azure and dark yellow fillets. Dorsal interspinous membrane pale blue, edged with yellow; the other fins azure striped with dusky yellow.

Habitat—Seas of India, Malaysia, and China.

Genus GENYOROGE, *Cantor*.

Diacope, *Cuv. & Val.*

Branchiostegals, seven. Preopercle with a notch above its angle as deep as broad, receiving a more or less spinous knob of the interopercle. Opercle with two or three flat spines. Dorsal fin single, with from ten to eleven, rarely more, spines; anal with three. Teeth villiform, with canines in both jaws: teeth on palatines: tongue smooth, scales moderate.

Genyoroge cœruleopunctata.

Kallee maee, *Russell*, pl. 96.

Diacope cœruleopunctata, *Cuv. & Val.* ii. p. 424.

Genyoroge cœruleopunctata, *Günther*, Catal. i. p. 182.

B. vii. D. $\frac{10}{15}$. P. 16-17. V. $\frac{1}{5}$. A. $\frac{3}{8\text{-}9}$. C. 17. L. l. 45-50. L. tr. $\frac{9}{15}$.

Length of head $\frac{1}{3}$, of pectoral $\frac{1}{4}$, of caudal $\frac{1}{5}$, of base of dorsal $\frac{1}{2}$, of base of anal $\frac{1}{6}$ of total length. Height of head $\frac{1}{4}$, of body $\frac{1}{3}$, of hard dorsal $\frac{1}{9}$, of soft dorsal $\frac{1}{7}$, of ventral $\frac{1}{5}$, of anal $\frac{1}{5}$ of the total length.

Eyes—Transversely oval, horizontal diameter $3\frac{3}{4}$, and vertical diameter $4\frac{3}{4}$ in the length of the head, rather more than 1 diameter from the end of snout, and $\frac{1}{2}$ a diameter apart.

The profile rises considerably to the commencement of the dorsal fin, the eye is close to the summit of the head.

The maxilla extends backwards as far as the anterior margin of orbit: openings of nostrils in front of upper quarter of orbit. Preorbital with an irregular lower margin. Preopercle, vertical limb finely serrated, even in its notch which is situated close to where it makes its inferior curve, angle rounded, lower limb rather oblique, more coarsely serrated than its vertical margin. Sub- and interopercles entire, the latter with a large triangular tuberosity directed a little upwards and backwards and received into the preopercular notch; opercle with two flattened spines, the lower the largest.

Teeth—Villiform in both jaws in three or four rows, with an external series about three times the size of the others: two large canines in each intermaxillary. Villiform teeth on vomer and palate.

Fins—Dorsal spines very strong, increasing in length to the third, whilst from the fifth they decrease. Ventral spine moderately strong. First anal spine rather strong, half as long as second, which is very strong and slightly longer than the third, which is also weaker. Pectoral triangular, pointed. Caudal slightly emarginate. Soft portions of dorsal and anal rounded. Ventral pointed, first soft ray prolonged.

Scales—Above lateral line pass backwards and upwards, below it in horizontal parallel rows.

Lateral line—In upper quarter of body.

Colours—Back above the lateral line olive, with a bluish slate coloured spot in the centre of each scale, thus forming lines passing backwards and upwards. Abdomen greyish slate colour, with horizontal golden lines along the centre of each scale, and vertical dark ones passing along their bases, several beautiful blue lines pass downwards and backwards over the preopercle and are continued on to the opercle: two larger ones run horizontally along the preorbital and suborbital bones. A large white finger mark on the lateral line opposite the third, fourth, and fifth soft dorsal rays having a wide anterior black margin, and also a posterior superior one of the same colour. The white mark covers four scales transversely, and is one scale below and three above the lateral line; the anterior black margin is from three to four scales transversely, but posteriorly it only covers two. Dorsal fin slate coloured with the superior margin of the interspinous membrane orange red, membrane between the rays reddish, its external border pink with a narrow white margin. Pectoral with a reddish tinge. Ventral slate coloured with darkish margin. Caudal slate coloured tipped with red. Anal with some white spots, and the first portion of the soft rays edged with white. Eye golden, with a brownish red margin to the pupil. After death the colours fade, and it appears olivaceous with a large white finger mark edged with black on the side.

Grows to at least two feet in length.

Habitat—Seas of India and Malaysia.

GENYOROGE NOTATA.

ANTIKA DOONDIAWAH, *Russell*, pl. 98.
DIACOPE NOTATA, *Cuv. & Val.* ii. p. 422.
GENYOROGE NOTATA, *Cantor*, Catal. p. 12; *Günther*, Catal. i. p. 181.
VELLA CHEMBOLAY, *Mal.*

B. vii. D. $\frac{10}{14}$. P. 15-16. V. $\frac{1}{5}$. A. $\frac{3}{8}$. C. 19. L. l. 52. L. tr. $\frac{8}{14}$.

Length of head $\frac{1}{4}$, of pectoral $\frac{1}{5}$, of caudal $\frac{2}{15}$, of base of dorsal $\frac{1}{2}$, of base of anal $\frac{1}{9}$ of total length. Height of head $\frac{1}{5}$, of body $\frac{1}{3}$, of hard dorsal $\frac{1}{10}$, of soft dorsal $\frac{1}{9}$, of ventral $\frac{1}{6}$, of anal $\frac{1}{9}$ of total length.

Eyes—Transversely oval, horizontal diameter $\frac{1}{5}$, and vertical diameter $\frac{1}{4}$ of length of head, $\frac{1}{2}$ a transverse diameter apart, slightly more than 1 diameter from end of snout.

Maxilla extends backwards as far as anterior margin of the orbit: openings of nostrils in front of upper third of orbit. Preorbital with an irregular lower margin. Preopercle, vertical limb finely serrated, even in its deep notch for the reception of the tuberosity of the interopercle, and which is situated close to where it makes its inferior curve; angle rounded, inferior limb horizontal, convex, serrated but not so finely as its vertical limb. Sub- and interopercles entire, the latter with a large triangular tuberosity directed upwards and outwards, and received into the preopercular notch. Opercle with a small point, nearly concealed.

Teeth—A single external row of teeth in both jaws about three times the size of the three or four internal ones, which are villiform: two large canines in each intermaxillary. Teeth villiform on vomer and palate.

Fins—Dorsal spines rather strong, increasing in length to the third and fourth, from whence they decrease. Ventral spine moderately strong. First anal spine a little more than half the height of second, which is one-fifth longer than the third, whilst the third is weaker than the second. Pectoral, triangular, pointed. Caudal emarginate. Ventral with first ray prolonged.

Scales—Above lateral line pass backwards and upwards, below it in parallel rows.

Lateral line—In upper third of body.

Colours—Pinkish golden, superior surface of head and eye pink: cheeks, especially sub- and interopercles golden. Back pinkish, with oblique lines passing upwards and backwards, and which are sometimes of an orange colour. A large black spot on the lateral line opposite the fifth, sixth, and seventh rays of the dorsal, two-thirds of it being above the lateral line. Abdomen golden tinged with yellow, having a darker line running along the centre of each scale. Dorsal margined with white, beneath which is a line of black, the remainder reddish violet, with the exception of a light band running longitudinally along its centre. Caudal tipped with white, the remainder greyish red, with a light bar passing vertically across its centre. Anal tipped with white, reddish inferiorly, divided by a white line from a golden base. Ventrals and pectorals golden. The colours vary with age.

Does not appear to grow to a large size. *Russell* mentions one eleven inches.

Habitat—Seas of India and Malaysia.

* Genyoroge rivulata.

Diacope rivulata, *Cuv. & Val.* ii. p. 414, pl. 38.
Genyoroge rivulata, *Günther*, Catal. i. p. 182.

B. vii. D. $\frac{10}{14\text{-}16}$. P. 16. V. $\frac{1}{5}$. A. $\frac{3}{8\text{-}9}$. C. 16. L. l. 54.

Length of head $\frac{3}{11}$ of the total. Height of body $\frac{3}{10}$ of total length. Caudal fin slightly emarginate.

Colours—Violet, with white (blue ?) spots on the head, and oblique white lines which are irregularly tortuous, forming islands and rings on the opercles. Each of the scales on the body has a blue mark upon it. Abdomen rosy, the soft portions of the fins blackish. The anal and the ventrals have their margins stained blackish. *Dr. Günther* states that there is "a white spot above the lateral line, above the front edge of the anal fin, more or less visible in dried specimens;" but such is neither mentioned by *Cuv. & Val.* in their description, nor shown in their plate.

Grows to three and a half feet in length.

Habitat—Seas of India, Malaysia, and China.

* Genyoroge alboguttata.

Diacope alboguttata, *Cuv. & Val.* vii. p. 445.

B. vii. D. $\frac{10}{13}$. A. $\frac{3}{9}$.

Colours—Body grey, with purplish reflections, having a white spot on the side, which is traversed in the middle by the lateral line. Fins greyish, the spinous portion of the dorsal bordered with red.

This may be the *G. cæruleopunctata.* C. & V.

Habitat—Malabar.

GENUS MESOPRION, *Cuv.*

Branchiostegals, seven. Preopercle finely serrated, without or with a very open notch. Opercle with three, or two, more rarely with one indistinct point. Dorsal fin single, with from nine to twelve spines, anal with three. Teeth villiform in both jaws with canines, teeth on the vomer and palate. Scales moderate.

MESOPRION RANGUS.

RANGOO, *Russell*, pl. 94.

MESOPRION RANGUS, *Cuv. & Val.* ii. p. 481; *Cantor*, Catal. p. 14; *Günther*, Catal. i. p. 199.

B. vii. D. $\frac{10}{13\text{-}15}$. P. 16. V. $\frac{1}{5}$. A. $\frac{3}{8}$. C. 16-17. L. l. 46. L. tr. $\frac{7}{15}$.

Length of head $\frac{1}{3}$, of pectoral $\frac{1}{4}$, of caudal $\frac{1}{5}$, of base of dorsal $\frac{2}{5}$, of base of anal $\frac{1}{8}$ of total length. Height of head $\frac{1}{4}$, of body $\frac{1}{3}$, of hard dorsal $\frac{1}{8}$, of soft dorsal $\frac{1}{8}$, of base of caudal $\frac{1}{10}$, of ventral $\frac{1}{6}$, of anal $\frac{1}{7}$ of total length.

Eye—Transversely oval, horizontal diameter $\frac{1}{4}$, and vertical diameter $\frac{1}{5}$ of the length of the head, $1\frac{1}{3}$ diameter from end of snout, $\frac{2}{3}$ of a diameter apart.

Maxilla extends to beneath the anterior margin of orbit. Openings of nostrils rather wide apart, in front of upper fourth of orbit. Preorbital entire. Preopercle emarginate and finely serrated on its vertical limb, angle rounded, lower limb oblique and serrated, the largest serratures being on its posterior half. Sub- and interopercles entire, in the latter is a slight tuberosity at its superior part. Opercle with two points. Suprascapular lineated and serrated.

Teeth—An external conical row in both jaws, with several bands of villiform ones behind. A pair of canines at the external margin of each intermaxillary, the outer much the largest. Villiform teeth on vomer and palate.

Fins—Dorsal spines moderately strong, first slightly more than one-third height of second, which is a little above three quarters as long as the third, from thence they decrease, the spinous portion occupies nearly three fourths of the length of the fin. Ventral spine weak. Second anal spine longest, and much the strongest, being twice as long as the first, and four-fifths longer than the third. Soft portions of dorsal and anal rather pointed. Caudal truncated and slightly emarginate. Ventral pointed, first ray prolonged.

Scales—None between or before orbits, two broad rows, separated by several smaller ones, pass over the shoulders. Above the lateral line the rows are a little irregular, at first parallel to the back, they subsequently turn upwards to the soft dorsal, beyond which their course is straight. Below the lateral line the first five rows terminate in it, those below passing horizontally.

Lateral line—In upper fourth of body, parallel with the back.

Colours—Back of a dark reddish brown, which below the lateral line becomes of a dull cherry red: the bases of the scales darker than their circumference. Pectoral orange, edges of caudal reddish brown, the other fins greyish brown. A blue line runs along the suborbital ring of bones. Eye dark red. The young have eight or nine irregular and very narrow vertical white bands on the body, a reddish orange streak along the margin of the hard dorsal, the ventrals externally with a broad white margin, and the lower part of the cheeks tinged with golden.

Common; esteemed for food in Malabar and Pinang, not at Vizagapatam. Grows to upwards of two feet in length.

Habitat—Seas of India and Malaysia.

MESOPRION RUBELLUS. Plate II. Fig. 2.

MESOPRION RUBELLUS, *Cuv. & Val.* ii. p. 475.
? JAHNGARAH, *Russell*, pl. 90.

B. vii. D. $\frac{10}{14}$. P. 16. V. $\frac{1}{5}$. A. $\frac{3}{8\text{-}9}$. C. 17. L. l. 46. L. tr. $\frac{7}{13}$.

Length of head $\frac{2}{7}$, of pectoral $\frac{1}{4}$, of caudal $\frac{2}{11}$, of base of dorsal $\frac{2}{5}$, of anal $\frac{1}{9}$ of total length. Height of head $\frac{2}{9}$, of body $\frac{2}{7}$, of hard dorsal $\frac{1}{9}$, of soft dorsal $\frac{1}{9}$, of ventral $\frac{1}{6}$, of anal $\frac{1}{9}$ of total length.

Eyes—Transversely oval, horizontal diameter $\frac{1}{5}$, vertical diameter $\frac{1}{6}$ of length of head, nearly 2 diameters from end of snout, $\frac{3}{4}$ of a diameter apart.

Maxilla extends to beneath the anterior third of orbit. Preopercle, vertical limb finely serrated in the whole of its extent, it is slightly emarginate, angle moderately rounded, with three or four blunt denticulations; lower limb oblique, entire. Sub- and interopercles entire, no protuberance on the latter. Opercle with two blunt points, no distinct spines. Suprascapular serrated.

Teeth—An external row of conical teeth in both jaws, smallest in the upper: several bands of villiform teeth in upper, but not so numerous in lower jaw still existing in its entire length. Canines in each intermaxillary. Villiform teeth on vomer and palate.

Fins—Dorsal spines moderately strong, the first nearly one-third height of second which is about one-sixth shorter than the third, the fourth is a little shorter, and they gradually decrease. Ventral spine weak. Second anal spine much the strongest, twice the length of the first but three-thirteenths shorter than the third. Pectoral pointed. Anal rather pointed. Caudal truncated, emarginate.

Scales—In horizontal rows both above and below lateral line.

Colours —Back greyish brown, chest orange, abdomen and sides of a light violet, each scale tipped with white. Cheeks orange, scales with a white exterior. Hard dorsal greyish, soft dorsal yellowish grey. Caudal brownish. Pectoral with a tinge of red. Hard portion of anal greyish, soft portion yellowish grey. Ventrals greyish, with an orange base. Eye silvery with a golden rim round the pupil.

Grows to a large size, and is excellent eating.

Habitat—Seas of India and Red sea.

MESOPRION JOHNII.

ANTHIAS JOHNII, *Bloch*, t. 318.
DOONDIAWAH, *Russell*, pl. 97.
COIUS CATUS, *Ham. Buch.* pp. 90, 369, pl. 38, f. 30.
MESOPRION UNIMACULATUS, *Cuv. & Val.* ii. p. 441.
MESOPRION JOHNII, *Cuv. & Val.* ii. p. 443; *Cantor*, Catal. p. 13; *Günther*, Catal. i. p. 200.
CHEMBOLAY, *Mal.*

B. vii. D. $\frac{10}{14}$. P. 16-18. V. $\frac{1}{5}$. A. $\frac{3}{8}$. C. 16-17. L. l. 48. L. tr. $\frac{7}{10}$.

Length of head $\frac{1}{3}$, of pectoral $\frac{1}{4}$, of caudal $\frac{1}{5}$, of base of dorsal $\frac{2}{5}$, of base of anal $\frac{1}{8}$ of the total length. Height of head $\frac{1}{4}$, of body $\frac{2}{7}$, of hard dorsal $\frac{1}{8}$, of soft dorsal $\frac{1}{7}$, of ventral $\frac{1}{5}$, of anal $\frac{1}{6}$ of the total length.

Eyes—Diameter $\frac{1}{5}$ of length of head, more than $\frac{1}{2}$ a diameter apart, 1 diameter from end of snout.

Maxilla extends to beneath the anterior margin of orbit: in young specimens to its anterior third; openings of nostrils wide apart, opposite upper third of orbit, which is close to the profile. Preorbital with an irregular lower margin. Preopercle, vertical limb finely serrated above, more coarsely along its concavity, angle rounded, inferior limb nearly horizontal, having from eight to ten serratures. Sub- and interopercles entire, the latter with a tuberosity, the size of which varies. Opercle with two flat spines, the lowest the largest. Suprascapular serrated.

Teeth—Villiform in both jaws, in two or three rows, with an external conical band about three times the size of the others: two large canines in either intermaxillary: villiform teeth on vomer and palate.

Fins—First dorsal spine half the height of second, which is two thirds the length of the next, which is one-thirteenth shorter than the fourth, the highest in the fin, from thence they decrease to the last; all the spines are moderately strong. Ventral spine pretty strong. First anal spine rather strong, two-fifths the length of the second which is the longest and strongest, the third being one-eleventh shorter. Soft portions of dorsal and anal rounded. Caudal slightly emarginate. Ventral pointed, first ray prolonged.

Scales—None between or before the eyes. Above the opercle they run upwards and backwards to the first six dorsal spines, beyond this they proceed in five horizontal rows parallel to the back, the superior row terminating at the end of dorsal fin. Below the lateral line the scales are in horizontal rows, the first three terminating on the lateral line, which passes parallel to the back.

Colours—Back greenish, abdomen yellowish, a large black finger mark on the lateral line, between the twenty-second and thirtieth scales, extending to one below, and three above it. Head and cheeks rather lighter than the rest of the body, and of a golden tinge shot with purple, a lighter line passes over the broad scales on the shoulder. Along the centre of each row of scales is a dark mark which is more apparent in some fish than in others; in the Ganges, at Pinang and elsewhere it is nearly black, dependant upon the character of the water. In some specimens each scale is tipped with a metallic golden colour. Dorsal spinous portion grey: soft dorsal, caudal, ventral, and anal yellowish dashed with red Pectoral yellowish.

Common, grows to five feet in length, and is fair eating.

Habitat—Seas and estuaries of India, Malaysia, China, Australia, and the Pacific Occan.

MESOPRION SILLAOO. Plate II. Fig. 1.

MESOPRION SILLAOO, *Cuv. & Val.* ii. p. 476.
SILLAOO, *Russell*, pl. 100.

B. vii. D. $\frac{10}{15}$. P. 16. V. $\frac{1}{5}$. A. $\frac{3}{8}$. C. 17. L. l. 50. L. tr. $\frac{7}{12}$.

Length of head $\frac{2}{7}$, of pectoral $\frac{1}{4}$, of caudal $\frac{1}{6}$, of base of dorsal $\frac{2}{5}$, of base of anal $\frac{1}{9}$ of total length. Height of head $\frac{1}{4}$, of body $\frac{2}{7}$, of hard dorsal $\frac{2}{19}$, of soft dorsal $\frac{1}{4}$, of ventral $\frac{2}{13}$, of anal $\frac{1}{9}$ of total length.

Eye—Transversely oval, its transverse diameter $\frac{1}{5}$, and its vertical $\frac{1}{6}$ of length of head, nearly 2 diameters from end of snout, $\frac{5}{6}$ of a diameter apart.

Maxilla extends to beneath the anterior third of orbit. Preopercle, vertical limb widely but not deeply emarginate in its lower half, where it is finely serrated, angle rounded with about six very blunt denticulations, lower limb very short and horizontal. Sub- and interopercles entire, a protuberance in the upper angle of the latter. Opercle with two blunted points, no distinct spines. Suprascapular veined but entire.

Teeth—An external row of conical teeth in both jaws, with two or three villiform bands in each intermaxillary and upper jaw, but only a few in the anterior portion of the lower jaw. Large canines in each intermaxillary. Numerous fine villiform teeth on vomer and palate.

PLATE II.

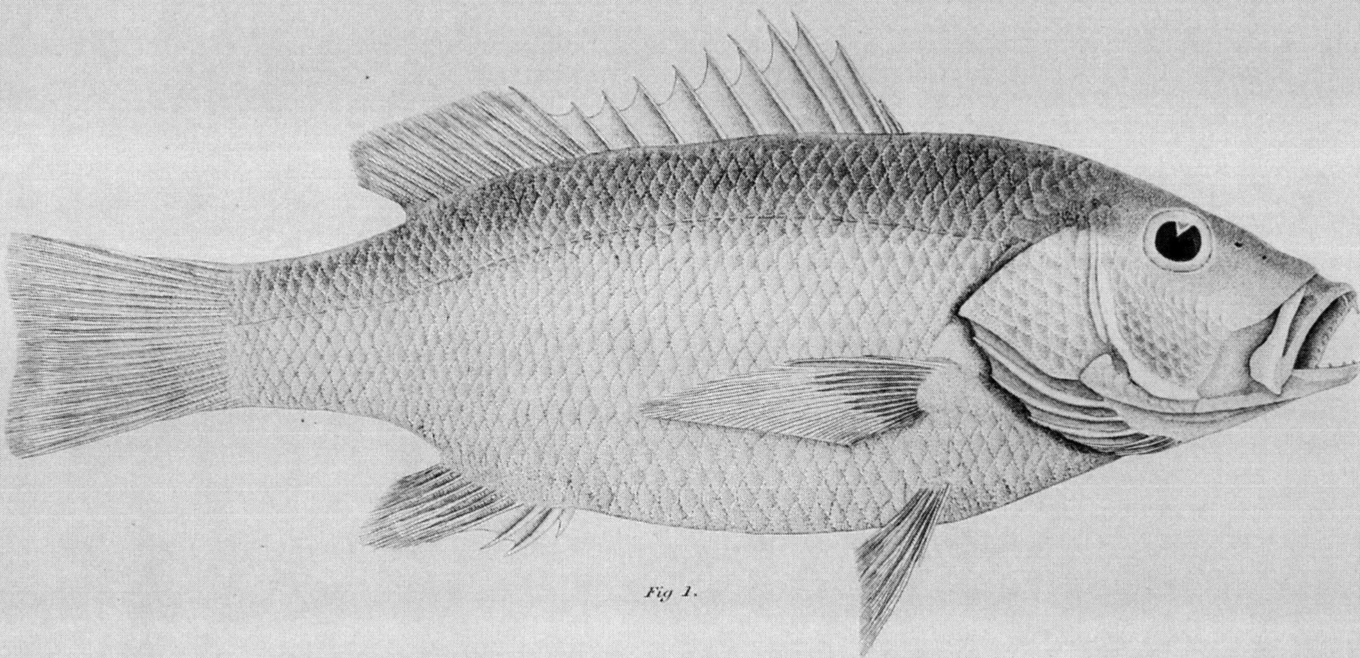

Fig 1.

Fig 2.

F. Day, del. et sculp.

1. MESOPRION SILLAOO. 2. MESOPRION RUBELLUS.

Fins—Dorsal spines not very strong, they occupy above half the length of the base of the fin, interspinous membrane rather deeply notched. Third and fourth spines the longest, from these they decrease to the ninth, whilst the last is slightly produced. Ventral spine weak. First anal spine not quite half the height of second which is slightly the strongest, whilst the third is the longest.

Scales—None between or before the orbits, an arched very conspicuous double row over the nape. Those on the body both above and below the lateral line pass horizontally, but opposite the termination of the soft dorsal the rows become undulating in their course.

Lateral line—Situated in upper fourth of body, parallel to the back.

Colours—Back brownish red, with the base of each scale greyish brown or ash coloured. Below the lateral line bright deep lake. Each scale rather darker at its base than at its margin. Cheeks orange scarlet. Under surface of throat and chest scarlet, with a shade of orange. A bright blue zig-zag line passes along either side of the snout over preorbital and suborbital ring of bones. Dorsal, hard portion brownish grey: the soft orange scarlet. Anal, hard portion greyish: the soft scarlet. Pectoral scarlet, deepest at its margin. Eye, bluish grey with a golden red centre. In the young fish the colours are rather brighter, but they soon fade after death.

Common, grows to a large size, and is excellent eating.

Habitat—Seas of India.

MESOPRION FULVIFLAMMA.

SCIÆNA FULVIFLAMMA. *Forskål, p.* 45.

MESOPRION FULVIFLAMMA, *Cuv. & Val.* ii. p. 423; *Günther*, Catal. i. p. 201.

B. vii. D. $\frac{10}{13\text{-}14}$. P. 16. V. $\frac{1}{5}$. A. $\frac{3}{8}$. C. 17. L. l. 43-50. L tr. $\frac{7}{16}$. Cæc. pylor. 5.

Length of head $\frac{1}{3}$, of pectoral $\frac{1}{4}$, of caudal $\frac{1}{5}$, of base of dorsal $\frac{1}{2}$, of base of anal $\frac{1}{7}$ of total length. Height of head $\frac{1}{4}$, of body $\frac{1}{3}$, of hard dorsal $\frac{1}{7}$, of soft dorsal $\frac{1}{7}$, of ventrals $\frac{2}{11}$, of anal $\frac{1}{7}$ of total length.

Eyes—Horizontal diameter $\frac{1}{3}$, and vertical diameter $\frac{2}{7}$ of length of head, 1 diameter from end of snout, $\frac{1}{2}$ a diameter apart.

Maxilla extends to beneath the centre of the orbit. Preorbital entire. Preopercle, vertical limb indistinctly emarginate and finely serrated, angle rounded where the serratures are stronger, lower limb oblique and rather coarsely serrated. Sub- and interopercles entire; no knob on the latter. Two rather strong but blunt spines to opercle.

Teeth—In jaws villiform, with an external larger row, and canines in each intermaxillary. Villiform teeth on vomer and palate.

Fins—First dorsal spine half the height of second, which is two-thirds that of the third which is nearly equal with fourth and fifth, from thence they gradually decrease: they are moderately strong, and the interspinous membrane is deeply notched. Second anal spine slightly longest and strongest. Ventral pointed. Caudal truncated.

Scales—Above lateral line pass backwards and upwards, below it in horizontal rows.

Colours—Back yellowish olive and in some specimens rose colour, abdomen yellow with oblique olivaceous lines passing upwards and backwards above the lateral line and longitudinal ones below it. A black spot on lateral line from twenty-third to twenty-sixth transverse scales. Fins yellowish. Dorsal tipped with black, pectoral olive, last half of caudal stained blackish grey. Eye golden.

Habitat—Red Sea, and Seas of India, Malaysia, China, and Seychelles.

MESOPRION AUROLINEATUS. PLATE III.

MESOPRION AUROLINEATUS, *Cuv. & Val.* iii. p. 496.

B. vii. D. $\frac{10}{13\text{-}14}$. P. 16. V. $\frac{1}{5}$. A. $\frac{3}{8}$. C. 17. L. l. 46. L. tr. $\frac{7}{13}$.

Length of head $\frac{4}{15}$, of pectoral $\frac{2}{9}$, of caudal $\frac{1}{6}$, of base of dorsal $\frac{1}{3}$, of base of anal $\frac{1}{8}$ of total length. Height of head $\frac{1}{6}$, of body $\frac{1}{3}$, of hard dorsal $\frac{1}{4}$, of soft dorsal $\frac{1}{6}$, of ventral $\frac{1}{6}$, of anal $\frac{1}{8}$ of total length.

Eyes—Situated close to the margin of prôfile: its diameter $\frac{2}{7}$ in length of head, upwards of 1 diameter from end of snout, $\frac{1}{2}$ a diameter apart.

Maxilla extends to beneath the anterior margin of the orbit: openings of nostrils wide apart opposite its upper fourth. Preorbital entire. Preopercle, vertical limb very slightly emarginate, finely serrated, angle rounded where the serratures become coarser, but they diminish in size as they approach the anterior end of the lower limb, which is slightly oblique. Sub- and interopercles entire. Opercle with two points. Suprascapular denticulated.

Teeth—An external row of conical teeth in both jaws, with several villiform rows behind: each intermaxillary crowded with villiform teeth and having two canines, the external of which is curved and very large in comparison to the size of the fish.

Fins—First dorsal spine half the length of the second, which is one-tenth shorter than the third, whilst the fourth is slightly the longest, from thence they very gradually decrease to the last, they are all rather strong. Ventral spine weak. Anal, second spine much the longest and strongest. Pectoral pointed. Soft portions of dorsal and anal rounded. Caudal slightly emarginate. Ventral pointed, first ray prolonged.

Scales—Above the lateral line they pass in an ascending backward series of rows to the base of the dorsal, beyond the end of that fin they proceed parallel to the back: below the lateral line the first four rows pass horizontally, and terminate in it, whilst the next five or six pass direct to the caudal.

Lateral line—Is situated in the upper third of the body parallel to the back.

Colours—Back olive shot with yellow: abdomen yellow with several brilliant, horizontal, golden lines, which are divided by a darker one running along the centre of each row of scales, so that each golden one is on part of two rows. A large black finger mark is situated on the lateral line from the twenty-second to the thirty-first scales, extending for three scales below and one and a half above it. Dorsal and pectoral olive. Caudal and anal olive yellow. Ventrals golden. Iris golden.

Very rare, has not been taken of a large size.

Habitat—Malabar and Ceylon; in *Sir Emerson Tennent's* drawings of the "Fishes of Ceylon," already referred to, is one apparently of this species marked "Taloorvah."

* MESOPRION MADRAS.

MESOPRION MADRAS, *Cuv. & Val.* vii. p. 446; *Günther*, Catal. i. p. 200.

B. vii. D. $\frac{10}{13}$. A. $\frac{3}{9}$. L. l. 55-60.

Length of head $\frac{2}{7}$ of total length. Height of body $\frac{4}{15}$ of total length. Diameter of eye $\frac{2}{7}$ of length of head. Preopercle finely serrated not emarginate. Interopercle entirely covered with scales. Spines of dorsal and anal fins rather feeble, fourth dorsal spine longest. Caudal truncated.

Colours—Yellowish red, with reddish brown longitudinal streaks, cheeks reddish, fins yellow.

Attains one foot in length at Mahé, and is good eating.

Habitat—Malabar, Batavia, and the Seychelles.

PLATE III.

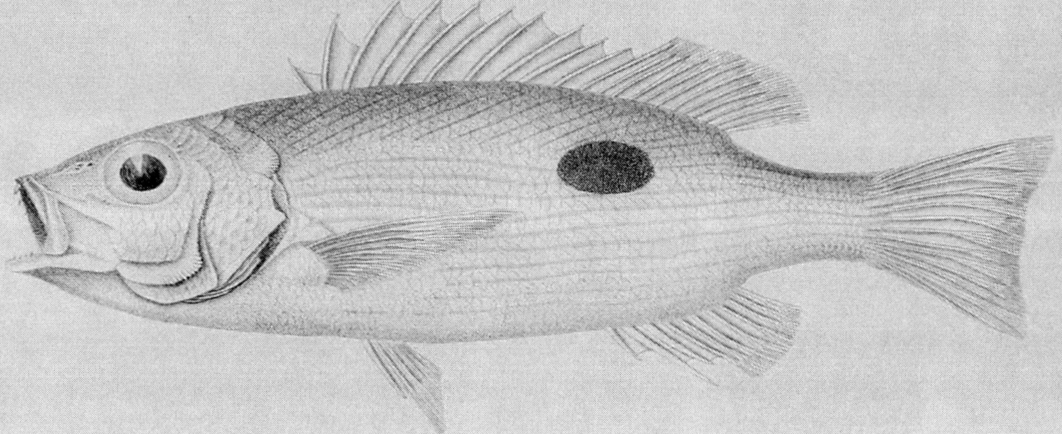

F. Day, del, et sculp.

MESOPRION AUROLINEATUS

GENUS AMBASSIS, *Cuv. and Val.*

CHANDA, *Ham. Buch.*
BAGODA, pt. *Bleeker.*

Branchiostegals, six: two dorsals, the first with seven spines, the anal with three. A recumbent spine in front of dorsal fin, pointing forwards. Lower limb of preopercle with a double denticulated edge. Opercle without a prominent spine. Body compressed, more or less diaphanous. No canines, but teeth on vomer and palatine bones. Scales large or moderate, frequently deciduous.

AMBASSIS COMMERSONII.

AMBASSIS COMMERSONII, *Cuv. & Val.* ii. p. 176, pl. 25; *Günther*, Catal. i. p. 223.

B. vi. D. 7 | $\frac{1}{9\text{-}11}$. P. 15. V. $\frac{1}{5}$. A. $\frac{3}{9}$. L. l. 30-33. L. tr. $\frac{5}{12}$. Vert. $\frac{9}{15}$.

Length of head $\frac{2}{7}$, of pectoral $\frac{1}{5}$, of caudal $\frac{1}{4}$, of base of dorsal $\frac{1}{3}$, of base of anal $\frac{1}{6}$ of total length. Height of head $\frac{1}{6}$, of body $\frac{1}{3}$, of first dorsal $\frac{1}{6}$, of second dorsal $\frac{1}{9}$, of ventral $\frac{1}{7}$, of anal $\frac{1}{6}$ of total length.

Eyes—Diameter $\frac{1}{4}$ length of head, 1 diameter from end of snout, nearly 1 diameter apart.

Maxilla extends to beneath the anterior third of orbit. Nostrils comparatively large. Preorbital rather strongly denticulated, denticulations passing downwards and slightly backwards. Preopercle, vertical limb finely denticulated, inferior limb with its double edge denticulated, the posterior teeth the coarsest with the exception of two or three large ones at the angle of the anterior edge. Inferior margin of interopercle very finely serrated at its posterior angle: in young specimens these serratures are only visible with the aid of a magnifying glass. Subopercle entire. Two or three very blunt and small spinous processes at posterior superior angle of orbit.

Teeth—Villiform, an external series of conical ones, about three times as large as the posterior rows, exists in both jaws and each intermaxillary. Teeth on vomer and palatines, in a single sharp series.

Fins—Dorsal spines moderately strong, straight, or curved slightly backwards, second the longest, from whence they decrease to the last. Ventral spine not very strong. First anal spine two-sevenths of length of the second and third which are equal, but the second spine is at least twice as broad as the third. First dorsal triangular. Pectoral rather pointed, reaching as far as first spine of anal. Ventral triangular, it does not extend so far as the anal by the length of the diameter of the orbit.

Scales—Deciduous. Lateral line at first convex, becoming nearly horizontal opposite posterior third of second dorsal.

Colours—Beautifully silvered with purplish reflections, a bright silvery metallic band of colour passes from orbit to centre of caudal. Opercle of burnished silver, back slightly greenish; the silvery peritoneum is visible through the abdominal walls. In some specimens there is a blackish mark between the first and second spines of dorsal, and also between the upper part of the second and third.

Common, grows in Malabar to seven inches in length. Found in fresh and brackish water.

Habitat—Fresh waters and estuaries of the East Indies, sometimes in the sea. Also the Red Sea, Mauritius, and the shores of North Australia.

AMBASSIS NALUA.

AMBASSIS NALUA, *Cuv. & Val.* ii. p. 182; *Günther*, Catal. i. p. 225.
CHANDA NALUA, *Buch. Ham.* pp. 107, 371, pl. 6, f. 36; *Cantor*, Catal. p. 6.

B. vi. D. 7 | $\frac{1}{10\text{-}11}$. P. 15. V. $\frac{1}{5}$. A. $\frac{3}{9\text{-}10}$. L. l. 30. L. tr. $\frac{5}{12}$.

Length of head $\frac{1}{3}$, of pectoral $\frac{2}{9}$, of caudal $\frac{1}{4}$, of base of dorsals $\frac{1}{3}$, of base of anal $\frac{1}{6}$ of total length. Height of head $\frac{2}{9}$, of body $\frac{2}{7}$, of first dorsal $\frac{2}{9}$, of second dorsal $\frac{1}{6}$, of ventral $\frac{1}{5}$, of anal $\frac{1}{6}$ of total length.

Eyes—Diameter $\frac{1}{3}$ length of head, $\frac{5}{7}$ of a diameter from end of snout, rather more than $\frac{1}{2}$ a diameter apart.

Maxilla extends to beneath the anterior third of orbit. Nostrils comparatively large. Preorbital with strong denticulations passing downwards and slightly backwards, and being largest posteriorly. Preopercle, vertical limb finely denticulated, inferior limb with its double edge denticulated, the posterior teething the coarsest, with the exception of one large tooth at the anterior angle. Inferior margin of interopercle strongly denticulated; thus with the double denticulated edge of the preopercle there are three parallel lines of teeth in this species. Subopercle entire. One sharp spine directed backwards at posterior superior angle of orbit, and two or three more along its posterior edge, separated from the first by a notch.

Teeth—Villiform, small, equal, on jaws, vomer, and palatines.

Fins—Dorsal spines moderately strong, curved slightly upwards in their external third; the second anal spine is also curved slightly forwards. Second spine of first dorsal very slightly the longest, its last spine half the length of that of the second dorsal. Ventral spine comparatively long, and reaches close to the first anal spine, whilst its soft rays extend as far as the third anal spine. First anal spine one-third the length of the second and third, which are equal, the second being slightly the strongest. First dorsal triangular. Pectoral rather pointed, and reaching as far as third or fourth anal ray. Ventral triangular. Caudal deeply forked.

Scales—Hardly deciduous. Lateral line convex to opposite termination of second dorsal, where it becomes horizontal.

Colours—Back greyish green with minute brown points, abdomen silvery, with a silver longitudinal band, and having pinkish reflections; opercles silvery, fins greyish, first and second spine of first dorsal with a blackish anterior margin: fine grey points on fin membrane more especially between second and third spines. Caudal minutely spotted. Eye silvery.

Does not appear to exceed five inches in length.

Habitat—Rivers and estuaries of Malabar, Bengal and Malaysia.

Ambassis Dussumieri.

Ambassis Dussumieri, *Cuv. & Val.* ii. p. 181, vi. p. 503, ix. p. 431; *Günther*, i. p. 225.
Chanda Dussumieri, *Cantor*, Catal. p. 6.

B. vi. D. 7 | $\frac{1}{9\text{-}10}$. P. 15. V. $\frac{1}{5}$. A. $\frac{3}{9\text{-}10}$. C. 17. L. l. 27. L. tr. $\frac{3}{8}$.

Length of head $\frac{1}{4}$, of pectoral $\frac{1}{6}$, of caudal $\frac{1}{4}$, of base of dorsals, $\frac{2}{7}$, of base of anal $\frac{1}{5}$ of total length. Height of head $\frac{1}{6}$, of body $\frac{1}{4}$, of first dorsal $\frac{1}{5}$, of second dorsal $\frac{1}{8}$, of ventral $\frac{1}{6}$, of anal $\frac{1}{7}$ of total length.

Eyes—Diameter not quite $\frac{1}{3}$ of length of head, $\frac{1}{2}$ a diameter from end of snout, and the same distance apart.

Maxilla extends to beneath the anterior margin of orbit, its extremity being pointed. Nostrils rather large. Preorbital with six strong denticulations directed downwards and a little backwards on its anterior margin, whilst its posterior edge next to the orbit is also serrated. Preopercle, vertical limb entire, inferior limb with a double denticulated edge, the anterior having the largest teeth, the posterior one of which is large and triangular. Sub-

and interopercles entire. Two strong spines directed backwards at posterior superior angle of orbit.

Teeth—Villiform, small, and equal.

Fins—Dorsal spines strong, the second slightly the longest, and very minutely serrated on its posterior margin, as is also that of the second dorsal: all the spines are transversely striated. Third anal spine slightly longer, but not quite so strong as second, which is about five times as long as the first. Ventral spine moderately strong and reaches only half way to base of anal. Fins shaped as in the last species *A. nalua*.

Scales—Scales not very deciduous. A row at the base of dorsal and anal rays.

Lateral line—Passes straight for eleven scales along the third row, is then interrupted and continued along fifth row to the tail. No cœcal appendages.

Colours—Back and summit of head greenish, minutely dotted with fine black points, fading to silvery along the sides and abdomen, with a bright silvery line passing from opercle to centre of tail. Cheeks silvery. Fins transparent with a yellowish tinge, blackish between second and third dorsal spines, due to numerous fine dots. Caudal with a blackish margin. Iris silvery, upper half blackish.

Eaten by the Natives. Grows to four inches in length. Not uncommon.

Habitat—Seas and estuaries of Malabar, Malaysia, China, the Celebes, Mauritius, and Seychelles.

Genus THERAPON, *Cuvier*.

Pelates, *Cuvier*.

Datnia, *Cuv. & Val.*

Branchiostegals, six: pseudobranchiæ. Eyes of moderate size. One dorsal with twelve, rarely thirteen, spines; interspinous membrane more or less emarginate. Preopercle serrated. Opercle spiniferous. Teeth villiform in both jaws, sometimes with an external conical series; deciduous on vomer and palate. Scales moderate. Air bladder divided by a contraction. Cœcal pylorica in moderate numbers.

Therapon trivittatus.

Keelputa, *Russell*, pl. 126.

Coius trivittatus, *Ham. Buch.* pp. 92, 370.

Therapon puta, *Cuv. & Val.* iii. p. 131.

Therapon trivittatus, *Cantor*, Catal. p. 19; *Günther*, Catal. i. p. 280.

Keetcha, *Mal.*

B. vi. D. $\frac{11\text{-}12}{10}$. P. 13-15. V. $\frac{1}{5}$. A. $\frac{3}{8\text{-}9}$. C. 17. L. l. 95-100. L. tr. $\frac{15}{24}$. Cœc. pylor. 7.

Length of head $\frac{1}{4}$, of pectoral $\frac{1}{6}$, of caudal $\frac{1}{6}$, of base of dorsal $\frac{1}{2}$, of base of anal $\frac{1}{6}$ of total length. Height of head $\frac{2}{11}$, of body $\frac{1}{4}$, of dorsal spines $\frac{1}{6}$, of dorsal rays $\frac{1}{9}$, of ventral $\frac{1}{6}$, of anal $\frac{1}{9}$ of total length.

Eyes—Transversely oval, horizontal diameter $\frac{1}{3}$, vertical diameter $\frac{1}{4}$ of length of head, $\frac{1}{2}$ a diameter apart, $\frac{3}{4}$ of a diameter from end of snout.

Maxilla extends to beneath the anterior margin of the orbit. Preorbital strongly denticulated, more especially at its posterior portion. Preopercle, with five strong spines on its vertical limb, the middle of which is generally the largest, and the two inferior larger than the two superior ones: lower limb with about ten comparatively fine denticulations. Sub- and interopercles entire. Opercle with two spines, the inferior the longest and strongest, and about equal to the largest of those of the preopercle.

Teeth—Villiform in the jaws, with an external slightly larger row. Vomer without teeth, except in the very young.

Fins—Dorsal spines rather slender, the fourth and fifth equal and the longest, from whence they decrease to the last but one, the last being a little higher. Ventral spine slender, first soft ray elongated. Second anal spine twice the length of the first, and the strongest, but a little shorter than the third: spinous portion, exclusive of the last spine, forming a long triangle. Pectoral rounded. Ventral pointed. Caudal emarginate.

Scales—None on summit of head, opercle scaled.

Lateral line—Follows the curve of the back in its upper fourth in rather an irregular course.

Colours—Back dark grey with a greenish tinge, becoming much lighter towards the abdomen, which is dirty white. Three longitudinal brownish black bands, the inferior passing direct from the eye, between the two spines of opercle to the centre of caudal: the superior from the back of the head to the commencement of soft dorsal, and continued along the last spine and the summit of the first five rays; the middle band begins at the posterior superior angle of the orbit, and passes direct to the soft dorsal, where it is continued on to its seventh and eighth rays. A black mark extends on the margin of the dorsal interspinous membrane from the third to seventh spines. Two oblique bands pass across the upper half of caudal, and one—sometimes two—across its lower lobe. Posterior half of anal, and anterior half of ventral, dull yellow. Iris golden. Pupil broad, lanceolate, apex in front.

None of the Therapons are esteemed as food. This species is common, and grows to eight inches in length.

Habitat—Seas and estuaries of India, Ceylon and Malaysia.

Therapon servus.

Therapon servus, *Cuv. & Val.* iii. p. 125, vii. p. 479; *Günther*, Catal. i. p. 278.

B. vi. D. 10-11 | $\frac{1}{10}$. P. 13. V. $\frac{1}{5}$. A. $\frac{3}{8}$. C. 17. L. l. 82. L. tr. $\frac{12}{27}$. Vert. $\frac{10}{15}$.

Length of head $\frac{1}{4}$, of pectoral $\frac{2}{15}$, of caudal $\frac{1}{5}$, of base of dorsal $\frac{2}{5}$, of base of anal $\frac{1}{7}$ of total length. Height of head $\frac{1}{5}$, of body $\frac{2}{7}$, of first dorsal $\frac{2}{15}$, of second dorsal $\frac{1}{9}$, of ventral $\frac{1}{7}$, of anal $\frac{1}{11}$ of total length.

Eyes—Transversely oval, horizontal diameter $\frac{2}{7}$, vertical $\frac{2}{8}$ of length of head, $\frac{1}{2}$ a diameter apart, 1 diameter from end of snout.

Maxilla extends backwards to opposite anterior third of orbit. Preorbital moderately serrated in the posterior half of its lower margin. Preopercle, vertical limb with about fourteen denticulations, the two at its rounded angle being very much the strongest, in the lower limb they are less strong and number about eight. In young specimens there are sometimes three conspicuously larger teeth at the angle, and the comparative size of the denticulations on the lower limb is greater. Sub- and interopercles entire. Opercle with two spines, the superior small, the inferior large, long and strong. Suprascapular and coracoid bones toothed.

Teeth—Several rows of villiform in both jaws, with an external conical band. A transverse narrow band of fine teeth on vomer.

Fins—Dorsal spines moderately strong, third and fourth equal and the longest. Ventral spine weak. Second anal spine the strongest, nearly twice as long as the first, and slightly shorter than the third. Fins as in the last species.

Scales—Smaller above than below the lateral line, which follows the curve of back in its upper fourth.

Colours—Back bluish grey, becoming silvery white on the abdomen; a tinge of gold along cheeks and snout. On the body three longitudinal dark reddish brown lines, which have a slight convexity downwards. In a fresh state a fourth line is occasionally perceived along the abdomen. The superior commences a little in front of first dorsal, curving downwards it passes in a concave direction to between the eighth and ninth dorsal spines. The second passes from the occiput, first downwards as low as the lateral line, subsequently curving upwards it reaches the back at the end of the soft dorsal. The third commencing at the back of the head, passes as low as the inferior spine of opercle, and is continued in a curved direction to the centre of caudal. Pectoral transparent. Ventral and anal with a yellow tinge along their centres. Dorsal, hard portion milk-white, with a very black mark in the upper two-thirds of the interspinous membrane between its third and sixth spines. A second black mark commences at the eighth spine, and is continued along the whole length of the base of the soft dorsal. Upper margin of first three rays tipped with black. Caudal with two oblique bands across both lobes. Eye yellowish red.

Common, not esteemed, grows to twelve or thirteen inches in length.

Habitat—Seas and estuaries of India and Ceylon, Red Sea, East Coast of Africa, and North Coast of Australia.

Therapon theraps.

Therapon theraps, *Cuv. & Val.* iii. p. 129, pl. 53; *Günther*, Catal. i. p. 274.

B. vi. D. $\frac{12}{10}$. P. 15. V. $\frac{1}{5}$. A. $\frac{3}{8}$. C. 17. L. l. 50-55. L. tr. $\frac{10}{14}$. Vert. $\frac{10}{15}$.

Length of head $\frac{1}{4}$, of pectoral $\frac{1}{5}$, of caudal $\frac{1}{5}$, of base of dorsal $\frac{1}{2}$, of base of anal $\frac{1}{7}$ of total length. Height of head $\frac{1}{5}$, of body $\frac{2}{7}$, of hard dorsal $\frac{1}{6}$, of soft dorsal $\frac{1}{10}$, of ventral $\frac{1}{5}$, of anal $\frac{1}{10}$ of total length.

Eyes—Diameter $\frac{1}{3}$ length of head, $\frac{3}{4}$ of a diameter apart, the same distance from end of snout.

Maxilla extends to beneath the anterior margin of the orbit. Preorbital very finely serrated, and lineated. Preopercle, vertical limb finely and evenly serrated, its angle rounded where the serratures are larger, along the lower limb they decrease in size. Sub- and interopercles entire. Opercle with two spines, the lowest much the largest, but not nearly so great as in the *T. servus*. Suprascapular serrated, also the lower portion of the coracoid bone.

Teeth—Several rows of villiform, and an external series of fine even conical ones. Bands of deciduous villiform teeth on vomer and palate.

Fins—Dorsal spines moderately strong, the fourth slightly the longest. Ventral spine pretty stout, first ray prolonged. Second anal spine the strongest, nearly twice as long as the first, but rather shorter than the third. Pectoral and ventral rather pointed; caudal emarginate.

Scales—None between or before the orbits, cheeks scaled, those above lateral line smaller than those below it.

Lateral line—In upper fourth of body.

Colours—Silvery, with a deep purple gloss along the back, and golden along the abdomen. Three horizontal dark brown lines pass along the sides, the first from the second to the last dorsal spine, the second from the nape to the second and third soft dorsal rays, on to which fin it is continued; the third line from opposite the eye to the upper third of the tail. Nape of an intense purple. Dorsal with a jet black mark on the upper two-thirds of the fin membrane between the third and sixth spines. Soft dorsal, upper portion barred with brown, and a brown bar between

D 2

its second and fourth rays. Caudal white, with one brown central bar and two oblique ones across either lobe. Ventral white. Pectoral yellow.

Common, not esteemed as food, grows to six inches in length.

Habitat—Seas and estuaries of India, China, and South Africa.

Genus PRISTIPOMA, *Cuvier*.

Branchiostegals, seven: pseudobranchiæ. Body oblong, compressed. Eyes of moderate size. Mouth horizontal, not very wide, jaws nearly equal, a central groove below the chin. One dorsal with from eleven to fourteen spines, anal with three; vertical fins without scales or only at their bases. Preopercle serrated, opercle with indistinct points. Villiform teeth in both jaws, no canines. Scales moderate. Air bladder simple. Pyloric appendages in small number.

Pristipoma hasta.

Lutjanus hasta, *Bloch*, t. 246, f. 1.
Pristipoma kaakan, *Cuv. & Val.* v. p. 244.
Pristipoma commersonii, *Cuv. & Val.* v. p. 252; *Cantor*, Catal. p. 72.
Pristipoma hasta, *Cuv. & Val.* v. p. 247; *Günther*, Catal. i. p. 289.
Pristipoma chrysobalion, *Cuv. & Val.* v. p. 248.

B. vii. D. $\frac{12}{14}$. P. 17. V. $\frac{1}{5}$. A. $\frac{3}{7\text{-}8}$. C. 17. L. l. 47. L. tr. $\frac{7}{10}$.

Length of head $\frac{2}{7}$, of pectoral $\frac{1}{4}$, of caudal $\frac{2}{11}$, of base of dorsal $\frac{3}{7}$, of base of anal $\frac{1}{9}$ of total length. Height of head $\frac{1}{5}$, of body $\frac{3}{10}$, of hard dorsal $\frac{1}{6}$, of soft dorsal $\frac{1}{8}$, of ventral $\frac{1}{5}$, of anal $\frac{1}{8}$ of total length.

Eyes—Transversely oval, horizontal diameter $\frac{3}{10}$, vertical diameter $\frac{1}{4}$ in length of head, $1\frac{1}{2}$ diameter apart, 1 diameter from end of snout.

Maxilla reaches to beneath the anterior margin of orbit. Preopercle rather deeply emarginate, serrated in its whole extent, angle rounded, produced, and having the coarsest serratures. Sub- and interopercles entire. Opercle ending in two rounded points, connected by a crescentic margin. Preorbital entire. Suprascapular and coracoid bones serrated. A deep groove beneath the centre of lower jaw.

Teeth—Villiform in jaws, with an external conical series, also some large ones in each intermaxillary.

Fins—Spinous portion of dorsal fin two-thirds of its entire length, fourth spine the longest. Ventral spine moderately strong. Second anal spine longest and strongest, nearly four times as long as first, and one-third longer than the third.

Scales—On body opercles, preorbital, and interorbital space: those above the lateral line are smaller than those below it.

Lateral line—Follows the curve of the back.

Colours—Generally silvered, with a beautiful purplish violet reflection along the whole of the nape and back. Pre- and suborbital space greenish golden. Opercle with a large black mark on its most posterior portion. A series of three or four lines of blotches of a dark grey colour exists along the sides, two above the lateral line, one on it, and one below it, sometimes coalescing and forming bands, but these marks are generally more apparent in the dry than in the fresh fish. Fins diaphanous, the dorsal sometimes stained yellow, margined with black, and having two or three rows of brownish black spots between its spines, which are sometimes extended on to the spines themselves: between the fourth and fifth rays they form two short longitudinal lines, then the lowest ceases but the upper is continued to the termination of the fin. Caudal stained with black. Ventral and anal with a reddish golden tinge. Eye with a violet reflection.

Common, does not grow to a large size, is eaten by the Natives.

Habitat—From the Red Sea, along the East Coast of Africa, through the seas of India to the northern shores of Australia.

PRISTIPOMA MACULATUM.

ANTHIAS MACULATUS, *Bloch*, t. 326. f. 2.
CARIPE, *Russell*, pl. 124.
PRISTIPOMA CARIPE, *Cuv. & Val.* v. p. 261; *Cantor*, Catal. p. 75.
PRISTIPOMA MACULATUM, *Günther*, Catal. i. p. 273.
ERRUTTUM CORAH, *Mal.*

B. vii. D. 11. | $\frac{1}{11\text{-}14}$. P. 17. V. $\frac{1}{5}$. A. $\frac{3}{7}$. C. 17. L. l. 52. L. tr. $\frac{8}{12}$.

Length of head $\frac{1}{4}$, of pectoral $\frac{1}{4}$, of caudal $\frac{1}{6}$, of base of dorsal $\frac{2}{5}$, of base of anal $\frac{1}{10}$ of total length. Height of head $\frac{1}{5}$, of body $\frac{1}{4}$, of hard dorsal $\frac{1}{8}$, of soft dorsal $\frac{1}{12}$, of ventral $\frac{1}{6}$, of anal $\frac{1}{10}$ of total length.

Eyes—Close to upper profile, transversely oval, horizontal diameter $\frac{1}{3}$, vertical diameter $\frac{1}{4}$ of length of head, 1 diameter from end of snout, $\frac{5}{6}$ of a diameter apart.

Maxilla extends to nearly opposite anterior margin of orbit. Preorbital entire. Preopercle, vertical limb slightly emarginate and finely serrated, angle rounded, with two or three very inconspicuous serratures, inferior limb entire. Sub- and interopercles entire. Opercle with two indistinct blunted points. Suprascapular, scapular, and coracoid bones entire.

Teeth—Villiform, with an external conical series in both jaws, not much larger than the posterior ones.

Fins—Dorsal spines strong, the fourth slightly the longest. Ventral spine weak, first soft ray prolonged. Second anal spine the strongest, more than three times as long as the first, and slightly longer than the third. Dorsal interspinous membrane deeply notched. Pectoral pointed. Caudal emarginate.

Scales—Cover preorbitals, cheeks, and to between the orbits. A long scale at origin of ventral. Those above lateral line considerably larger than those below it, passing upwards and backwards from lateral line as far as the end of dorsal, whilst below it they proceed horizontally.

Lateral line—In upper fourth of body, following the curve of back till opposite the end of dorsal, from whence it passes straight.

Colour—Greyish with a silvery abdomen, and in the monsoon months with a beautiful purplish tinge on the nape. A vertical black band about eight scales wide passes over the nape and descending backwards crosses the lateral line terminating about three scales below it. Posterior to this are six black spots, three above and three below the lateral line, which do not form bands, but are slightly united, being placed like squares in a chess board. The first dorsal has a yellowish buff base, otherwise stained with black, and minutely dotted with grey, and a large black mark in its centre between the fourth and seventh spines. Soft dorsal yellowish, finely dotted with grey, and the upper half stained with black. Pectoral, ventral, and caudal yellowish, the last stained with black. "Over the infraorbitals an oblique blackish band edges the orbit, a second from the occiput edges the margin of the preopercle and the opercle," (Cantor). Opercles bluish. Iris golden.

Common, not esteemed as food, grows to sixteen inches in length.

Habitat—Red Sea and seas of India to New Guinea.

* Pristipoma dussumieri.

Pristipoma dussumieri, *Cuv. & Val.* v. p. 259; *Günther*, Catal. i. p. 291.

B. vii. D. $\frac{12}{14}$. A. $\frac{3}{7}$. L. l. 46. L. tr. $\frac{6}{12}$.

Length of head $\frac{2}{7}$, of pectoral $\frac{1}{4}$ of total length. Height of body nearly $\frac{2}{7}$ of total length.

Eyes—Diameter nearly $\frac{1}{4}$ of length of head, rather more than 1 diameter from end of snout.

Maxilla hardly extends as far as anterior margin of orbit, cleft of mouth narrow. Preopercle, vertical limb emarginate, angle not projecting.

Fins—Dorsal spines strong, interspinous membrane notched, the fourth spine the longest and three-fourths of length of head. Second anal spine much the longest and strongest. Caudal truncated.

Colours—Body silvery, slightly tinged with brown on the back, and with six longitudinal golden lines. The membrane of the spinous dorsal brownish, with a brown spot between each of the soft rays. The caudal blackish brown. The other fins are of a bright yellow, as is also the iris: the pectorals are pale.

Grows to six inches in length.

Habitat—Malabar Coast.

* Pristipoma guoraka.

Pristipoma guoraka, *Cuv. & Val.* v. p. 256; *Cantor*, Catal. p. 73.
Guoraka, *Russell*, pl. 132.

B. vii. D. $\frac{12}{14}$. P. 18. V. $\frac{1}{5}$. A. $\frac{3}{8}$. C. 17.

Form closely resembles the *P. hasta*, only slightly more elevated, the vertical limb of the preopercle more rectangular, and the scales smaller. The second anal spine excessively thick, striated on its anterior surface, in length rather more than half the vertical diameter of the body above it, and comparatively shorter than in the *P. hasta*.

Air vessel elongated, nearly one-third of the total length, swelling in the middle, and terminating in a point; the anterior extremity blunt, and appears to have on each side a pointed process a little less than one-third of the length of the vessel itself, which is restricted at the origin of the lateral processes.

Colours—Upper surface of head and back pale blackish olive; cheeks, opercles and sides silvery grey, with blue and golden reflections; abdomen yellowish silvery; most of the scales have the edges minutely dotted with brown, and those above the lateral line a pale brown spot at the root, forming six or seven indistinct parallel lines; fins pale yellowish; membrane of dorsal minutely dotted with brown, between the spines one or two series of large clouded brown spots, and a single series of smaller between the rays; margins of dorsal and caudal blackish; the membrane of the latter and of the anal slightly dotted with brown. Iris golden. (Cantor.)

Good eating, air vessel very thin, and consequently furnishes isinglass of but little value. Grows to two feet in length.

Habitat—Seas of India and Malaysia; said occasionally to enter fresh water.

Genus, DIAGRAMMA, *Cuvier*.

Plectorhynchus, *Lacép.*

Branchiostegals, six or seven: pseudobranchiæ. Body oblong, compressed, with the upper profile of head parabolic. Eyes of moderate size. Mouth small, horizontal, with lips folded and turned back. Four or six pores on under surface of lower jaw, but no large groove. One dorsal with from nine to fourteen spines, anal with three. Preopercle serrated, suborbitals entire. No canine teeth. Scales rather small, rarely of moderate size. Air bladder simple. Pyloric appendages few.

Diagramma nigrum.

Pristipoma nigrum, *Cantor*, Catal. p. 74; ? *Cuv. & Val.* v. p. 258; *Günther*, Catal. i. p. 289.

Diagramma affine, *Günther*, Catal. i. p. 319.

B. vii. D. $\frac{14}{16}$. P. 16. V. $\frac{1}{5}$. A. $\frac{3}{7}$. C. 17. L. l. 47. L. tr. $\frac{10}{17}$.

Length of head $\frac{2}{7}$, of pectoral $\frac{1}{6}$, of caudal $\frac{1}{6}$, of base of dorsal $\frac{1}{2}$, of base of anal $\frac{1}{9}$ of total length. Height of head $\frac{1}{4}$, of body $\frac{1}{3}$, of hard dorsal $\frac{1}{9}$, of soft dorsal $\frac{2}{11}$, of ventral $\frac{1}{6}$, of anal $\frac{2}{11}$ of total length.

Eyes—Transversely oval, horizontal diameter $\frac{1}{5}$, vertical diameter $\frac{1}{6}$ of length of head, $1\frac{1}{2}$ diameter from end of snout, more than 1 diameter apart.

Lips fleshy, folded, and turned back. Snout short, rather elevated. Cleft of mouth horizontal, rather narrow. Maxilla extending only two-thirds of the distance to the orbit, in young specimens it goes rather further back. Nostrils approximating, situated close to anterior superior margin of orbit. Preopercle, vertical limb finely serrated, angle rather produced, rounded and denticulated, also about half the horizontal limb sparingly denticulated. Sub- and interopercles and preorbital entire. Opercle with two bluntish spines, the lower of which is the largest and serrated. Suprascapular serrated: scapular and coracoid bones entire.

Teeth—Two villiform bands in either jaw separated by a narrow interspace.

Fins—Dorsal with a scaly sheath, the base of spinous portion two-thirds the entire length of that of the fin. Spines strong, interspinous membrane deeply notched. The thickness of each spine varies on the different sides of the body, the fourth the longest. Ventral spine moderately strong. Anal arises opposite third or fourth dorsal ray, the spines which are very strong have a scaly sheath at their base, the second much the strongest, more than two and a half times as long as the first, and one-third longer than the last. Pectoral rounded. Ventral and caudal both moderately rounded.

Scales—Above lateral line passing obliquely upwards and backwards, below it in horizontal rows: the whole of the head except the snout scaled.

Lateral line—In upper third of body, passing parallel with the back until opposite end of soft dorsal.

Air bladder large: intestinal canal short, pyloric appendages rather numerous.

Colours—Generally greyish or slate colour, with a golden brassy tint towards the back and abdomen, and a violet tinge over the head and remainder of the body, especially about the forehead. A few bright coppery spots are irregularly dispersed over some scales, and a coppery tinge over the hard rays of the dorsal. All the fins of a violet slate colour, stained darker along their margins, and with a dark band at the base of each, so that the centre is the lightest colour. Throat and breast white. Eyes silvery, with a copperish dash.

Excellent eating, captured in Malabar about July; and commonly known as the "Black rock fish." It grows to two feet and upwards in length.

Habitat—Seas of India and Malaysia as far as coasts of N. W. Australia.

* Diagramma griseum.

Diagramma griseum, *Cuv. & Val.* v. p. 306; *Günther*, Catal. i. p. 321.

D. $\frac{12}{21}$. A. $\frac{3}{7}$. Vert. $\frac{10}{16}$.

Length of head $\frac{1}{4}$ of total length. Height of head $\frac{1}{3}$ of total length.

Fins—Second anal spine strong. Caudal truncated.

Colours—Interior of mouth orange: body clear brown or grey. Fins grey, tinged with rose colour.

Length to eight inches.

Habitat—Malabar.

Genus LOBOTES, *Cuvier*.

Branchiostegals, six: pseudobranchiæ. Body and fins rather elevated. Eyes rather small, snout blunt, lower jaw longest, cleft of mouth oblique. One dorsal with twelve, anal with three spines. Preopercle denticulated. Opercle with obtuse points. No canine teeth: inferior pharyngeal bones separated. Scales moderate, ctenoid. Air bladder simple. Pyloric appendages few.

Lobotes surinamensis.

Holocentrus surinamensis, *Bloch*, t. 243.
Lobotes surinamensis, *Cuv. & Val.* v. p. 319.
Lobotes Farkharii et L. somnolentus, *Cuv. & Val.* v. p. 324.
Lobotes erate, *Cuv. & Val.* v. p. 319; *Cantor*, Catal. p. 80.
Lobotes auctorum, *Günther*, Catal. i. p. 338.
Parrandee, *Mal.*

B. vi. D. $\frac{12}{15\text{-}16}$. P. 15-17. V. $\frac{1}{5}$. A. $\frac{3}{11\text{-}12}$. C. 17-18. L. l. 48. L. tr. $\frac{8}{11}$. Vert. $\frac{13}{11}$.

Length of head $\frac{2}{7}$, of pectoral $\frac{1}{8}$, of caudal $\frac{1}{6}$, of base of dorsal $\frac{1}{2}$, of base of anal $\frac{1}{6}$ of total length. Height of head $\frac{1}{5}$, of body $\frac{2}{7}$, of hard dorsal $\frac{1}{9}$, of soft dorsal $\frac{2}{13}$, of ventral $\frac{1}{6}$, of anal $\frac{1}{6}$ of total length.

Eyes—Situated near upper profile, diameter $\frac{1}{7}$ of length of head, 1 diameter from end of snout, nearly 2 diameters apart.

Maxilla extends to beneath anterior third of orbit. Snout elevated. Preorbital entire. Preopercle, vertical limb strongly denticulated, the strongest teeth being at the angle, which is rounded, and slightly produced; inferior limb nearly horizontal. Sub- and interopercles entire. Opercle with a blunt point. Suprascapular serrated, scapular entire, coracoid finely serrated.

Teeth—Villiform, with an external conical row.

Fins—Dorsal spines strong, the spinous portion occupies a little more than half the fin, membrane deeply emarginate, third spine the longest. Ventral spine strong. Third anal spine one-fifth longer than the second, which is three-tenths longer than the first. Soft portions of dorsal, anal, pectoral, and caudal fins rounded.

Scales—Above lateral line smaller than those below.

Lateral line—First slightly descends, then ascends and follows the curve of the back.

"Air vessel very large, about one-third of the total length, silvery white, and of a lanceolate shape. It is excessively thin and so firmly adherent to the back, that but a small portion can be removed." (Cantor.) The quality of the isinglass made from it is good, but the quantity small.

Colours—The young are more or less of a brassy brown colour, blotched with darker markings, and having the extremity of the caudal dirty white. The adult is of a slate colour, blotched with a darker tinge. Pectorals yellowish white. The other fins slate colour, darkest at their margins except the caudal, the extremity of which, in specimens up to thirteen inches, is of a dirty white. Iris bluish silvery.

Very good eating, are dried in some places, and good isinglass is obtained from them in small quantities. They grow to two and a half feet in length. Small ones are common.

Habitat—Seas of India, Malaysia, and China, also the Atlantic Coasts of America from New York to Surinam.

Genus SCOLOPSIS, *Cuvier*.

Branchiostegals five: pseudobranchiæ. Form of body oblong. Eyes large. Snout moderate, jaws equal, cleft of mouth horizontal. One dorsal with ten, anal with three spines: caudal more or less forked. Infraorbital arch with a spine directed backwards. Preopercle mostly denticulated. Opercle with an indistinct spine. Scales moderately ctenoid. Air bladder simple. Pyloric appendages few.

Scolopsis japonicus.

Anthias japonicus, *Bloch*, t. 325, f. 2.
Kurite, *Russell*, pl. 106.
Scolopsis kate, *Cuv. & Val.* v. p. 329.
Scolopsis Rüppelii, *Cuv. & Val.* v. p. 332.
Scolopsis kurite, *Cuv. & Val.* v. p. 331.
Scolopsis japonicus, *Günther*, Catal. i. p. 354.

B. vi. D. $\frac{10}{9}$. P. 15. V. $\frac{1}{5}$. A. $\frac{3}{7}$. C. 17. L. l. 44. L. tr. $\frac{5}{12}$.

Length of head $\frac{1}{4}$, of pectoral $\frac{1}{6}$, of caudal $\frac{1}{6}$, of base of dorsal $\frac{1}{2}$, of base of anal $\frac{1}{8}$ of total length. Height of head $\frac{2}{7}$, of body $\frac{1}{3}$, of hard dorsal $\frac{1}{9}$, of soft dorsal $\frac{1}{9}$, of ventral $\frac{1}{6}$, of anal $\frac{1}{7}$ of total length.

Eyes—Transversely oval, horizontal diameter $\frac{1}{2}$, vertical diameter $\frac{1}{3}$ of length of head, $\frac{1}{2}$ a diameter from end of snout, and the same distance apart.

Maxilla extends to beneath the anterior fourth of orbit. Infraorbital ring with two prominent spines, the posterior largest and directed backwards, the anterior elevated and directed forwards, the plate serrated below. Preopercle slightly emarginate, denticulated, with the strongest teeth at its angle; lower limb, horizontal, entire. Sub- and interopercles entire. Opercle with a blunt point. Shoulder bones entire.

Teeth—In jaws in villiform bands.

Fins—Dorsal spines moderately strong, the spinous portion upwards of half the length of the fin, interspinous membrane moderately notched. Fourth and fifth spines slightly the longest.

Ventral spine rather weak, first ray prolonged. Second anal spine much the longest, and slightly stronger than the third. Caudal moderately forked.

Scales—In parallel rows above the lateral line, but passing upwards and backwards below it. None on snout, pre- or infraorbital bones, but present on cheeks and between orbits.

Lateral line—In upper fourth of body.

Colours—Back of a dull reddish yellow, shot with greenish, the rest of the body orange, brightest on the abdomen. A light buff band passes over the back of the head and extends itself over the opercle. The base of each scale on the body rather darker than its margin. Fins dusky yellow. Iris yellow.

Grows to eight inches in length.

Habitat—Red Sea, Seas of India and China.

GENUS DENTEX, *Cuvier*.

Branchiostegals, six: pseudobranchiæ. Body compressed, oblong, rather elevated. Eyes moderate. Cleft of mouth more or less horizontal, jaws nearly equal, usually with strong canines in each. One dorsal from ten to thirteen spines, anal with three, caudal more or less forked. Preorbital and preopercle entire, opercle without prominent spine. Scales moderate, ctenoid, more than three rows on preopercle. Air bladder notched posteriorly. Pyloric appendages few.

* DENTEX HASTA.

DENTEX HASTA, *Cuv. & Val.* vi. p. 255; *Günther*, Catal. i. p. 373.

B. vi. D. $\frac{11}{11}$. P. 15. V. $\frac{1}{5}$. A$\frac{3}{8}$. C. 17.

Height of body $\frac{1}{3}$ of total length. Eyes large, central. Mouth slightly protractile.

Teeth—Six strong canines in each jaw, those below weaker than those above, an external series of large triangular and compressed teeth, with villiform ones behind.

Colours—Greenish brown on the back, becoming silvery on the abdomen. Ten to twelve violet lines along the sides. Fins, blue, shot with violet.

Grows to eight inches in length.

Habitat—Malabar.

GENUS SYNAGRIS, *Günther*.

DENTEX, SP. *Cuvier*.

Branchiostegals, six: pseudobranchiæ. Form of body elongate: eyes moderate. Jaws nearly equal. Mouth more or less horizontal. One continuous dorsal with ten feeble spines, anal with three. Caudal deeply forked. Infraorbital arch entire: preopercle entire, or finely serrated. Opercle without prominent spine. Canine teeth in upper jaw. Scales of moderate size, ctenoid, with three rows on preopercle. Swimming bladder notched posteriorly. Pyloric appendages few.

SYNAGRIS GRAMMICUS. Plate IV.

SYNAGRIS GRAMMICUS, *Day*, Proceed. Zool. Soc. 1865, p. 14.

B. vi. D. $\frac{10}{10}$. P. 17. V. $\frac{1}{5}$. A. $\frac{3}{7}$. C. 17. L. l. 48. L. tr. $\frac{4}{10}$.

PLATE IV.

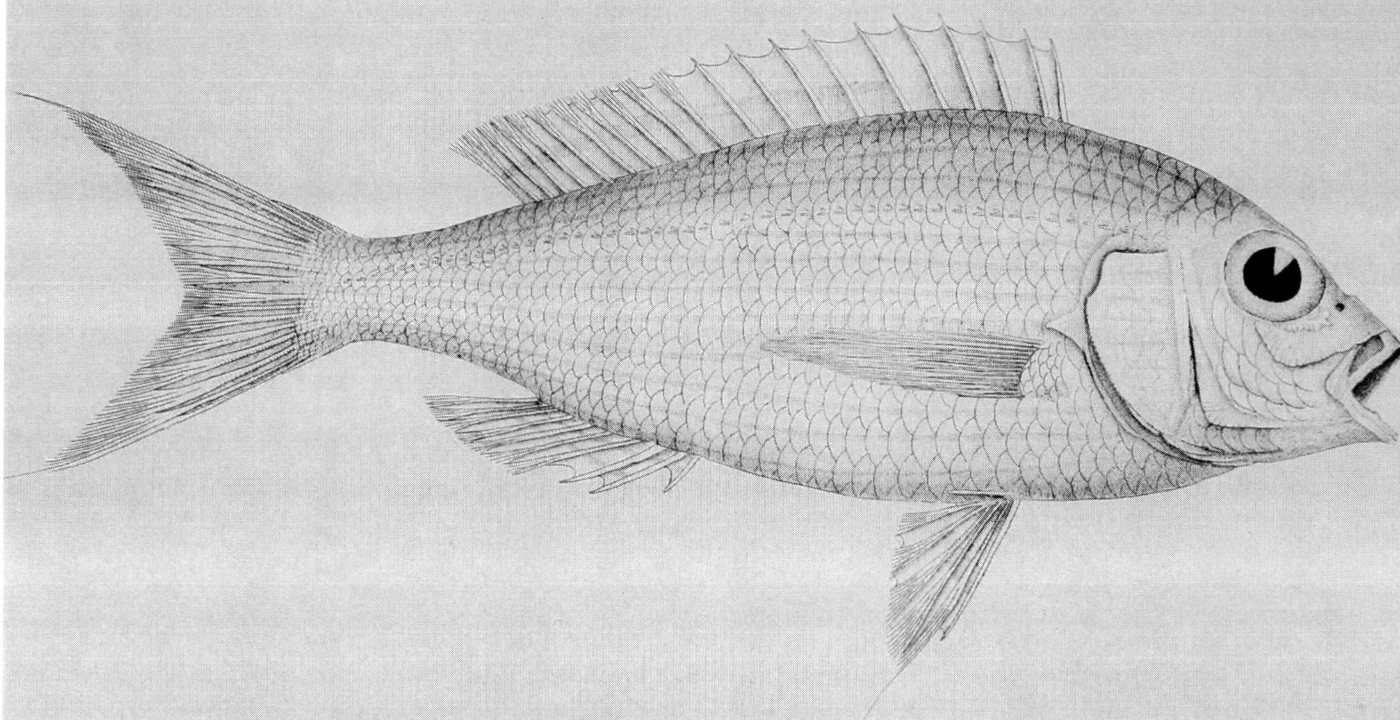

F. Day, del. et sculp.

SYNAGRIS GRAMMICUS

Length of head $\frac{2}{9}$, of pectoral $\frac{1}{5}$, of caudal $\frac{1}{4}$, of base of dorsal $\frac{1}{3}$, of base of anal $\frac{1}{9}$ of total length. Height of head $\frac{1}{5}$, of body $\frac{1}{4}$, of hard dorsal $\frac{1}{10}$, of soft dorsal $\frac{1}{9}$, of ventral $\frac{1}{9}$, of anal $\frac{1}{10}$ of total length.

Eyes—Close to profile, and transversely oval, horizontal diameter $\frac{1}{3}$, vertical diameter $\frac{1}{4}$ in length of head, $\frac{2}{3}$ of a diameter from end of snout.

Nape short, profile convex from snout to dorsal. Lower jaw longest.

Maxilla extends as far as to below anterior third of orbit. Preopercle, vertical limb finely serrated in its lower half, whilst from between each serrature a fine furrow runs forwards and downwards; angle rounded, entire: lower limb horizontal, entire. Sub- and interopercles entire. Opercle ending in a dull point. Preorbital half the diameter of the eye in width, entire, but furrowed downwards and backwards. Nostrils approximating and close to orbit. Shoulder bones entire. Three rows of scales between orbit and margin of preopercle, none between or before the orbits. Three oval facets on under surface of lower jaw, the posterior the largest.

Teeth—An external row of six curved canines in intermaxillaries, with villiform ones behind, and covering both upper and lower jaws in about five rows.

Fins—Dorsal spines weak, and extending over more than half the base of the fins. Interspinous membrane not notched: second spine one tenth longer than first, and the same amount shorter than the third, from thence they continue much the same length. Ventral spine weak, first ray prolonged. Anal spines weak, second one-third longer than the first, but one-twentieth shorter than the third. There are scaly grooves in which the hard portions of the dorsal and anal, and also a portion of the rays can be laid flat. Caudal deeply emarginate, the first and second rays on either side being prolonged. Pectoral pointed, reaching nearly as far as the first ray of anal.

Scales—Large, arranged in horizontal rows, a few extend over the base of the caudal; they are rather smaller above than below the lateral line, which runs parallel with the back in the upper fifth of the body.

Colours—Yellowish, with reddish longitudinal lines passing along each row of scales. Upper portion of head and opercles dull reddish. Throat, chin and chest yellowish, the colours below the lateral line lighter than those above it. Dorsal fin yellowish, with a grey base and pinkish exterior. Caudal reddish, stained with grey externally. Anal yellowish with a grey base, and two reddish stripes along its foremost part. Ventral yellowish with a grey base. Pectoral reddish yellow. Eyes golden.

Rare. Length $7\frac{2}{10}$ inches.

Habitat—Cochin on the Malabar Coast.

Genus UPENEOIDES, *Bleeker*.

Upeneus, sp. *Cuv. & Val.*

Branchiostegals, four: pseudobranchiæ. Form of body elongate, slightly compressed. Eyes moderate, lateral. Mouth in front of snout rather small. Hyal apparatus with two long barbels. Fine teeth on jaws, vomer, and palatine bones. Two dorsals. Scales large and deciduous. Air bladder absent. Stomach siphonal.

Upeneoides vittatus.

Mullus vittatus, *Forskål*, Faun. Arab. p. 31.

BANDI GOOLIVINDA, *Russell*, pl. 158.
UPENEUS VITTATUS, *Cuv. & Val.* iii. p. 448.
UPENEOIDES VITTATUS, *Günther*, Catal. i. p. 397.
CHEERUL, *Mal.*

B. iv. D. 8 | $\frac{1}{8}$. P. 17. V. $\frac{1}{5}$. A. 7. C. 15. L. l. 38. L. tr. $\frac{2}{5}$.

Length of head $4\frac{1}{5}$, of pectoral $\frac{2}{11}$, of caudal $\frac{2}{11}$, of base of first dorsal $\frac{1}{8}$, of base of second dorsal $\frac{2}{19}$, of base of anal $\frac{2}{23}$ of total length. Height of head $\frac{2}{11}$, of body $\frac{5}{21}$, of first dorsal $\frac{2}{11}$, of second dorsal $\frac{1}{8}$, of ventral $\frac{1}{6}$, of anal $\frac{1}{10}$ of total length.

Eyes—Transversely oval, horizontal diameter $\frac{1}{4}$, vertical diameter $\frac{1}{5}$ in length of head: 1 diameter apart, $1\frac{1}{4}$ from end of snout.

Maxilla extends to beneath the anterior margin of orbit. The barbules reach to rather beyond the posterior margin of the preopercle. Preopercle entire, as are also the sub- and inter-opercles. Opercle with two very obtuse points separated by a crescentic emargination. Preorbital entire, its width equalling two-thirds of the diameter of the eye. Three small glandular orifices on the inferior surface of the lower jaw.

Teeth—Villiform on jaws, vomer, and palatines.

Fins—Dorsal spines weak, interspinous membrane scarcely notched, second spine of first dorsal the longest. Ventral spine weak, first ray prolonged, an elongated scale at base of fin. First dorsal triangular. Pectoral pointed. Caudal deeply lobed.

Scales—Large and deciduous, in horizontal rows, extending in front as far as the snout, and covering the jaws and opercles, some also on base of caudal.

Lateral line—In upper fourth of body, nearly straight, and in diverging tubes.

Colours—Back and summit of head iron blue, becoming silvery on the cheeks and along the sides, whilst inferiorly it has a golden tinge. A dark band passes along the superior surface of the back. A bright metallic golden line commences opposite the upper third of the opercle, and passes direct to the upper third of the tail. There are two reddish brown lines, the first between the line on the back and the first golden one, the second dividing the two golden ones, the lowest of which last proceeds from the pectoral to the lower third of the tail. Ventrals and anal gamboge yellow. Pectorals silvery. First dorsal tipped with black, and having a horizontal brown line along its centre, and a lighter one at its base. Second dorsal with a blackish brown margin, a second brown line running along its centre, and a third smaller one at the posterior part of its base. Caudal with two horizontal brown lines on either side of its centre, and three oblique bands running across the upper lobe, and two across the lower one. Eye golden, with a tinge of red.

Common, grows to seven inches in length. Is eaten by the Natives.

Habitat—Red Sea, seas of India, Malaysia, and Philippine Islands.

GENUS UPENEUS, *Bleeker*.

UPENEUS, SP. *Cuv. & Val.*

Characters as in the *Upeneoides*, except that in the *Upeneus* the teeth in both jaws form a single series, and the palate is edentulous.

UPENEUS INDICUS.

MULLUS INDICUS, *Shaw*, Zool. iv. pt. ii. p. 614.
RAHTEE GOOLIVINDA, *Russell*, pl. 157.

UPENEUS RUSSELLII, *Cuv. & Val.* iii. p. 465.
UPENEUS INDICUS, *Günther*, Catal. i. p. 406.

B. iv. D. 8 | 9. P. 16. V. $\frac{1}{5}$. A. $\frac{1}{7}$. C. 14. L. l. 30. L. tr. $\frac{3}{7}$.

Barbels reach beyond angle of preopercle. Space between the orbits rather flat. Opercle has two small spinous points. Snout scaleless. Nostrils small, approximating, rather distant from orbit. Caudal lobed.

Colours—Upper part of head and back dark purple, with some light violet lines. Cheeks pink variegated with yellow, and tortuous light blue lines. A dark spot at corner of mouth. Two oblong oval spots on lateral line, the first white shot with gold, the second beyond the end of second dorsal, and of a dark purple, lighter in the centre. Abdomen white, with horizontal golden lines. Dorsal fins purplish streaked with blue, pectoral pink, anal white and pink with a few yellowish cross bars, caudal purplish, the membrane between the rays greenish.

Grows to thirteen inches in length.

Habitat—Seas of India and China.

* UPENEUS MALABARICUS.

UPENEUS MALABARICUS, *Cuv. & Val.* iii. p. 467; *Günther*, Catal. i. p. 407.

B. iv. D. 8 | 9. A $\frac{1}{7}$ — 7. L. l. 30. L. tr. $\frac{3}{7}$.

Head oblong, its barbels extend beyond the angle of the preopercle. Preorbital longer than wide, and marked with numerous pores. Teeth thin and short.

Colours—Rosy, a pale line traverses the forehead in front of eyes. A large pale or golden spot on the lateral line opposite the interval between the two dorsals. A round black spot on the side of the root of the tail.

Length up to six inches.

Habitat—Malabar, Philippine Islands.

GENUS CHRYSOPHRYS, *Cuvier*.

Branchiostegals, six: pseudobranchiæ. Body oblong, compressed. Four or six conical or blunt teeth in front, and three or more series of rounded molars in both jaws. One continuous dorsal with eleven or twelve spines, which can be received into a groove. Three anal spines. Scales of moderate size, extending over the cheeks. Air bladder sometimes notched, or with very short appendages. Pyloric appendages few.

CHRYSOPHRYS HASTA.

SPARUS HASTA, *Bloch, Schn.*, p. 275.
COIUS DATNIA, *Ham. Buch.* pp. 88, 369. pl. 9. f. 39.
CHRYSOPHRYS LONGISPINIS, *Cuv. & Val.* vi. p. 116.
CHRYSOPHRYS BERDA, *Cuv. & Val.* vi. p. 113.
CHRYSOPHRYS HASTA, *Günther*, Catal. i. p. 490.

B. vi. D. $\frac{11-12}{11-10}\left(\frac{13}{9}\right)$. P. 15. V. $\frac{1}{5}$. A. $\frac{3}{8-9}$. C. 17. L. l. 48. L. tr. $\frac{5}{9}$.

Length of head $\frac{1}{4}$, of pectoral $\frac{1}{4}$, of caudal $\frac{1}{5}$, of base of dorsal $\frac{3}{7}$, of base of anal $\frac{1}{8}$ of total length. Height of head $\frac{1}{5}$, of body $\frac{2}{7}$, of hard dorsal $\frac{1}{9}$, of soft dorsal $\frac{1}{11}$, of ventral $\frac{1}{6}$, of anal $\frac{1}{7}$ of total length.

Eyes—Situated close to profile, diameter $\frac{2}{7}$ of length of head, $\frac{3}{4}$ of a diameter apart, rather more than 1 diameter from end of snout.

Maxilla extends to beneath the anterior third of orbit. Preopercle furrowed but entire. Sub- and interopercles entire. Opercle ending in a spine. Suprascapular furrowed. Preorbital entire, more than twice as long as high, with its lower margin nearly horizontal, and in large specimens considerably notched to receive the superior extremity of the maxilla. There is a slight protuberance above the anterior superior angle of the orbit. Five facets exist on the inferior surface of the lower jaw.

Teeth—Six sharp curved teeth in the front of both jaws, with numerous molars posterior to them, above in four or five series, below in three or four rows.

Fins—Dorsal spines moderately strong, compressed, broader on one side, fourth spine the longest; interspinous membrane deeply notched. Ventral spine weak, equal to fourth dorsal, first ray prolonged, an elongated scale at the base of the fin. Second anal spine much the strongest, and above three times the length of the first, and one-seventh longer than the third. Pectoral pointed, extending on the body to opposite second anal spine, but if the fin is deflected it only reaches to commencement of anal. The distances between the terminations of the dorsal and anal fins to the commencement of the caudal are the same, and equal to the length of the base of the anal.

Scales—Moderate extending as far as the orbits, and over the cheeks: on the body they pass in horizontal rows, and some cover the base of the caudal.

Lateral line—In upper third of body, very slightly curved, and in single tubes.

Colours—Silvery, with a greenish shade along the back. Each scale with its base darker than its margin. Abdomen, silvery with indistinct horizontal golden lines. Dorsal, caudal and anal, greyish tipped with black.

Not common in Malabar; good eating, grows to ten inches in length.

Habitat—Seas and estuaries of India, China and Japan.

Chrysophrys calamara.

Calamara, *Russell*, pl. 92.

Chrysophrys calamara, *Cuv. & Val.* vi. p. 117; *Cantor*, Catal. p. 48; *Günther*, Catal. i. p. 493.

Aree, *Mal.*

B. vi. D. $\frac{11}{11}$. P. 15. V. $\frac{1}{5}$. C. 17. L. l. 45. L. tr. $\frac{5}{10}$.

Length of head $\frac{1}{4}$, of pectoral $\frac{4}{13}$, of caudal $\frac{2}{13}$, of base of dorsal $\frac{1}{2}$, of base of anal $\frac{2}{13}$ of total length. Height of head $\frac{1}{4}$, of body $\frac{1}{3}$, of hard dorsal $\frac{2}{13}$, of soft dorsal $\frac{1}{8}$, of ventral $\frac{1}{6}$, of anal $\frac{2}{13}$ of total length.

Eyes—Close to profile, diameter $\frac{1}{4}$ of length of head, $1\frac{1}{2}$ diameter from end of snout, 1 diameter apart.

The profile rises very considerably from snout to base of dorsal, the mouth being opposite the central ray of pectoral, and in the lower fourth of the body. Upper jaw protrusible. The maxilla extends to beneath the anterior third of orbit. There is no enlargement, or else a very slight one, of the anterior margin of the orbit. Pre- sub- and interopercles entire: coracoid furrowed. Opercle with a small, but rather sharp spine. Preorbital entire, about twice as broad as high, its lower margin horizontal.

Teeth—Six conical ones in the anterior portion of each jaw, with four rows of molars in the posterior portion of the lower, and five in the same part of the upper jaw.

Fins—Spinous portion of dorsal, occupies more than half the base of the fin, where it can be received into a groove. Spines strong, each alternate one being broadest on the opposite side of the fin. Interspinous membrane deeply notched. Fourth spine slightly longer than third or fifth, which are equal in height. Pectoral pointed, fifth ray the longest, and reaching (when the fin is deflected) to second anal spine, but when resting in its natural position extending to opposite fifth anal ray. Ventral spine moderately strong, and equalling the fourth dorsal in length, first ray prolonged. Second anal spine the longest and strongest, being five-sevenths longer than the first, and nearly the length of the first spine longer than the third; the spinous portion and first few rays can be received into a groove at their base. The anal commences opposite first ray of dorsal, and ends opposite its termination, between this and the commencement of the caudal the finless portion equals the base of the soft rays of the anal. Caudal rather deeply emarginate.

Scales—Widest from above downwards, placed in horizontal rows, some extending forward as far as the orbits and over the cheeks, and some covering the base of the soft rays of dorsal, caudal and anal fins.

Lateral line—Proceeds backwards and upwards for the first nine scales, then curves downwards to opposite end of dorsal, from whence it proceeds direct to the caudal on to which fin it is continued about half its length, curving upwards and crossing the lowest rays of the upper lobe.

Colours—Greyish, the external margin of each scale being marked with a darker tinge. Abdomen silvery. Fins margined with dark grey, also a line of the same colour passes along the centre of the soft portions of the dorsal, and anal. Pectoral dirty yellow. Eyes silvery. Specimens captured in October appear greyish black, but become brighter after death, and the pectoral is of a dirty reddish yellow.

Very common in Malabar until July, when it gives place to the *Diagramma nigrum,* both of which are known as "Black rock fish," and are excellent eating. The *C. Calamara* grows to twelve inches and upwards in length.

Habitat—Seas of India and Malaysia.

GENUS CHÆTODON, *Artedi.*

Branchiostegals, six: pseudobranchiæ. Body much compressed and elevated. Eyes moderate. Mouth small, with lateral cleft: muzzle short or of moderate length. One dorsal, with the spinous and soft portions equally developed, none of the spines elongated. Anal with three or four spines and equally developed with the soft dorsal. Ventral with one spine and five rays. The vertical fins more or less covered with scales. Preopercle either entire or finely serrated, no spines. Teeth villiform, none on palate. Scales large or of moderate size, finely ctenoid or smooth. Lateral line continuous. Air bladder with horns or two divisions. Intestines with many convolutions. Pyloric appendages in moderate numbers.

CHÆTODON PRÆTEXTATUS.

CHÆTODON PRÆTEXTATUS, *Cantor*, Catal. p. 156, pl. 3; *Günther*, Catal. ii. p. 22.

B. vi. D. $\frac{12}{26\text{-}28}$. P. 15. V. $\frac{1}{5}$. A. $\frac{3}{20\text{-}22}$. C. 17. L. l. 20. L. tr. 16.

Length of head $\frac{2}{7}$, of pectoral $\frac{1}{4}$, of caudal $\frac{2}{11}$, of base of dorsal $\frac{2}{3}$, of base of anal $\frac{1}{3}$ of total length. Height of head $\frac{1}{3}$, of body $\frac{1}{2}$, of hard dorsal $\frac{1}{4}$, of soft dorsal $\frac{1}{4}$, of ventral $\frac{1}{5}$, of anal $\frac{1}{4}$ of total length.

Eyes—Diameter slightly exceeding $\frac{1}{3}$ of length of head, nearly $\frac{1}{2}$ diameter from end of snout, $\frac{5}{7}$ of a diameter apart.

Form of body rounded, strongly compressed. Snout rather produced. Mouth small, slightly protractile. Maxilla extends two-thirds of the distance to orbit. Preorbital with elevated margins, forming a slight tubercle anteriorly. Preopercle narrow, finely serrated at its angle, lower limb slightly oblique and two-thirds the height of the vertical one. Interopercle large, entire, and produced downwards in a somewhat triangular form. Subopercle entire. Opercle with two obtuse points, divided by a long but shallow emargination.

Teeth—Slender and close like the hairs of a brush.

Fins—Spinous portion of dorsal occupying just half of the base of the fin, spines broad: interspinous membrane deeply notched. Fifth and sixth spines longest; central rays of soft portion the longest. Ventral spine moderately strong, equalling the length of the third dorsal. Third anal spine strongest, but second slightly the longest. Dorsal fin evenly rounded from commencement of spines to the last soft ray. Pectoral short. Ventral triangular, first ray produced, with an elongated scale at its base. Soft portion of anal equally rounded with the soft portion of the dorsal. Caudal nearly straight.

Scales—Large, and deciduous, extending to the snout over the pre- and suborbitals and opercles. The dorsal is scaled in an oblique arched line, commencing at the root of the third spine, and continued so that only the points of the three last are visible; whilst its soft rays, those of the anal and sometimes the base of the caudal, are likewise scaled. The scales on the anal begin at the base of the first spine, and are continued in a curved line so that merely the outer third of the last spine is visible.

Lateral line—First ascends to the root of the last dorsal spine, then follows the base of the soft rays.

Colours—Generally brownish olive, each scale with a light citron spot in its centre. One bluish white band passes in front of the dorsal fin, over the opercle and downwards to the throat, where it expands. A second band passes across the preorbital, and over the cheek to the throat, opposite the orbit it gives off another small bluish white band, which passes to the angle of the mouth, and then downwards to the throat. A bluish white line exists on the forehead, and passes to the eye, where it is lost. Dorsal and anal fins tinged with reddish violet, the upper fourth of the soft portion is margined with six bands in the following order from without, white, black, scarlet, black, pearl white and black, the colours are slightly extended on to the spines. Anal, tipped with three rows, white, black and scarlet. Caudal, posterior half pearly white, divided by a black band from a scarlet base. Pectoral diaphanous. Ventral black. Eyes hazel.

Common in Malabar for about a fortnight in June subsequent to the commencement of the monsoon. Grows to six inches in length. Cantor observes that it is esteemed at Pinang as food.

Habitat—Malabar, Pinang.

Genus HENIOCHUS, *Cuv. & Val.*

Taurichthys, *Cuv. & Val.*

Branchiostegals, five: pseudobranchiæ. Body compressed and elevated. One dorsal with from eleven to thirteen spines, the fourth of which is much elongated and filiform. Vertical fins more or less scaled. Snout short, or of moderate length. Preopercle entire, or finely serrated. Teeth villiform, none on palate. Scales of moderate size, finely ctenoid, or smooth. Lateral line continuous. An air bladder. Pyloric appendages few.

HENIOCHUS MACROLEPIDOTUS.

CHŒTODON MACROLEPIDOTUS, *Artedi*, p. 94.
HENIOCHUS ACUMINATUS, *Cuv. & Val.* vii. p. 98.
HENIOCHUS PERMUTATUS, *Cuv. & Val.* vii. p. 99.
HENIOCHUS MACROLEPIDOTUS, *Cuv. & Val.* vii. p. 93; *Günther*, Catal. ii. p. 39.
DIPHREUTES MACROLEPIDOTUS, *Cantor*, Catal. p. 159.
PURROAMEE, *Mal.*

B. v. D. $\frac{11-12}{24-25}$. P. 17. V. $\frac{1}{5}$. A. $\frac{3}{17}$ $\frac{3}{18}$. C. 17. L. l. 60. L. tr. $\frac{9}{22}$. Vert. $\frac{10}{14}$. Cœc. pylor. 6.

Length of head $\frac{2}{7}$, of pectoral $\frac{1}{4}$, of caudal $\frac{1}{4}$, of base of dorsal $\frac{2}{3}$, of base of anal $\frac{2}{7}$ of total length. Height of head $\frac{1}{4}$, of body $\frac{4}{5}$, of hard dorsal (excluding the fourth spine which equals the total length) $\frac{1}{4}$, of soft dorsal $\frac{1}{6}$, of ventral $\frac{1}{4}$, of anal $\frac{1}{4}$ of total length.

Eyes—Close to profile, diameter slightly more than $\frac{1}{3}$ of length of head, 1 diameter from end of snout, $\frac{5}{6}$ of a diameter apart.

Snout moderately produced, profile rises direct from orbits to dorsal fin. Maxilla extends half way to anterior margin of orbit. A small protuberance above each orbit, but none on nape of neck. Preorbital large, entire, with its anterior superior angle elevated. Preopercle, vertical limb narrow, more than twice as long as inferior one, posterior margin straight and finely serrated, especially at its angle, horizontal limb straight. Sub- and interopercles entire. Opercle with two obtuse points widely separated, and connected by a shallow emargination.

Teeth—In jaws villiform, none on palate.

Fins—Dorsal spines moderately strong, they occupy rather more than half the base of the fin, the fourth filamentous at its extremity, the sixth longer than the third, and the fifth longer than either. Ventral spine rather strong. Two last anal spines about the same length and strength. Pectoral rather rounded. Ventral triangular. Anal opposite soft portion of dorsal, and its anterior rays much the longest. Caudal nearly square at its extremity.

Scales—Longest diameter from above downwards: some cover most of the dorsal and anal spines, and the soft rays, also the base of the caudal, and are extended on to the snout and cheeks.

Lateral line—Curves upwards to upper fourth of body, and opposite the end of the soft dorsal it takes a straight direction.

Colours—Pearl white with a purplish bar on the summit of the snout, another over the eye, and a third broad one extending from the dorsal to the abdominal surface, its posterior half includes the first three dorsal spines and the posterior two-thirds of the opercle, and passing downwards includes the whole of the ventral fin and extends as far backwards as the anal. The last band commences at the summit of the fifth dorsal spine, passes downwards to the base of the seventh, and is as wide as to the first ray; it then passes downwards over the posterior third of the abdomen, and includes the posterior half of the anal fin. The soft portions of the dorsal and caudal are of a bright gamboge colour. Pectoral yellow. Iris gamboge, purplish towards the orbit.

Common, said to grow to eighteen inches in length.

Habitat—From the Mauritius through all the East Indian seas to the N.W. Coast of Australia.

GENUS SCATOPHAGUS, *Cuv. and Val.*

CACODOXUS, *Cantor.*

Branchiostegals, six; pseudobranchiæ. Body much compressed and elevated. Two dorsals united at their base, the first with ten or eleven spines, and having anteriorly a recumbent one directed forwards: the second dorsal covered with scales. Anal with four spines. Snout much compressed and elevated; preopercle spineless. Scales very small. Air bladder simple. Pyloric appendages many.

SCATOPHAGUS ARGUS.

CHÆTODON ARGUS, *Linn. Gm.* p. 1248.
CHITSILLOO, *Russell*, pl. 78.
CHÆTODON PAIRATALIS, *Ham. Buch.* pp. 122, 372. pl. 16, f. 41.
CHÆTODON ATROMACULATUS, *Bennett*, Fishes of Ceylon, pl. 18.
CACODOXUS ARGUS, *Cantor*, Catal. p. 163.
SCATOPHAGUS ARGUS, *Cuv. & Val.* vii. p. 136; *Günther*, Catal. ii. p. 56.
NUTCHAR CHAR, *Mal.*

B. vi. D. 10 | $\frac{1}{16}$. P. 15. V. $\frac{1}{5}$. A. $\frac{4}{14}$. C. 16. Vert. $\frac{11}{12}$.

Length of head $\frac{1}{4}$, of pectoral $\frac{1}{8}$, of caudal $\frac{1}{6}$, of base of dorsals $\frac{1}{2}$, of base of anal $\frac{1}{3}$ of total length. Height of head $\frac{2}{7}$, of body $\frac{5}{6}$, of hard dorsal $\frac{2}{9}$, of soft dorsal $\frac{1}{6}$, of ventral $\frac{1}{5}$, of anal $\frac{1}{5}$ of total length.

Eyes—Diameter $\frac{1}{3}$ length of head, $\frac{1}{2}$ diameter from end of snout, $1\frac{1}{2}$ diameters apart.

The body is somewhat quadrangular, strongly compressed, with its upper margin more curved than its abdominal one. The profile is convex from the snout to above the orbits, then it ascends at an acute angle to the first dorsal fin, along the base of which it is nearly horizontal. Muzzle broad, lips do not cover the jaws. Maxilla extends about half way to the orbit. Preorbital half longer than broad, with the posterior portion of its lower margin finely denticulated. Posterior nostril oval, close to orbit, and a short distance from the anterior which is rounded. Preopercle entire, as are also the sub- and interopercles. Opercle ending in a spine.

Teeth—In jaws villiform, none on the palate.

Fins—Dorsal spines moderately strong with a groove at their base into which they can be received. The first dorsal occupies three-tenths more of the back than does the second dorsal. Interspinous membrane deeply notched: fourth spine the highest: anterior rays much the longest. Ventral spine strong and as long as sixth dorsal, first ray prolonged. Anal opposite second dorsal, its third spine the strongest, but all about the same length, and can be received into a groove at their base, anterior rays the longest. Caudal fanshaped, its central rays slightly the longest. Upper pectoral rays the longest.

Scales—Very minute, covering the soft portions of the dorsal, anal, and caudal fins, and extending over the head and opercles.

Lateral line—Rather wavy in its course, first slightly ascending, then following the curve of the back as far as the end of second dorsal, from whence it proceeds straight.

Colours—Of a reddish purple, becoming silvery on the abdomen. Large round brownish spots are scattered over the whole of the body, but most thickly along the back. The cheeks and snout have bluish reflections. First dorsal brownish blue, having a few minute spots; second dorsal yellowish with slight brown markings between the rays, the soft portion of the anal being similarly coloured. Pectorals and ventrals yellowish. Eyes golden.

The colours depend on the season of the year in which captured, and whether taken in fresh or salt water. In the monsoon time the back becomes greenish, and the purple colour is deeper.

Common, grows to one foot in length. Owing to its being reputed to be a very foul feeder, only the lowest classes will eat it. *Bennett* states that in Ceylon it is caught on hooks baited with seaweed "Pendah," of which it is particularly fond.

Habitat—East Indian and Chinese seas, entering the mouths of rivers and backwaters.

GENUS EPHIPPUS, *Cuvier*.

ILARCHES, *Cantor*.

Branchiostegals, six: pseudobranchiæ. Body much compressed and elevated. Dorsal with eight or nine spines, receivable into a groove at its base, the third and sometimes more, are elongated and flexible; interspinous membrane deeply notched. Three anal spines. Pectoral short. Snout short, upper profile parabolic. Preopercle without a spine. No teeth on palate. Scales moderate or small. Air bladder bifurcated in front, with two horns posteriorly.

EPHIPPUS ORBIS.

CHÆTODON ORBIS, *Bloch*, t. 202, f. 2.
EPHIPPUS ORBIS, *Cuv. & Val.* vii. p. 127; *Günther*, Catal. ii. p. 62.
ILARCHES ORBIS, *Cantor*, Catal. p. 160.

B. vi. D. 8 | $\frac{1}{19}$. P. 19. V. $\frac{1}{5}$. A. $\frac{3}{15}$. C. 19. L. r. 35. L. tr. $\frac{7}{15}$.

Length of head $\frac{1}{4}$, of pectoral $\frac{1}{6}$, of base of dorsals nearly $\frac{1}{2}$, of base of anal $\frac{1}{3}$, of caudal $\frac{1}{5}$ of total length. Height of head $\frac{2}{7}$, of body nearly $\frac{1}{2}$, of first dorsal $\frac{1}{3}$, of second dorsal $\frac{1}{5}$, of ventral $\frac{1}{5}$, of anal $\frac{1}{4}$ of total length.

Eyes—Diameter $\frac{1}{2}$ length of head, 1 diameter from end of snout, nearly 1 diameter apart.

The upper profile is much elevated, rising abruptly from the snout to the first dorsal fin: the abdominal contour is much less convex. The maxilla extends to opposite anterior margin of orbit. Preopercle narrow, finely denticulated on its vertical limb and at its angle. Sub- and interopercles entire. Opercle half as wide as long, ending in two obtuse points, connected by a shallow emargination.

Teeth—Villiform in jaws, none on palate.

Fins—Dorsal spines moderately strong at their bases; interspinous membrane of first fin deeply emarginated, but not that between spine of second fin and soft rays. The spines of the first dorsal can be received into a groove at their base, which is slightly more than two-thirds of the extent of that of the second dorsal. The third, fourth and fifth spines are elongated and filiform at their extremities, especially the third spine. The anterior rays of the second dorsal are the longest. Ventral spine weak but rather long, first ray elongated. Anal opposite soft dorsal, second spine the longest and strongest, equal to the seventh dorsal in length, the spines can be received into a groove at their base anterior rays the longest. Pectoral short rounded. Ventral pointed.

Second dorsal rounded. Anal longest in front. Caudal slightly produced in the centre, and somewhat emarginate above and below.

Scales—Moderate in size, some over base of caudal and anal rays.

Lateral line—First ascends backwards to opposite eighth dorsal spine, from thence it curves downwards.

Colours—Back and head greyish green, sides and abdomen silvery shot with pink. Fin membranes diaphanous, finely dotted with black, more especially in their marginal halves. The rays pale yellow. Iris golden, with some fine black points.

Not common. Eaten but not esteemed. Grows to six inches in length.

Habitat—Seas of India, Malaysia and China.

Genus DREPANE, *Cuv. and Val.*

Harpochirus, *Cantor.*

Branchiostegals, six: pseudobranchiæ. Body much compressed and elevated. Dorsal with eight or nine spines receivable into a groove at its base, with a concealed spine anteriorly, and directed forwards. Interspinous membrane deeply notched. Anal with three spines. Pectoral elongated, falciform. Preopercle spineless. No teeth on palate. Scales of moderate size. Air bladder prolonged into two horns posteriorly. Pyloric appendages few.

Drepane punctata.

Chætodon punctatus, *Linn. Gmel.* p. 1243.
Latte-Terla, A. & B. *Russell*, pl. 79, 80, 81.
Drepane punctata, *Cuv. & Val.* vii. p. 132. pl. 179; *Günther*, Catal. ii. p. 62.
Drepane longimana, *Cuv. & Val.* vii. p. 133.
Harpochirus punctatus, *Cantor*, Catal. p. 162.
Harpochirus longimanus, *Cantor*, Catal. p. 163.
Piindthee, *Mal.*

B. vi. D. $\frac{8-9}{20-21}$. P. 17. V. $\frac{1}{5}$. A. $\frac{3}{17-18}$. C. 15. L. l. 50. L. tr. $\frac{14}{33}$. Cœcal pylor. 2-3.

Length of head $\frac{1}{4}$, of pectoral rather more than $\frac{1}{3}$, of base of dorsal $\frac{1}{2}$, of base of anal $\frac{1}{3}$ of total length. Height of head $\frac{1}{3}$, of body $\frac{1}{2}$, of hard dorsal $\frac{1}{6}$, of soft dorsal $\frac{1}{5}$, of ventral $\frac{1}{6}$, of anal $\frac{1}{5}$ of total length.

Eyes—Close to profile, diameter $\frac{2}{5}$ length of head, $\frac{2}{3}$ of a diameter apart, 1 from end of snout.

The profile rises abruptly from snout to commencement of dorsal fin, whilst that of the abdomen is nearly straight. The maxilla extends backwards to opposite the anterior margin of the orbit, mouth small. Intermaxillaries protrusible. Preorbital very broad, entire. Preopercle long and narrow, its horizontal limb is denticulated, and only one-third the length of the vertical one which is entire. Sub- and interopercles entire.

Teeth—Villiform in jaws, none on palate.

Fins—Dorsal spines strong, compressed, pointed, their base equals one-third of that of the entire fin, having a groove into which they can be partially received: the third spine the longest: interspinous membrane deeply notched: the rays longer than the spines. Pectoral falciform, extending as far as last dorsal rays, and sometimes to root of caudal. Ventral spine moderately strong, as long as that of fourth dorsal, its first rays prolonged. Anal opposite posterior three-fourths of dorsal, second spine much the strongest and longest, its spines can be received into a groove at their base, the length of the rays equals those of the dorsal fin. Central rays of caudal the longest.

Scales—Extend as far forwards as centre of eye, none on opercles, between the eyes, or on the snout.

Colours—Silvery with a gloss of bluish violet. Fins yellowish, stained darker at their margins, about six dark greyish bands pass downwards from the back, in which are several round, brown, or black spots, none of which descend below the middle of the body. The older the specimens the more decided the spots, the less marked the stripes. In some old specimens there are no spots.

Not rare in Malabar, or much esteemed as food. Grows to one foot three inches in length.

Habitat—Aden, Seas of India, Malaysia, China, New Holland, New Guinea, N. W. Coast of Australia.

GENUS TOXOTES, *Cuvier.*

Branchiostegals, seven: pseudobranchiæ. Body compressed, oblong. One dorsal with five strong spines, situated on posterior part of the back: anal with three spines, its soft portion and that of the dorsal scaled. Snout rather produced, lower jaw the longest. Eyes of moderate size. Villiform teeth on jaws, vomer, and palatine bones. Scales cycloid, of moderate size. Air bladder simple. Pyloric appendages in moderate number.

* TOXOTES JACULATOR.

SCIÆNA JACULATRIX, *Pallas*, Spicil. Fas. viii. p. 41.

COIUS CHATAREUS, *Ham. Buch.* pp. 101, 370, pl. 14, f. 34.

TOXOTES JACULATOR, *Cuv. & Val.* vii. p. 314, pl. 192; *Cantor*, Catal. pl. 176; *Günther*, Catal. ii. p. 67.

B. vii. D. $\frac{5}{11\text{-}13}$. P. 13-14. V. $\frac{1}{5}$. A. $\frac{3}{15\text{-}17}$. C. 17. L. l. 28. L. tr. $\frac{3\text{-}4}{7\text{-}8}$. Vert. $\frac{10}{14}$. Cœc. pylor. 7-9.

Length of head $\frac{4}{13}$, of base of dorsal $\frac{2}{7}$, of pectoral $\frac{1}{4}$ of total length. Height of body a little more than $\frac{2}{5}$ of total length.

Eyes—With axis of pupils vertical, diameter $\frac{2}{9}$ of length of head.

Body irregularly oval and compressed, its greatest width is behind the middle, and it is more prominent below than above: back rounded, upper surface of skull flattened. Thickness above pectorals equals more than half its height. The profile is a little oblique from the dorsal fin to the mouth, and descends in a straight line.

The length of the snout equals the width of the interorbital space, lower jaw slightly the longest. Maxilla extends to beneath the posterior border of eye. Preorbital, lower border straight, and finely serrated. Preopercle, horizontal border finely denticulated. Orifices of nostrils close to anterior superior margin of orbit, the upper oval and larger than the lower which is circular.

Teeth—A straight band of fine sharp and closely set villiform teeth in both jaws, vomer, palatines, pterygoids, and tongue.

Fins—Dorsal spines very strong, the last three the longest and half the height of body, the second one-third, and the first two-thirds shorter. Interspinous membrane deeply notched, soft portion covered with small scales, as are also the soft rays of the anal. Caudal with a concave edge.

Scales—Extend over head, larger above than below.

Lateral line—In a single tube at centre of each scale, at first straight and near the back, just before reaching opposite the dorsal fin it curves downwards to centre of body.

Colours—Vary in different localities, head and back silvery olive green, brown or blackish, the remainder silvery buff or greyish. Scales with minute brown spots in their centres, thus forming longitudinal lines. Five large rounded spots along the sides, with a series of smaller intermediate ones above. Dorsal greyish, minutely dotted with black, with two large oblique black spots on the soft dorsal, which is margined with black. Caudal bright gamboge yellow, with a more or less distinct black band, arched backward behind its root. Anal silvery margined with black. Pectorals and ventrals white, the latter with a large black spot. Iris bright gamboge, blackish towards orbit.

Uncommon in Malabar, said to be indifferent food. Grows to one foot in length.

Habitat—Seas of India, Malaysia, China, and Polynesia.

Genus PTEROIS, *Cuvier*.

Branchiostegals, seven: pseudobranchiæ. Head and body compressed, the former armed with spines on its upper and lateral surfaces. No groove on occiput. One dorsal with twelve or thirteen spines, the membrane deeply notched. Anal with three spines. The rays generally elongate, free, but branched. Villiform teeth in jaws and vomer, none on the palatines. Scales moderate or small. Air bladder large. Pyloric appendages few.

Pterois volitans.

Gasterosteus volitans, *Linn.* i. p. 491.
Kodipungi, *Russell*, pl. 133.
Scorpœna volitans, *Bennett*, pl. i.
Pterois volitans, *Cuv. & Val.* iv. p. 352, pl. 88; *Günther*, Catal. ii. p. 122.
Purrooah, *Mal.*

B. vii. D. $\frac{13}{10\text{-}11}$. P. 14. V. $\frac{1}{5}$. A. $\frac{3}{6}$. C. 13. L. r. 90. Cœc. pylor. 3 Vert. $\frac{10}{14}$.

Length of head $\frac{2}{9}$, of pectoral $\frac{2}{3}$, of caudal $\frac{1}{4}$, of base of dorsal $\frac{1}{2}$, base of anal $\frac{1}{9}$ of total length. Height of head $\frac{1}{6}$, of body $\frac{1}{4}$, of hard dorsal $\frac{1}{5}$, of soft dorsal $\frac{1}{5}$, of ventral $\frac{2}{7}$, of anal $\frac{1}{5}$ of total length.

Eyes—With upper wall of orbit much raised above the line of the profile, diameter $\frac{2}{7}$ of length of head, 1 diameter from end of snout, nearly 1 diameter from the summit of one superorbital ridge to that of the opposite one.

Profile convex over snout, from nostrils to base of dorsal nearly straight, but the upper margin of the orbit projects considerably above it.

Maxilla extends to beneath the anterior margin of the orbit. Symphysis of lower jaw projects a little downwards. Intermaxillaries notched in centre and protrusible. Preorbital broad, rather elevated in front, and roughened by ridges and grooves which radiate from its centre. Preopercle with two strong spines (the upper the largest) on its vertical limb, a third less strong on its angle, and one—sometimes two—indistinct points on its oblique lower limb. A spiny ridge from angle of preopercle to preorbital. Opercle ending in a soft point. Sub- and interopercles entire. A short sharp spine close above the anterior opening of the nostrils. A blunt spine on posterior superior angle of orbit. Two sharp blade-like flattened spines on either side of occiput. Scapular spiny: coracoid entire. Above the centre of the orbit is a long fleshy filament two-thirds the diameter of the eye; other shorter but broader ones arise as follows, one from below the nasal spine, one from each intermaxillary, two from preorbital, three from lower limb of preopercle. Two orifices of nostrils wide apart, in front of centre of orbit.

Teeth—Fine, villiform, on jaws and vomer.

Fins—Dorsal spines moderately strong, and extend over more than two-thirds of the base of the fin, membrane only existing just at the posterior margin of each spine, and notched almost to its base: rays branched into two. Pectorals elongated so as to extend a short distance beyond the base of the caudal, the membrane between the rays deeply notched, covering both sides of the ninth or tenth, but the under side only of those above, and the upper side of those below: none of the rays branched. Ventral spine weak, rays branched, elongated, and the membrane deeply notched, being least so between sixth and seventh rays. Anal spines weak, the third the longest: rays branched, membrane not deeply cleft. Caudal, central rays longest, branched, membrane moderately cleft.

Scales—Small, and covering the cheeks and head, except the snout and interopercle.

Lateral line—Tubular in each scale and situated in upper fourth of body.

Colours—Generally of a fawn colour, with vertical bands of reddish brown, the outer portion of which is the darkest. The first dark band on the body commences opposite the second dorsal spine: the second opposite the fourth: the third opposite the sixth: the second and third bands coalesce a little below the lateral line. The fourth commences opposite the tenth spine: the fifth opposite the second and third rays, passing down to first anal ray. Another dark band passes mid-way between the termination of the dorsal and the commencement of the caudal, whilst an eighth exists at the base of the caudal fin: between all these dark bands there are lighter ones. The head is also striped like the body, one dark band passes from the anterior portion of the orbit to the middle of the upper jaw, a second from the centre of the orbit over the cheek to the anterior termination of the inferior limb of preopercle: a third from the posterior margin of the orbit to the angle of preopercle: whilst the last broad stripe commences at the anterior spine at the side of the occiput, and passing over the opercle ends in the upper part of the base of the pectoral fin. Besides these there are numerous narrower and lighter intermediate bands. All the filaments have dark centres and brownish margins. Dorsal spines leaden colour with whitish markings, rays white spotted with black, and some black markings opposite the vertical dark bands already described. Caudal and anal whitish spotted with black, the latter marked with the continuation of the two dark bands that go to its base. Pectoral slate colour, irregularly barred with white: one small round white spot on the body just above the base of the pectoral. Ventrals slate colour, with brown and white markings.

It is not uncommon. Grows to nine inches in length; is said to be eaten.

Habitat—From eastern coasts of Africa, through the Indian, to the Australian seas.

PTEROIS MILES.

SCORPÆNA MILES, *Bennett*, pl. 9.
PTEROIS MURICATA, *Cuv. & Val.* iv. p. 363.
PTEROIS MILES, *Cantor*, Catal. p. 42; *Günther*, Catal. ii. pp. 125, 521.

B. vii. D. $\frac{13}{11\text{-}12}$. P. 12. V. $\frac{1}{5}$. A. $\frac{3}{7}$. C. 14. Vert. $\frac{10}{14}$.

Length of head $\frac{1}{4}$, of pectorals $\frac{1}{2}$, of caudal $\frac{2}{9}$, of base of dorsal $\frac{1}{2}$, of base of anal $\frac{1}{10}$ of total length. Height of head $\frac{1}{5}$, of body $\frac{1}{4}$, of hard dorsal $\frac{2}{9}$, of soft dorsal $\frac{1}{5}$, of ventral $\frac{1}{4}$, of anal $\frac{1}{5}$ of total length.

Eyes—The upper margin of orbit somewhat raised above the profile, its diameter $\frac{1}{4}$ the length of the head, $1\frac{1}{2}$ diameter from end of snout, 1 diameter apart.

Profile very slightly convex over snout, straight from thence to dorsal, but the upper margin of the orbit projects slightly, and the spines on the side of the occiput very much above it.

Mouth horizontal, the maxilla does not reach as far as the anterior margin of the orbit. Symphysis of lower jaw projects a little downwards. Intermaxillaries deeply notched in centre, and protrusible. Preorbitals broad, rather elevated in front, and roughened by ridges and grooves which radiate from their centres. Preopercle with two strong spines on the vertical limb, the upper being the largest: a third, less strong on its angle. Lower limb nearly horizontal, entire. Sub- and interopercles entire. Opercle with a blunt spinous extremity. Between and internal to the two nasal orifices is a sharp spine directed upwards and backwards, there are also some rugosities along the upper margin of the orbit which in old specimens become spiniferous, and one large spine at the posterior superior angle of the orbit. The temporal ridge, commencing about the centre of the posterior margin of the orbit, is spiny in the whole of its course towards the lateral line. The interorbital space is shallow and rather concave from side to side, a deep groove continued anteriorly as far as the intermaxillary bones, runs down its centre, whilst posteriorly it expands over the occiput, where it is bordered on either side by an outwardly curved blade-like crest, flattened from side to side, and terminates in its posterior superior part in two large flat spines, which in old specimens become several badly developed spines. A spiny ridge proceeds from the preorbital over the cheeks to the angle of the preopercle; in old subjects it becomes very rugged, the single row of spines is augmented into two or three lesser ones, while its width is much increased. At the centre of the upper margin of the orbit arises a fleshy filament half the diameter of the eye in length, but which in old subjects appears to become still shorter: there is generally another at the angle of the mouth, and some others along the inferior margin of the preorbital and preopercle.

Teeth—In jaws and vomer villiform.

Fins—Dorsal spines pretty strong and extend over more than two-thirds of the base of the fin, the membrane merely connects them close to their origin, whilst the rays are connected at their summits, and are only divided into two branches, the third spine is equal to the highest. In the pectorals the membrane is extended as in the *P. volitans*, and the other fins resemble those of that fish.

Scales—Small.

Lateral line—In upper fourth of body.

Colours—Brilliant scarlet, the bars darker, but distributed as in the last species, rays of dorsal, anal, and caudal unspotted. In fact an old *Pterois volitans* and a young *P. miles* are still desiderata.

Not uncommon in Malabar, where it arrives about the commencement of the monsoon. From one, 21 specimens of the *Atherina Forskâlii* were taken, so gorged was it,—its entire length being only 11½ inches,—that the tail of one was protruding from its mouth. Not esteemed for eating. Length from eleven to twelve inches.

Habitat.—Red Sea, and seas of India.

GENUS TETRAROGE.

APISTUS, SP. *Cuv. & Val.*

Branchiostegals, from five to seven: pseudobranchiæ. Head and body compressed, naked or with rudimentary scales. One dorsal with from seven to seventeen spines: no pectoral appendage. Preorbital and preopercle armed. Teeth in jaws, vomer, and generally on the palatines. No cleft behind the fourth gill. Air bladder present. Pyloric appendages few.

* TETRAROGE BELENGERII.

APISTUS BELENGERII, *Cuv. & Val.* iv. p. 412.

D. $\frac{12}{8}$. P. 13. V. $\frac{1}{5}$. A. $\frac{3}{6}$. C. 11.

Body elevated in the centre where its height equals one-third of its length. Profile oblique, the mouth descending posteriorly. Preorbital spine hardly extends as far as the centre of the orbit, with a small one in front of its base. Preopercular spine nearly equals that of preorbital, and is directed backwards; two very short ones exist on the lower limb. Opercle ends in three points.

Fins—The first dorsal spine arises opposite the posterior border of the orbit, and is nearly as high as the second. The interspinous membrane beyond the fifth spine is deeply cleft. Between the last dorsal ray and the caudal there is an interval. Caudal cut square, and is comprised four and a-half times in the total length. Pectorals slightly longer, ventrals rather less.

Scales—Very small.

Lateral line—Parallel with the back, and marked by elevations which appear like little points lying in the mucus.

Colours—Grey, finely dotted with brown, except the chest and abdomen, which are whitish. The fins are the same colour as the body, and there is a black spot on the dorsal from the fifth to the eighth spine.

Grows to two and a quarter inches in length.

Habitat—Mahé in Malabar.

GENUS PROSOPODASYS, *Cantor.*

APISTUS, SP. *Cuv. & Val.*

PROSOPODASYS, *Cantor.*

Branchiostegals, five to seven: pseudobranchiæ. Head and body more or less compressed, naked, or with minute rudimentary scales. Three anterior dorsal spines divided from the others by a deep notch.

The second dorsal with from nine to twelve, the anal with three spines. No pectoral appendages. Preorbital and preopercle armed. Villiform teeth on jaws, vomer, and usually on the palatines. No cleft behind the fourth gill.

PROSOPODASYS DRACÆNA.

APISTUS DRACÆNA, *Cuv. & Val.* iv. p. 403.
PROSOPODASYS DRACÆNA, *Günther*, Catal. ii. p. 140.

B. vii. D. 3 | $\frac{9}{8}$. P. 13. V. $\frac{1}{5}$. A. $\frac{3}{6}$. C. 12.

Length of head more than $\frac{1}{4}$, of pectoral above $\frac{1}{4}$, of caudal $\frac{1}{4}$, of base of dorsals $\frac{1}{2}$, of base of anal $\frac{1}{6}$ of total length. Height of head $\frac{1}{4}$, of body $\frac{1}{3}$, of first dorsal $\frac{1}{6}$, of second dorsal $\frac{1}{6}$, of ventral $\frac{1}{4}$, of anal $\frac{1}{6}$ of total length.

Eyes.—Diameter slightly above $\frac{1}{3}$ the length of head, rather above $\frac{1}{2}$ a diameter from end of snout, $\frac{2}{5}$ of a diameter apart.

The maxilla extends to beneath the anterior third of orbit. Lower jaw longest, with a tubercle at its symphysis. Intermaxillaries slightly protrusible, and notched in their centre. Preorbital with a strong spine, directed backwards, three quarters of the diameter of the orbit in length. Preopercle with a long spine the length of the orbit, directed backwards, and four dull points formed by an equal number of concave emarginations on its angle, and one on its inferior limb. Opercle ending in two spines. A concave channel along the summit of the head, between the eyes.

Teeth—Villiform in jaws, vomer, and palate.

Fins—Dorsal spines sharp but slender, the first arises over the centre of the orbit, the interspinous membrane is deeply notched, the second spine the longest, but all three are longer than the spines of the second dorsal, the membrane of which is deeply notched, and the rays are branched. Pectoral reaches to fourth dorsal ray. Ventral spine strong, slightly longer than second dorsal spine, rays branched. Third anal spine longest, rays branched. Central caudal rays slightly the longest.

Lateral line—In upper fourth of body.

Colours—Greyish brown along the back, and pinkish along the chest and abdomen. The whole of the body, dorsal, pectoral, ventral, and anal fins more or less dotted with brown. The caudal immaculate. A large black blotch between the third and sixth spines of the second dorsal.

Grows to three inches in length.

Habitat—Seas and estuaries of Malabar.

GENUS MINOUS, *Cuv. and Val.*

CORYTHOBATUS, *Cantor.*

Branchiostegals, six to seven: pseudobranchiæ. Head and body compressed, scaleless. Several bones of head, especially preorbital, armed. One dorsal with from nine to eleven spines. Anal with from one to three spines. Pectoral rather large, with one appendage. Villiform teeth on jaws and vomer, none on palate. Air bladder present. Pyloric appendages few.

MINOUS MONODACTYLUS.

SCORPÆNA MONODACTYLA, *Bl. Schn.* p. 194.
WORRAH MINOO, *Russell*, pl. 159.
MINOUS WOORA, *Cuv. & Val.* iv. p. 421.
MINOUS MONODACTYLUS, *Cuv. & Val.* iv. p. 424, pl. 59, f. 2; *Günther*, Catal. ii. p. 148.
CORYTHOBATUS WOORA, *Cantor*, Catal. p. 45.

B. vii. D. $\frac{9-11}{12-9}$. P. 11. V. $\frac{1}{5}$. A. 9-11. C. 10.

Length of head $\frac{1}{3}$, of pectoral $\frac{2}{7}$, of caudal $\frac{1}{4}$, of base of dorsal $\frac{1}{2}$ of total length. Height of head $\frac{1}{4}$, of body $\frac{1}{4}$, of hard dorsal $\frac{1}{8}$, of soft dorsal $\frac{1}{8}$, of ventral $\frac{1}{6}$, of anal $\frac{1}{8}$ of total length.

Eyes—Diameter $\frac{2}{9}$ of length of head, 1 diameter from end of snout, 1 diameter apart.

The maxilla extends to beneath the anterior margin of orbit. Intermaxillary rather deeply notched. Lower jaw with tubercle at symphysis. Spinous elevations over nostrils. Smooth ridges radiating from a common centre on the suborbital ring of bones. A strong spine on preorbital equal to the diameter of the eye. Preopercle with a strong spine, at angle three others shorter and blunter, and one more on its lower limb. Temporal and occipital ridges spinous; three moderate sized spines at anterior superior margin of orbit, superciliary ridge rough, nodulated, or spinous.

Teeth—Villiform on jaws and vomer: none on palatines.

Fins—Dorsal spines moderately strong, first spine situated over vertical limb of preopercle, interspinous membrane deeply cleft. Pectoral rather large, extending to the commencement of soft dorsal. One pectoral appendage, nearly the length of the fin, which in dried specimens often separates into two. Caudal rays undivided, membrane notched.

Scales—None.

Colours—Head greyish brown above, sides and abdomen rather lighter. Dorsal fin light brown, with the external margins of spines and outer half of rays deep black. Anal buff, external half black. Pectoral black, appendage white. Caudal buff coloured, with three vertical dark brown bars. Iris grey, minutely dotted with brown.

Common in Malabar, grows to four or five inches in length. Is not esteemed as food.

Habitat—Seas of India, Malaysia, and China.

GENUS PLATYCEPHALUS, *Bl. Schn.*

Branchiostegals, seven: pseudobranchiæ. Head broad, depressed, more or less armed with spines, body subcylindrical posteriorly. Eyes superior or lateral. Cleft of mouth wide. Two dorsals, with a small isolated spine in front of first. Anal equally developed to soft dorsal. Ventrals thoracic. No pectoral appendage. Villiform teeth in jaws, vomer, and palatines, sometimes with larger ones intermingled. Body scaled. Lateral line present, spined in some species. No air bladder. Pyloric appendages in moderate number.

PLATYCEPHALUS INSIDIATOR.

COTTUS INSIDIATOR, *Forskål*, p. 25.

PLATYCEPHALUS INSIDIATOR, *Cuv. & Val.* iv. p. 227; *Cantor*, p. 37; *Günther*, ii. p. 177.
IRRWA, *Russell*, pl. 46.
CALLIOMORUS CHACA, *Ham. Buch.*, pp. 133, 373.
PLATYCEPHALUS CHACCA, *Gray*, Ill. Indian Zool. ii. pl. 93, f. 2.

B. vii. D. 1 | 7 | 13. P. 17. V. $\frac{1}{5}$. A. 13. C. 15. L. r. 94. L. tr. $\frac{12}{24}$.

Length of head nearly $\frac{1}{4}$, of pectoral $\frac{1}{7}$, of caudal $\frac{1}{7}$, of base of first dorsal $\frac{1}{7}$, of base of second dorsal $\frac{3}{10}$, of base of anal $\frac{3}{10}$ of total length. Height of head $\frac{1}{13}$, of body $\frac{1}{7}$, of first dorsal $\frac{1}{7}$, of second dorsal $\frac{1}{9}$, of ventral $\frac{1}{5}$, of anal $\frac{1}{19}$ of total length.

Eyes—Diameter $\frac{2}{17}$ of length of head, $1\frac{1}{2}$ diameters apart, 2 diameters from end of snout. Head strongly compressed and flattened above, its superior surface being almost triangular, the base of which is between the spines of the preopercle, and its apex at the snout. Width of head between preopercular spines is three-fourths of its length. The body subcylindrical.

Lower jaw slightly the longest, the maxilla extends to beneath the centre of orbit. Interobital space flat, or slightly concave from side to side, eyes on the upper surface of the head, which has two spiniferous ridges extending backwards, one internal, which bifurcates over the occiput: the second or temporal from the posterior margin of the orbit terminates at the suprascapular in two flattened blade-like spines. One small sharp spine at the anterior superior angle of the orbit, no spines at nostrils. Preorbital with three raised grooves starting in a stellated form from a common centre. Intermaxillary bones protrusible. Preopercle with most of its surface forming a portion of the flattened upper plane of the head, and having two very strong spines at its angle, the inferior of which is the largest and equals the diameter of the eye. Opercle forming a portion of the flattened upper surface of the head, and having two minute spines.

Teeth—Numerous, and fine in the upper jaw, and a large triangular toothed space at the internal extremity of each intermaxillary, where some larger teeth are intermingled with villiform ones. Three rows of sharp teeth in lower jaw. A convex band of sharp teeth on vomer, and a single series in the palate.

Fins—First dorsal triangular, spines weak, the first slightly the longest, interspinous membrane very slightly emarginate. A small, stout, single spine before the first dorsal, and sometimes another fine one between it and second dorsal. Origin of pectoral partially hidden by the opercle, whilst it covers the commencement of the ventral, which extends to below the third ray of second dorsal. Caudal emarginate, lower lobe the longest. No swimming bladder.

Scales—Small, ctenoid, extending in front to between the orbits, and over the opercular pieces.

Lateral line—Smooth.

Colours—Dirty brown above, and dirty white below, the darker colours being sometimes banded on the head and body, and having a yellowish tinge. Pectoral greyish brown, spotted with dark brown, more especially at its base. Dorsal, ventral, and anal diaphanous, spotted with light brown. Caudal bright yellow, spotted with brown, which is most apparent at its base, and having a deep black band bordered with pure white, crossing obliquely the posterior third of the upper lobe of caudal, whilst another very deep black band bordered with white extends along the whole of the outer side of the lower lobe, between these two bands are one or two lighter ones variously disposed in different individuals.

Known as the "Crocodile Fish" in Malabar: as wounds from its spines are dreaded, it is immediately on being captured knocked on the head. Is eaten by the Natives. Said to grow to eighteen inches in length.

Habitat—Red Sea to the coast of South Africa, and through all the Indian seas to N. W. Australia.

Platycephalus Malabaricus.

Platycephalus Malabaricus, *Cuv. & Val.* iv. p. 245; *Günther*, Catal. ii. p. 181.
Platycephalus carbunculus, *Cuv. & Val.* ix. p. 461; *Cantor*, Catal. p. 39.

B. vii. D. 1 | 8 | 11-12. P. 19. V. $\frac{1}{5}$. A. 12. C. 15. L. r. 85. L. tr. $\frac{9}{20}$.

Length of head $\frac{2}{7}$, of pectoral $\frac{2}{13}$, of caudal $\frac{2}{13}$, of base of first dorsal $\frac{2}{13}$, of base of second dorsal $\frac{1}{4}$, of base of anal $\frac{2}{13}$ of total length. Height of head $\frac{1}{11}$, of body $\frac{1}{9}$, of first dorsal $\frac{2}{13}$, of second dorsal $\frac{1}{12}$, of ventral $\frac{1}{6}$, of anal $\frac{1}{13}$ of total length.

Eyes—Situated on the upper and outer surface of the head, their superior margins forming a portion of its upper surface. Horizontal diameter $\frac{1}{5}$, vertical diameter $\frac{1}{6}$ of length of head, $\frac{1}{2}$ a diameter apart, $1\frac{1}{2}$ from end of snout.

Body subcylindrical; head depressed and flattened, but not nearly so much as in the last species.

Lower jaw longest; the maxilla extends to beneath the anterior margin of orbit. Interorbital space slightly concave from side to side. At the anterior superior angle of the orbit a sharp spine exists, and five more directed backwards, are placed along the superciliary ridge, which is continued over the occiput, and has a sharp spine about its centre. From the upper third of the posterior margin of the orbit commences the temporal ridge, which contains five or six spines; and at the suprascapular it terminates in two broad flattened spines. Nostrils rather wide apart, not defended by spines. Preorbital large, rather rugose. Intermaxillaries protrusible. Two sharp spines at lower margin of orbit, directed backwards, from the posterior of which runs a crest to the angle of the preopercle, where there are two strong spines, the largest and superior of which equals half the diameter of the eye, is directed backwards, and has a small spinous projection at its base; the lowest is directed backwards and downwards. Opercle with two spines, not very wide apart, the lower being the termination of a smooth ridge.

Teeth—Villiform on each intermaxillary, also on vomer, and palate.

Fins—As in the last species, except that the interspinous membrane of first dorsal is more deeply emarginate, and the caudal is nearly square.

Scales—Small, ctenoid, extending as far forwards as the orbits, and over opercles.

Lateral line—Smooth and a little above the central half of the body.

Colours—Greenish buff; head, cheeks, and sides spotted with blackish brown, and sometimes having numerous black points intermingled. Irregular dark bands on head and body. Throat and abdomen dirty white. First dorsal diaphanous, upper half blackish. Second dorsal, pectoral, ventral, and caudal dirty white, the rays spotted with brown. Posterior half of caudal blackish, with sometimes two or three vertical wavy white lines. Anal white, with some brown spots at its external margin. Iris greenish golden, spotted with brown.

Common in Malabar, along with the last; grows to eleven inches in length. Is eaten by the Natives.

Habitat—Seas of India and Malaysia.

* Platycephalus suppositus.

Platycephalus scaber, *Cuv. & Val.* iv. p. 249.

Platycephalus suppositus, *Trosch*, Wiegm. Arch. 1840, p. 269; *Günther*, Catal. ii. p. 187.

B. vi. D. 1 | 8 | 12. P. 22. V. $\frac{1}{5}$. A. 12. C. 18.

Length of head $\frac{5}{16}$ in its total: width between preopercular spines $\frac{5}{9}$ in length of head. Second dorsal spine $\frac{5}{13}$ in that of head. Each nostril is defended by a small spine, there is one also before the orbit, and five or six on the superciliary ridge; four larger ones on its continuation, which is prolonged posteriorly. There are four spines on the temporal ridge, which extends from the eye to the suprascapular, and five or six on a ridge which passes from the preorbital to the angle of the preopercle, the superior of which is three or four times larger than the one below it, and equals its distance from the orbit, beneath which is a third still shorter, having a very small one at its base. Interorbital space slightly concave, and its width equals the diameter of the orbits. Opercle with two widely separated spines, the inferior of which is situated at the end of a ridge which traverses the length of that bone.

Eyes—Smaller and less approximating than in the *P. insidiator*.

Scales—Those on opercular pieces and back of head have a small projection in their centres.

Lateral line—Armed with from 44 to 50 small pointed spines directed backwards, like those on the head; it is nearer the back than in the *P. insidiator*.

Colours—Reddish grey above, whitish beneath. First dorsal with a black band. Second dorsal, caudal, and pectoral spotted with brown on a pale ground; posterior half of caudal black, end of ventral blackish, pectorals deeply spotted with brown, anal white.

Habitat—Indian seas.

Genus ANEMA, *Günther*.

Uranoscopus, sp. *Cuv. & Val.*

Branchiostegals, six: pseudobranchiæ. Body elongate, low. One dorsal, the spinous portion having its base shorter than that of the soft. Anal developed equally to soft dorsal. Ventral jugular. Pectoral rays branched. Cleft of mouth vertical. Eye on upper side of head. Villiform teeth on jaws, vomer, and palatines. No filament below or before the tongue, or a superior opening of the gills as in the genus *Uranoscopus*. Some of the bones of the head armed. Infraorbital ring does not articulate with the preopercle. Body covered with very fine scales. Air bladder none. Pyloric appendages in moderate numbers.

* Anema inerme.

Uranoscopus inermis, *Cuv. & Val.* iii. p. 310, pl. 65.

Anema inerme, *Günther*, Catal. ii. p. 230.

B. vi. D. $\frac{3\text{-}4}{16\text{-}18}$. P. 18. V. $\frac{1}{5}$. A. 16-19. C. 11. Cœc. pylor. 8.

Length of head $3\frac{2}{7}$ in total.

Surface of head with irregular or radiating granulated lines. Preorbital large, its anterior border divided into three lobes. Preopercle large, entire, finely granulated, and radiated in its inferior portion. Opercle radiated below, finely granulated or vermiculated over the rest of its surface, its posterior superior border fringed. Spine on shoulder small and flat. No spine on sub- or preopercles. Posterior margin of occipital straight, unnotched. Posterior orifice of nostril long, and with a fringed border, anterior round.

Teeth—In upper jaw villiform: strong, crooked, and rather distant apart in the lower jaw.

Scales—Small, and in oblique lines.

Colours—Brownish in spirit, with large oval spots forming two series on either side, and three in front: those in the same rows sometimes coalescing and forming bands. Below the lateral line of a whitish colour. Dorsal with two series of spots as on the back. Pectoral whitish, with a brown transverse band across its centre, and also a spot near its base. Caudal whitish with a large irregular brownish transverse band. Ventral and anal whitish. When fresh the colours are said to be reddish and the spots orange.

Not eatable, grows to two feet in length.

Habitat—Seas of India.

GENUS SILLAGO, *Cuv.*

Branchiostegals, six: pseudobranchiæ. Body elongate, somewhat cylindrical. Head rather pointed. Two dorsals, the first with from nine to twelve spines, the spinous portion with its base shorter than that of the soft. Anal developed like soft dorsal. Ventral thoracic, one spine and five rays, the lower of which are branched. Cleft of mouth small, upper jaw slightly the longest. Eyes lateral. Gill opening wide. Villiform teeth in jaws and vomer, none on palate. Preopercle denticulated: opercle ending in a point. Bones of head with a developed muciferous system. Infraorbital ring of bones do not articulate with preopercle. Body scaled, scales ctenoid. Air bladder simple. Pyloric appendages few.

SILLAGO SIHAMA.

ATHERINA SIHAMA, *Forsk.*, p. 70.
SORING, *Russell*, pl. 113.
SILLAGO ACUTA, *Cuv. & Val.* iii. p. 400.
SILLAGO ERYTHRÆA, *Cuv. & Val.* iii. p. 409.
SILLAGO MALABARICA, *Cantor*, Catal. p. 21.
SILLAGO SIHAMA, *Günther*, Catal. ii. p. 243.
CUDEERAH, *Mal.*

B. vi. D. 10-11 | $\frac{1}{20\text{-}22}$. P. 15-16. V. $\frac{1}{5}$. A. $\frac{1}{22\text{-}23}$. C. 17. L. l. 74. L. tr. $\frac{6\text{-}7}{14}$.

Length of head $\frac{3}{10}$, of pectoral $\frac{1}{8}$, of caudal $\frac{1}{8}$, of base of first dorsal $\frac{1}{6}$, of base of second dorsal $\frac{2}{7}$, of base of anal $\frac{3}{10}$ of total length. Height of head $\frac{1}{8}$, of body $\frac{2}{13}$, of first dorsal $\frac{2}{13}$, of second dorsal $\frac{1}{11}$, of ventral $\frac{1}{8}$, of anal $\frac{1}{14}$ of total length.

Eyes—Oval, upper margin close to profile, horizontal diameter $\frac{2}{9}$, vertical diameter $\frac{1}{6}$ of length of head, 2 diameters from end of snout, 1 diameter apart.

Head cone-shaped, ending in an obtuse point where the mouth is situated, the snout being long. Body most compressed at its posterior third.

Upper jaw the longest, and in front forming a semicircle, the maxilla extends nearly half as far as the anterior margin of orbit. Mouth small, upper jaw moderately protrusible. A large pore under symphysis of lower jaw. Interorbital space flat or slightly convex, covered with small scales, which do not extend over snout. Nostrils approximating and near to anterior superior angle of orbit. Posterior limb of preopercle vertical, and only half as long as the inferior horizontal limb which is covered by a row of large scales, angle rounded, its upper half crenated. Opercle with a short sharp spine. Shoulder bones unarmed.

Teeth—Villiform and numerous in both upper and lower jaws, and vomer, where they form a crescentic band.

Fins—Ventrals attached a little further back than the pectorals; first dorsal arises opposite centre of pectoral: anal opposite second ray of second dorsal. Spines of first dorsal weak, the first three about equal in length, and one third longer than the fourth, from thence they gradually decrease: interspinous membrane slightly emarginate. The first soft ray in second dorsal equals the fourth spine of the first dorsal, from this they gradually decrease. Ventral spine weak, first ray prolonged. Pectoral rounded. Caudal slightly crescentic.

Scales—Rough on their free border, their longest diameter from above downwards, equal to about twice their transverse length. They are placed in oblique rows on the body. Anteriorly they extend to between the orbits, and cover the suborbital ring, and pieces of opercle. Each spine in the fins has a very fine row of scales behind it, some exist on the pectoral fin, and over the base of the caudal.

Lateral line—First curves slightly upwards to upper fourth of body, then descends and when opposite the middle of the second dorsal is below the centre of the body, and is continued on to the caudal fin. The scales forming the lateral line are smaller than those above or below. The tube is single and elevated.

Colours—Greyish, lighter below than above, and with pinkish reflections, a silvery longitudinal stripe below lateral line: very minute black points on membranes of dorsal and anal fins. Pectoral, ventral and anal with a tinge of yellow. Iris pale golden.

This fish, which is known to Europeans under the name of "Whiting," is excellent eating; it arrives in Malabar about January, and is never salted. It is said to grow to three feet in length.

Habitat—From the Red Sea, through the seas of India, Malaysia and China.

Genus UMBRINA, *Cuv.*

Branchiostegals, seven: pseudobranchiæ. Body oblong, upper jaw overlapping lower, a short barbel under symphysis of inferior jaw. Two dorsals, the first with nine or ten flexible spines, soft dorsal more developed than spinous one. Anal with one or two spines. Ventrals thoracic, with one spine and five rays. Opercle unarmed, or feebly so. Teeth on jaws in villiform bands with sometimes conical ones intermixed, none on palate. Scales moderate, lateral line continuous. Air bladder with or without appendages, or absent. Pyloric cœca few.

Umbrina Dussumieri.

Umbrina Dussumieri, *Cuv. & Val.* ix. p. 481.

? UMBRINA DUSSUMIERI, *Günther*, Catal. ii. p. 278.

B. vii. D. $\frac{1}{23\text{-}24}$. P. 17. V. $\frac{1}{5}$. A. $\frac{2}{7}$. C. 17. L. l. 48. L. tr. $\frac{7}{19}$.

Length of head $\frac{1}{4}$, of pectoral $\frac{1}{5}$, of base of first dorsal $\frac{1}{6}$, of base of second dorsal $\frac{2}{7}$, of base of anal $\frac{1}{12}$, of caudal $\frac{1}{6}$ of total length. Height of head $\frac{1}{6}$, of body $\frac{1}{4}$, of first dorsal $\frac{1}{4}$, of second dorsal $\frac{1}{10}$, of ventral $\frac{1}{7}$, of anal $\frac{1}{8}$ of total length.

Eyes—Diameter $\frac{1}{4}$ of length of head, 1 diameter apart, 1 diameter from end of snout.

Snout and cheeks much inflated. Lower jaw shorter than the upper which overlaps it : below the symphysis of the lower jaw is a short fleshy cirrus about half the diameter of the eye in length, with two pores external to it on either side, the outer of which is the largest. The maxilla extends to beneath the anterior third of the orbit. Preopercle entire, its angle rounded. Opercle without spines, shoulder bones entire. Nostrils close to the centre of the anterior margin of orbit, the posterior oval and the largest. Preorbital rather produced in front.

Teeth—Villiform in several rows in both jaws, with an outer strongly curved series in the upper jaw. No teeth on vomer, or on palate.

Fins—Origin of pectoral slightly in advance of ventral, whilst the first dorsal commences above ventral. Anal commences opposite centre of second dorsal. Caudal cut square, in the young fish its central rays are produced. Dorsal spines weak, the first very short, the second the longest and equal to the height of the body. Interspinous membrane moderately emarginate. Second dorsal rays of nearly equal length in the entire fin. First anal spine short, second equals three-eighths of the length of the head.

Scales—Body and head scaled, on the former they pass in oblique rows backwards and upwards.

Lateral line—First in upper fourth of body, then gently curves downwards, and opposite end of anal becomes central.

Colours—Back and upper surface of the head and cheeks of a copper tinge, which below the lateral line becomes silvery. Fins reddish brown, first dorsal stained with black. Ventrals yellow. In the dried specimens a brownish horizontal band is seen along the suborbital ring of bones, and the fins are more or less dotted with black points.

Captured of sizes up to six and a half inches in length.

Habitat—Seas of India.

GENUS SCIÆNA.

SCIÆNA, SP. *Cuvier.*
JOHNIUS, *Bloch*, *Schn.*
LEIOSTOMUS, *Cuv. & Val.*
HOMOPRION, *Holb.*
BOLA, pt. *Ham. Buchanan.*

Branchiostegals, seven ; pseudobranchiæ. Body rather elongate, oblong, and compressed ; eyes lateral, and of moderate size, interorbital space rather convex. Muzzle convex, mouth in front of snout, its cleft horizontal or slightly oblique, with the upper jaw overhanging the lower, or else the two of the same length anteriorly. Two dorsal fins, the soft portion more developed than the spinous or than the anal. Anal fin with two spines of varying strength, the second the longest, and not above two-thirds the length of the first ray. Teeth villiform in both jaws, with an external conical row, but without large canines; no teeth on the palate. Scales ctenoid. Air bladder with appendages. Cæca pylorica in small numbers.

SCIÆNA MACULATA.

JOHNIUS MACULATUS, *Bl. Schn.* 75.
SARI KULLAH, *Russell*, pl. 123.
CORVINA MACULATA, *Cuv. & Val.* v. p. 126.
SCIÆNA MACULATA, *Günther*, Catal. ii. p. 291.
CUTLAH, *Mal.*

B. vii. D. 10 | $\frac{1}{23\text{-}24}$. P. 16. V. $\frac{1}{5}$. A. $\frac{2}{7}$. C. 17. L. l. 45. L. tr. $\frac{11}{16}$.

Length of head $\frac{1}{3}$, of pectoral $\frac{1}{5}$, of caudal $\frac{1}{5}$, of base of first dorsal $\frac{1}{5}$, of base of second dorsal $\frac{3}{8}$, of base of anal $\frac{1}{10}$ of total length. Height of head $\frac{1}{5}$, of body $\frac{1}{3}$, of first dorsal $\frac{1}{7}$, of second dorsal $\frac{1}{10}$, of ventral $\frac{1}{7}$, of anal $\frac{1}{7}$ of total length.

Eyes—Close to profile, oval, horizontal diameter nearly $\frac{1}{4}$, vertical diameter $\frac{1}{5}$ in length of head, 1 diameter from end of snout, $\frac{4}{5}$ of a diameter apart.

Upper jaw the longest, overlapping the lower. Two large pores on either side of the symphysis of lower jaw. Maxilla small, extending nearly to beneath centre of orbit. Preopercle with its posterior margin nearly vertical, its angle rounded and with about six strong teeth: inferior border only half the length of the vertical one, and with its edges crenated. Opercle with two feeble spines. Interorbital space slightly convex. Preorbital large and rather inflated. Shoulder bones entire.

Teeth—In upper jaw villiform, with an external curved band of conical ones: villiform in lower jaw, none on palate.

Fins—The first dorsal and pectoral commence opposite each other, the ventral slightly behind, the anal beneath centre of second dorsal, extending from about the tenth to sixteenth rays. Spines of first dorsal ending in elastic points: second to fifth of nearly equal lengths: membrane rather deeply cleft. Ventral spine weak, first ray prolonged. First anal spine very short, second moderately strong and two-thirds the length of rays. Caudal rhomboidal.

Air bladder with fourteen or fifteen lateral processes on either side.

Scales—Cover the whole of the body, head, and lower jaw. A row exists at the base of the second dorsal and anal, also over base of pectoral and caudal fins. Their longest diameter is vertical.

Lateral line—Has a very slight curve for little more than the first half of its extent; it is continued on the caudal fin nearly to its termination.

Colours—Silvery grey, abdomen whitish. Five broad black bands extend over the back, the first from the nape passes backwards and downwards, and shortly after crossing the lateral line terminates abruptly. The second commences opposite from fifth to seventh spines of dorsal, passes backwards and downwards, and terminates opposite base of ventral fin. The third commences opposite second and third rays of second dorsal, and passes downwards parallel to the second band. The fourth commences below centre of second dorsal, and passes downwards as low as the lateral line.

The fifth which is opposite the last few rays of the second dorsal, takes the same course. Sometimes there is a sixth over the caudal. The upper two-thirds of the first dorsal is stained black, deepest in colour posteriorly, and terminating opposite its eighth spine. The upper half of the second dorsal is stained black along its whole extent. Caudal slightly tinged with black. The other fins yellowish.

Not considered good eating; grows to one foot in length.

Habitat—Seas of India.

SCIÆNA DUSSUMIERI.

CORVINA DUSSUMIERI, *Cuv. & Val.* v. p. 119.
JOHNIUS DUSSUMIERI, *Cantor*, Catal. p. 64.
SCIÆNA DUSSUMIERI, *Günther*, Catal. ii. p. 292.

D. 9-10. | $\frac{1}{28\text{-}29}$. P. 18. V. $\frac{1}{5}$. A. $\frac{2}{7}$. C. 15. L. l. 52. L. tr. $\frac{6}{15}$. Vert. $\frac{10}{14}$.

Length of head $\frac{3}{13}$, of pectoral $\frac{2}{13}$, of caudal $\frac{2}{13}$, of base of first dorsal $\frac{2}{13}$, of base of second dorsal $\frac{2}{5}$, of base of anal $\frac{1}{9}$ of the total length. Height of head $\frac{2}{11}$, of body nearly $\frac{1}{4}$, of first dorsal $\frac{1}{7}$, of second dorsal $\frac{1}{9}$, of ventral $\frac{2}{13}$, of anal $\frac{1}{8}$ of the total length.

Eyes—Oval, horizontal diameter $\frac{1}{4}$, vertical diameter $\frac{1}{5}$ of length of head, 1 diameter from end of snout, 1 diameter apart.

Body elongated, the profile from ventrals to anterior extremity of the first dorsal forms an obtuse angle. The dorsal profile is rather more convex than that of the abdomen.

Head rounded anteriorly, upper jaw the longest, the snout projects over the mouth, the cleft of which is somewhat oblique. The posterior extremity of the maxilla reaches to opposite the posterior third of the orbit. Preopercle descends rather obliquely backwards, its angle rounded, its inferior limb at first very oblique, and not one half of the length of the posterior one: both are finely serrated. The opercle has a fine point, and ends in a soft extremity. Interorbital space convex. Posterior nostril vertically oval, close to centre of orbit, the anterior midway between snout and orbit. Five moderately sized pores under centre of mandibulæ.

Teeth—Villiform with an external row of crooked conical ones in the upper jaw, whilst in the lower the posterior row is the largest on each ramus.

Fins—First dorsal slightly in advance of pectoral, and ventral slightly behind it. The second dorsal commences over the end of the pectoral. The anal arises under eleventh ray of dorsal. The last dorsal ray reaches as far as the base of the caudal; the distance from the root of the last anal ray to the base of the caudal equals the length of the caudal fin. Pectoral rounded. Ventral spine weak, ending in a thin point, and rather longer than the transverse diameter of the orbit. First dorsal forms a long triangle, first spine short, the second the longest in the fin; interspinous membrane deeply notched. Spine of second dorsal nearly half the length of the rays, which are about equal, except the last four or five which are shorter. First anal spine short, second moderately strong, and three fifths of length of first ray, and rather longer than the base of the fin: it equals the distance from the posterior extremity of orbit to anterior nostril: its first ray longest: the fin rounded. Caudal rounded.

Scales—They cover the head, the jaws and the body; and their exposed portions are lozenge-shaped. A low band exists along the base of the first dorsal, and along the lower half of the second dorsal, whilst fine ones are continued on the latter fin as far as its external margin; the anal and caudal are equally scaled, and there are a few on the pectoral and the ventral. Above the lateral line the rows of scales pass at first obliquely upwards and backwards, becoming more horizontal opposite its curve, and quite so from opposite the posterior extremity of the anal. Below the lateral line they first pass upwards and backwards, but not quite so obliquely as the rows above the lateral line: on the chest, and beyond the posterior extremity of pectorals they are nearly horizontal.

Lateral line—First curves upwards, and opposite fifth dorsal spine it is slightly above the upper third of the height of the body, from thence it gradually sinks to opposite the posterior extremity of the base of the anal, where it becomes straight, and is so continued to the end of the caudal.

Air vessel—About one fourth of the total length, dilated in its anterior part, forming a rounded lateral process on each side of the vertebral column. Immediately behind them the body of the vessel is constricted, and the rest presents a broad lanceolate form, tapering backwards into a sharp point. From each side proceed ten processes, of which eight are branched, but the two posterior pairs, which are the longest, are either simple or bipartite. (Cantor.)

Colours—A golden silver, the back dark purplish, cheeks tinged with golden violet. The abdominal surface yellow. First dorsal tipped with black, second dorsal and caudal also margined with the same colour; these marks are due to numerous fine dark points; pectoral brownish yellow, dotted with black. Ventral and anal yellowish. Eye silvery with violet reflections.

Grows to six and a half inches in length. Is good eating. From its air vessel good isinglass can be prepared.

Habitat—Malabar, Malaysia, and China.

* Sciæna sina.

Corvina sina, *Cuv. & Val.* v. p. 122.

Sciæna sina, *Günther*, Catal. ii. p. 292.

B. vii. D. 10. | $\frac{1}{27-28}$. P. 17. V. $\frac{1}{5}$. A. $\frac{2}{7-8}$. L. l. 46.

Length of head $\frac{1}{4}$ of total length. Height of body $\frac{1}{4}$ to $\frac{4}{17}$ of total length.

Eyes—Diameter $\frac{1}{3}$ to $\frac{2}{7}$ of length of head, not quite 1 diameter from end of snout.

Upper jaw rather the longest, the maxilla extends to beneath the posterior half of orbit: there are four pores on lower surface of mandibles. Preopercle indistinctly denticulated, its angle rounded.

Teeth—Villiform, with an external larger and pointed row.

Fins—Pectoral longer than the ventral. Second anal spine one third to one fourth of length of head. Caudal pointed.

Colours—Greyish green above, silvery below, with a dark blotch behind opercle.

Grows to one foot in length: it is little esteemed as food.

Habitat—Seas of India and Japan.

Genus CORVINA.

Corvina, *Cuvier.*

Bola, pt. *Ham. Buchanan.*

Artificially divided from the Genus *Sciæna*, because its second anal spine is stronger, and from two-thirds, to as long as the first ray.

* Corvina semiluctuosa.

Corvina semiluctuosa, *Cuv. & Val.* v. p. 97, pl. 106; *Günther*, Catal. ii. p. 304.

B. vii. D. 10 | 31. P. 18. V. $\frac{1}{5}$. A. $\frac{2}{7}$. C. 17.

Length of head $\frac{2}{7}$ of total length. Height of body nearly equal to length of head.

Upper jaw convex, overlapping the lower. The membraneous border of preopercle very indistinctly crenulated. Opercle ending in two points.

Fins—Second anal spine very strong and one fourth shorter than the first ray. Caudal rounded or slightly rhomboidal. Pectoral of moderate size, semi-oval. Ventral with first ray rather prolonged.

Colours—Of a silvery ground colour with oblique brown-black lines passing backwards and upwards along the centre of each row of scales. There are about forty above the lateral line, and twenty or twenty-one below it. All the fins are blackish brown.

Is good eating. Grows to six inches in length.

Habitat—Seas of India and Malaysia.

* Corvina carutta.

Johnius carutta, *Bloch*, t. 356; *Cantor*, Catal. p. 66.
Corvina carutta, *Cuv. & Val.* v. p. 124; *Günther*, Catal. ii. p. 302.
? Corvina carouna, *Cuv. & Val.* v. p. 125.

B. vii. D. 10 | $\frac{1}{27\text{-}28}$. P. 16. V. $\frac{1}{5}$. A. $\frac{2}{8}$. C. 17. L. l. 50.

Length of head $\frac{3}{13}$ in total length. Height of body nearly $\frac{3}{13}$ of total length.

Eyes—Diameter $\frac{1}{4}$ of length of head, 1 diameter from end of snout.

Snout convex, upper jaw overhanging the lower. Preopercle indistinctly crenulated: posterior limb vertical. Four pores on lower surface of mandibles.

Teeth—Villiform, with the external row slightly enlarged in the upper, whilst the band of teeth is wider in the lower jaw.

Fins—Second anal spine very strong, and two thirds the length of the first ray. Caudal rounded or rhomboidal.

Colours—Upper surface of head and back dark brown claret colour, lighter and silvery on the cheeks, sides, and abdomen. Scales minutely dotted with black, and their margins of a deeper brown than the ground colour. Fin membranes pale yellowish white, minutely dotted with black, the upper half of spinous dorsal—from second to seventh spines—black, the soft dorsal with four equidistant, large, oblique black spots: the marginal half of caudal, ventral and anal fins blackish. Iris golden, orbital half, bluish black.

Grows to one foot in length.

Habitat—Seas and rivers of Malabar and Malaysia.

* Corvina axillaris.

Corvina axillaris, *Cuv. & Val.* v. p. 113; *Günther*, Catal. ii. p. 302.

B. vii. D. 10 | $\frac{1}{27\text{-}28}$. A. $\frac{2}{7}$. L. l. 52. L. tr. $\frac{8}{14}$. Cæc. pylor. 9.

Length of head $\frac{1}{4}$ of total length. Height of body $\frac{5}{18}$ to $\frac{4}{13}$ in total length.

Eyes—Diameter $\frac{2}{9}$ of length of head, 1 diameter from end of snout, $1\frac{1}{2}$ diameters apart.

Mouth short and rounded, jaws nearly equal in front; cleft of mouth very oblique, maxilla extending to below the middle of orbit. Four pores on lower surface of mandibles. Preopercle with two or more small spines at its angle, the lowest being the largest, and four or five smaller ones along its inferior margin. Opercle ends in two fine points.

Teeth—Villiform.

Fins—Anal spine striated, of moderate strength, two fifths of the length of the head, and shorter than the first ray. Caudal rounded. Second dorsal covered for some distance with scales.

Air vessel large, rounded anteriorly, ending posteriorly in a long and sharp point.

Colours—Silvery, tinged with brownish towards the back. A black spot above the axil of the pectoral. First dorsal blackish, the rest of the fins grey.

Grows to three inches in length.

Habitat—Malabar.

* Corvina albida.

Corvina albida, *Cuv. & Val.* v. p. 93; *Günther*, Catal. ii. p. 304.

B. vii. D. 10 | $\frac{1}{24\text{-}25}$. P. 16. V. $\frac{1}{5}$. A. $\frac{2}{7}$. C. 19. L. l. 75. L. tr. $\frac{7}{19}$.

Length of head $\frac{2}{9}$ of total length. Height of body nearly equal to length of head.

Eyes—Diameter $\frac{1}{7}$ of length of head.

Snout rather obtuse and convex; jaws of equal length in front, five pores on the lower surface of mandibles. Preopercle denticulated, most visibly in the young. Suprascapular crenated, coracoid bone entire.

Teeth—Villiform, with an external larger row, in both jaws.

Fins—Ventral and pectoral fins of nearly equal length. Second anal spine strong, slightly shorter (in some specimens one fifth) than the first ray. Caudal rounded, or slightly pointed.

Air bladder with fringed appendages on either side.

Colours—Greyish on the back, silvery white on sides and abdomen: the centre of each scale rather the darkest, forming lines. Fins clear white.

Grows to two feet in length and termed "Sapé-katelé" at Pondicherry; is good eating.

Habitat—Seas of India and China.

Corvina Belengerii.

Corvina Belengerii, *Cuv. & Val.* v. p. 120; *Günther*, Catal. ii. p. 303.
Johnius Belengeri, *Cantor*, Catal. p. 65.

D. 9-10 | $\frac{1}{28\text{-}31}$. P. 15. V. $\frac{1}{5}$. A. $\frac{2}{7}$. C. 15. L. l. 45-48. L. tr. $\frac{6}{11}$.

Length of head $\frac{2}{9}$, of pectoral $\frac{1}{6}$, of caudal $\frac{1}{6}$, of base of first dorsal $\frac{1}{8}$, of base of second dorsal nearly $\frac{1}{3}$, of base of anal $\frac{1}{10}$ of the total length. Height of head rather more than $\frac{1}{5}$, of body $\frac{1}{4}$, of first dorsal $\frac{1}{8}$, of second dorsal $\frac{1}{10}$, of ventral $\frac{1}{6}$, of anal $\frac{1}{7}$ of the total length.

Eyes—Oval, horizontal diameter $\frac{1}{4}$, vertical diameter $\frac{2}{9}$ of length of head, $\frac{2}{3}$ of a diameter from end of snout, $\frac{3}{4}$ of a diameter apart.

Snout hardly projects beyond the upper jaw, which is in advance of the lower: the posterior extremity of the maxilla extends to beneath the centre of the orbit. Preopercle distinctly denticulated. Five pores under the lower jaw.

Teeth—In upper jaw are numerous and villiform, with an external series of curved conical ones which are rather wide apart. In the lower jaw the teeth are villiform, largest opposite the symphysis, those of the anterior row are directed obliquely outwards, the teeth of the posterior series are rather larger than the others.

Fins—First dorsal slightly in advance of the pectoral: and the ventral opposite its first quarter: the anal arises under the fourteenth dorsal ray. The third and fourth spines of first dorsal the longest, the membrane deeply emarginate. The second anal spine five-sevenths of the length of the first ray, and rather longer than the base of the fin, it equals the distance from the posterior margin of the orbit, to the posterior extremity of the opercle. First ventral ray with a filamentous prolongation. Caudal wedge-shaped. The shape of the fins much the same as in the *Sciæna Dussumieri,* but rather more pointed.

Scales and lateral line, as in the *Sciæna Dussumieri.*

Air bladder large, thick, lanceolate, with ten branching processes.

Colours—Rather similar to the *Sc. Dussumieri,* but darker. The body is dotted with fine brown spots, and all the fins with closely placed, minute, black points causing the first dorsal, the lower half of the anal, and the posterior portion of the caudal to be almost black. A spot of brilliant gold colour exists on the preopercle. Iris silvery, upper half bluish black.

Grows to seven inches in length. Isinglass from this species is reputed to be good.

Habitat—Seas of Malabar, and Malaysia.

* CORVINA LOBATA.

CORVINA LOBATA, *Cuv. & Val.* v. p. 122, pl. 107; *Günther*, Catal. p. 304.

B. vii. D. 9-10 | $\frac{1}{28\text{-}31}$. A. $\frac{2}{7}$. Cæc. pylor. 8.

Length of head $\frac{2}{9}$ of total length. Height of head $\frac{2}{9}$ of total length.

Snout convex, upper jaw overhanging the lower, cleft of mouth nearly horizontal. Preopercle appears entire.

Fins—Second anal spine strong and two-fifths of length of head: first ventral ray prolonged into a filament: caudal rhomboidal.

Air vessel bulges out and appears as if it were constricted into two at its anterior part.

Colours—Silvery, with five large rather obscure cross bands, passing downwards to slightly below the lateral line. Fins yellowish. The anterior portion of the first dorsal, the external margins of the second, of the caudal, anal, and ventral are blackish.

Grows to five inches in length.

Habitat—Malabar.

CORVINA NEILLI.*

B. vii. D. 9 | $\frac{1}{25}$ P. 17. V. $\frac{1}{5}$. A. $\frac{2}{7}$. C. 17. L. r. 53. L. tr. 24.

Length of head $\frac{1}{4}$, of pectoral nearly $\frac{1}{7}$, of caudal $\frac{2}{13}$, of base of first dorsal $\frac{2}{13}$, of base of second dorsal $\frac{1}{3}$, of base of anal $\frac{1}{13}$ of total length. Height of head $\frac{1}{6}$, of body $\frac{1}{4}$, of first dorsal $\frac{1}{9}$, of second dorsal $\frac{1}{11}$, of ventral $\frac{1}{7}$, of anal $\frac{1}{9}$ of total length.

* I have named this species after *A. C. B. Neill, Esq.*, Retired list, Medical Department, Madras Army, from whom I have received most valuable assistance during the progress of this work through the press.

Eyes—Horizontal diameter $\frac{2}{11}$, vertical diameter $\frac{2}{13}$ of length of head, $1\frac{1}{3}$ diameters from end of snout, $1\frac{1}{2}$ diameters apart anteriorly, further posteriorly.

Body most elevated opposite commencement of first dorsal, and gradually tapering towards the tail. Profile from snout to dorsal rather convex: the upper profile more convex than that of the abdomen.

Snout obtuse, upper jaw rather oblique, lower nearly horizontal. The large orifice of a gland exists under the symphysis of lower jaw, which has two others of equal size on either side. The maxilla extends to below the posterior third of the orbit. Posterior margin of preopercle vertical, entire: inferior limb convex and also entire, very slightly roughened along its edge but nowhere serrated; its angle irregularly rounded. Interopercle entire, a very small portion visible. Opercle ending in a soft extremity. Interorbital space convex, snout laterally rather bulging. Posterior nostril transversely oval and the largest, situated close above the centre of the anterior margin of the orbit; anterior small, oval, nearer the orbit than the end of the snout. Suprascapular entire.

Teeth—Villiform in both jaws, with an external row of curved conical ones in each intermaxillary, and a posterior row of larger ones on either side of mandibles.

Fins—First dorsal and pectoral arise on a line, close behind the termination of opercle; ventral slightly posterior: the anal commences opposite the middle of the second dorsal and terminates opposite its fourteenth ray, thus leaving double the length on the abdominal surface of the tail finless, compared to what exists on that of the back. First spine of first dorsal fin very minute, the next four of about equal length, and the last hardly one quarter their height: the interspinous membrane rather deeply cleft. Second dorsal with its posterior extremity rounded. Pectoral rather pointed. Anal moderately square, its second spine very strong, four times the length of the first, and nearly three quarters that of the first ray.

Scales—Exist over the body, head, and jaws. They are placed in oblique rather irregular rows above the lateral line as far as opposite the base of the anal, beyond which they become horizontal. Below the lateral line they are at first oblique, becoming horizontal beyond the base of the anal. There are some at the base of second dorsal, anal, and caudal fins, especially over the last. Their longest diameter is from above downwards.

Lateral line—Consisting of single tubes dividing and subdividing posteriorly into numerous branches. First curved to opposite the base of the anal, from thence straight to the caudal, on to which it is continued to its termination.

Colours—General dark greyish silvery, with the upper surface of the head of a beautiful violet purple, which tint is continued, but less vividly, along its whole back: abdomen silvery with purplish reflections. Upper edge of dorsal slightly stained with black. Scales rather darkest in their centres, forming oblique and longitudinal lines. Eyes silvery, purple above.

Common in Cochin, where it is found to two feet or more in length.

Habitat—Malabar.

Genus OTOLITHUS, *Cuvier*.

Branchiostegals, seven: pseudobranchiæ. Body oblong, compressed. Bones of head with muciferous system well developed. Muzzle obtuse, or moderately pointed; mouth in front of snout. Preopercle denticulated or crenulated. Bony opercle ending in one or two flat points. Two dorsal fins, the first with nine or ten feeble spines, the soft portion more developed than the spinous or than the anal. Anal with two small spines. Pectoral rays branched. Ventral thoracic, with one spine and five soft rays. Teeth in villiform bands, with more or less distinct conical canines, either in both jaws or only in the upper. A large loose bone in each auricular cavity. Scales of moderate size, ctenoid. Air bladder present, and with lateral appendages. Pyloric appendages few.

OTOLITHUS RUBER.

JOHNIUS RUBER, *Bl. Sch.* p. 75, t. 17.

OTOLITHUS RUBER, *Cuv. & Val.* v. p. 60, pl. 102; *Cantor*, Catal. p. 59; *Günther*, Catal. ii. p. 309.

B. vii. D. 10 | $\frac{1}{30}$. P. 17. V. $\frac{1}{5}$. A. $\frac{1}{7}$. C. 17. L. l. 50. L. tr. $\frac{7}{17}$.

Length of head, from $\frac{1}{4}$ in the young to $\frac{2}{7}$ in the adult, of pectoral $\frac{2}{13}$, of caudal $\frac{2}{13}$, base of first dorsal $\frac{1}{8}$, base of second dorsal $\frac{3}{10}$, base of anal $\frac{1}{17}$ of total length. Height of head $\frac{1}{5}$, of body little more than $\frac{1}{5}$, of first dorsal $\frac{1}{9}$, of second dorsal $\frac{1}{14}$, of ventral $\frac{2}{17}$ of total length.

Eyes—Diameter rather more than $\frac{1}{5}$ of head, $1\frac{1}{4}$ diameters apart, 1 diameter from end of snout.

Body gradually decreases in size from the head to the tail, sides moderately compressed.

Mouth protrusible, lower jaw longest; when closed its extremity is received into an emargination in end of upper jaw. Maxilla very wide at its posterior extremity; it extends backwards to below the middle of orbit. Preorbital, long narrow; preopercle, posterior margin vertical, angle rounded, lower margin nearly horizontal, all with fine denticulations, which on the lower limb become very small and blunt. Opercle triangular, base in front, with one point moderately distinct at centre of posterior margin, and a smaller one above it. Sub- and interopercles entire, interorbital space rather convex. Nostrils opening at anterior superior margin of orbit, in rather a depressed triangular space, having an elevated margin above, and bounded below by continuations from the orbital rim.

Teeth—On either side of centre of upper jaw closely approximating, two conical teeth, the internal the shortest, with a row of villiform ones behind, and a very fine brush-like series posterior to them: a single external series of sharp short conical ones along the jaw, with an internal series of several rows of brush-like ones. Two large canines in lower jaw at its centre, with several rows of villiform ones behind, a single row of sharp short conical ones moderately far apart along either limb of lower jaw.

Fins—First dorsal and ventral arise on a line, slightly behind the origin of the pectoral. Second dorsal commences midway between snout and base of caudal. Anal commences opposite centre of second dorsal. First dorsal of a long triangular shape, spines weak, extending beyond the membrane which is rather deeply notched, first spine one-third the length of second, which is about the same length as the third, from whence they rapidly decrease. Second dorsal slightly highest in front, but its upper margin is parallel with curve of back. Pectoral pointed. Ventral triangular. Anal square, spine one-third the length of rays. Caudal pointed in the young, but becomes rounded with age.

Scales—Cover body, cheeks, snout and lower jaw, with some along the centre of caudal. The rows ascend backwards, and in rather an irregularly arched direction from above the lateral line, below it they pass more regularly upwards and backwards towards it.

Lateral line—Gradually descends, forming a sort of curve to a little beyond the commencement of the anal, where it becomes straight, and is so continued to the end of caudal fin. Each scale has a raised horizontal tube, which in some, especially those most anterior, have a horizontal depression along their centre as well as on each side, and posteriorly there are offsets from the tube of smaller tubular processes.

Stomach elongated, cylindrical, with four cæcopyloric appendages. Air vessel half length of body, large, flattened, broad, lanceolate, terminating behind in a short point, and having thirty-four processes, of which the anterior four or five divide into four branches, the next into three, the succeeding ones into two, while the posterior processes which are slightly longer than the preceding ones are simple: all again divide into minor ramifications. (Cantor.)

Colours—Dull brownish red with silvery reflections; sides of body, of head and abdomen whitish silvery; the upper portion of opercle steel blue. Dorsal with a tinge of dull red, externally minutely dotted with brown spots; the other fins yellow, with a dash of red. Eye golden, reddish brown superiorly.

Grows to two feet and a half in length. Good eating, fresh or salted, and from its air-vessel isinglass can be manufactured. Is not very common in Malabar. Termed *Péchepierre* at Pondicherry.

Habitat—Seas of India and Malaysia.

* OTOLITHUS ARGENTEUS.

OTOLITHUS ARGENTEUS, *Cuv. & Val.* v. p. 62; *Cantor*, Catal. p. 61; *Günther*, Catal. ii. p. 310.

B. vii. D. 9-10 | $\frac{1}{25\text{-}28}$. P. 20. V. $\frac{1}{5}$. A. $\frac{2}{7}$. C. 17. L. l. 70. Cæc. pylor. 6.

Length of head $\frac{1}{4}$ to $\frac{2}{9}$ of total length. Height of body nearly $\frac{1}{6}$ of total length.

Eyes—Diameter from $\frac{3}{16}$ to $\frac{3}{19}$ of length of head.

Preopercle with very small denticulations.

Teeth—Villiform, with two—sometimes three—canines on either side of symphysis of maxilla, of which the posterior, or centre one when three are present, is the longest; the canines are succeeded by a series of distant, conical teeth. On either side of symphysis of lower jaw is a small canine, and inside the villiform series a row of large conical ones, some of which in size exceed the lower canines.

Fins—Anal spine feeble, one third the length of the first soft ray. Caudal rhomboidal.

Scales—None on fins.

Colours—Upper surface of head and back iridescent greyish green, with pale reddish reflections. Sides of head and below lateral line reddish golden. Upper part and posterior margin of opercle blackish blue. Dorsal interspinous membrane reddish; caudal, reddish yellow minutely dotted with brown and having black margins. Pectoral, ventral and anal pale yellowish red. Iris golden, bluish black towards the orbit. The colours are lighter in the young.

Air bladder small, very narrow, lanceolate, about one quarter the length of the fish, and terminating in a fine point; from each side of the body of the air-vessel proceed twenty-five branched processes, of which the anterior are the largest, and have the greatest number of branchlets.

The quantity of isinglass yielded by this species is small but very good.

Grows to two feet seven inches in length.

Habitat—Seas of Malabar, Malaysia, and China.

Fam. POLYNEMIDÆ.

GENUS POLYNEMUS, *Linn.*

Branchiostegals, seven: pseudobranchiæ. Form of body oblong, compressed. Eyes, large lateral. Mouth below snout, with lateral cleft, snout prominent. Two separate dorsals, the second, the anal, and the caudal more or less covered with small scales. Dorsal spines weak. Second dorsal and anal of nearly equal extent. Several articulated free filiform appendages in front of base of pectoral fin. Preopercle serrated. Villiform teeth in jaws, vomer and palate. Scales moderate, ctenoid. Lateral line continued on to caudal. Air bladder varying in size and structure; in some species absent.

POLYNEMUS HEPTADACTYLUS.

POLYNEMUS HEPTADACTYLUS, *Cuv. & Val.* iii. p. 390; *Cantor*, Catal. p. 34; *Günther*, Catal. ii. p. 321.

B. vii. D. 7-8 | $\frac{1}{12}$. P. 15, vii. V. $\frac{1}{5}$. A. $\frac{3}{11\text{-}12}$. L. l. 50. L. tr. $\frac{5}{11}$. Cæc. pylor. 4.

Length of head $\frac{2}{11}$, of pectoral $\frac{1}{6}$, of caudal $\frac{1}{4}$, of base of anal $\frac{1}{7}$ of total length. Height of head $\frac{1}{6}$, of body $\frac{1}{4}$, of hard dorsal $\frac{1}{7}$, of soft dorsal $\frac{1}{7}$, of ventral $\frac{1}{7}$, of anal $\frac{1}{7}$ of the total length.

Eyes—Diameter $\frac{1}{3}$ of length of head, $1\frac{1}{2}$ diameters from end of snout, $2\frac{1}{2}$ diameters apart. External third of orbits surrounded by an adipose lid.

Profile rather elevated from snout to the first dorsal. Upper jaw rather oblique, the maxilla extends behind the orbit a distance of half its transverse diameter.

Preopercle, vertical limb slightly convex, denticulated, with a very strong spine at the lower termination of its denticulations, and opposite the upper margin of the mouth. Opercle ending in a soft point.

Teeth—Villiform in both jaws, none on their outer surfaces. A band of the same character on vomer and palate.

Fins—The first dorsal arises above, or slightly in advance of base of pectoral: ventral opposite second third of pectoral: the second dorsal midway between posterior margin of orbit and root of caudal: anal opposite fifth dorsal ray. First dorsal triangular, spines weak, the first very short, the second shorter than the third, which is the longest, from it they rapidly decrease: the spines are prolonged beyond the membrane which is moderately notched. The distance between the end of first and commencement of second dorsal, equals half the distance between end of second dorsal and commencement of caudal. Spine of second dorsal half the length of first ray, which is the longest; the fin is of a trapezoid shape, with its superior margin concave. Pectoral rather pointed, with seven appendages, the two highest and lowest equal, and shorter than the other four which extend to the third and fourth anal rays. Ventral triangular, its spine weak. Anal, first spine short, second half the length of third, which is half as long as first ray; shape of fin trapezoid. Caudal deeply lobed.

Scales—Deciduous, and placed as in the *P. Indicus*, p. 61.

Lateral line—First ascends, from opposite the end of the first dorsal it descends, above extremity of anal it proceeds straight to the base of the caudal, where it passes downwards over the upper margin of the highest ray of the lower lobe, and divides into two, one being continued straight to the end of the fin, the other passing to between the two inner rays of the lower lobe.

Colours—General colour silvery, with a yellowish tinge, and light yellowish-brown stripes along its sides and back. Pectorals deep black, a black spot on upper margin of opercle. All the fins finely dotted with black points, the tips of the dorsal and caudal appear blackish, as do also the extremities of the free pectoral filaments.

No air bladder.

Common in Malabar during the monsoon, but does not appear ever to exceed five inches in length.

Habitat—Seas of India, Malaysia, China, and the Moluccas.

POLYNEMUS SEXTARIUS.

POLYNEMUS SEXTARIUS, *Bloch*, Syst. p. 18, t. 4; *Cuv. & Val.* iii. p. 388, vii. p. 514; *Cantor*, Catal. p. 32; *Gunther*, Catal. ii. p. 326.

B. vii. D. 8 | $\frac{1}{12}$. P. 15, vi. V. $\frac{1}{5}$. A. $\frac{3}{12}$. C. 17.

Length of head $\frac{1}{4}$, of pectoral $\frac{2}{13}$, of caudal $\frac{2}{9}$, of base of first dorsal $\frac{1}{11}$, of base of second dorsal $\frac{1}{7}$, of base of anal $\frac{1}{8}$ of total length. Height of head more than $\frac{1}{5}$, of body $\frac{2}{9}$, of first dorsal $\frac{2}{13}$, of second dorsal $\frac{1}{8}$, of ventral $\frac{1}{8}$, of anal $\frac{1}{8}$ of the total length.

Eyes—Horizontal diameter $\frac{1}{3}$, and vertical diameter $\frac{1}{4}$ of length of head, $\frac{2}{5}$ of a diameter from end of snout, nearly 1 diameter apart.

The posterior extremity of the maxilla extends to beyond the posterior margin of the orbit. Preopercle, posterior margin strongly denticulated, with a very strong tooth just above its angle.

Teeth—Villiform, in about three rows, none exist in the outer surface of either jaw.

Fins—First dorsal arises slightly behind the pectoral, ventral opposite centre of first dorsal. Second dorsal commences midway between summit of preopercle and base of caudal. Anal arises under third ray of dorsal. The outer pectoral filaments reach beyond the end of the ventral. The fins are shaped as in the last species, with the caudal lobes pointed.

Colours—The upper half of first dorsal black, also the remainder of its interspinous membrane between the first and fifth spines, but not quite so dark. Pectoral and ventral dark-spotted, nearly black. External half of second dorsal and anal, as well as most of the caudal finely dotted with minute black points. A black mark on the shoulder. Palate covered with large black spots.

Lateral line—Is almost straight as far as the base of the caudal, from whence it passes to the posterior margin of the lower lobe.

Air bladder—Very small.

Not rare, up to four inches in length during the monsoon time in Malabar. Appears to be quite a small species.

Habitat—Seas of India, and Malaysia.

POLYNEMUS INDICUS.

POLYNEMUS INDICUS, *Shaw*, Zool. v. pt. 1, p. 155; *Cantor*, Catal. p. 29; *Günther*, Catal. ii. p. 326.

MAGA-BOSHÉE, *Russell*, pl. 184.

POLYNEMUS SELE, *Ham. Buch.* pp. 226, 381; *McClelland*, Journal Asiatic Society, viii. 1839, p. 203; Calcutta Journal of Natural History, ii. p. 450, iii. pp. 179, 181, pl. 6.

POLYNEMUS PLOTEUS, PLEBEJUS, LINEATUS, ET GELATINOSUS, *McClelland*, Ibid. ii. p. 450, iii. p. 179, &c.

Polynemus uronemus, *Cuv. & Val.* iii. p. 385.

B. vii. D. 8 | $\frac{1}{13-14}$. P. 20, v. V. $\frac{1}{5}$. A. $\frac{2-3}{11-12}$. C. 17. L. l. 62-65. L. tr. $\frac{7}{13}$. Cæco-pyloric appendages numerous.

Length of head $\frac{2}{9}$, of pectoral $\frac{1}{6}$, of caudal $\frac{1}{4}$, of base of first dorsal $\frac{1}{9}$, of base of second dorsal $\frac{1}{8}$, of base of anal $\frac{1}{8}$ of the total length. Height of head $\frac{1}{7}$, of body $\frac{1}{4}$, of first dorsal $\frac{1}{6}$, of second dorsal $\frac{1}{6}$, of ventral $\frac{1}{8}$, of anal $\frac{1}{6}$ of the total length.

Eyes—External third on either side covered by an adipose lid; diameter $\frac{1}{3}$ of length of head, $\frac{1}{2}$ diameter from end of snout; 1 diameter apart.

Body of a rather elliptical form, more prominent below than above.

Mouth with an oblique cleft, the posterior extremity of maxilla extending to one quarter of a diameter behind the orbit: lower jaw shortest, snout overhanging, and advanced beyond both jaws. Preopercle, its posterior limb nearly vertical, slightly convex in its upper portion and with its angle produced: moderately strong serratures, with a prominent tooth above the angle. Lower limb short, horizontal and entire. Opercle rounded posteriorly. Interorbital space rather convex. Snout produced, diaphanous. Openings of nostrils oval, rather large, approximating: anterior on a lower level than the posterior one.

Teeth—Villiform, in about five rows in the upper, and four in the lower jaw. Villiform teeth on vomer in a transversely oval spot, and in a row on the palate.

Fins—First dorsal commences slightly behind the origin of the pectoral: ventral arises opposite centre of pectoral. Second dorsal commences rather nearer to the base of caudal, than it does to the posterior margin of the orbit. Anal begins opposite fourth dorsal ray. First dorsal triangular, spines weak and prolonged beyond the membrane which is also emarginate: first spine very short, second the longest, from which they rapidly decrease to the last. Second dorsal trapezoid, the distance between it and the posterior extremity of the first dorsal equals that from the end of the snout to the posterior margin of the orbit: the distance from the posterior extremity of second dorsal to base of caudal equals the distance from the commencement of first dorsal to that of the second dorsal. Pectoral rather rounded, with five articulated filaments arising a short distance below and in front of its base, the first of which is the longest and extends as far as the commencement of the anal fin, the inferior one is the shortest only extending as far as the end of the pectoral. Ventral spine weak, a long wide free scale at its base: distance from commencement of fin to base of anal nearly equals the space from the anterior margin of the orbit to the posterior extremity of opercle. Anal trapezoid, first spine small, second nearly half the length of first ray which is the longest: this fin extends the same distance posteriorly beyond the end of the second dorsal, as it arises behind its origin. Caudal with long rather crescentic shaped pointed lobes, which sometimes end in filamentous prolongations, the lowest is usually the longest.

Scales—Ctenoid extending over body and head, but none on snout, they cover the lower jaw, and exposed portion of maxilla as well as the base of the caudal, and there are a few between the spines of the first dorsal fins. A few finer ones over pectoral, second dorsal, and anal fins.

Lateral line—Nearly straight, in single tubes along the centre of each scale. At the base of the caudal it curves downwards over the internal ray of lower lobe and is thus continued to the posterior extremity of the fin.

Colours—Back greyish green: abdomen silvery white, with a very indistinct stripe along the centre of each line of abdominal scales. First dorsal stained with black, and its anterior portion closely dotted with minute black points: the inferior half of opercle also minutely dotted with black. Second dorsal dotted with black, and darkest anteriorly. Caudal darkest posteriorly especially at the points of its lobes. Anal finely dotted in the same way as the second dorsal. Pectoral, its appendages, and ventral nearly white.

Air bladder present, "its form is oval and the membrane is silvery and thick. It occupies the whole length of the abdomen, terminating posteriorly in a very sharp point, which penetrates the muscles of the tail over the first interspinal of the anal. It adheres to the abdominal vertebræ from the third to the seventh. From either side towards the ventral surface proceed from twenty-eight to thirty-five appendages, which with the exception of the three last have two roots, but terminate in a single sharp point. Above each of these, towards the dorsal surface, appear one or two others. All the appendages penetrate the thick of the muscles, and are slightly directed towards the back of the fish." *Cuv. & Val.* iii. p. 285.

Grows to three feet in length, but rarely exceeds 20 lbs. in weight. As an article of diet it is inferior to the *P. tetradactylus,* both of which are termed *Rowball* at Vizagapatam. Its great value consists in the isinglass which is obtained from its air bladder, a large fish yielding about two ounces of good quality. It is probable that much of the isinglass exported from Malabar under the designation of "fish maws" is produced from this species.

Habitat—Seas of India, Malaysia, and extending to the coasts of Australia.

Polynemus tetradactylus.

POLYNEMUS TETRADACTYLUS, *Shaw*, v. p. 155; *Cuv. & Val.* iii. p. 375. vii. p. 514; *McClelland*, J. A. S. viii. 1839, p. 206; *Cantor*, Catal. p. 25; *Günther*, Catal. ii. p. 329.

MAJA-JELLEE, *Russell*, pl. 183.

POLYNEMUS TERIA, *Ham. Buch.* pp. 224, 381; *Gray*, Illust. I. Z., i. pl. 92, f. 2.

POLYNEMUS SALLIAH, ET QUADRIFILIS, *Cantor*, Catal. J. A. S., v. p. 166.

B. vii. D. 8 | $\frac{1}{13\text{-}15}$. P. 16, iv. V. $\frac{1}{5}$. A. $\frac{2}{16\text{-}17}$. C. 17. L. l. 75-85. L. tr. $\frac{10}{14}$.
D. 8-9 | $\frac{1}{14\text{-}15}$. P. 17, iv. V. $\frac{1}{5}$. A. $\frac{3\text{-}4}{15\text{-}16}$. C. 17. according to *Cantor*.

Length of head $\frac{1}{5}$, of pectoral $\frac{1}{6}$, of caudal $\frac{1}{5}$, of base of first dorsal $\frac{1}{13}$, of base of second dorsal $\frac{1}{8}$, of base of anal $\frac{1}{7}$ of total length. Height of head $\frac{1}{6}$, of body $\frac{1}{5}$, of first dorsal $\frac{1}{7}$, of second dorsal $\frac{1}{7}$, of ventral $\frac{1}{10}$, of anal $\frac{1}{7}$ of total length.

Eyes—Oval, with adipose lids, covering nearly half their width. Horizontal diameter $\frac{2}{9}$, vertical diameter $\frac{2}{11}$ of length of head, $\frac{1}{2}$ transverse diameter from end of snout, 1 transverse diameter apart.

Body long, rather compressed and tapering towards both extremities.

Mouth oblique, deeply cleft, and not protrusible, the maxilla extends the length of transverse diameter of the orbit behind its posterior margin. Lower jaw shortest, snout diaphanous, overhanging, and advanced before the jaws: nostrils at its outer margin: under surface of lower jaw nearly flat. Preopercle, its ascending limb obliquely convex, slightly produced just above the angle, the whole being finely and evenly serrated except on the angle where the serratures are finer and less distinct, its lower limb short and entire. Interorbital space nearly flat.

Teeth—Exceedingly numerous and very fine, covering the whole of the exposed and inferior edges of the intermaxillaries, making them appear rough like a file. The lower jaw on its upper and external margins is similarly covered to beneath the posterior margin of the orbit. Teeth of the same description on vomer and palate.

Fins—A short distance in front and below the level of the base of the pectoral fin arise four articulated filaments, the two posterior of which are usually longest, and equal the length of the head: in one specimen there were three free rays on the left side, and four on the right. The first dorsal arises over the first third of the pectoral, the ventral opposite its posterior third. The second dorsal commences a little nearer the base of the caudal than it does to the orbit, the anal arises opposite to it. The distance between the root of the ventral and the commencement of the anal, equals the extent from the anterior margin of the orbit to the end of the opercle. First dorsal triangular, its spines weak, membrane slightly emarginate: first spine very short, the second the longest, from whence they rapidly decrease. Second dorsal highest in front, first ray the longest, its upper margin slightly concave, its general form trapezoid. Pectoral slightly pointed, an elongated scale at its base. Ventral small and triangular with a badly developed but elongated scale at its base. Anal rather larger than second dorsal, but of the same shape. Caudal lobed in its posterior two-thirds, the upper one slightly the longest.

Scales—Moderate, ctenoid, disposed the same as in the last species.

Lateral line—Consists of single well marked tubes, its direction is nearly straight, with a very slight downward curve from opposite the first dorsal, and a moderate rising opposite the end of second dorsal, at the base of the caudal it divides into two branches which slightly diverge, and again subdivide each into two more.

Colours—Head and back silvery green, becoming silvery white on the sides and abdomen. Dorsal and caudal greyish with minute black points, and darkest—nearly black—at their margins. Pectoral, ventral, and anal fins, pale orange, filaments white. A dark mark on upper portion of opercle. Cheeks and suborbital region golden. Iris silvery with a golden green tinge on its upper surface.

No air bladder. Pyloric appendages very numerous.

Grows to six feet in length in the Gangetic estuaries, but rarely above three feet in Malabar. Is excellent eating. It appears to be very numerous in Cochin, especially in the months of December and January, when numbers are taken by trolling. Of course, having no air bladder it is useless for the manufacture of isinglass.

Habitat—Seas of India, Malaysia, and China.

Fam. SPHYRÆNIDÆ.

Genus SPHYRÆNA, *Artedi.*

Branchiostegals, seven: pseudobranchiæ. Body elongated, subcylindrical. Eyes lateral, of moderate size: cleft of mouth wide, armed with large strong trenchant teeth in both jaws and on the palatine bones. Preopercle entire. Opercle without spines. Two dorsal fins, remote, similar to and opposite second dorsal. Ventrals abdominal. Scales small, cycloid: lateral line continuous. Air bladder large, sometimes bifurcated anteriorly. Pyloric appendages many.

Sphyræna jello.

Jellow, *Russell*, pl. 174.

Sphyræna jello, *Cuv. & Val.* vi. p. 349; *Cantor*, Catal. p. 24; *Günther*, Catal. ii. p. 337.

Cheelahoo, *Mal.*

B. vii. D. 5 | $\frac{1}{9}$. P. 14. V. $\frac{1}{5}$. A. $\frac{1}{8\text{-}9}$. C. 17. L. l. 90-100. L. tr. $\frac{10}{22}$. Vert. $\frac{12}{12}$.

Length of head nearly $\frac{1}{4}$, of pectoral $\frac{1}{11}$, of caudal $\frac{1}{6}$, of base of first dorsal $\frac{1}{17}$, of base of second dorsal $\frac{1}{14}$, of base of anal $\frac{1}{14}$ of total length. Height of head $\frac{1}{11}$, of body $\frac{2}{13}$, of first dorsal $\frac{1}{11}$, of second dorsal $\frac{1}{8}$, of ventral $\frac{1}{12}$, of anal $\frac{1}{8}$ of total length.

Eyes—Close to profile, oval, horizontal diameter $\frac{1}{9}$, vertical diameter $\frac{1}{8}$ of length of head, $2\frac{1}{2}$ transverse diameters from end of snout, 1 diameter apart.

Body elongated, tapering towards both extremities, head depressed, sides compressed. There is a gradual rise from snout to first dorsal, from whence to termination of second dorsal the profile is nearly horizontal.

Mouth deeply cleft, jaws compressed, almost ending in a point, the anterior extremity of maxilla having a shallow notch to receive the tip of the lower jaw: posterior extremity of maxilla extending to beneath anterior margin of the orbit: lower jaw slightly the longest, with a fleshy tubercle at symphysis. Preorbital produced, narrow anteriorly, with stellated ridges arising from its posterior and extending towards its anterior margin; the superior four are directed horizontally, the inferior five downwards, or backwards and downwards. Preopercle, its posterior and inferior limbs of nearly equal length, angle obliquely rounded. Opercle rather narrow, terminating in two flat membraneous points and forming with the subopercle a semicircle posteriorly. Upper surface of head has raised irregular longitudinal ridges. The gills are cleft to below the anterior margin of the orbits. The branchiostegal rays are rather wide apart. The orifice of the nostrils approximate, and are close to the angle of the preorbital.

Teeth—An external series of numerous sharp teeth in the upper jaw, and two large canines in the anterior portion of either intermaxillary. A row of large canines along the palate. Lower jaw with large teeth placed rather wide apart, their size augmenting posteriorly, and with two large canines anteriorly.

Fins—Pectoral arises close to the anterior margin of the opercle, ventral on the abdominal surface under its posterior third. First dorsal opposite ventral. Second dorsal commences midway between the commencement of first dorsal and base of caudal; the anal is placed beneath it: there is a space between these fins and the base of the caudal equal to the distance from the anterior margin of the orbit to the posterior margin of the opercle: whilst the distance between the two dorsal fins is somewhat more. The distance from the base of ventral to the commencement of anal, equals the length of the head. First dorsal square, spines weak, protruding beyond the membrane, which is rather deeply cleft. Second dorsal produced in front, with a concave superior margin; the spine is rather more than one-third the length of the first ray, which is rather the longest. Pectoral rather pointed. Ventral abdominal. Anal of the same shape as the second dorsal. Caudal lobed in its posterior two-thirds.

Scales—Extend over the body and opercles, but there are none on the summit of the head, preorbital, or on the jaws.

Lateral line—Consisting of single tubes: at first slightly concave, forming an obtuse curve opposite the centre of the pectoral, then bending gradually downwards until opposite the origin of the second dorsal, from whence it proceeds direct to the centre of the caudal.

Air vessel long and cylindrical.

Colours—Greyish green above, white beneath. Fins greyish. Dorsal, caudal and anal tipped with white. Some cloudy bands pass from the back downwards towards the abdomen. Iris pale golden, dark above.

Grows to four feet in length, and is sometimes eaten by Europeans, but is not esteemed.

Habitat—Red Sea, Seas of India, Malaysia, China, and the Cape of Good Hope.

* Sphyræna obtusata.

Sphyræna obtusata, *Cuv. & Val.* iii. p. 350. *Cantor*, Catal. p. 24; *Günther*, Catal. ii. p. 339.

B. vii. D. 5 | $\frac{1}{9}$. P. 12. V. $\frac{1}{5}$. A. $\frac{1}{9}$. C. 17. L. l. 90.

Length of head $\frac{3}{10}$ of total length. Height of body from $\frac{1}{7}$ to $\frac{2}{17}$ of total length.

Eyes—Oval, the horizontal diameter $\frac{1}{4}$ of length of head.

Lower jaw either deficient in, or with a very slight fleshy appendage at symphysis. Preopercle almost rectangular, with angle slightly produced. Opercle terminates in a single flat membraneous point.

Teeth—Small but with three longer ones (the second, third and fourth) anteriorly on either side of palatine bones.

Fins—The ventrals are situated in front of the first dorsal, opposite the posterior half of the pectorals. The caudal is less deeply cleft than in the last species.

Colours—The upper surface of the head and back of a dark greyish green, paler on the upper part of the sides, and clouded beneath the lateral line, the cheeks and the remainder of the sides of a pale silvery colour; the abdomen white; pectorals and ventrals whitish; the other fins and the iris the same as in the *S. jello.*

Grows to two feet six inches in length.

Habitat—Red Sea, Seas of India, Mauritius, Malaysia, to Port Jackson in Eastern Australia.

Fam. TRICHIURIDÆ.

Genus TRICHIURUS, *Linn.*

Branchiostegals, seven: pseudobranchiæ. Body elongate, bandlike, compressed, with the tail tapering to a point. Eyes lateral. Muzzle elongate. Cleft of mouth wide. One dorsal extending along the whole length of the back: no caudal: ventrals thoracic, reduced to a pair of scales or absent: anal spines numerous, minute, sometimes concealed in the skin. Gill openings wide. Strong teeth in the jaws and on the palatine bones, none on the vomer. No scales. Air bladder present. Pyloric appendages numerous.

Trichiurus malabaricus, Plate V.

Trichiurus Malabaricus, *Day*, Proc. Zool. Society, 1865, p. 20.

B. vii. D. 132 P. 11.

Length of head $\frac{1}{7}$, of pectoral $\frac{1}{24}$ of total length. Height of body $\frac{1}{17}$, of head $\frac{1}{20}$ of total length.

Eyes—Diameter $\frac{1}{5}$ of length of head, rather more than $\frac{1}{2}$ a diameter apart, nearly $1\frac{1}{2}$ diameters from end of snout.

Lower jaw longest, the maxilla extends to beneath the first quarter of orbit. Preorbital large, lineated, but entire. Opercle finely lineated and extending backwards to above pectoral fin. Openings of nostrils large, rather close to anterior margin of orbit, the superior margin of which is nearly horizontal, and close to the profile of the head.

Teeth—Three large canines in intermaxillaries, the anterior the largest, curved, directed forwards, downwards, and barbed at its extremity: the two posterior ones arising from the external extremities of the intermaxillaries, are curved backwards and downwards; they are also slightly barbed at their extremities. An external row of about five fine teeth exists in the intermaxillaries, and a single row of about seven sharp, pointed, and flattened laterally is found in the maxilla. A row similar to that in the upper jaw exists in the lower, but the teeth are finer. In young specimens the dental arrangement is slightly different.

Fins—Dorsal fin commences opposite the anterior margin of opercle: spines weak, they become gradually longer until they nearly equal the height of the body. Anal spines are very fine and short in young specimens, or else truncated at their extremities; in the adult fish all are truncated as shown magnified in the plate.

Lateral line—Curves downwards behind the pectoral, and at first passes along the inferior third of the body, subsequently still lower.

Colours—Silvery white with a slight pinkish tinge: back a little the darkest. The first three or four dorsal spines have a black spot upon them. A line of greenish black formed of very minute dots, extends along the upper third of the dorsal fin in its whole extent. Caudal extremity with a dark margin. Eyes silvery: tongue smooth and of a golden tinge. Pectoral greyish yellow. Skin of a metallic silver.

Is very common at Cochin. Grows to twelve inches or more in length, and is good eating.

Habitat—Malabar.

* TRICHIURUS HAUMELA.

CLUPEA HAUMELA, *Forsk.* p. 72.

SAWALA, *Russell*, pl. 41.

TRICHIURUS LEPTURUS, *Ham. Buch.* pp. 31, 364.

TRICHIURUS HAUMELA, *Cuv. & Val.* viii. p. 249; *Cantor*, Catal. p. 113; *Günther*, Catal. ii. p. 348.

B. vii. D. 127-133. P. 11.

Length of head from $\frac{1}{6}$ to $\frac{1}{7}$ of the total length. Height of body from $\frac{1}{15}$ to $\frac{1}{17}$ of the total length.

Eyes—Diameter $\frac{1}{6}$ of the length of head, $2\frac{1}{3}$ diameters from end of snout.

Teeth—In the upper jaw, according to *Cantor*, are upwards of fifteen distant teeth on either side, of which the anterior pair, which are present in only the very young, are directed forwards. Behind these appear a pair, or a single arched tooth, the posterior part of the point of which is barbed. Next follow three or four very small and lancet shaped, behind which is a very long

PLATE V.

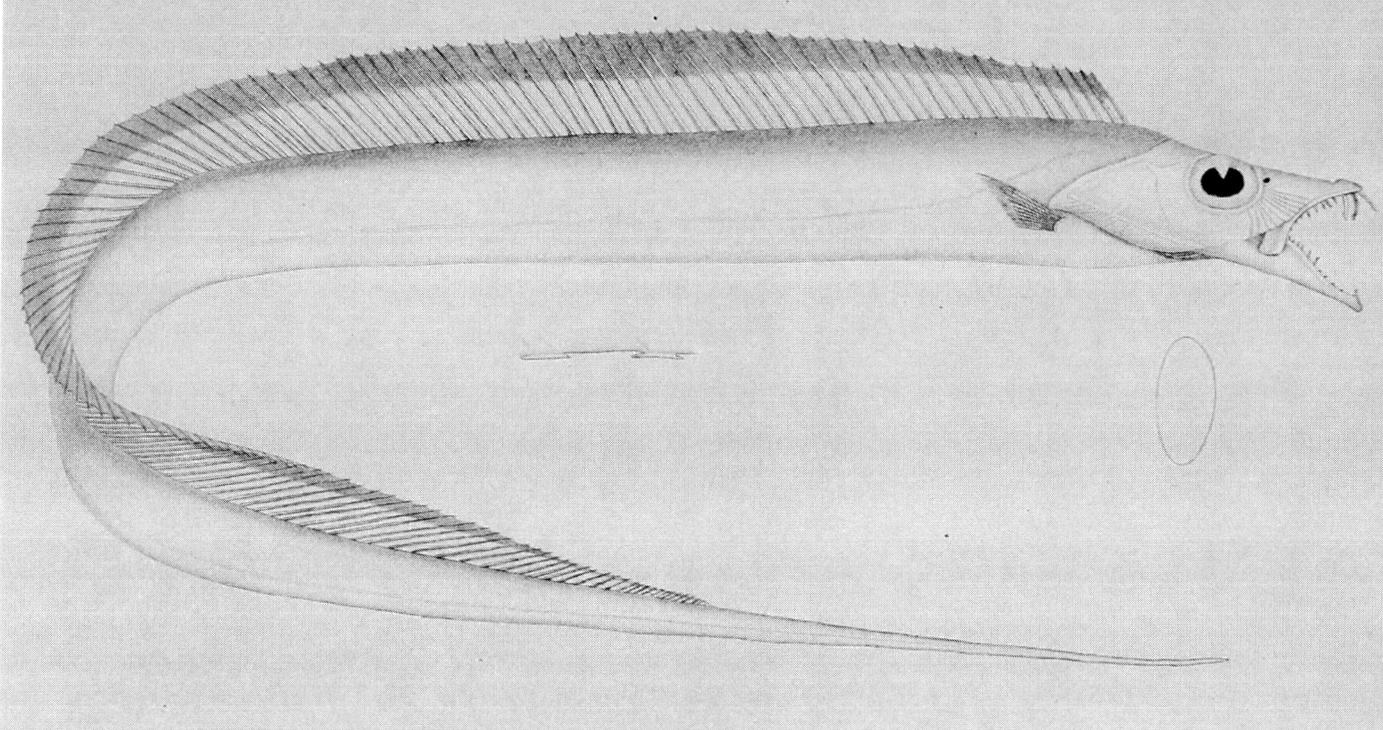

F. Day, del, et sculp.

TRICHIURUS MALABARICUS

arched, half-barbed tooth. The rest of the space is occupied by some distant lancet shaped teeth, of which those in the middle are the largest. On each side of the symphysis of the lower jaw appears an arched tooth, like the corresponding one in the lower jaw, but shorter. Behind the tooth is a vacant space, followed by upwards of twelve lancet shaped teeth, which with the exception of one or two half barbed in the middle, are smaller than the corresponding ones in the upper jaw. Along the margin of each palatine bone is a series of velvety teeth. Tongue smooth.

Fins—The anterior dorsal ray is one-fourth of length of head.

Colours—Upper surface of head, back, and naked point of tail bluish black, light silvery on the jaws, sides of head, and body: abdomen of a brilliant silver. Dorsal rays and membrane pale reddish yellow, the whole of the latter to the twelfth ray, and from thence only its upper half minutely dotted with black. Anterior third of pectorals pale reddish yellow, the rest blackish. Iris silvery blue, blackish towards the orbit. The young are lighter in colour.

Grows to two feet eight inches in length, is eaten fresh or salted. It is of voracious habits, devouring its own kind as well as other fishes and crustacea.

Habitat—Seas and estuaries of India, Malaysia and China.

* Trichiurus savala.

Trichiurus savala, *Cuv. & Val.* viii. p. 251; *Cantor*, Catal. p. 115; *Günther*, Catal. ii. p. 347.

Trichiurus armatus, *Gray*, Ill. I. Z. pl. 93, f. 1.

B. vii. D. 112-120. P. 11.

Length of head $\frac{2}{13}$ to $\frac{4}{27}$ of the length of body. Height of body $\frac{1}{13}$ to $\frac{1}{16}$ of total length.

Eyes—Diameter $\frac{2}{17}$ to $\frac{1}{9}$ of length of head, $3\frac{1}{2}$ diameters in length of snout, 1 diameter apart. Interorbital space flat.

Teeth—The lancet shaped teeth of the jaws are proportionably smaller than in the *T. haumela*, which species it much resembles.

Colours—Upper surface of head, back, and naked point of the tail bluish, all the other parts of a shining silver. Dorsal and pectoral rays yellowish white, their membranes diaphanous. Iris silvery, bluish towards the orbit.

Grows to one foot four inches in length, and is eaten both fresh and salted by the Natives. Is captured most abundantly in April and May.

Habitat—Seas and estuaries of India, Malaysia, and China.

Fam. SCOMBRIDÆ.

Genus SCOMBER, *Artedi*.

Branchiostegals, seven: pseudobranchiæ. Body rather elongate and compressed. Eyes lateral. Cleft of mouth wide. Infraorbital bones do not articulate with the preopercle. Two dorsals, the first spinous and separated by an interspace from the second, behind which and also behind the anal are five or six finlets: the spinous dorsal is less developed than the soft dorsal, or than the anal: ventrals thoracic; two slight ridges on either side of root of caudal; gill openings wide. Teeth small on jaws, vomer, and palatine bones. Scales small. Air bladder simple, but absent in some species. Pyloric appendages very numerous.

SCOMBER KANAGURTA.

KANAGURTA, *Russell*, pl. 136.

SCOMBER KANAGURTA, *Cuv. & Val.* viii. p. 49; *Günther*, Catal. ii. p. 360.

ILA, *Mal.*

B. vi. D. 8-10. | $\frac{1}{11}$ | v. P. 21. V. $\frac{1}{5}$. A. 1. | $\frac{1}{11}$ | v. C. 25. Vert. $\frac{14}{16}$.

Length of head rather more than $\frac{1}{4}$, of pectoral $\frac{1}{7}$, of caudal $\frac{1}{6}$, of caudal lobes $\frac{1}{5}$, of base of first dorsal $\frac{1}{6}$, of base of second dorsal (exclusive of finlets) $\frac{1}{8}$, of base of anal (exclusive of finlets) $\frac{1}{10}$ of total length. Height of head $\frac{1}{5}$, of body $\frac{1}{4}$, of first dorsal $\frac{1}{7}$, of second dorsal $\frac{1}{12}$, of ventral $\frac{1}{8}$, of anal $\frac{1}{12}$ of total length.

Eyes—Upper margin close to profile, diameter $\frac{1}{4}$ length of head, with an adipose lid on either side extending across $\frac{1}{4}$ of the diameter: 1 diameter from end of snout: 1 diameter apart.

Lower jaw rather the longest, with a tubercle at the symphysis: gape of mouth wide: the maxilla extends almost to beneath the posterior margin of the orbit, it is concealed by a large elliptical preorbital which has a line of pores opening along its upper third. Preopercle large, its posterior margin oblique, its angle rounded and forming its widest part, its inferior margin horizontal and about half the length of the vertical, the lower margin with about fifteen shallow canals passing downwards. Opercle triangular, its base above, posterior border with an emargination as deep as it is high. Upper surface of the head with a central ridge that extends from opposite the anterior margin of the orbit backwards to the occipital: several other smaller ones run parallel with, or towards it. Snout rather elevated. Nostrils midway between eye and snout.

Teeth—Minute in the jaws, vomer and palate.

Fins—Pectoral arises below and a short distance in advance of the emargination of the opercle: the first dorsal begins opposite middle of pectoral: ventral under first dorsal: the second dorsal commences midway between opercle and base of caudal: anal under fourth ray of second dorsal terminating opposite the end of that fin. First dorsal triangular, its spines weak, and it can be received into a groove on the back: the second spine one quarter longer than the first, and very slightly longer than the third, posteriorly they rapidly decrease in height, interspinous membrane entire. The distance between the first and second dorsal fins equals half the base of the latter. First ray of second dorsal the longest, upper margin of fin rather concave: the finlets commence just posterior to second dorsal and anal fins and are opposite one another, they consist of a single stem with branched rays. Pectoral short, nearly triangular. Caudal deeply lobed, each lobe being pointed, and with two raised crests along either side of its base.

Scales—Extend over body to between the orbits, also on the cheeks: they are smaller above than below the lateral line, and largest just beneath the pectoral fin: the first few rows below the lateral line run parallel to it, those under pectoral are irregularly concave: there are some minute scales over second dorsal and anal fins.

Lateral line—First describes a very slight curve, and then proceeds direct to the centre of the caudal.

Colours—Back greenish, sides and abdomen iridescent, a row of sixteen spots along the back, close to the base of the dorsal fin. Summit of head spotted: sides shot with bluish purple. Dorsal fins yellowish, tipped with black. Caudal bright yellow, stained with black at its extremity. Pectoral bright yellow. Ventral and anal finely dotted with black, which fades soon after death, when all the shot colours also disappear, and it becomes of a dull green with the abdomen of a lighter colour.

An air bladder present.

Grows to about ten inches in length. It is captured in Cochin in enormous numbers from January until May, its average size is about seven and a half inches. Although excellent eating when quite fresh, it soon taints and is rarely brought to the table of Europeans. It is commonly salted, dried in the sun, and exported in bundles of about one thousand each, mostly to Ceylon.

Habitat—Red Sea, Seas of India, Malaysia and China.

GENUS CYBIUM, *Cuvier*.

Branchiostegals, seven: pseudobranchiæ. Body oblong or rather elongate. Eyes lateral. Cleft of mouth wide. Infraorbital bones do not articulate with the preopercle. Two dorsals, the first extending to commencement of the second, spinous, and not so developed as the second: seven or more pairs of finlets behind second dorsal and anal fins. A slight ridge on either side of root of caudal lobes. Teeth large and strong on jaws, villiform on vomer, palatine bones, and tongue. Air bladder present.

All the species of this genus are comprised under the common appellation of *Seir fish* by European residents in British India.

CYBIUM COMMERSONII.

SCOMBER COMMERSONII, *Lacép.* ii. p. 600, pl. 20, f. 1.

KONAM, *Russell*, pl. 135.

CYBIUM COMMERSONII, *Cuv. & Val.* viii. p. 165; *Cantor*, Catal. p. 108; *Günther*, Catal. ii. p. 370.

CHUMBUM, *Mal.* SEIR FISH.

B. vii. D. 16-17. | $\frac{2\text{-}4}{15\text{-}13}$ | ix-x. P. 20-23. V. $\frac{1}{5}$. A. $\frac{2\text{-}4}{15\text{-}13}$ | ix-x. C. 17.

Length of head $\frac{2}{11}$, of pectoral $\frac{1}{8}$, of caudal $\frac{1}{5}$, of base of first dorsal $\frac{2}{11}$, of base of second dorsal (excluding finlets) $\frac{1}{11}$, of anal (excluding finlets) $\frac{1}{10}$ of total length. Height of head $\frac{1}{8}$, of body $\frac{2}{11}$, of first dorsal $\frac{1}{20}$, of anal $\frac{1}{10}$ of total length.

Eyes—Oval, surrounded by a small circular adipose membrane. Horizontal diameter $\frac{2}{9}$, vertical $\frac{2}{11}$ of length of head, 2 transverse diameters from end of snout, $1\frac{1}{2}$ transverse diameters apart.

Body elongate, tapering towards either extremity, both it and sides of head strongly compressed, the latter also depressed: anteriorly the snout comes to a sharp point.

Mouth deeply cleft, upper jaw with rather a concave lower margin, produced in front; lower jaw nearly horizontal, with a fleshy protuberance at the symphysis. Vertical limb of intermaxillaries very broad, the two conjoined having somewhat the appearance of the upper bill of a rasorial bird. Maxilla extends to beneath the centre of the orbit. Preorbital narrow. Preopercle, its posterior border rather concave along its centre, so that its angle, which is rounded appears rather produced, its lower border rather more than half the length of its vertical one. Opercle narrow. Cleft of gills very wide, extending to under the centre of the lower jaw. Upper surface of head flat with a raised ridge along its centre. Nostrils in front of upper third of orbit, in a depressed triangular space surrounded by rather raised margins.

Teeth—Strong, lancet shaped, laterally compressed, those in the upper jaw varying in number from fifteen to twenty-five, the posterior ones being rather the smallest. In the lower jaw there are from ten to fifteen of the same shape, but the posterior ones are the largest. Villiform teeth exist on the vomer in a small triangular space, which is somewhat rounded anteriorly, and a long narrow band of two or three rows is found on the palatine bones.

Fins—Ventral arises opposite the first third of the pectoral and on a line with the first dorsal: the second dorsal commences opposite the anal and midway between the centre of caudal fin and the anterior extremity of the snout. The spines of the first dorsal are weak, and end in thin filamentous points projecting beyond the membrane, which is deeply notched. *Cantor* observes that "the anterior dorsal and anal fin rays are preceded by four spines, which however cannot be distinctly perceived without removing the covering scales and integuments." The second dorsal is highest in front with its upper margin concave, it is situated opposite the anal which it resembles, the finlets commence just behind them, and are continued opposite each other to the root of the caudal. Ventral small. Pectoral pointed. Caudal with pointed lobes, its posterior margin forming a semicircle; each lobe with a raised soft ridge along its base, between which is the termination of the lateral line in the form of a raised soft horizontal keel.

Scales—Small, elongated, some exist on the second dorsal, caudal, and anal fins, and from the infraorbitals round to the posterior margin of the orbit, also extending for a short distance over the upper margin of the preopercle.

Lateral line—At first in upper third of body, makes a gradual and not very distinct curve to opposite the twelfth or thirteenth dorsal ray, where it forms a sort of angle and then bends down, making a second curve from opposite the first to the third pairs of finlets, beyond which it passes direct to the centre of the caudal, where it ends in a soft raised keel between the bases of the lobes.

Colours—Summit of head and back of a deep bluish purple, with golden green reflections, lighter on the sides and body to a little beneath the lateral line; the rest of the sides, the abdomen, opercles and cheeks, shining silvery with lilac reflections; membrane of anterior dorsal fin pale greyish lilac, minutely dotted with brown, upper margin black: second dorsal, anal, and their spurious fins pale silvery lilac; anal and its spurious fins with white margins: caudal silvery, blackish; ventrals white; anterior half of pectorals white, posterior blackish; between the gill opening and the root of the upper margin of the pectorals a large black spot. Iris silvery, bluish black near the orbit. After death the sides above the lateral line acquire a number of close, vertical, undulating lines and spots; beneath the lateral line there are black lines, but fewer and more distant.

Grows to four feet in length, and is inferior eating to the *C. guttatum*; it should be dressed when quite fresh; salts well.

Habitat—From east and south coasts of Africa through the Red Sea, Seas of India, Malaysia and China.

* Cybium lineolatum.

Cybium lineolatum, *Cuv. & Val.* viii. p. 170; *Cantor*, Catal. p. 110; *Günther*, Catal. ii. p. 370.

B. vii. D. 16 | 16 | ix. P. 21. V. $\frac{1}{5}$. A. $\frac{2-5}{15-14}$ | x. C. 15.
Length of head $\frac{1}{5}$ of total length. Height of body $\frac{2}{13}$ of total length.

Eyes—Each having rather a broad circular adipose membrane, diameter $\frac{2}{9}$ of length of head, $1\frac{1}{4}$ diameters apart.

Teeth—On either side of both jaws are upwards of eighteen lancet shaped teeth, many of which however are often absent. The middle ones in the lower jaw are the largest. On the anterior part of the vomer appears a pointed triangular spot with velvety teeth, and on each palatine and pterygoid bone a rather broad continued line of similar teeth. Others exist at the root of the small oval flattened tongue, and on the margin and internal surface of each hyoid.

Fins—The spines of the dorsal fin are very slender, and the membrane is easily detached, so as to leave the filamentous points of the anterior and the whole of the posterior five or six very short spines unconnected. The anterior spine, scarcely equal to the diameter of the eye, is two-thirds of the length of the second, which is shorter than the third. The fourth, the longest, is one-fourth of the length of the head; the rest gradually decrease; the sixteenth is so short and slender that it may easily escape observation. The anterior spurious fin is often connected by a short membrane to the second dorsal and anal. Each caudal lobe equals the length of the head. The length of the pectorals is two-seventeenths of the total length; the ventrals one-third of the pectorals.

Scales—Are placed as in the last species.

Lateral line—Consists of a series of short rectangular elevations, at first in upper fourth of body, from whence it gradually deviates towards the termination of the second dorsal, and again declines to below the middle of the body opposite the fifth finlet, where it ascends on to the lateral keel.

Colours—The same as in the last species, the *C. Commersonii*. After death several series of irregularly disposed black spots appear above the lateral line, whilst beneath it there are three or four rows of longitudinal short linear spots, each resembling an interrupted line.

Grows to two feet in length.

Habitat—Seas of India and Malaysia.

CYBIUM GUTTATUM.

SCOMBER GUTTATUS, *Bl. Schn.* p. 23. t. 5.

WINGERAM, *Russell*, pl. 134.

CYBIUM GUTTATUM, *Cuv. & Val.* viii. p. 173; *Cantor*, Catal. p. 3; *Günther*, Catal. ii. p. 371.

CYBIUM KUHLII, *Cuv. & Val.* viii. p. 178, (*young.*)

ARRAKEEAH, *Mal.* SEIR FISH.

B. vii. D. 16-18 | 19-21 | viii-x. P. 15-21. V. $\frac{1}{5}$. A. 20-22 | vii-ix. C. 26.

Length of head $\frac{3}{16}$, of pectoral $\frac{1}{10}$, of caudal $\frac{1}{5}$, of base of second dorsal (exclusive of finlets) $\frac{1}{10}$, of base of anal (exclusive of finlets) $\frac{1}{10}$ of total length. Height of head $\frac{1}{8}$, of body $\frac{1}{5}$, of first dorsal $\frac{1}{10}$, of second dorsal $\frac{1}{10}$, of ventral $\frac{1}{20}$, of anal $\frac{1}{10}$ of total length.

Eyes—Oval, each surrounded by a circular adipose membrane, horizontal diameter $\frac{2}{11}$, vertical $\frac{1}{6}$ of length of head, nearly 2 diameters from end of snout, $1\frac{1}{2}$ diameters apart.

Body oblong, tapering off to both extremities, sides and head compressed.

Mouth wide, gradually expanding posteriorly: upper jaw very slightly convex, from about its centre it is produced anteriorly when it tapers to a point: lower jaw longest, rather convex along its extent, and slightly prominent at symphysis: the posterior extremity of maxilla extends to beneath the posterior third of the orbit. Preorbitals, and opercles as in the *C. Commersonii.* A moderately raised ridge extends along the centre of the head. Nostrils rather wide apart; the posterior, which is the largest, rather higher than the orbit: the anterior which is round, on a still higher level.

Teeth—Lancet shaped and laterally compressed, about twenty in the upper, and fifteen in the lower jaw in which latter they are the largest, whilst they increase in size posteriorly. Numerous villiform teeth on vomer and palate.

Fins—First dorsal and ventral arise on a line, slightly posterior to the origin of the pectoral: the second dorsal commences midway between the snout and the posterior margin of centre of caudal fin: anal rather behind it. First dorsal spines weak and ending in soft points, the membrane deeply notched. Second dorsal highest in front, with a concave upper margin: anal of the same shape: the finlets commence close behind each of these fins and extend to the root of the caudal. Pectoral rather pointed. Ventral small. Caudal deeply lobed with a soft elevated keel running parallel with the base of either lobe.

Lateral line—Consisting of small rectangular elevations, proceeds nearly straight, at first in upper fourth of body, but becomes more undulating opposite the commencement of the second dorsal, and very much so opposite third and fourth finlets: between the keels along the base of either caudal lobe is a triangular horizontal keel.

Colours—Generally the same as in the *C. Commersonii,* but after death numerous round or oval spots of different sizes and irregularly scattered, appear in longitudinal rows along the back and upper half of the sides. The membrane of the first seven or nine spines of the first dorsal is black, that of the succeeding spines white minutely dotted with brown and edged with black.

Grow to three and a half feet in length, are good eating and salt well: but when under a foot in length are dry, from two to two and a-half feet long they are in the best condition, above that they become coarse. They should be dressed when quite fresh. They are also one of the best fish for making "Tamarind fish." Are found in Malabar from October throughout the cold months.

Habitat—Seas of India, Malaysia, and China.

Genus NAUCRATES, *Cuvier.*

Branchiostegals, seven: pseudobranchiæ. Body oblong, subcylindrical. Eyes lateral. Cleft of mouth moderate. Infraorbital bones do not articulate with the preopercle. Two dorsals, the first reduced to a few free spines; ventrals thoracic: no spurious fins: a keel on each side of tail. Villiform teeth on jaws, vomer, and palatine bones. Air bladder small. Cæcal appendages in moderate numbers.

* Naucrates ductor.

Gasterosteus ductor, *Linn.* Syst. Nat. i. p. 489.
Naucrates ductor, *Cuv. & Val.* viii. p. 312. pl. 232; *Günther*, Catal. ii. p. 374.
Naucrates noveboracensis, *Cuv. & Val.* viii. p. 325.
Naucrates Indicus, *Cuv. & Val.* viii. p. 326.
Naucrates Koelreuteri, *Cuv & Val.* viii. p. 327.
The Pilot fish.

B. vii. D. 3-6 | $\frac{1}{26\text{-}29}$. P. 18. V. $\frac{1}{5}$. A. $\frac{2}{16\text{-}17}$. C. 17. Cæc. pylor. 12-15. Vert. $\frac{10}{16}$.

Length of head $\frac{2}{9}$, of pectoral $\frac{2}{15}$, of ventral $\frac{2}{15}$, of caudal $\frac{1}{5}$ of the total length. Height of head $\frac{1}{6}$, of body $\frac{1}{5}$, of second dorsal $\frac{1}{15}$ of total length.

Eyes—Each surrounded by a circular adipose membrane, diameter $\frac{1}{5}$ of the length of head, and 1 diameter from end of snout.

The curve of the profile of the back is nearly equal to that of the abdomen.

Mouth moderately cleft, the lower jaw rather advanced beyond the upper: the posterior extremity of maxilla extends to beneath the anterior margin of the orbit. Angle of preopercle rounded, its border extremely finely crenulated: opercle striated in shallow grooves. The orifices of the nostrils approximate, are close to the upper profile, and rather nearer to the end of the mouth than they are to the eye.

Teeth—Villiform in both jaws, vomer, and palatine bones.

Fins—Pectoral oval and situated slightly below the middle line of the body; ventrals close together, and arise opposite the anterior third of the pectoral: first dorsal begins opposite end of pectoral; second dorsal, in middle of the body: anal, below centre of second dorsal. The first dorsal consists of very small spines. The spine of the second dorsal is one-third the length of the anterior rays which are the longest, and they gradually diminish to about the twelfth, the last two or three are slightly prolonged. Ventral pointed, its spine two-thirds the length of the first ray. Two small free spines before the anal.

Scales—Small on the top of the head, the cheeks, and over the body, except on a small spot above the base of the pectoral fin, which is destitute of scales.

Lateral line—Consists of a straight series of very small elevations: above the pectoral it forms a curve which descends to the centre of the body which it reaches below the anterior third of the second dorsal, from whence it is continued straight to the centre of the caudal, where it forms an horizontal elevated keel close to its base.

Colours—Bluish silvery grey, darkest towards the back; large vertical blue or violet bands pass down the body; the number is generally five on the body, one on the head, and one on the caudal fin. The first on the body is behind the opercle, the second passes down from the first dorsal, the third from the anterior third of the second dorsal to before the anal, and the two last from the second dorsal to the anal. Caudal dark blue tipped with black and margined with pure white. Pectoral white with violet tip, ventral nearly black, with white points. Iris golden.

Grows to one foot in length, and is good eating.

Habitat—Seas of India, and nearly all those of temperate and tropical regions.

GENUS ELACATE, *Cuvier*.

Branchiostegals, seven: pseudobranchiæ. Body elongated, fusiform; head depressed. Eyes lateral. Cleft of mouth moderately deep. Infraorbital bones do not articulate with the preopercle. Two dorsals, the first formed of eight small and free spines, the soft dorsal of greater extent than the spinous. Ventrals thoracic; no spurious fins, or keel on tail. Villiform teeth on jaws, vomer, and palatine bones. No air bladder. Cæcal appendages in enormous numbers, and subdividing into minute branches.

ELACATE NIGRA.

SCOMBER NIGER, *Bloch*, t. 337.

PEDDA-MOTTAH, *Russell*, pl. 153.

ELACATE PONDICERIANA, *Cuv. & Val.* viii. p. 329; E. MOTTA, *ibid.* p. 332; E. MALABARICA, *ibid.* p. 332; E. ATLANTICA, *ibid.* p. 334; E. BIVITTATA, *ibid.* p. 338; *Cantor*, Catal. p. 116.

ELACATE NIGRA, *Günther*, Catal. ii. p. 375.

B. vii. D. 8 | $\frac{2}{28\text{-}36}$. P. 21. V. $\frac{1}{5}$. A. $\frac{2}{25\text{-}28}$. C. 17. Vert. $\frac{12}{13}$.

Length of head $\frac{1}{5}$, of pectoral $\frac{1}{7}$, of caudal $\frac{3}{19}$, of base of first dorsal $\frac{1}{7}$, of base of second dorsal $\frac{3}{7}$, of base of anal $\frac{1}{3}$ of total length. Height of head $\frac{1}{9}$, of body $\frac{1}{7}$, of hard dorsal $\frac{1}{37}$, of soft dorsal $\frac{1}{9}$, of ventral $\frac{1}{10}$ of total length.

Eyes—Close to line of profile, transversely oval, and each surrounded by a large circular adipose membrane: horizontal diameter $\frac{1}{4}$, vertical diameter $\frac{1}{8}$ of length of head, $1\frac{1}{3}$ diameters from end of snout, nearly 2 diameters apart.

Mouth wide, maxilla extending to beneath the anterior margin of the orbit: mandibulæ flat beneath: a slight tubercle at symphysis. Preorbital small, narrow, and rugose. Preopercle with its inferior and posterior borders of equal length, and meeting at right angles, its surface rather roughened. Opercle also with rough lines which commence from its anterior superior angle, proceed downwards and backwards, and expand into a fan-shaped form. Upper surface of head flat and lineated from two points, both of which are behind the eye, separated from one another by a slight interval, but still not far from the central line of the head; from these two points fine raised lines radiate, joining behind at the occipital crest, and in front opposite the anterior margin of the orbit, thus enclosing a lozenge-shaped space. Nostrils have two orifices approximating, and in the first third of the distance between the eye and the end of the snout; gills open as far forwards as commissures of lips. Coracoid bone rough and well developed.

Teeth—In numerous villiform bands in both jaws, on a large oval space on vomer, and in a long band on each palatine. There also exists an oval patch on the tongue which is wide: skin of palate and side of tongue rough. Pharyngeal teeth villiform.

Fins—The commencement of the free dorsal spines in a line with the bases of the pectoral and ventral. The anal begins under about the twelfth dorsal ray. The dorsal spines are short and sharp with a very small membrane to each, they can be laid flat and extend as far as the base of the soft dorsal. The soft portion of the dorsal commences opposite the posterior margin of the pectoral, its anterior portion is the highest, and its upper margin is thus a little concave, whilst in the last three-fourths of its course it follows the curve of the back, the last rays which are a little prolonged do not extend quite as far as the base of the caudal. The anal is of the same form as the dorsal, and they terminate opposite each other, leaving about one eighth of the posterior extremity of the body finless. The pectoral is situated low down and is rather large and pointed. The ventrals are small and pointed, the spine fine and the external ray the longest. The caudal emarginate, with the lower lobe the shortest.

Scales—Minute, extending over the body, each side of occiput, opercles, cheeks, and base of caudal, also a few fine ones over the soft dorsal and anal.

Lateral line—With slight undulations, curved slightly downwards until opposite the commencement of the anal from whence it is continued to centre of caudal and on to its termination.

Colours—Ground colour of a dark olivaceous brown, with a light band from orbit to root of caudal, next a dark one from the shoulder to the caudal, below which it becomes lighter towards the abdomen, where it has a slight silvery tint. All the fins are brownish, the pectorals being stained with black, the ventrals with grey, the caudal also with blackish grey, and the external corners of the lobes tipped with white.

Grows to two feet in length: and is eaten by the Natives.

Habitat—Seas of India, Malaysia, China, and Japan. The tropical parts of the Atlantic, extending along the shores of the United States.

GENUS ECHENEIS, *Artedi.*

Branchiostegals, eight: pseudobranchiæ. Body elongate, fusiform. Eyes lateral or directed downwards and outwards. Cleft of mouth wide. Infraorbital bones do not articulate with the preopercle. Head depressed. The spinous dorsal modified to an adhesive disk on the summit of head and neck. Ventrals thoracic: no finlets, or keel on the tail. Teeth villiform on jaws, vomer, palatine bones, and generally on the tongue. Scales very small. No air bladder. Pyloric appendages in moderate numbers.

ECHENEIS NAUCRATES.

ECHENEIS NAUCRATES, *Linn.* Syst. i. p. 446; *Cantor*, Catal. p. 199; *Günther*, Catal. ii. p. 384.

ALA MOTTAH, *Russell*, pl. 49.

PUTTHOO MUDAY, *Mal.*

B. vii. D. 22-25 | 33-41. P. 20. V. $\frac{1}{5}$. A. $\frac{2\text{-}1}{32\text{-}36}$. C. 17.

Length of head rather more than $\frac{1}{6}$, of pectoral $\frac{1}{8}$, of base of second dorsal $\frac{1}{3}$, of base of anal $\frac{1}{3}$, of caudal $\frac{1}{8}$ of total length. Height of head $\frac{1}{19}$, of body $\frac{1}{8}$, of second dorsal $\frac{1}{12}$, of anal $\frac{1}{12}$, of ventral $\frac{1}{8}$ of total length.

Eyes—Oval, looking obliquely outwards and downwards, horizontal diameter $\frac{1}{5}$, and vertical diameter $\frac{1}{7}$ of length of head, $2\frac{1}{2}$ diameters apart superiorly, but inferiorly only 2: 2 diameters from end of upper jaw.

Body—Cylindrical, tapering off to the tail. Upper surface of head covered by a flattened oval disk, rather widest posteriorly, one fifth of the total length, and two and a-half times as long as wide, containing usually if not invariably in Malabar specimens twenty-two transverse laminæ with dentated or spiny teeth on the posterior margin of each, and also a central wide tooth, or smooth bony elevation between each near their centres, so that a vacuum can be created along the whole extent of the disk, or only in one-half. The most anterior of the laminæ are directed slightly forwards, the second quarter are nearly transverse, and the posterior go backwards, the difference between each succeeding one being very gradual. External to this disk is a wide fleshy membrane, which posteriorly extends over the occiput, but anteriorly does not reach to the end of the upper jaw; the whole acting as a sucker.

Mouth—Oblique, maxilla extending about as far as the anterior margin of orbit. Mandibulæ pointed and covered superiorly with numerous rows of villiform teeth in a triangular space in advance of the upper jaw, which is pointed. The lower jaw has a soft tip. Opercle rounded with some striated ridges on it. Nostrils rather nearer to angle of mouth than to the anterior superior angle of the orbit.

Fins—Pectoral situated over the posterior margin of the opercle, and opposite posterior quarter of the bony disk. Ventral slightly posterior to it. Second dorsal commences midway between anterior extremity and base of caudal, anal opposite to it. First dorsal forming portion of the disk. Second dorsal and anal opposite one another, both highest in front with rather concave margins, and the last rays slightly produced. Ventral pointed, and placed almost horizontally. Caudal with its posterior margin straight, but having four short notches at its extremity: one-ninth of the body finless, between the last dorsal and anal rays, and the base of the caudal fin.

Scales—Minute, closely adherent to the skin, their longest diameter transverse.

Lateral line—Rather undulating, passing slightly downwards to the centre of the body which it attains between the anal and second dorsal fins.

Colours—Generally brownish grey, with the external margins of the caudal, and the anterior tips of the dorsal and anal fins edged with white. Pectoral of a deep brown, centre of caudal nearly black.

Not rare in Malabar, where they are found of all sizes up to a foot, or even to two feet in length. Are frequently captured attached to sharks, and eaten by the Natives.

Habitat—Seas of India, and all those of temperate and tropical regions.

Genus STROMATEUS, *Artedi.*

Peprilus, *Cuvier.*
Apolectus, *Cuv. & Val.*
Rhombus, *Cuv. & Val.*
Seserinus, *Cuv. & Val.*

Branchiostegals, from five to seven: pseudobranchiæ. Body compressed, more or less elevated. Eyes lateral. Cleft of mouth narrow, or of moderate width. Infraorbitals do not articulate with preopercle. A single long dorsal and anal fin having rudimentary spines anteriorly. No ventral fins in the adult. Teeth in a single series on the margin of the jaws: palate and tongue smooth: œsophagus armed with numerous bony barbed teeth. Scales small, covering vertical fins. No air bladder. Pyloric appendages numerous.

Stromateus sinensis.

Stromateus sinensis, *Euphrasén,* Vetensk. Acad. Nya Handl. Stockh. ix. p. 49, t. 9; *Bl. Schn.* p. 492; *Cantor,* Catal. p. 140.
Atookoia, *Russell,* pl. 44.
Stromateus atous, *Cuv. & Val.* ix. p. 389; *Günther,* Catal. ii. p. 399.
Stromateus albus, *Cuv. & Val.* ix. p. 388.
Vella arwoolee, *Mal.* White Pomfret.

B. vi. D. $\frac{1}{43\text{-}49}$. P. 23-27. V. $\frac{1}{5}$. A. $\frac{1}{39\text{-}42}$. C. 17.

Length of head $\frac{1}{5}$, of pectoral $\frac{3}{10}$, of caudal $\frac{1}{5}$, of base of dorsal upwards of $\frac{1}{2}$, of base of anal $\frac{1}{2}$ of total length. Height of head $\frac{1}{4}$, of body $\frac{2}{3}$, of dorsal $\frac{1}{4}$, of anal $\frac{1}{4}$ of total length.

Eyes—Diameter $\frac{1}{4}$ of length of head, $\frac{2}{3}$ of a diameter from end of snout, $1\frac{2}{3}$ diameters apart.

Mouth in central line: the maxilla extends to beneath the anterior third of the orbit. Opercles striated from above downwards and backwards, the preopercle downwards and forwards. Nostrils approximating, overhanging the snout, and placed above the level and in front of the orbit.

Teeth—A single row of excessively minute and closely set teeth in each jaw.

Fins—Dorsal commences over the pectoral, and anal opposite the posterior third of the pectoral. The dorsal rays gradually increase, the tenth being the longest, from whence the fin descends, and has a concave upper margin: four spines are hidden in the flesh before the anal and dorsal fins. The anal is the same shape as the dorsal. The caudal lobed, with the lobes of equal size: the pectoral rather pointed.

Scales—Small and very deciduous, extending over the vertical fins and head.

Lateral line—In upper fifth of body, at first it irregularly ascends, and curves slightly upwards, but opposite the end of dorsal it passes straight to the centre of the caudal fin.

Colours—Upper surface of head and body as far as the lateral line of a deep neutral tint, the rest of the body with a mixture of brownish grey, having metallic reflections, lighter and silvery towards the abdomen. It is dotted all over with brown, the larger spots having a silvery point in their centres. Fins silvery grey, marginal half blackish. Cavity of the mouth and tongue pale bluish grey with brown dots, silvery in the centre. Iris reddish silver or copper coloured, minutely dotted with brown.

This species of Pomfret is that most esteemed for eating: in Malabar it is by no means rare during the S.W. monsoon (from June till September). It should be cooked when quite fresh.

Habitat—Seas of India, Malaysia, and China.

Stromateus argenteus.

Stromateus argenteus, *Bloch*, xii. p. 92, t. 421; *Russell*, pp. 31, 35; *Cuv. & Val.* ix. p. 393; *Cantor*, Catal. p. 142; *Günther*, Catal. ii. p. 400.

Stromateus securifer, *Cuv. & Val.* ix. p. 394, pl. 273 (*young*).

Stromateus candidus, *Cuv. & Val.* ix. p. 391.

Tella sandawa, *Russell*, pl. 42.

Silver Pomfret.

B. vii. D. 5-9 | $\frac{1}{39\text{-}43}$. P. 25-27. A. 6 | $\frac{1}{34\text{-}41}$. C. 16.

Length of head $\frac{2}{9}$, of pectoral $\frac{1}{3}$, of caudal $\frac{1}{3}$ of total length. Height of body $\frac{1}{2}$, of dorsal $\frac{1}{3}$, of anal $\frac{1}{3}$ of the total length.

Eyes—Diameter $\frac{2}{7}$ of length of head, 1 diameter from end of snout, 1 diameter apart.

Lower jaw the longest, the maxilla extends to beneath the anterior third of orbit. Snout projecting over the mouth.

Teeth—In a close single row in either jaw, largest in the inferior.

Fins—The second dorsal commences slightly posterior to the origin of the pectoral, and opposite the anal. The spines of the first dorsal in the adult are truncated superiorly, as are also those of the anal. The anterior extremities of the dorsal and anal are elevated and falcated, whilst the posterior portion of each is parallel to the profiles of the back and the abdomen. Pectoral rather prominent in the adult, rounded in the young. Caudal deeply lobed. No ventral fin in adult specimens.

Scales—Small and very deciduous.

Lateral line—As in the *S. sinensis.*

Colours—Upper surface of head and back as low as the lateral line of a greyish neutral tint with purplish reflections, sides of head and body silvery grey, fading to white on the abdomen, and everywhere covered with minute black dots. A dark spot on upper portion of opercle. Dorsal and anal grey minutely dotted with black, the outer half being the darkest. Caudal and pectoral yellowish white also minutely dotted with black, the outer half being the darkest. Iris silvery.

Grows to ten inches in length, and is much esteemed for eating, but is not so good as the *S. sinensis.*

Habitat. Seas of India, Malaysia, and China.

Stromateus cinereus.

Stromateus cinereus, *Bloch*, xii. p. 90, t. 420, (*middle age*); *Cantor*, Catal. p. 143; *Günther*, Catal. ii. p. 400.

Sudi sandawah, *Russell*, pl. 45, (*young*).

Stromateus griseus, *Cuv. & Val.* ix. p. 395.

Grey Pomfret.

B. vii. D. 7-8 | $\frac{1}{38\text{-}41}$. P. 23-25. A. 5. | $\frac{1}{32\text{-}39}$. C. 17-19.

Length of head $\frac{1}{8}$, of pectoral $\frac{3}{8}$, of lower lobe of caudal $\frac{1}{2}$, of upper lobe of caudal $\frac{1}{4}$, of base of second dorsal $\frac{3}{8}$, of base of anal $\frac{1}{4}$ of total length. Height of head $\frac{1}{7}$, of body $\frac{1}{3}$, of second dorsal $\frac{3}{8}$, of anal rather more than $\frac{1}{2}$ of total length.

Eyes—Diameter rather more than $\frac{1}{5}$ of length of head, $\frac{1}{2}$ a diameter from end of snout, rather more than 1 diameter apart.

Lower jaw considerably the longest, the maxilla extends to beneath the anterior third of the transverse diameter of the orbit. Nostrils projecting over the snout.

Teeth—In a fine single row in each jaw.

Fins—The spines of the first dorsal appear above the skin in a truncated form, as do also those of the anal. Both the dorsal and anal are pointed anteriorly, the latter being the most produced. The pectoral is long and pointed. The lower lobe of the caudal equals the length of the body and head.

Scales—Small, very deciduous and extended over the vertical fins.

Lateral line—As in *S. sinensis.*

Colours—Upper surface of head and back, also the sides above the lateral line of a leaden grey: cheeks and opercles silvery, an irregular black spot on opercle. Sides of body beneath the lateral line light grey, becoming silvery white on the abdomen. Dorsal and anal grey with minute black dots, their margins and points blackish. Pectoral buff. Caudal of a light orange with minute black dots: margins and points of lobes blackish. Iris silvery, orbital half, leaden grey.

Grows to eight inches in length: is good eating, but inferior to the *S. argenteus.* It is not rare in Malabar.

Habitat—Seas of India, and Malaysia.

STROMATEUS NIGER.

STROMATEUS NIGER, *Bloch*, xii. p. 93. t. 422; *Cuv. & Val.* xi. p. 385; *Cantor*, Catal. p. 139; *Günther*, Catal. ii. p. 401.

NALA SANDAWAH, *Russell*, pl. 43.

APOLECTUS STROMATEUS, *Cuv. & Val.* viii. p. 439, pl. 328, *(young)*; *Cantor*, Catal. p. 123.

KAR ARWOOLEE, *Mal.* BLACK POMFRET.

B. vii. D. $\frac{5}{42\text{-}44}$. P. 22. A. $\frac{3}{35\text{-}39}$. C. 19.

Length of head $\frac{2}{9}$, of pectoral nearly $\frac{1}{3}$, of caudal $\frac{1}{4}$, of base of dorsal $\frac{1}{2}$, of base of anal $\frac{3}{7}$ of total length. Height of head $\frac{2}{9}$, of body $\frac{1}{3}$, of dorsal $\frac{3}{14}$, of anal $\frac{3}{14}$ of total length.

Eyes—Diameter $\frac{1}{5}$ of length of head, 1 diameter from end of snout, nearly 2 diameters apart.

The profiles of the back and of the abdomen are about equally curved: the body from the posterior extremities of the dorsal and anal fins to the base of caudal is cylindrical.

Mouth situated opposite about the centre of the body, the lower jaw the longest: the maxilla extends to beneath the anterior margin of the orbit. Preopercle entire. Opercle ending in a dull obtuse point. Nostrils anterior and superior to orbit.

Teeth—In a fine single series in both jaws.

Fins—The dorsal commences a little behind the pectoral, and opposite the anal. The dorsal and anal are much elevated anteriorly, very low posteriorly, with concave external margins. Pectorals long and falciform. Ventrals only apparent in the young, in a specimen $3\frac{3}{10}$ inches in length, the ventrals are jugular and one eighth of the total length. The spines before the dorsal and anal fins, which are concealed in the adult fish, are apparent in the immature.

Scales—Small, extending over body, head, opercles, and vertical fins, but not over snout, or on the lower jaw.

Lateral line—At first in upper third of body from whence it gently curves downwards, and in its last fourth passes straight to the centre of the caudal, in the form of a raised keeled line with lateral shields as is perceived in the *Carangidæ*.

Colours—Deep brown or greyish brown with blue reflections. Cheeks, opercles and abdomen pale neutral tint or brownish neutral. Dorsal and anal greyish brown, stained black towards the margins. Pectoral and caudal brownish, edged with black. Iris brownish blue. The young is grey, the dorsal and anal fins black and the caudal yellow, with three brown cross bands, the most posterior of which is at its base.

Grows to two feet in length, is excellent eating. In the Straits it is dried and largely exported to India and elsewhere. It appears in Malabar about the same time as the *S. sinensis*, it comes in shoals and disappears as suddenly as it arrives.

Habitat—Seas of India, Malaysia, and China.

Fam. CARANGIDÆ.

GENUS CARANX, *Cuv. & Val.*

OLISTUS, SCYRIS, BLEPHARIS, GALLICHTHYS, et HYNNIS, *Cuv. & Val.*

MEGALASPIS, DECAPTERUS, SELAR, CARANGOIDES, LIEGLOSSUS, URASPIS, SELAROIDES et GNATHANODON, *Bleeker.*

CARANGUS, *Girard.*

Branchiostegals, seven: pseudobranchiæ. Body oblong or elevated, and more or less compressed. Eyes lateral. Cleft of mouth moderate. Infraorbital bones do not articulate with the preopercle. Two dorsals, the first having in front of it a recumbent immoveable spine directed forwards, the spinous less developed than the soft dorsal or anal, which are of nearly equal extent: whilst several of the posterior rays of both these last fins may be detached from the rest (***Megalaspis***, Bleeker), or only one (***Decapterus***, Bleeker). Two spines separated by an interspace from but in front of anal fin. Ventrals thoracic. Teeth disposed in various manners, and in some species the dentition changing with age. Scales small. Lateral line continuous, and curved anteriorly, with its posterior portion straight, and mailed with scaly plates, each of which is keeled and has a spinate termination. Air bladder bifurcated posteriorly. Pyloric appendages numerous.

a. With eight or nine detached rays, behind dorsal and anal fins.

CARANX ROTTLERI.

SCOMBER ROTTLERI, *Bloch*, x. p. 40, t. 346.

WORAGOO, *Russell*, pl. 143.

CARANX ROTTLERI, *Cuv. & Val.* ix. p. 29; *Cantor*, Catal. p. 124; *Günther*, Catal. ii. p. 424.

B. vii. D. 8 | $\frac{1}{10\text{-}11}$ viii.-ix. P. 21. V. $\frac{1}{5}$. A. 2 | $\frac{1}{8\text{-}9}$ vii.-viii. C. 18. Keel 55. Vert. $\frac{10}{14}$.

Length of head $\frac{2}{9}$, of pectoral $\frac{1}{4}$, of caudal $\frac{1}{5}$, of base of first dorsal $\frac{1}{9}$, of base of second dorsal (excluding free rays) $\frac{1}{9}$, of base of anal (excluding free rays) $\frac{1}{11}$ of total length. Height of head $\frac{1}{6}$, of body $\frac{2}{9}$, of first dorsal $\frac{1}{11}$, of second dorsal $\frac{1}{9}$, of anal $\frac{1}{9}$, of ventral $\frac{1}{9}$ of total length.

Eyes—Rather close to profile, diameter $\frac{1}{5}$ of length of head, 1 diameter from end of snout, 1 diameter apart.

Body compressed, with a raised keel along the vertical portion of the lateral line. A gradual rise from the snout to the first dorsal.

Lower jaw the longest: the maxilla extends to beneath the centre of the orbit.

Teeth—Villiform in a single series except at the centre of the jaw.

Fins—Pectoral and ventral in a line. First dorsal arises over the anterior fourth of pectoral, second dorsal over posterior fourth of pectoral: anal opposite ninth ray of dorsal. First dorsal triangular, with a procumbent spine in front, the interspinous membrane scarcely notched; both it and the anal spines can be received into grooves. Second dorsal highest in front, with from eight to nine free rays extending posteriorly as far as the root of the caudal. Pectoral falciform extending to the twenty-fifth plate of lateral line. The second of the two spines before the anal the longest: the anterior rays of the anal higher than the posterior: eight or nine free rays behind the anal fin. Caudal deeply lobed.

Scales—Small on the body, but not so over the head or before the ventral fin.

Lateral line—First passes in the form of small round scales upwards, then below the third spine of the first dorsal bends suddenly downwards, and from opposite the first third of the pectoral proceeds straight to the caudal, in the form of a raised sharp keel, which becomes more prominent as the tail is approached, where each of these scales have broad lateral processes.

Colours—Back glossy green, abdomen silvery white tinged with yellow. A large black spot on the upper and posterior part of opercles. Pectoral, ventral, and anal yellow. Dorsals and caudal tipped with black, and the posterior edge of the caudal also stained dark.

Common, but not frequently seen above nine inches in length, although sometimes it attains eleven. Not much esteemed as food by Europeans, but employed for such by the Natives.

Habitat—Red Sea, Seas of India and Malaysia.

b. With one detached ray behind dorsal and anal fins.

CARANX KURRA.

KURRA WODAGAWAH, *Russell*, pl. 139.

CARANX KURRA, *Cuv. & Val.* ix. p. 44 (not *Günther*).

B. vii. D. 8 | $\frac{1}{30}$ | i. P. 25. V. $\frac{1}{5}$. A. 2 | $\frac{1}{27}$ | i. C. 17. L. l. 33.

Length of head rather above $\frac{1}{4}$, of pectoral $\frac{1}{5}$, of caudal $\frac{1}{6}$, of base of first dorsal $\frac{1}{8}$, of base of second dorsal $\frac{1}{3}$, of base of anal $\frac{2}{7}$ of the total length. Height of head $\frac{1}{6}$, of body $\frac{1}{6}$, of first dorsal $\frac{1}{7}$, of second dorsal $\frac{1}{11}$, of anal $\frac{1}{11}$, of ventral $\frac{1}{9}$ of the total length.

Eyes—Diameter $\frac{1}{4}$ of length of head, 1 diameter from end of snout, 1 diameter apart.

Body and head of equal height, tapering off opposite the commencement of the second dorsal.

Mouth oblique, lower jaw compressed and the longest: the posterior extremity of the maxilla extends to beneath the anterior margin of the orbit: the intermaxillaries considerably protractile. Preorbital broad, with four or five radiating ridges. Preopercle as broad as high, its angle rounded. Opercle with an emargination on its posterior border, and six ridges arising from its anterior superior margin proceeding backwards and downwards. A moderately strong longitudinal ridge extends along the centre of the upper surface of the skull. Nostrils approximating: the posterior bean-shaped and larger than the anterior, which is round.

Teeth—A single row of sharp recurved teeth in both jaws: a triangular spot of teeth at anterior extremity of vomer, with a narrow row proceeding posteriorly from its centre, a row of teeth on either palatine bone: three rows of sharp recurved teeth along the centre of the tongue.

Fins—The first dorsal commences opposite the anterior fourth of the pectoral, which last is falcate, and reaches as far as opposite the free anal spines: ventral arises rather posterior to the origin of the pectoral; its spine is weak: anal free spines of equal length: anal fin commences opposite the sixth ray of the second dorsal. First dorsal nearly triangular, spines weak, the third the longest. Third ray of second dorsal the longest, as is also the third ray of the anal. The last ray of both the second dorsal and of the anal detached. Caudal with deeply pointed lobes.

Scales—Exist over the whole of the body, chest, upper surface of the head as far as to opposite the orbits, and the upper portions of both opercle and preopercle.

Lateral line—Nearly straight until opposite the end of the first dorsal, it then slopes downwards, and under the fifteenth ray of the second dorsal passes direct in a keeled line to the centre of the caudal: the mailed scales are at first but moderately so, the broadest equal one quarter of the height of the body.

Colours—Deep bluish green or plumbaceous above, and silvery white beneath. A deep black spot exists on the upper margin of the opercle, and the upper surface of the head is minutely dotted with black. Fins yellow, the dorsal and caudal fins with some fine black dots, especially at their margins. Iris golden.

Habitat—Seas of India and Red Sea.

c. None of the posterior rays of dorsal or anal fins detached.
1. *None of the fin rays elongated.*

Caranx mate.

Caranx mate, *Cuv. & Val.* ix. p. 54; *Cantor*, Catal. p. 125.
Caranx xanthurus, *Cuv. & Val.* ix. p. 55; *Günther*, Catal. ii. p. 434.
Batta parra, *Mal.*

B. vii. D. 8 | $\frac{1}{24}$. P. 20. V. $\frac{1}{5}$. A. 2 | $\frac{1}{19}$. L. l. 40-45.

Length of head $\frac{2}{9}$, of pectoral nearly $\frac{1}{4}$, of caudal more than $\frac{1}{4}$, of base of first dorsal $\frac{1}{11}$, of base of second dorsal $\frac{1}{3}$, of base of anal $\frac{2}{7}$ of total length. Height of head $\frac{1}{5}$, of body nearly $\frac{1}{4}$, of first dorsal $\frac{1}{11}$, of second dorsal $\frac{1}{8}$, of ventral $\frac{1}{10}$, of caudal $\frac{1}{12}$ of total length.

Eyes—Each with an adipose covering extending for one third across either side, and a vertical elliptical opening: diameter $\frac{1}{3}$ length of head, $\frac{3}{4}$ of a diameter from end of snout, 1 diameter apart.

Body elliptical, but becoming more elongated posteriorly. Upper and lower profile equally curved.

Mouth rather oblique, lower jaw longest, a tubercle at symphysis, the posterior extremity of the maxilla reaches to under the anterior third of the orbit. Opercle twice as high as broad, lower or posterior-inferior margin rather concave in the centre: subopercle very narrow superiorly: preopercle wide; preorbital rather wide, with three or four radiating ridges. A rather high long ridge runs along the centre of the skull, and above the orbit there is another parallel with it, which at the summit of the orbit divides posteriorly into two. Nostrils single, at the anterior superior margin of the orbit, and at a short distance from it, close to the origin of the elevated ridges on the head.

Teeth—A fine single band of villiform ones in both jaws, a single row in palatines, and the same in a triangular spot on the vomer. Some fine teeth along the centre of the tongue.

Fins—Pectoral arises opposite the most concave portion of the lower margin of the opercle, and on a line with the ventral; the first dorsal being slightly posterior to it, and the second dorsal rather nearer the snout than the base of the caudal. Anal commences opposite eighth dorsal ray. First dorsal triangular, with a horizontal spine in front: first spine half the height of the second, which is the longest, from whence they decrease rapidly to the last: membrane rather deeply notched. First two rays of the second dorsal undivided; the upper margin of the fin slopes off gradually backwards, the last ray is rather prolonged. Pectoral falcate, and reaching to opposite the eleventh ray of the second dorsal. Ventral spine weak. Of the free anal spines, the first is rather more than twice as long as the second. The lower border of the anal fin is at first rather concave, but after the sixth ray it is parallel to the abdomen; its last ray is prolonged. Caudal rather deeply lobed, the upper one being usually the longest, and rather exceeding the length of the head. The portion of the tail, which is finless, equals the base of the first dorsal fin.

Scales—Small, covering the body and chest, and a few exist on the upper part of the opercle, also a row along the bases of the soft dorsal and anal.

Lateral line—Rather strongly curved anteriorly, where the height it rises to is equal to more than one-third of its length, this curved portion ceases opposite about the fifth ray of the second dorsal, where it becomes straight and keeled, but the alteration to the commencement of the plates is so gradual that it is difficult to decide exactly where they begin; they become gradually broader, the widest being one-eighth the height of the body; the ridge is elevated, and especially sharp near the tail.

Colours—Generally silvery gold, with bluish green on the back and a large round black spot at the upper and posterior surface of the opercle. Fins yellow, except the first dorsal which has a dark tinge, as has also the upper lobe of the caudal. Iris silvery, the adipose lid to eye of a pale amber.

Grows to ten inches in length; very common in Malabar, and is good eating.

Habitat—Seas of India and Malaysia, also from the Seychelles to New Guinea.

* Caranx kalla.

Caranx kalla, *Cuv. & Val.* ix. p. 49.
Caranx calla, *Günther*, Catal. ii. p. 433.

B. vii. D. 8 | $\frac{1}{23\text{-}24}$. V. $\frac{1}{5}$. A. 2 | $\frac{1}{19\text{-}20}$. L. l. 42-44.

Length of head $\frac{1}{5}$ of total length. Height of head $\frac{1}{5}$, of body $\frac{2}{7}$ of total length. It is three times as thick as high, and the abdominal profile is more convex than that of the back.

The lower jaw extends very slightly beyond the upper, and the maxilla reaches to beyond the anterior margin of the orbit.

Teeth—In the jaws are disposed in a single row: there are teeth on the vomer, the palatine bones, and on the tongue.

Fins—The last ray of the dorsal, and also of the anal, is slightly longer than the rest, from which it is rather detached.

Scales—Small and extending over the chest.

Lateral line—Curved to opposite the commencement of the second dorsal, becoming straight under the third or fifth ray; the plates are well developed and occupy the whole of its horizontal portion.

Colours—Bluish green above, shot with silver, sides and abdomen silvery, with nacreous reflections. The tail and the caudal fin brilliant yellow, the upper lobe being tinged with green: the other fins white, excepting the dorsal which has some black upon it. *Dr. Günther* states that the opercular spot is distinct.

Grows to two feet in length.

Habitat—Red Sea, Seas of India and China.

Caranx melanostethos. Plate VI.

Caranx melanostethos, *Day*, Proc. Zool. Soc. 1865, p. 23.

B. vii. D. 8 | $\frac{1}{23}$. P. 19. V. $\frac{1}{5}$. A. 2 | $\frac{1}{19}$. C. 19. L. l. 28.

Length of head $\frac{2}{9}$, of pectoral $\frac{1}{5}$, of base of first dorsal $\frac{2}{17}$, of base of second dorsal $\frac{1}{3}$, of caudal $\frac{2}{9}$ of total length. Height of body $\frac{1}{4}$, of head $\frac{1}{5}$, of first dorsal $\frac{1}{11}$, of second dorsal $\frac{1}{10}$, of ventral $\frac{1}{10}$, of anal $\frac{1}{11}$ of total length.

Eyes—Horizontal diameter $\frac{1}{3}$, vertical diameter $\frac{1}{4}$ of length of head, $\frac{4}{5}$ of a diameter apart, and the same distance from end of snout. A membraneous curtain extends $\frac{1}{5}$ across either side of eye.

Lower jaw slightly the longest, intermaxillaries moderately protrusible. The superior maxillary extends to beneath the anterior margin of the orbit. Preorbital small, with two slightly raised straight lines on its posterior part. Preopercle oblique, angle rounded, inferior margin convex. Subopercle large and entire.

Teeth—Two to three bands of fine villiform teeth in intermaxillaries, and superior half of upper jaw, the same also exist in the lower jaw. A triangular space—convex anteriorly—of rather sharp teeth on vomer, and commencing from its posterior margin a straight single row of sharp teeth, the two thus covering a somewhat T-shaped spot. A fine row on the palatine bones.

Fins—Pectorals rather in advance of the origins of dorsal and ventral. Anal arises under second dorsal. First dorsal triangular: second dorsal highest in front, where it exceeds that of the first dorsal. Pectoral falciform, reaching to nearly opposite anal. Caudal deeply lobed. Dorsal spines weak, third slightly the longest. First ray of second dorsal the longest. Fifth or sixth ray of pectoral longest. Ventral spine weak. Of the two anal spines, the second is the longest and strongest. Spine of anal fin weak, first ray the longest. There is a deep membraneous sheath at the base of the dorsal and of the anal fins.

Scales—Cover the whole of the body, as well as under the eye and upper part of opercle.

Lateral line—Is at first moderately curved, from opposite the eighth dorsal ray it passes direct, but the laminated scales do not begin until opposite the thirteenth ray, they are well marked but not very strong, the widest being nearly equal to half the diameter of the eye.

Colours—Back leaden blue, which below the lateral line becomes silvery white. The forepart of the chest, throat, the opercles, summit of head, and upper jaw, deep brownish black, which sometimes remains after death, on all these places there are numerous black spots, and dots. Fins tinged with yellow. Second dorsal deeply stained with black and margined with white on its first eight rays, the rest of the fin and anal stained with brown, and dotted with black points, as are also the membraneous sheaths to the fins. Eyes silvery: curtains brown.

Grows to upwards of a foot in length and is good eating. Mostly taken in Malabar during the cold season.

Habitat—Malabar, where it is common. It is also found on the Coromandel coast.

Caranx speciosus.

Scomber speciosus, *Forsk.* 54, No. 70.

Poloosoo parah, *Russell*, pl. 149.

Caranx speciosus, *Cuv. & Val.* ix. p. 130; *Cantor*, Catal. p. 133; *Günther*, Catal. ii. p. 444.

B. vii. D. 7-8 | $\frac{1}{18\text{-}20}$. P. 20-22. V. $\frac{1}{5}$. A. 2 | $\frac{1}{15\text{-}16}$. L. l. 34.

Length of head $\frac{1}{4}$, of pectoral $\frac{2}{9}$, of base of first dorsal $\frac{2}{13}$, of base of second dorsal $\frac{1}{3}$, of base of anal $\frac{2}{7}$ of total length. Height of head $\frac{2}{9}$, of body $\frac{1}{3}$, of first dorsal $\frac{1}{8}$, of second dorsal $\frac{1}{7}$, of ventral $\frac{1}{8}$, of anal $\frac{1}{9}$ of total length.

Eyes—With a narrow adipose lid on anterior and posterior sides, diameter $\frac{1}{3}$ of length of head, 1 diameter from end of snout, 1 diameter apart.

PLATE VI.

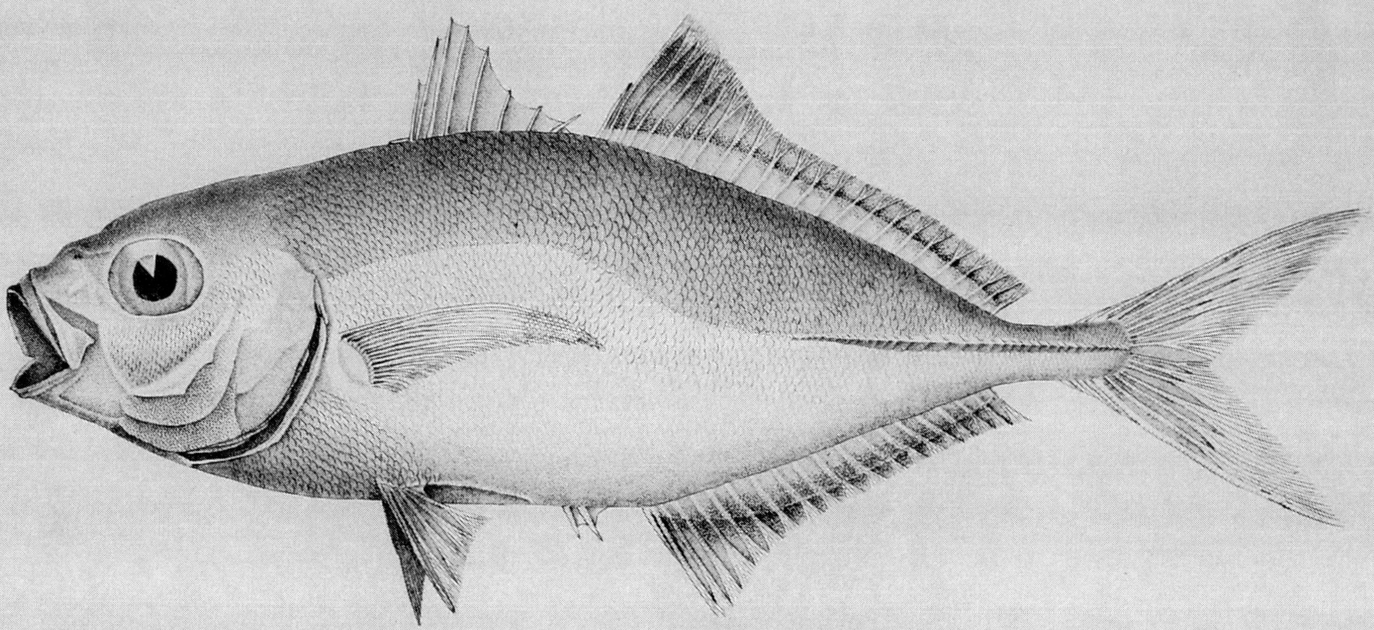

F. Day, del. et sculp.

CARANX MELANOSTETHOS

Body elliptical, the upper and lower profiles equally convex, but its caudal end more produced than its anterior extremity.

Mouth oblique, upper jaw rather concave laterally: the posterior extremity of the maxilla reaches to below the centre of the orbit. Preorbital wide, its upper portion having a festooned edge of ridges directed downwards. Opercle, its lower margin straight. Subopercle high and narrow. Preopercle rather concave posteriorly, owing to its angle being slightly produced, lower margin forming a curve continuous with the angle. Nostrils approximating and near the upper third of the orbit. Longitudinal crest along upper surface of head well developed, lateral ridges but moderately so.

Teeth—In young specimens several rows of villiform teeth in upper jaw, with an external row of strong ones: a single row of irregularly sized ones in the lower jaw: small and villiform on vomer and palate. *Cantor* observes that when "nine inches in length no teeth appear except a small distinct one on either side of symphysis of the lower jaw."

Fins—The pectoral arises under the inferior third of opercle, and extends posteriorly to opposite the second anal ray: the first dorsal commences over the first third of the pectoral, and the second rather nearer to the snout than to the base of the caudal: the anal begins under the fifth dorsal ray. Pectoral pointed, scarcely falcate. First dorsal triangular, its spines weak, and its membrane deeply notched; a procumbent spine in front of its base very distinct in the young: its first spine is half the height of the second, which is one third shorter than the third, the longest in the fin. Second dorsal, with its first rays undivided and the highest portion of the fin, it decreases in height as far as the ninth, from whence it is parallel to the back. Ventral spine weak. Anal free spines, the second longest and strongest. Anal fin, its spine moderately strong and one-third the length of the first ray, the first six of which are the highest portion of the fin, decreasing obliquely and posteriorly, whilst the rest of the rays are parallel to the abdomen. Caudal rather deeply lobed. The portion of the tail uncovered by fin equals in length the diameter of the eye.

Scales—Small, extending over body, chest and cheeks.

Lateral line—First proceeds obliquely upwards and backwards to opposite sixth spine of the dorsal, it then curves downwards to opposite the sixth dorsal ray, from whence it becomes straight and keeled, the size of the scales increasing in strength, and the edges more raised, the height of the widest plate being equal to one-ninth of the height of the body.

Colours—Generally of a beautiful bright golden, having a greenish tinge along the upper surface of the back: six vertical greenish grey bands pass downwards to the abdomen, and a seventh is situated at the base of the caudal: the first vertical band commences above the eye: the upper and posterior part of opercle with a dark spot. The first dorsal dark, minutely and closely dotted with fine brown points, the centre of the last five interspinous membranes having the least. Second dorsal and caudal tipped with darkish grey. The anal golden. Eye with a shade of brown. As the age of the fish increases its colours fade considerably.

Grows to three feet in length.

Habitat—Red Sea, Seas of India, Malaysia, and Philippine islands.

* Caranx para.

Caranx para, *Cuv. & Val.* ix. p. 58.

B. vii. D. 7 | $\frac{1}{25}$. A. 2 | $\frac{1}{21}$. L. l. 36-40.

Length of head $\frac{3}{14}$, of pectoral $\frac{1}{4}$ of the total length. Height of head $\frac{3}{13}$, of body $\frac{3}{13}$ of the total length. The thickness of the body is $\frac{2}{7}$ in its height.

Eyes—Diameter more than $\frac{1}{3}$ length of head.

Teeth—With difficulty to be perceived.

Lateral line—Moderately curved, and under the anterior fifth of second dorsal passes straight towards the centre of the caudal: there are from thirty-six to forty mailed and keeled scales along this last portion of the lateral line.

Grows to four and a half inches in length.

Habitat—Seas of India.

* Caranx ekala.

Caranx ekala, *Cuv. & Val.* ix. p. 117.
Ekalah para, *Russell*, pl. 146.

B. vii. D. 7 | $\frac{1}{19}$. P. 20. V. $\frac{1}{5}$. A. 2 | $\frac{1}{16}$. C. 25. L. l. 26.

Length of head nearly $\frac{1}{4}$, of pectoral more than $\frac{1}{3}$, of caudal $\frac{2}{9}$ of total length. Height of body $\frac{1}{3}$ of total length.

Teeth—In upper jaw form a villiform band, with an external larger row; those in the lower jaw form a single series stronger than the external row in the upper jaw.

Fins—Pectoral falcate: the anterior margins of both second dorsal and anal elevated, rather exceeding half the height of the body; caudal deeply forked.

Scales—Small, extending over body, chest, and along the suborbital ring of bones.

Lateral line—Forms a curve to opposite the anterior third of the second dorsal, from whence there are about twenty-six mailed and keeled scales along its straight portion.

Colours—Summit of head green, the cheeks, opercles, and breast pearly. The back golden shot with green, blue, and purple: sides pearly: abdomen yellowish white: dorsal and upper lobe of caudal an obscure green: pectorals transparent: ventral, anal, and lower lobe of caudal yellow.

Grows to upwards of a foot in length.

Habitat—Seas of India.

Caranx hippos.

Scomber hippos, *Linn.* Sys. Nat. i. p. 494.
Wotim parah, *Russell*, pl. 148.
Caranx sem, *Cuv. & Val.* ix. p. 105.
Caranx Forsteri, *Cuv. & Val.* ix. p. 107; *Cantor*, Catal. p. 127.
? Caranx Peronii, *Cuv. & Val.* ix. p. 112.
Caranx Lessonii, *Cuv. & Val.* ix. p. 113.
Caranx Belengerii, *Cuv. & Val.* ix. p. 116.
Caranx Heberi, *Cuv. & Val.* ix. p. 119.
Scomber Heberi, *Bennett*, pl. 26.
Caranx hippos, *Günther*, Catal. ii. p. 449.

B. vii. D. 7-8 | $\frac{1}{19-22}$. P. 20. V. $\frac{1}{5}$. A. 2 | $\frac{1}{16-17}$. C. 21. L. l. 27-31.

Length of head $\frac{1}{4}$, of pectoral $\frac{2}{7}$, of caudal $\frac{2}{9}$, of base of first dorsal $\frac{1}{7}$, of base of second dorsal rather more than $\frac{1}{3}$, of anal $\frac{1}{4}$ of total length. Height of head $\frac{1}{4}$, of body $\frac{1}{3}$, of first dorsal $\frac{1}{9}$, of second dorsal $\frac{1}{6}$, of ventral $\frac{2}{9}$, of anal $\frac{2}{13}$ of total length.

Eyes—Each with a small adipose lid along their anterior and posterior margins. Diameter $\frac{3}{11}$ of length of head, 1 diameter from end of snout, 1 diameter apart.

Body elliptical, decreasing considerably posteriorly; profile, from the snout to the horizontal spine in front of the first dorsal fin, forming the segment of a circle; from the commencement of the second dorsal there is a gradual slope. The finless portion of the tail is straight and cylindrical: the lower profile of the head and abdomen not so much curved as that of the back.

Mouth oblique and deep: the maxilla extends backwards to opposite the posterior third of orbit: the lower jaw has a tubercle at its symphysis. Preorbital twice as long as deep, with a raised portion in its upper half, which is stellated inferiorly. Preopercle rather more than twice as high as wide, posterior limb nearly vertical, and the angle rounded: inferior limb slightly oblique. Opercle twice as high as wide with a slight emargination in the upper portion of its posterior margin. Central crest on the head well developed and the lateral ridges more moderately so. Nostrils approximating, situated opposite the upper third of the orbit, from whence they are only one-third of the distance from the orbit to the snout.

Teeth—In upper jaw an external rather widely separated conical row, with a villiform series posteriorly; in the lower jaw a single series intermixed with conical ones.

Fins—Pectoral and ventral commence on a line, the first dorsal slightly posteriorly, and the second dorsal midway between the snout and the external margin of the centre of the caudal. The two anal spines are situated under the commencement of the second dorsal, and the anal fin opposite the sixth or seventh dorsal ray. First dorsal triangular, spines weak, the whole being capable of being laid flat in a groove; the third spine is the highest, the upper margin rather rounded, and the last spine terminates close to the second dorsal. In front of the first dorsal is a horizontal spine hidden in the integument. The first ray of the second dorsal is the longest, after which they rapidly decrease to the seventh, from whence they continue about the same height, the last being slightly prolonged: its upper margin is at first concave: a low sheath exists along its base. Pectoral falcate, the fourth and fifth rays the longest. Ventral spine weak. The second of the two anal spines the longest. Spine of anal fin rather more than one-third the height of the first ray: shape of the fin the same as that of the second dorsal, with a short sheath along its base. Caudal deeply lobed in its posterior three-fifths, with a slight soft raised keel along the base of each lobe. The length of the finless portion of the tail equals the diameter of the eye.

Scales—Cover the body, chest and summit of head to opposite the nostrils, also the cheeks and the upper portions of the preopercle and opercle.

Lateral line—Forms a curve to opposite the fifth dorsal ray, but in this course is at first a little concave as far as the fifth dorsal spine. The last or straight portion of the lateral line is covered with armed plates, the widest of which equals one-seventh of the height of the body.

Colours—Body golden with a tinge of grey along the back, and also on the upper surface and front of the head. When alive this fish has a bright bluish silvery reflection shot with gold. Some darkish blotches on the first dorsal, and the summit of the second dorsal greyish black. Point of the upper lobe of the caudal of a deep black, and in some specimens the black border is continued round the whole of the posterior margin of the fin: after death these last mentioned dark markings fade. Eye bright orange.

Very common, and enters the mouth of the river at Cochin, but the largest specimens, which attain to two feet and a half in length, are captured in the deep sea. When taken it gives a grunt like a young pig, and this is repeated whenever it is moved as long as it has any life remaining. It is first captured at the end of the S. W. monsoon, and continues off Malabar through the whole of the cold months.

Habitat—Seas of India, Malaysia, and China, through the Pacific to the shores of Australia, and the Atlantic coasts of temperate and tropical America.

2. *One or more of the dorsal or anal rays elongated.*

Caranx atropus.

Brama atropus, *Bl. Schn.* p. 98, t. 23.
Mais-parah, *Russell*, pl. 152.
Caranx nigripes, *Cuv. & Val.* ix. p. 122; *Cantor*, Catal. p. 129.
Olistus atropus, *Cuv. & Val.* ix. p. 141.
Caranx atropus, *Cantor*, Catal. p. 130; *Günther*, Catal. ii. p. 450.

B. vii. D. 8 | $\frac{1}{22}$. P. 19. V. $\frac{1}{5}$. A. 2 | $\frac{1}{18}$. C. 16. L. l. 32-35. Vert. $\frac{10}{14}$.

Length of head $\frac{1}{4}$, of pectoral $\frac{2}{7}$, of caudal $\frac{1}{4}$, of base of first dorsal $\frac{1}{14}$, of base of second dorsal $\frac{1}{3}$, of base of anal $\frac{1}{3}$ of total length. Height of head $\frac{1}{4}$, of body $\frac{2}{5}$, of first dorsal $\frac{1}{14}$, of second dorsal $\frac{1}{7}$, of ventral $\frac{1}{5}$, of anal $\frac{1}{7}$ of total length.

Eyes—Large and round, diameter $\frac{3}{10}$ of length of head, $\frac{2}{3}$ of a diameter from end of snout, $\frac{2}{3}$ of a diameter apart.

Body compressed, with an elevated crest commencing from the anterior extremity of the frontal bones and extending over the occiput. Ventral fins elongated and occasionally some of the rays of the dorsal, especially in male specimens.

Cleft of mouth very oblique. Lower jaw much the longest: the upper appearing as if it had been partially cut off. The maxilla extends to beneath the anterior margin of the orbit. Preopercle high and narrow, with an oblique rounded angle, its horizontal limb only half the length of its vertical one. Opercle short and high, sub- and interopercles rather broad and large. Gill openings very wide. Intermaxillaries slightly protrusible. Nostrils large and opposite the anterior superior angle of orbit, behind them is a rather high narrow crest.

Teeth—Villiform in jaws, a triangular patch on vomer, and a narrow band on the palatine bones.

Fins—Pectoral and ventral arise on a line, and the first dorsal rather posterior to them; the second dorsal commences opposite the centre of the pectoral, and the anal opposite about the eighth dorsal ray. The first dorsal fin, and the two spines before the anal, can be received into a groove at their bases. First dorsal triangular, its spines very weak, and the membrane rather notched. The second ray of the second dorsal the longest, the upper margin of the fin is at first concave, and subsequently straight. Pectoral falciform, third and fourth rays the longest, it extends to opposite the thirteenth dorsal ray. Ventral spine weak, the rays elongated. Second anal ray the longest, the inferior border of the fin is at first concave, subsequently straight. Caudal deeply lobed.

Scales—Fine, and extending forwards to between the bases of the pectoral and ventral fins; the head, nape, and chest scaleless.

Lateral line—At first forms a strong curve, opposite the commencement of the anal, and in the upper two-fifths of the body passes direct in a keeled line to the centre of the caudal.

Colours—Bluish silvery above, silvery shot with pink and purple on the sides. A black mark on the upper third of opercle which fades after death: and another under the branchiostegal membrane. Ventrals deep black with a white anterior border. First dorsal with some fine black points: second dorsal stained dark at its upper margin, and with some fine dots along its interspinous membrane, also on that of the caudal the ground colour of which is bright yellow. Iris silvery.

Grows to twelve inches in length.

Habitat—Seas of India, Malaysia, and China.

CARANX ARMATUS.

SCIÆNA ARMATA. *Forsk.* p. 53.
TCHAWIL PARAH, *Russell*, pl. 151 (*young*).
CARANX CITULA, *Cuv. & Val.* ix. p. 126, pl. 250.
CARANX ARMATUS, *Cuv. & Val.* ix. p. 127; *Cantor*, Catal. p. 131; *Günther*, Catal. ii. p. 453.
CARANX CILIARIS, *Cuv. & Val.* ix. p. 129 (*young*).
OLISTUS MALABARICUS, *Cuv. & Val.* ix. p. 137, pl. 251.
OLISTUS RÜPPELLII, *Cuv. & Val.* ix. p. 144.

B. vii. D. 7-8 | $\frac{1}{20\text{-}21}$. V. $\frac{1}{5}$. A. 2 | $\frac{1}{16\text{-}17}$. C. 19. L. l. 20.

Length of head $\frac{3}{11}$, of pectoral $\frac{4}{17}$, of base of first dorsal $\frac{1}{8}$, of base of second dorsal $\frac{1}{3}$, of base of anal rather more than $\frac{1}{4}$ of total length. Height of head $\frac{1}{3}$, of body $\frac{1}{2}$, of first dorsal $\frac{1}{7}$, of second dorsal $\frac{2}{11}$, of ventral $\frac{2}{7}$, of anal $\frac{2}{11}$ of total length.

Eyes—Diameter $\frac{2}{5}$ of length of head, $\frac{1}{2}$ diameter from end of snout, nearly 1 diameter apart.

Body elliptical, the upper and lower profile equally curved, but the anterior extremity more obtuse than the posterior.

Mouth oblique, lower jaw the longest, the maxilla extending to beneath the anterior fourth of the orbit. Preorbital wide, its upper portion having a festooned edge of ridges directed downwards. Lower margin of opercle rather concave. Preopercle nearly vertical posteriorly, its angle rounded, and lower margin equal in length to about half its height. Nostrils approximating and near to upper third of orbit. Longitudinal crest along upper surface of the head well developed, as are also the lateral ridges.

Teeth—Villiform in both jaws, vomer and palate.

Fins—The pectoral arises below posterior extremity of opercle, and extends to opposite seventh dorsal ray: the first dorsal commences slightly behind the origin of the pectoral, and opposite the ventral: the second dorsal commences midway between the mouth and centre of base of caudal: the anal begins opposite posterior extremity of the pectoral. First dorsal triangular, spines moderately strong, the first very short, the second one quarter as long as the third, which is the highest: a procumbent spine is very apparent anterior to the fin in the young specimens. Second dorsal and anal highest anteriorly, in some specimens the rays are elongated and filiform, as are also those of the ventral. Caudal rather deeply lobed.

Scales—Small: none on the chest, but covering the body and cheeks.

Lateral line—Moderately bent, becoming straight under posterior third of second dorsal. The plates are very little developed.

Colours—Upper surface of head and back bluish green, sides of the head and body golden with purplish reflections, fading to white on the abdomen. Opercular spot moderately distinct in immature, absent in adult specimens. First dorsal blackish; second dorsal, caudal, and anal yellowish, stained darker at their margins. Pectoral whitish at its base, the rest of a greyish black. Iris silvery. In young specimens there are six vertical dark bands passing from the back to the abdomen.

Grows to six inches or upwards in length.

Habitat—Red Sea, Seas of India, and Malaysia, to the coast of New Guinea.

3. *One or more of the dorsal, ventral, or anal rays elongated, and the first dorsal slightly developed, or disappearing with age.*

Caranx ciliaris.

Zeus ciliaris, *Bloch*, vi. p. 29, t. 191.
Blepharis Indicus, *Cuv. & Val.* ix. p. 154.
Gurrah parrah, *Russell*, pl. 57 (*young*).
Chewolah parrah, *Russell*, pl. 58 (*young*).
Gallicthys major, *Cuv. & Val.* ix. p. 168, pl. 254 (*young*); *Cantor*, Catal. p. 136.
Gallicthys chevola, *Cuv. & Val.* ix. p. 175.
Caranx ciliaris, *Günther*, Catal. ii. p. 454.

B. vii. D. 6 | $\frac{1}{19}$. P. 18. V. $\frac{1}{5}$. A. 2 | $\frac{1}{16}$. C. 19. L. l. 15.

Length of head $\frac{2}{7}$, of pectoral $\frac{2}{7}$, of caudal $\frac{1}{4}$, of base of first dorsal $\frac{1}{13}$, of base of second dorsal $\frac{2}{5}$, of base of anal $\frac{1}{3}$ of total length. Height of head $\frac{1}{3}$, of body $\frac{1}{2}$ of total length.

Eyes—Diameter $\frac{1}{4}$ of length of head, nearly 2 diameters from end of snout, rather more than $\frac{1}{2}$ a diameter apart.

Body of an oval shape, strongly compressed, and rather elevated at the commencement of the dorsal and anal fins. Profile to first dorsal convex: the lower profile not so convex as the upper. The tail produced posteriorly.

Mouth in front, upper jaw protrusible and oblique; the lower horizontal and compressed. The maxilla extends posteriorly rather more than half the distance to the anterior margin of the orbit. Preopercle vertical, narrow and high, the width at the angle one-fifth its height, inferior margin very oblique. Opercle rather more than twice as high as broad, with a shallow emargination at the centre of the posterior margin. Preorbital large and smooth. Summit of the orbit one diameter from the upper profile. Gill openings large.

Teeth—Villiform in both jaws; fine teeth on vomer and palatine bones.

Fins—Pectoral falciform, extending to nearly opposite the fifteenth dorsal ray. Ventral arises slightly in front of pectoral: first dorsal opposite the first third of the pectoral, and the base of anal opposite its second third. The first dorsal merely short spines, with one anteriorly directed forwards. Spine of second dorsal very short; the first ray wide and strong, and the first four very prolonged, the filaments reaching some distance beyond the end of the caudal fin: the anterior portions of the next five rays also prolonged into filaments, but decreasing in width. The two first rays of the ventral small, prolonged, and extending in some specimens as far as those of the dorsal. Between the ventral and anal there is a trenchant space, where there are vestiges of two spines, which are apparent in the very young. Spines of anal fin short and flattened, first three rays prolonged as in the second dorsal, but not quite so far; remainder of the fin of the same shape as the second dorsal. Finless portion of the tail cylindrical, and equals half the length of the orbit. Caudal with pointed lobes, and cleft in its posterior two thirds.

Lateral line—With a high curve in front to opposite midway between the posterior margin of the orbit and the base of the caudal, from whence it passes obliquely downwards to opposite the sixteenth ray of the second dorsal, and then direct to the centre of the caudal; in this last part of its course some fine round scales begin to appear, after the eleventh they become larger, and the last nine constitute a kind of keel, as in the rest of the Caranx genus.

Pyloric appendages very numerous.

Colours—Silvery white, with a yellowish tint on the back, which gradually darkens towards the tail. The filamentous prolongations of the dorsal are black, as are also the longer rays of the ventrals. There are six wide vertical bands passing from the back to the abdomen, most apparent in the very young. Immature specimens have a pinkish tinge.

Esteemed as food. Grows to six inches in length. Large ones have not been recorded, unless the *C. gallus* is the mature of this species.

Habitat—Red Sea, Seas of India, Malaysia, and China.

Caranx gallus.

Zeus gallus, *Lin.* Sys. Nat. i. p. 454.
Scyris Indica, *Cuv. & Val.* ix. p. 145, pl. 252; *Cantor*, Catal. p. 134.
Caranx gallus, *Günther*, Catal. ii. p. 455.

B. vi. D. $\frac{1}{19}$. P. 17. V. $\frac{1}{5}$. A. $\frac{1}{16}$. C. 19. L. l. 8-10. Vert. $\frac{10}{14}$.

Length of head $\frac{1}{4}$, of pectoral more than $\frac{1}{4}$, of caudal more than $\frac{1}{4}$, of base of second dorsal nearly $\frac{1}{2}$, of base of anal nearly $\frac{1}{3}$ of total length. Height of head nearly $\frac{1}{4}$, of body $\frac{1}{2}$ of total length.

Eyes—Diameter $\frac{1}{4}$ length of head, 2 diameters from end of snout, nearly 1 diameter apart.

The difference between the *C. gallus* and *C. ciliaris*, if any exists, is that the first dorsal is not present in large specimens of the former (small ones are not recorded), and only moderately so in middle sized ones: anal spines absent: pectorals not elongated: lateral line rather more distinct in the last part of its course, whilst it has fewer scales to the keel.

Colours—As in the *C. ciliaris.*

Grows to five feet in length.

Habitat—Red Sea, Seas of India, Malaysia, and China.

Genus CHORINEMUS, *Cuv. and Val.*

Scomberoides, *Lacép.*

Branchiostegals, seven or eight: pseudobranchiæ. Body oblong and compressed. Eyes lateral. Cleft of mouth moderate or wide. Infraorbital bones do not articulate with the preopercle Two dorsals, the first—preceded by an immoveable recumbent spine, directed forwards—is formed by a few free spines, and of less extent than the soft dorsal, and anal, the posterior rays of both of which last are either detached or semi-detached. Two spines in front of, but separated by an interspace from, the anal fin. Ventrals thoracic. Teeth villiform on jaws, vomer, and palatine bones. Scales small. Lateral line continuous, not keeled. Air bladder bifurcated posteriorly. Pyloric appendages numerous.

CHORINEMUS LYSAN.

SCOMBER LYSAN, *Forsk.*, pl. 54, no. 67.
CHORINEMUS LYSAN, *Cantor*, Catal. p. 118; *Günther*, Catal. ii. p. 471.
CHORINEMUS LYZAN, *Cuv. & Val.* viii. p. 387.
CHORINEMUS COMMERSONIANUS, *Cuv. & Val.* viii. p. 370.
? CHORINEMUS FARKHARII, *Cuv. & Val.* viii. p. 388.
CHORINEMUS ACULEATUS, *Cuv. & Val.* viii. p. 384.
AKEN PARAH, *Russell*, pl. 141.

B. viii. D. 7 | $\frac{1}{20}$. P. 19. V. $\frac{1}{5}$. A. 2 | $\frac{2}{18}$. Vert. $\frac{10}{16}$.

Length of head $\frac{1}{6}$, of pectoral $\frac{2}{19}$, of caudal $\frac{1}{7}$, of base of first dorsal $\frac{2}{13}$, of base of second dorsal $\frac{1}{3}$, of base of anal $\frac{1}{3}$ of total length. Height of head $\frac{3}{19}$, of body $\frac{1}{4}$, of first dorsal $\frac{1}{33}$, of second dorsal $\frac{1}{7}$, of ventral $\frac{1}{10}$, of anal $\frac{1}{7}$ of total length.

Eyes—Transversely oval with an adipose lid on each side, diameter $\frac{2}{9}$ of length of head, $\frac{3}{4}$ of a diameter from end of snout, rather more than 1 diameter apart.

Body elliptical, and compressed, jaws compressed and sharp.

Mouth large, the lower jaw the longest. The maxilla extends to a distance, equalling one-third of the diameter of the orbit, behind its posterior margin; the intermaxillaries are rather convex in their first third, concave in the last half of their extent, and equal tw thirds the length of the head. Symphysis of lower jaw slightly tubercular. Preorbital narrow the width of its upper portion equal to that of the lower end of the maxilla. Preopercle long and narrow, its lower margin nearly horizontal and only one quarter the length of the posterior, which is rather oblique, making a gradual curve at the angle, its limbs forming an arc of a circle. Opercle with an obtuse point. Nostrils large, and close to the anterior superior angle of the orbit, with a very slight crest over them. Central and side crests of skull moderately prominent.

Teeth—In two rows in both jaws, the external row in the lower directed upwards and outwards, and the internal one upwards and inwards: near the symphysis and close to the end of each row, there is a large canine like tooth, and also an additional row of smaller ones. The upper jaw has two rows and numerous villiform ones near its centre. Teeth on the vomer in a spot largest in front, and in the palate a long band which narrows posteriorly.

Fins—Ventral commences slightly in advance of pectoral; first dorsal over posterior third of pectoral, second dorsal opposite anal, at an equal distance between the snout and base of caudal. Spines of first dorsal strong and pointed, flattened anteriorly, and sharp at the sides, whilst they can be received into a groove at their bases. No interspinous membrane. The horizontal spine before the first dorsal can scarcely be seen in the adult fish, being hidden by the integuments. The first soft ray of the second dorsal is the longest, the superior margins of the first seven are concave, and the last half of the rays are joined very slightly to each other, almost forming finlets, the last two rays are rather prolonged, and reach to the base of the caudal. The anal free spines are triangular, the second rather the longest. The anal fin opposite the second dorsal and of the same shape. Caudal deeply lobed, in its posterior three-fourths. Pectoral rather pointed. Ventral, first ray very strong, flattened towards its base, and connected to the body by two membranes;

the external and shortest passing from the fourth ray to the body, the second and longest, extending from the last nearly as far as the vent.

Scales—Small and ovoid, with long central furrows. None on the head.

Lateral line—At first concave; opposite the first dorsal spine it forms a very obtuse angle, from whence it gradually and rather irregularly sinks, until opposite the last spine, and then proceeds direct to the centre of the caudal.

The air bladder extends some distance backwards.

Colours—Summit of head and back of a golden olive, the rest of the head and back of a brilliant gold colour. Second dorsal, anal, pectoral, and caudal fins greenish olive; posterior margin of the caudal blackish, anterior dorsal, ventrals and posterior anal spines white. Iris golden, greenish towards the orbit. After death the golden tint disappears, and there are six or seven large oval greyish spots above the lateral line.

This *Chorinemus* appears in Malabar about July, and is considered good eating, although rather dry, especially the larger fish.

Grows to three feet in length.

Habitat—Red Sea, Seas of India, Malaysia, and China, as far as the N. W. coast of Australia, also Madagascar.

* CHORINEMUS TOL.

TOL PARAH, *Russell*, pl. 138.

CHORINEMUS TOL, *Cuv. & Val.* viii. p. 385; *Günther*, Catal. ii. p. 473.

B. vii. D. 7 | $\frac{1}{20}$. P. 17. V. $\frac{1}{5}$. A. 2 | $\frac{1}{19}$. C. 21.

Length of head $\frac{1}{6}$ of total length. Height of body $\frac{2}{11}$.

Its form is more elongated than that of *C. lysan;* its upper profile descends in a straight line, or is even slightly concave.

The lower jaw is longer than the upper: the maxilla extends posteriorly to beneath the anterior margin of the orbit.

Fins—Pectorals and ventrals of equal length: the second dorsal and anal are elevated anteriorly: the caudal lobed. The free spines forming the first dorsal fin are more equal than, and not so flat as in the *C. lysan.* The twelve last rays of the second dorsal and anal are almost free.

Scales—Very minute, appearing like little points pressed into the skin.

Lateral line—Is marked by a series of very straight small elevations, and makes an obtuse angle above the posterior third of the pectoral.

Colours—Blue above and silvery over the rest of the body. Four or five small vertically oval deep blue spots exist along the lateral line, the last a little above it opposite the commencement of the second dorsal. Fins yellowish, the extremity of the dorsal blackish, and a black spot exists on the point of the second dorsal.

Moderately good for eating; grows to fifteen inches in length.

Habitat—Seas of India and Malaysia.

CHORINEMUS TALA.

TALA PARAH, *Russell*, pl. 140.

CHORINEMUS TALA, *Cuv. & Val.* viii. p. 377; *Günther*, Catal. ii. p. 473.

B. viii. D. 7 | $\frac{1}{20}$. P. 20. V. $\frac{1}{5}$. A. 2 | $\frac{1}{17}$. C. 19.

Length of head $\frac{1}{6}$, of pectoral $\frac{1}{8}$, of caudal $\frac{1}{4}$, of base of first dorsal $\frac{1}{6}$, of base of second dorsal $\frac{1}{3}$, of base of anal $\frac{1}{3}$ of total length. Height of head $\frac{1}{6}$, of body $\frac{2}{7}$, of first dorsal $\frac{1}{22}$, of second dorsal $\frac{1}{6}$, of ventral $\frac{1}{9}$, of free spines $\frac{1}{22}$, of anal $\frac{1}{6}$ of total length.

Eyes—Diameter, $\frac{1}{4}$ length of head, rather more than $\frac{1}{2}$ a diameter from end of snout, 1 diameter apart.

Body elliptical, compressed, and rather extended towards the tail. There is a gradual rise to the first dorsal.

Mouth wide and obtuse. The maxilla extends to below the posterior margin of the orbit. Upper jaw rather wide, slightly convex towards its centre, and more concave inferiorly: intermaxillaries equal to two-thirds the length of the head. The symphysis of the lower jaw, when the mouth is closed, is received into an emargination in centre of upper jaw, and so forms a portion of the superior profile. Preorbital narrow. Preopercle narrow, the lower limb hardly more than a fourth the length of the posterior one, it is finely lineated inferiorly; the lower portions of the posterior limb and angle rounded. Opercle triangular and slightly produced in the centre of its posterior edge. Nostrils approximating, large, and surmounted by a crest. Central and lateral crests of the skull distinct.

Teeth—Two or three rows of sharp ones in both jaws, but those in the lower having the outer row directed rather outwards, as well as a large canine on each side. Fine teeth on vomer and palatine bones, on the first in the form of a circular spot, and on the latter in that of a long ellipsis. The upper surface of the tongue is covered with teeth.

Fins—Pectoral arises opposite the ventral, first dorsal opposite the posterior third of pectoral, and second dorsal midway between the snout and the base of the caudal. First dorsal with a flat recumbent spine in front, equal to the third spine of the fin in length: the dorsal spines are sharp, strong and moveable, flat anteriorly, cutting laterally, and receivable into a groove at their bases: the first is the shortest, and the last three about equal in length, the interspinous membrane is deeply emarginate, and connects each spine with the one posterior to it. Anterior portion of the second dorsal the highest, its spine equals one third of the length of the first soft ray; first and second rays the longest: upper margin of the second dorsal at first concave, but from twelfth ray equal, and having rather the appearance of finlets. The first soft ray of the anal is the longest, then they decrease to the eighth, from whence they continue as in the second dorsal. Both the anal and second dorsal have their three or four last rays with sheaths covering a small portion of their bases. Of the free anal spines the second is the longest, being equal to one-sixth the height of the body, they have a short connecting membrane. Caudal rather deeply lobed, but not so much so as in the *C. lysan*. Ventral triangular, and the membrane the same as in the *C. lysan*.

Scales—Small and oval in their exposed portion, none on the head or fins.

Lateral line—Irregular and jagged, rising to a sharp angle under the first dorsal spine, then gradually sinking to opposite the third dorsal ray, from thence continued straight.

Colours—Bright orange over the whole surface, with a slight greenish tinge on the summit of the head, and along the back nearly as low as the lateral line; from six to eight circular, dull, almost indistinct spots on the side a short distance above the lateral line, commencing at the shoulder. Pectoral, ventral, and anal bright orange. Dorsal and caudal diaphanous stained with greenish brown, and the lower lobe of the caudal with yellow: a spot of a darkish colour at the tip of the lower jaw, which when closed comes on to the profile of the back. Iris silvery, with a purplish tinge.

Grows to two feet in length. It appears in Malabar during the S.W. monsoon, and is moderately good eating.

Habitat—Seas of India.

CHORINEMUS SANCTI PETRI.

CHORINEMUS SANCTI PETRI, *Cuv. & Val.* viii. p. 379, pl. 236; *Günther*, Catal. ii. p. 473.

CHORINEMUS MOADETTA. *Cuv. & Val.* viii. p. 382.

CHORINEMUS MAURITIANUS, *Cuv. & Val.* viii. p. 382.

CHORINEMUS TOL, *Cantor*, Catal. p. 119.

PALLAGAY, *Mal.*

B. viii. D. 7 | $\frac{1}{20-21}$. P. 17. V. $\frac{1}{5}$. A. 2 | $\frac{1}{18}$. C. 15.

Length of head $\frac{2}{11}$, of pectoral $\frac{1}{10}$, of caudal $\frac{2}{11}$, of base of dorsal spines $\frac{2}{13}$, of base of second dorsal $\frac{1}{3}$, of base of anal $\frac{1}{3}$ of total length. Height of head $\frac{1}{8}$, of body $\frac{2}{11}$, of dorsal spines $\frac{1}{21}$, of second dorsal $\frac{1}{12}$, of ventral $\frac{1}{10}$, of anal $\frac{1}{16}$ of total length.

Eyes—Diameter $\frac{1}{4}$ to $\frac{1}{5}$ of length of head, nearly 1 diameter from end of snout, $\frac{3}{4}$ of a diameter apart. *Dr. Günther* observes that "the snout in mature fishes is nearly twice as long as the diameter of the eye."

Body long and flat; the upper profile rather concave opposite the orbits, then horizontal to the base of the first dorsal.

Mouth deep, the maxilla triangular and nearly flat posteriorly, extending to beneath the centre of the orbit: a tubercle on each ridge of the symphysis; intermaxillaries half the length of the head: their posterior processes large and broad. Preopercle with the posterior limb nearly vertical, and the angle rounded; the inferior limb one third shorter than the posterior, and nearly horizontal, with some openings of glands which pass in narrow shallow grooves downwards, and divide into numerous branches, taking the same direction. Opercle triangular, base above, posterior margin with a slight emargination. Preorbital narrow. Central and lateral crests of the skull scarcely elevated. Nostrils situated midway between the orbit and the commencement of the intermaxillary process.

Teeth—Numerous and sharp in several rows, the posterior ones being curved backwards.

Fins—Procumbent spine in front of the first dorsal, usually concealed. First dorsal spines free, broad, strong, sharp, and can be received into a groove: they commence over the posterior third of the pectoral; the interspinous membrane when it exists is very small; the last spine reaches as far as the second dorsal, which commences half way between the snout and the base of the caudal; the first soft ray is the longest, and the first portion of the fin the highest, and concave above. Anal opposite the second dorsal; the two free spines are strong, and do not quite reach to the anal fin. Pectoral triangular and commencing close to the opercle, just below the emargination; ventral long, and can be received into a groove: it extends nearly to the orifice of the anus. Caudal deeply lobed and pointed.

Scales—Minute, rhomboidal, appearing like the points of needles, none on the head.

Lateral line—Consists of single tubes, and makes a very obtuse angle opposite the third dorsal spine, from whence it slopes gradually downwards to opposite the third or fourth dorsal ray, and then proceeds nearly straight to the centre of the caudal.

The air bladder extends far backwards on each side of the hæmal spines.

Colours—Upper surface of head and back bluish grey, fading to silvery on the opercles and abdomen. A bluish grey spot on the upper portion of the opercle, and a series of from six to eight, or sometimes a double row, above the lateral line. Pectoral and caudal yellowish, the last stained with black at its margin. Summit of the second dorsal blackish, the rest of the fins white. Iris silvery.

Grows to twenty inches in length.

Habitat—Eastern coast of Africa, Seas of India, Malaysia, and China.

* CHORINEMUS TOOLOO.

TOOLOO PARAH, *Russell*, pl. 137.
CHORINEMUS TOOLOO, *Cuv. & Val.* viii. p. 377; *Günther*, Catal. ii. p. 473.

B. vii. D. 7 | $\frac{1}{19\text{-}20}$ P. 18. V. $\frac{1}{5}$. A. 2 | $\frac{1}{18\text{-}19}$ C. 19.

Length of head $\frac{2}{11}$ of total length. Height of body $\frac{1}{4}$ of total length.

Eyes—Their diameter equals their distance from the anterior extremity of the snout.

The maxilla does not extend posteriorly so far as to beneath the posterior margin of the orbit.

The mouth is like that of the *C. tala, C. & V.*, but the limb of the preopercle has more resemblance to that of the *C. lysan.*

Teeth—Resembling those of the *C. tala, C. & V.*

Lateral line—Scarcely curved.

Colours—A series of about six small spots exists along the lateral line. Superiorly the head is of a deep blue, and the back of a lighter tint: the abdomen of a yellowish white. The tips of the dorsal and anal, also the lobes of the caudal, blackish: the other fins transparent.

Grows to eighteen inches in length.

Habitat—Red Sea, and Seas of India.

GENUS TRACHYNOTUS, *Cuv. & Val.*

TRACHINOTUS, *Lacép.*
CÆSIOMORUS, *Lacép.*
ACANTHINION, *Lacép.*

Branchiostegals seven: pseudobranchiæ none. Body more or less elevated, and compressed. Eyes lateral. Cleft of mouth rather small, muzzle swollen and very obtuse. Infraorbital bones do not articulate with the preopercle. Two dorsals, the first composed of free spines, with a small interspinous connecting membrane, and a horizontal procumbent spine directed forwards anterior to the fin, the base of which is of less extent than that of the soft dorsal or of the anal, the anterior margins of each of the latter fins are pointed and elongated: no finlets. Two spines, in front of but separated by an interspace from the anterior margin of the anal fin. Ventral thoracic. Teeth small on jaws, vomer, and palatine bones, usually lost with age. Scales small. Lateral line continuous and unarmed. An air bladder bifurcated posteriorly. Pyloric appendages numerous or in moderate numbers.

Trachynotus ovatus.

Gasterosteus ovatus, *Lin.* Syst. Nat. i. p. 490.
Mookalee-parah, *Russell*, pl. 154.
Trachinotus falcatus, *Cuv. & Val.* viii. p. 430.
Trachinotus mookalee, *Cuv. & Val.* viii. p. 423; *Cantor*, Catal. p. 120.
Trachinotus Blochii, *Cuv. & Val.* viii. p. 425.
Trachinotus affinis, *Cuv. & Val.* viii. p. 428.
Trachinotus falcifer, *Cuv. & Val.* viii. p. 428.
Trachinotus drepanis, *Cuv. & Val.* viii. p. 429.
Trachynotus ovatus, *Günther*, Catal. ii. p. 481.

B. vii. D. 6 | $\frac{1}{19}$. P. 17. V. $\frac{1}{5}$. A. 2 | $\frac{1}{17}$. C. 17.

Length of head $\frac{1}{5}$, of pectoral $\frac{1}{7}$, base of first dorsal $\frac{1}{8}$, base of second dorsal $\frac{1}{3}$, of caudal $\frac{1}{4}$, of base of anal $\frac{1}{3}$ of total length. Height of head $\frac{1}{4}$, of body $\frac{1}{2}$, of first dorsal $\frac{1}{17}$, of second dorsal $\frac{1}{5}$, of ventral $\frac{1}{8}$, of anal $\frac{1}{5}$ of total length.

Eyes—Diameter $\frac{1}{3}$ length of head, $\frac{3}{4}$ of a diameter from end of snout, $1\frac{1}{4}$ diameters apart.

Body elliptical, sides compressed; snout obtuse; a considerable rise from it to the first dorsal, but superior and inferior profile of body equally convex.

Mouth oblique, its angle under anterior margin of orbit, the posterior extremity of the maxilla reaching to beneath the centre of orbit: snout vertical. Preorbital rather broad, rounded anteriorly, and tapering almost to a point beneath centre of orbit: preopercle broad, horizontal portion half the height of its narrow vertical one: its external surface is divided into two parts by an elevation down the centre, sending off long radiating ridges towards its angle and horizontal margin: angle slightly produced. Opercle half as wide as high: interopercle rather large. Anterior opening of nostrils smaller than the posterior.

Teeth—In young specimens there is a band of card-like teeth in both jaws, but as the fish increase in size (as eight inches in length) they lose them, as well as those on the vomer and palatine bones.

Fins—Pectoral broad and rounded, it commences behind the upper margin of the subopercle; first dorsal and ventral on a line opposite its centre; second dorsal opposite its termination: anal spines opposite commencement of second dorsal: and anal fin below sixth ray of second dorsal. First dorsal with a horizontal spine before it: first spine small, from whence the others gradually increase in size: in specimens up to five inches in length there is a deeply cleft interspinous membrane which connects the first and second dorsal fins, but this is wanting in older fish. Spine of second dorsal strong, first ray highest, and more than four times as long as the last; anterior portion of upper margin concave, but for its last two thirds parallel with the curve of the back. Ventral pointed, the second of the anal spines the strongest and longest. Spine of anal fin strong. Caudal with deeply pointed lobes.

Scales—Minute.

Lateral line—At first very slightly ascends and then forms a slight curve to opposite the eleventh dorsal ray, from whence it proceeds straight to the centre of the caudal.

Colours—The upper surface of the head and back silvery green, on the sides golden green, whilst the opercles and abdomen are brilliant gambnge, as are all the fins. The upper half of the first five rays of the dorsal tipped with black, and the whole of the fin dotted with minute black spots, as are also the bases and anterior portions of the anal and pectoral fins and the outer edge of the caudal. Iris golden and green towards the orbit.

Grows to twenty inches in length, but is dry and insipid eating.

Habitat—Seas of India, Malaysia, and as far as the coast of Australia. Atlantic coasts of tropical and temperate America, crossing over to the Western coast of Africa.

TRACHYNOTUS BAILLONI.

BOTLA PARAH, *Russell*, pl. 142.

CÆSIOMORUS BAILLONI, *Lacép.* iii. p. 93, pl. 3, fig. 1.

TRACHINOTUS QUADRIPUNCTATUS, *Cuv. & Val.* viii. p. 434; *Cantor*, Catal. p. 122.

TRACHINOTUS RUSSELLI, *Cuv. & Val.* viii. p. 436.

TRACHINOTUS BAILLONI, *Cuv. & Val.* viii. p. 431; *Günther*, Catal. ii. p. 484.

VELLA OODOO, and PARRUVU, *Mal.*

B. vii. D. 6 | $\frac{1}{22\text{-}23}$. P. 17. V. $\frac{1}{5}$. A. 2 | $\frac{1}{22\text{-}23}$. C. 17.

Length of head $\frac{3}{16}$, of pectoral $\frac{1}{8}$, of caudal $\frac{2}{7}$, of base of first dorsal $\frac{1}{9}$, of base of second dorsal $\frac{1}{4}$, of base of anal $\frac{2}{7}$ of total length. Height of head $\frac{1}{6}$, of body $\frac{2}{7}$, of first dorsal $\frac{1}{34}$, of second dorsal $\frac{1}{4}$, of anal $\frac{1}{4}$, of ventral $\frac{1}{14}$ of total length.

Eyes—Diameter rather more than $\frac{1}{4}$ length of head; 1 diameter from end of snout, $1\frac{1}{4}$ diameters apart.

Body ovoid, elevated, and strongly compressed, its width not exceeding one third of its height.

Jaws of equal length, the maxilla extending backwards until it nearly reaches to beneath the centre of the orbit. Snout obtuse: nostrils between orbit and snout, but rather above the level of the former, the posterior nostril large and oval, the anterior round and small. Preopercle, vertical limb directed rather backwards, with the angle rounded and produced: inferior margin oblique. Opercle of moderate size.

Teeth—Card-like in both jaws, and on vomer and palate.

Fins—The first dorsal consists of six free spines, preceded by a recumbent one directed forwards: these spines can be laid flat, and have also an irregular lateral movement. The first dorsal spine is situated over the posterior third of pectoral, the ventral arises under its centre. The second dorsal commences about midway between snout and base of caudal: the anal under the fourth ray of second dorsal: both are very much produced in front, whilst the last fifteen rays are parallel with the back and abdomen: a small portion only of the tail is uncovered by fin. Pectoral and ventral small: caudal with deeply produced lobes, the upper slightly the longest. Two free spines before the anal fin of moderate strength.

Scales—Small, external portions oval, they are placed in sinuous lines, and below the level of the pectoral are much smaller than those above it.

Lateral line—In simple tubes: it is slightly arched at first, but from opposite the last third of the pectoral proceeds straight to the centre of the caudal.

Colours—Upper surface of head and back of a silvery yellowish green, becoming lighter on the sides, and silvery white on the abdomen, opercles, and cheeks. The first two or three rays of the dorsal and anal, and the external half of each lobe of the caudal, are black. On the lateral line there are four or five large black spots, more or less distant, the first one is opposite the end of the pectoral. Fins diaphanous. Iris silvery, and greenish towards the orbit.

This fish is uncommon, and usually captured by cast nets in the surf where the fishermen assert it always swims; it is very rarely taken in the deep sea, and never in the rivers. It grows to one foot seven inches in length.

Habitat—Red Sea, Seas of India, Malaysia, and Madagascar.

GENUS PSETTUS, *Cuv. and Val.*

MONODACTYLUS, *Lacép.*

Branchiostegals, six: pseudobranchiæ. Body much compressed and elevated. Eyes lateral. Cleft of mouth moderate, snout short. Infraorbital bones do not articulate with the preopercle. One dorsal with seven or eight spines: anal with three: ventrals rudimentary. Teeth velvety on jaws, vomer, and palate. Scales small, covering the vertical fins. Lateral line continuous, simple. Air bladder present, bifurcated posteriorly. Pyloric appendages numerous.

PSETTUS ARGENTEUS.

CHÆTODON ARGENTEUS, *Lin.* Amœn. Acad. iv. p. 249.
KAUKI SANDAWA, *Russell*, pl. 59.
PSETTUS RHOMBEUS, *Cuv. & Val.* vii. p. 245.
MONODACTYLUS RHOMBEUS, *Cantor*, Catal. p. 172.
PSETTUS ARGENTEUS, *Günther*, Catal. ii. p. 487.

B. vi. D. $\frac{8}{28\text{-}30}$. P. 16. V. $\frac{1}{3\text{-}5}$. A. $\frac{3}{28\text{-}30}$. C. 17. L. l. 75. Vert. $\frac{9}{14}$.

Length of head $\frac{1}{4}$, of pectoral $\frac{1}{5}$, of base of dorsal $\frac{1}{2}$, of base of anal $\frac{1}{2}$, of caudal $\frac{1}{5}$ of total length. Height of head $\frac{2}{7}$, of body $\frac{1}{2}$, of dorsal $\frac{1}{3}$, of anal $\frac{1}{3}$, of base of caudal $\frac{1}{9}$ of total length.

Eyes—Diameter rather more than $\frac{1}{3}$ length of head, $\frac{1}{2}$ diameter from end of snout, $\frac{2}{3}$ of a diameter apart.

Body elevated and compressed; the distance from the posterior margin of the orbit to the base of the caudal fin, equals the distance from the base of the dorsal to the base of the anal.

Lower jaw slightly the longest, and when the mouth is open forms the base of a semicircle, the remainder being completed by the upper jaw, which is rather protrusible. Preorbital long and narrow, with a raised festooned line rather nearer its anterior than its posterior edge. Preopercle high; vertical border nearly straight and entire; the angle slightly produced and finely serrated; the lower margin nearly horizontal and two thirds the length of the vertical one. Opercle ending in two blunt spines separated by a semi-circular margin, and sometimes a third minute spine is perceived below.

Teeth—Villiform in several rows in both jaws; some small ones on the vomer, and a lancet-shaped line broadest in front on the palate: teeth also along the centre of the tongue.

Fins—The pectoral commences slightly anterior to the commencement of the dorsal and ventrals, which last are placed close together, and appear like two strong spines, the rays being indistinct: the dorsal and anal terminate opposite one another; the extremity of the dorsal rays usually extends as far as the commencement of the caudal fin. The dorsal spines are nearly concealed, the three first being most apparent; the soft portion is elevated in front, then becomes concave, and in its last third is parallel to the curve of the back. The anal is of the same form as the dorsal, but not so concave. The ventral spines are short and strong, each one tenth the length of head; at their base both are in contact, but their points diverge; they can be received into a groove. The caudal is broad and very slightly emarginate, sometimes square. The pectoral rounded.

Scales—Small and rather adherent; from an irregular line commencing at the centre of the opercle to the caudal passing upwards and backwards: below the line they proceed downwards and backwards. They cover almost the whole of the dorsal and anal fins, also the base of the caudal, the opercles, the cheeks, and summit of the head as far as the snout.

Lateral line—Forms a long irregular curve in the upper half of the body; from opposite the last four dorsal rays it passes straight.

Colours—Silvery with purplish reflections, especially about the anal fin: the back is of a yellowish green, which after death rapidly assumes a leaden hue. One rather wide black band passes directly downwards from the nape to the centre of the eye; a second from opposite the three first hard rays of the dorsal fin as far as the opercle. Some of the dorsal is stained with black, as is also the anterior portion of the anal, though to a less extent. Pectoral and ventral colourless: caudal yellow.

Is most common in Malabar during the monsoon months. Grows to about seven inches in length.

Habitat—Red Sea, Seas of India, to the coasts of Australia and Polynesia.

PSETTUS FALCIFORMIS.

MONODACTYLUS FALCIFORMIS. *Lacép.* iii. pp. 131, 132, 133.
PSETTUS COMMERSONII, *Cuv. & Val.* vii. p. 250.
PSETTUS FALCIFORMIS, *Günther*, Catal. ii. p. 488.
PURRANDEE, *Mal.*

B. vi. D. $\frac{8}{27\text{-}29}$. P. 17. A. $\frac{3}{29}$. C. 17. L. r. upwards of 120.

Length of head $\frac{1}{4}$, of pectoral $\frac{1}{6}$, of base of dorsal $\frac{1}{2}$, of base of anal $\frac{1}{2}$ of total length. Extreme height $1\frac{1}{3}$, height of head $\frac{1}{3}$, of body $\frac{1}{2}$, of dorsal $\frac{1}{4}$, of anal $\frac{1}{3}$ of total length.

Eyes—Diameter $\frac{1}{2}$ length of head, $\frac{2}{10}$ of a diameter from end of snout, $\frac{4}{10}$ of a diameter apart.

Jaws of equal length. The maxilla extends to below the anterior half of the orbit; the preorbital is narrow and festooned; the vertical border of the preopercle entire, and passing rather backwards: the angle produced, rounded, and very finely serrated: inferior margin rather oblique, and four fifths of the length of the vertical margin: the opercle has an obtuse spine; the distance from the angle of the orbit to that of the preopercle equals more than half the length of the pectoral fin.

Fins—The pectoral rounded: the dorsal commences above its centre, and the ventral beneath its base. The anal arises opposite the first dorsal ray. The dorsal is elevated in front, then concave, and its last quarter is parallel to the curve of the back. The anal somewhat resembles the dorsal, but is not so concave, and for its last two thirds its margin is parallel to the line of the abdomen. Caudal deeply lunated. Ventrals as in the last species.

Scales—Disposed as in the last species, and the fins scaled in the same manner.

Lateral line—In a regular curve to opposite the last ray of dorsal, from whence it proceeds direct.

Colours—Very similar to the last, but rather more golden, and without the purple tinge, whilst the bands are neither so wide nor so well marked.

Habitat—Red Sea, Seas of Malabar, and China.

Genus PLATAX, *Cuvier*.

Branchiostegals, six: pseudobranchiæ. Body compressed and elevated. Eyes lateral. Cleft of mouth rather small: snout short. Infraorbital bones do not articulate with the preopercle. One dorsal, with from three to seven spines: anal with three: ventrals well developed. Teeth setiform, with an external larger series, trilobed at their summits: villiform on vomer. Scales of moderate size or small, extended on to the vertical fins. Lateral line continuous, simple. Air bladder simple.

Platax teira.

Chætodon teira, *Forsk.* p. 60, no. 82, t. 22.

Platax teira, *Cuv. & Val.* vii. p. 226; *Cantor*, Catal. p. 168; *Günther*, Catal. ii. p. 492.

B. vi. D. $\frac{5}{31-32}$. P. 16. V. $\frac{1}{5}$. A. $\frac{3}{23-27}$. C. 17. L. r. 86.

Length of head nearly $\frac{1}{4}$, of pectoral $\frac{2}{9}$, of caudal $\frac{1}{4}$, of base of dorsal $\frac{1}{2}$, of base of anal $\frac{1}{3}$ of total length. Height of head nearly $\frac{1}{3}$, of body $\frac{2}{3}$, of hard dorsal $\frac{1}{3}$, of soft dorsal more than $\frac{1}{6}$, of anal more than $\frac{1}{6}$, of ventral $\frac{5}{6}$ of total length.

Eyes—Diameter $\frac{1}{3}$ length of head, 1 diameter from end of snout, 1 diameter apart.

Body elliptical, and strongly compressed: profile rising abruptly to dorsal, from whence it rapidly sinks.

Mouth broad, snout obtuse, posterior extremity of maxilla extends to under the anterior margin of orbit: preorbital large, with three or four ridges: preopercle twice as high as wide, angle rounded, opercle ending in a soft point.

Teeth—Villiform in both jaws, the inner row being slightly larger than the external. A small spot covered by sharp villiform teeth on the vomer.

Fins—Pectoral arises in the lower third of body, opposite the lower margin of the preopercle. Dorsal commences over the opercle, and opposite the ventral: the anal opposite the nineteenth dorsal ray. Only a very short portion of the tail finless. Of the spines of the dorsal the first is short, but they rapidly increase, the fourth not being half the length of the fifth; the first ray is very long and the last very short; the dorsal and anal fins are of the same shape, whilst the caudal is cut square at its extremity. The ventral is shorter in the adult than in young specimens.

Scales—Small, on body, opercles, cheeks and summit of head.

Lateral line—First curves upwards, but opposite the dorsal begins to bend downwards, and opposite its last rays passes straight towards the caudal, but ceases a short distance before reaching its base.

Colours—Brown with dark bands, one of which passes through the eye, a second from the hard dorsal to behind the ventral, and a third from the centre of the dorsal to the anal, whilst there is a fourth at the base of the caudal. Pectoral and caudal yellow. Dorsal, ventral, and anal black. Eye golden. The bands become more indistinct as the age of the fish increases.

Grows to eight inches in length.

Habitat—Red Sea, Seas of India, Malaysia, and China.

Genus EQUULA, *Cuvier*.

Branchiostegals, from four to five: pseudobranchiæ. Body oblong or elevated, more or less compressed. Eyes lateral. Mouth very protractile. Lower margin of preopercle serrated. Infraorbital bones do not articulate with the preopercle. One dorsal with from eight to ten spines, and fifteen to seventeen rays: anal with three spines, and from thirteen to fourteen rays. Edges of back and abdomen dentated along the base of the fins. Ventrals thoracic. Minute teeth on jaws, none on the palate. Scales cycloid, small, deciduous. Lateral line continuous, unarmed: in some species ceasing abruptly beyond the end of the dorsal fin. Air bladder ending posteriorly in two horns. Pyloric appendages few.

Equula insidiatrix.

Zeus insidiator, *Bl.* t. 192, f. 2-3.

Equula insidiatrix, *Cuv. & Val.* x. p. 98; *Cantor*, Catal. p. 151; *Günther*, Catal. ii. p. 504.

Paarl coorchee, *Mal.*

B. iv. D $\frac{8-9}{16}$. P. 15. V. $\frac{1}{5}$. A. $\frac{3}{14}$. C. 19.

Length of head $\frac{1}{5}$, of pectoral $\frac{1}{6}$, of caudal $\frac{1}{5}$, of base of dorsal $\frac{1}{2}$, of base of anal $\frac{2}{9}$ of total length. Height of head $\frac{1}{5}$, of body $\frac{2}{5}$, of hard dorsal $\frac{1}{10}$, of soft dorsal $\frac{1}{2.9}$, of anal spines $\frac{1}{15}$, of anal rays $\frac{1}{29}$ of total length. The ventral is of various lengths in different specimens, being sometimes prolonged.

Eyes—Diameter nearly $\frac{1}{2}$ length of head, $1\frac{1}{3}$ diameters from end of snout, nearly 1 diameter apart.

Body oval, and compressed, abdominal profile much more convex than that of the back.

Mouth—Placed horizontally, the opening small, intermaxillaries very protractile, equal to one-eighth of the length of the body: when fully protracted the mouth is still slightly directed upwards, and when closed the mandibula is quite vertical; the interorbital space, or rather the cavity on the summit of the head, is triangular; the middle third of the superciliary margin is finely serrated. The two supraorbital spines are small but distinctly visible and directed backwards, the external being the strongest; the lower preopercular margin is finely serrated, the serratures being largest anteriorly. Nostrils close to orbit.

Teeth—Minute in the jaws.

Fins—The dorsal is placed over the centre of the pectorals, and the ventral on a line with it. The anal commences opposite the soft portion of the dorsal. The first dorsal spine is small, the second wide, compressed, and the longest of all. The pectoral is rather pointed, the ventral minute, and the caudal deeply lobed. The second anal spine is rather strong, sharp, and much the longest and strongest, the first is the smallest.

Scales—Very minute.

Lateral line—Passes nearly level with the back but approaching it, and is generally lost near the tail, but sometimes as far forwards as below the last third of the dorsal fin.

Colours—Back bluish silver, abdomen whitish silver, the whole being glossed over with a slightly golden tint. Three or four horizontal lines of black spots, with bronze reflections, form from eight to ten vertical bands descending along the upper half of the body. The upper surface of the head, cheeks, and lower jaw, all of burnished silver. Dorsal tipped with black: ventral white. Pectoral light yellow. Caudal yellowish, and stained at the end with brown.

This is an exceedingly common fish in Malabar, and quantities of it, along with other species of the same genus, are kept for consumption during the monsoon, as owing to the small amount of intestines and the compressed form of the body very little salt is necessary for their preservation. As the salt tax falls heavily on the poor classes of Natives, they evade it, along the coast (at least in the Native States of Malabar), by opening and cleansing this little fish, soaking it in the sea, and drying it in the sun. It is of course but partially salted, and when eaten during the monsoon is in a semi-putrid state, thereby giving rise to attacks of diarrhœa and dysentery.

Habitat—Seas of India and Malaysia. Said to be occasionally captured in fresh water.

Equula edentula.

Scomber edentulus, *Bloch*, t. 428.
Komah karah, *Russell*, pl. 63.
Equula ensifera, *Cuv. & Val.* x. p. 66.
Equula coma, *Cuv. & Val.* x. p. 76.
Tottah karah, *Russell*, pl. 62.
Equula caballa, *Cuv. & Val.* x. p. 73; *Cantor*, Catal. p. 146.
Equula edentula, *Günther*, Catal. ii. p. 498.

B. v. D. $\frac{8}{16}$. P. 17. V. $\frac{1}{5}$. A. $\frac{3}{14}$. C. 17.

Length of head $\frac{1}{4}$, of pectoral $\frac{1}{6}$, of caudal $\frac{1}{5}$, base of dorsal $\frac{4}{9}$, base of anal $\frac{1}{3}$ of total length. Height of head $\frac{1}{4}$, of body $\frac{1}{3}$, of hard dorsal $\frac{1}{5}$, of soft dorsal $\frac{1}{13}$, of ventral $\frac{1}{9}$, of anal spines $\frac{1}{6}$, of anal rays $\frac{1}{12}$ of total length.

Eyes—Diameter $\frac{1}{3}$ length of head, $\frac{5}{6}$ of a diameter from end of snout, 1 diameter apart.

Upper profile rather more curved than the lower.

Mouth directed nearly horizontally, opening moderate; intermaxillaries rather convex superiorly and equal to one and a quarter diameters of the orbit. Mandibulæ very concave below; interorbital cavity rather broad, coming to a point opposite the posterior end of the orbit, and having a longitudinal ridge along the anterior portion of the groove. A slight roughness exists along the superior superciliary ridge, where there are two rather strong supraorbital spines directed backwards. Opercle narrow, posteriorly angular, and its greatest width not equalling half its height. Lower margin of the horizontal line of the preopercle rather strongly serrated, its length being rather more than half that of its vertical limb; angle scarcely rounded.

Teeth—Small, and concealed by rather thick lips.

Fins—Pectoral arises just below the end of opercle, and scarcely in advance of the dorsal and ventral which are on a line. Anal commences opposite the eighth spine of the dorsal. First spine of the dorsal very short; second rather more than half the height of the body, with a deep groove down its anterior margin, and two sevenths longer than the third spine, which has on its lower half anteriorly a flat serrated bony expansion, becoming gradually wider inferiorly, so that it extends as far as the next spine. Fourth spine somewhat shorter, and serrated anteriorly.

All the spines have horizontal striæ on their posterior halves, as have also those of the ventral and anal fins. Ventral spine moderately strong and sharp. First anal spine short; the second broader than the second dorsal spine, and one sixth longer than the third dorsal spine; the third weak, and one third shorter that the second, with a bony serrated expansion anteriorly, the same as in the third dorsal spine. Caudal deeply lobed.

Scales—Minute.

Lateral line—At first slightly concave, then very slightly convex to opposite the end of the dorsal fin, from whence it proceeds straight in the direction of the centre of the caudal, but ceases before reaching it.

Colours—Summit of head and back silvery green, minutely dotted with black; the remainder of the head and body bright silvery, muzzle greenish grey, minutely dotted with black; dorsal and anal spines of a pale shining silvery tinge, and as well as their membranes dotted with black; the base of the dorsal and anal membrane reddish yellow, the remainder transparent; margin of the dorsal blackish; caudal yellowish white; ventral white, reddish yellow at the base: pectoral transparent, with a dark silvery band along its base; a black spot in axilla. Iris silvery, orbital half blackish.

Very common: grows to six inches in length.

Habitat—Seas of India and Malaysia.

* Equula splendens.

Gomorah karah, *Russell*, pl. 61.

Equula splendens, *Cuvier*, Reg. Anim. ii. p. 212; *Cantor*, Catal. p. 149.

Equula gomorah, *Cuv. & Val.* x. p. 80.

B. v. D. $\frac{8}{16}$. P. 19. V. $\frac{1}{5}$. A. $\frac{3}{14}$. C. 17.

Length of head $\frac{3}{11}$ to $\frac{1}{4}$ in the total length. Height of body $\frac{4}{5}$ to $\frac{3}{8}$ in total length.

Eyes—Diameter, a little more than $\frac{1}{3}$ of the length of the head.

The upper profile is more convex than the lower, and the muzzle when protracted projects very slightly downwards, forming a short truncated cone.

A pair of small spines exists above the anterior margin of the orbit, and the cavity on the head is about twice as long as broad. The lower margin of preopercle is finely serrated, and its length four fifths of that of the mandibula which is slightly concave, and ascends at an angle of about 35°.

Teeth—A single series of fine setaceous ones in both jaws, concealed by rather fleshy lips.

Fins—The second spine of the dorsal is one fifth of the total length, and three quarters the length of the head; the third spine is somewhat less in length. The second anal spine is two thirds the length of the second spine of the dorsal, and the third is slightly shorter than the second.

Colours—Upper surface of head and back golden green, minutely dotted with black, and forming a blackish line along the base of the dorsal fin: the rest of the body of a silvery satin. The muzzle minutely dotted with black. A little above the lateral line is an arched pale reddish line joining the posterior third of the lateral, which itself forms the superior border of a broad pale reddish band. Cheeks and opercles shining silvery. Membrane of dorsal hyaline, the upper half between the second and sixth spine black, the rest edged with black. Caudal pale reddish yellow. Ventrals and pectorals white. Iris silvery, orbital margin black (*Cantor*).

Grows to four inches in length.

Habitat—Red Sea, Seas of India, Malaysia and China.

* EQUULA BLOCHII.

EQUULA BLOCHII, *Cuv. & Val.* x. p. 84.

B. v. D. $\frac{8}{16}$. V. $\frac{1}{5}$. A. $\frac{3}{14}$.

Body oblong: head higher and shorter than in the *E. daura, Cuv.* Lower jaw concave inferiorly.

Fins—Spines of dorsal and anal nearly as strong as in the *E. edentula, Bl.*

Colours—Silvery, with a grey or leaden tinge on the back, and a longitudinal silvery band along its centre. A black spot on the dorsal fin.

Grows to three and a quarter inches in length.

Habitat—Malabar.

EQUULA DAURA.

DACER KARAH, *Russell*, pl. 65.

EQUULA DAURA, *Cuv.* Reg. Anim; *Cantor*, Catal. p. 150; *Günther*, Catal. ii. p. 502.

EQUULA DACER, *Cuv. & Val.* x. p. 83.

B. v. D. $\frac{8}{15}$. P. 17. V. $\frac{1}{5}$. A. $\frac{3}{14}$. C. 17.

Length of head $\frac{1}{5}$, of pectoral $\frac{3}{10}$, of caudal $\frac{1}{5}$, of base of dorsal $\frac{3}{7}$, of base of anal nearly $\frac{1}{3}$ of total length. Height of head $\frac{1}{5}$, of body $\frac{1}{3}$, of hard dorsal $\frac{1}{6}$, of soft dorsal $\frac{1}{15}$, of anal spines $\frac{1}{10}$, of anal rays $\frac{1}{15}$ of total length.

Eyes—Transverse diameter $\frac{1}{2}$, vertical diameter $\frac{2}{5}$ of length of head, $\frac{1}{2}$ diameter from end of snout, $\frac{3}{4}$ of a diameter apart.

Upper and lower profile equally convex, and general appearance the same as in the *E. insidiatrix.*

Mouth as in the *E. insidiatrix,* the intermaxillaries equal in length to the transverse diameter of the orbit; the lower preopercular margin finely serrated, the serratures being largest anteriorly; the mandibulæ rather concave inferiorly. No serratures on the superciliary ridge or spines in my specimen from Malabar, but they are said to be sometimes present. There is a triangular shallow cavity on the summit of the head.

Teeth—In a fine single series in the jaws.

Fins—Dorsal commences opposite the posterior third of the pectoral. Ventral under its first quarter. Anal opposite the seventh dorsal spine. The second dorsal spine the longest and broadest; first anal spine very short, the second rather broad, strong, and longer than the third which is feebler. The caudal deeply lobed.

Scales—Comparatively small.

Lateral line—In upper quarter of the body parallel to the back.

Colours—Generally of a silvery satin; back bluish green, a greenish line passes along the centre of the back; abdomen bluish golden. From ten to twelve fine darkish bands descend from the dorsal to the lateral line. On the shoulder there is a deep greenish black mark; the opercles and summit of head are like burnished silver; a dark tinge exists along the supraorbitals. The dorsal fin is orange above and silvery beneath, with a deep black mark occupying the upper half of the membrane between its second and sixth spines. Pectoral with a black mark at its axil. Anal tipped anteriorly with orange.

Grows to eight inches in length, and is esteemed for eating by the Natives, it is also dried in the same manner as the *E. insidiatrix.*

Habitat—Seas of India, and Malaysia.

* EQUULA OBLONGA.

EQUULA OBLONGA, *Cuv. & Val.* x. p. 85; *Günther*, Catal. ii. p. 502.
EQUULA BERBIS, *Cuv. & Val.* x. p. 85.

B. v. D. $\frac{8}{16\text{-}17}$. P. 16. V. $\frac{1}{5}$. A. $\frac{3}{14\text{-}15}$. C. 16.

Length of head $\frac{1}{4}$ of total length. Height of body $\frac{2}{7}$ of its total length.

" A pair of spines above the anterior margin of the orbit. The mandibula is very slightly concave; the lower preopercular margin serrated." *Günther*.

Fins—The second spine of the dorsal is of moderate strength, and half as high as the body: the second spine of the anal is a little stronger but not quite so long.

Scales—Inconspicuous.

Lateral line—Ceases before reaching the base of caudal fin.

Colours—Silvery with a brownish or violet tinge towards the back. The upper half of each side is scattered with round or oval blackish spots, unequal and irregular. Iris greyish yellow, without any black spot.

Habitat—Red Sea, Malabar, and Malaysia.

* EQUULA FASCIATA.

KARAH, *Russell*, pl. 66.

CLUPEA FASCIATA, *Lacép.* v. p. 463.

EQUULA FILIGERA, LONGISPINIS, CARAH, et FASCIATA, *Cuv. & Val.* x. pp. 92, 94, 95, 96, pl. 284.

EQUULA FILIGERA, *Cantor*, Catal. p. 150.

EQUULA FASCIATA, *Günther*, Catal. ii. p. 498.

B. v. D. $\frac{8}{16}$. P. 19. V. $\frac{1}{5}$. A. $\frac{3}{14}$. C. 17.

Length of head $\frac{1}{4}$ of total length. Height of body $\frac{3}{7}$ of the total length.

Eyes—Diameter $\frac{3}{10}$ of the length of head.

The mandibula concave and ascends at an angle of 40°: the fleshy lips entirely hide the teeth. The cavity of the head is nearly quadrangular, and four ninths as long as broad. The lower margin of the inferior limb of preopercle indistinctly serrated, and its length four fifths of that of the mandibula. A pair of small spines above the anterior margin of the orbit.

Teeth—In a narrow setaceous band.

Fins—The second spine of dorsal flexible, and one seventh less than the greatest height of the body, or three quarters in the length of the head: the third spine is rather more than half the height of the second, and about one third the length of the second anal; the third anal spine is two thirds the length of the second.

Scales—Small but conspicuous.

Colours—Upper surface of head and back pale greyish green, minutely dotted with brown, the rest of the body and head shining silvery. Fins yellowish white; dorsal spines and their membranes as well as the muzzle dotted with pale brown. Iris silvery: orbital margin blackish. (Cantor.)

Grows to five inches in length.

Habitat—Red Sea, Seas of Malabar, Malaysia, Seychelles, the Moluccas, and Philippine Islands.

GENUS LACTARIUS, *Cuv. and Val.*

Branchiostegals, seven: pseudobranchiæ. Body oblong, compressed. Eyes lateral. Cleft of mouth wide and oblique, the lower jaw prominent. Infraorbital bones do not articulate with the preopercle. Margins of preopercle entire. Two dorsals, the first with seven or eight feeble spines; the second and the anal more developed, scaly, and without finlets. Anal fin with three spines, no free spines anterior to fin. Ventral thoracic. Teeth in jaws small, with one or two pairs of strong canines. Scales of moderate size, cycloid. Lateral line continuous, simple. Air bladder bifurcated both anteriorly and posteriorly. Pyloric appendages few.

LACTARIUS DELICATULUS.

SCOMBER LACTARIUS, *Bl. Schn.* p. 31.

CHUNDAWAH, *Russell*, pl. 108.

LACTARIUS DELICATULUS, *Cuv. & Val.* ix. p. 238, pl. 261; *Cantor*, Catal. p. 138; *Günther*, Catal. ii. p. 507.

PURRUWAH, *Mal.*

B. vii. D. 7-8 | $\frac{1}{21\text{-}22}$. P. 17. V. $\frac{1}{5}$. A. $\frac{3}{25\text{-}28}$. C. 17. L. l. 74. Cæc. py. 6.

Length of head $\frac{1}{4}$, of pectoral $\frac{2}{11}$, of caudal $\frac{1}{4}$, of base of first dorsal $\frac{1}{11}$, of base of second dorsal $\frac{1}{4}$, of base of anal $\frac{2}{7}$ of the total length. Height of head $\frac{1}{4}$, of body $\frac{2}{7}$, of first dorsal $\frac{1}{8}$, of second dorsal $\frac{1}{9}$, of ventral $\frac{1}{9}$, of anal $\frac{1}{8}$ of the total length.

Eyes—Diameter $\frac{1}{3}$ length of head, $\frac{1}{2}$ a diameter from end of snout, $\frac{4}{5}$ of a diameter apart.

Body elliptical, broadest in front: profile with a gradual rise from the summit of lower jaw to the first dorsal. Sides and head compressed. The point of the lower jaw when the mouth is closed appears on the upper profile.

Mouth oblique and large: the lower jaw prominent, the upper extending backwards to below the centre of the orbit. Jaws protrusible. Preorbital narrower than the maxillary: preopercle narrow, with its margin entire and angle rounded, the lower limb being half the length of the vertical one. Opercle ending in a soft point, with its inferior border concave and an emargination near its angle. Interorbital space convex: openings of nostrils close to the anterior superior angle of the orbit. Occipital crest well developed, the lateral ridges moderately so.

Teeth—One or two long and curved on each side of the symphysis of the upper and lower jaws, and a single series of fine curved teeth in both jaws. Teeth on vomer and palatine bones.

Fins—Ventral arises a little behind the pectoral; first dorsal opposite the centre of the pectoral; anal rather nearer the snout than the base of the caudal; the second dorsal midway between the base of the caudal and the centre of the orbit; the anal continued rather further posteriorly than the second dorsal. First dorsal triangular, spines weak, the third the longest, membrane rather deeply notched. Second dorsal spine about half the length of the first ray, which is the longest, after which the rays gradually decrease in length, the last two being a little prolonged, but not nearly half way to the base of the caudal fin. Pectoral rather pointed. Ventral triangular, and not reaching so far as the anal. Anal of the same shape as the second dorsal, but rather larger. In many specimens taken in Malabar the fin rays were invariably A. $\frac{3}{26}$; but in several taken in Madras they were in all A. $\frac{3}{28}$. Caudal rather deeply lobed.

Scales—Cycloid, large, and deciduous.

Lateral line—In the upper third of the body following the curve of the back.

Colours—The upper surface of the head and the back as low as the lateral line of a leaden colour: a black spot exists on the upper and posterior part of opercle. Fins diaphanous, marginal halves of dorsals and caudal minutely dotted with black. Iris silvery, upper portion darkish.

Grows to ten inches in length, is eaten by the Natives either fresh or salted, but is insipid. It appears in Malabar in shoals during the months of February and March.

Habitat—Seas of India, Malaysia, and China.

Genus PEMPHERIS, *Cuv. and Val.*

Branchiostegals, seven: pseudobranchiæ. Body oblong, compressed. Eyes large, lateral. Cleft of mouth oblique, lower jaw prominent, snout short. Opercle with a small spine. Infraorbital bones do not articulate with the preopercle. One short elevated dorsal with five or six spines and from nine to ten rays. Anal elongated, with three spines, scaly. Villiform teeth in jaws, vomer, and palatine bones. Scales of moderate size, or small. Lateral line simple. Air bladder divided into an anterior and posterior portion. Pyloric appendages in moderate numbers.

* Pempheris Molucca.

Pempheris Molucca, *Cuv. & Val.* vii. p. 306; *Cantor*, Catal. p. 175; *Günther*, Catal. ii. p. 509.

Pempheris Malabarica, *Cuv. & Val.* vii. p. 308.

B. vii. D. $\frac{6}{9}$. P. 19. V. $\frac{1}{5}$. A. $\frac{3}{42\ 46}$. C. 17. L. l. 60.

Length of head $\frac{3}{13}$ of total length. Height of body $\frac{1}{3}$ of total length.

Eyes—Nearer to the snout than to the gill opening. Diameter nearly $\frac{1}{2}$ length of head.

The profile between the eyes is somewhat concave, owing to a projection of the upper margin of the orbit, impinging on the line of the profile.

Teeth—Villiform in jaws, vomer, and palatine bones.

Colours—Violet brown above, fading to silvery on the abdomen and with golden reflections. Fins rose colour or reddish yellow, upper half of dorsal spines and membrane of a dark brown. Axil and base of pectoral white. Iris with a golden rim round the pupil.

Grows to six inches in length.

Habitat—Seas of India, Malaysia, the Moluccas, and Japan.

Fam. GOBIIDÆ, *Owen.*

Gobioidei, pt. *Cuvier.*

Branchiostegals, five: pseudobranchiæ. Body low, and elongated. Infraorbital bones do not articulate with the preopercle. Two dorsal fins, the anterior with from five to nine flexible spines, the posterior soft the most developed and of the same character as the anal. Ventrals each with one spine and five rays united, the two forming a disk. Teeth in several rows in the jaws, canines present in some species. Anal papilla generally distinct. Gill openings of moderate width, the membranes united to the isthmus. Scales over the body or absent. Air bladder small or absent. Pyloric appendages none.

Gobius giurus.

Korah-mottah, *Russell*, pl. 50.

? Koku, *Russell*, pl. 51.

Gobius giurus, *Ham. Buch.* pp. 51, 366, pl. 33, f. 15; *Cuv. & Val.* xii. p. 72; *Günther*, Catal. iii. p. 21.

Gobius kokius, *Cuv. & Val.* xii. p. 68; *Jerdon*, Madras Journ., xv. p. 148; *Cantor*, Catal. p. 180.

Gobius catebus, *Cuv. & Val.* xii. p. 76.

Gobius kora, *Cuv. & Val.* xii. p. 77.

Wartee poollah, and pooan, *Mal.*

B. iv. D. 6 | $\frac{1}{9}$. P. 18-20. V. $\frac{4}{4}$. A. $\frac{1}{8\text{-}9}$. C. 17. L. l. 26-34. Vert. $\frac{11}{16}$.

Length of head $\frac{3}{13}$, of pectoral $\frac{1}{7}$, of caudal $\frac{1}{5}$, of first dorsal $\frac{1}{8}$, of second dorsal $\frac{1}{6}$, of anal $\frac{1}{8}$ of total length. Height of head $\frac{1}{8}$, of body $\frac{2}{13}$, of first dorsal $\frac{1}{8}$, of second dorsal $\frac{2}{19}$, of ventral $\frac{1}{8}$, of anal $\frac{2}{19}$ of total length.

Eyes—On upper surface of the head, directed upwards and forwards; diameter $\frac{2}{15}$ of length of head, $2\frac{1}{2}$ diameters from end of snout, not quite $\frac{1}{2}$ a diameter apart.

Body elongated, subcylindrical and rather compressed towards the tail; the profile from the snout to the dorsal is in a straight line; the head rather wider than the body.

Mouth wide; lower jaw the longest, the upper extends to beneath the anterior margin of the orbit; intermaxillaries rather large and protrusible. Preopercle broad, its vertical limb about equal in length to the horizontal, and its angle rounded. Cheeks puffed. Opercle triangular, with the base above. Subopercle rather broad. The distance from the snout to the posterior margin of the preopercle rather more than that from the base of the first dorsal to the posterior margin of the orbit. Interorbital space concave from side to side. Openings of nostrils situated midway between the eyes and snout.

Teeth—Several rows of villiform with an external row of widely separated conical ones in each jaw. Some large canines in the upper jaw.

Fins—Pectoral arises behind the opercle, its base being broad and equal to about one-third the height of the body: the ventrals commence under it, and the first dorsal opposite its first third; the second dorsal begins rather beyond the posterior extremity of the pectoral. The anal commences under the third ray of the second dorsal. Spines of the first dorsal weak, and prolonged, the membrane rather deeply notched, its base occupying two-elevenths less space than the base of the second dorsal. Pectoral rounded. Ventrals united into a disk, the distance from their posterior extremity to the vent being equal to half their length. A considerable portion of the tail (equal to the base of the first dorsal) is finless. Caudal pointed.

Scales—Large and quadrangular, rather smaller anterior to the first dorsal, and considerably so opposite the opercles.

Colours—Vary in different specimens according to the waters they inhabit; they are usually of a fawn colour, with slight cloudy markings of a darker colour, and having purplish reflections on the body. The head has a cloudy band passing over the eyes and forehead, down towards the corner of the mouth: another dark band passes along the lower border of the cheek, which is met by two other narrower bands, one of which proceeds from behind the eye, and the other from the back of the head. The lower surface of the body is white, and the sides have golden reflections, owing to the edges of each scale being covered with little golden dots; the same golden gloss is also apparent at the base of the pectoral. The pectoral fin has some dark marks at the base of its rays, which have a gloss of purple in them, the fin is barred in spots, most apparent in its centre. The first dorsal, which is diaphanous, is tipped with deep brown, its first and second rays have a bar near their base, and some slighter markings higher up, which are continued in the form of spots on to the other rays. The second dorsal has six rows of spots along it, and is also tipped with a dark shade. Caudal barred in ten or twelve irregular stripes. Ventral and anal yellowish, stained with grey at their extremities. Caudal with grey margin and dark base. Eyes hazel.

Grows to one foot and a half in length, and is found in all pieces of fresh and brackish water, and even within the influence of the tides. Its taste is rather insipid, and muddy in some waters, but it is highly esteemed by the Natives as food. It is a voracious fish which takes a bait freely.

Habitat—Fresh waters of Hindustan, Ceylon, Malaysia, China, and the Philippine islands.

GOBIUS VIRIDI-PUNCTATUS.

NUNA-MOTTAH, *Russell*, pl. 52.

GOBIUS VIRIDI-PUNCTATUS, *Cuv. & Val.* xii. p. 62; *Günther*, Catal. iii. p. 24.

B. iv. D. 6 | $\frac{1}{10}$. P. 17. V. $\frac{1}{5}$ A. $\frac{1}{9}$. C. 15. L. l 28. L. tr. 13.

Length of head $\frac{1}{5}$, of pectoral $\frac{1}{8}$, of caudal $\frac{1}{6}$, of base of first dorsal $\frac{1}{10}$, of base of second dorsal $\frac{1}{5}$, of base of anal $\frac{1}{7}$ of total length. Height of head $\frac{1}{8}$, of body $\frac{1}{5}$, of first dorsal $\frac{1}{12}$, of second dorsal $\frac{1}{10}$, of anal $\frac{1}{12}$, of ventral $\frac{1}{6}$ of total length.

Eyes—Partly on the upper surface of the head, directed upwards and outwards: diameter $\frac{1}{4}$ of length of head, rather more than 1 diameter from end of snout, $\frac{1}{3}$ of a diameter apart.

Body elongated, slightly tapering off towards either extremity: profile from snout to first dorsal very slightly elevated: muzzle rounded, obtuse anteriorly.

Lower jaw slightly the longest: gape of mouth wide: the maxilla extends backwards to below centre of orbit. Upper jaw rather protrusible. Preopercle wide, its horizontal margin of equal length with its vertical. Opercle narrow superiorly, one fifth of the length of the head, and narrowing inferiorly. Anterior margin of orbit raised, as is also the superciliary ridge. Interorbital space narrow and concave from side to side. Openings of nostrils just anterior to and opposite the lower margin of the orbit.

Teeth—In jaws villiform, with an external row of larger and distant ones in the upper jaw, and some large conical external ones in the lower, some of which are as large as canines.

Fins—Ventrals united, short, and arising on the lower surface rather behind the commencement of the pectoral: the first dorsal arises opposite the posterior fourth of the pectoral, and the second dorsal rather behind the middle of the total length. First dorsal triangular, its spines weak, and their terminations almost filamentous: the interspinous membrane rather deeply notched. Second dorsal and anal cut square, their posterior extremities slightly produced owing to the last rays being rather prolonged, reaching almost to the root of the caudal. Pectoral bluntly pointed. Caudal wedge-shaped, its central rays the longest.

Scales—Of a quadrangular form, longest diameter from above downwards. They cover the body, upper portion of opercle, and base of caudal: each is striated in very fine raised lines converging posteriorly. The scales on the nape are smaller than those on the body.

Colours—Greyish brown above, some irregular bands or blotches of brown along the sides, abdomen dirty white. The whole of the dark portion of the body is covered with small metallic emerald green spots. Fins dusky, upper third of dorsal brownish grey. Eyes metallic emerald green. After death many of the spots disappear.

Grows to five inches in length. Is captured in the sea, and also in the mouths of the rivers. Is not uncommon.

Habitat—Seas of India.

* Gobius criniger.

Gobius criniger, *Cuv. & Val.* xii. p. 82; *Cantor*, Catal. p. 184; *Günther*, Catal. iii. p. 29.

B. v. D. 6 | $\frac{1}{9}$. P. 17. V. $\frac{1}{5}$. A. $\frac{1}{9}$. C. 13. L. l. 34.

Length of head $\frac{1}{4}$ of the total length. Height of body $\frac{1}{6}$, of head $\frac{1}{8}$, of first dorsal $\frac{3}{4}$, of second dorsal $\frac{1}{6}$ of the total length.

Eyes—Diameter $\frac{1}{4}$ of length of head, $\frac{1}{2}$ a diameter apart, 1 diameter from end of snout.

Teeth—Minute, velvety, and of nearly equal length.

Fins—The second ray of the anterior dorsal is the longest, and terminates in a filament; its length is nearly three quarters of the total length. Nine rows of scales between the second dorsal and anal fins. Caudal rounded.

Scales—None on head or neck: the rest of the body covered with large ctenoid and faintly striated ones.

Colours—"Pale ochreous, with faint silvery lustre; abdomen whitish; head and upper jaw black; three round black spots on the cheeks; a fourth larger at posterior angle of the orbit; a similar on the opercle; on the sides three large rounded black spots: the anterior behind the pectoral fin, spreading on the back; the second below the posterior part of the second dorsal, and the third at the root of the tail. Between the spots are several smaller, irregular black marks. The fin membranes whitish, that of the ventral minutely dotted with black. That of the two dorsals and the caudal with large black spots: the free margin of the caudal and anal black."—*Cantor.*

Grows to five inches in length.

Habitat—Seas of India, Malaysia, North-west coast of Australia, and New Guinea.

Gobius Malabaricus. Plate VII. f. 2.

Gobius Malabaricus, *Day*, Proc. Zool. Soc. 1865. p. 27.

B. iv. D. 6 | $\frac{1}{10}$. P. 13. V. 4. A. $\frac{1}{10}$. C. 13. L. l. 50. L. tr. 10.

Length of head $\frac{1}{4}$, of pectoral $\frac{1}{6}$, of caudal $\frac{1}{4}$, of base of first dorsal $\frac{1}{8}$, of base of second dorsal $\frac{1}{4}$, of base of anal $\frac{1}{4}$ of total length. Height of head $\frac{1}{6}$, of body $\frac{1}{4}$, of first dorsal $\frac{1}{7}$, of second dorsal $\frac{1}{7}$, of ventral $\frac{1}{4}$, of anal $\frac{1}{8}$ of total length.

Eyes—Diameter $\frac{1}{6}$ of length of head, 1 diameter from end of snout, $\frac{1}{2}$ a diameter apart.

Snout obtuse, its upper profile descending abruptly, from it to the first dorsal there is only a slight rise. Maxilla extends backwards as far as the anterior third of orbit. A moderately strong prominent crest at the nape. The bony ridge between the orbits narrow, with a low crest along its centre. Orbits very closely approximating at their upper surface: a well developed projecting angle at their anterior and posterior margins, the anterior the strongest. A bony ring around nasal apertures.

Teeth—Conical: an external row in upper jaw the largest. Smaller but conical in lower jaw;

Fins—Origin of ventral in front of pectoral, of first dorsal over anterior third of pectoral. Distance between first and second dorsal equals diameter of eye. Dorsal spines weak. Caudal wedge-shaped.

Scales—Nearly quadrangular, elevated along their centres: none on the head.

Colours—Of a general light brown, with some irregularly disposed dusky vertical bands on the sides and back. A dark bar runs directly downwards from the eye, and several irregular brown bands exist about the opercles and on the head. The first dorsal has a deep black crescentic mark, commencing between its second and third spine, and being continued to its last, above it is a curved white band bordered superiorly by black. Second dorsal, caudal and anal brownish, with several rows of spots of a darker colour.

Common in the Kurriavanoor river north of Cochin, when the freshes from the ghauts rush down to the sea. The size does not appear to exceed three inches.

Habitat—Rivers of Malabar.

* Gobius neglectus.

Gobius neglectus, *Jerdon*, Madras Journal, xv. p. 148.
? Bullee kokah, *Russell*, pl. 53.

B. iv. D. 6 | 11. A. 10-11. L. l. about 50.

Length of head $\frac{1}{4}$ of total length. Diameter of eye $\frac{1}{5}$ length of head, nearly 1 diameter apart.

Profile of head sloping from eye to muzzle.

Colours—Nearly uniformly fulvous, with occasionally some dark markings on the back: second dorsal and caudal spotted.

Grows to eight inches in length.

Habitat—Rivers of Malabar and Coromandel.

Gobius acutipinnis.

Gobius acutipinnis, *Cuv. & Val.* xii. p. 80; *Günther*, Catal. iii. p. 44.
Gobius setosus, *Cuv. & Val.* xii. p. 81.

B. iv. D. 6 | $\frac{1}{10\text{-}11}$. P. 19. V. $\frac{4}{4}$. A. $\frac{1}{11}$. C. 19. L. l. 25. L. tr. 6.

Length of head $\frac{1}{6}$, of pectoral $\frac{2}{9}$, of caudal $\frac{1}{3}$, of base of first dorsal $\frac{1}{7}$, of base of second dorsal $\frac{1}{4}$, of base of anal $\frac{1}{4}$ of the total length. Height of head $\frac{1}{7}$, of body $\frac{1}{5}$, of first dorsal $\frac{1}{3}$, of second dorsal $\frac{1}{7}$, of ventral $\frac{1}{6}$, of anal $\frac{1}{3}$ of the total length.

Eyes—Directed upwards and outwards, diameter $\frac{1}{3}$ length of head, $\frac{1}{2}$ a diameter apart, 1 diameter from end of snout.

Body elongated, rather compressed, abdominal profile rather more curved than that of the back.

Muzzle rounded, maxilla extending posteriorly to beneath the anterior margin of the orbit. Opercle rounded. Preopercle rectangular, its angle rounded.

Teeth—Villiform, with a larger external row.

Fins—Dorsal and ventral arise slightly in advance of the pectoral: the second dorsal opposite the ninth row of scales: the anal opposite the third dorsal ray. First dorsal spines weak, prolonged into filaments, the fourth and fifth being of equal length and the longest: the interspinous

Fig 1.

Fig 2.

Fig 3.

F. Day, del, et sculp.

1. PUNTIUS PUNCTATUS. 2. GOBIUS MALABARICUS. 3. PUNTIUS PARRAH.

membrane deeply notched. Second dorsal trapezoid, its rays branched. Caudal wedge-shaped, its central rays the longest. Pectoral pointed, its central rays produced. Ventrals joined together. Anal trapezoid, its rays filamentous.

Scales—Exposed portions quadrangular, longest diameter from above downwards, striated in very fine raised lines converging posteriorly. No scales on cheek, a very few over base of caudal.

Colours—Greyish brown above, whitish brown underneath: four or five dull blotches, almost forming bands, pass from the back to the sides, and a deep brown mark exists at the base of the caudal. A brownish line descends from the lower margin of the eye to the angle of the mouth. The first dorsal has four rows of brown spots, almost forming lines, the colour and size of which are most distinct on the first spine, and less so towards the last; the rows of spots again become well-marked on the anterior portion of the second dorsal, but are lost towards its posterior extremity. There are some obscure brownish bars on the posterior half of the caudal, which are most distinct on its central rays. Pectoral, ventral and anal are stained with darkish slate colour, which tint also forms the ground of the other fins.

Grows to four inches in length.

Habitat—Seas and estuaries of India.

GENUS APOCRYPTES, *Cuvier*.

Branchiostegals, five: pseudobranchiæ rudimentary. Body elongated. Infraorbital ring of bones does not articulate with the preopercle. The first dorsal fin separated from or continuous with the second dorsal. Ventrals united. Gill openings of moderate width, united to the isthmus. Scales small, generally larger posteriorly.

APOCRYPTES RICTUOSUS.

APOCRYPTES RICTUOSUS, *Cuv. & Val.* xii. p. 151; *Günther*, Catal. iii. p. 82.

B. iv. D. 6 | 24-27. P. 20. V. $\frac{1}{5}$. A. 26-29. L. l. about 75.

Length of head $\frac{2}{11}$, of pectoral $\frac{1}{9}$, of caudal $\frac{1}{3}$ to $\frac{1}{4}$, of base of first dorsal $\frac{2}{19}$, of base of second dorsal $\frac{1}{3}$, of base of anal $\frac{1}{3}$ of total length. Height of head $\frac{2}{19}$, of body $\frac{2}{13}$, of first dorsal $\frac{1}{19}$, of second dorsal $\frac{1}{19}$, of anal $\frac{1}{19}$, of ventral $\frac{1}{19}$ of total length.

Eyes—Looking upwards and outwards, horizontal diameter $\frac{1}{7}$, vertical diameter $\frac{1}{9}$ of length of head, $\frac{1}{4}$ of a transverse diameter apart, rather more than 1 diameter from end of snout.

Body elongated, rather compressed, head depressed.

Mouth rounded anteriorly, cleft oblique, its depth one quarter greater than its width, and extending to beneath the posterior margin of the orbit: upper jaw notched anteriorly: lower jaw slightly prominent. Preopercle, its vertical and horizontal limbs of equal length, angle rounded. Opercle large, rounded posteriorly. An elevated longitudinal crest extends backwards from the centre of the interorbital space. Nostrils opposite the anterior superior angle of the orbit.

Teeth—Rather long and curved, in a single closely set series in both jaws, about twenty-eight in the lower, and thirty-two in the upper. Two large teeth inside the lower jaw on either side of the symphysis.

Fins—Pectoral and ventral arise on a line; the first dorsal opposite the middle third of the pectoral, and the second dorsal opposite its posterior extremity. The anal arises under the second dorsal. All the spines and rays of the fins are weak. Caudal wedge-shaped.

Scales—Rather larger in the posterior than in the anterior part of the body.

Colours—Greyish, lighter towards the abdomen, with oblique bands passing downwards and forwards from the bases of the dorsal fins half way to the abdomen. Pectoral, ventral, and anal whitish; the first and second dorsals grey, stained with brown, caudal and posterior third of dorsal dark grey spotted with brown. The inside of the mouth spotted with black points.

Grows to seven inches in length, and is not uncommon in Malabar.

Habitat—Seas and estuaries of India.

GENUS ELEOTRIS, *Gronov.*

PHILYPNUS, *Cuvier.*
BOSTRICHTHYS, (*Duméril*) *Gill.*
CULIUS, BUTIS, VALENCIENNEA, BELOBRANCHUS, et ELEOTRIODES, *Bleeker.*
LEMBUS, *Günther.*

Branchiostegals, from four to six: pseudobranchiæ. Body subcylindrical. Eyes moderate, lateral. Infraorbital bones do not articulate with the preopercle. Two dorsal fins, the anterior with from five to eight spines: the posterior soft, the most developed, and of the same character as the anal. Ventrals with their bases approximating but not united. Teeth variously disposed, or even absent on vomer and palate: villiform in the jaws. Gill opening of moderate width. Scales over body and head. Air bladder large.

ELEOTRIS BUTIS.

CHEILODIPTERUS BUTIS, *Ham. Buch.* pp. 57, 367; *Gray*, Ill. I. Z. ii. pl. 93, f. 3.
ELEOTRIS HUMERALIS, *Cuv. & Val.* xii. p. 246.
ELEOTRIS BUTIS, *Cantor*, Catal. p. 196; *Günther*, Catal. iii. p. 116.
KULLAHRAY, *Mal.*

B. vi. D. 6 | $\frac{1}{8}$. P. 17. V. $\frac{1}{5}$. A. $\frac{1}{8}$. C. 15. L. l. 28. L. tr. 12. Vert. $\frac{12}{14}$.

Length of head $\frac{1}{3}$, of pectoral $\frac{1}{5}$, of caudal $\frac{1}{5}$, of base of first dorsal $\frac{2}{17}$, of base of second dorsal $\frac{1}{7}$, of base of anal $\frac{2}{17}$ of total length. Height of head $\frac{1}{6}$, of body $\frac{1}{4}$, of first dorsal $\frac{2}{17}$, of second dorsal $\frac{2}{17}$, of anal $\frac{2}{17}$, of ventral $\frac{1}{6}$ of total length.

Eyes—Diameter $\frac{1}{6}$ of length of head, $2\frac{1}{2}$ diameters from end of snout, 2 diameters apart.

There is a considerable rise from the snout to the first dorsal, the profile of the back being arched, whilst that of the abdomen is straight. The greatest width of the body is opposite the base of the pectoral fin.

Gape of mouth wide, upper jaw protrusible, snout broad and depressed, the posterior extremity of the maxilla extends to opposite the anterior margin of the orbit: interorbital space rather convex. Preopercle with its horizontal border nearly one and a half times as long as its vertical, angle rounded and destitute of spines: nine series of scales exist between it and the orbit.

Opercle wider above than below, and ending posteriorly in a blunt point: it has six transverse rows of scales. Nostrils midway between the orbit and the snout.

Teeth—In villiform bands in both jaws.

Fins—The ventral arises rather in front of the pectoral, the first dorsal over its anterior fourth, and the second dorsal over its posterior fourth. First dorsal spines weak, its membrane deeply notched, and its form triangular: the second trapezoid with the last rays rather prolonged. Pectoral rounded, and extending as far as the commencement of the anal. Ventral triangular. Anal of the same shape as the second dorsal. Caudal wedge-shaped.

Scales—Cycloid, quadrangular, their longest exposed portions from above downwards, those on the head smaller than those over the body; they are extended over the opercles and summit of the head as far as the nostrils.

Colours—Greenish black, with vermilion spots irregularly disposed over the body. Pectoral, second dorsal, and caudal tipped with scarlet: first dorsal dark, more especially at its base. Second dorsal with four or five black bars on a deep grey ground. Caudal also barred with brown, but having some scarlet spots mostly at its upper part, occasionally it has a black base. Pectoral black, with its base margined with bright scarlet, and with some irregular transverse black bands and red blotches upon it. Anal deep grey barred with brown, and margined with scarlet. Eyes hazel. In the monsoon time the dark red on the fins becomes more of an orange colour, and numerous orange dots appear on the body below the lateral line, also on the throat and under surface of the abdomen. As the monsoon continues the upper half of the caudal becomes whitish, and the scarlet margin to the anal also becomes white.

Grows to six inches in length; common in the sea and also in the backwaters. Is eaten by the Natives.

Habitat—Seas of India, Malaysia, China, and the Philippine Islands.

ELEOTRIS FUSCA.

PÆCILIA FUSCA, *Bl. Schn.* p. 453.
CHEILODIPTERUS CULIUS, *Ham. Buch.* pp. 55, 367, pl. 5, f. 16.
ELEOTRIS NIGRA, *Cuv. & Val.* xii. p. 233.
ELEOTRIS FUSCA, *Günther*, Catal. iii. p. 125.
POOLLAN, *Mal.*

B. vi. D. 6 | $\frac{1}{8}$. P. 17. V. $\frac{1}{5}$. A. $\frac{1}{8}$. C. 15. L. l. 60-65. L. tr. 21-23. Vert. $\frac{11}{14}$.

Length of head rather more than $\frac{1}{4}$, of pectoral $\frac{1}{6}$, of caudal $\frac{1}{6}$, of base of first dorsal $\frac{1}{12}$, of base of second dorsal $\frac{1}{8}$, of base of anal $\frac{1}{10}$ of total length. Height of head $\frac{1}{8}$, of body $\frac{1}{4}$, of first dorsal $\frac{1}{12}$, of second dorsal $\frac{1}{8}$, of ventral $\frac{1}{6}$, of anal $\frac{1}{8}$ of total length.

Eyes—Transversely oval, situated near the profile; horizontal diameter rather more than $\frac{1}{6}$, vertical diameter $\frac{1}{7}$ of the length of head, $1\frac{1}{4}$ diameters apart, 1 diameter from the end of the snout.

Body broad in front, compressed behind, and nearly as wide across the shoulder as it is high: the abdominal profile more curved than that of the back, which is nearly straight.

Head depressed, upper jaw oblique and slightly protrusible, extending posteriorly to beneath the centre of the orbit: lower jaw horizontal. Preopercle, with the posterior limb directed slightly backwards, its angle rounded, and a sharp spine directed downwards and a little forwards; the horizontal limb rather longer than the vertical one. Opercle rather inflated, and rounded posteriorly. Interorbital space nearly flat. Anterior nostril tubular. Snout short and depressed.

Teeth—Fine, short, sharp, and recurved, irregular in size and forming bands in both jaws, which decrease in width posteriorly.

Fins—Ventral arises under pectoral; first dorsal opposite the first third of the pectoral; second dorsal midway between the snout and the posterior extremity of the caudal, and the anal opposite the third ray of the second dorsal. The last quarter of the body finless. First dorsal quadrangular, its spines weak, and membrane notched. Second dorsal trapezoid, with the posterior rays somewhat prolonged. Anal the same as the second dorsal. Ventral, with its second, third, and fourth rays prolonged. Pectoral rounded, the central rays the longest. Caudal rhomboidal or rounded, the central rays being the longest.

Scales—Exposed portions quadrangular: they extend over the body and upper surface of the head as far as the snout, where they are small, and on the opercles minute.

Colours—Leaden black, lighter on the abdomen, with sometimes a yellowish tinge. Pectoral and ventral occasionally yellowish. Some fine horizontal bars on the dorsal fin, which is also covered with some fine spots; sometimes the sides are barred. The colours depend on the waters the fish inhabits; if very clear, the back is sometimes lighter than the abdomen. Pectoral fin with a black base.

Inhabits most of the muddy ditches and tanks in Malabar, is often found in the paddy fields, and sometimes in the backwater. Much esteemed for eating in the Mauritius when fried. Grows to four inches in length.

Habitat—The fresh waters of the whole of the Peninsula of India; also found in Madagascar, the Mauritius, and Polynesia.

GENUS AMBLYOPUS, *Cuv. and Val.*

GOBIOIDES, *Lacép.*

Branchiostegals, four or five: pseudobranchiæ none. Body elongated, head oblong, no cavity above opercle; cleft of mouth directed upwards, and lower jaw prominent. Eyes lateral, small, more or less hidden. Infraorbital bones do not articulate with the preopercle. One dorsal, the first portion consisting of five undivided rays, separated from the soft portion by an interval, in the centre of which is situated a sixth simple ray: the dorsal and anal fins are more or less continuous with the caudal. Ventrals united. Teeth small, with an external row of large conical curved distant ones. Scales rudimentary or absent. Air bladder small or none.

AMBLYOPUS HERMANNIANUS.

? CEPOLA HERMANNIANA, *Shaw*, Zool. iv. p. 191.

GOBIOIDES RUBICUNDUS, *Ham. Buch.* pp. 37, 365, pl. 5, f. 9.

AMBLYOPUS HERMANNIANUS, *Cuv. & Val.* xii. p. 159, pl. 350; *Günther*, Catal. iii. p. 135.

AMBLYOPUS MAYENNA, *Cuv. & Val.* xii. p. 163.

B. v. D. $\frac{6}{43\text{-}46}$. P. 15. V. $\frac{1}{5}$. A. $\frac{1}{43\text{-}45}$. C. 13.

Length of head $\frac{2}{15}$, of pectoral $\frac{1}{15}$, of caudal $\frac{2}{15}$, of base of hard dorsal $\frac{1}{15}$, of base of soft dorsal above $\frac{1}{2}$, of base of anal nearly $\frac{1}{2}$ of total length. Height of head $\frac{1}{10}$, of body $\frac{1}{9}$, of hard dorsal $\frac{1}{37}$, of soft dorsal $\frac{1}{30}$, of ventral $\frac{1}{18}$, of anal $\frac{1}{30}$ of total length.

Eyes—Minute.

Body eel-shaped, with the sides and cheeks rather compressed.

Mouth directed upwards, very wide, one fourth more so than deep. Lower jaw the longest, with a tubercle at symphysis. Preopercle as wide as high, angle oblique: opercle rounded posteriorly. The centre third of the summit of the head triangular, the apex of the triangle which is posterior, being rounded: a longitudinal ridge down its mesial line, whilst its sides are elevated, and occipital crest sharp. Lower jaw without barbels.

Teeth—Vary in different specimens. In the upper jaw there is a single posterior row of villiform ones, with some curved conical ones externally, one or two near the symphysis being more especially large; posteriorly they decrease in size, and there are about eight on each side. Lower jaw with two rows of villiform teeth internally, and four or more curved conical ones externally, the two posterior of which are usually the largest; the whole of this external row is outside the upper jaw when the mouth is closed.

Fins—Pectoral and ventral on a line: hard dorsal commences over the middle of the pectoral, and soft dorsal in the second third of the body, between the snout and base of caudal. Anal begins under the third dorsal ray. The sixth dorsal spine is some distance in front of the fifth: its soft portion and the anal are joined to the caudal, but the distinctions between them are apparent. Caudal pointed.

Scales—In crypts anteriorly, and not very distinct, but posteriorly some are more apparent than others. They extend over the body, but there are none on the bases of the fins.

Lateral line—Depressed, and where the superior and inferior muscular insertions join it, there are small orifices like pin holes.

Colours—Of a bright rosy pink, with the lateral line and all the muscular insertions whitish. The divisions between the opercles, interopercles, and subopercles, are all marked by dotted lines; there is also a line of glands along the side of the lower jaw. Fins yellowish; caudal at times with a few red markings, and its base stained with a darkish tint. After the fish has been sodden in water a short time, the colours change to a general bluish grey.

Grows to seven inches in length.

Habitat—Estuaries of India and China.

AMBLYOPUS CÆCULUS.

? CEPOLA CÆCULA, *Bl. Schn.* p. 241, t. 54.
AMBLYOPUS CÆCULUS, *Cuv. & Val.* xii. p. 165; *Günther*, Catal. iii. p. 133.
AMBLYOPUS HERMANNIANUS, *Cantor*, Catal. p. 190.

B. v. D. $\frac{6}{40\text{-}44}$. P. 15. V. $\frac{1}{5}$. A. 38-45. C. 13.

Length of head $\frac{1}{7}$ to $\frac{1}{8}$, of pectoral $\frac{1}{28}$, of caudal $\frac{1}{15}$ of total length. Height of body $\frac{1}{15}$ of total length.

Eyes—Minute.

Body elongated and scaleless. Head as wide as the body.

Mouth directed upwards, its gape wide: lower jaw the longest, with some barbels on it. Each nostril has a small aperture near the orbit.

Teeth—A band of villiform ones posteriorly and of curved conical ones externally.

Fins—Dorsal and anal united with the caudal, and enveloped in a thick skin. Ventrals united.

Colours—Head and back of a brownish ochre. Sides dullish red, becoming dirty whitish with a red tinge on the abdomen. All the fins of a dirty reddish tint.

Grows to one foot two inches in length. Is employed as food.

Habitat—Seas and estuaries of India, Malaysia, and China.

GENUS TRYPAUCHEN, *Cuv. and Val.*

Branchiostegals, four. Body elongated, head moderately compressed, a deep cavity above opercle not communicating with the branchial. Infraorbital bones do not articulate with the preopercle. Eyes minute. One dorsal, which as well as the anal are continuous with the caudal. Ventrals united. Teeth without canines. Scales minute.

TRYPAUCHEN VAGINA.

GOBIUS VAGINA, *Bl. Schn.* p. 73, no. 20.

GOBIOIDES RUBER, *Ham. Buch.* pp. 38, 365.

TRYPAUCHEN VAGINA, *Cuv. & Val.* xii. p. 153, pl. 351; *Cantor*, Catal. p. 190; *Günther*, Catal. iii. p. 137.

B. iv. D. $\frac{6}{40\text{-}49}$. P. 25. V. $\frac{1}{5}$. A. $\frac{1}{39\text{-}46}$. C. 13.

Length of head $\frac{1}{8}$, of pectoral $\frac{1}{11}$, of caudal $\frac{1}{5}$, of base of dorsal $\frac{3}{5}$, of base of anal $\frac{1}{2}$ of total length. Height of head $\frac{1}{11}$, of body $\frac{1}{11}$, of dorsal $\frac{1}{22}$, of anal $\frac{1}{22}$, of ventral $\frac{1}{10}$, of the total length.

Eyes—Apparently small black points, $\frac{1}{4}$ length of head from snout, and about the same distance apart.

Body—Elongated and compressed, the head rather wide.

Mouth wide and oblique; the lower jaw the longest, broad and shallow. Preopercle wide, the angle rounded, its horizontal limb being one third longer than its vertical. Opercle wide, and with radiated raised lines upon it; both it and the subopercle covered with narrow depressions, as is also the upper surface of the head.

Teeth—An external row of long curved teeth in each jaw, with a row of shorter ones internally. None on the palate or tongue.

Fins—Pectoral and ventral arise on a line: dorsal opposite the posterior third of the pectoral. Caudal produced and pointed.

Scales minute.

Lateral line central.

Colours—Dirty white, with a slightly rosy tint, the back darker, almost of a dirty brown. Dorsal and anal stained black in their external halves. Caudal dirty brownish black. Pectoral and ventral colourless.

Not rare at Cochin, where it enters the backwaters. It grows to six inches in length.

Habitat—Seas and estuaries of India, Malaysia, and China.

Fam. BATRACHIDÆ.

GENUS BATRACHUS, *Klein.*

Branchiostegals, six: pseudobranchiæ none. Head broad depressed, body subcylindrical anteriorly, compressed posteriorly. Eyes lateral or approximating superiorly. Mouth widely cleft, lips frequently surmounted by tentacles. Gill covers spinate. Two dorsals, the anterior spinous and short; the posterior long and similar to the anal. Ventrals jugular with three rays, the anterior of which is simple, elongated and flattened. Teeth on the jaws, vomer, and palatine bones. Scales absent or rudimentary. Air bladder present, constricted into two lateral portions.

BATRACHUS GRUNNIENS.

COTTUS GRUNNIENS, var. B. *Linn. Gmelin*, i. p. 1209.
BATRACHUS GRUNNIENS, *Bloch*, pl. 179; *Günther*, Catal. iii. p. 168.
BATRACHOIDES GANGENE, *Ham. Buch.* pp. 34, 365, pl. 14, f. 1.

B. vi. D. 3 | 20. P. 25. V. $\frac{1}{2}$. A. 14-18. C. 12. Opercular spines iv.

Length of head $\frac{2}{7}$, of pectoral $\frac{1}{7}$, of caudal $\frac{1}{6}$, of base of first dorsal $\frac{1}{20}$, of base of second dorsal $\frac{3}{8}$, of base of anal $\frac{1}{4}$ of the total length. Height of head $\frac{1}{7}$, of body $\frac{1}{5}$, of first dorsal $\frac{1}{16}$, of second dorsal $\frac{1}{11}$, of anal $\frac{1}{11}$, of ventral $\frac{1}{5}$ of total length.

Eyes—On upper and outer side of head, diameter $\frac{2}{9}$ of length of head, 1 diameter apart, $\frac{1}{2}$ a diameter from end of snout.

Body longest in front, widest opposite the end of the opercle, where it is nearly two thirds the height of body. Head flat, depressed, and obtuse in front. Body rather compressed posteriorly.

Lower jaw the longest, rather pointed in front, and with a tubercle on symphysis. Gape of mouth very wide. The maxilla rather notched in the centre and extending to beneath the posterior margin of the orbit. Lips fleshy, and surrounded by a wreath of short tentacles. Intermaxillaries protrusible. Preopercle as long as high. Opercle with two strong spines on its posterior margin, the largest equal to two thirds of the diameter of the orbit, they are connected at their bases, the superior passes upwards, backwards, and slightly outwards, the inferior directly backwards and slightly outwards. From the subopercle proceed two more spines also connected together at their bases, neither so long, nor so strong as the upper two, but passing in the same direction. Preorbital small. Upper surface of the head lineated in ridges. The posterior processes of the intermaxillaries extend backwards to opposite the centre of the orbit. A groove passes from the posterior margin of one orbit to that of the other. At the anterior superior margin of the orbit exists a blunt elevation, sometimes surmounted by a tentacle.

Teeth—In numerous, sharp, pointed, irregular rows in both upper and lower jaws, which become a single series posteriorly. Teeth also on the vomer and palatines, forming a single semicircular band rather larger than those in the jaws.

Fins—The ventral arises under the throat: the pectoral which has a long muscular base, commences from behind the opercles: it has no foramen in the axil. The first dorsal commences opposite the posterior margin of the origin of the pectoral: the anal opposite the fourth ray of the dorsal. Ventral pointed. Pectoral wedge-shaped. First dorsal triangular: spines moderately strong, the second being the longest: second dorsal, and anal trapezoid. Caudal wedge-shaped.

Colours—Of a dirty olive brown, with irregular vertical brown and black bands or marblings. Fins yellowish brown, with cloudy black markings. Eyes reddish.

Grows to six inches in length. Is common in the backwaters within the influence of the tides. It emits a croaking noise when captured, and can live some time out of water. Is not eaten. Fishes of this genus, *Cantor* observes, are considered so poisonous in Pinang that they are rejected even as manure.

Habitat—Seas and estuaries of India and Malaysia.

BATRACHUS TRISPINOSUS.

BATRACHUS GRUNNIENS, *Cuv. & Val.* vii. p. 466; *Cantor*, Catal. p. 205.
BATRACHUS TRISPINOSUS, *Günther*, Catal. iii. p. 169.

B. vi. D. 3 | 20-22. P. 25. V. $\frac{1}{2}$. A. 14-16. C. 12. Opercular spines iii.

Length of head $\frac{2}{7}$, of pectoral $\frac{1}{5}$, of caudal $\frac{1}{5}$, of base of first dorsal $\frac{1}{14}$, of base of second dorsal $\frac{3}{7}$, of base of anal $\frac{1}{4}$ of total length. Height of head $\frac{2}{11}$, of body $\frac{1}{4}$, of first dorsal $\frac{1}{18}$, of second dorsal $\frac{1}{8}$, of anal $\frac{1}{11}$, of ventral $\frac{2}{11}$ of total length.

Eyes—On upper and outer surface of the head, diameter $6\frac{1}{2}$ times in length of head, $1\frac{1}{2}$ diameters apart, $\frac{1}{2}$ a diameter from the end of the snout.

General appearance the same as in the *Batrachus grunniens*, but the lower jaw is more rounded, the maxilla passing beyond the posterior margin of the orbit; the remainder of the head, however, is very similar in both.

Teeth—In the lower jaw a single series of strong conical teeth, which becomes double on the symphysis. A double row of strong conical teeth on the vomer and palatine bones, extending posteriorly beyond the intermaxillaries. Intermaxillary teeth minute, in a double series, extending from the symphysis to opposite the eyes.

Colours—Summit of head, back and sides light greenish, or brownish olive. Abdomen greenish or brownish white; head marbled and spotted with black; body with more or less distinct oblique and vertical broad bands edged and spotted with black, and darker than the ground colour: fleshy filaments buff, fins of the ground colour of the body; dorsals and anal indistinctly clouded with black, or with very oblique blackish bands; caudal, pectoral, and ventral with blackish spots or narrow vertical bands. Iris silvery olive; orbital part blackish.

Air bladder separated into two lateral divisions, united by a narrow transverse channel.

Grows to ten inches in length, and is said to be eaten in Bombay.

Habitat—Seas and estuaries of India and Malaysia.

* BATRACHUS DUSSUMIERI.

BATRACHUS DUSSUMIERI, *Cuv. & Val.* xii. p. 474, pl. 367; *Günther*, Catal. iii. p. 169.

B. vi. D. 3 | 20. A. 16. V. $\frac{1}{2}$. Opercular spines iii.

Said to differ from the last chiefly in having straight bands of villiform teeth in the palate and lower jaw instead of strong and conical ones, and a very short tentacle above the orbit instead of a large one.

Colours—Above deep brown, side and abdomen grey olive brown; three large dark brown bands pass downwards, ending in an irregular manner on the sides. In the fresh state the tints are said to be of a dark green marbled with dirty yellow. Fins greyish olive, blackish towards their borders.

Air bladder the same as in the last species.

Grows to ten inches in length.

Habitat—Malabar.

Fam. PEDICULATI, Cuvier.

GENUS ANTENNARIUS, *Commerson.*

CHIRONECTES, pt., *Cuvier.*

Branchiostegals, six: pseudobranchiæ none. Head and anterior portion of body large, high, and compressed. Eyes lateral. Mouth vertical or subvertical. Two dorsals, the first with three spines, the anterior of which is modified into a tentacle situated above the snout. The soft dorsal of moderate length, and more developed than the anal. Ventrals jugular, with four or five soft rays. Pectoral arising from a species of arm formed by the prolongation of the carpal bones. Teeth in cardiform or villiform bands on jaws, vomer, and palatine bones. Skin naked, or covered with minute spines. Gill opening reduced to a small foramen situated in or near the axil. Air bladder present. Stomach wide. Pyloric appendages none.

* ANTENNARIUS MARMORATUS.

CHIRONECTES MARMORATUS, *Cuv. & Val.* xii. p. 402; *Günther*, Catal. iii. p. 185.
CHIRONECTES NESOGALLICUS, *Cuv. & Val.* xii. p. 401.
ANTENNARIUS RANINUS, *Cantor*, Catal. p. 292.

D. 3 | 12. P. 10. A. 7. Vert. $\frac{8}{9}$.

The variations in this species due to age or locality are so considerable that two specimens are very rarely found possessing complete similarity. The skin may be smooth, minutely or distinctly granulated: whilst the length of the third dorsal spine varies from one-half to less than one-third of the height of the body.

The anterior dorsal spine is short, slender, and terminates in a small knob with a minute tentacle attached to it, which is sometimes very short, or it may be entirely absent: the second and third spines are fringed on their summits. The last dorsal ray, if laid backwards, extends to or slightly beyond the root of the caudal.

Head and body with cutaneous tentacles, those at the angle of the mouth and on the abdomen being the largest.

Colours—Vary, generally reddish yellow marbled with brown: and brown spots mostly edged with white radiate from the eye. Round white spots on sides, and abdomen. In some the fins are banded. Iris golden, with radiating brown lines.

Habitat—Seas between the Tropics.

* ANTENNARIUS NUMMIFER.

CHIRONECTES NUMMIFER, *Cuv. & Val.* xii. p. 425; *Günther*, Catal. iii. p. 195.

D. 3 | 12. P. 9-10. V. 5-6. A. 7.

Anterior dorsal spine short, having a cuneiform extremity. Cutaneous fringes not numerous. Skin rough, covered with small spines.

Colours—Violet or red, with yellowish or nacreous spots, one below the posterior portion of the dorsal fin being the largest. Abdomen with numerous brown spots. Fins marbled with brown.

Habitat—Red Sea, Seas of India and Malaysia.

Fam. BLENNIIDÆ, Owen.

GOBIOIDEI, pt., *Cuvier*.
BLENNIOIDEI, *Müller*.

GENUS SALARIAS, *Cuvier*.

Branchiostegals, six: pseudobranchiæ. Body moderately elongated. Eyes lateral. Cleft of mouth transverse, snout short. The infraorbital bones do not articulate with the preopercle. One dorsal, occupying most of the extent of the back, in some species divided into two by a notch. Anal fin long. Ventrals jugular, with a hidden spine and from two to four rays. Tentacle above orbit more or less developed. Teeth small, numerous, moveable in the jaws where they are implanted into the gums, usually a curved canine on either side of lower jaw behind the smaller rows. Palate usually smooth. Skin naked. Gill openings wide. Air bladder and pyloric appendages absent.

SALARIAS FASCIATUS.

BLENNIUS FASCIATUS, *Bloch*, p. 1076, t. 162, f. 1.
SALARIAS FASCIATUS, *Cuv. & Val.* xi. p. 324; *Günther*, Catal. iii. p. 244.

B. vi. D. $\frac{12}{20}$. P. 15. V. $\frac{1}{4}$. A. 24. C. 11.

Length of head $\frac{1}{6}$, of pectoral $\frac{1}{8}$, of caudal $\frac{1}{5}$, of base of dorsal $\frac{2}{3}$, of base of anal $\frac{1}{3}$ of total length. Height of head $\frac{1}{8}$, of body $\frac{1}{6}$, of hard dorsal $\frac{1}{12}$, of soft dorsal $\frac{1}{8}$, of ventral $\frac{1}{7}$, of anal $\frac{1}{12}$ of total length.

Eyes—Upper margins close to profile, diameter $\frac{1}{4}$ length of head, $\frac{1}{4}$ of a diameter apart, 1 diameter from end of the snout.

Body elongated, almost rhomboidal, largest in front, where the head has a rounded external profile, which is considerably sloped, forming a curve from the snout to the first dorsal. Mouth almost on the lower surface. From the commencement of the dorsal to that of the caudal the line of the profile is straight, and is parallel to the abdominal surface.

Mouth anterior and very low down: its gape extends one-third the distance to the orbit, and the posterior extremity of the maxilla to beneath the orbit. Opercle rounded posteriorly. Preopercle wide, with a rounded angle. Two elongated simple tentacles arise between the orbits, on the anterior half of the head. Gill openings very small, situated above and in front of the pectoral fin.

Teeth—A single row of fine ones in each jaw, two large recurved sharp canines in lower jaw.

Fins—Dorsal arises over the opercle: pectoral opposite the fourth dorsal spine: ventral in front of it: anal opposite the commencement of the soft dorsal. Dorsal spines weak, membrane scarcely emarginate, the third spine higher than the first two, from whence they continue the same. Soft dorsal rather longer than the unbranched portion: pectoral rounded. Ventral pointed, with two elongated rays, the outer one being a third shorter than the inner one, the most elongated one reaches to the anterior extremity of the pectoral fin. Anal parallel to the back. Caudal square.

Body naked, covered with mucous secretions.

Lateral line—Straight, and in upper third of the body.

Colours—Of a light brownish tint, with twelve vertical markings along the base of the dorsal fin, passing downwards towards the abdomen in the form of light cloudy bands, which disappear below the lateral line: on these bands, where they meet the lateral line, there is generally a spot, and an intermediate one between that and the upper one. The head of a light yellowish brown colour, with a dark streak passing down the snout, and another from the side of the eye forwards, whilst other well-defined bands radiate about the throat, and the base of the pectoral fin. A beautiful fine line of a lustrous metallic green passes directly downwards behind the eye. Fins colourless, excepting the first thirteen rays of the dorsal, which are tipped with bright yellow.

Grows to about three inches in length, and is found in Malabar during the monsoon.

Habitat—Red Sea, Seas of India, Malaysia, the Philippine Islands, and through the Indian Archipelago to Polynesia.

Fam. TEUTHIDIDÆ. Günther.

TEUTHYES, pt., *Cuvier.*

GENUS TEUTHIS, *Linn.*

SIGANUS, *Forskål.*
CENTROGASTER, *Houttuyn.*
AMPHACANTHUS, *Bl. Schn.*

Branchiostegals, five: pseudobranchiæ. Body oblong and compressed. Eyes lateral. Mouth slightly cleft and little protractile. One dorsal, with a horizontal spine in front of it, and the spinous portion more developed than the soft. Ventral fins with three soft rays in each, and an external and internal spine. Teeth small, trenchant, and in a single row on the jaws, none on the vomer or palatine bones. Scales very small. Lateral line continuous. Air bladder large, forked both anteriorly and posteriorly. Pyloric appendages few.

TEUTHIS VERMICULATA.

AMPHACANTHUS VERMICULATUS, *Cuv. & Val.* x. p. 126.
TEUTHIS VERMICULATUS, *Günther*, Catal. iii. p. 317.
KUTERAH, *Mal.*

B. v. D. $\frac{13}{9\text{-}10}$. P. 16. V. $\frac{2}{4}$. A. $\frac{7}{8\text{-}9}$. C. 17.

Length of head $\frac{1}{4}$, of pectoral $\frac{1}{5}$, of caudal $\frac{1}{5}$, of base of dorsal $\frac{3}{5}$, of base of anal $\frac{2}{5}$ of total length. Height of head $\frac{1}{4}$, of body $\frac{1}{2}$, of hard dorsal $\frac{1}{8}$, of soft dorsal $\frac{1}{5}$, of ventral $\frac{1}{6}$, of anal spines $\frac{1}{8}$, of anal rays $\frac{1}{5}$ of total length.

Eyes—Their upper margins close to the profile: diameter $\frac{1}{3}$ length of head, $1\frac{1}{4}$ diameters from end of snout, rather more than 1 diameter apart.

Body oval, with superior and inferior profile about equally convex. From the snout to the dorsal there is a considerable rise, the upper jaw being elevated like a parrot's bill.

The upper jaw if anything is slightly the longest; the maxilla extends about half way to the orbit. The mouth is narrow and the lips fleshy. The margins of the orbits are roughened in places, owing to several furrows terminating there, but are not denticulated. Preorbital roughened in irregular lines. Preopercle high and narrow, with its angle slightly produced and rounded, its horizontal length being two thirds that of its vertical, the whole is roughened in lines which are deepest about the angle and the horizontal portion, where they coalesce. Opercle narrow, about twice as high as wide, and ending in a dull point. Branchiostegal rays entirely hidden by the gill covers. Interorbital space with a ridge down its centre, and also along each side, approaching each other closely at the snout. Nostrils rather wide apart, the distance of the anterior one from the superior margin of the upper jaw equals the distance of the posterior one from the margin of the orbit, whilst they are slightly less than this distance apart. Shoulder bones furrowed but entire.

Teeth—In jaws, in a single sharp and compressed row.

Fins—Pectoral commences under opercle: dorsal opposite its middle third: ventral opposite third dorsal spine, and the anal opposite the eighth dorsal spine. Dorsal spines strong, sharp, and capable of being laid flat, but no groove exists on the back for their reception: their base occupies five sevenths of the entire fin, interspinous membrane deeply notched: from the fourth spine all are of nearly equal height excepting the last, which is rather produced. In the soft portion the second, third and fourth rays are the longest, and this portion of the fin is of rather a triangular shape, but rounded at its posterior extremity. Anal of the same shape as the dorsal, but the spines are rather stronger, and occupy three fifths of the entire fin. Ventral with the external spine stronger than the internal one: the fin of the generic type. Pectoral of an obtuse triangular form, the second ray the longest. A very short portion of the base of the tail finless. Caudal deeply emarginate.

Scales—Small and cycloid extending over the whole body, and to the suborbital region.

Lateral line—Conspicuous, in upper fifth of body, following the curve of the back: opposite the end of dorsal it becomes straight, and central.

Colours—Light brownish, running into a bluish green on the back, and light bluish on the abdomen. The whole of the body, head, forehead, and lips are lineated with undulating, narrow blue lines, some few of which end in thick rounded points; as a rule they are about a fourth the width of the ground colour which they encircle, but towards the abdomen the blue portion becomes wider and lighter, so that it appears as if the lower surface of the fish were blue, with brown undulating lines which are rounder, and shorter than those of the back. The tail and the caudal fin also appear as if they were blue, with brown lines. The dorsal, ventral, and anal, brownish, and the first and last stained with a dark slate colour. The caudal of a more or less slate coloured tint, and also stained with black at its termination. Pectoral a light slate colour, which after death rapidly turns yellowish. Eyes light coloured. In the young specimens the convolutions are wider, and the back greener.

It grows to eleven inches in length, and is asserted by the Natives to be good eating.

Habitat—Seas of Malabar, Malaysia, and the Mauritius.

TEUTHIS JAVA.

TEUTHIS JAVUS, *Linn.* Sys. i. p. 507; *Cantor*, Catal. p. 207.
WORAHWAH, *Russell*, pl. 102.
AMPHACANTHUS JAVUS, *Cuv. & Val.* x. p. 118.
TEUTHIS JAVUS, *Günther*, Catal. iii. p. 315.

B. v. D. $\frac{13}{10}$. P. 18. V. $\frac{2}{4}$. A. $\frac{7}{9}$. C. 17.

Length of head $\frac{2}{9}$, of pectoral $\frac{1}{6}$, of caudal $\frac{1}{6}$, of base of dorsal $\frac{2}{5}$, of base of anal $\frac{2}{5}$ of total length. Height of head $\frac{1}{5}$, of body $\frac{2}{5}$, of hard dorsal $\frac{1}{7}$, of soft dorsal $\frac{1}{8}$, of ventral $\frac{1}{7}$, of anal $\frac{1}{9}$ of total length.

Eyes—Rather oblique and oval, being lowest in front; at the anterior third of the superior margin they are defended by an elevated finely serrated crest. Transverse diameter $\frac{1}{3}$, vertical diameter $\frac{2}{7}$ of length of head, $1\frac{1}{2}$ diameters from the anterior end of the intermaxillaries.

Body elliptical, rather prolonged at either extremity. Upper and lower profiles equally convex. Intermaxillaries forming a raised knob at the anterior point of the superior profile. Sides of body and head strongly compressed.

Mouth small, its depth rather less than its width. Posterior extremity of the maxilla extends to beneath the posterior nostril. Appearances of the head the same as in the *T. vermiculata.* Preorbital roughened superiorly in lines running into one another, and smooth on its anterior inferior portion. Horizontal margin of the preopercle with a few very fine serratures, its length is rather more than three fourths of its vertical limb. Opercle about two thirds as long as wide, ending in a dull rounded extremity. Interorbital space with a tongue-shaped shallow depression, rounded superiorly opposite the anterior third of the orbit, broadest opposite the anterior margin of the orbit: whilst a very indistinct ridge runs along its centre, and in its anterior half throws out lateral branches. Above the orbit there are some raised (but not well developed) coalescing ridges. Nostrils rather wide apart, the distance of the anterior one from the end of the preorbital equals the distance of the posterior one from the anterior margin of the orbit, whilst they are nearly as far asunder.

Teeth—In one flat compressed row in the jaws.

Fins—Pectoral commences under opercle, dorsal opposite its middle third; ventral opposite third dorsal spine; and anal opposite eighth dorsal spine. Dorsal spines strong, sharp, and capable of being laid flat, but no groove exists in the back to receive them, their base occupies five sevenths of the entire fin: interspinous membrane deeply notched; from the fourth all the spines are nearly of equal length, but the last is somewhat higher: of the soft portion the second, third, and fourth rays are the longest, it is of rather a triangular shape with a rounded extremity. Anal of the same shape as the dorsal, the spines rather stronger, and occupying three fifths of the entire fin. A very short portion of the base of the tail finless. Caudal deeply emarginate.

Lateral line—First passes along the upper fifth of the back following its curve, but rather approaching it; towards the end of the dorsal it becomes central.

Colours—Head, back, and sides lightish brown with a tinge of blue, becoming paler towards the abdomen. On the head and back there are numerous pale bluish grey rounded spots, which towards the lateral line become oval, and below it are produced forming lines, the ground colour between, being of about equal width: they here and there coalesce, but towards the abdomen are in alternate bands. Sides of the head of a lightish brown, shot with sulphur. Pectorals transparent; the other fins minutely spotted with black, and tinged with sulphur. Iris pale yellowish, the upper half brownish.

Said to be considered poisonous in Malaysia, but is not found to be so in Malabar. It grows to eleven inches in length.

Habitat—Seas of India, Malaysia, and Australia.

* Teuthis sutor.

? Buro brunneus, *Comm.* v.
Amphacanthus sutor, *Cuv. & Val.* x. p. 148.
Teuthis sutor, *Günther*, Catal. iii. p. 317.

B. v. D. $\frac{13\text{-}14}{10}$. A. $\frac{7}{9\text{-}10}$.

Height of body not quite $\frac{1}{3}$ in the total length.

Colours—Greenish grey, with dull blue spots; towards the abdomen it becomes more grey. Fins greenish: pectorals with a tinge of yellow.

Grows to one foot in length. Flesh blackish, but esteemed for food: it also salts well.

Habitat—Coast of Malabar, and the Seychelles.

Fam. ACRONURIDÆ, Günther.

Teuthyes, pt., *Cuvier.*
Acanthuroidei, *Bleeker.*

Genus ACANTHURUS, *Bl. Schn.*

Branchiostegals, five: pseudobranchiæ. Body oblong, or elevated and compressed. Eyes lateral. Mouth slightly cleft. One dorsal, the spinous less developed than the soft portion. Anal with three spines. Ventrals thoracic. Tail on either side, armed with a strong moveable spine directed anteriorly. Teeth in a single row in each jaw, trenchant, with crenulated margins, and sometimes moveable: none on vomer or palatine bones. Scales minute, ctenoid. Lateral line continuous. Air bladder large, and forked posteriorly. Pyloric appendages few.

Acanthurus matoides.

? Acanthurus rasi, *Cuv. & Val.* x. p. 203.
Acanthurus matoides, *Cuv. & Val.* x. p. 204; *Günther*, Catal. iii. p. 330.
Acanthurus annularis, *Cuv. & Val.* x. p. 209 (*immature, with whitish caudal ring*).
Acanthurus Blochii, *Cuv. & Val.* x. p. 209 (*immature, without whitish caudal ring*).

B. v. D. $\frac{9}{25\text{-}28}$. P. 17. V. $\frac{1}{5}$. A. $\frac{3}{25\text{-}28}$. C. 16. Vert. $\frac{9}{13}$.

Length of head $\frac{3}{13}$, of pectoral $\frac{1}{5}$, of caudal $\frac{3}{13}$, of base of dorsal $\frac{12}{25}$, of base of anal $\frac{3}{7}$ of total length. Height of head $\frac{1}{3}$, of body $\frac{4}{9}$, of hard dorsal $\frac{2}{13}$, of soft dorsal $\frac{1}{6}$, of ventral $\frac{2}{11}$, of spines of anal $\frac{1}{8}$, of rays of anal $\frac{2}{13}$ of total length.

Eyes—Diameter $\frac{3}{11}$ of length of head, $2\frac{1}{4}$ diameters from end of snout, 1 diameter apart.

Body oblong, compressed: profile from snout to dorsal fin much elevated, with a depression opposite the orbits. The height of the body opposite the posterior extremities of the dorsal and anal fins, equals one third the height opposite the ventral and commencement of dorsal.

Mouth small, upper jaw slightly the longest. Preopercle long and narrow, its inferior margin rather oblique, and more than one third the length of its posterior border, which slopes downwards and forwards. Opercle narrow. The distance from the nostril to the anterior edge of the upper jaw equals two thirds the length from the posterior margin of the opercle to snout.

Teeth—In a single compressed row in both jaws.

Fins—Origins of dorsal, pectoral, and ventral on a line: anal commencing opposite seventh dorsal spine. Dorsal spines weak; they occupy two-fifths of the base of the fin, interspinous membrane very slightly emarginate. Second ray of pectoral the longest. Ventral pointed. Anal similar to dorsal. Caudal emarginate.

Scales—Small.

Lateral line—At first in upper fifth of back following its course to opposite the end of the dorsal fin, from whence it passes direct to the centre of the caudal. It curves upwards in its course over a lancet-shaped moveable spine, which is situated at the side of the tail, directed forwards, and receivable into a sheath.

Colours—Leaden black, with several badly marked yellow stripes or lines passing longitudinally along the body in the young, but which in the adult are of a yellowish brown, with bluish margins; when the fish is dead it is of a dull leaden grey, and the abdomen lighter. Dorsal and anal fins grey, with four longitudinal rusty bands. Pectoral in some specimens yellow, in others dark grey. Ventral and caudal grey, the last usually margined with white. Iris golden.

Grows to eighteen inches in length, and is eaten by the lower classes.

Habitat—Seas of India and Polynesia.

Genus ACRONURUS, *Gronow.*

Acanthurus, sp., *Cuv. & Val.*

Branchiostegals, five: pseudobranchiæ. Body oblong, compressed. Eyes lateral. One dorsal, the spinous portion less developed than the soft. Anal with three spines. Ventrals thoracic. Tail on either side armed with a strong moveable spine, directed forwards. Teeth in a single trenchant row in each jaw and lobate superiorly: none on the vomer or palatine bones. Skin with vertical striæ, in some species having fine pointed elevations. No scales.

Acronurus melanurus.

Acronurus melanurus, *Cuv. & Val.* x. p. 240; *Günther*, Catal. iii. p. 346.

B. v. D. $\frac{10}{14}$. P. 15. V. $\frac{1}{5}$. A. $\frac{3}{24}$. C. 17.

Length of head nearly $\frac{1}{4}$, of pectoral nearly $\frac{1}{4}$, of caudal $\frac{1}{5}$, of base of dorsal rather more than $\frac{1}{2}$, of base of anal $\frac{2}{5}$ of total length. Height of head $\frac{1}{3}$, of body $\frac{1}{2}$, of hard dorsal $\frac{2}{15}$, of soft dorsal $\frac{2}{15}$, of ventral $\frac{1}{10}$, of anal $\frac{2}{15}$ of total length.

Eyes—Diameter $\frac{1}{2}$ length of head, $\frac{3}{4}$ of a diameter from end of snout, $\frac{1}{2}$ a diameter apart.

Body nearly oval, widest opposite the opercles, and strongly compressed. Mouth situated opposite the centre of the body. Profile much elevated.

Mouth anteriorly compressed, gape small, situated a short distance below the level of the orbit. Lips fleshy. Cleft of mouth extending half way to below the anterior margin of the orbit. Preopercle narrow, the posterior margin oblique, and nearly three times as long as the inferior which is horizontal, its angle rounded. Opercle ending in an obtuse point. Orifices of nostrils large, circular, and approximating, situated in a furrow at the anterior superior margin of the orbit, and having a rather strong overhanging ridge, with a slighter one below.

Teeth—In a single compressed series in each jaw.

Fins—Pectoral situated rather behind the origins of the dorsal and ventral, which are on a line. Anal commences opposite the end of the ventral. A short portion of the tail finless. First dorsal spines strong, and the membrane deeply emarginate: second spine the longest, being three times higher than the first (it is serrated in front in its middle third); from thence the spines decrease in thickness and length to the last: the rays are articulated, not branched. Caudal rather emarginate. Pectoral pointed. Anal, second spine the longest and strongest, it is rather rugose anteriorly; the third spine is nearly as long, but much more slender. The margin of the fin is parallel to the abdominal profile.

Body and head with a rugose cuticle, forming distinct horizontal lines, which on the body under a magnifying glass are seen covered with triangular points, projecting backwards.

Lateral line—In upper fifth of the body, forming a curve parallel to that of the back; opposite the dorsal fin it passes straight to the centre of the caudal, in this horizontal portion there is a sharp lancet-shaped spine directed forwards and receivable into a sheath on the lateral line.

Colours—Uniform, ventral fin stained blackish. A silvery band along the opercles, and part of the abdomen.

Rare in Malabar, where it grows to about four inches in length: but *Sir Emerson Tennent*, in his drawings of the "Fishes of Ceylon," has one of this species of at least twelve inches in length.

Habitat—Seas of India, and China.

Fam. NANDIDÆ, Günther.

PSEUDOCHROMIDES, pt. MÆNOIDEI, pt. *Müller & Troschel.*

GENUS NANDUS, *Cuv. and Val.*

BEDULA, *Gray.*

Branchiostegals, six: pseudobranchiæ present or absent. Body oblong, compressed. Opercle with two spines: preopercle more or less serrated: preorbital entire. The infraorbital bones do not articulate with the preopercle. Eyes lateral. Mouth very or moderately protractile. One dorsal the spinous portion being slightly more developed than the soft. Anal with three spines. Teeth villiform in the jaws on the vomer, and palatine bones, tubercular on the pterygoid and base of the tongue. Scales ctenoid and of moderate size. Lateral line interrupted. Air bladder large, simple. Pyloric appendages none.

NANDUS MARMORATUS.

COIUS NANDUS, *Ham. Buch.* pp. 96, 370, pl. 30, f. 32.

NANDUS MARMORATUS, *Cuv. & Val.* viii. p. 482, pl. 207; *Cantor*, Catal. p. 17; *Jerdon*, Madras Journal, 1848, p. 141; *Günther*, Catal. iii. p. 367.

BEDULA HAMILTONII, *Gray*, Ill. I. Z., ii. pl. 88, f. 3.
BEDULA NEBULOSA, *Gray*, Ibid. f. 2.
MOOTAHREE, *Mal.*

B. vi. D. $\frac{12}{11}$-$\frac{14}{13}$. P. 16. V. $\frac{1}{5}$. A. $\frac{3}{7-9}$. C. 15. L. l. 46-55. L. tr. $\frac{7}{13}$-$\frac{7}{15}$. Vert. 24.

Length of head $\frac{1}{3}$, of pectoral $\frac{2}{15}$, of caudal $\frac{2}{11}$, of base of dorsal $\frac{2}{5}$, of base of anal $\frac{1}{10}$ of total length. Height of head $\frac{1}{5}$, of body $\frac{3}{10}$, of hard dorsal $\frac{1}{12}$, of soft dorsal $\frac{2}{15}$, of ventral nearly $\frac{1}{9}$, of anal $\frac{2}{15}$ of total length.

Eyes—Rather transversely oval, nearly bordering on the profile. Diameter $\frac{1}{6}$ of length of head, rather more than 1 diameter from end of snout, and 1 diameter apart.

Snout rather elevated, and profile slightly concave opposite the orbits, from whence it rises to the dorsal fin, the abdominal line not being so curved as that of the back. Body compressed, especially towards the tail, opposite the commencement of the dorsal fin, its thickness equals half its height.

Mouth wide, lips thin, extremity of the upper jaw reaching to opposite the posterior margin of the orbit. Intermaxillaries very protrusible, extending the length of the orbit, behind its posterior border. Preopercle very finely serrated, especially about its angle, which is rounded: horizontal limb two-thirds the length of the vertical one. Opercle with one well-marked fine sharp spine posteriorly, above its centre. Sub- and interopercles with some very fine serratures at their approximating portions, which are continued a short distance along the inferior margin of the interopercle. Between the centre of the superior orbital margin and the muzzle there are three distinct fossæ, and three more on the preorbital, whilst below the symphysis of the lower jaw there are two pores and two fossæ posteriorly on each ramus. Between the orbit and the angle of the preopercle are fourteen series of scales, and across the opercles about thirteen. Nostrils close to the orbit, and opposite its superior third.

Teeth—Minute, in villiform bands on the jaws, vomer and palate. In the lower jaw there are several rows at the centre, but only one or two on each ramus. In the upper jaw the teeth are villiform and most numerous at its centre, but they decrease in width at the sides; intermixed with these there are a few larger ones in each jaw.

Fins—Origins of dorsal, pectoral and ventral on a line: anal commences opposite the soft dorsal. Dorsal spines rather strong, their base occupying rather more than three fourths of the fin, and are receivable into a groove: the interspinous membrane is deeply notched: soft portion square. Pectoral short and rounded. Ventral spine weak and the fin short. Anal spines moderately strong, the centre one the longest and two thirds the length of the rays: there is a groove at its base: soft portion square. Caudal large, and cut square.

Scales—Ctenoid, covering the body, head, and even the upper jaw: none on the lower jaw; they are rather smaller on the nape than on the body. There are some on the bases of the soft dorsal and anal fins.

Lateral line—Consists of minute tubes bifid at each extremity. At first it proceeds in the upper fourth of the body for about thirty-six scales, where it abruptly ceases, but is subsequently continued four rows lower down to the centre of the caudal.

Colours—Greenish brown with brassy reflections, marbled vertically with three wide patchy streaks, whilst a fourth dark one passes across the base of the caudal fin. Hard portion of the dorsal diaphanous: the soft spotted with transverse bands of brown. Caudal darkest near its base, but with a light line dividing it from the vertical dark marking. Caudal and soft portion of the anal spotted in transverse bars.

No pseudobranchiæ.

Grows to six inches in length. Common in the rivers and paddy fields. It is a voracious fish, preys on small cyprinidæ, and is very tenacious of life.

Habitat—Fresh waters of India and Malaysia.

NANDUS MALABARICUS. Plate VIII.

CATOPRA MALABARICA, *Günther*,* Annals Nat. Hist. 1864, p. 375; *Day*, Proc. Zool. Society, 1865, p. 30.

B. vi. D. $\frac{14}{12}$. P. 15. V. $\frac{1}{5}$. A. $\frac{3}{8}$. C. 16. L. l. 25. L. tr. $\frac{4}{8}$. Vert. $\frac{13}{11}$.

Length of head about $\frac{1}{4}$, of pectoral $\frac{1}{5}$, of caudal $\frac{1}{5}$, of base of dorsal $\frac{1}{2}$, of base of anal $\frac{1}{7}$ of total length. Height of head $\frac{1}{4}$, of body $\frac{1}{3}$, of hard dorsal $\frac{1}{9}$, of soft dorsal $\frac{1}{7}$, of ventral $\frac{1}{7}$, of anal $\frac{1}{7}$ of total length.

Eyes—Diameter $\frac{2}{7}$ length of head, 1 diameter from end of snout, nearly 1 diameter apart.

Body compressed; mouth situated below the central line of the body; there is a considerable rise to the dorsal fin.

Jaws equal: intermaxillaries protractile, their posterior process being two-thirds the length of the diameter of the orbit: upper lip rather fleshy. The superior maxilla extends to slightly behind the anterior margin of the orbit. Upper surface of eye nearly close to profile. Preopercle, posterior limb almost vertical, roughened, angle rounded and finely serrated, inferior limb horizontal, entire, and little more than half the length of posterior limb. Sub- and interopercles with a few very fine serratures at their approximating extremities. Opercle with two rather strong flat spines, and ending in a membraneous point. Preorbital entire. Nostrils rather wide apart, posterior the largest. Pseudobranchiæ present. Branchiostegal rays covered: gills three and a half.

Teeth—Several rows of fine teeth in the intermaxillaries, with an external larger band of curved ones. In the mandibulæ several rows of nearly equal sized villiform ones, and four large curved teeth external to them at the symphysis. On the front of the vomer is a transverse oval patch of villiform ones, divided by a short interspace from a narrow band of the same description which exists on the palatine bones. Pterygoid bones, and root of the tongue covered by rounded teeth, which posteriorly become roughened and even pointed. Sharp villiform teeth on the pharyngeal bones.

Fins—Origins of pectoral and dorsal on a line, ventral slightly behind: anal arises opposite commencement of soft dorsal. Spinous dorsal can be laid flat on the back, in a groove, its base occupies nearly four-fifths of that of the entire fin. Dorsal spines rather strong, shorter than the rays, the third the longest, the remainder nearly the same. Interspinous

---

* *Dr. Günther* affixed the name of "Catopra Malabarica" to a specimen of this fish which I had given to the British Museum. In deference to the expressed opinion of that excellent ichthyologist, I adopted his designation in my "Fishes of Cochin:" but its preorbital being entire, &c., I, at the suggestion of the late *Sir John Richardson*, forwarded a specimen to *Dr. Bleeker* for his opinion, who pronounced it to be undoubtedly a "Nandus" as at present constituted, but which will probably at a future date have to be placed in a distinct, but nearly allied genus. Having been furnished by the *Rev. H. Baker* with four more specimens from India, I have been enabled to obtain a skeleton, which fully confirms the views entertained by *Dr. Bleeker*. Should more species be discovered, I would suggest the generic term of *Paranandus*, differing from the Nandus by its mouth being moderately protrusible, by its having two opercular spines, pseudobranchiæ, &c.

PLATE VIII.

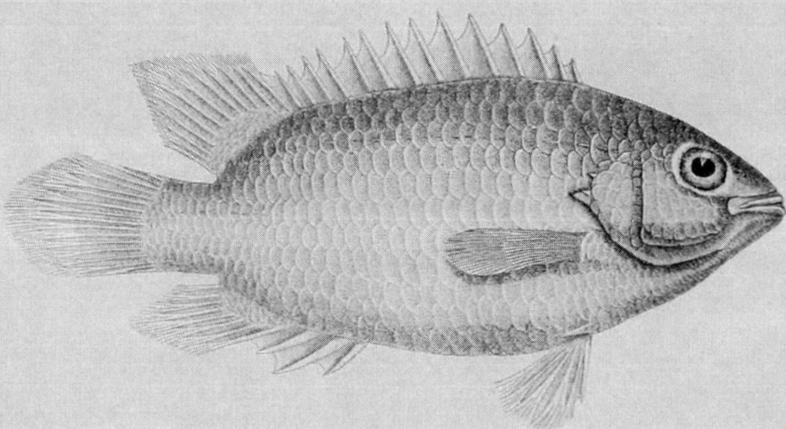

F. Day, del, et sculp.

NANDUS MALABARICUS

membrane deeply notched, and extending slightly beyond the points of the spines. Central dorsal rays the longest. Ventral spine moderately strong. Anal spines strong, second the strongest, but not quite so long as third, they can be received into a groove the same as the dorsal spines; central rays the longest, as are also those of the caudal.

Scales—Ctenoid, greatest diameter from above downwards, they cover body, opercles and head, but there are none between or before the eyes, or on the preorbital; some are continued over the soft portions of the dorsal, anal, and base of caudal.

Lateral line—Interrupted, at first in upper fourth of body, opposite fourth dorsal ray it ceases on the twenty-first scale, and before the last portion of the soft dorsal it is continued along the mesial line as far as, but not on to, the caudal fin.

Colours—Of a rifle green with purplish reflections: darker on the back than on the abdomen. Fins greenish. Eyes yellowish green.

I am indebted to the Rev. H. Baker, junior, for six specimens of this fish from the Hill ranges of Travancore.

Grows to four inches in length.

Habitat—Hill streams of Malabar.

GENUS PRISTOLEPIS.

PRISTOLEPIS, *Jerdon*, Madras Journal, xv. 1848, p. 141.
CATOPRA, *Bleeker*, Borneo, iii. 1851, p. 65.

Branchiostegals, six. Body rather short, compressed. Preopercle and preorbitals serrated: opercle with two flat spines. Mouth protractile. One dorsal with from thirteen to fifteen spines, anal with three. Teeth villiform on jaws, vomer, palatine and pterygoid bones, also on the tongue. Scales ctenoid. Lateral line interrupted.

* PRISTOLEPIS MARGINATUS.

PRISTOLEPIS MARGINATUS, *Jerdon*, Madras Journal, xv. p. 141.

B. vi. D. $\frac{15}{12}$. P. 15. V. $\frac{1}{5}$. A. $\frac{4}{8}$? $\frac{3}{8}$.

Length of head $\frac{1}{3}$ of body, not including caudal fin. Height of body $\frac{1}{2}$ its length.

Body broadly oval, compressed. Jaws nearly equal. Preopercle finely serrated. Opercle with two flat spines.

Teeth—Villiform in both jaws, vomer, palate, and base of tongue, with a row of larger pointed ones of unequal size in front of upper jaw.

Fins—Pectoral rather large, somewhat rounded: soft portions of dorsal and anal rounded, much longer than the spinous. Caudal rounded.

Scales—Large, ctenoid, some extend over bases of the dorsal and caudal fins.

Lateral line—Interrupted, at first on third scale, subsequently central and on seventh row.

Colours—Sap green, palest beneath; dorsal and anal fins with a streak of orange on the interspinous membrane.

Grows to four inches and upwards.

Habitat—Hill streams of Malabar.

Fam. LABYRINTHICI, Cuvier.

LABYRINTHIBRANCHII, pt., *Owen.*
OSPHROMENOIDEI, *Bleeker.*

GENUS ANABAS, *Cuvier.*

Branchiostegals, six; pseudobranchiæ none. Body oblong, compressed: opercles and preorbital serrated. A superbranchial organ, composed of thin laminæ, situated in a cavity above the gills, and resting upon the upper part of the third branchial arch. Eyes lateral. Mouth moderately cleft. Branchial arches with toothed tubercles. Gill openings narrow, membranes join below isthmus. One dorsal fin, the spinous portion more developed than the soft. Anal spines many, but less than those of the dorsal fin, the soft rays nearly equal in extent. Ventrals thoracic. Teeth villiform in jaws, on the anterior and posterior extremity of the vomer; none on the palatine bones. Scales ctenoid, of moderate size. Lateral line interrupted. Air bladder bifid, and produced posteriorly. Pyloric appendages few.

ANABAS SCANDENS.

PERCA SCANDENS, *Daldorf*, Trans. Linn. Soc. iii. p. 62.
COJUS COBOJIUS, *Ham. Buch.* pp. 98, 370, pl. 13, f. 33.
ANABAS SCANDENS, *Cuv. & Val.* vii. p. 333, pl. 193 & 205; *Cantor*, Catal. p. 82; *Jerdon*, Madras Journ. xv. p. 144; *Günther*, Catal. iii. p. 375.
ANABAS SPINOSUS, *Gray*, Ill. I. Z. ii. p. 189, f. 1.
UNDEE COLLEE, *Mal.*

B. vi. D. $\frac{17\text{-}18}{8\text{-}10}$ P. 15. V. $\frac{1}{5}$. A. $\frac{9\text{-}10}{9\text{-}11}$. C. 16. L. l. 27-32. L. tr. $\frac{5}{9}$. Vert. $\frac{10}{16}$. Cæc. py. 3.

Length of head $\frac{1}{4}$, of pectoral $\frac{1}{6}$, of caudal $\frac{1}{5}$, of base of hard dorsal $\frac{1}{2}$, of base of anal $\frac{1}{3}$ of total length. Height of head $\frac{1}{5}$, of body above $\frac{1}{3}$, of hard dorsal $\frac{1}{11}$, of soft dorsal $\frac{1}{7}$, of hard anal $\frac{1}{11}$, of soft anal $\frac{1}{8}$, of ventral $\frac{1}{4}$ of total length.

Eyes—Diameter $\frac{1}{5}$ length of head, nearly $\frac{1}{2}$ a diameter from end of snout, $1\frac{3}{4}$ to 2 diameters apart.

Body oblong, and slightly compressed in its posterior third, but elevated opposite the dorsal. Head rounded, cheeks and gullet inflated, whilst the head is wider than the body.

Lower jaw rather the longest. Upper jaw extending backwards to beneath the middle of the orbit. Preorbital strong, and denticulated. Preopercle, with the posterior margin nearly straight, and about twice as long as the inferior: angle with some strong teething. Opercle strongly spined on its posterior margin, also on the angle of the sub-opercle, which is very moveable, and hides the branchiostegal rays. The spines may be said to exist in three distinct patches on the vertical limb of the opercle, and on the subopercle: the superior consists of four or five, with some smaller ones which are above the centre of the opercle: the middle is a little beneath the centre of the opercle, and has a large one above and some smaller ones below; whilst the inferior patch is placed entirely on the subopercle, and has the greatest number of spines and rather the longest, which are continued, but less strongly, along the lower margin of the subopercle. Nostrils at anterior superior angle of the orbit, the anterior is slightly tubular. Suprascapular serrated.

Teeth—Villiform in jaws, with an external rather conical row. Also villiform on the front of vomer, and on its posterior part. None on palate.

Fins—The dorsal commences over the posterior margin of the opercle, its spinous portion lower than its soft, which is rather pointed. Pectoral rounded, arising opposite the third dorsal spine. Ventral commences opposite the first quarter of the pectoral. Anal of the same shape as the dorsal, and begins below the tenth dorsal spine. Caudal large and rounded. Dorsal spines strong, occupying nearly five sixths of the base of the fin: the membrane deeply notched: the third spine is higher than the two first, which are about even in length; a groove exists along the back, into which the spines may be laid. Anal spines and groove the same as in the dorsal fin: its spinous portion occupies two thirds of the entire length of the fin.

Scales—Ctenoid, erectile, longest diameter from above downwards, extending over the body, and bases of soft dorsal, anal, and caudal fins, whilst the head is covered with rhomboidal or polygonal scales: there are some also on the mandibula.

Five pores exist at the posterior extremity of the orbit, and pass in a line over the occiput: others are placed below the snout, also along the lower margin of the preopercle, on its vertical border, and on the mandibulæ.

Lateral line—Interrupted, for its first two thirds being on the sixth scale, and for its last third on the eighth: it is not continued on to the caudal fin.

Colours—Rifle green becoming lighter on the abdomen: four dark, vertical, diffused bands pass from the back to the abdomen. In the young fish a dark spot is generally present at the base of the tail. Fins of a dark green, but in clear water they become reddish, and the body more yellow. Eyes reddish hazel.

Habits—The climbing properties attributed to this fish in other portions of India and Ceylon, are fully believed in by the inhabitants of Malabar. Certainly it is with difficulty that they can be retained in a vivarium, as unless it is covered, or its summit upwards of a foot from the water they invariably escape. They are able to progress along the ground in two ways, either by lying on their sides, flapping their tails, and moving their pectoral fins: or else chiefly by the aid of the latter fins, first one being advanced and then the other. They can erect their fins and likewise their scales at pleasure, even down to those along the bases of the caudal fin. This power of erection, especially as it also exists in the gill covers, would be a great assistance did they employ the latter in climbing.

Its hollow superbranchial organ, with from two to six laminæ (the number of which depends on the age of the specimen), with fringed valances, enables the *climbing perch* to retain water for a considerable time, so that it can moisten its gills and live whilst out of its native element. *Hamilton Buchanan* observes that he has known it to retain vitality under these conditions for six days. That it travels from pond to pond when its means of subsistence fail is a well known fact; but that it buries itself in the mud as tanks dry up and remains there until the monsoon of the next year again fills them with water, is a subject that requires further research.

It should be remarked that the comparative size of many of the parts of the body varies with the age of the fish, its state of health at the time captured, and the supply of food which it has been obtaining. Likewise the number of scales along the lateral line differs considerably in various specimens, as do also the number of its fin rays, and its colours.

Are common in most pieces of fresh water in Malabar, and esteemed very good eating by the Natives, who invariably when catching them bite their heads, in order to destroy life. On one occasion this practice led to a fatal result; the fish having slipped down the throat of the fisherman, it could not be withdrawn owing to the erectile nature of the gill covers and scales, and the man was suffocated before reaching the hospital.

Habitat—Fresh waters of India, Malaysia, and the Philippine Islands.

GENUS POLYACANTHUS, *Cuv. and Val.*

Branchiostegals, six: pseudobranchiæ none. Body oblong, compressed: opercles without spines: sub- and interopercles and preorbital serrated. A superbranchial organ as in the Genus *Anabas*. Eyes lateral. Mouth small, oblique, little protractile. Branchial arches with toothed tubercles. One dorsal fin, the spinous portion much more developed than the soft. Anal spines numerous, and more developed than its soft portion. Ventrals of one spine and five well developed rays, some of which are usually elongated. Teeth villiform in both jaws. Scales ctenoid. Lateral line interrupted, partially or entirely absent. Air bladder simple. Pyloric appendages few.

POLYACANTHUS CUPANUS.

POLYACANTHUS CUPANUS, *Cuv. & Val.* vii. p. 357; *Günther*, Catal. iii. p. 381.
CARINGANAH, and WUNNUTTEE, *Mal.*

B. vi. D. $\frac{14-15}{6}$. P. 10. V. $\frac{1}{5}$. A. $\frac{16-18}{11}$. C. 13. L. l. 30-32. L. tr. $\frac{4}{7}$.

Length of head $\frac{1}{5}$, of pectoral $\frac{2}{13}$, of caudal nearly $\frac{1}{4}$, of base of dorsal spines nearly $\frac{1}{4}$, of base of soft dorsal $\frac{1}{13}$, of base of anal spines above $\frac{1}{4}$, of base of soft anal $\frac{1}{6}$ of the total length. Height of head $\frac{1}{5}$, of body $\frac{1}{4}$, of hard dorsal $\frac{1}{13}$, of soft dorsal $\frac{1}{5}$, of ventral $\frac{1}{5}$, of anal spines $\frac{1}{16}$, of anal rays $\frac{1}{13}$ of the total length.

Eyes—Diameter $\frac{1}{5}$ of length of head, 1 diameter from end of snout, 2 diameters apart.

Body rather oblong, and compressed.

Mouth transverse; lower jaw rather the longest: intermaxillaries slightly protrusible. Angle and posterior half of the horizontal margin of the preopercle finely serrated. The opercle ending in a fleshy point. Subopercle very finely serrated, also the posterior half of the interopercle. Preorbital serrated in its external extremity. Openings of the nostrils wide, approximating, the posterior being close to the anterior superior margin of the orbit, and the anterior close to the edge of the snout.

Teeth—In two or three rows of villiform ones in the upper jaw: in several opposite the symphysis of the lower, and in two rows along either side.

Fins—The dorsal commences above the posterior third of the pectoral, and terminates opposite the last spine of the anal, where the rays are elongated and the fin becomes pointed: the ventral arises under the pectoral, its first ray is elongated into two filaments which reach to opposite the eighth anal spine: the anal begins opposite the anterior third of the pectoral. The dorsal spines increase in length to the last, and there exists a groove along the back for their reception into which they can be laid flat: the last spine equals the distance between the posterior extremity of the orbit and the posterior extremity of the opercle: the last rays are likewise longer than the first, and extend to opposite the anterior third of the caudal fin. The anal is similar to the dorsal, but continued further posteriorly, its rays are longer than its spines. The central caudal rays are elongated.

Scales—Ctenoid, covering the body, head, and jaws, whilst some fine ones are also present along the base of the dorsal and anal rays.

Numerous glandular openings exist on the head, one is present at the angle near the centre of the lower margin of the preopercle, another about the centre of its vertical limb.

Lateral line—At first on the fifth row, then on the fourth to the fourteenth scale where it ceases.

Colours.—Deep rifle green with the prolonged ray of the ventral of a bright scarlet. Caudal barred in lines of spots, as is also the dorsal especially in its soft portion. A round black spot exists at the base of the caudal. Eyes hazel.

In one specimen of an inch in length and having one spine in the dorsal and one ray in the anal less than in any of the others, the colours differ, being of a beautiful rose colour, and rather dark brown along the back and base of the anal fin. Two deep black horizontal lines pass one from above the orbit direct to the caudal, and a second from the angle of the mouth, through the eye to the caudal. Head and cheeks spotted.

Grows to about three inches in length, and is eaten by the Natives. Is found in ditches and frequently remains under stones in the water, in which situation it is readily captured by the hand.

Habitat—Fresh waters of Malabar, and Coromandel.

Fam. ATHERINIDÆ.

GENUS ATHERINA, *Artedi.*

Branchiostegals, five or six: pseudobranchiæ. Body subcylindrical and elongated. Eyes large, lateral. Cleft of mouth rather deep. Upper jaw protractile. Snout obtuse. Two dorsals widely separated, the spines of the first feeble: anal resembling the soft dorsal or slightly larger. Ventrals abdominal with one spine and five rays. Teeth minute, those on palate sometimes indistinct. Scales cycloid, of moderate size. Air bladder present. Pyloric appendages none.

ATHERINA FORSKÅLII.

? ATHERINA HEPSETUS, *Forsk.* p. 69.

ATHERINA FORSKÅLII, *Rüp.* N. W. F., p. 132, t. 33, f. 1; *Cantor*, Catal. p. 103; *Günther*, Catal. iii. p. 397.

B. vi. D. 5 | $\frac{1}{9-10}$. P. 17. V. $\frac{1}{5}$. A. $\frac{1}{13-14}$. C. 15. L. l. 40. L. tr. 6-7.

Length of head $\frac{1}{5}$, of pectoral $\frac{1}{8}$, of caudal $\frac{1}{5}$, of base of first dorsal $\frac{1}{15}$, of second dorsal $\frac{1}{10}$, of base of anal $\frac{1}{10}$ of total length. Height of head $\frac{1}{8}$, of body $\frac{1}{6}$, of first dorsal $\frac{1}{12}$, of second dorsal $\frac{1}{10}$, of ventral $\frac{1}{9}$, of anal $\frac{1}{10}$ of total length.

Eyes—Very large, nearly circular, the upper margin of the orbit forming part of the profile. Diameter from $\frac{1}{2}$ length of head to $\frac{2}{5}$, $\frac{1}{3}$ of a diameter from end of snout, and 1 diameter apart.

Body elongated and compressed, tapering towards the caudal extremity: upper profile nearly straight—excepting where the upper margin of the orbit causes a slight bulging—and beyond the second dorsal, where it slightly sinks: the lower profile is more convex than the upper.

Snout short, mouth oblique, upper jaw slightly protractile. Maxilla extends to beneath the anterior third of the orbit. Lower jaw very slightly the longest: along its lower margin there are the openings of five or six pores, and two or three more on the preorbitals. Preopercle narrow and rectangular, with the angle rounded, and horizontal limb nearly as long as the vertical. Opercle ending in a soft point. Summit of head almost flat, on the vertex there is a raised triangular space, which is continued in the form of a narrow elevation as far as the anterior third of the interorbital space. Passing backwards from the posterior superior margin of the orbit, is a rather deep longitudinal groove, which extends above the upper margin of the opercle and contains the openings of two or three pores.

Teeth—Bands of fine villiform ones in both jaws, on the vomer, palatine, and pterygoid bones.

Fins—Pectoral arises close to the posterior margin of the opercle, and above the central line of the body: ventral opposite the posterior extremity of the pectoral; first dorsal opposite the posterior end of the ventral, and the breadth of one scale nearer the commencement of the anal than to that of the ventral; the second dorsal commences six scales behind the posterior extremity of the first dorsal, and the anal arises rather in front of it. The spines of the first dorsal are fine, with hair-like terminations, and the membrane is rather deeply cleft; the first four are close together, and the fifth rather further apart. Pectoral slightly pointed, with a rather broad base. Second dorsal highest in front, with the upper margin rather concave: anal of the same shape. Caudal rather deeply lobed.

Scales—Cycloid, and large, vertical diameter the greatest. The lateral line in the third row and in the centre of its course consists of two parallel tubes, above them is a semicircular notch excavated from the posterior margin of the scales: both anteriorly and posteriorly it consists of badly marked circular orifices.

Colours—Silvery, with the upper surface of the head and back of a pale sea green, and with numerous fine points of black. A steel blue line, darkest above, extends along the third row of scales and also the upper third of the fourth. Cheeks and opercles shining silvery: muzzle and lips blackish. Fins diaphanous: margins of dorsal spines, and the rays of the pectoral and caudal finely dotted with black. Iris silvery.

Very abundant in Malabar during the monsoon months, but a few are always present. It is one of several genera which are known to the Europeans as "Whitebait," like which it is dressed, especially for the breakfast table. It rarely exceeds four inches in length.

Habitat—Red Sea, Malabar, and Malaysia.

Fam. MUGILIDÆ.

Genus MUGIL, *Artedi.*

Branchiostegals, from five to six: pseudobranchiæ. Body more or less oblong and compressed. Eyes lateral. Cleft of mouth transverse and laterally short. Anterior margin of mandible sharp. Teeth in jaws feeble or absent. Two dorsals widely separated; the first with four spines, the second longer but not so long as the anal, which is opposite it. Ventral abdominal, with one spine and five rays suspended from an elongated coracoid bone. Gill openings wide. Scales cycloid, and of moderate size. Lateral line absent. A portion of stomach very muscular. Vertebræ twenty-four.

a. With adipose eyelids.

Mugil cunnesius.

Cunnesee, *Russell*, pl. 181.

Mugil cunnesius, *Cuv. & Val.* xi. p. 114; *Cantor*, Catal. p. 100; *Günther*, Catal. iii. p. 434.

Mahlah, *Mal.*

B. v. D. 4. | $\frac{1}{8}$. P. 17. V. $\frac{1}{5}$. A. $\frac{3}{9}$. C. 14. L. l. 41-43. L. tr. 13-15.

Length of head $\frac{3}{14}$, of pectoral $\frac{2}{15}$, of caudal $\frac{1}{6}$, of base of first dorsal $\frac{1}{11}$, of base of second dorsal $\frac{1}{16}$, of base of anal $\frac{1}{10}$ of total length. Height of head $\frac{2}{15}$, of body $\frac{3}{14}$, of first dorsal $\frac{1}{16}$, of second dorsal $\frac{1}{9}$, of ventral $\frac{2}{13}$, of anal $\frac{1}{9}$ of the total length.

Eyes—With adipose lids covering $\frac{1}{3}$ of each side, with vertical elliptical openings. Horizontal diameter of eye $\frac{1}{4}$, vertical diameter $\frac{1}{5}$ of length of head, $\frac{3}{4}$ of a diameter from end of snout, rather more than 2 diameters apart.

The upper profile is more convex than the lower. The upper surface of the head rather compressed and slightly convex from side to side. The width of the body equals two thirds its height.

Mouth small, lower jaw slightly the shortest, angle situated opposite the anterior opening of the nostril. A slight tubercle at the centre of the lower jaw, fitting into a notch in the centre of the upper. Preorbital truncated externally, and thin interiorly, forming a long triangle, the inferior margin is nearly straight, and neither serrated or notched but with a slight roughness along the posterior two thirds of its lower edge: its posterior margin has four or five very fine serratures, and does not quite cover the maxilla, the angle of which is perceptible opposite the anterior margin of the orbit. Intermandibular space tongue-shaped. Anterior nostril close to the posterior margin of the preorbital, and some distance from the posterior nostril, which is opposite the anterior superior angle of the orbit. There is a large gland opposite the centre of the vertical border of the preopercle, another just above its angle, and three above its horizontal border. Several other wide glandular openings exist on various parts of the head, and many fine longitudinal grooves.

Teeth—None apparent: on each side of the vomer is a transverse tubercle.

Fins—Pectoral obtuse, almost entirely situated in the upper half of the body, the lowest ray equal to a fourth the length of the highest, the fin extends to opposite the eleventh scale of the lateral line. Ventral commences opposite the last fourth of the pectoral, its spine is weak, and the first ray sometimes prolonged. First dorsal begins midway between the snout and the base of the external ray of the caudal, and about opposite the tip of the ventral spine, and the twelfth scale of the lateral line: it is highest in front: the three anterior rays arise close together, the fourth is distant rather above half its height from the third and is more than a third shorter than the first. Second dorsal commences midway between the origin of the first dorsal and the base of the external caudal ray, opposite the twenty-fifth scale of the lateral line: its anterior margin is the highest, its superior border concave, and its last ray double and elongated: its spine is half the height of the first ray. Anal arises opposite the second dorsal, its spines are weak, the first half as long as the second, which is nearly a third less than the third, and the first ray is twice its length: the form of the fin is like that of the second dorsal. Caudal emarginate.

Scales—Not very regular in size, they cover the body, head, cheeks, and lower jaw. Some fine ones exist in the adult, on the rays of the pectoral, ventral, and caudal fins, and on the anterior margins of the second dorsal and anal. Each scale has a smooth edge equal to about a fifth of its exposed portion; along the mesial line there is a narrow furrow, generally running longitudinally, and extending for four fifths of the exposed part. Below the pectoral fin these lines run very irregularly (except in the two or three lowest rows where they are longitudinal) some being vertical and some oblique. There is a long scale at the base of the first dorsal, also a large axillary one, and another elongated one at the base of the ventral.

Colours—Bluish silvery-green on the back and sides, becoming silvery white on the abdomen. Each row of scales marked by a broad parallel longitudinal line, equal to a third of its width, and darkest at their bases. Cheeks and opercles shining silvery, the latter with steel blue reflections, most apparent on the upper portion. Pectoral fin with a light base, dark at its outer third owing to the membrane being minutely dotted with black. Ventral and anal white, the latter greyish near its anterior extremity, but with a white margin. Both dorsals appear grey, owing to their being minutely dotted with black points, the outer margin of the second dorsal is lighter than its basal half. Caudal light coloured, with the external and posterior margins grey, due to the presence of minute black dots.

It is from this species of mullet that the fine fish roes are obtained for which Cochin is so famous. The roe is removed as soon as the fish is captured, and is then dried in the sun. The season commences about the middle of October, or beginning of November, when these fish swarm into the river to deposit their spawn. By the month of February mullets known as *Cunnumboo, Mal.* begin to be scarce, and by April they are almost unprocurable.

This species is excellent eating when not more than a foot and a half in length, for the larger ones are dry. It grows to three feet in length.

Habitat—Red Sea, Seas of India and of Malaysia.

* Mugil subviridis.

Mugil subviridis, *Cuv. & Val.* xi. p. 115; *Günther*, Catal. iii. p. 423.

D. 4 | $\frac{1}{8}$. A. $\frac{3}{8}$. L. l. 30. L. tr. 11.

Length of head $\frac{3}{16}$ of the total length, and pectoral rather shorter than the length of the head, the snout not included. Height of body $\frac{2}{9}$ of the total length.

Eyes—With adipose lids well developed: the distance between the eyes is equal to $\frac{4}{9}$ of the length of the head.

Snout broad, obtuse, depressed, and as long as the eye; its anterior margin is formed by the upper lips which are moderately thick. The maxilla is bent downwards behind and below the angle of the mouth, where its extremity is visible. A very obtuse angle made by the anterior margins of the mandibular bones. Cleft of mouth at least thrice as broad as deep. The intermandibular space is rather short and cuneiform. Preorbital angularly bent, its extremity subtruncated and denticulated.

Fins—Eighteen scales between the snout and the origin of the first dorsal fin. Pectoral is inserted above the middle of the height of the body, it has a very obtuse and rudimentary scale in its axil (absent according to Dr. Günther) and extends to the seventh horizontal row of scales. The eleventh and twentieth scales of the lateral line correspond to the origins of the dorsal fins. Nearly the whole of the anterior half of the anal is before the second dorsal. Caudal emarginate.

Scales—Extend over body, cheeks, lower jaw, summit of head, and the soft dorsal and anal fins.

Colours—Back greyish green: sides silvery, shot with golden: caudal stained with black.

Grows to eight inches in length.

Habitat—Seas of India.

Mugil Sundanensis.

Mugil Sundanensis, *Bleeker*, Sumatra, ii. p. 265; *Günther*, Catal. iii. p. 425.

B. v. D. 4 | $\frac{1}{8}$. P. 15. V. $\frac{1}{5}$. A. $\frac{3}{9}$. L. l. L. tr. 9.

Length of head $\frac{1}{5}$, of pectoral $\frac{1}{7}$, of caudal $\frac{2}{11}$, of base of first dorsal $\frac{1}{12}$, of base of second dorsal $\frac{1}{12}$, of base of anal $\frac{1}{10}$ of total length. Height of head $\frac{1}{6}$, of body $\frac{2}{9}$, of first dorsal $\frac{}{7}$, of second dorsal $\frac{2}{17}$, of ventral $\frac{1}{10}$, of anal $\frac{2}{17}$ of total length.

Eyes—Slightly wider than high, and with narrow anterior and posterior adipose lids. Diameter a little more than $\frac{1}{3}$ the length of head, $\frac{2}{3}$ of a diameter from the end of snout, and $1\frac{1}{3}$ diameters apart.

Body comparatively short. Upper and lower line of profile equally convex. Head slightly depressed. Snout rather obtuse.

Mouth wide, having at the symphysis of the mandibula a tubercle which is received into a notch in the intermaxillary. Preorbital with a well-marked notch anteriorly. Extremity of maxilla uncovered and apparent below the angle of the mouth. Upper lip rather thick. Preopercle with three wide glands opening along its vertical margin, one opposite the lower margin of the orbit, another just above the angle, and a third between the other two: along its horizontal limb there are three more, one at the angle just before and below the lowest of the vertical ones, another at its anterior extremity, and a central one. On the upper line of the opercles there are three more, and an oblique line of three rather superior to them. On the summit of the head there are some others.

Teeth—Some exceedingly fine ones in both jaws.

Fins—Pectoral extends to the eighth scale on the lateral line. First dorsal situated opposite the tenth scale of the lateral line: second dorsal opposite the nineteenth scale and the centre of the anal, which is opposite the seventeenth scale. Pectoral rather pointed. The anterior three spines of the dorsal strong, the first the highest and strongest, the fourth weak. Upper border of second dorsal concave. Ventral spine strong, equal in length to the third spine of the dorsal. Anal arises in front of the second dorsal, and has a concave inferior edge. Caudal emarginate in its posterior third.

Scales—With longitudinal shallow grooves, which below the pectoral are irregular in their direction: they extend over the body and head, and between the rays of the pectoral, second dorsal, anal, and caudal fins. An elongated scale at the base of the first dorsal, and another small one at that of the ventral.

Colours—Greyish, darkest on the back, and silvery white towards the abdomen: opercles tinged with a golden colour. Each scale darkest at the margin, and with a darkish grey line along its centre, forming longitudinal stripes. All the fins minutely spotted with black, giving them a greyish appearance. Caudal and pectoral the darkest, their edges being almost black, especially those of the caudal.

This does not appear to be a very common mullet in Malabar. Still it is occasionally taken with the others, but is not often seen more than five or six inches in length.

Habitat—Seas of Malabar and Malaysia.

MUGIL ENGELI.

MUGIL ENGELI, *Bleeker*, Nat. Tijds. Ned. Ind. xvi. p. 277; *Günther*, Catal. iii. p. 430.

B. v. D. 4 | $\frac{1}{8}$ P. 15. V. $\frac{1}{5}$. A. $\frac{3}{9}$. C. 14. L. l. 33-34. L. tr. 10-11.

Length of head $\frac{1}{6}$, of pectoral $\frac{1}{5}$, of caudal $\frac{1}{5}$, of base of first dorsal $\frac{1}{10}$, of base of second dorsal $\frac{1}{10}$, of base of anal $\frac{1}{9}$ of total length. Height of head $\frac{1}{7}$, of body $\frac{1}{5}$, of first dorsal $\frac{1}{10}$, of second dorsal $\frac{1}{8}$, of ventral $\frac{1}{7}$, of anal $\frac{1}{7}$ of total length.

Eyes—With adipose anterior, and posterior lids. Diameter rather more than $\frac{1}{3}$ length of head, $\frac{1}{2}$ a diameter from end of snout, $1\frac{1}{4}$ diameters apart.

Body with the superior and inferior profiles equally convex, snout rather rounded. Head slightly compressed.

Mouth transverse. Intermaxillaries very protractile, making an obtuse angle and having an emargination to receive the notch on the symphysis of the mandibulæ. Maxilla quite hidden by the preorbital, which is scaled, emarginate, and indistinctly serrated: preopercle with three glands on its vertical margin, the superior and largest being opposite the lower margin of the orbit, and the inferior and smallest opposite the angle: there are also three small ones along its horizontal margin. Several glands exist on the summit of the head. Intermandibular space lanceolate.

Teeth—None visible in the specimens obtained at Cochin.

Fins—Pectoral pointed and reaching to the tenth scale on the lateral line. Ventral large, and arising under the middle of the pectoral, its spine strong and rather longer than the third spine of the dorsal. First dorsal arises beyond the eighth scale on the lateral line, and opposite the end of the pectoral; its spines are moderately slender, the first the longest and strongest, and the last weak and half the length of the first. The second dorsal arises midway between the commencement of the first dorsal and the base of the upper caudal ray, opposite the fifth ray of the anal, and on the nineteenth scale of the lateral line: its upper margin is concave. Anal arises in front of the second dorsal. Caudal lunated in its posterior fourth.

Scales—Over the body and head, none on the fins excepting at the base of the caudal. They have fine longitudinal grooves, excepting below the pectoral, where they are irregular in their course. An elongated scale at the bases of the dorsal, pectoral, and anal fins.

Colours—Silvery, with a slight bronzed golden tint. Upper surface of the preopercle bright golden. Cheeks with a slightly golden tint. Base of pectoral jet black at its upper margin, the colour fading after death; posteriorly it is of a deep brown. Fins greyish, excepting the ventral which is colourless. Upper margin of iris bright golden.

Grows in Malabar to about nine inches in length, and is employed as food by the Natives.

Habitat—Malabar and the Seas of Malaysia.

MUGIL POICILUS. Plate IX.

MUGIL POICILUS, *Day*, Proceed. Zool. Society, 1865, p. 33.

B. v. D. 4 | $\frac{1}{8}$. P. 15. V. $\frac{1}{5}$. A. $\frac{3}{9}$. C. 14. L. l. 32. L. tr. 10.

Length of head about $\frac{1}{5}$, of pectoral $\frac{1}{7}$, of caudal $\frac{1}{5}$, of base of second dorsal $\frac{1}{14}$, of base of anal $\frac{1}{14}$ of total length. Height of head $\frac{1}{8}$, of body $\frac{1}{5}$, of first dorsal $\frac{1}{9}$, of second dorsal $\frac{1}{10}$, of ventral $\frac{1}{7}$, of anal $\frac{1}{10}$ of total length.

Eyes—An adipose membrane extends over about one third of either side in the adult fish, in the young the anterior curtain is broader than the posterior one. Diameter $\frac{2}{7}$ of length of head, $\frac{3}{4}$ of a diameter apart, $1\frac{1}{2}$ diameters from end of snout.

There is not much rise from the snout to the first dorsal. Lower jaw slightly the shortest, curved a little upwards, and having a notch in the centre of its extremity. Upper lip broad. Upper jaw considerably protractile. The superior maxilla is bent downwards below and behind angle of mouth, where its extremity is visible. Preorbital angularly bent, with a rounded and finely serrated margin. Nostrils rather wide apart, the posterior the largest, and nearer the orbit than it is to the anterior one. Interorbital space nearly flat. Snout broad, somewhat pointed in

PLATE IX.

F. Day, del. et sculp.

MUGIL POICILUS

the centre. Cleft of mouth rather more than twice as broad as deep. The free intermandibular space tongue-shaped, and moderately long.

Teeth—A fine row in the upper jaw, more apparent in the young than the adult.

Fins—Pectoral fin a little above the central line of the body, and extending to the eighth scale. No elongated scale at its base. Twenty scales from snout to origin of first dorsal, which commences nearer the snout than the caudal fin, and above the eighth scale on the lateral line. Eight scales between the two dorsal fins. First dorsal spines strong, the first the strongest and equal in length to the second: when laid flat they scarcely extend more than half way from their origin to the base of the second dorsal. Second dorsal, pectoral, anal, and caudal with some fine scales at their bases. Caudal emarginate. Pectoral rounded. Ventral with a pointed scale at its origin.

Scales—Rather irregular in size, highest from above downwards, each scale on the body and bases of the fins in the adult fish with a round or irregular cavity or gland in its centre of a deep black colour; in the young fish these are not so apparent, and until they are about three inches in length the black central spot is hardly discernible. The scales on the head vary much in shape, the posterior ones being irregularly quadrilateral, and the central ones between the orbits nearly round, but with deeply emarginated sides.

Colours—Greyish shot with silver, lightest on the sides and abdomen, each scale with a deep black central spot; fins stained with grey: pinkish golden about the cheeks.

Common in Cochin. Grows to eight inches in length; is good eating.

Habitat—Malabar.

MUGIL CUNNUMBOO.

B. v. D. 4 | $\frac{1}{7}$. P. 15. V. $\frac{1}{5}$. A. $\frac{3}{10}$. C. 15. L. l. 34. L. tr. 11.

Length of head $\frac{1}{5}$, of pectoral $\frac{1}{7}$, of caudal $\frac{3}{16}$, of base of first dorsal $\frac{1}{10}$, of base of second dorsal $\frac{1}{15}$, of base of anal $\frac{2}{23}$ of total length. Height of head $\frac{1}{9}$, of body $\frac{1}{5}$, of first dorsal $\frac{1}{9}$, of second dorsal $\frac{1}{9}$, of ventral $\frac{1}{8}$, of anal $\frac{1}{8}$ of the total length.

Eyes—With an adipose lid on either side $\frac{1}{3}$ their width. Horizontal diameter $\frac{2}{9}$, vertical diameter $\frac{2}{10}$ of the length of head: $\frac{1}{2}$ a diameter from the end of snout: 2 diameters apart.

Body rather broad, the upper profile more convex than that of the abdomen, which is nearly straight. Head compressed so that a distinct ridge exists from the posterior superior angle of the orbit to the upper edge of the base of the pectoral fin.

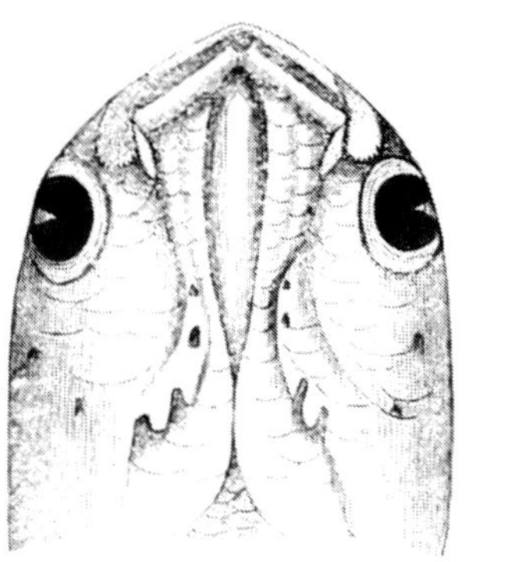

Mouth rather pointed, the centre of the intermaxillaries forming superiorly a rather broad knob, which inferiorly is notched in the centre to receive the tubercle of the lower jaw. Upper jaw longest, and the depth of the mouth one half of its width. Mandibulæ broad and flattened, the two meeting at an angle where there is a deep emargination, free space tongue-shaped. Preorbital triangular, strongly bent at its external end, the extremity of which is rounded and serrated, a few more serratures likewise exist along its inferior margin which is notched near its extremity. Lower end of maxilla not covered. Opercle ending superiorly in a fine point just above the lateral ridge. Interorbital space flat. Posterior nostril broad, oval: the anterior the smallest and circular, both situated rather above the level of the orbit. Preopercle with a broad glandular opening opposite the lower third of the orbit, a second at its angle directed backwards and downwards, whilst there is a third intermediate:

another is present on the horizontal limb close to the angle, a second small one at its anterior extremity, and a third intermediate. The rest of the glands on the head are as in the ***M. cunnesius, C. & V.***

No teeth apparent.

Fins—Pectoral arises in the centre of the height of the body, and extends to the eighth scale on the lateral line, it is rather pointed, and has a very small elongated scale at its axil. The first dorsal arises on the twenty-first scale from the snout, and on the eighth of the lateral line, its second spine is midway between the snout and the base of the caudal fin: spines strong, especially the first, the length of which equals the distance from the posterior margin of the orbit to the posterior margin of the opercle: the second spine is slightly and the last half shorter than the first: the fin has an elongated scale at its base extending to just beyond its last spine, whilst the groove for its reception is very shallow. The ventral arises about midway between the base of the pectoral and the base of the first dorsal, and on the ninth scale of the lateral line, it has a small elongated scale at its base. The second dorsal arises opposite the twentieth scale of the lateral line and the third soft ray of the anal: its spine is not quite half the length of the first ray: fin rhomboidal, its anterior margin the highest, its upper border straight, and its last ray double, and scarcely a fourth as long as the first: base of rays almost entirely hidden by scales. Anal with the first spine minute and short, and the second nearly as long as the third, which is more than half as long as the first ray: the fin is covered with scales excepting on its extremity, its last ray is double, and a third the height of the first. Caudal lunated in its posterior third.

Scales—Rather irregular in size, covering the posterior three fourths of the caudal, and most of the soft dorsal, anal, pectoral and ventral fins: most of the scales have fine longitudinal grooves, but those under the base of the pectoral pass downwards and backwards. The scales on the summit of the head are more regular than in most of the other species of mullets found in Malabar.

Colours—Silvery, upper surface of body of a greenish blue, darkest on the back, and becoming whitish on the abdomen, the edges of the scales being of the lightest tint. The whole fish is longitudinally striped with grey along the centre of each scale. Cheeks tinged with golden: a dark spot over the summit of the base of the pectoral fin. Dorsal greyish, very minutely dotted with dark grey. Second dorsal whitish with a dark grey tip, being minutely dotted with fine points of a darker tint. Caudal with a white base, and its posterior third grey, dotted with spots of the same colour. Ventral and anal white, pectoral with a dark margin to its upper rays.

Grows to two feet in length, and is excellent eating.

Habitat—Malabar.

MUGIL PARSIA.

MUGIL PARSIA, *Ham. Buch.* pp. 215, 380, pl. 17, f. 71; *Cuv. & Val.* xi. p. 144; *Günther*, Catal. iii. p. 426.

B. vi. D. 4 | $\frac{1}{8}$. P. 14. V. $\frac{1}{5}$. A. $\frac{3}{8\text{-}9}$. C. 14. L. l. 35. L. tr. 12.

Length of head $\frac{1}{5}$, of pectoral $\frac{2}{11}$, of base of second dorsal $\frac{1}{11}$, of base of anal $\frac{1}{11}$, of caudal $\frac{2}{9}$ of the total length. Height of head $\frac{2}{11}$, of body $\frac{2}{9}$, of first dorsal $\frac{2}{13}$, of second dorsal $\frac{2}{13}$, of anal $\frac{2}{13}$ of the total length.

Eyes—With adipose lids on their posterior fourth. Diameter $\frac{1}{3}$ of length of head, $\frac{1}{2}$ diameter from end of snout, $1\frac{1}{4}$ diameters apart.

Snout short, broad, depressed, with its anterior margin acute: lips thin: the maxilla bent behind the angle of the mouth and its extremity not covered by the preorbital. The anterior margin of the mandibula forms a rather obtuse angle, and is slightly emarginate at the symphysis. The cleft of the mouth is more than twice as wide as deep. Interorbital space slightly convex. Preorbital distinctly denticulated. Free space between mandibulæ lanceolate.

Teeth—In a specimen $3\frac{1}{10}$ inches in length, a row of fine teeth in the upper jaw is very distinctly visible.

Fins—The pectoral arises just below the middle of the height of the body, is rounded and extends to the eighth scale. The first dorsal is triangular, its spines moderately strong and it arises opposite the tenth scale of the lateral line. The second dorsal commences opposite the twenty-first scale, and above the fifth ray of the anal. Caudal emarginate.

Scales—Over body, head, base of soft dorsal, and anal rays.

Colours—Silvery, with a greenish tinge along the back and golden reflections on the head.

Grows to about four inches in length.

Habitat—Seas and estuaries of India, entering rivers.

B. Without adipose eyelids.

Mugil suppositus.

Mugil suppositus, *Günther*, Catal. iii. p. 437.
Mugil borbonicus, *Cantor*, Catal. p. 101.

B. v. D. 4 | $\frac{1}{8}$. P. 15. V. $\frac{1}{5}$. A. $\frac{3}{9}$. C. 14. L. l. 39. L. tr. 14.

Length of head $\frac{1}{5}$, of pectoral $\frac{1}{6}$, of caudal $\frac{1}{6}$, of base of first dorsal $\frac{1}{12}$, of base of second dorsal $\frac{1}{12}$, of base of anal $\frac{1}{11}$ of total length. Height of head $\frac{2}{13}$, of body $\frac{1}{5}$, of first dorsal $\frac{1}{10}$, of second dorsal $\frac{1}{9}$, of ventral $\frac{1}{9}$, of anal $\frac{1}{9}$ of total length.

Eyes—Without adipose lids; horizontal diameter $\frac{2}{7}$, and vertical diameter $\frac{2}{8}$ of length of head, rather more than $\frac{1}{2}$ diameter from end of snout, $1\frac{1}{3}$ diameters apart.

Body equally convex on its superior and inferior profiles. Head rather broad, and a slight ridge from the upper surface of orbit to the base of the pectoral, the interorbital space rather convex.

Mouth transverse, its depth a fourth of its width. Upper jaw more rounded than angular, with a notch in its centre to receive the knob of the lower jaw, which is elevated in its centre, and concave along either side. The free space is rather narrow and lanceolate in shape. Preorbital irregularly triangular, with the base in front: it is convex as far as its bent angle, whilst its superior margin has a hollow rounded notch, and its inferior angle is bent down, rounded, and denticulated; an oblique line of three open glands exists from between the notch to its external angle. Preopercle, with a deep glandular notch opposite the lower margin of the orbit, and two approximating just above its angle; on its horizontal margin there is one at its angle directed backwards, and one at its posterior extremity, and a third intermediate: there are also two or three smaller and more circular ones, three along the lower edge of the mandibula, and two larger ones along its inferior limb. Opercle with a notch on its posterior margin, close to the ridge. Glands on the upper surface disposed as in the *M. cunnesius*.

Teeth—None apparent in the lips: but on either side of the vomer is a strong, rounded, smooth, transverse ridge.

Fins—The upper margin of the pectoral is in the upper third of the body, and it has an elongated scale at its axil: the fin is pointed, and extends to the tenth scale on the lateral line. First dorsal spines not strong: the membrane rather emarginate; the fin commences on the twenty-first scale from the snout, and on the twelfth of the lateral line: its second spine is midway between the snout and base of caudal fin: its first three spines are of about equal length, the third is weak, and rather more than half as long as the first: an elongated scale extends the whole length of the base of the fin. Ventral spine moderately strong, and nearly as long as the third of the dorsal ones. The second dorsal commences opposite the second ray of the anal, and the twenty-fourth scale of the lateral line. The distance between the two dorsals, equals the anterior margin of the second dorsal, which is twice as high as the posterior; upper edge of fin concave, its last ray double and rather prolonged. Anal slightly in advance of the second dorsal, the third spine rather more than twice as long as the first ray, the last ray being double and longer than the preceding one: its inferior margin concave. Caudal lunated in its posterior fourth.

Scales—Over body and head: some fine ones on the base of the caudal, and between the ventral rays; a few along the bases of the second dorsal, anal, and between their first few rays. A fine longitudinal groove on all those except below the pectoral fin, which have vertical grooves, excepting the three rows in the centre of the abdominal line. The scales on the opercles and subopercles are very thin.

Colours—Silvery, with the summit of head and back bluish green: the fin membrane of the first and second dorsals, caudal, anal, and pectoral pale yellow, dotted with black. The first spine of the dorsal blackish; the spine and the upper half of the first ray of the second dorsal black, and also the margins of the caudal. A black mark in the axil, ventrals white. Iris silvery round the pupil, but dark green towards the orbit.

Not rare at Cochin. Grows to six inches in length.

Habitat—Seas of Malabar and Malaysia.

MUGIL WAIGIENSIS.

MUGIL WAIGIENSIS, *Quoy & Gaim.* Voy. Freyc. Poissons, p. 337, pl. 59, f. 2; *Günther*, Catal. iii. p. 435.

MUGIL MACROLEPIDOTUS, *Cuv. & Val.* xi. p. 134; *Cantor*, Catal. p. 95.

FRESH WATER MULLET.

B. vi. D. 4 | $\frac{1}{8}$. P. 17. V. $\frac{1}{5}$. A. $\frac{3}{8}$. C. 15. L. l. 26-27. L. tr. 8-9.

Length of head $\frac{1}{5}$, of pectoral $\frac{2}{11}$, of caudal $\frac{2}{11}$, of base of first dorsal $\frac{2}{25}$, of base of second dorsal $\frac{1}{14}$, of base of anal $\frac{2}{25}$ of total length. Height of head $\frac{1}{8}$, of body $\frac{1}{5}$, of first dorsal $\frac{1}{10}$, of second dorsal $\frac{1}{7}$, of ventral $\frac{2}{15}$, of anal $\frac{1}{7}$ of total length.

Eyes—Without adipose membranes, horizontal diameter $\frac{2}{9}$, vertical diameter $\frac{2}{11}$ of the length of head, $1\frac{1}{4}$ diameters from end of snout, and 2 diameters apart.

General appearance short and stout. The line of the profile from the snout along the back being almost straight. Head rather compressed. The width of the body is more than the height of the head.

Mouth broad, lips thin, intermaxillaries wide, meeting superiorly at an angle, slightly notched in the centre to receive the knob of the symphysis of the mandibulæ. Maxilla thin, rounded, and angular, apparent under the preorbital. Preorbital irregularly pyramidal, its base being towards the orbit, ending in a point anteriorly: lower margin denticulated, its anterior two-thirds convex, and separated by a deep notch from its external angle which is rounded and denticulated. The inferior angle of the maxilla is perceptible below the angle of the mouth. Interorbital space nearly flat. Intermandibular space broadly lanceolate. On the vertical margin of the preopercle exist three large wide glandular orifices, and a fourth just below the angle. Superiorly from the centre of the orbit there is a line of four of these glands which passes along the upper margin of the opercles, two others go towards the occiput, across which is a concave line of four more. Posterior nostril large and close to the anterior superior margin of the orbit, the anterior one round and close to the margin of the preorbital.

Teeth—Not to be seen in a specimen twelve inches long.

Fins—Pectoral broad, obtuse and situated rather nearer the back than the abdomen, it extends to the eighth scale of the lateral line. Ventral arises under the posterior third of pectoral, its spine strong. Spines of first dorsal strong, the fin is situated nearer to the snout than it is to the base of the caudal: it arises opposite the end of the pectoral on the eighth row of scales of the lateral line, and a deep groove along the back exists for its reception. The second dorsal commences opposite the sixteenth scale of the lateral line, and nearer to the caudal than to the anterior margin of the first dorsal; the fin is highest in front and rounded posteriorly. The anal arises opposite to the second dorsal and corresponds with it. Caudal slightly emarginate.

Scales—Cover body, head, and bases of soft portions of dorsal, anal, and caudal fins; they are large, and the transverse series on the opercle consists of only three rows. On the body they are twice as high as broad, and each has one or two fine longitudinal grooves along its centre; below the pectoral fin some of these grooves run downwards and outwards. An elongated scale is present at the bases of the pectoral and ventral, and also along the side of the dorsal fin.

Colours—Greyish, each scale darkest at its margin, and with a dark raised line along the centre. Fins dark greyish, edged with white. Pectoral nearly black. Eye silvery and greyish above.

Grows to twelve inches in length. Captured during the S. W. monsoon, when it ascends high up the rivers, and is considered by the Natives to be a "fresh water mullet." It is good eating.

Habitat—Red Sea, Seas of India, Malaysia and China to Australia and Polynesia.

* Mugil carinatus.

Mugil carinatus, *Cuv. & Val.* xi. p. 148.

D. 4 | $\frac{1}{8}$. A. $\frac{3}{9}$.

Mouth much depressed: preorbital sloping, and making a very projecting angle on each side of the mouth. The maxilla is visible at the angle of the mouth.

Eyes—It is not stated whether adipose lids are present or absent.

Fins—Small and scaled; the caudal is slightly emarginate.

Colours—Greenish on the back, silvery on the rest of the body.

Grows to three and a half inches in length.

Habitat—Red Sea, Seas of India, Seychelles, and the island of Guam.

Fam. OPHIOCEPHALIDÆ, Günther.

LABYRINTHICI, pt., *Cuvier.*
LABYRINTHIBRANCHII, pt., *Owen.*
OPHIOCEPHALOIDEI, *Bleeker.*

GENUS OPHIOCEPHALUS, *Bloch.*

Branchiostegals five: pseudobranchiæ none. Body elongated, subcylindrical anteriorly. Head depressed, covered superiorly with shield like scales. Cleft of mouth lateral, wide. Gill opening wide, the membrane of both sides connected below the isthmus. A labyrinthiform cavity accessory to the gill cavity for the purpose of retaining water. Villiform teeth on jaws, vomer, and palate, sometimes with larger ones intermixed. One long spineless dorsal and anal fin. Ventral thoracic, six rays, the outer one not branched but articulated at its extremity. Scales usually large. Lateral line abruptly curved or sub-interrupted. An air bladder. Pyloric appendages two.

OPHIOCEPHALUS MARULIUS.

SOWARAH, *Russell*, pl. 163.
OPHIOCEPHALUS MARULIUS, *Ham. Buch.* pp. 65, 367, pl. 17, f. 19; *Cuv. & Val.* vii. p. 432; *Jerdon*, Madras Jour. xv. 1848, p. 146; *Günther*, Catal. iii. p. 478.
OPHIOCEPHALUS GRANDINOSUS, *Cuv. & Val.* vii. p. 434, pl. 203.
OPHIOCEPHALUS LEUCOPUNCTATUS, *Sykes*, Trans. Zool. Soc. ii. p. 352, pl. 60, f. 3.
? OPHIOCEPHALUS PSEUDOMARULIUS, *Günther*, Catal. iii. p. 478 (? *young*).
CHOAREE VERARL, and COORAVOO, *Mal.*

B. v. D. 49-55. P. 18. V. 6. A. 31-36. C. 14. L. l. 59-64. L. tr. $\frac{6\text{-}9}{9\text{-}6}$.

Length of head $\frac{1}{4}$, of caudal $\frac{3}{19}$, of base of dorsal $\frac{1}{19}$, of base of anal $\frac{1}{3}$ of total length. Height of head $\frac{1}{10}$, of body $\frac{1}{7}$, of dorsal fin in front portion $\frac{2}{33}$, in posterior portion $\frac{1}{10}$, of anal fin in front portion $\frac{1}{19}$, in posterior portion $\frac{1}{10}$, of ventral $\frac{1}{11}$ of total length.

Eyes—Situated laterally, but a small portion on upper surface of the head, and they look upwards and outwards. Diameter $\frac{1}{8}$ length of head, 1 diameter from end of snout, nearly 2 diameters apart.

Head depressed and widest opposite the opercles, where it equals the height of the body. Body elongated with rather compressed sides. Cheeks slightly bulging. Cleft of mouth wide. Upper jaw rather protrusible. Maxilla extends half the length of the orbit behind its posterior margin. Between the orbit and the angle of the preopercle are a series of from ten to eleven very irregular scales. Opercle terminating in a bluntish point, and having about five transverse series of scales. Lower jaw flat below, with a knob at the symphysis. Posterior nostril just in advance of, and inferior to the orbit.

Teeth—Numerous and villiform in jaws, vomer, and palate. In lower jaw they are most numerous in the centre, whilst along each ramus there exists a single row of larger teeth posterior to the villiform ones.

Fins—Dorsal commences over the pectoral, and the ventral below its anterior third. Pectoral does not quite extend to opposite the commencement of the anal, which arises under about the seventeenth dorsal ray. There is a very short portion of the tail finless between the termination of the vertical fins and the commencement of the caudal, but it is rather longer below than above. Dorsal fin lowest in front, its extremity being twice the height of its anterior portion, the same also obtains in the anal. Pectoral and caudal rounded.

Scales—Cover body, opercles, and the summit of the head. Between the orbits and the posterior margin of the preopercles is a large irregularly quadrangular scale, with a semicircular one posterior to it; and anteriorly from its outer third a very irregularly shaped scale enlarging exteriorly; the whole of the scales on the head are of very irregular shapes, being lineated with roughened tubercular lines, and having numerous glandular openings.

Lateral line—In a groove along each side, it first passes along about sixteen rows, then bends downwards along two rows, and from thence passes straight to the centre of the caudal, but in this deflection the scales alter so much that the second portion of the lateral line is only one scale below where the upper portion would have been had its course been unchanged. The rows however are irregular, and not the same in all the specimens examined.

Colours—These vary with the waters in which it is captured. Back greenish grey, passing downwards in five or six digitations below the lateral line. Abdomen (when from clear and rather shallow streams) of a bright orange, with some dusky markings at the bases of the scales. On the posterior third of the body, of the dorsal and anal fins, and on the whole of the caudal are some fine pearly white spots. Dorsal, caudal, anal and pectoral grey: ventral orange.

In some specimens, especially in the young, the dorsal fin is barred, and there is an ocellus at its extremity: the same also sometimes exists on the root of the caudal. In the very young an orange stripe runs from the eye to the caudal fin, whilst the dorsal fin has pale stripes directed backwards.

This is considered the best of the genus for the table, because as it resides in streams it rarely has the muddy flavour of the *O. striatus*.

It grows to about two feet in length.

Habitat—Rivers of India, Ceylon and China.

OPHIOCEPHALUS DIPLOGRAMME, Plate X.

OPHIOCEPHALUS DIPLOGRAMME, *Day*, Proc. Zool. Soc. 1865, p. 36.

B. v. D. 43. P. 15. V. 6. A. 27. C. 15. L. l. 84. L. tr. $\frac{7\text{-}8}{13\text{-}12}$.

Length of head about $\frac{2}{7}$, of pectoral $\frac{1}{10}$, of base of dorsal $\frac{1}{2}$, of base of anal $\frac{2}{7}$, of base of caudal $\frac{2}{7}$ of total length. Height of body $\frac{1}{8}$, of head $\frac{1}{10}$, of dorsal $\frac{1}{16}$, of ventral $\frac{1}{10}$, of anal $\frac{1}{16}$ of total length.

Eyes—Diameter $\frac{2}{11}$ of length of head, 1 diameter from end of snout, nearly $1\frac{1}{2}$ diameters apart.

Body anteriorly subcylindrical, head depressed above, and laterally: orbit close to profile.

Cleft of mouth wide, the maxilla extends to below the posterior third of orbit: lower jaw the longest. Thirteen rows of scales between orbit and angle of preopercle. Interorbital space flat, covered with six rows of irregularly rounded scales, having raised margins. Nostrils rather wide apart, the superior the largest. A spinous process on either side of the occipital space. The labyrinthiform cavity above the gills large.

Teeth—Several rows of sharp villiform teeth in lower jaw, with some larger ones internal to them. Some bands of sharp teeth in upper jaw, but without larger ones. The same on vomer and palate, interspersed posteriorly with larger ones.

Colours—Back grey, sides scarlet, abdomen white. A black band passes through the eye direct to the upper half of caudal, a second from the angle of the mouth to the lower half of caudal. Dorsal grey. Caudal scarlet, with two black horizontal stripes. Ventral and anal yellowish, with dark grey bases. Pectoral yellowish.

A single specimen was captured at the mouth of the Cochin river, it was nearly four inches long. Its small scales and two spines might probably constitute this a sub-genus.

Habitat—Malabar.

OPHIOCEPHALUS STRIATUS.

OPHIOCEPHALUS STRIATUS, *Bloch*, t. 359; *Cuv. & Val.* vii. p. 417, pl. 202, 206; *Cantor*, Catal. p. 92; *Jerdon*, Madras Journal, xv. p. 146; *Günther*, Catal. iii. p. 474.
MUTTAH, *Russell*, pl. 162.
OPHIOCEPHALUS WRAHL, *Ham. Buch.* pp. 60, 367, pl. 31, f. 17; *McClelland*, Calcutta Journal of Natural History, ii. p. 575.
OPHIOCEPHALUS CHENA, *Ham. Buch.* pp. 62, 367.
? OPHIOCEPHALUS PLANICEPS, *Cuv. & Val.* vii. p. 424.
VERARL, and WRAHL, *Mal.* MORRUL, *Hindustani.*

B. v. D. 37-40. P. 17. V. 6. A. 23-26. C. 13. L. l. 51-57. L. tr. $\frac{5-7}{9-7}$.

Length of head $\frac{2}{7}$, of pectoral $\frac{2}{13}$, of caudal $\frac{1}{6}$, of base of dorsal $\frac{1}{2}$, of base of anal $\frac{1}{3}$ of total length. Height of head $\frac{1}{8}$, of body $\frac{1}{5}$, of dorsal $\frac{1}{12}$, of anal $\frac{1}{12}$, of ventral $\frac{1}{9}$ of the total length.

Eyes—Situated near the profile. Diameter $\frac{1}{7}$ of length of head, 1 diameter from end of snout, $1\frac{3}{4}$ diameters apart.

Body long, sub-cylindrical, head depressed, body laterally compressed, wider opposite opercle, where it about equals the height of the body. Under surface of the head flat: cheeks rather inflated.

Mouth obtuse, cleft wide, maxilla extending the width of the orbit behind it; upper jaw slightly protrusible, wider than the lower, which is rather the longest. A tubercle at the symphysis of the lower jaw, and a glandular orifice just behind and below it. Four clusters of glandular openings along the inferior margin of the lower jaw, and many other similar clusters in various other places on the body and head. Interorbital space flat, and covered with large polygonal scales. Between the eye and the angle of the preopercle are eight rows of scales. The opercle ends in an obtuse point. The opening of the posterior nostril are just in front of, and above the eyes.

Teeth—Numerous, sharp and pointed in jaws, vomer, and palate, with some large curved ones along the sides and in the posterior row on the lower jaw.

Fins—The dorsal commences just over the pectoral, and terminates slightly posterior to the termination of the anal: ventral arises opposite the fourth ray of the dorsal, and the anal beneath the thirteenth dorsal ray. Dorsal rays weak, membrane rather deeply cleft. Pectoral rounded, and does not extend so far as the origin of the anal. Ventral small. Anal the same shape as the dorsal. Caudal rounded.

Scales—Cover body and head: those on the body are irregularly circular and horizontally lineated; whilst on the head they are semicircular, and on its vertex irregularly shaped, one large one existing midway between the orbits. Several glands open on some of the scales.

Lateral line—Consists of short central, bifurcating tubes on each scale; at first it is on the fifth row, but opposite the twelfth dorsal ray it bends down to the seventh, from whence it proceeds direct to the centre of the caudal fin.

PLATE X.

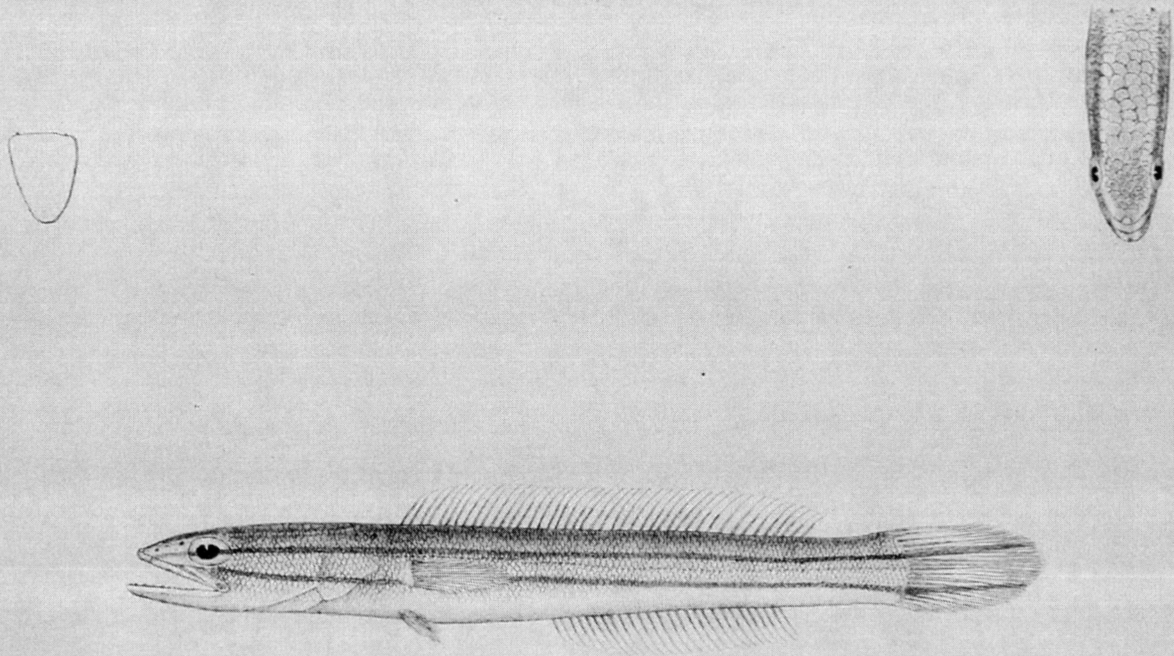

F. Day, del. et sculp.

OPHIOCEPHALUS DIPLOGRAMME

Colours—Dark greyish above, dirty white beneath, with bands of grey passing vertically from the sides on to the abdomen: besides these streaks, there are some small dark grey spots intermingled. Cheeks and lower surface of the mouth streaked and spotted with grey. Ventral white, spotted with black or dark grey. Anal deep grey, with a line of greyish white at its base, which is also spotted.

In a young specimen, captured June 17th, 1863, the posterior margin of the dorsal has a large black ocellus, and an orange tinge, whilst the bands of the body are continued on to the dorsal and anal fins.

These fish are said to attain three feet in length, and inhabit all stagnant pieces of water and rivers, whilst their young may be found in every paddy field. They are able to progress to some distance along the ground, especially in moist places, and thus readily change their locality at the commencement of the monsoon. In progression they move by the aid of the pectoral and caudal fins. Owing to the cavity, capable of retaining water which is accessary to the gill cavity, they can live many hours out of their native element. I am informed that *Captain Mitchell* of the Madras Museum endeavoured in 1864 to try experimentally whether, if the *O. striatus*, the *anabas scandens*, and the *saccobranchus singio* were placed in suitable localities, and the superincumbent water were gradually removed, they would endeavour to force themselves into the mud beneath. Several inches of soft mud from a neighbouring tank was put inside a large vessel, and this was covered by a few inches of water. Here the fish were placed, and the water was permitted to gradually drain away, until only mud remained. All the fish died without attempting to bury themselves, the *O. striatus* being the last retaining vitality, and they rubbed for themselves a depression into which water drained whilst any remained, and then they also died without attempting to force their way into the mud.

This fish is very good eating, but muddy in some pieces of water. It is very voracious, and takes a bait freely.

Habitat—Fresh waters of India, Ceylon, Burmah, Siam, Malaysia, China, and the Philippine Islands.

OPHIOCEPHALUS GACHUA.

OPHIOCEPHALUS GACHUA, *Ham. Buch.* pp. 68, 367, pl. 21, f. 21; *Günther*,* Catal. iii. p. 471.

* *Dr. Günther* is of opinion that the *O. aurantiacus, Ham. Buchanan*, is identical with this species, but considering the latter comes from a mountain stream, whilst the *O. gachua* is from the low country, and the colours widely differ, I have not inserted it amongst the present synonyms, but would suggest that it is a subject for further investigation. In justice to the researches of that talented naturalist, *Dr. Hamilton Buchanan*, I would observe that *Dr. Günther* is mistaken in asserting of this fish (pl. 23, f. 22) that "in fact the drawing is taken from the *Hardwicke* collection," for the work of the former preceded that of the latter by eight years; whilst he died a year before the commencement of the publication of "Illustrations of Indian Zoology." It can hardly be considered a good reason that because the specimen does not now exist in *Dr. Buchanan's* collection, that he never possessed it, especially as he distinctly states, "I found it in a pure mountain stream near Goyalpara, in the N. E. frontier of Bengal." Any one desirous of ascertaining how the two sets of drawings became intermixed may do so by referring to *Dr. McClelland's* paper in the *Asiatic Researches*, xix. p. 218, et seq., and *Sir John Richardson's* "Report on the Ichthyology of the Seas of China and Japan," in the report of the fifteenth meeting of "the British Association for the Advancement of Science," p. 188.

KORAH MOTTAH, *Russell*, pl. 49.
OPHIOCEPHALUS CORA-MOTA, *Cuv. & Val.* vii. p. 414.
OPHIOCEPHALUS MARGINATUS, *Cuv. & Val.* vii. p. 411; *Jerdon*, Madras Journal, xv. p. 145.
OPHIOCEPHALUS FUSCUS, *Cuv. & Val.* vii. p. 414; *Jerdon*, ibid. p. 149.
OPHIOCEPHALUS KELARTII, *Günther*, Catal. ii. p. 472 (*? young*).
KURAVU, *Mal.*

B. v. D. 32-33. P. 13. V. 6. A. 21-23. C. 11. L. l. 40-45. L. tr. $\frac{4}{7}$.

Length of head $\frac{1}{4}$, of pectoral $\frac{1}{6}$, of caudal $\frac{1}{6}$, of base of dorsal $\frac{1}{2}$, of base of anal $\frac{1}{4}$ of the total length. Height of head $\frac{1}{8}$, of body $\frac{1}{6}$, of dorsal $\frac{1}{12}$, of ventral $\frac{1}{20}$, of anal $\frac{1}{12}$ of the total length.

Eyes—Close to profile directed upwards and outwards. Diameter $\frac{2}{13}$ of length of head, 1 diameter from end of snout, 2 diameters apart anteriorly, rather more posteriorly.

Body elongated and compressed, head depressed, cheeks puffed out, their transverse width being rather more than the height of the body.

Mouth deeply cleft, rather rounded anteriorly, lips fleshy: the maxilla extends to beneath the posterior margin of the orbit. The posterior nostril round, and situated close to the anterior superior margin of the orbit, the anterior close to the snout, tubular, and its exposed width equal to half that of the orbit. Two glands on lower surface of mandibula, the posterior the largest: some circular glandular orifices at posterior margin of the orbit, also on the cheeks and various other parts of the head.

Teeth—Villiform, in both jaws, with several rows opposite the symphysis, the internal of which is rather conical and longer than the others. Those on vomer and palate villiform, and in one crescentic band, with some larger ones interspersed, especially on the vomer: the width of this band varies in different specimens, whilst in some the larger teeth on the palate are wanting.

Fins—The pectoral arises a short distance posterior to the opercle, and extends to opposite the commencement of the anal: the minute ventral is situated under the middle third of the pectoral, whilst the dorsal commences opposite the origin of the pectoral. Dorsal low, parallel to the back, and ceasing five scales anterior to the base of the caudal: anal parallel to the abdomen, and ceasing eight scales anterior to the base of the caudal, which latter fin is wedge-shaped, sometimes rounded, and in the young is one-fifth of the total length.

Scales—Broad and irregular on the summit of head, higher than wide on the body. There are three rows of scales between the anterior, and four between the posterior margins of the orbit: the central scale on the head has four in the mesial line anterior to it. Five rows between angle of orbit and that of the preopercle. Lower jaw with a long oval scale, beneath and opposite to the end of the maxilla.

Lateral line—In single elevated tubes, the scale being also emarginate and with two or three small orifices at its base. It passes along the upper third of the body until it arrives opposite the last quarter of the pectoral where it bends downwards to the centre of the body and is so continued to the caudal.

Colours—Differ most materially in fishes of this species in accordance with the waters in which they reside, and the season of the year. Those in paddy fields where the water is clear are light and barred, if the water be muddy they are dark, but some taken out of a well were of a dark greenish with orange margins to their fins.

They are generally greenish, abdomen dirty green barred with darker stripes. Dorsal, caudal, and anal tipped with reddish orange. Pectoral barred, and having a black base and a slight tinge of red. Eyes orange.

In the monsoon time they become of a dark brown: the orange markings are deeper and wider, the under surface of the throat and chest bluish: and some irregular bars exist on the lower fourth of the dorsal fin.

In the young (? *O. Kelaartii, Günther*) the colours are greyish brown with superiorly lighter bars running from behind forwards to the lateral line, and from before backwards below it. The whole of the head with fine black spots. Dorsal grey irregularly barred, and with a large ocellus having a white margin covering the last five dorsal rays. Caudal barred. Pectoral and ventral immaculate.

This fish grows to one foot in length in Bengal, but not to above six inches in Malabar. It is found in almost every pond of fresh water. It takes a bait freely, and is eaten by the Natives.

Habitat—Fresh waters of India and Ceylon.

Ophiocephalus punctatus.

Ophiocephalus punctatus, *Bloch*, t. 358; *Cuv. & Val.* vii. p. 404; *Jerdon*, Madras Journal, xv. p. 145; *Günther*, Catal. iii. p. 469.

Ophiocephalus latus, *Ham. Buch.* pp. 63, 637, pl. 34, f. 18.

Ophiocephalus Indicus, *McClelland*, Cal. J. N. H., ii. p. 533.

B. v. D. 29-31. P. 16. V. 6. A. 31. C. 12. L. l. 40. L. tr. $\frac{4}{9}$.

Length of head $\frac{2}{7}$, of pectoral $\frac{1}{7}$, of caudal nearly $\frac{1}{6}$ of the total length. Height of head $\frac{1}{7}$, of body $\frac{1}{6}$, of ventral $\frac{1}{9}$ of the total length.

Eyes—Close to profile, diameter $\frac{1}{6}$ of the length of the head, 1 diameter from end of snout, more than 1 diameter apart.

Body elongated, cylindrical, compressed posteriorly: head depressed, cheeks puffed out, its transverse width three-fifths of its length.

Mouth widely cleft, rather rounded anteriorly, and the maxilla extending to nearly as far as the posterior margin of the orbit, and slightly protractile. Opercle ends in an obtuse angle. There are five rows of scales between the eye and the angle of the preopercle which is rounded. The anterior nasal orifice is furnished with a short fleshy tentacle. Numerous well marked glandular orifices exist on the scales of the head: there are three a little behind the eyes, three in a vertical line on the preopercle, and three larger ones on each ramus of the lower jaw.

Teeth—Numerous and villiform, with a posterior row of four or five conical ones on either side of the lower jaw, villiform ones on vomer and palatine bones.

Fins—The ventrals arise very near together and slightly posterior to the pectoral. The pectoral rounded and extends to the origin of the anal fin. The dorsal commences above the origin of the ventrals and is continued nearly to the caudal, the finless portion of the tail equal to one-fifteenth of the length of the fish: the length of the dorsal rays is nearly the same and equals about half the height of the body. The anal commences opposite the anterior third of the dorsal. Caudal rounded.

Scales—Large, about one quarter longer than they are high. Those on the head are irregular in their shape.

Lateral line—Is nearly straight, with the exception of a curve behind the end of the pectoral fin. Its anterior portion is in the upper third of the body, its last portion central, it is marked by a straight elevation along the centre of each scale.

Colours—Back dirty green, fading to yellowish white on the abdomen. A dark stripe extends from the eye to the tail, and from it several irregular bands pass towards the back, these are most numerous in those taken in dirty water. These markings are often wanting in the young. There are also some spots along the abdominal surface and on the dorsal and anal fins. Pectorals grey. Ventrals whitish and without spots.

Grows to one foot in length, and is esteemed for eating by the Natives.

Habitat—Fresh waters of India, Ceylon, and Burmah.

Fam. FISTULARIDÆ, *Müll.*

AULOSTOMATOIDEI, et FISTULAROIDEI, *Bleeker*.

GENUS FISTULARIA, *Lin.* SP.

SOLENOSTOMUS, SP. *Klein & Gronow.*

CANNORHYNCHUS, *Cantor.*

Branchiostegals, five: pseudobranchiæ. Body elongated, depressed, anterior bones of skull elongated forming a long depressed tube which ends in a narrow mouth, jaws slightly cleft, nearly horizontal. Eyes lateral. Teeth small. One dorsal of moderate length and resembling the anal. Ventrals abdominal with six rays. Caudal forked, the two middle rays ending in long filamentous prolongations. Scales absent. Lateral line continuous. Air bladder large. Pyloric appendages in small numbers. Intestinal tract short.

FISTULARIA SERRATA.

FISTULARIA SERRATA, *Cuvier*, Reg. Anim.; *Günther*, Catal. iii. p. 533.

GOORUM, *Russell*, pl. 173.

CANNORHYNCHUS IMMACULATUS, *Cantor*, Catal. p. 211.

B. vii. D. 13-17. P. 15. V. 6. A. 14-15. C. 2 + 6 | 2 | 6 + 2.

Length of head $\frac{1}{3}$, of pectoral $\frac{1}{26}$, of caudal without including its prolongation $\frac{1}{22}$, of caudal including its prolongation $\frac{1}{4}$, of base of dorsal $\frac{1}{30}$, of base of anal $\frac{1}{30}$ of the total length not including the prolongation of its caudal fin. Height of head $\frac{1}{36}$, of body $\frac{1}{30}$, of dorsal $\frac{1}{20}$, of anal $\frac{1}{18}$, of ventral $\frac{1}{45}$ of the total length not including the prolongation of its caudal fin.

Eyes—Close to upper profile. Horizontal diameter $\frac{1}{12}$, vertical diameter $\frac{1}{20}$ of the length of the head, 9 horizontal diameters from end of snout, nearly 1 horizontal diameter apart.

Body cylindrical, with an elongated flattened tubular snout.

Orifice of mouth oblique, situated at the anterior tenth of the snout, lower jaw the longest, and having a tubercle at the symphysis: the posterior half of the external margin of the snout strongly denticulated, the most posterior denticulations being the longest and widest apart. Some sharp denticulations along the anterior and posterior margins of the orbit, and the anterior margin of which is extended into a sharp spine. There are two grooves along the upper surface of the snout which is elevated at its extremity. Some elevated, radiating lines commence from a short distance in front of the anterior margin of the orbit, and coalesce with those from the opposite side at the anterior fifth of the snout. Behind the orbits are irregular radiating lines coalescing on the summit of the head with those from the opposite side. Opercle also with radiating raised lines, and above it a longitudinal serrated ridge. An elevated, sharp, bony, lateral ridge extends from the dorsal to the side of the caudal, it is most indistinct anteriorly.

Teeth—Villiform, unequal, small in jaws, also on palatines, and from four to six on the vomer.

Fins—Pectoral rounded, it arises just behind opercle. Dorsal in posterior fourth of the distance from the orbit to the base of the caudal, its sixth ray the longest, its upper margin concave. Anal opposite the dorsal and of the same shape. Caudal lobed, with its two central rays prolonged into long filiform processes.

Lateral line—Commences above opercle, it consists of a number of linear tubes, deeply cleft at both ends, which behind the dorsal fin change to short, bony, spine-like ridges, as already described.

Colours—Reddish brown above, becoming greyish on the sides, and white on the abdomen. Numerous fine black points exist along the back. A silvery white band borders the lateral line. Fins transparent, caudal filament brownish olive. Iris golden round the pupil. *Dr. Rüppell* observed a lateral series of blue spots in some of his specimens.

Grows to two feet in length.

Habitat—Seas of India. From the Coast of Mosambique to the Seas of China, and New Holland.

Fam. MASTACEMBELIDÆ, Günther.

SCOMBEROIDEI, pt. *Cuvier.*
NOTACANTHI, pt. *Müll.*
RHYNCHOBDELLOIDEI, *Bleeker.*

GENUS MASTACEMBELUS, *Cuv. & Val.*

Branchiostegals, six: pseudobranchiæ. Body elongated, eel-shaped. Eyes lateral. Head elongated, the upper jaw terminating in a soft, moveable, fleshy appendage which is not transversely striated inferiorly. Cleft of mouth narrow. Preopercle generally with spinous teeth at its angle. Dorsal fin long, the anterior portion composed of free spines. No ventrals. Anal generally with three spines. Dorsal, caudal, and anal continuous. Teeth minute. Scales small. Air bladder present. Pyloric appendages two.

MASTACEMBLUS ARMATUS.

MACROGNATHUS ARMATUS, *Lacép.* ii. p. 286; *Ham. Buch.* pp. 28, 364, pl. 37, f. 6.
MASTACEMBLUS ARMATUS, *Cuv. & Val.* viii. p. 456, pl. 240; *Sykes*, Trans. Zool. Soc. ii. p. 350, pl. 60, f. 2; *Günther*, Catal. iii. p. 542.
MASTACEMBLUS PONTICERIANUS, *Cuv. & Val.* viii. p. 460.
MASTACEMBLUS MARMORATUS, *Cuv. & Val.* viii. p. 461; *Jerdon*, Madras Journ. xv. p. 147.
MACROGNATHUS UNDULATUS et HAMILTONII, *McClelland*, Cal. J. N. H. iv. pp. 393, 398, pl. 22, f. 1.

B. vi. D. 35-39 | 74-87. P. 23. A. 3 | 79-87. C. 15. Cæc. pylor. 2. Vert. $\frac{39}{53}$.

Length of head $\frac{3}{22}$, of pectoral $\frac{1}{26}$, of caudal $\frac{1}{20}$, of base of first dorsal $\frac{4}{10}$, of base of second dorsal $\frac{1}{3}$, of base of anal a little more than $\frac{1}{3}$ of total length. Height of head $\frac{1}{17}$, of body $\frac{1}{8}$, of first dorsal about $\frac{1}{46}$, of second dorsal $\frac{1}{37}$, of anal $\frac{1}{37}$ of total length.

Eyes—Horizontal diameter $\frac{1}{10}$, vertical diameter $\frac{1}{16}$ of length of head, $2\frac{1}{2}$ diameters from end of snout, rather more than $\frac{1}{2}$ a horizontal diameter apart.

Body elongated and eel-like, laterally compressed, head pointed.

Mouth rather oblique, cleft narrow, jaws not protractile, the upper the longest, with a soft elongated snout trilobed at its end, and about equal to one diameter and a quarter of the orbit in length; lips fleshy. Posterior margin of the maxilla extends to rather behind the anterior margin of the orbit. Opercle rounded posteriorly, without any spine. Preopercle with the posterior border short and rather vertical; the angle and lower limb forming an oblique curve; at the angle there are two sharp spines directed backwards, the superior nearly twice as long as the inferior. Nostrils large and opposite the centre of the orbit. Two small spines beneath the orbit.

Teeth—Villiform, and in several sharp rows.

Fins—First dorsal commences over the posterior third of the pectoral, and the anal rather in front of the second dorsal and continuous with the caudal. Pectoral short and rounded. The first dorsal consists of a series of sharp spines,—connected in their posterior lower halves by a short membrane,—increasing very gradually in length from the first to the last, which is strong, rounded, and nearly as long as the rays of the second dorsal. The second dorsal is continuous with the caudal and consists of branched rays. Caudal with a square base and a rather rounded extremity. Anus midway between the posterior border of the opercle and the base of the caudal, behind it there are two spines, the first being short, the second strong and tapering, one third longer than the last dorsal spine, they can be received into a sheath: anteriorly, and nearer to the commencement of the anal fin, there is a third very short sharp spine hidden in the flesh.

Scales—Very minute, they cover the opercles and head.

Lateral line—Nearly straight.

Colours—Dark green, marbled in about twenty stripes, and with a yellowish tinge; the anterior portion of the abdomen dirty white, and the under surface of the throat white. Caudal and pectoral fins barred.

Air vessel simple, lengthened and pointed at both extremities.

Common in the rivers of Malabar, and is good eating, especially when curried. It is dangerous to handle on account of its spines.

Grows to two feet and upwards in length.

Habitat—Fresh waters of India, Ceylon, and China.

Mastacemblus Güntheri. Plate XI.

Mastacemblus Güntheri, *Day*, Proc. Zool. Soc. 1865, p. 37.

B. vi. D. 27-28 | 60-64. P. 15. A. 3 | 62-64. C. 9.

Length of head $\frac{1}{7}$, of pectoral $\frac{1}{23}$, of caudal $\frac{1}{17}$, of base of hard dorsal $\frac{2}{5}$, of soft dorsal $\frac{1}{3}$, of anal $\frac{2}{5}$ of total length. Height of head $\frac{1}{23}$, of body $\frac{1}{9}$, of soft dorsal $\frac{1}{23}$, of anal $\frac{1}{12}$ of total length.

Eyes—Diameter $\frac{1}{10}$ length of head, rather more than 1 diameter apart, and 4 diameters from end of snout.

Upper jaw longer than the lower. The soft snout extends one tenth of the length of the

PLATE XI.

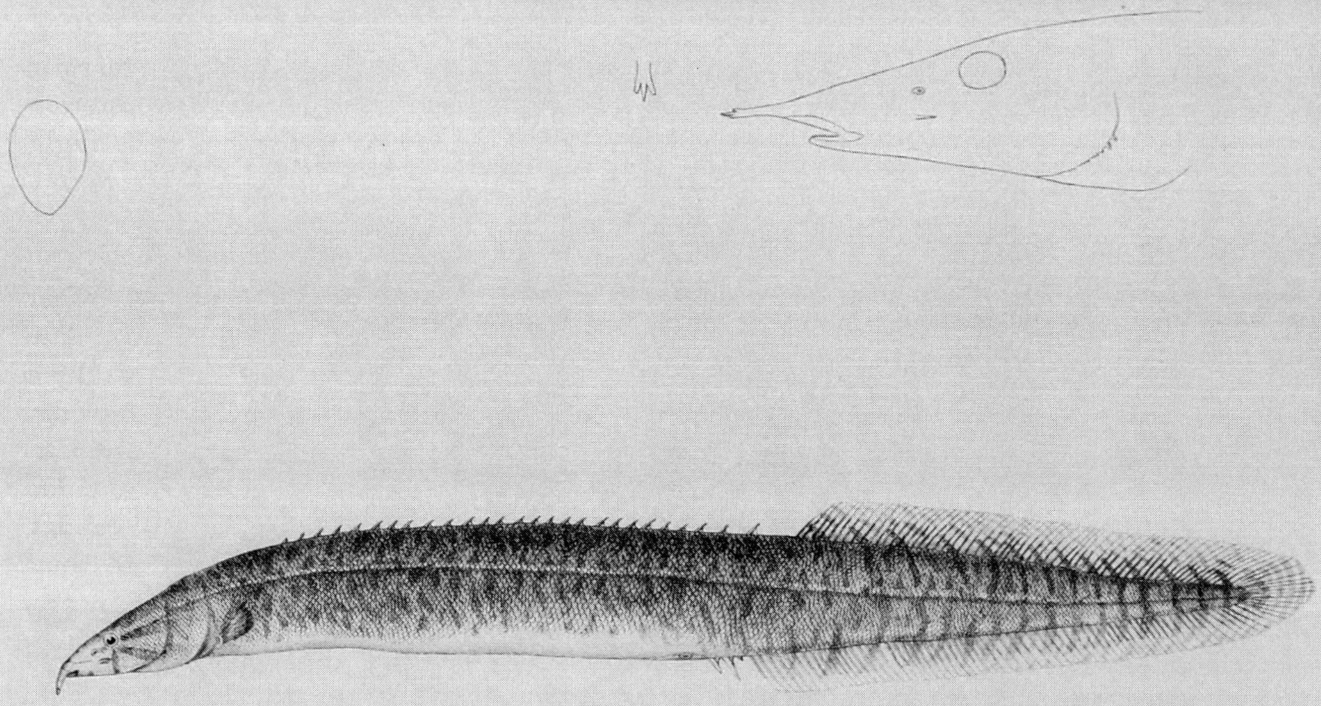

F. Day. del. et sculp.

MASTACEMBLUS GÜNTHERI

head beyond the end of the jaw. Cleft of mouth small, and extending about half-way to the orbit. Preopercle with two spines at its angle directed backwards and downwards, and some fine serratures along its lower limb. A rather long, strong, sharp, and erectile preorbital spine.

Teeth—Several rows of sharply pointed teeth, directed backwards, in both upper and lower jaws.

Fins—Dorsal spines strong, short and sharp, commencing about the termination of the first fifth of the body. Soft dorsal, caudal and anal united. Anal spines strong, the central one the longest and strongest, the third nearly hidden; they can be laid flat in a kind of sheath.

Scales—Cover the whole of the head, including the interorbital space, and to the end of the snout. There are thirteen rows between the orbit and the angle of the preopercle.

Lateral line—As in the last species.

Colours—Greenish brown. A yellowish white streak passes from just above the eye, along the lateral line to the centre of the caudal. Abdomen from vent to head of dull yellowish white, with a number of blotchy markings extending on to it from the sides. Opercles greyish brown, and the throat of the same colour. Preopercle of a lighter tint, and the lower jaw of a dirty white. Soft portion of the dorsal dotted with brown, and with fourteen irregular blotches along its base, extending on to the back. Caudal with a black bar at its base, and four or five lighter ones between that and its extremity. Anal irregularly spotted.

Very common in the paddy fields and in the backwater at Trichoor.

Grows to seven inches in length. Is good eating.

Habitat—Malabar.

ORDER.—PHARYNGOGNATHI.

SUB-ORDER.—PHARYNGOGNATHI ACANTHOPTERYGII.

Fam. POMACENTRIDÆ, Günther.

SCIÆNOIDEI, pt. *Cuvier.*
LABROIDEI CTENOIDEI, *Müll.*
CTENOLABRIDÆ, *Owen.*

GENUS GLYPHIDODON, *Lacép.*

EUSCHISTODUS et HYPSYPOPS, sp. *Gill.*

Branchiostegals, five or six: pseudobranchiæ. Body short, more or less compressed. Eyes lateral. Cleft of mouth small. Preopercle entire. Teeth compressed and in a single row, sometimes every alternate one being similar. One dorsal, with the spinous as well developed or more so than the soft portion. Two spines to anal fin. Ventrals thoracic, with one spine and five rays. Scales of moderate size over body and head. The lateral line either ceases below the posterior portion of the dorsal fin, or is continued in the form of small circular orifices. Air bladder present. Pyloric appendages three.

GLYPHIDODON COCHINENSIS. Plate XII.

GLYPHIDODON COCHINENSIS, *Day*, Proc. Zool. Soc. 1865, p. 38.

B. v. D. $\frac{13}{11}$. P. 15. V. $\frac{1}{5}$. A. $\frac{2}{10}$. L. l. 28. L. tr. $\frac{3}{8}$.

Length of head $\frac{2}{11}$, of pectoral $\frac{1}{6}$, of caudal $\frac{1}{3}$, of base of dorsal $\frac{2}{5}$, of base of anal $\frac{2}{11}$ of total length. Height of head $\frac{2}{11}$, of body $\frac{2}{6}$, of hard dorsal $\frac{2}{15}$, of soft dorsal $\frac{2}{6}$, of base of caudal $\frac{1}{9}$, of ventral $\frac{1}{6}$, of anal $\frac{1}{8}$ of the total length.

Eyes—Diameter $\frac{2}{7}$ length of head, $\frac{3}{4}$ of a diameter from end of snout, 1 diameter apart.

Body ovoid and compressed, the width at the shoulder being scarcely equal to half its height: profile from the snout to the dorsal fin convex. Soft portions of dorsal, anal, and caudal fins much elongated.

Maxilla extends to opposite the anterior margin of the orbit: jaws of equal length. Preopercle entire; posterior limb slightly oblique, and half as long again as the inferior, which is horizontal, the angle being rounded. Sub- and interopercles entire. Opercle ending in a flat moderately strong spine a little below the level of the lower margin of the orbit; a second exists a short distance above, and in one specimen a third about an equal distance below the central one. Nostrils a short distance apart, and near the anterior surface of the orbit slightly above its mesial line: the posterior is round, the anterior transversely oval. All the opercles and the interorbital space scaled. Suprascapular, scapular, and humeral bones entire.

Teeth—In a single flattened and compressed row, decreasing in size from the centre of the jaws to their circumference.

Fins—Dorsal commences opposite the end of the opercle: pectoral slightly behind: and the ventral a little more posteriorly: anal begins about opposite the tenth dorsal spine. Spinous portion of dorsal occupies three-fourths of the base of the fin, its spines moderately strong: interspinous membrane slightly longer than the spines, and deeply notched; soft portion elongated, first spine one third shorter than the second, from whence they gradually increase to the last, which is two and a half times as long as the first. Pectoral rounded. Ventral spine moderately strong, two thirds the length of the anterior rays, the first of which is prolonged. First spine of anal

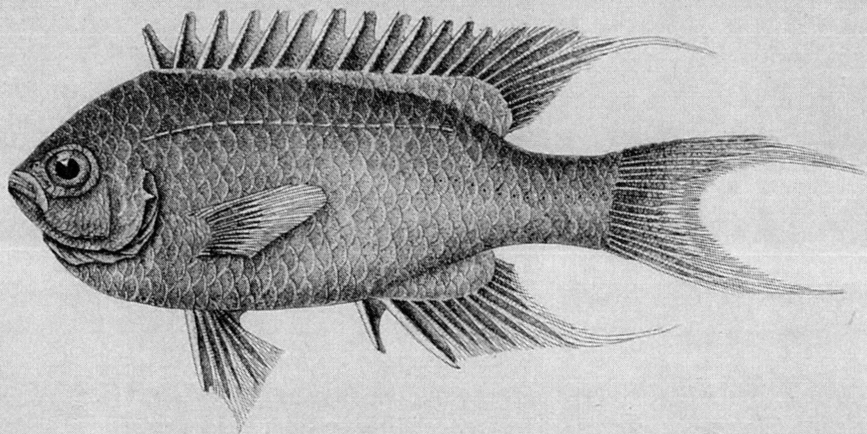

F. Day, del. et sculp.

GLYPHIDODON COCHINENSIS

half the height of the second, the soft rays are prolonged. Caudal deeply lunated and the outer rays much prolonged.

Scales—Greatest diameter from above downwards; some of them are continued over the soft portions of the dorsal, anal, and the commencement of the caudal fins.

Lateral line—At first passes along the third scale, on which it is continued for about eighteen, when it apparently ceases opposite the end of the dorsal fin, but is in reality continued on the sixth row, in the form of round glandular cavities, in the centre of each scale.

Colours—Of a deep purplish black: the margins of some of the scales having a whitish shade. It is lightest on the abdomen. Pectoral fins not so deeply stained as the others. Eyes dark hazel.

Only three specimens were observed at Cochin, and they were all captured in one net. Grows to about four inches in length.

Habitat—Cochin on the Malabar Coast.

Fam. LABRIDÆ, Cuvier.

LABROIDEI CYCLOIDEI, *Müll.*
CYCLOLABRIDÆ, *Owen.*

Sub-Fam. JULIDINA, Günther.

XIPHOCHILUS, *Bleeker.*

GENUS PLATYGLOSSUS, *Klein*, SP.

HALICHÆRES, SP. *Rüppell.*
JULIS, SP. *Cuv. & Val.*
PLATYGLOSSUS, HALICHÆRES, MACROPHARYNGODON, GUNTHERIA, et HEMITANTOGA, *Bleeker.*
CHÆROJULIS, *Gill.*

Branchiostegals, five or six: pseudobranchiæ. Body oblong and compressed. Eyes lateral. Cleft of mouth small. Only one inferior pharyngeal bone without median suture. Teeth conical on jaws with a posterior canine. One dorsal fin, the spinous portion as well developed or more so than the soft: soft anal similar to soft dorsal. Ventral thoracic with one spine and five rays. Scales cycloid and of moderate size, none (or a very few) on the head. Lateral line continuous, forming a curve opposite end of dorsal fin. Air bladder present. Pyloric appendages none.

PLATYGLOSSUS NIGRESCENS.

LABRUS NIGRESCENS, *Bloch Schn.* p. 263.
SAHNEE MOIA, *Russell*, pl. 120.
JULIS DUSSUMIERI, *Cuv. & Val.* xiii. p. 476, pl. 387; *Cantor*, Catal. p. 236.
HELICHÆRES NIGRESCENS, *Bleeker*, Atlas Icthyologique des Indes Orientales Néêrlandaises, i. p. 118, t. 37, f. 4.
PLATYGLOSSUS DUSSUMIERI, *Günther*, Catal. iv. p. 143.
KULLARAY MEEN, *Mal.*

B. vi. D. $\frac{9}{12}$. P. 15. V. $\frac{1}{5}$. A. $\frac{3}{12}$. C. 15. L. l. 29. L. tr. $\frac{3}{10}$.

Length of head $\frac{1}{4}$, of pectoral $\frac{1}{6}$, of caudal $\frac{2}{11}$, of base of dorsal $\frac{1}{2}$, of base of anal $\frac{1}{3}$ of total length. Height of head $\frac{2}{11}$, of body $\frac{2}{7}$, of hard dorsal $\frac{1}{11}$, of soft dorsal $\frac{1}{7}$, of ventral $\frac{1}{6}$, of total length.

Eyes—Diameter $\frac{1}{4}$ of length of head, $1\frac{1}{3}$ diameters from end of snout, 1 diameter apart.

Body elongated and compressed, snout rather produced, profile rising to the dorsal but rather concave between the snout and the middle of the orbit. Head rather pointed in front.

Mouth moderately protrusible, lower jaw the longest. Maxilla does not extend as far as below the anterior margin of the orbit: lips rather fleshy. Posterior margin of the preopercle rather oblique, angle rounded, lower limb horizontal and scarcely more than half the height of the vertical one. Opercle irregularly triangular, ending in a soft fleshy termination. Interorbital space moderately flat.

Teeth—Sharp and conical, two or three rather large ones about the centre of the upper jaw. A row of rounded teeth posteriorly. Those on each side of the symphysis larger than the succeeding seven which gradually decrease in length. Some on the palate.

Fins—Dorsal and ventral situated on a line, and slightly in advance of the pectoral: the anal opposite the end of the pectoral. Dorsal spines slender, the membrane slightly notched, the third spine the longest; the rays but little longer than the spines, the last ones rather prolonged. A very short interspace exists between the end of the dorsal and the base of the caudal. Pectoral rounded. Ventral pointed, its spine weak, and the first ray ending in a filamentous prolongation. The third anal spine the longest, all are weak, the rays a little longer than the spines, and slightly produced. Caudal with a broad base, and a broadly rounded extremity.

Scales—Large, none on the head.

Lateral line—In upper fourth of body, and composed of a single tube on each scale having four or more smaller ones branching off posteriorly: opposite the ninth or tenth dorsal ray, it suddenly bends downwards to the centre of the body, and passes direct to the middle of the caudal.

Colours—Green, with five or six bars of rather a deep blue, checquered with a deep dull reddish purple. A black spot at the base of the pectoral, in front of which there is a vivid green mark. Eye of a light cœrulean blue, with an inner golden margin round the pupil. Some irregular bands of red between the eyes, one passing downwards and forwards to the centre of the snout: a line of red passes along the lower margins of the opercle, sub- and preopercles; and two or three other irregular lines on the different opercles. The pectoral fin has no markings except at its base; on the ventral there is a red streak between the first and second soft rays, and in the dorsal an oval yellow spot between each ray, the rest of the fin being reddish margined with a lighter tint, and tipped with white. The anal of the same colour as the dorsal. The caudal tipped with blue, its angles being orange with a red base, and a lilac band passing across the fin from one angle to the other: posterior to this it has a red pavement the same as on the body. There is a black spot on the dorsal, between the fifth and sixth rays.

Habitat—Seas of India, Malaysia, and China.

Fam. GERRIDÆ, Günther.

Genus GERRES, *Cuvier*.

Catochænum, *Cantor*.

Diapterus et synistius, *Gill*.

Branchiostegals, six: pseudobranchiæ. Body compressed, oblong, or elevated. Eyes large, lateral. Mouth very protractile downwards. Angle and inferior margin of preopercle toothed or entire. One dorsal fin, with the spinous and soft portions equally developed, and having, as well as the anal, a scaly sheath along its base. Anal with three—sometimes two—spines, and its soft portion similar to the soft dorsal. Ventral thoracic, with one spine and five rays. Caudal forked. Scales large, and deciduous. The lower pharyngeal bones are firmly united by a suture. Teeth in jaws velvety. Air bladder simple. Pyloric appendages in small numbers. Vertebræ $\frac{10}{14}$.

Gerres filamentosus.

Woodawahah, *Russell*, pl. 68.
Gerres filamentosus, *Cuv. & Val.* vi. p. 482; *Günther*, Catal. i. p. 345, iv. p. 261.
Catochænum filamentosum, *Cantor*, Catal. p. 56.

B. vi. D. $\frac{9}{10}$. P. 15. V. $\frac{1}{5}$ A. $\frac{3}{7}$. C. 17. L. l. 42-45. L. tr. $\frac{5}{9}$-$\frac{6}{12}$.

Length of head $\frac{1}{4}$, of pectoral $\frac{2}{7}$, of caudal $\frac{2}{9}$, of base of dorsal $\frac{2}{5}$, of base of anal $\frac{2}{17}$ of total length. Height of head $\frac{2}{9}$, of body $\frac{2}{5}$, of hard dorsal $\frac{1}{2}$, of soft dorsal $\frac{1}{9}$, of ventral $\frac{1}{9}$, of anal $\frac{1}{9}$ of total length.

Eyes—Large and near the profile; diameter $\frac{1}{3}$ length of head, $\frac{4}{5}$ of a diameter from end of snout, and the same distance apart.

Body compressed and elevated.

Maxilla extends to beneath the first fourth of the orbit. Snout elevated. Preopercle entire, its horizontal margin about half as long as its vertical; angle rounded. Opercle with two blunt points, separated by a crescentic margin. Subopercle narrow. Interopercles rather wide.

Teeth—Velvety in the jaws; none on vomer or palate.

Fins—Dorsal commences slightly behind the pectoral, but opposite the origin of the ventral; and the anal opposite the fourth ray of the dorsal. Dorsal spines strong, and flattened laterally; the first short, the second prolonged, its size varying, that of the third equals the distance from the snout to the posterior margin of the eye; the membrane is slightly notched: the base of the spinous portion equals that of the soft; a scaly sheath extends along its base: the hard portion concave above, and the soft short and straight. Pectoral pointed, and extends to above the first anal ray. Ventral spine weak, first ray prolonged. First spine of anal weak, and slightly longer than the third; the rays gradually decrease in length: this fin has a sheath the same as the dorsal. Caudal deeply lobed.

Scales—Cover the body and opercles.

Lateral line—In single tubes on each scale, and following the curve of the back.

Colours—Summit of head and back pale greenish grey, the rest of the body silvery with reddish reflections. Above and following the lateral line, there are two parallel series of large oval blackish spots, and below the line one or two straight series of similar but smaller spots. Dorsal, anal, and caudal fins pale yellow: the spines, rays, and membranes of the dorsal and caudal minutely dotted with brown; the superior margin of the dorsal black; the posterior margin of the caudal pale blackish; ventrals and pectorals white. Iris pale golden.

Grows to eight inches in length. Is eaten by the Natives.

Habitat—Seas of India and Malaysia.

Gerres punctatus.

Woodan, *Russell*, pl. 68.
Gerres punctatus, *Cuv. & Val.* vi. p. 480; *Günther*, Catal. i. p. 346, iv. p. 260.

B. vi. D. $\frac{9}{10}$. P. 15. V. $\frac{1}{5}$ A. $\frac{3}{7}$ C. 17. L. l. 42. L. tr. $\frac{5}{8}$.

Length of head $\frac{1}{4}$, of pectoral $\frac{1}{3}$, of caudal $\frac{1}{4}$, of base of dorsal $\frac{2}{5}$, of base of anal $\frac{1}{7}$ of total length. Height of head $\frac{1}{4}$, of body $\frac{1}{3}$, of hard dorsal $\frac{1}{6}$, of soft dorsal $\frac{1}{11}$, of base of caudal $\frac{1}{9}$, of ventral $\frac{1}{6}$, of anal $\frac{1}{8}$ of total length.

Eyes—In upper part of the head, and close to the profile. Horizontal diameter $\frac{2}{5}$, vertical diameter $\frac{1}{3}$ of length of head, $\frac{6}{7}$ of a horizontal diameter from end of snout, and the same distance apart.

Body compressed, and of a long ovoid shape, broadest in front: the rise from the snout to the first dorsal is abrupt. There is a slight elevation on the snout, another just in front of the orbits, and a depression over the centre of the orbits. From the mouth to the ventrals, the profile is nearly straight.

Mouth comparatively small, compressed, and wide. Maxilla extends to beneath the anterior third of the orbit, and is overlapped by the anterior portion of the preorbital. Upper jaw protrusible. Preorbital nearly triangular. Preopercle finely serrated, with the vertical limb rather oblique, and the angle produced and rounded; the horizontal limb half the height of the vertical one. Opercles narrow, three times higher than wide. Nostrils over the anterior third of the orbits, approximating behind, the largest with a bony ridge over it, and an oval depression posteriorly.

Fins—Pectoral and dorsal arise on a line, ventral slightly behind; anal opposite the fifth dorsal ray. Dorsal highest in front, the second spine the longest, from whence they gradually decrease to the last: the membrane rather deeply notched. Pectoral long, pointed, and extending nearly to the end of the anal fin. Ventral spine moderately strong. The second spine of the anal much the strongest, and of the same length as the third. Caudal deeply lobed. Dorsal and anal with a scaly sheath along each of their bases.

Scales—Rather deciduous.

Lateral line—Follows the curve of the back in its upper third.

Colours—Greyish silvery above, with a purplish reflection, and fading to silvery on the abdomen. A row of dark spots extends along the base of the dorsal fin. Iris yellowish, with some minute black points. The young have indistinct cross bands.

Grows to eight inches in length, and is eaten by the Natives.

Habitat—Seas of India and China.

* GERRES LIMBATUS.

GERRES LIMBATUS, *Cuv. & Val.* vi. p. 476; *Günther*, Catal. iv. p. 259.
CATOCHÆNUM LIMBATUM, *Cantor*, Catal. p. 55.

B. vi. D. $\frac{9}{10}$. P. 15. V. $\frac{1}{5}$. A. $\frac{3}{7\text{-}8}$. C. 17. L. l. 37. L. tr. $\frac{5}{10}$.

Height of body $\frac{3}{10}$ of total length.

Eyes—Diameter $\frac{2}{7}$ of length of head, rather more than 1 diameter from end of snout, 1 diameter apart.

Mouth very protractile. The preorbital and preopercle entire, but in the young the lower margin of the latter is toothed. The groove for the processes of the intermaxillaries is devoid of scales, and extends rather beyond the anterior margin of the orbit.

Teeth—Velvety in the jaws.

Fins—The second spine of the dorsal is much longer than the third, in the adult being above half the height of the body in length: but in the young the two spines are of equal length: the scaly sheath to the fin is moderately developed. The second anal spine is stronger and a little longer than the third, being more than half the length of the second dorsal spine.

Scales—Deciduous.

Lateral line—Follows the curve of the back.

Colours—Silvery with lilac reflections; dorsal, caudal, and anal fins pale yellow; dorsal spines, rays, and membrane, minutely dotted with brown, their upper margins black: caudal with a broad blackish margin: ventrals and pectorals white. Iris silvery, or pale golden.

Grows to seven inches in length. Is considered good eating: the young are dried at Penang and used for food.

Habitat—Seas of India and Malaysia.

Fam. CHROMIDES, *Müll.*

GENUS ETROPLUS, *Cuv. and Val.*

Branchiostegals, six: pseudobranchiæ absent. Body oblong, elevated, and compressed. Eyes lateral. Cleft of mouth short. Teeth in one or two rows, compressed and lobate, none on palate. One dorsal fin with a developed spinous portion: anal spines also numerous. Ventral thoracic with one spine and five rays. The inferior pharyngeal bones triangular with a median suture. Anterior prominences of branchial arches few, short, conical, and hard. Scales of moderate size, ctenoid. Lateral line interrupted. Air bladder present. Pyloric appendages none. Stomach with a cæcal appendage.

ETROPLUS SURATENSIS.

CHÆTODON SURATENSIS, *Bloch*, t. 217.
CHÆTODON CARIS, *Ham. Buch.* pp. 125, 372.
ETROPLUS MELEAGRIS, *Cuv. & Val.* v. p. 486.
ETROPLUS MACULATUS, *Jerdon*, Madras Journ. xv. p. 142.
ETROPLUS SURATENSIS, *Günther*, Catal. iv. p. 266.

B. vi. D. $\frac{18-19}{14}$. P. 17. V. $\frac{1}{5}$. A. $\frac{13}{11}$. C. 16. L. l. 45. L. tr. 21.

Length of head $\frac{4}{17}$, pectoral $\frac{1}{5}$, base of dorsal a little above $\frac{1}{2}$, base of anal $\frac{3}{8}$, of caudal $\frac{1}{4}$ of total length. Height of head $\frac{1}{4}$, of body nearly $\frac{1}{2}$, of hard dorsal $\frac{1}{17}$, of soft dorsal $\frac{1}{4}$, of anal spines $\frac{1}{17}$, of anal rays $\frac{1}{5}$, of ventral $\frac{2}{13}$ of total length.

Eyes—High, not far from the profile. Diameter $\frac{1}{4}$ length of head, 2 diameters from end of snout, and $1\frac{3}{4}$ diameters apart.

Mouth oval, very compressed, and situated below the centre of the body. Profile rises abruptly to the base of the dorsal, but is rather concave between the snout and the upper margin of the orbit. Lower profile not quite so rounded as the upper.

Lower jaw slightly the longest. Maxilla extends more than half way to the orbit. Preopercle oblique and entire. Opercle entire. Shoulder bones entire. Nostrils situated about midway between the eye and the snout.

Teeth—In two rows in each jaw, compressed, and sharp in the centre, with a small lobe on each side; no teeth on the palate.

Fins—Pectoral arises close behind the central line of the opercle; the commencement of the dorsal fin is in a line above it: the ventral is beneath the fourth dorsal spine, and there is a very short finless space between the terminations of the dorsal and anal, and the commencement of the caudal. Dorsal spines strong, the spinous portion occupying seven tenths of the length of the base of the fin; the interspinous membrane deeply notched and longer than the spines: the fourth ray is the longest, and extends to three fourths the length of the caudal: the last is the shortest, being not quite a fourth of the length of the longest ray. The anal spines occupy seven tenths of the length of the base of the fin, and both spines and rays are the same as in the dorsal. Both dorsal and anal spines can be laid flat in a groove. Pectoral rather pointed. Ventral spine moderately strong, and a third longer than any of the dorsal spines. Caudal broad at its extremity and slightly emarginate.

Scales—Ctenoid, covering the opercles, none on the snout, between the eyes, or on the preorbitals, but they are extended on to the caudal, and along the base of dorsal and anal fins in the form of a scaly sheath.

Lateral line—In upper fourth of body, extending along about sixteen scales, and ceasing opposite the twelfth dorsal spine.

Colours—Light green, with eight vertical bands, the first passes over the occiput, the last across the base of the caudal, and the other six are intermediate. Most of the scales above the lateral line have a central white pearly spot, whilst there are some irregular black spots over the abdomen. The dorsal, caudal, ventral, and anal are of a dark leaden colour, the pectoral yellowish, with a jet black base.

Specimens from the salt water are of a deep purple colour, the bands almost black, and the white spots very distinct.

During the monsoon time the colours of this fish are most beautiful, the eight vertical bands are more distinctly marked, the abdomen is nearly white, the back of a deep green, and the round white spot on nearly every scale gleams like a small pearl.

Very young fish have a large black ocellus surrounded by a white margin, extending from the fourth to the tenth soft rays of the dorsal fin.

Very common in all pieces of fresh water. Excellent eating, especially when of a large size. It grows to upwards of a foot in length. It takes a bait freely, but is not so easily captured in a net, as it appears to bury itself in the mud.

Habitat—Fresh waters of Southern India and Ceylon.

Etroplus maculatus.

Chætodon maculatus, *Bloch*, t. 427, f. 2; *Cuv. & Val.* v. p. 489; *Günther*, Catal. iv. p. 266.

Etroplus coruchi, *Cuv. & Val.* v. p. 491, pl. 136; *Jerdon*, Madras Journ. xv. p. 142.

Pụlluttay, *Mal.*

B. vi. D. $\frac{18}{10}$. P. 14. V. $\frac{1}{5}$. A. $\frac{13}{9}$. C. 16. L. l. 35. L. tr. 21.

Length of head $\frac{2}{7}$, of pectoral $\frac{2}{9}$, of base of dorsal $\frac{1}{2}$, of base of anal $\frac{2}{5}$, of caudal $\frac{1}{4}$ of total length. Height of head $\frac{2}{7}$, of body $\frac{2}{5}$, of hard dorsal $\frac{1}{11}$, of soft dorsal $\frac{1}{7}$, of ventral $\frac{1}{6}$, of anal spines $\frac{1}{11}$, of anal rays $\frac{1}{7}$ of total length.

Eyes—Diameter $\frac{1}{3}$ length of head, slightly more than 1 diameter from end of snout, 1 diameter apart.

Body oval and strongly compressed. Mouth situated in the lower third of the body. Profile rises abruptly to the dorsal, and is slightly concave between the snout and the upper margin of the orbit. Lower profile not quite so convex as the upper.

Lower jaw rather the longest. Maxilla extends two-thirds of the distance to the orbit. Preopercle oblique and entire. Opercle entire. Shoulder bones entire.

Teeth—As in the ***Etroplus Suratensis***, but rather more pointed.

Fins—Pectoral arises close behind the opercle, and the commencement of the dorsal is slightly in advance of it. The finless space on the tail is short. Dorsal spines strong and occupying eleven fourteenths of the entire fin: interspinous membrane deeply notched and longer than the spines: the fourth ray the most produced, extending to the posterior third of the caudal. Anal spines strong, and occupying seven tenths of the entire base of fin; the rays are the same as in the dorsal. Both dorsal and anal spines can be laid flat in a groove. Ventral spine moderately strong, slightly exceeding the longest dorsal spine in length. Pectoral rather pointed. Caudal lunated and emarginate.

Scales—Ctenoid, and in other respects the same as in the ***E. Suratensis.***

Colours—Yellowish with a greenish back, and about seventeen horizontal lines of deep golden spots along the dorsal fin, the back, and the abdomen, occasionally a few also exist on the anal. Between the dorsal spines and rays there are more spots, some being brown and others yellow. Along the lateral line are three black finger marks, the central one being the largest. Ventral and anal fins stained with a deep black. In specimens taken from January to May there is occasionally a reddish tinge at the extremity of the caudal fin, and a leaden or violet hue over the body, and the number of the golden spots is apparently less.

Having captured about fifty specimens on July 15, 1863, in the fort ditch at Cochin, for the purpose of minutely examining their coloration, I found that no two could be said to be identical. The seventeen lines of golden spots were more or less apparent in all; in some the three blotches on the side were black, in others of a light emerald green, whilst all intermediate shades were perceptible: some were glossed over with purple, which tint was absent in others.

Common in every paddy field, tank, or piece of fresh water, and even occasionally found in the backwater within the influence of the tides. Eaten by the Natives; but as it rarely, if ever, exceeds three inches in length, it is not employed as food by Europeans.

Habitat—Fresh waters of India and Ceylon.

SUB-ORDER.—MALACOPTERYGII PHARYNGOGNATHI.

Fam. SCOMBERESOCIDÆ, *Müll.*

GENUS BELONE, *Cuvier*.

Branchiostegals, from about ten to fifteen. Body subcylindrical and elongated. The jaws extended into a long beak, the upper portion principally formed of the intermaxillaries, and its base by the maxillæ. Under the symphysis of the lower jaw is a soft fleshy appendage. Eyes lateral. A single dorsal situated in the posterior portion of the body, opposite an anal of the same description. Ventral six-rayed, anterior to the dorsal. Caudal generally lobed, the lower being usually the longest. Teeth in both jaws, in two or three rows of different sizes: pharyngeal teeth conical; absent on the vomer, except in the *Belone vulgaris*. Scales small. Bones green. Gill openings very wide. Air vessel large. Cæcal appendages absent.

Belone caudimaculata.

Belone caudimaculata, *Cuv. & Val.* xviii. p. 452; *Cantor*, Catal. p. 246.
Kuddera, A. *Russell*, pl. 176.
Coplah, *Mal.*

B. xii. D. 13-14. P. 11. V. 6. A. 16-17. C. 15.

Length of head $\frac{1}{3}$, of pectoral $\frac{1}{12}$, of base of dorsal $\frac{1}{10}$, of base of anal $\frac{1}{8}$, of caudal $\frac{1}{10}$ of total length. Height of head $\frac{1}{17}$, of body $\frac{1}{14}$, of dorsal $\frac{1}{14}$, of anal $\frac{1}{10}$ of total length.

Eyes—Diameter $\frac{1}{11}$ of length of head, 1 diameter apart.

Mouth from the gape to extremity three-tenths of the total length. Upper and lateral surfaces of snout compressed. The posterior margin of the maxilla reaches to beneath the centre of the orbit. Central line of lower jaw elevated, and covered with transverse rough plates. Preopercle wide; opercle posteriorly rounded. Infraorbital space nearly flat, with a wide longitudinal groove.

Teeth—In upper jaw widely separated, sharp, straight, and directed slightly backwards; in the last ninth they are smaller, and more closely set; between, or rather anterior to them, there is a series of villiform ones, which are in two rows in the centre, and in three or more at the base. In the lower jaw the large teeth are anteriorly the same as in the upper; there are two external rows of villiform, one directed upwards, and the other rather outwards: which posteriorly increase to two, three, or even more.

Fins—Pectoral just behind the opercle, in the centre of the body: ventral rather nearer the posterior extremity of the pectoral than to the commencement of the anal: anal in the last third of body rather in advance of the dorsal, which last is highest in front, with the upper margin concave: anal of the same shape. Caudal with rounded lobes.

Scales—Over the body and opercles.

Lateral line—Double; the upper one passes from the superior margin of the opercle along the upper fourth of the back, gradually rising until opposite the ventral, when it descends to the centre and proceeds straight to the middle of the caudal. The lower lateral line at first commences some distance before the pectoral in the lower fourth of the body, then rises to midway between the termination of the pectoral and the commencement of the anal, and sinks again until it is close to the base of the latter fin, from whence it gradually ascends, and joins the upper line close to the caudal.

Colours—Summit of head and back yellowish green, with minute brown dots, fading into silvery on the sides, and white on the abdomen. Cheeks and opercles silvery. A deep blue longitudinal band, bordered beneath by another broader one of silver, passes along the posterior half of the sides. Dorsal, and sometimes the anal, bright yellow, and the rays dotted with brown. Pectorals and ventral diaphanous, the latter occasionally with a black spot at the base. Caudal yellowish or greenish, minutely dotted with black, and having a round bluish-black spot in the centre near the root. Iris silvery; upper surface of eye bluish-black.

Grows to about two feet in length. It is only captured in the sea at Cochin, and at the mouth of the river within the influence of the tides. The Natives consider it good eating, but it is not much esteemed by Europeans, on account of the large number of bones it contains.

Habitat—Seas and estuaries (fresh water ?) of India, Malaysia, China, and North Australia.

BELONE ANNULATA.

BELONE ANNULATA, *Cuv. & Val.* xviii. p. 447, pl. 550; *Cantor*, Catal. p. 244.
WAHLAH KUDDERA, *Russell*, pl. 175.

B. xiii. D. 20-23. P. 12. V. 6. A. 21-23. C. 15.

Length of head more than $\frac{1}{3}$, of pectoral $\frac{1}{13}$, of base of dorsal $\frac{1}{8}$, of base of anal $\frac{1}{8}$, of caudal $\frac{1}{10}$ of total length. Height of head about $\frac{1}{19}$, of body $\frac{1}{13}$, of dorsal $\frac{1}{13}$, of anal $\frac{1}{12}$ of total length.

Eyes—Diameter $\frac{1}{11}$ of length of head, 1 diameter apart.

Mouth from gape to the extremity one-fifth of the total length: upper and lateral surface of snout compressed. Lower jaw with a row of glands near its inferior margin. Head as in the *Belone caudimaculata*, but the interorbital groove is wider and shallower. The maxilla extends to beneath the anterior third of the orbit. The comparative size of the parts varies with age.

Teeth—Upper jaw with small sharp teeth disposed laterally along the margin of the side of the jaw; they are some distance asunder, but become smaller towards the orbit: between them and under the margin of the jaw are numerous sharp teeth.

Scales—On the head and opercles, scarcely perceptible.

Lateral line—Double; the superior passes along the upper third of the body, and reaches the mesial line about the centre of the body, from whence it is continued on to the caudal: the inferior line proceeds from near the under surface of the throat, and passes to slightly below the anterior margin of the ventral, which it curves round, and beyond it passes to above the anterior margin of the anal, from whence it proceeds direct to the centre of the caudal.

Fins—Pectoral arises close behind the opercle: ventral midway between the posterior extremity of the pectoral and the centre of the anal: anal in the posterior third of the body, and the dorsal rather behind the anal. The last ray of the anal almost touches the base of the caudal, and the last rays of the dorsal extend nearly to the base of the caudal. Lower lobe of caudal the longest. The anterior extremities of the dorsal and anal the highest.

Colours—Upper surface of the head and back green, with steel blue reflections, minutely dotted with black, fading into silvery white on the abdomen. The side of the upper jaw of a dark olive, of the lower silvery. A black line passes from the angle of the mouth along the base of the teeth. Cheeks and opercles silvery. Membranes of the dorsal, caudal, and pectoral fins of a light greenish grey, minutely dotted with black, especially at the margins. Anal and ventral anteriorly white, dotted with black. Iris silvery, the margin of the orbit black. In young specimens the colours vary, the upper surface is more of a yellowish green, there is a large black spot on the opercle, and the lower jaw is also black: a narrow silvery greenish band passes longitudinally above the lateral line. The posterior two-thirds of the dorsal is black, and there is a large black spot on the centre of the caudal.

Grows to two feet in length, and is found in the same localities as the *Belone caudimaculata*.

Habitat—Seas and estuaries of India, Malaysia, China, and North Australia.

BELONE CANCILA.

ESOX CANCILA, *Ham. Buch.* pp. 213, 380, pl. 37, f. 70; *Cuv. & Val.* xviii. p. 455.
BELONE GRAII, *Sykes*, Proc. Zool. Soc. 1841, p. 367, pl. 63, f. 4; *Jerdon*, Madras Journal, xv. p. 345.
COAHLAN and MORRAHLOO, *Mal.*

B. x. D. 16-17. P. 11. V. 6. A. 16-17. C. 15.

Length of head nearly $\frac{1}{3}$, of pectoral $\frac{1}{14}$, of caudal $\frac{1}{10}$, of base of dorsal $\frac{1}{8}$, of base of anal $\frac{2}{15}$ of total length. Height of head $\frac{1}{11}$, of body $\frac{1}{10}$, of dorsal $\frac{1}{16}$, of anal $\frac{1}{11}$, of ventral $\frac{1}{27}$ of total length.

Eyes—Oval, upper margins close to the profile, horizontal diameter $\frac{1}{10}$, vertical diameter $\frac{1}{15}$ of length of head, 6 horizontal diameters from end of snout, 1 horizontal diameter apart.

Body elongated, slightly compressed, and tapering towards the extremities.

Jaws elongated, depressed, and compressed, the lower ends in a soft symphysis, it is deep at its base. Preopercle rather longer than high. Opercle forming the arc of a circle; its anterior margin vertical. No roughened elevation along the centre of the lower jaw, nor glands along its external margin. The maxilla extends to below the anterior third of the orbit. Nostrils single, opposite the anterior superior margin of the orbit, in a triangular depression with the base behind.

Teeth—No lateral ones. A row of widely separated sharp conical teeth directed downwards in each jaw, with an external series of villiform much the smallest in the mandibulæ.

Fins—Pectoral commences a short distance behind the centre of the opercle; ventral rather nearer the anal than to the end of the pectoral; anal in the posterior third of body; and the dorsal slightly behind it. Second and third rays of the dorsal the highest, upper margin of the fin concave, the end of the last ray reaches the base of the caudal fin. The third ray of the anal the longest: the upper margin concave: the termination of the last ray not quite extending to the caudal. Caudal with rounded lobes, the lower being slightly the longest.

Scales—Small and deciduous, none on the opercles and cheeks.

Lateral line—Double, the upper one being at first in the superior third of the body, but it gradually sinks, and passes along the central line of the body, but is very indistinct. The lower branch commencing under the throat, passes straight along the lower fourth of the body parallel with the abdomen, opposite the posterior end of the anal, it curves upwards to gain the centre of the body, and from thence proceeds to the middle of the caudal fin.

Colours—Back greenish, abdomen silvery. A line resembling burnished silver, commences at the upper part of the opercle, and passes direct to the upper part of the caudal fin; at first it is narrow, but opposite the dorsal it widens, and beyond it again decreases: on each side of the tail, above and below the silver line, there are occasionally four irregular black spots. Caudal with a black crescentic mark, a short distance from the commencement. Cheeks of burnished silver. Eyes yellowish white; bones greenish.

Found in the Kurriavanoor river, near Cochin. Said to be very destructive to small fish. It does not appear to grow to more than fourteen inches in length.

Habitat—Fresh waters of India.

GENUS HEMIRAMPHUS, *Cuvier.*

Branchiostegals, about twelve or thirteen. Body subcylindrical and elongated. Eyes lateral. Upper jaw very short, formed by the intermaxillaries, the symphysis of the lower jaw extended into a long beak, at upper and posterior portion of which beneath the upper jaw is the margin of the mouth. A single dorsal situated in the posterior portion of the body opposite to an anal of a similar description. Ventral six-rayed, anterior to the dorsal. Caudal generally lobed, the lower usually the longest. Teeth villiform in both jaws in several rows. Scales of moderate size or large. Gill openings very wide. Air vessel large. No cæcal appendages.

HEMIRAMPHUS REYNALDI.

HEMIRAMPHUS REYNALDI, *Cuv. & Val.* xix. p. 39.
MORRUL, *Mal.*

B. xii. D. 16. P. 12. V. 6. A. 15. C. 15. L. l. 50-58. L. tr. 6-7.

Length of head excluding beak nearly $\frac{1}{7}$, including beak $\frac{1}{3}$, of pectoral $\frac{1}{9}$, of caudal $\frac{1}{8}$, of base of dorsal $\frac{1}{8}$, of base of anal $\frac{1}{9}$ of total length. Height of head $\frac{1}{12}$, of body $\frac{1}{9}$, of dorsal $\frac{1}{15}$, of ventral $\frac{1}{15}$, of anal $\frac{1}{15}$ of total length.

Eyes—Oval, superior margins close to profile. Horizontal diameter $\frac{1}{3}$, and vertical diameter $\frac{1}{4}$, 1 horizontal diameter to end of snout, $\frac{4}{5}$ of a horizontal diameter apart in the centre, but further posteriorly.

Body elongated, moderately compressed, head slightly depressed.

The intermaxillaries form an obtuse triangle, the base behind, the apex in front, rounded, and its length a fourth less than its width at its base: a furrow passes longitudinally down its centre, its edges are slightly raised, and its external margin is a little convex at its centre. The posterior extremity of the maxilla reaches to opposite the anterior margin of the orbit. The width of the mouth is a fourth greater than its length, and the length of the beak from the end of the intermaxillaries to the tip, is equal to the length from the base of the pectoral to the anterior extremity of the mouth, consequently the end of the snout is midway between the base of the pectoral and the tip of the beak: it is thin and straight. From the centre of the beak at its base, a ridge arises which from its first third is continued along the upper surface of the beak in the form of a groove as far as its tip. Interorbital space flat. Preopercle rectangular, angle slightly produced. Opercle a third higher than wide, and all the edges nearly straight. The openings of the nostrils are placed in a shallow oval depression, in front and rather internal to the upper margins of the orbit.

Teeth—Villiform, placed in close bands, wider in the mandibulæ than in the upper jaw. Opposite the centre of the lower jaw there is a short edentulous interval where a ridge exists.

Fins—Pectoral arises a short distance posterior to, and on a level with, the superior margin of the opercle: ventral commences midway between the anterior margin of the orbit and the base of the caudal: anal arises the width of one scale nearer the caudal than it does to the ventral, and is slightly behind the dorsal. Dorsal highest in front, upper margin rather concave: anal of the same shape. Caudal lobed, the lower a third longer and much larger than the upper.

Scales—Deciduous, covering the body and summit of head.

Lateral line—Proceeds parallel to the abdomen, passing just above the ventral, and two scales above the anal, from whence it reaches the centre of the fin by crossing the base of the upper ray of the lower lobe.

Colours—Silvery, greenish blue on the back, and whitish grey on the abdomen. The silver band is quite straight, widest opposite the commencement of the dorsal fin. Dorsal and caudal margined with blackish, and some minute black dots exist between the caudal rays.

Exceedingly common after the S. W. monsoon, and through the cold weather. Much esteemed for eating by the Natives, and the roes highly prized by Europeans for curries. Grows to eight inches in length.

Habitat—Malabar, Ceylon, and the tanks around Calcutta.

HEMIRAMPHUS XANTHOPTERUS.

HEMIRAMPHUS XANTHOPTERUS, *Cuv. & Val.* xix. p. 47.

? HEMIRAMPHUS TRIDENTIFER, *Cantor*, Catal. p. 249.

B. xii. D. 15. P. 13. V. 6. A. 16. C. 15. L. l. 56. L. tr. 9.

Length of head to the end of intermaxillaries $\frac{1}{6}$, of beak from opening $\frac{1}{6}$, of caudal $\frac{2}{13}$, of pectoral $\frac{1}{11}$, of dorsal $\frac{1}{9}$, of anal $\frac{1}{10}$ of total length. Height of head $\frac{1}{13}$, of body $\frac{1}{9}$ of total length.

Eyes—Oval. Upper margins form part of the profile. Horizontal diameter $\frac{4}{13}$ and vertical diameter $\frac{1}{4}$ of length of head. Not quite 1 horizontal diameter apart, $1\frac{1}{4}$ horizontal diameters from the end of intermaxillaries.

Body elongated, subcylindrical; head compressed and depressed.

Mouth formed by the intermaxillaries and a portion of the mandibulæ, its extended prolongation or beak being beyond the mouth: the exposed portion of the intermaxillaries form a triangle, with the base behind, and having a slight longitudinal keel along its centre, with rather raised edges: it opens something like the lid of a box. The posterior extremity of the maxilla does not extend to beneath the anterior margin of the orbit. The mandibular portion of the mouth is rather wide. The length of the mandibles from the end of the snout nearly equals the distance from the posterior margin of the orbit to the end of the mouth, consequently the extremity of the mouth is slightly nearer the posterior margin of the orbit than the end of the snout. In front of the centre of the lower jaw the suture forms a ridge which proceeds a very short distance and ends in rather a broad groove, which is continued along the whole of the upper surface of the mandibles to about their extremity: the tip is fleshy. The interorbital space nearly flat. Preopercle narrow and rectangular. Opercle large, the upper third of the posterior margin ending in a rounded point. Posterior margins of orbits rather raised. Nostrils opposite the anterior superior angle of the orbit in a depressed oval space, having raised edges. Intermaxillaries form a very pointed angle at their junction.

Teeth—In a very wide band in both jaws, especially in the lower one and in the mesial line, owing to the commencement of a ridge: the bands of the two sides are only connected half the width of the band posteriorly. The internal teeth a little longer than the others.

Fins.—Dorsal commences a little behind the posterior third of the body: anal opposite dorsal; both fins of the same shape, highest in front, with their margins rather concave. Caudal not deeply cleft, the lower lobe much the largest and longest.

Scales—On body, summit of head, and the base of the intermaxillaries.

Lateral line—Descends until close to the ventral fin, and then passing parallel to the abdomen, it gradually ascends opposite the anterior end of the anal, and from thence passes to the base of the fifth ray of the lower lobe, over which it crosses, and ascending over the next, is lost.

Colours—Silvery greenish-blue on the back, whitish on the abdomen. A silver band passes from opposite the commencement of the dorsal fin to the centre of the caudal. Tip of beak of a brilliant scarlet. Dorsal and caudal margined with black. Some fine black points below the caudal rays.

Occasionally arrives in vast numbers at Cochin, and is captured at the mouth of the river, in the backwater, and even in fresh water. Grows to about eight inches in length.

Habitat—Seas, estuaries, and sometimes fresh waters of Malabar and Malaysia.

HEMIRAMPHUS LIMBATUS.

HEMIRAMPHUS LIMBATUS, *Cuv. & Val.* xix. p. 44.

B. xii. D. 15. P. 12. V. 6. A. 13-15. C. 15. L. l. 52. L. tr. 7.

Length of head excluding beak $\frac{1}{6}$, of head including beak $\frac{2}{7}$, of pectoral $\frac{1}{10}$, of caudal $\frac{2}{13}$, of base of dorsal $\frac{1}{8}$, of base of anal $\frac{1}{10}$ of total length. Height of head $\frac{1}{13}$, of body $\frac{1}{11}$, of dorsal $\frac{1}{17}$, of ventral $\frac{1}{22}$, of anal about $\frac{1}{20}$ of total length.

Eyes—Oval, upper margins close to the profile. Horizontal diameter $\frac{3}{10}$, vertical diameter $\frac{1}{4}$ of length of head, 1 transverse diameter from end of snout, and nearly the same distance apart.

The body of the same character as in the previous specimens.

The intermaxillaries form a triangle, the base being behind and a third wider than it is long, having a longitudinal ridge above, and a slight elevation along its margins: its anterior extremity not quite pointed. The posterior extremity of the maxilla reaches half way from the angle of the mouth to the orbit: the width at its gape slightly exceeds the length of the mouth. The length of the beak from the end of intermaxillaries to its tip, equals the distance from the centre of the opercle to the end of the intermaxillaries, consequently the anterior extremity of the mouth is midway between the centre of the opercle and end of beak. Beak weak, and curving in its middle for one third of its length. A very slight ridge at the symphysis, where the two portions of the lower jaw join: a groove along its centre. Interorbital space flat. Preopercle rectangular. Opercle nearly triangular, becoming pointed just above its centre, its width is nearly equal to its height. Nostrils in very shallow oval depressions, at anterior superior margin of orbit.

Teeth—In villiform bands, widest in the upper, being narrow in the anterior portion of the lower jaw, with a slight interval between those of the two sides.

Fins—Pectoral pointed, and arising just above the posterior angle of the opercle: dorsal opposite the thirty-first scale, and slightly in advance of the anal: both fins are highest in front: ventral midway between the posterior margin of the orbit and the base of the caudal. Caudal with its posterior margin rounded, and its lower portion, which can scarcely be termed a lobe, the longest.

Scales—As in the *H. Reynaldi.*

Lateral line—As in the *H. Reynaldi.*

Colours—Silvery, greenish blue on the back, and whitish grey on the abdomen. The silver band is widest opposite the commencement of the dorsal fin, and quite straight, but rather indistinct under the scales. Caudal and dorsal finely edged with black, small black points between the rays. Intermaxillaries and mandibulæ black. A black mark along the branches of the lower jaw. Pectoral, ventral, and anal colourless.

Habitat—Seas of India.

* Hemiramphus Georgii.

Hemiramphus Georgii, *Cuv. & Val.* xix. p. 37, pl. 555; *Cantor*, Catal. p. 248.

B. xii. D. 15-17. P. 12. V. 6. A. 15. C. 15.

Length of head from apex of intermaxillaries $\frac{2}{11}$, beak to angle of the mouth $\frac{3}{11}$ to $\frac{3}{7}$ in the total length. Height of body equals half the length of the head.

Eyes—Diameter $\frac{1}{4}$ of length of head, 1 diameter apart.

The roof of the orbits being arched, occasions the middle of the orbit to appear excavated: the depth at the occiput equals half the length of the head.

Teeth—The band of villiform ones on the intermaxillaries is very narrow at the angle of the mouth, but gradually widens towards its apex: the inner row are somewhat larger than the others. A single row in the lower jaw of very minute teeth, behind which the anterior half of the mouth is lined with a black crescent-shaped membrane.

Fins—Pectorals five-eighths of the length of the head. Ventrals placed opposite the posterior third of the distance between the occiput and the root of the caudal. Caudal moderately cleft; lower lobe slightly longer than the upper, and three-quarters as long as the head.

Colours—Greenish grey above, minutely dotted with black, particularly on the intermaxillaries and on the occiput. Back and sides pale greenish grey, the margins of the scales minutely dotted with black: along each side a shining silvery band, divided in the middle by the lateral line, and edged above by a deep blue line: abdomen faint silvery white: opercles shining silvery, with steel-blue reflections: lower jaw greenish grey, with a black marginal membrane: dorsal and caudal pale greenish grey, marginal half dotted with black: rest of the fin diaphanous. Iris silvery: orbital margin bluish black.—(*Cantor.*)

Grows to ten and a half inches in length.

Habitat—Seas of Malabar and Malaysia.

ORDER ANACANTHINI.

Fam. GADIDÆ, *Owen*.

GADOIDEI, pt. *Cuvier*.

GENUS BREGMACEROS, *Thompson*.

CALLOPTILUM, *Richardson*.

Branchiostegals, seven: pseudobranchiæ none. Body fusiform posteriorly compressed. Mouth anterior and oblique. Eyes lateral. Two dorsal fins, the first consisting of an elongated ray arising from the occiput, the second and the anal having each a central depressed portion almost forming a distinct fin. Ventrals jugular, and long, consisting of five or six rays. Teeth in jaws moveable, also teeth on vomer, none on palate. Scales cycloid. Lateral line continuous. Gill openings very wide, the gill membranes united beneath the throat but not attached to the isthmus. No air bladder or pyloric appendages.

BREGMACEROS MACCLELLANDI.

BREGMACEROS MACCLELLANDI, *Thompson*, Charlest. Mag. Nat. History, 1840, iv. p. 184; *Günther*, Catal. iv. p. 368.

B. vii. D. 1 | 16+X+15. P. 25. V. 5-6. A. 22+X+15. C. 15. L. l. 64. L. tr. $\frac{8}{8}$.

Length of head $\frac{1}{7}$, of pectoral $\frac{1}{5}$, of caudal $\frac{2}{11}$ of the total length. Height of head $\frac{1}{8}$, of body $\frac{1}{7}$, of first dorsal $\frac{2}{11}$, of anal $\frac{2}{11}$ of the total length.

Eyes—Oval: horizontal diameter $\frac{2}{5}$, vertical diameter $\frac{1}{4}$ of the length of the head, $\frac{1}{2}$ a horizontal diameter from end of snout, and 1 diameter apart.

Body fusiform, posteriorly compressed. There is a slight rise in the profile from the snout to the first dorsal fin, from whence it gradually sinks to the caudal. The abdominal profile is nearly straight.

Mouth anterior, rather oblique, upper jaw slightly the longest, extending posteriorly to behind the centre of the orbit. Mandibula rather concave. Opercle rounded.

Teeth—Villiform and moveable in jaws, a few on the vomer, but none on the palatine bones.

Fins—The first dorsal arises from the occiput in the form of a slender ray, which is rather longer than the head. The second dorsal commences in the middle third of the total length, its fourth ray the longest and the fin being highest in front, each ray is unbranched but articulated, and very slender, the membrane is deeply notched: the succeeding ten rays are very short and slender appearing almost like a distinct fin: whilst the last fifteen are lengthened and extend nearly to the base of the caudal: the fin can be laid flat in a groove which exists on the back. The pectoral is situated in the upper third of the body, and just posterior to the opercle, its rays are articulated but unbranched. The anal is of much the same shape as the second dorsal. The ventral which arises under the throat, consists of six rays, the outer three of which are elongated so as to reach as far as about the twenty-first anal ray.

Scales—Cycloid, small.

Lateral line—Continuous.

Colours—Silvery, the back shaded with green. Occiput and upper half of pectoral black; the first half of the dorsal spotted with black.

Grows to about three inches in length, and is rare in Malabar.

Habitat—The mouths of rivers and Coasts of Malabar, Bengal, China, and the Philippine Islands.

Fam. PLEURONECTIDÆ, *Flem.*

HETEROSOMATA, *Bon.*

GENUS PSEUDORHOMBUS, *Bleeker.*

Branchiostegals, seven: pseudobranchiæ. Body laterally compressed and very flat, one side coloured, the other colourless or only spotted. Eyes placed on the left which is the upper side, and though the bones on either side of the head are developed, they are not symmetrical. Mouth wide, cleft deep. Teeth in each jaw in a single row of unequal sizes; none on vomer or palate. The dorsal fin commences on the snout and is continued along the upper profile nearly as far as the caudal fin: the anal continued most of the extent of the lower profile, the rays in both fins are simple. Scales small. Lateral line with a strong curve anteriorly. Gill membranes united below the throat. Gill rakers lanceolate. No air bladder.

PSEUDORHOMBUS RUSSELLII.

PLATESSA RUSSELLII, *Gray*, Ill. Ind. Zool. pl. 94, f. 2; *Cantor*, Catal. p. 214.
PSEUDORHOMBUS RUSSELLII, *Günther*, Catal. iv. p. 424.

B. vii. D. 71. P. 12. V. $\frac{1}{5}$. A. 59. C. 17. L. l. 75.

Length of head $\frac{2}{9}$, of pectoral $\frac{2}{17}$, of base of dorsal $\frac{4}{5}$, of base of anal nearly $\frac{1}{2}$ of total length. Height of body $\frac{2}{5}$, of head $\frac{1}{5}$, of dorsal $\frac{1}{10}$, of ventral $\frac{1}{16}$, of anal $\frac{1}{12}$ of total length.

Eyes—Lower orbit slightly in advance of the upper one. Horizontal diameter $\frac{1}{5}$, and vertical diameter $\frac{1}{6}$ of length of head. Margins of orbits closely approximating and near to end of snout.

Body elliptical, and sinistral.

Mouth forming a very oblique curve with the lower jaw, which is the longest. The posterior extremity of the maxilla extends to under the centre of the orbit. Preopercle slightly convex vertically, lower margin oblique two-thirds as long as posterior one, angle rounded. Opercle ending in a soft point. Interorbital space a mere ridge. Gill rakers compressed, lanceolate, slightly apart, and half as long as the orbit. Posterior aperture of the nostrils in front of the orbit, and larger than the anterior one.

Teeth—Conical, pointed, and directed slightly inwards, about six in each side of the lower jaw, with some small ones posteriorly. About six also on the anterior portion of the upper jaw having a row of smaller ones between and internal, and posteriorly some fine villiform ones. None on vomer and palate.

Fins—Dorsal commences just above the anterior margin of the upper orbit, and extends nearly to the base of the caudal. The left ventral fin nearer the gill openings than the anal, arising under the centre of opercle and reaching as far as the second anal ray: its two first rays are unbranched; the right ventral is situated further back. Pectoral close to the opercle, and rather below the centre of the body, its two upper rays are unbranched, its posterior extremity is rather rounded. Anal arises under the pectoral, and is continued close to the caudal. The longest dorsal rays are in the posterior third of the fin, all excepting the last three are undivided, they project slightly beyond the end of the membrane. The posterior five anal rays are branched. Caudal pointed in the centre.

Scales—Large, ctenoid, and extending over the body, opercles, cheeks, and to the end of the maxilla. They are smaller on the cheeks, the anterior surface of the body and near the base of the dorsal fin. There is a row along the anterior margin of each ray smaller in size but otherwise ctenoid, like those on the rest of the body. Some also over the dorsal, anal, and caudal fins.

Lateral line—Forms a strong curve, equal to half its length, and extending to opposite the posterior fourth of the pectoral, it then proceeds slightly downwards, but soon passes quite horizontally to the centre of the caudal on to which fin it is continued. The depth between the lateral line—just posterior to the end of its curve—and the anal fin, equals the distance from the anterior extremity of the snout to the centre of the base of the pectoral.

Colours—Left side reddish brown, with the base of each scale rather darker than its margin, and numerous black spots irregularly scattered over the body. Opercles and anterior third of the abdomen of a dull neutral tint; fins finely dotted with brown. Iris silvery, brown along its upper margin. Left side whitish or stained with light brown, bluish anteriorly.

Grows to upwards of a foot in length. Not common. Is eaten by the Natives.

Habitat—From the east coast of Africa through the Seas of India, Malaysia, and China to Australia.

Genus SYNAPTURA, *Cantor.*

Achiroides, *Bleeker.*

Æsopia, euryglossa et eurypleura, *Kaup.*

Branchiostegals, six: pseudobranchiæ. Body compressed, flat, right side coloured. Eyes on right side, the upper in advance of the lower. Cleft of mouth narrow, twisted round to the left side. No dilated nostril on left side. Teeth small only on the left side, none on vomer or palate. Vertical fins confluent. Pectoral fin on both sides. Scales ctenoid, small. Lateral line straight.

Synaptura foliacea.

Solea foliacea, *Richardson*, Ich. China, p. 279.

Synaptura foliacea, *Günther*, Catal. iv. p. 481.

Sappatee, *Mal.*

B. vi. D. 62. P. 7. V. 6. A. 46. C. 15. L. l. 75.

Length of head $\frac{1}{5}$, of right pectoral $\frac{1}{16}$, of caudal $\frac{2}{13}$, of base of dorsal $\frac{3}{5}$, of base of anal $\frac{2}{3}$ of total length. Height of head $\frac{1}{4}$, of body $\frac{3}{8}$, of dorsal $\frac{1}{13}$, of anal $\frac{1}{13}$, of ventral $\frac{1}{26}$ of total length.

Eyes—Upper eye $\frac{1}{2}$ a diameter in advance of the lower: lower orbit just above the level of the angle of the mouth, to which half of it is posterior. Diameter $\frac{1}{6}$ of length of head, $1\frac{3}{4}$ diameters from end of snout, and nearly 1 diameter apart.

Mouth cleft to beneath the posterior extremity of the superior orbit, it is narrow and twisted round to the left side. Upper jaw the longest, overlapping the lower. Interorbital space concave. From the anterior angle of the upper orbit is a raised ridge, which is continued two-thirds of the distance to the end of the snout, terminating just above the upper lip. Snout sharp. The posterior aperture of the nostrils a little in front of the lower orbit, the anterior a little before it and tubular. Lower lip of right side fleshy.

Teeth—Fine, and only apparent on the left side.

Fins—Dorsal commences over the centre of the superior orbit, and terminates close to the base of the caudal; the anal arises just behind the ventral, and is also continued to the base of the caudal. Right pectoral short rounded, and equal to a third the length of the head; left pectoral rather shorter. Caudal wedge-shaped. Ventral short.

Scales—Strongly ctenoid, extending over the body, head, dorsal, anal, and caudal fins: largest in size along each side of the lateral line nearly as far as the head, but for the external fourth of the body very much smaller.

Lateral line—Composed of single well developed tubes. It passes straight from the head to the centre of the caudal along the mesial line, and is continued on the caudal fin to its posterior extremity. Interorbital space scaled.

Colours—Leaden above, fins dark blackish grey, under or left surface dirty white.

Grows to six inches or more in length, and is good eating.

Habitat—Malabar and China.

GENUS PLAGUSIA, pt. *Cuvier*.

Branchiostegals, six: pseudobranchiæ. Body compressed, flat, the left side coloured. Mouth rather narrow and unsymmetrical, the upper part of the snout produced backwards, covering the mandibulæ; lips on the left side with tentacles. One nostril on the left side before the angle of the lower orbit. Teeth minute, and only on the right side, none on vomer or palate. Vertical fins confluent. No pectorals. Gill opening narrow. Scales small, ctenoid. Lateral line on left side, double or triple.

PLAGUSIA BILINEATA.

PLEURONECTES BILINEATUS, *Bloch*, pl. 188.

JERREE POTOO, E. *Russell*, pl. 74.

PLAGUSIA BILINEATA, *Cantor*, Catal. p. 227; *Günther*, Catal. iv. p. 492.

B. vi. D. 96. A. 73. C. 8. L. l. 85.

Length of head $\frac{2}{9}$ of total length. Height of body $\frac{2}{9}$, of dorsal $\frac{1}{17}$, of anal $\frac{1}{23}$ of total length.

Eyes—Situated on the upper surface of the head, the left one being behind the centre of the head, just above the posterior extremity of the opening of the mouth, and the lower orbit posterior to the upper one. Diameter $\frac{1}{10}$ of length of head.

Body elongate and lanceolate. Muzzle bluntly pointed. A single nostril in front of the lower eye close to the lip. Lips fleshy.

Teeth—The left side of the jaw toothless. The teeth in the right side are fine and setaceous.

Fins—Dorsal commences before the orbits, the fifth ray being over the upper eye; the anal arises a short distance posterior to the opercle, and both fins are joined to the caudal, which is pointed: the points of the rays project slightly above the membrane. Left ventral situated at the gill opening and above the anal.

Scales—Ctenoid.

Lateral line—Commences at the muzzle, and proceeds straight to the upper margin of the opercle, where it ascends slightly, then again bends downwards to opposite the commencement of the second third of the body, from whence it proceeds nearly straight to the centre of the caudal. Above the preopercle it gives an oblique ascending branch to the second lateral line, the anterior branch of which commences at the snout, ascends to close to the anterior margin of the dorsal, from whence it continues a short distance below it to nearly the base of the caudal. There are fifteen rows of scales between the upper and lower lateral line.

Colours—Left side pale reddish brown. Scales with rather iridescent reflections. Opercles with a bluish tinge. Fin membrane light brown: rays buff. Iris golden round the pupil, the rest blackish lilac. The right side is brownish white, opercles and over anterior part of abdomen bluish yellow.

Grows to nine inches in length, and is very good eating.

Habitat—Red Sea, Seas of India, and Malaysia.

ORDER PHYSOSTOMI.

SUB-ORDER SILURIDÆ.

Fam. SILUROIDEI, *Bleeker.*

Sub-Fam. BAGRIFORMES, *Bleeker.*

GROUP BAGRINI, *Bleeker.*

SUB-GROUP ARII, *Bleeker.*

GENUS NETUMA, *Bleeker.*

ARIUS, pt. *Cuv. & Val.*

Branchiostegals, five or six. Opercular bones with moveable articulations. No lateral groove on the head: bones on summit of head granulated, roughened, and covered with very thin skin. Mouth anterior: the upper jaw generally the longest. Eyes with free orbital margin. Cirri six, one maxillary and two mandibular pairs. Nostrils approximating, the posterior provided with a valve. Teeth in jaws villiform; also present (usually villiform) on vomer and palate, disposed in six patches, which may be either distinct or confluent: four of these patches form an anterior row, two of them being on the vomer, whilst the posterior row is composed of one pair, which are behind the internal portion of the anterior palatine row. Two dorsals, the first with one strong serrated spine and seven rays; it is situated above or before the ventrals: second dorsal adipose, well developed or moderate. Pectoral spine strong and serrated. Caudal forked or emarginate. An air bladder.

NETUMA NETUMA.

ARIUS NETUMA, *Cuv. & Val.* xiv. p. 438, pl. 417; *Day*, Proc. Zool. Soc. 1865, p. 292.

B. vi. D. $\frac{1}{7}$ | 0. P. $\frac{1}{12}$. V. 6. A. 19. C. 17.

Length of head $\frac{1}{4}$, of pectoral $\frac{1}{5}$, of caudal $\frac{1}{5}$, of base of dorsal $\frac{2}{25}$, of base of adipose dorsal $\frac{1}{4}$, of base of anal $\frac{1}{4}$ of the total length. Height of head $\frac{1}{6}$, of body $\frac{2}{9}$, of first dorsal $\frac{1}{5}$, of second dorsal $\frac{1}{21}$, of ventral $\frac{2}{19}$, of anal $\frac{1}{6}$ of the total length.

Eyes—Oval, situated in the anterior half of the head: horizontal diameter $\frac{2}{13}$, vertical diameter $\frac{1}{11}$ in length of head, 2 horizontal diameters from end of snout, 3 horizontal diameters apart.

Gape of mouth wide and semi-elliptical, upper jaw rather the longest: the maxillary pair of cirri extend to the root of the pectoral, and the two pairs of mandibular two-thirds the length of the maxillary. Opercular bones roughened in lines, shoulder bones in numerous small circular or oval depressions: the whole of the upper surface of the head nodulated as far forwards as orbits. Occipital process broader at its base than it is long, slightly keeled along its centre: basal bone of dorsal spine strong, the central longitudinal groove widest opposite the posterior margin of orbit, but does not extend much beyond the posterior margin of preopercle, where the raised longitudinal keel of the occipital process commences. Nostrils large, approximating, and midway between orbit and snout.

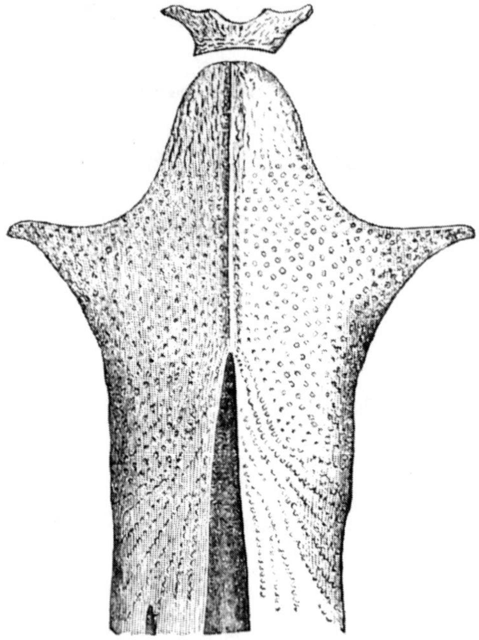

Teeth—In intermaxillaries sharp, in a straight band of several rows, and which are rather smaller in the lower jaws. Those on vomer and palate form two patches on either end of the mesial line, the internal pair being small and level with the front portion of the large patches: the external largest portions are each evidently formed of two confluent patches, a long anterior one and a short posterior one behind the inner portion of the anterior patch: thus the vomero-palatine teeth may be considered to be three patches on either side more or less confluent with one another.

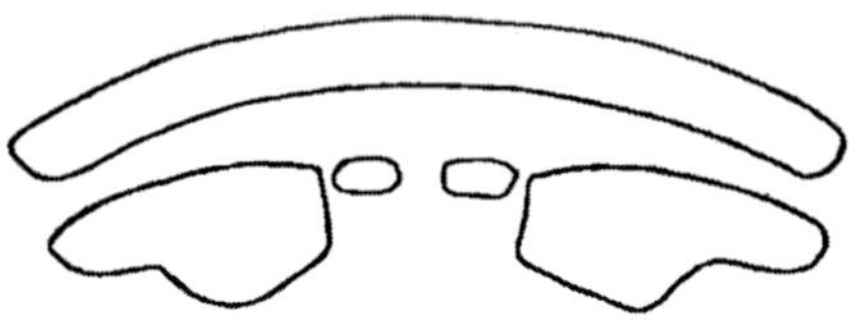

Fins—The dorsal fin commences opposite to the posterior third of the pectoral: ventral arises midway between the centre of the orbit and the base of the caudal: the anal arises nearer the end of the pectoral than it does to the base of the caudal. Dorsal spine very strong, granulated in front, serrated in its upper posterior half, it and the pectoral spine are of equal length, the latter also being granulated in front and serrated in its upper third, whilst posteriorly it is strongly denticulated: the length of these spines equals the distance from the posterior margin of the orbit to the end of the opercle. The dorsal rays are two thirds as high as the body. The caudal is lobed, the superior lobe being slightly the longest.

Lateral line—First ascends, opposite the first dorsal spine it bends downwards, and above the ventral it becomes straight; at the base of the caudal it divides into two branches, the upper crossing over the base of three, the lower of four caudal rays: a second raised line passes from the commencement of the last, and downwards to the base of the anal fin. The lateral line consists of raised, long and wide parallel tubes decreasing in size posteriorly.

Colours—Brownish silvery, slightly plumbaceous on the back. Head bronzed. Fins greyish with a yellowish tinge.

Grows to a large size, and is eaten by the Natives.

Habitat—Red Sea, and Seas and estuaries of India and Burmah.

Genus ARIUS, *Cuv. and Val.*

Branchiostegals, from five to six. Opercular bones with moveable articulations. No lateral groove on head: bones on summit of head rugose, with very thin skin. Mouth anterior, the upper jaw generally the longest. Eyes with a free orbital margin. Cirri six, one maxillary pair and two mandibular pairs. Nostrils approximating, the posterior provided with a valve. Teeth in jaws villiform, and in two distant patches on the palatines. Two dorsals, the first inserted above or before the ventrals, and with one strong serrated or roughened spine and six or seven rays: second dorsal adipose, well developed or moderate. Anal of moderate length. Pectoral spine strong and serrated. Caudal forked or emarginate. An air bladder.

Arius subrostratus.

Arius subrostratus, *Cuv. & Val.* xv. p. 62; *Day*, Proc. Zool. Soc. 1865, p. 293.

B. vi. D. $\frac{1}{7}$ | 0. P. $\frac{1}{11}$. V. 6. A. 20. C. 17.

Length of head $\frac{3}{10}$, of pectoral $\frac{1}{5}$, of base of first dorsal $\frac{1}{18}$, of base of second dorsal $\frac{1}{22}$, of base of anal $\frac{1}{10}$, of caudal $\frac{1}{5}$ of total length. Height of head $\frac{1}{6}$, of body $\frac{1}{5}$, of dorsal $\frac{1}{4}$, of anal $\frac{1}{10}$ of total length.

Eyes—Diameter $\frac{1}{5}$ of length of head, $\frac{5}{7}$ of a diameter apart, and nearly 2 diameters from end of snout.

Mouth spatuliform, extending across the anterior surface of head, its depth nearly equals a third of its width. Maxillary cirri rather fleshy at their origin, and do not extend so far as the orbit, whilst the external mandibular ones are not quite so long as, and the internal half the length of the external ones. Upper profile of head granulated, occipital process rather longer than broad, moderately keeled along its centre, and with a rounded extremity, where it articulates with a narrow nasal bone, which is convex anteriorly, and very rough. Central groove of head long and narrow, widest opposite the orbits, becoming quite sharp at both extremities; anteriorly it extends as far as the snout, and posteriorly to opposite the end of the opercles. The skull is roughened by raised nodules, in some places passing in lines as far forwards as the orbits, and laterally over summit of opercles. The shoulder bones are rough with small depressions. Opercle terminates posteriorly in a sub-acute angle, roughened by raised lines and depressions. Nostrils large, circular, and approximating, both situated in the anterior third of the snout, and at equal distances from the central line of the head and the margin of the snout.

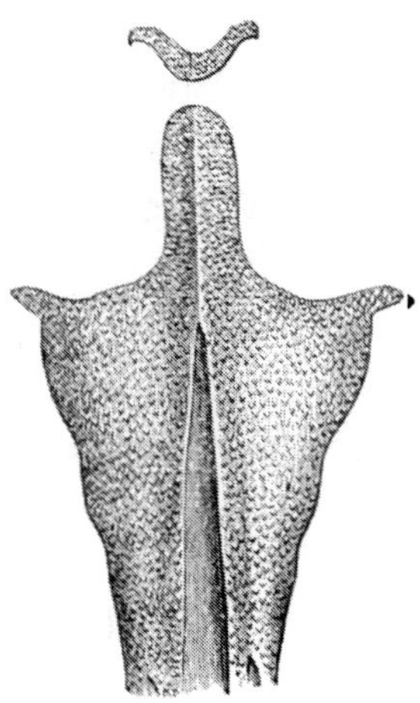

Teeth—Villiform in both jaws. On intermaxillaries the band is more than a fourth as wide as long. No teeth on vomer. In palate they are in two oval patches, placed wide apart, and diverging posteriorly.

Fins—First dorsal commences opposite the posterior fourth of the pectoral: ventral midway between the base of the pectoral and the posterior extremity of the anal: anal between the posterior extremity of the pectoral and the centre of the base of the dorsal: adipose dorsal situated over the posterior half of anal. Dorsal fin pointed, its spine long, equal to the distance from the centre of the orbit to the end of the snout: it is flattened laterally and lineated, nodulated anteriorly, becoming almost serrated in its upper three fourths, the serratures below being much less developed than those above: it terminates in a soft point; the first ray does not extend so far as the end of the soft termination of the spine, and the last ray is only a third the length of the spine. Pectoral spine very slightly shorter than that of the dorsal, laterally compressed and slightly roughened in lines: it is nodulated externally, and semi-serrated in its external half: internally it is serrated for its whole extent: it ends in a soft point. Anal with the sixth or seventh ray the longest, its external margin is rather concave. Base of soft dorsal equal to about half that of the anal, it is higher than wide. Caudal lobed, but not deeply: fin rather expanded: the distance between the end of the anal and commencement of caudal equals the base of the anal.

Lateral line—In pairs of short parallel tubes, at first curving upwards, below the dorsal spine it begins to sink, and from opposite the end of the ventral it passes direct to the centre of the caudal, where it divides into two branches, the superior passing upwards, crossing the base of two rays, and the inferior downwards crossing the base of three.

Colours—Brilliant silvery blue as far as the lateral line: silvery white below: a golden gloss over the cheeks. Fins yellowish: very fine black spots on the tip of the dorsal, over the adipose dorsal and the caudal.

Common, and is captured principally during the S. W. monsoon. Is eaten by the Natives. Grows to a foot in length.

Habitat—Malabar.

* Arius rostratus.

Arius rostratus, *Cuv. & Val.* xv. p. 63.

D. $\frac{1}{6}$ | 0. P. $\frac{1}{10}$. V. 7. A. 18. C. 18.

Length of head $\frac{1}{3}$ of the body excluding the caudal fin, measured to the summit of the interparietal prominence it is $\frac{3}{7}$. The distance from the end of the mouth to the angle of the frontal is half the length from the end of the snout to the angle of the opercle, which is more than obtains in the *Ar. subrostratus.*

The interorbital space is more flat than in the last, and the central longitudinal groove on the head straighter and longer, whilst the interparietal ridge is narrower and its granulations stronger.

The maxillary cirrus does not extend so far as the projecting angle of the frontal: the others are a third or half shorter.

The shoulder bones are smooth and without any striæ or granulations.

Teeth—Are villiform and fine in the jaws, and on a very small patch on the palatines they are blunt and granulated.

Colours—Plumbaceous, blackish on the back and silvery below.

Habitat—Allepey in Malabar.

Arius cœlatus.

Arius cœlatus, *Cuv. & Val.* xv. p. 66; *Bleeker*, Atl. Ich. ii. p. 35, t. 53; *Günther*, Catal. v. p. 158.

Arius æquibarbis, *Cuv. & Val.* xv. p. 68.

Arius granosus, *Cuv. & Val.* xv. p. 69.

B. v. D. $\frac{1}{7}$. | 0. P. $\frac{1}{9}$. V. 6. A. 19. C. 15.

Length of head $\frac{1}{5}$, of pectoral $\frac{1}{6}$, of caudal $\frac{1}{5}$, of base of dorsal $\frac{1}{15}$, of base of second dorsal $\frac{1}{10}$, of base of anal $\frac{1}{8}$ of total length. Height of head $\frac{1}{7}$, of body $\frac{1}{6}$, of first dorsal $\frac{1}{4}$, of second dorsal $\frac{1}{19}$, of anal $\frac{1}{10}$, of ventral $\frac{1}{7}$ of total length.

Eyes—Oval, situated midway between the posterior extremity of the opercles and the end of snout. Horizontal diameter $\frac{1}{4}$, vertical diameter $\frac{1}{6}$ of length of head, 1 diameter from end of snout, 2 diameters apart.

Mouth wide, upper jaw rather the longest. Maxillary cirrus extends to half the length of the pectoral, the two mandibular cirri to its base. Opercle striated in rough lines. Central longitudinal groove of head broad, extending in front to the snout, and behind to opposite the posterior extremity of the opercle. Occipital process longitudinally keeled, narrow, one and a fourth times as high as wide, basal bone narrow, both covered with nodules—most apparent in the adult—as is also the skull as far forwards as the orbits, and laterally as the opercles. Shoulder bone also similarly roughened. Nostrils, the posterior the largest, oval, and with a valve: the anterior round, close to the anterior margin of the snout.

Teeth—In intermaxillaries villiform and numerous in a band about a sixth as wide as long, and which is rather expanded at its extremity. They are also villiform in the mandibles. In either palatine bone is an irregularly triangular patch containing numbers of villiform teeth, they are nearer together anteriorly, than posteriorly.

Fins—Dorsal commences opposite the centre of the pectoral; ventral midway between the snout and base of caudal: anal midway between the base of pectoral and the posterior extremity of the lower lobe of the caudal. Dorsal pointed, spine in the adult much thicker below than above, but weaker in the young; anteriorly granulated in its basal half, and semi-serrated in its upper portion: serrated posteriorly, laterally compressed and rough: its rays rapidly decrease in length to the last; its spine equals the distance from the posterior extremity of the opercle to the posterior extremity of the anterior nostril. Pectoral spine rather shorter and not so strong as the dorsal, it is laterally compressed, roughened anteriorly, and serrated posteriorly. The sixth anal ray the longest, its external margin concave. Caudal deeply lobed.

Lateral line—Consists of short parallel longitudinal tubes. First it rises slightly to the upper fourth of the body, opposite the first dorsal spine it curves downwards, and then nearly above the commencement of the anal it proceeds straight: at the base of the caudal it divides into two branches, the upper crossing the base of three rays, and the lower the base of two.

Air vessel of a silvery tint, with a thick fibrous covering, and very adherent. The lining membrane is very thin.

Colours—In the adult steel blue, with a gloss of golden. Adipose fin black, with its posterior margin yellow. Dorsal, anal, and caudal grey, finely spotted with minute black points, as is also the under surface of head and abdomen. Upper surface of head blackish. The young have no black spot to the adipose dorsal.

Grows to eleven inches or more.

Habitat—Seas of India, Burmah, and Malaysia.

ARIUS GAGORA.

PIMELODUS GAGORA, *Ham. Buch.* pp. 167, 376, pl. 10, f. 54.
ARIUS GAGORA, *Cuv. & Val.* xv. p. 99; *Günther*, Catal. v. p. 168.

B. v. D. $\frac{1}{7}$ | 0. P. $\frac{1}{10-11}$. V. 6. A. 18-19. C. 15. Vert. $\frac{16}{29}$.

Length of head $\frac{2}{7}$, of caudal $\frac{2}{11}$, of base of first dorsal $\frac{1}{11}$, of base of second dorsal $\frac{1}{16}$, of base of anal $\frac{1}{8}$ of total length. Height of head $\frac{2}{13}$, of body $\frac{1}{4}$, of first dorsal $\frac{1}{3}$, of anal $\frac{1}{8}$ of total length.

Eyes—Oval and situated in the anterior half of the head. Horizontal diameter $\frac{2}{11}$, vertical diameter $\frac{1}{7}$ of length of head, 2 diameters from end of snout, $2\frac{1}{2}$ diameters apart.

Head broader than high, rather flattened above and its width equal to three quarters of its length.

Snout obtuse, opening of mouth transverse, its cleft equals half the distance to the anterior margin of the orbit, upper jaw the longest. Opercle radiated, with some irregular roughened lines crossing the radiations. Central longitudinal groove rather shallow anteriorly, but deep posteriorly: widest opposite the posterior margin of the orbits, passing anteriorly as far as to opposite the posterior nostril, and posteriorly to the opposite posterior end of the opercles. Occipital process longitudinally keeled, as high as wide, its superior extremity rather convex where it joins the basal bone of the dorsal fin, which is rather broad, and as well as the whole of the occipital process is covered with raised nodules, which extend nearly as far forwards as the orbit, and down towards the shoulder. Nostrils approximating, situated in the anterior half of the distance between the orbit and the end of snout; the anterior one circular, the posterior crescent-shaped and covered by a valve. Shoulder bone covered with round and oval depressions. Maxillary cirri reach to the posterior extremity of opercle. There are two pairs of mandibular cirri extending as far as the base of the pectoral or slightly further.

Teeth—By an evident misprint, *Hamilton Buchanan* states, that the palatine teeth are sharp and those in the jaw granular, which statement should be reversed. The teeth in the intermaxillaries are in a sharp crowded band, about a fourth as wide as long: in the lower jaw they are also sharp and crowded. The palatine teeth are rounded, and placed like a pavement, in two large rhomboidal patches, converging behind, but rather more widely separated in front.

Fins—Dorsal commences opposite the middle of the pectoral, and the ventral midway between the angle of the mouth and the centre of the base of the caudal: the anal arises about midway between the posterior extremity of the pectoral, and the base of the caudal: the adipose dorsal is situated over the last half of anal. Dorsal fin pointed, spine strong, equal to the distance from the posterior nostril to the posterior extremity of the opercle, it is flattened, roughened by lines laterally, and extended into a soft point longer than the rays; its spine is nodulated anteriorly, and serrated in its upper half: also serrated posteriorly. Pectoral spine equal to the distance from the anterior angle of the orbit, to the posterior extremity of the opercle, it is shorter than that of the dorsal, and ends in a soft point: it is flattened and roughened in lines laterally, and serrated in its whole anterior and posterior extents. The sixth anal ray is the highest, and the external margin of the fin is slightly concave. Caudal lobed, and extended laterally, so that its posterior margin is semicircular.

Lateral line—At first curves slightly upwards, opposite the dorsal spine bends downwards to opposite the commencement of the anal, from whence it proceeds direct to the base of the caudal, where it divides into two branches, the upper one crossing over the three rays above it, and the lower one over the bases of the three rays below.

Colours—Back of a dusky bluish purple, which becomes almost white below the lateral line, the whole shining with silvery reflections. Dorsal, anal, pectoral, and caudal finely and minutely dotted with small black points, as is also the abdomen: ventral, anal, and caudal stained with red. Adipose fin with a large blackish spot.

Not uncommon. Eaten by the lower classes. Grows to three feet in length.

Habitat—Seas and estuaries of India.

GENUS OSTEOGENIOSUS, *Bleeker.*

Branchiostegals, five. Opercular bones with moveable articulations. No lateral groove on head: bones on summit of head granulated, and covered with a very thin skin. Mouth anterior, very wide, the upper jaw generally the longest. Cirri consisting of one bony maxillary pair. Nostrils approximating, the posterior provided with a valve. Teeth in jaws villiform: on palate obtusely conical, in two oblong widely separated patches. Two dorsals, the first with a strong serrated spine and seven rays, it is placed before the ventrals: second dorsal adipose, small. Pectoral spine strong and serrated. Caudal forked or emarginate. Air bladder present.

OSTEOGENIOSUS MILITARIS.

SILURUS MILITARIS, *Linn.* Sys. Nat. i. p. 503.
ARIUS MILITARIS, *Cuv. & Val.* xv. p. 114, pl. 430; *Cantor*, Catal. p. 259.
OSTEOGENIOSUS MILITARIS, *Bleeker*, Atl. Ich. iv. p. 46; *Günther*, Catal. v. p. 181.

B. v. D. $\frac{1}{7}$ | 0. P. $\frac{1}{10\text{-}11}$. V. 6. A. 20-23. C. 15. Vert. $\frac{18}{29}$.

Length of head $\frac{1}{4}$, of pectoral $\frac{1}{6}$, of caudal $\frac{1}{6}$, of base of first dorsal $\frac{1}{13}$, of base of second dorsal $\frac{1}{16}$, of base of anal $\frac{1}{7}$ of total length. Height of head $\frac{1}{7}$, of body more than $\frac{1}{4}$, of first dorsal $\frac{2}{9}$, of second dorsal $\frac{1}{16}$, of ventral $\frac{1}{8}$, of anal $\frac{1}{7}$ of total length.

Eyes—Oval. Horizontal diameter $\frac{1}{7}$, vertical diameter $\frac{1}{10}$ of length of head, 2 diameters from end of snout, $3\frac{1}{2}$ diameters apart.

Body broadest opposite the first dorsal. Width of head nearly twice its height, width of interorbital space equal to half the length of the head.

Gape of mouth extends nearly across the end of the head, which is obtuse, and cleft half way from the snout to the orbit. Lower jaw slightly the shortest. Central longitudinal groove having its widest portion not quite midway between the snout and first dorsal, it rapidly narrows superiorly, but much more gradually inferiorly; it is of a lanceolate shape, extending from the snout nearly to the base of the occipital process. Occipital process nearly three times as high as broad, roughened in longitudinal lines, and extending as far as the basal bone of the first dorsal fin. Between the upper end of the central groove of the head and the base of the occipital process, there are some very distinct elevated nodules, external to which are roughened lineated elevations. Upper surface of orbits covered by a fleshy curtain. Nostrils large, approximating, situated near the snout, the anterior round close to the margin of snout, the posterior one oval. Maxillary barbel, long, flexible, compressed, and furrowed, becoming fine at its external point, and extending slightly beyond the centre of the pectoral fin: from its posterior margin near its root, extends a small triangular membrane, which is so short, that the cirrus cannot be extended at a right angle to the head.

Teeth—In the upper jaw in a band one-third as wide as long, not reaching the angle of the mouth, but terminating near the root of the bony maxillary cirrus: they are small, placed close together, and curved. In the lower jaw they are of the same description, but extend further laterally, whilst there are none opposite the symphysis. On the palate they are obtusely conical, placed in two large rhomboidal patches, wide apart, but converging posteriorly.

Fins—First dorsal commences over the posterior extremity of the pectoral spine: ventral opposite the posterior end of the dorsal: anal midway between the base of the pectoral and the posterior extremity of the centre of the caudal: adipose dorsal opposite the centre of the anal.

First dorsal spine laterally compressed, serrated on both sides in its upper third, the serratures on the posterior margin being the strongest: it is also roughened anteriorly to its base: its rays are longer than its spines, the posterior of which are the shortest. Pectoral spine rather shorter than that of the dorsal, it is also compressed, serrated on both sides of its external third, and rugose along the rest of its outer margin. Anal with the fifth ray the longest, from whence they rapidly decrease to the last. Caudal lobed, but not deeply. Adipose dorsal twice as long as wide.

Lateral line—Proceeds straight to opposite the commencement of the first dorsal, then obliquely downwards to opposite the commencement of the ventral; from thence it takes an undulating course to the centre of the caudal where it divides into two branches, one passing obliquely upward, crossing over the base of three rays, and ending between them and the next; the lower branch takes the same course downwards over the lower lobe of the caudal.

Colours—Of a beautiful leaden silvery tint on the upper surface of the body and sides, which fades into a silvery white on the abdomen and chest. The first dorsal has a slight pinkish tinge, and is stained darker on its margin. Adipose dorsal slate colour, darkest at its margins. Caudal pinkish, stained with grey posteriorly. Maxillary cirri, and snout rose-coloured. Pectoral, ventral, and anal also of a rose colour. Eye of a rosy tint.

Dr. Jerdon states, that the air vessel "yields a coarse isinglass, which is exported to Bombay:" and *Cantor* observes that he believes in the Straits "their air vessels are preserved."

Habitat—Seas and estuaries of India, Burmah, and Malaysia.

Genus BATRACHOCEPHALUS, *Bleeker*.

Branchiostegals, five. Head broad, depressed. Opercular bones articulated and moveable. Summit of head granulated. Mouth very wide, anterior, cleft extending to under eyes. Lower jaw the longest. Nostrils approximating, the posterior provided with a valve. Eyes with a free orbital margin. Cirri, one pair of mandibular, fine and rudimentary. Teeth in jaws conical, with rounded summits, and placed in two bands with a short interspace: a broad longitudinal band on either palate; none on the vomer. Two dorsals, the first with one strong serrated spine and seven rays: it is situated before the ventrals: second dorsal adipose, and short. Pectoral spine strong, serrated. Anal fin short. Caudal forked or emarginate. Gill membranes united under the throat without a notch. Air bladder present.

Batrachocephalus mino.

Ageneiosus mino, *Ham. Buch.* pp. 158, 375.

Batrachocephalus mino, *Bleeker*, Atl. Ich. iv. p. 48, t. 65, f. i.; *Günther*, Catal. v. p. 182.

B. v. D. $\frac{1}{7}$ | 0. P. $\frac{1}{9}$. V. 6. A. 20. C. 17.

Length of head $\frac{1}{4}$, of pectoral $\frac{1}{5}$, of caudal $\frac{1}{5}$, of base of first dorsal $\frac{1}{14}$, of base of second dorsal $\frac{1}{17}$, of base of anal $\frac{1}{6}$ of total length. Height of head $\frac{1}{6}$, of body $\frac{2}{9}$, of first dorsal $\frac{1}{5}$, of second dorsal $\frac{1}{11}$, of ventral $\frac{1}{6}$, of anal $\frac{1}{7}$ of total length.

Eyes—Oval. Horizontal diameter $\frac{2}{7}$, vertical diameter $\frac{1}{6}$ in length of head, $\frac{3}{5}$ of a diameter from end of snout, $1\frac{1}{2}$ diameters apart.

Body widest opposite the opercles, profile rises to the first dorsal, and from thence gradually sinks to the caudal. Abdominal surface more convex than that of the back.

Gape of mouth extends across the front of the head, and its cleft to beneath the posterior third of the orbit. Lower jaw rather the longest, roughened below. Central longitudinal groove on head lanceolate, widest opposite the posterior extremity of the orbit; extending anteriorly to the snout, posteriorly to midway between the snout and the base of the occipital process. Occipital process rugose, as wide at the base as it is high, and extending to the basal bone of the first dorsal. Sides of head roughened. Opercles slightly lineated, and covered with small round depressions. Apertures of nostrils circular, approximating, the posterior one covered by a valve, close to the anterior superior angle of the orbit, and the anterior one situated just in front of it. Two short mandibular cirri exist, equal in length to a fourth of the diameter of the eye. Shoulder bones almost naked, marked with depressions. Basal bone of dorsal spine crescent-shaped, and narrow.

Teeth—In upper jaw in from four to five rows, with long rather obtuse heads, the two anterior rows—which contain the largest teeth—separated by a short interspace from three posterior ones. The outer band of the upper jaw extends furthest laterally. Teeth in lower jaw the same as in the upper: those in the palate rather smaller but of the same description, placed in two straight widely separated patches.

Fins—First dorsal arises opposite the middle of the pectoral: ventral midway between the snout and the posterior extremity of the lower lobe of the caudal: anal opposite end of ventral: adipose dorsal over the fifth anal ray. The first spine of the dorsal is equal to the distance from the angle of the mouth to the posterior extremity of the bony opercle: it is laterally compressed and not quite so high as the first ray: also serrated posteriorly in the upper half, and anteriorly rugose in its whole extent; the rays decrease in length from the first to the last. The adipose dorsal is one and a half times as long as wide. Pectoral spine compressed, stronger, and one sixth longer than that of the dorsal, serrated interiorly, rugose in its whole extent externally. Ventral rounded. Anal with the fifth ray the longest, from which they decrease to the last. Caudal lobed, the lower lobe the longest.

Lateral line—Gradually sinks to opposite the base of the anal, being almost concave above, and from thence it proceeds direct to the base of the caudal, where it divides into two branches, the upper of which crosses over the base of the two rays above, and then goes direct to the end of the caudal, the lower branching downwards in the same manner.

Colours—Upper surface of head and body silvery, becoming white on the abdomen. Dorsal dark grey, tipped with black. Superior half of the upper lobe of the caudal black. Pectoral with a slightly greyish tint: other fins yellowish. Eyes golden.

By no means rare at Cochin, especially in the cold months. Grows to a foot and a half in length, but is not esteemed for eating, although the lower classes of Natives employ it as food.

Habitat—Seas of India and Malaysia.

Sub-Group BAGRI, *Bleeker.*

Genus HARA, *Blyth.*

Branchiostegals, ten. Head broad, depressed. Opercular bones articulated and moveable. A separate bone between basal bone of dorsal fin and end of occipital process: in adults an interspace between the end of occipital process and anterior extremity of intermediate bone, which is not apparent in the young: these bones and summit of head granulated or rough. Eyes without free orbital margins, below the skin. Mouth wide, anterior. Cirri eight: one pair arises at posterior nasal orifice which is some distance apart from the anterior which is tubular: one maxillary pair, widest at their basal halves, and two pairs of mandibular ones. Teeth villiform in intermaxillaries and lower jaw, and an uninterrupted band across vomer and palate. First dorsal with one sharp spine—sometimes denticulated—and seven rays, it is inserted before the ventral which has six rays. Adipose dorsal longer than the anal, which last is short. Pectoral spine strongly denticulated. Caudal emarginate or forked. Interbranchial membrane deeply cleft. Air bladder present.

Hara Malabarica. Plate XIII. Fig. 3.

B. x. D. $\frac{1}{7}$ | 0. P. $\frac{1}{9}$. V. 6. A. 10. C. 18.

Length of head $\frac{2}{11}$, of pectoral $\frac{1}{6}$, of caudal $\frac{1}{7}$, of base of first dorsal $\frac{1}{9}$, of base of second dorsal from $\frac{1}{9}$ to $\frac{2}{9}$, of base of anal $\frac{2}{11}$ of total length. Height of head $\frac{1}{9}$, of body $\frac{1}{6}$, of first dorsal $\frac{2}{11}$, of ventral $\frac{1}{7}$, of anal $\frac{1}{8}$ of total length.

Eyes—Close to profile below the skin, diameter $\frac{2}{9}$ of length of head, $1\frac{1}{2}$ diameters from end of snout, $1\frac{3}{4}$ diameters apart.

Form of body compressed, head broad and strongly depressed, its width being equal to the height of the body. There is a slight rise from the snout to opposite the orbits, from whence the upper profile is nearly straight: the abdominal profile is more convex than that of the back.

Mouth anterior, gape nearly four times as wide as its cleft which does not extend so far as to beneath the orbits. The upper surface of the head is granulated and rather convex transversely, with a longitudinal central groove, extending from opposite the posterior extremity of the opercle to the snout, it is widest between the orbits. The occipital process in the adult is above twice as long as wide, and an interval equal to its length exists between it and the interneural bone which reaches the base of the basal one, in the immature they touch one another. The maxillary cirri are long, rather thick at their bases and extend as far as the centre of the ventral fins: the nasal pair reach as far as the end of the opercle: the external mandibular pair go as far as the end of the opercle: the internal pair not quite so far. Gill membranes deeply cleft, one slightly overlapping the other: gills four. Anus under posterior third of ventral fins.

Teeth—A wide band of villiform teeth in intermaxillaries, also a semilunar uninterrupted one about one quarter as wide as long passes across the vomer and palate.

Fins—Pectoral arises under the last quarter of the opercle: the first dorsal over the posterior third of the pectoral spine: the ventral opposite the posterior extremity of the first dorsal, and the anal commences twice the length of the base of the ventral fin behind its posterior margin. First dorsal spine weak, and not quite half the length of the rays which are branched: the length of the spine equals the distance between the posterior margin of the orbit and the posterior extremity of the opercle. First ventral ray undivided, the rest branched, the fin situated horizontally. Pectoral spine strong, laterally compressed, its length equals the distance from the anterior extremity of the orbit to the posterior extremity of the opercle: it is armed internally with eight sharp curved

PLATE XIII.

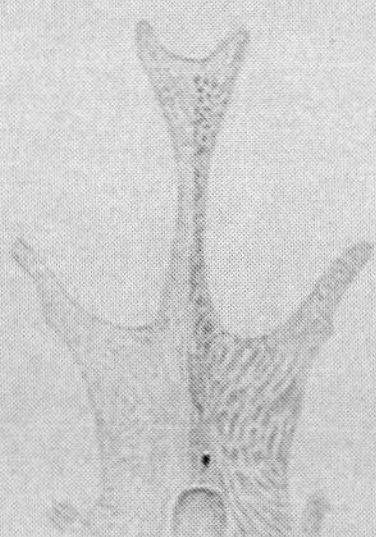

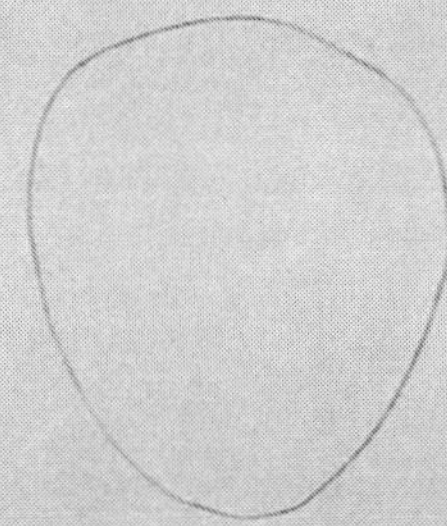

Fig 1.

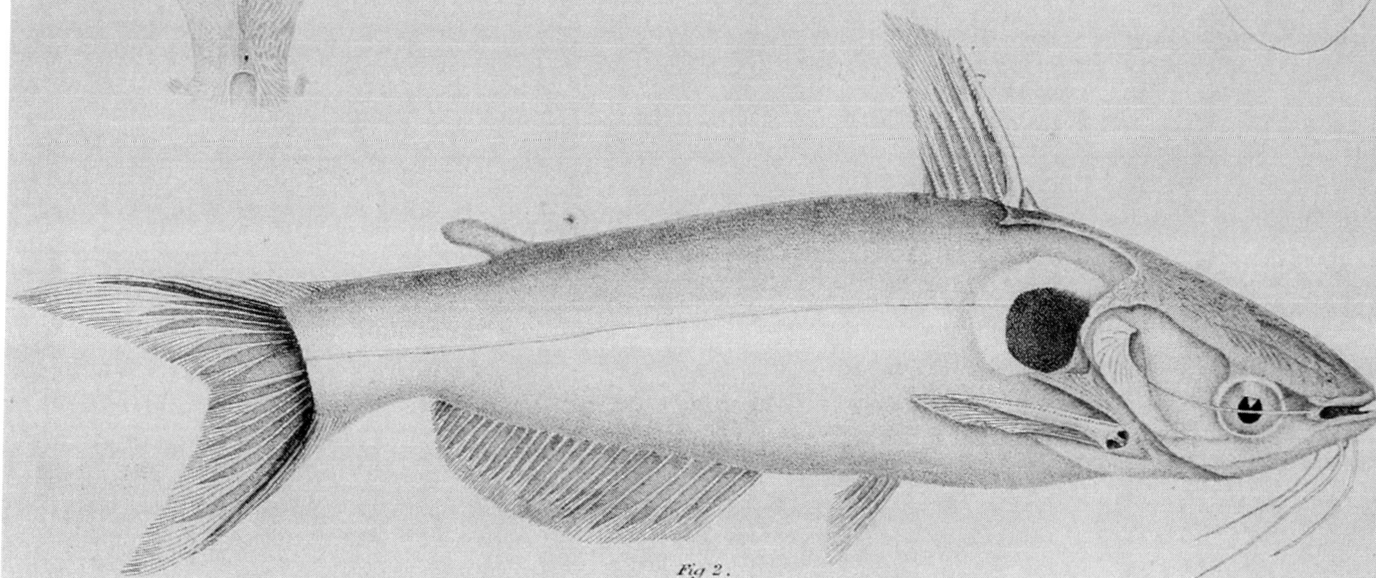

Fig 2.

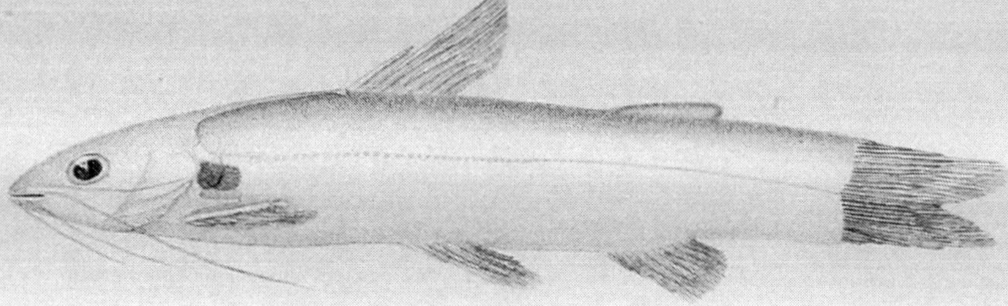

Fig 3.

F. Day, del, et sculp.

1. PUNTIUS VITTATUS. 2. PSEUDOBAGRUS CHRYSEUS. 3. HARA MALABARICA.

teeth, decreasing in size from the first to the last: it is also finely serrated externally and ends in a strong tooth directed forwards, between which and the most anterior tooth of its internal margin is a trefoil-shaped membraneous prolongation as seen in the *Hypselobagrus armatus* (page 188). The adipose dorsal appears as if it contained the rudiments of rays. Anal with its first three rays unbranched, the remainder branched, a fleshy sheath extends along the base of the fin. Caudal lobed in the adult, deeply lunated in the immature.

Lateral line—Proceeds direct to opposite centre of caudal, and ceases just before reaching it: it is formed of pairs of very short parallel tubes, more distinct in the anterior than in the posterior portion of the body.

Colours—Deep leaden, with a dark brown spot on the shoulder surrounded by a lighter margin: abdomen silvery. Cheeks and under surface of head of a yellowish tinge. Bases of pectoral and anal yellowish. Fins grey, covered with minute dark points.

I received some specimens of this fish from the Rev. H. Baker (junior) from the mountain streams of Travancore, the largest being rather less than four inches in length.

Habitat—Mountain streams of Malabar.

Genus PSEUDOBAGRUS, *Bleeker*.

Branchiostegals, from eight to ten. Head depressed, roughened, and covered with very thin skin. Opercular bones articulated and moveable: occipital process scarcely reaches the basal bone of dorsal fin. Back wide. Eyes of moderate size or small. Mouth anterior. Cirri eight, one nasal, one maxillary, and two mandibular pairs. Teeth form a continuous transverse villiform band on the vomer and palate; those in jaws also villiform, and in several rows. Dorsal with one sharp, sometimes serrated spine, and seven rays: it is inserted before the ventral, which has six rays. Adipose dorsal short, as long as high. Pectoral spine strong and denticulated. Anal of moderate length, of twenty or more rays. Caudal emarginate or forked: the external rays sometimes produced. Interbranchial membrane deeply cleft. An air bladder present.

Pseudobagrus chryseus. Plate XIII. Fig. 2.

Pseudobagrus chryseus, *Day*, Proc. Zool. Soc. 1865, p. 290.

B. x. D. $\frac{1}{7}$ | 0. P. $\frac{1}{6}$. V. 6. A. 27. C. 17.

Length of head about $\frac{2}{9}$, of base of first dorsal $\frac{1}{13}$, of base of adipose dorsal $\frac{1}{13}$, of caudal $\frac{2}{9}$, of base of anal $\frac{2}{9}$ of total length. Height of head $\frac{1}{9}$, of body $\frac{2}{9}$, of dorsal fin $\frac{1}{6}$, of anal $\frac{1}{10}$ of total length.

Eyes—Diameter $\frac{9}{20}$ of length of head, $1\frac{1}{2}$ diameters apart, upwards of 1 diameter from end of snout.

Gape of mouth wide, its transverse width being equal to half the length of the head. Jaws equal in length. Summit of head depressed, both it and the shoulder bone furrowed; occipital process narrow, twice as long as wide; basal bone considerably produced, so as nearly to touch the occipital process, and extended in front on either side of the dorsal spine. A flat lance-shaped groove in the central line of the head, between the orbits, pointing downwards and forwards, reaching in front nearly to the intermaxillaries, and superiorly only extending to a short distance behind the orbits. Nasal cirri equal to half the length of the head, the maxillary pair slightly longer; the external of the mandibular pairs reaches as far as the base of the pectoral, whilst the internal pair is one-fourth shorter.

Teeth—Very fine and villiform in both intermaxillaries and lower jaw; on the vomer and palate they are considerably longer and stronger, and are arranged in a transverse band, slightly crescentic posteriorly.

Fins—The first dorsal arises opposite the middle of the pectoral, and the ventral just beyond its termination, and reaching as far as the commencement of the anal. Pectoral situated in the lower quarter of the body. The adipose dorsal commences opposite the middle of the anal. Dorsal spine strongly serrated, having about ten teeth posteriorly in its upper two-thirds, and three serratures in the front of its summit anteriorly, its extremity ending in a soft filament: its rays are longer than its spine. The pectoral spine is stronger than that of the dorsal, slightly roughened, serrated anteriorly, and more strongly so posteriorly, with from sixteen to eighteen teeth: when laid flat this spine is protected by an overhanging bony arch, formed by the process of the shoulder bone. Adipose dorsal soft and rounded. Anal rather rounded posteriorly. Caudal deeply lunated; outer rays the longest.

Lateral line—Passes from the summit of the opercle direct to the centre of the caudal.

Colours—Back greenish yellow; sides golden; a large round black finger mark situated just behind the opercle, and surrounded by a light yellow margin. The first and adipose dorsals are yellowish, with a dusky tinge. Caudal with a deep black base and a blackish margin, the ground colour being of a reddish orange, slightly stained with black at its extremity. Anal of a deep orange red, slightly margined with black. Eyes orange.

Exceedingly common in the Kurriavanoor river, near Cochin, where they appear to prefer the deepest pools; four or five are frequently taken out at one haul of a cast-net. They are also occasionally captured during the monsoon in the backwater at Kurriapudnam, and in the river at Cochin. Said by the fishermen rarely to exceed sixteen inches in length. Esteemed for eating; but the wounds inflicted by their pectoral spines are dreaded.

Habitat—Fresh waters and occasionally backwaters of the Malabar coast.

Genus HEMIBAGRUS, *Bleeker*.

Branchiostegals, from eleven to twelve. Head depressed. Opercular bones with moveable articulations. An interspace between the posterior extremity of occipital process, and the anterior extremity of the basal bone of the dorsal fin; bones rough or granulated. Back wide, fleshy. Eyes with free circular lids. Mouth anterior. Cirri eight, one pair at posterior nasal orifices, which are some distance from the anterior which are tubular: one maxillary and two mandibular pairs, the last being near the corner of the mouth. Teeth in intermaxillaries and lower jaw in several villiform rows; those on vomer and palatines form a semicircular undivided patch. Two dorsals, the first with one denticulated spine and seven rays: the second adipose and of moderate size. Pectoral with a strong denticulated spine. Anal of medium size. Caudal bilobed. Interbranchial membrane deeply cleft. Air bladder present.

* Hemibagrus oculatus.

Bagrus oculatus, *Cuv. & Val.* xiv. p. 424; *Jerdon*, Madras Journal, xv. p. 339.

B. vi. (?) D. $\frac{1}{7}$ | 0. A. 12.

Eyes—Diameter $\frac{1}{3}$ of length of head, 1 diameter apart.

Front of mouth rounded, Upper surface of head granulated, and twice as long as wide. Occipital process long, straight, and extending half way to the base of the dorsal. Maxillary cirri pass the anal.

Fins—First dorsal pointed, higher than the body: the adipose dorsal equals the anal in its length. Lobes of caudal pointed, the superior the longest.

Colours—Grey above, silvery on the sides and white beneath. The dorsal black at its base, and superiorly; the other fins blackish. Ventrals fawn colour, with white edges.

Grows to three inches in length.

Habitat—Rivers and fresh waters of Malabar.

GENUS HYPSELOBAGRUS, *Bleeker.*

MACRONES, pt. *Dumeril.*

Branchiostegals, from eight to ten. Head conical, compressed. Opercular bones articulated and moveable. The occipital process which is rugose touches the basal bone of the dorsal fin, or should there be an intermediate shield they articulate one with the other, and there is no intermediate free space. Back compressed. Eyes free with subvertical lids. Mouth anterior. Cirri eight, one pair to posterior nasal orifice which is some distance apart from the anterior which is tubular; one pair to maxillaries: and two pairs to mandibulæ. Teeth in both jaws sharp and in many rows, those on the vomer and palate villiform and continuous in one semilunar band. Dorsal inserted before ventral, with a sharp serrated spine and seven rays: adipose dorsal in length equal to, or of greater extent than the anal which is short. Pectoral spine denticulated. Caudal bilobed. Interbranchial membrane deeply cleft. Air bladder present.

HYPSELOBAGRUS ARMATUS.

MACRONES ARMATUS, *Day*, Pro. Zool. Soc. 1865, p. 289.

B. ix-x. D. $\frac{1}{7}$ | 0. P. $\frac{1}{6}$. V. 6. A. 11-12. C. 15.

Length of head above $\frac{1}{5}$, of pectoral $\frac{1}{6}$, of caudal $\frac{1}{4}$, of base of dorsal $\frac{1}{9}$, of base of adipose dorsal $\frac{1}{7}$, of base of anal $\frac{1}{9}$ of total length. Height of head $\frac{1}{7}$, of body $\frac{1}{5}$, of first dorsal $\frac{1}{5}$, of anal $\frac{1}{9}$ of total length.

Eyes—Transversely oval: horizontal diameter $\frac{2}{5}$, vertical diameter $\frac{1}{3}$ of length of head, $\frac{3}{4}$ of a horizontal diameter apart, $\frac{1}{2}$ a diameter from end of snout.

Head compressed, a gradual rise from snout to first dorsal. Upper jaw the longest overlapping the lower, the cleft of the mouth hardly exceeds one-fourth of its gape, and does not extend posteriorly so far as the anterior margin of the orbit, the inferior surface of the intermaxillaries is on a level with the lower margin of the orbit. Upper surface of head rugose with a central longitudinal groove extending nearly but not quite to the base of the occipital process which is rugose. The occipital process (including its second bone) is three times as long as wide, the second bone is closely articulated to it and also touches the basal bone of the dorsal fin. The nostrils are wide apart, the posterior having a cirrus. The nasal cirri extend to as far as the posterior margin of the orbit: the

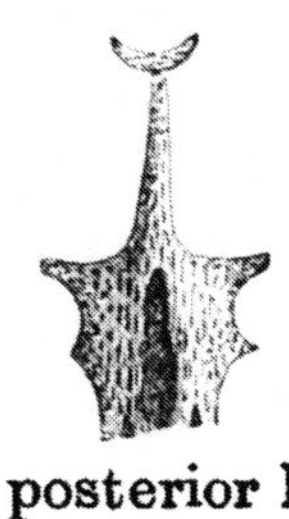

maxillary to the middle or end of anal: and the external mandibular which arises just under the angle of the mouth extends to the middle of the pectoral, whilst the internal pair arise near together under symphysis and do not reach quite so far posteriorly as the external ones.

Teeth—Villiform in both jaws in several rows: those on vomer and palate also villiform and

disposed in a single uninterrupted crescentic band.

Fins.—Pectoral arises under the extremity of the opercle and in the lower fourth of the body: the dorsal is situated over the posterior third of the pectoral spine: the anal midway between the base of the ventral and base of the caudal: the adipose dorsal commences a short distance anterior to the anal. Pectoral spine strong, curved, laterally compressed, its length equals the distance between the angle of the mouth and the posterior extremity of the opercle: it has about ten very

strong curved denticulations along its internal border, whilst its anterior border ends in a point directed forwards, between which and the first tooth—on its internal border—is a membraneous prolongation in the form of a trefoil leaf. The dorsal spine is of the same length but more slender than that of the pectoral, it is finely serrated posteriorly and ends superiorly in a soft prolongation. The three first anal rays are undivided; the caudal deeply lobed, the superior being generally the longest whilst both frequently terminate in filamentous prolongations.

Lateral line—Passes direct from the upper margin of the opercle to the centre of the caudal fin.

Colours—Bright leaden silvery, lightest along the sides and with a purplish gloss over the cheeks. A black spot just anterior to the root of the dorsal spine. Fins finely dotted with minute black points.

Not uncommon in the rivers and tanks of fresh water, and occasionally found in the back-water. Immediately on being captured the fishermen break off its pectoral and dorsal spines, as wounds from them are dreaded. It takes a bait freely, and is eaten by the Natives, but does not appear to exceed five inches in length.

Habitat—Malabar.

HYPSELOBAGRUS CAVASIUS.

PIMELODUS CAVASIUS, *Ham. Buch.* pp. 203, 379, pl. 11, f. 67.

BAGRUS CAVASIUS, *Cuv. & Val.* xiv. p. 209; *Jerdon*, Madras Journal, xv. p. 337.

PIMELODUS SEENGTEE, *Sykes*, Trans. Z. S. ii. p. 374, pl. 66, f. 2.

MACRONES CAVASIUS, *Günther*, Catal. v. p. 76.

D. $\frac{1}{7}$ | 0. P. $\frac{1}{8}$. V. 6. A. 11. C. 15.

The length of the head rather more than $\frac{1}{6}$, base of adipose dorsal $\frac{2}{5}$ of total length. Height of body $\frac{1}{5}$ of total length.

Head as broad as high, its greatest width being equal to two-thirds of its length. Upper jaw the longest: snout slightly depressed. Central longitudinal groove narrow extending posteriorly to the anterior extremity of the base of the occipital process: on either side are raised ridges which from opposite the orbits pass irregularly forward, and behind them in a stellated form. Occipital process narrow, and extending to the basal bone of the dorsal fin. Nasal cirri short: maxillary cirri reaching to the base of the caudal fin: mandibular ones short, the external being longer than the head, the internal slightly shorter. Both apertures of nostrils are nearer to the snout than they are to the orbits.

Teeth—None on jaws, but in a narrow uninterrupted crescentic band on the vomer.

Fins—Dorsal fin pointed, higher than the body, its spine one-third shorter than its rays, of moderate strength, and entire: the soft dorsal commences just behind the first dorsal, and gradually increases in height, ending a short distance below the base of the caudal. Caudal deeply emarginate, upper lobe the longest, and both pointed. Pectoral spine shorter than that of the dorsal, strongly denticulated interiorly and its extremity soft and reaching slightly beyond the base of the first dorsal. Ventral commencing posterior to the end of the pectoral and not reaching so far as the anal.

Colours—Brownish above, with a green and purplish reflection on the sides, becoming pure white on the abdomen. All the fins except the anal are dotted with black, as are also the maxillary cirri.

Grows to about six inches in length.

Habitat—Fresh waters of Hindustan.

* HYPSELOBAGRUS MONTANUS.

BAGRUS MONTANUS, *Jerdon*, Madras Journal, xv. p. 337.

Head rather more than $\frac{1}{4}$, and height about $\frac{1}{5}$ of length of body. Second dorsal about $\frac{1}{4}$ of total length.

Eyes—Diameter about $\frac{1}{4}$ of length of head, $1\frac{1}{2}$ diameters apart.

The maxillary cirri extend to the anal fin.

Fins—Dorsal spine toothed. Pectoral spine with seven or eight moderately strong teeth on its terminal half.

Colours—Greenish above and on the fins: yellow on the cheeks and beneath.

Grows to six inches in length.

Habitat—Manantoddy river in the Wynaad.

* HYPSELOBAGRUS MALABARICUS.

BAGRUS MALABARICUS, *Jerdon*, Madras Journal, xv. p. 338.

D. $\frac{1}{7}$ | 0. A. 11.

Head slightly shorter than in the *Hyp. montanus*, being about $\frac{2}{9}$ of length of body, and about the same length as the height of the body.

Maxillary cirri reach to beyond the ventrals.

Fins—Pectoral spine with fifteen teeth.

Colours—Bluish-leaden above, silvery beneath.

Habitat—Mountain streams of Malabar.

HYPSELOBAGRUS TENGARA.

PIMELODUS TENGARA, *Ham. Buch.* pp. 183, 377, pl. 3, f. 61.

BAGRUS TENGGARA, *Cuv. & Val.* xiv. p. 414.

MACRONES TENGARA, *Günther*, Catal. v. p. 81.

B. x. D. $\frac{1}{7}$. | 0. P. $\frac{1}{8}$. V. 6. A. 12.

Length of head $\frac{2}{9}$, of pectoral $\frac{2}{11}$, of caudal $\frac{1}{5}$, of base of first dorsal $\frac{1}{11}$, of base of second dorsal $\frac{1}{13}$, of base of anal $\frac{1}{10}$ of total length. Height of head $\frac{1}{7}$, of body $\frac{1}{5}$, of first dorsal $\frac{1}{5}$, of second dorsal $\frac{1}{13}$, of ventral $\frac{2}{17}$, of anal $\frac{2}{17}$ of total length.

Eyes—Oval, situated near the profile, and in the anterior half of the head. Horizontal diameter $\frac{1}{4}$, vertical diameter $\frac{1}{5}$ of length of head, $\frac{1}{4}$ of a diameter from end of snout, and 2 diameters apart.

Profile rather convex from the snout to the first dorsal, from whence it sinks to the anal. Abdominal profile straighter than that of the back. Thickness of body greatest opposite the opercles.

Head obtuse and rounded in front. Width of the head rather more than the height of the body. Mouth forming nearly a semicircle, and cleft midway to the anterior margin of the orbit. Upper jaw slightly the longest. Opercle ending in an obtuse point, which is rather produced: its whole surface roughened in lines. Upper surface of head as far as the centre of the orbits roughened in small sinuous closely approximating elevations. Occipital process long and narrow, half as wide at the base as it is high, and divided from the basal bone of the dorsal by a bone shaped like an arrow-head, directed forwards, and meeting the summit of the occipital process. Basal bone nearly triangular, concave in front and posteriorly; all are roughened the same as the summit of the head. Central longitudinal groove broad posteriorly, where it commences opposite the posterior margin of the orbit; it is continued to opposite the posterior nostril; between the upper end of the groove on the head and the base of the occipital process, and a short distance on either side, is an irregular depression, the two rather converging posteriorly, and rather expanded externally. Shoulder bone nodulated. Nasal cirri as long as the head: maxillary widest at their base, and extended as far as the posterior extremity of the ventral. The two pairs of mandibular cirri reaching to the posterior extremity of the opercles. Nostrils, posterior one round, not far from the mesial line, and a short distance from the anterior one, which is more external.

Teeth—In intermaxillaries numerous, and in a small, fine, sharp band: vomerine teeth in a narrow crescentic band sub-interrupted in the centre.

Fins—Dorsal arises opposite the posterior third of the pectoral: ventral slightly beyond the extremity of the dorsal: second dorsal opposite anal. First dorsal spine rather feeble, half as long as the head, its sides smooth, with one or two serratures at its upper and anterior extremity, whilst its upper third is posteriorly serrated, it ends in a soft prolongation: the fin pointed. Pectoral spine stronger than that of the dorsal, and equal to the distance from the anterior margin of the orbit to the posterior margin of the opercles: anterior edge rugose, posterior strongly serrated. Caudal deeply lobed.

Lateral line—Curves down to opposite the end of the ventral fin, then proceeds direct to the base of the caudal, where it divides into two very indistinct branches, the upper curving over the bases of three rays above it, and the lower over the bases of two below it.

Colours—Greenish olive, with three brown longitudinal bands, the centre one of which commences from a large black ocellus behind the head: the bands and ocellus are more distinct in young specimens than in adults. There is sometimes a dark spot on the middle of the root of the caudal.

I have with some hesitation considered this fish to be *Hamilton Buchanan's* "Pimelodus tengara," but it is without doubt *Dr. Günther's* "Macrones tengara," and as he has probably described his specimen from *Hamilton Buchanan's* typical one, I conclude some mistake may have arisen in the "Fishes of the Ganges," especially as it is there asserted that the fish is small and inhabits ponds, that its dorsal spine is smooth, and that its maxillary cirri reach to the end of the caudal fin. I should also remark that this can hardly be identical, as *Dr. Günther* suggests, with *Ham. Buchanan's* "Pimelodus batasius," pl. 23, f. 60, the figure of which is incorrect, for in the description, pp. 179, 377, it is expressly stated that it has eight cirri *shorter than the head,* and only grows to about three inches in length. Again it can scarcely be the "Pimelodus carcio" of the same author, which is a pond fish of about three inches in length, from North Bengal, in which the maxillary cirrus does not extend to the posterior extremity of the first dorsal fin, whilst the dorsal spine is said to have a strong prickle barbed behind, &c. &c.

Common. Grows to at least a foot and a half in length, and is eaten by the poorer classes.

Habitat—Seas and estuaries of India and Ceylon.

Group PANGASINI, *Bleeker.*

Sub-Group PANGASII, *Bleeker.*

Genus PSEUDEUTROPIUS, *Bleeker.*

Branchiostegals from (? five) nine to ten. Abdominal profile more convex than that of the back: opercular bones with moveable articulations; body compressed. Eyes large, situated behind; occasionally a portion rather below the level of the mouth. Mouth anterior, in some the lower jaw the longest, in others the upper, according to the age of the fish. Head covered with soft skin. Nostrils patent, transverse, the posterior pair nearer to one another than they are to the anterior pair. Cirri eight, one pair to posterior nostrils, one maxillary pair, and two mandibular pairs close to margin of lower jaw. Two dorsals, the anterior placed before the ventral, short with a sharp, often serrated spine, and from four to eight rays: the second adipose, rudimentary, and opposite the anal, which latter is elongate and many-rayed, terminating some distance from the caudal which is forked. Ventral with six or seven rays. Pectoral with a serrated spine. Teeth villiform in several rows in intermaxillaries and mandibles, those on vomer and palatines in one undivided transverse band. Branchial aperture wide, interbranchial membrane deeply emarginate. An air bladder present.

Pseudeutropius Sykesii.

Schilbe Sykesii, *Jerdon*, Madras Journal, xv. p. 335.
Pseudeutropius Mitchelli, *Günther*, Catal. v. p. 59.

B. viii. or ix. D. $\frac{1}{7}$ | 0. P. $\frac{1}{8}$. V. 6. A. 35.

Length of head $\frac{2}{13}$, of pectoral $\frac{1}{8}$, of caudal $\frac{1}{5}$, of base of dorsal $\frac{1}{19}$, of base of anal more than $\frac{1}{3}$ of total length. Height of head $\frac{1}{10}$, of body $\frac{2}{11}$, of dorsal $\frac{1}{10}$, of ventral $\frac{1}{12}$, of anal $\frac{1}{12}$ of total length.

Eyes—Diameter rather exceeding $\frac{1}{5}$ of length of head, 1 diameter from end of snout, rather more than 1 diameter apart.

Body elongated, compressed, decreasing in size from the head to the caudal. Profile of head slightly elevated over the snout and nape, causing the central portion to appear rather concave; from thence to the caudal the line is nearly straight: the profile of the abdomen is more convex than that of the back.

Mouth, in young specimens up to about four inches and a half in length the upper jaw is slightly the longest, but in adults the lower is the longest, and curved upwards at its extremity. Preopercle narrow, a third as broad as high. Posterior nostril the largest, nearly circular, and situated near the mesial line: the anterior rather below and in front on the anterior surface of the snout. Occipital process covered by very thin skin, slender, and joining the basal bone of the dorsal fin, which is triangular, and half as long as the occipital process. A central longitudinal groove, which becomes almost imperceptible in the adult, exists along the central line of the skull to the base of the occipital process. The pair of maxillary cirri extend as far as the anterior margin of the anal fin: the nasal pair are fine, and not so long as the head: the two pairs of labial cirri arise close together, nearly under the symphysis, and are as long as the head.

Teeth—In both jaws sharp and villiform, in two rows along the sides, but more numerous in the centre. Teeth on palate in two small oval patches.

Fins—Dorsal arises opposite the posterior third of the pectoral: ventral under the termination of the dorsal: anal about midway between the snout and the base of the caudal: adipose dorsal arises over the thirtieth ray of anal. First dorsal rounded, spine slender, two-thirds the length of the head, and finely serrated posteriorly: interspinous membrane deeply notched. Pectoral spine strong, much more so than that of the dorsal, and as long as the head without the snout; its internal margin has from twenty to twenty-five serratures. Ventral very small, not extending as far as the anal. The first ray of the anal the longest: the distance between the end of the anal and the commencement of the caudal fin, equals two-thirds of the depth of the base of the caudal. Caudal rather deeply lobed.

Lateral line—First curves downwards, and then passes direct to the centre of the caudal.

Colours—Upper surface of head of a deep grey. Body green, abruptly changing a short distance above the lateral line, where it becomes a beautiful silvery white, which is continued on to the abdomen. Dorsal, pectoral, anal, and caudal white, the last two fins being stained with grey at their bases.

By no means rare in the rivers of Malabar. In two instances the second or adipose dorsal fin was deficient, perhaps lost by some accident. No doubt it was from some such deformed specimen that *Dr. Jerdon* has described this fish.

Does not grow to above eight inches in length.

Habitat—Rivers of Malabar.

Sub-Fam. SILURIFORMES, *Bleeker*.

GROUP SILURINI, *Bleeker*.

GENUS WALLAGO, *Bleeker*.

Branchiostegals, fifteen to twenty-one. Neck not elevated, the upper profile of the head being straight. Eyes above or on a level with the angle of the mouth. Snout rather produced; head covered with soft skin: nostrils remote. Cirri four, one on each supramaxillary, and one on either mandibula. One very short dorsal above or before ventrals, and without any sharp spine. No adipose dorsal. Anal elongated, and terminating near the caudal, which is long and has two rounded lobes. The pectoral spine moderately strong; serratures weak or absent. Teeth villiform, in many rows in the jaws, and in an oblong patch on either side of vomer, but separated by an interspace: none on the palate.

WALLAGO ATTU.

SILURUS ATHU, *Bloch*, *Schn.* p. 378, t. 75.
WALLAGOO, *Russell*, pl. 165.
WALLAGO ATTU, *Bleeker*, Atl. Ich. ii. p. 79, t. 86, f. 1; *Günther*, Catal. v. p. 36.
SCHILBE BOALIS, *Sykes*, T. Z. S. ii. p. 368, pl. 64, f. 3.
SILURUS BOALIS, *Ham. Buch.* pp. 154, 375, pl. 29, f. 49; *Jerdon*, Madras Journal, xv. p. 335.
SILURUS WALLAGOO, *Cuv. & Val.* xiv. p. 354.
WAHLAH, *Mal.*

B. xix-xxi. D. $\frac{1}{4}$. P. $\frac{1}{13\text{-}14}$ V. 8-10. A. 86-93. C. 17.

Length of head $\frac{2}{11}$, of pectoral $\frac{1}{7}$, of caudal $\frac{1}{7}$, of base of dorsal about $\frac{1}{90}$, of base of anal $\frac{1}{2}$ of total length. Height of head $\frac{1}{10}$, of body $\frac{1}{7}$, of dorsal $\frac{1}{7}$, of anal $\frac{1}{15}$, of ventral $\frac{1}{15}$ of total length.

Eyes—Transversely oval. Horizontal diameter $\frac{1}{6}$, vertical diameter $\frac{1}{8}$ of length of head, nearly 2 diameters from end of snout, $2\frac{1}{2}$ diameters apart.

Body compressed from side to side: head depressed. A slight rise from the snout to the first dorsal, from thence a gradual descent to the caudal. Abdominal profile more curved than that of the back.

Gape of mouth oblique, wide, and its cleft extending the width of the orbit behind its posterior extremity. Lower jaw the longest, with eight pores along each ramus. Nostrils round, placed midway between the orbits and snout. Nasal cirri broad, fleshy, and extending to about the thirtieth anal ray. Mandibular cirri one-fourth length of head.

Teeth—Villiform, in many rows in the upper and lower jaws, also in two oblong and rather widely separated spots on vomer.

Fins—Dorsal commences over the posterior third of pectoral: ventral under the dorsal: anal at about a third of the distance between the snout and the base of the caudal. Dorsal high. Pectoral spine moderately strong and rough, but can scarcely be said to be toothed; its oblique articulations are very distinct, and its termination soft: the extremity of the fin reaches to opposite the sixth anal ray. Caudal lobed, the upper the longest, and the lower the widest. A short interval exists between the anal and caudal fins.

Lateral line—At first curves downwards, but from opposite the tenth ray of the anal proceeds direct to the centre of the caudal.

Colours—Upper surface of body greenish, sides and abdomen silvery white. All the fins with the exception of the dorsal yellowish white. The upper portion of the anal fin has a purplish tinge along its whole extent. Dorsal greenish yellow.

Common in the rivers, and excellent eating, although rather rich; it salts well, and is especially adapted for curries. Usually found to about three and a half feet in length, but said to attain six feet. The jaw bones of this fish when dried, are stated by *Russell* to be used at Vizagapatam for carding the finest kinds of cotton. It is very voracious, and takes a bait freely.

The number of branchiostegous rays varies exceedingly in this species. In three examined in one day all differed.

Habitat—Fresh waters of India, Burmah, and Malaysia.

Wallago Malabaricus.

Silurus Malabaricus, *Cuv. & Val.* xiv. p. 353; *Jerdon*, Madras Journal, xv. p. 334; *Günther*, Catal. v. p. 34.

Mungee wahlah, *Mal.*

B. xv. D. 4. P. $\frac{1}{13}$. V. 9. A. 68. C. 17.

Length of head $\frac{1}{7}$, of base of dorsal about $\frac{1}{125}$, of pectoral $\frac{1}{9}$, of base of anal $\frac{2}{3}$, of caudal $\frac{1}{9}$ of total length. Height of head $\frac{1}{14}$, of body $\frac{1}{7}$, of dorsal $\frac{1}{16}$, of ventral $\frac{1}{21}$, of anal $\frac{1}{16}$, of base of caudal $\frac{1}{25}$ of total length.

Eyes—Diameter $\frac{1}{5}$ of length of head, $1\frac{1}{2}$ diameters apart, nearly 1 diameter from end of snout.

Gape of mouth very wide, being three times its antero-posterior length. Muzzle rounded in front. Lower jaw the longest, curving upwards in the centre, so that when closed its extremity is completely in advance of the upper jaw, and even higher. The cleft of the mouth only extends half the distance to the eye, where it ascends to opposite the centre of the orbit. The maxillary cirri are situated opposite its angle, and reach to the end of the pectoral fin: the mandibular pair are short and only equal to a third the length of the head. Head fleshy.

Teeth—Sharp, carded, and recurved, in six or eight rows on the intermaxillary bone and the lower jaw, and also in two oblique oval spots on the vomer, separated by an interspace: none on palate.

Fins—Dorsal arises above the commencement of the ventral: the pectoral reaches just beyond the origin of the anal, which is divided from the caudal by a notch, and for two-thirds of its distance from the abdomen is covered by a fleshy sort of sheath. Dorsal fin weak and expanded in the centre. Pectoral spine serrated on its inferior aspect. Caudal lobed, the superior the longest.

Lateral line—Passes direct from the upper margin of the opercle to the centre of the caudal.

Colours—Greenish along the back, and white with a purplish tinge along the sides, abdomen and chest. The whole of the body minutely studded with fine black dots. A large round dark finger mark on the shoulder, opposite the centre of the opercle.

This fish is found in the same localities as the *Wallago attu*, but is said never to exceed two feet in length. It is equally good for salting and eating.

Habitat—Rivers of Malabar.

Fam. CHACOIDEI, *Bleeker*.

Sub-Fam. PLOTOSIFORMES, *Bleeker*.

Genus PLOTOSUS, *Lacép.*

Branchiostegals from nine to twelve. Head conical, depressed. Opercular bones with immoveable articulations. Eyes small, with free lids. Mouth transverse. Cirri eight, one pair to posterior nasal orifices, which are some distance apart from the anterior, which are on the margin of the snout or perforating the upper lip: one maxillary and two mandibular pairs. Teeth in jaws, unequal in size, in several rows, those on the vomer obtuse and in a semilunar patch. Two dorsals, the first short and having a sharp spine, the second long and confluent with the caudal and anal, which last also consists of many rays; Pectoral spine moderately strong and denticulated. Branchial aperture large, and divided as far forwards as the eyes: membranes not attached to the isthmus. The branchial arches are without any posterior processes or membrane.

Plotosus Arab.

Silurus Arab, *Forskål*, p. xvi. No. 36.
Ingelee, *Russell*, pl. 166.
Plotosus anguillaris, *Cantor*, Catal. p. 264; *Günther*, Catal. v. p. 24.
Plotosus Arab, *Bleeker*, Atl. Ich. ii. p. 98, t. 95, f. 2.
Plotosus lineatus, *Cuv. & Val.* xv. p. 412.
? Plotosus castaneus, *Cuv. & Val.* xv. p. 421.
Moorghee, *Mal.* .

B. xi.-xii. D. $\frac{1}{4\text{-}5}$ | 93. V. 12. A. 66. C. 13. Vert. $\frac{12}{35}$.

Length of head $\frac{2}{9}$, of pectoral $\frac{1}{8}$, of caudal $\frac{1}{15}$, of base of first dorsal $\frac{1}{18}$, of base of second dorsal above $\frac{1}{2}$, of base of anal $\frac{1}{2}$ of total length. Height of head $\frac{1}{8}$, of body $\frac{1}{5}$, of first dorsal $\frac{1}{8}$, of second dorsal $\frac{1}{15}$, of anal $\frac{1}{5}$, of ventral $\frac{1}{8}$ of total length.

Eyes—Oval, situated near the upper profile. Horizontal diameter $\frac{1}{5}$, vertical diameter $\frac{1}{8}$ of length of head, 2 diameters from end of snout, and the same distance apart.

Body elongated and compressed: head depressed, obtuse, and widest opposite the opercles, the width forming almost a semicircle.

Mouth directed forward with fleshy lips: its gape equal to half the length of the head. Numerous papillæ on both lips. Upper jaw slightly the longest. The posterior limb of the preopercle slopes a little downwards and forwards: angle rounded. Opercle ending in rather an obtuse point. Summit of head rough, with a lanceolate central longitudinal groove from opposite the orbits to the snout. Nodulated lines exist above the orbits. Occipital process long and very narrow. Four pairs of cirri, the maxillary and external mandibular pairs equal to about half the length of the head: nasal and internal mandibular pairs also equal in length but shorter than the others. Nostrils close to the lips, and near the central line of the head.

Teeth—Irregularly disposed in three rows, in the intermaxillaries and lower jaw they are large, sharp, pointed, and directed a little backwards: the anterior ones the strongest. Two outer teeth in the upper jaw, large, curved, and directed slightly inwards. There are more teeth in the lower than in the upper jaw. Vomerine teeth rounded, with one or two sharp ones externally. Tongue fleshy, without teeth.

Fins—First dorsal and pectoral arise on a line: ventral commences opposite the end of the pectoral, and the second dorsal above it: anal begins opposite the end of the ventral. First dorsal pointed, and its rays prolonged; its spine rather strongly toothed on the anterior and posterior margins. The distance between the first dorsal and the second equals two-thirds of the height of the body: it is rather lower in front than towards its centre; it, the caudal, and the anal are united, but as each ends in a point, of which that of the caudal is the shortest, it appears as if two V-shaped notches had been nipped out of the extremity of the caudal fin, which however occasionally is rounded. The pectoral spine is moderately strong, half the length of the fin, denticulated on either edge.

Lateral line—Commences at the upper margin of the opercles, first curves slightly upwards, and then gradually downwards to opposite about the sixteenth anal ray, from whence it passes straight.

Colours—Chestnut, tinged with green on the back, and lighter on the abdomen. A fine bluish-white line commences on the summit of the snout, passes upwards over the back of the eye, and then runs onwards to its termination at the tail, midway between the lateral line and the base of the dorsal fin. A second and much broader bluish-white line passes from the upper angle of the jaw, under the eye, across the centre of the opercle, meets the lateral line opposite the commencement of the second dorsal, and proceeds under it to the tail. Occasionally a third white line skirts the base of the anal fin. Fins brownish edged with black.

Not uncommon in the backwater and estuaries of Malabar. Eaten by the lower classes. Grows to two feet seven inches in length.

Habitat—Seas and estuaries of India. It is found from the Eastern coast of Africa to Japan and Polynesia.

* Plotosus limbatus.

Plotosus limbatus, *Cuv. & Val.* xv. p. 422; *Günther*, Catal. v. p. 25.

D. 112. A. 101. C. 11.

Length of head from $\frac{2}{11}$ to $\frac{1}{6}$ of the total length.

The nasal cirrus reaches as far as the posterior border of the orbit: and the maxillary to the border of the opercle.

Colours—Of an uniform maroon; or dark with a greenish tinge. The fins are bordered with black.

Habitat—Seas of India.

Fam. HETEROBRANCHOIDEI, *Bleeker*.

Sub-Fam. HETEROBRANCHIFORMES, *Bleeker*.

Genus CLARIAS, *Gronov.*

Macropteronotus, *Lacép.*

Cossyphus & phagorus, *McClelland.*

Branchiostegals, from seven to nine. Upper and lateral portion of head—which is broad and depressed—osseous, and if covered with skin it is extremely thin. Opercular bones articulated together, moveable. Cirri eight, fleshy, two nasal, two maxillary and four mandibular. Cleft of mouth transverse. Eyes small, with a free orbital margin. A dendritic accessory respiratory apparatus is attached to the convex side of the second and fourth branchial arches and is received into a cavity behind the gill-cavity proper. Dorsal fin long, and without a spine, it extends from the neck nearly to the caudal: no adipose fin. Anal long, extending almost to caudal. Pectoral with a sharp spine. Ventral with six rays. Teeth in jaws in villiform bands, and a transverse band of villiform or granular ones on the vomer: villiform also on palate.

Clarias magur.

Marpoo, *Russell*, pl. 168.

MACROPTERONOTUS MAGUR, *Ham. Buch.* pp. 146, 374, pl. 26. f. 45.
CLARIAS MARPUS, *Cuv. & Val.* xv. p. 378.
CLARIAS MAGUR, *Cuv. & Val.* xv. p. 381; *Günther*, Catal. v. p. 17.
CLARIAS PUNCTATUS, *Cuv. & Val.* xv. p. 284; *Cantor*, Catal. p. 263.

B. ix. D. 64-70. P. $\frac{1}{8}$. V. 6. A. 50-53. C. 17.

Length of head $\frac{1}{6}$ of the total length.

Eyes—Situated in the anterior fourth of the head: diameter $\frac{1}{9}$ of length of head: the distance apart equals $\frac{1}{7}$ of the length of head.

Mouth anterior and of moderate width. Head finely granulated superiorly, and covered with a thin skin, its width opposite the gill covers equals two-thirds of its length. In the centre of the helmet are two ovoid depressions, the anterior—which is the longest and equals about one-fifth of the entire length of the head—is situated so that its lower portion is between the orbits: the upper depression is half the size of the lower one, situated in the mesial line of the head, and opposite the base of the pectoral fins. The occipital process is not prominent, and is rounded posteriorly.

The maxillary cirri are thick and fleshy at their bases, rather more than one quarter of the entire length of the fish, and extend to opposite the end of the pectoral spine: the nasal cirri reach to the base of the occipital process: the outer mandibular ones are one-fifth and the inner one-eighth of the entire length of the fish.

Teeth—Card-like, those in intermaxillaries forming a broad band which extends nearly as far as opposite the base of the maxillary cirri: those on vomer and palate form a villiform crescentic band in width about equalling those in the intermaxillaries.

Fins—Dorsal commences at the neck and extends nearly as far as the caudal: it is rather highest posteriorly. The pectoral commences under opercle, its spine is strong, three-fourths the length of the fin, and finely serrated internally, but the serratures are concealed in the skin. Ventral abdominal, commencing rather posterior to the end of the pectoral. Anal arises under posterior extremity of first fourth of the dorsal. Caudal rounded.

Lateral line—Nearly straight.

Colours—Olive green above with purplish reflections, the body with lighter spots or blotches, (in a specimen captured in Cochin, but since mislaid), and of a dirty yellowish white inferiorly. Cirri black.

Is eaten by the Natives. Grows to ten inches in length.

Habitat—Fresh waters of India and Malaysia.

* CLARIAS DUSSUMIERI.

CLARIAS DUSSUMIERI, *Cuv. & Val.* xv. p. 382; *Jerdon*, Madras Journal, xv. p. 342.

D. 69. A. 50.

Head smooth. Pectoral spine denticulated.

Teeth—Those on the vomer like a pavement and placed in an arc-shaped spot.

Colours—Greenish-black above, fading to greyish white beneath.

Grows to eight inches in length.

Habitat—Fresh waters of Malabar.

Sub-Fam. SACCOBRANCHIFORMES, *Bleeker*.

Genus SACCOBRANCHUS, *Cuv. and Val.*

Heteropneustes, *Müller*.

Branchiostegals, from six to eight. Eyes small. Opercular bones articulated together, moveable. Upper and lateral part of head osseous, or covered by a very thin skin. Cleft of mouth transverse, moderate, anterior. Gill cavity with an accessory posterior sac, extending backwards between the muscles on either side of the vertebral column, to beneath the dorsal fin. Cirri eight, two nasal, two maxillary and four mandibular. One dorsal, short, and composed of few rays: no adipose fin. Pectoral spine moderately strong. Ventral of six rays, situated behind or below the dorsal. Jaws with bands of villiform teeth, disposed on the vomer in two oblong widely separated patches.

Saccobranchus singio.

Silurus singio, *Ham. Buch.* pp. 147, 347, pl. 37, f. 46.
Saccobranchus singio, *Cuv. & Val.* xv. p. 400, pl. 448; *Günther*, Catal. v. p. 30.
Saccobranchus fossilis, *Jerdon*, Madras Journal, xv. p. 342.
Kahree meen, *Mal.*

B. vi-vii. D. 7. P. $\frac{1}{6}$. V. 6. A. 68-72. C. 15.

Length of head $\frac{1}{8}$, of pectoral $\frac{1}{10}$, of caudal $\frac{1}{8}$, of base of dorsal about $\frac{1}{30}$, of base of anal $\frac{4}{7}$ of total length. Height of head $\frac{1}{14}$, of body $\frac{1}{8}$, of dorsal $\frac{1}{14}$, of ventral $\frac{1}{14}$, of anal $\frac{1}{14}$ of total length.

Eyes—In the adult are situated on the external margin of the head, and directed upwards and outwards. Diameter $\frac{1}{6}$ of length of head, from $1\frac{2}{3}$ to 2 diameters from end of snout, and rather more than 3 diameters apart. In immature specimens the eyes are directed more laterally, and are proportionately larger.

Body long and compressed. Head broad and strongly depressed, its width being equal to the height of the body. A slight rise occurs from the snout towards the occiput.

Mouth anterior, with wide transverse nearly semicircular gape, but narrow cleft; its lips fleshy, and surrounded by four pairs of cirri. Maxillary cirri with fleshy bases; they extend to the termination of the pectoral fin, or sometimes slightly beyond it: nasal cirri small, extending to opposite the posterior third of the pectoral: the two pairs of mandibular cirri are of equal size, the external reaching to the posterior third of the pectoral, whilst the internal are slightly shorter; but it must be remarked, that these cirri vary irregularly in different specimens; in one ten inches in length the maxillary pair reach the commencement of the anal fin, and the remainder are comparatively produced to what is observable in the adult. On the summit of the head, which is rugose, osseous, or but slightly covered with skin, there is, between and rather behind the orbits, a smooth lanceolate depression, directed forwards, broader and shorter in the adult than in the immature. In the central line, and on the posterior extremity of the cranium, there is another smooth oval depression, about the size of the orbit in the adult, but larger in the immature. Nostrils in front and rather internal to the orbit, the anterior one tubular, the posterior oblong, and midway between the orbit and jaws.

Teeth—In crowded villiform bands in each jaw, and a semicircle of the same character on the vomer and palate. Tongue smooth.

Fins—Dorsal small, rounded, and rather expanded above, situated over the ventral and opposite the posterior extremity of the pectoral; it has a strong spine having a slightly convex external border, more so in the old than in the immature; to lay it against the body it makes a semi-curve. The pectoral spine is from two-thirds to three-fourths the length of the head, serrated internally and roughened externally in adults, but in immature specimens moderately serrated externally. Ventral small, and extends as far as the base of the anal, the third ray of which is the longest, from whence to the last there is a gradual but very slight decrease. There is a notch between the end of the anal and the commencement of the caudal fin. Caudal lobed, the lowest the largest, and extending the furthest: in some small specimens the lobing is not observable, the fin being rounded.

Lateral line—Faint, passing along the centre of the side.

Colours—Of a leaden black or dirty green, with dusky or reddish fins, lighter than the rest of the body. Under surface lighter than the back. In some localities there is a long yellow streak passing above the lateral line, and another below it. Eyes hazel. Immature specimens are of a much lighter colour.

This fish is held in great dread by the Natives of Malabar, and is commonly known amongst the Mahomedans as the *Bichu ka mutchee*, Hind, or "scorpion fish," so named from the injuries inflicted by its serrated pectoral spine. It is believed that lock-jaw is caused by a scratch from this spine, and I have personally witnessed most intense phlegmonous inflammation caused by wounds received from one of these fish. Consequently, as soon as captured the offensive spine is immediately broken off with a piece of stick, and a perfect specimen can for this reason be rarely procured. The fishermen dread it so much, that they would rather cut the meshes of their nets and let it escape, than endeavour to take it out uninjured. As this erectile spine can only be laid flat by a rounded movement, no direct pressure can have any effect on it.

It inhabits all sluggish pieces of water, and the immature are found in the paddy fields in the low country. It is eaten by the Natives, who consider it highly nourishing. It grows to a foot and a half in length.

Habitat—Fresh waters of India and Cochin China.

Fam. SCOPELIDÆ, *Günther*.

SCOPELINI, pt., *Müller*.

Sub-Fam. SAURINA, *Günther*.

GENUS SAURUS, *Cuvier*.

HARPODON, pt. *Lesueur*.
TRIURUS, *Swainson*.

Branchiostegals, from eight to sixteen. Body elongated, subcylindrical. Eyes of moderate size, lateral. Muzzle short. Gape of mouth wide, and cleft very deep, extending far behind the eyes: edge of upper jaw formed entirely by the intermaxillaries, which are long and thin: maxillary long, thin, and closely adherent to the intermaxillary. First dorsal of a moderate number of rays, nearly central; second or adipose dorsal small. Pectoral short. Ventral with eight rays, the internal being the longest, inserted before the dorsal and not far behind the pectoral. Anal short or of moderate length. Caudal forked. Teeth numerous and pointed, some being elongated and slender, and can be laid downwards and inwards; they exist on the jaws, tongue, and palatine bones, with a single row on the palate, but there are generally none or very few on the vomer. Body covered with moderately sized scales. Lateral line entire. A raised keel more or less developed along the central line of the side to the caudal. Gill-openings very wide, gill membrane not attached to the isthmus. Cæcal appendages few.

Saurida tumbil.

Salmo tumbil, *Bloch*, t. 430.

Badi mottah, *Russell*, pl. 172.

Saurida tombil, *Cuv. & Val.* xxii. p. 500; *Cantor*, Catal. pp. 270, 442.

Saurida tumbil, *Günther*, Catal. v. p. 399.

Arranna, *Mal.*

B. xiii. D. 12 | 0. P. 16. V. 10. A. 10. C. 19. L. l. 53-64. L. tr. $\frac{6}{5}$.

Length of head $\frac{2}{11}$, of pectoral $\frac{1}{10}$, of caudal $\frac{2}{11}$, of base of first dorsal $\frac{1}{9}$, of base of adipose dorsal about $\frac{1}{75}$, of base of anal $\frac{1}{14}$ of total length. Height of head $\frac{1}{11}$, of body $\frac{2}{15}$, of first dorsal $\frac{1}{7}$, of adipose dorsal about $\frac{1}{37}$, of ventral $\frac{1}{7}$, of anal $\frac{1}{11}$ of total length.

Eyes—Oval, with broad adipose lids; upper margins close to the profile: horizontal diameter $\frac{1}{5}$, vertical diameter $\frac{1}{7}$ of length of head, $1\frac{1}{4}$ diameters from end of snout, $1\frac{1}{4}$ diameters apart.

Body elongated, sub-cylindrical; head compressed. A raised keel of scales along either side of the body.

Cleft of mouth very wide, extending to nearly one diameter behind the posterior margin of the orbit. Posterior extremity of the maxilla reaches nearly to the angle of the preopercle. Intermaxillaries very long, tapering, extending to the angle of the mouth, and crowded with teeth. Mandibulæ broad, shallow, tapering almost to a point in front, and crowded with teeth. Lips absent. Posterior margin of the preopercle rather oblique, and convex. Opercles rounded. Preorbital and anterior suborbitals, festooned in radiating ridges, arising from two points, the anterior under the snout, the posterior under the centre of the orbit. Interorbital space and centre of the summit of head with rather a broad, shallow, longitudinal groove. Nostrils double.

Teeth—Several rows of card-like teeth in the upper jaw, the internal the largest, and the external smallest: the surface of the intermaxillaries on which they are placed is bevilled off, so as to look outwards. The teeth on the mandibulæ are of the same character as the largest internal and smallest external rows: they are more numerous than in the upper jaw, and placed on a surface looking upwards and outwards. Teeth on palate in two distinct rows, the internal series in each of which is the largest, whilst the inner is only one-third the length of the outer row. A small round patch of teeth on the vomer.

Fins—Pectoral commences rather behind the opercles, and opposite the angle of the mouth; first dorsal in the centre of the body, its anterior extremity being as far from the snout as its posterior is from the root of the caudal: ventral arises midway between the end of the pectoral and the commencement of the dorsal; and the anal midway between the end of the ventral and the base of the caudal: the adipose dorsal is situated over the last two anal rays. The second ray of the first dorsal is undivided and the longest, the last being not quite a third as long: upper margin of the fin concave, the last ray rather prolonged. Ventral placed horizontally, with a long elongated scale at its base, the last ray the longest. Anal with the second ray the longest. Caudal deeply forked, the upper lobe sometimes the longest.

Scales—With their exposed portions higher than wide: they are present over the body and head, with some on the base of the caudal fin. A broad triangular scale exists in the axilla.

Lateral line—Rather nearer the back than the abdomen, and on the sixth row of scales. The number of scales on this row appears to vary; in several specimens examined at Cochin none had more than fifty-six. The keel is most developed in the posterior third of the body.

Colours—Back brownish grey, abdomen silvery, the whole with greenish yellow reflections: the abdomen finely spotted with black. Dorsal fin diaphanous, with a blackish grey margin. Pectoral blackish grey. Soft portion of the dorsal with a darkish centre. Ventral greyish, tipped with white. Anal diaphanous, and tinged with yellow. Caudal tipped with black.

It is never common, but rarely absent in Cochin on the Malabar coast during the cold months of the year. Eaten by the Natives, but not esteemed as it is dry and insipid. It grows to a foot in length.

Habitat—Red Sea, Seas of India, Malaysia, and the Western Pacific.

Genus HARPODON, pt., *Lesueur*.

Branchiostegals, from twenty-three to twenty-five: pseudobranchiæ. Body elongated, rather compressed. Eyes small. Muzzle short, gape of mouth wide and cleft very deep, extending far behind the eyes: edge of upper jaw formed entirely by the intermaxillaries, which are thin and long: maxillaries absent (rudimentary according to Valenciennes). First dorsal with a moderate number of rays, central: second or adipose dorsal small. Pectoral long. Ventral with nine long rays inserted below the anterior ones of the dorsal. Anal of moderate length. Caudal with three lobes, the lateral line being continued along the central one. Teeth on the intermaxillaries and lower jaw, also on the palatine and hyoid bones, and on the tongue: the anterior palatine teeth are large and can be laid downwards. Body covered with thin diaphanous and deciduous scales: the bones of the head very soft, and partly modified into wide muciferous channels: the lateral canal along the body also wide, and having two openings, one above and one below on each scale. Gill openings wide. Air bladder absent. Pyloric appendages numerous.

* Harpodon nehereus.

Wana Motta, *Russell*, pl. 177 (*adult*).
Osmerus nehereus, *Ham. Buch.* pp. 209, 379 (*adult*).
Saurus ophiodon, *Cuv. & Val.* xxii. p. 490.
Saurus nehereus, *Cantor*, Catal. p. 273.
Harpodon nehereus, *Günther*, Catal. v. p. 401.
Bombay Duck. Bummaloh.

B. xxiii-xxv. D. 12-13 | 0. P. 11-12. V. 9. A. 14-15. C. 19. Vert. 38. Cæc. pyl. 22.

Length of head $\frac{1}{6}$, of pectoral from $\frac{1}{2}$ to $\frac{1}{7}$, varying with the age of the fish being shorter in the adult than in the immature, of caudal $\frac{1}{6}$ of the total length. Height of body $\frac{1}{6}$, of dorsal $\frac{4}{19}$, of ventral $\frac{1}{3}$, of anal $\frac{2}{15}$ of the total length.

Eyes—Diameter $\frac{1}{16}$ of length of head, 2 diameters from end of snout, 4 diameters apart.

Body elongated, rather compressed, at the occiput its height is one-eighth, opposite first dorsal one-sixth, and opposite root of caudal one-twelfth of the total length.

Jaws of equal length; the angle of the mouth is situated at the posterior fourth of the head. The opercles membraneous, diaphanous, and all apparently blended together. The branchiostegous membrane is narrow, but projects behind the posterior radiated angle of the opercle. The branchiostegous rays hair-like, gradually increasing in length backwards, the posterior are discernible through the lower portion of the opercle. The nostrils open vertically in front of the anterior margin of the orbit, the anterior the largest.

Teeth—"All are excessively slender, recurved, and like those of some of the gobioidæ, erectile, but not flexible. They may be raised or laid down in the manner in which Cuvier describes the teeth of the genus *Salarias,* like the keys of a piano. Those of the jaws and some of the palatals have a single barb at the posterior margin of the point: a few of the former are arrow-shaped. In both jaws appear three series of somewhat distant teeth: the external consists of excessively minute ones, the second of longer, and the internal series the longest of all. Those of the lower jaw are longer than those of the upper, particularly three or four on each side of the symphysis. The pharyngeal and palatals consist of two series. The fourth anterior tooth of each palatal is very long. The tongue is very short, linear, and covered with fine teeth, like those of the hyoid bone and the upper margin of the branchial arches."—(*Cantor.*)

Fins—The first dorsal is situated midway between the snout and the root of the caudal: the ventral opposite the dorsal, midway between the snout and the last ray of the anal: the first anal ray midway between the last ray of the dorsal and the root of the caudal: the adipose dorsal opposite the posterior third of the anal. The third dorsal ray is the longest, from it they gradually decrease, the last being but slightly more than one-third the length of the longest. The point of the ventral reaches to the middle of the anal, a thin elongated scale is situated at its base. The third anal ray is the longest, and twice the length of the last. The adipose dorsal is rather large. The caudal divided into three pointed lobes, of which the centre is rather the shortest. The pectorals are falciform, and in the young reach to the last dorsal ray, but become shorter with age.

Scales—All are diaphanous, and can but with difficulty be distinguished in the fresh fish.

Lateral line—Rather nearer to the back than to the abdomen: it is slightly keeled with about forty-four rectangular membraneous pieces, covered with scales like the rest of the body.

Colours—Head, back, and sides light grey, dust-coloured, or semi-transparent like gelatine, with minute star-like, black or brownish dots: anterior part of the abdomen pale silvery: rest whitish: cheeks and opercles pale silvery, dotted like the body: fins transparent, coloured like the body, but more closely dotted, so as to appear pale blackish. Iris bluish silvery, minutely dotted with black.—(*Cantor.*)

This fish, which is so exceedingly numerous in North Malabar and Bombay, rarely, if ever, extends its range so far South as Cochin. It is rich, but highly esteemed as a delicacy immediately after it is taken. Salted and dried it is exported in large quantities from Bombay under the denomination of ***Bummalohs*** or ***Bombay ducks.*** It grows to eleven inches in length.

Habitat—Seas and estuaries of India, Burmah, Malaysia, and China.

SUB-ORDER.—CYPRINIDÆ.

Fam. COBITIOIDES, *Bleeker.*

GENUS NEMACHEILUS, v. *Hasselt.*

ACOURA et ACOURUS, *Swns.*

Branchiostegals, three. Body elongated, anteriorly cylindrical, back low, without any adipose keel. Eyes with free lids. Lower jaw ending in a sharp point, but not tuberculated. No free suborbital spine. Cirri six or eight, four on snout, and from two to four on maxillæ. Anterior nostril tubular. Dorsal fins consisting of few rays, and entirely or mostly situated in the anterior half of the body and opposite the ventral. No scales on head. An air bladder, entirely enclosed in a cavity formed by the vertebral column.

Nemacheilus triangularis, Pl. XIV. fig. 1.

Nemacheilus triangularis, *Day*, Proc. Zool. Soc. 1865, p. 295.

B. iii. D. 9. P. 11. V. 9. A. 6. C. 19.

Length of head about $\frac{1}{5}$, of base of dorsal $\frac{1}{10}$, of base of anal about $\frac{1}{20}$, of pectoral $\frac{1}{6}$, of caudal $\frac{1}{5}$ of the total length. Height of head $\frac{1}{10}$, of body $\frac{1}{4}$, of dorsal $\frac{1}{4}$, of anal $\frac{1}{10}$ of the total length.

Eyes—Diameter $\frac{1}{4}$ of length of head, 1 diameter apart, 2 diameters from end of snout; no suborbital spine.

Body elongated, fusiform, cylindrical in front, compressed along the sides. From snout to frontal convex, thence to caudal straight; interorbital space convex.

Lower jaw shortest: opening of mouth below, and extending as far posteriorly as half the distance to the orbit; the end of snout fleshy, and overhanging the mouth; intermaxillaries produced downwards, and forming a knob, which is in advance of the lower jaw when the mouth is closed. Lips rather fleshy. Cirri, four on snout with their bases not united; two on superior maxillaries half the length of head. Eyes not covered by any adipose membrane. Nostrils nearer to the eye than the snout; anterior tubular, posterior broad and open. Opercle rounded posteriorly.

Fins—Dorsal arises slightly in front of the origin of the ventral, and most of it is situated in the anterior half of the body. Anal is entirely in the posterior third of the body. Dorsal square; anal slightly rounded; caudal deeply lobed.

Scales—Very distinct over the whole body; none on the head.

Lateral line—Passes straight from the head towards the centre of the caudal fin, but ceases abruptly opposite the termination of the anal.

Colours—Yellowish, banded, each band being edged with black; seven along the body, which meet at the lateral line, and consequently are disposed in a V-shape; one band passes over the opercle, a second through the eye, and a third from the orbit to the angle of the mouth. Dorsal with three irregular rows of black spots. Pectoral, ventral, and anal unspotted, but darkest at their margins. Three oblique black bands on the caudal, which has a black base.

I am indebted to the Rev. Henry Baker, jun., for this pretty little loach, of which he obtained two specimens on the hills at Mundikyum.

Habitat—Travancore Hills.

Nemacheilus rubripinnis.

Cobitis rubripinnis, *Jerdon*, Madras Journal, xv. p. 332.

B. iii. D. $\frac{2}{6}$. A. $\frac{2}{7}$. C. 13.

Length of head $\frac{1}{6}$, of pectoral $\frac{1}{8}$, of base of dorsal $\frac{1}{3}$, of base of anal $\frac{1}{8}$, of caudal $\frac{1}{6}$ of total length. Height of head $\frac{1}{8}$, of body $\frac{1}{5}$, of dorsal $\frac{1}{8}$, of anal $\frac{1}{16}$ of total length.

Eyes—Diameter $\frac{1}{6}$ of length of head, 2 diameters apart, 2 diameters from end of snout.

Profile ascends to the back of the head, from thence straight to the dorsal fin, from whence it descends gradually to the base of the caudal.

Mouth fleshy, with six cirri.

Fins—Dorsal commences just midway between the snout and the base of the caudal, and slightly in front of the commencement of the ventral: anal in posterior quarter of the body.

Scales—On the cheeks. Summit of head scaleless.

Lateral line—Straight.

Colours—Body olive green, becoming lightish brown on the sides, and dirty white on the abdomen. Nine brown bars pass from the back half way to the lateral line, and a number of smaller ones as well as some irregular bands descend along the sides to just below the lateral line. A black bar at the base of the caudal, and a black spot on the upper half of the opercle. Dorsal with two brown bars, the lowest of which is sometimes red. Caudal with three wide brown bars, and a dark brown tip.

Habitat—Malabar.

GENUS PLATACANTHUS, *Day*.

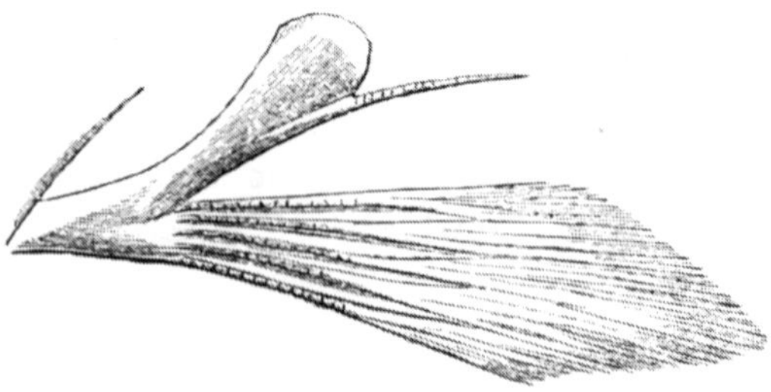

Branchiostegals three. Body elongate, and moderately compressed: back low: a fleshy keel midway between termination of the dorsal and commencement of the caudal fin, on to which it is continued for a short distance. Eyes veiled. A free bifurcated suborbital spine situated close to the lower margin of the orbit: snout obtuse, no tubercle on end of lower jaw. Eight cirri, two on snout, four on superior maxillaries, and two on lower jaw. Nostrils simple. Dorsal fin arises opposite the ventral in the centre of the body. The internal ray of the pectoral forming a large flattened spine, half the length of the soft rays. Caudal emarginate. Scales over opercular and suborbital region. No swimming bladder apparent.

PLATACANTHUS AGRENSIS. Pl. XIV. f. 2.

PLATACANTHUS AGRENSIS, *Day*, Proc. Zool. Soc. 1865, p. 296.

B. iii. D. 7. P. $\frac{1}{6}$. V. 7. A. 6. C. 16.

Length of head $\frac{1}{11}$, of pectoral $\frac{1}{4}$, of base of dorsal $\frac{1}{16}$, of base of anal $\frac{1}{32}$, of caudal $\frac{1}{8}$ of the total length. Height of head $\frac{1}{16}$, of body $\frac{1}{8}$, of dorsal $\frac{1}{12}$, of anal $\frac{1}{12}$ of the total length.

Eyes—Diameter $\frac{1}{3}$ of length of head, 1 diameter from end of snout, $\frac{1}{2}$ a diameter apart. A strong bifurcated suborbital spine arises below the orbit close to its anterior margin, and then passes backwards with a slight inward curve.

Body elongated and compressed. Profile curving considerably from the snout to opposite the orbits; from the back of the head to the caudal it is nearly straight: a raised adipose keel passes along the posterior sixth of the back, and extends on to the upper surface of the base of the caudal fin. Sides compressed, but with a slight bulging just before the commencement of the caudal.

Opening of the mouth below, transversely oval, and extending a very short distance posteriorly. End of snout fleshy and overhanging the mouth. Lips thick, and continuous, no enlargement of intermaxillaries, or tubercle on the lower jaw. Cirri, two fleshy ones on the snout with their bases not united; four on the superior maxillaries, and two on the lower jaw; the longest cirrus reaches as far as the eye. Nostrils midway between the orbit and the end of the snout; neither of them tubular. Upper margin of the orbit close to the profile. Eyes covered with a veil. Opercles rounded posteriorly. Interorbital space smooth and scaleless.

PLATE XIV.

Fig 1.

Fig 2.

F Day, del. et sculp.

1. NEMACHEILUS TRIANGULARIS. 2. PLATACANTHUS AGRENSIS

Fins—Dorsal arises midway between the snout and the base of the caudal; ventral under the commencement of the dorsal: whilst the anal is situated entirely in the posterior third of the total length. Pectoral large, the internal rays forming a broad spine, with a flattened extremity internally, and terminating externally in a soft filamentous and articulated prolongation: the flat portion of the spine, which is only about half the length of the soft rays, lies against the side when the fin is at rest. The anal with the first ray undivided, and the last divided to the root. Caudal slightly lobed.

Scales—Very distinct over the whole of the body and cheeks. None on the summit of the head.

Lateral line—Straight.

Colours—Light brown with irregular spots and bands. Dorsal spotted with brown. Caudal with four oblique bars of dark brown, and a brown bar at its base.

Habitat—Trichoor, near Cochin, on the Malabar coast.

Fam. CYPRINOIDES, *Bleeker.*

Sub-Fam. LABEONINI, *Bleeker.*

GROUP GARRÆ.

GENUS GARRA, *Ham. Buch.*

DISCOGNATHUS, *Heckel.*

DISCOGNATHICHTHYS et LISSORHYNCHUS, *Bleeker.*

Branchiostegals, three: pseudobranchiæ. Body elongated, subcylindrical. Mouth destitute of teeth, directed downwards, jaws protrusible: lower jaw not covered in front by lips, but those of the upper and lower jaw continuous. No lateral processes to the snout. A suctorial disk on the chin. Cirri four (*Garra*, Ham. Buch.) of which one pair are on the snout, the others on the maxilla: or only one pair present (*Discognathus*, Heckel) which are situated on the maxillæ. Pharyngeal teeth, sharp, conical, and curved at their extremities, situated in three closely approximating rows 2, 4, 5 | 5, 4, 2. Dorsal with few rays, no scales along its base: pectoral inserted sub-horizontally. Scales large, cycloid. Lateral line continuous.

GARRA MALABARICA. Plate XV. Fig. 1.

GARRA MALABARICA, *Day*, Proc. Zool. Soc. 1865, p. 297.

B. iii. D. $\frac{3}{9}$. P. 15. V. 10. A. $\frac{2}{5}$. C. 19. L. l. 31. L. tr. $\frac{4}{3}$. Vert. 29.

Length of head $\frac{1}{6}$, of pectoral $\frac{1}{7}$, of base of dorsal $\frac{1}{8}$, of base of anal $\frac{1}{16}$ of total length. Height of head $\frac{1}{10}$, of body $\frac{1}{6}$, of dorsal $\frac{1}{7}$, of anal $\frac{1}{8}$ of total length.

Eyes—Nearer the posterior than anterior extremity of the head, and with their superior surfaces on the upper profile looking upwards and outwards. Diameter nearly $\frac{1}{3}$ the length of the head, rather more than 1 diameter from end of snout, nearly 2 diameters apart.

The profile rises as far as the back of the head, from whence to the caudal it is nearly straight: the abdominal profile as convex as that of the back, sides compressed. Back rather broad, flat, and nearly as wide as the body is high.

Mouth below, snout broad and depressed, the upper jaw overlapping the lower: the two lips united, moderately thick and in the young covered with numerous pores which almost disappear in the adult. Below the mandibulæ is an oval suctorial disk, the transverse diameter of which is rather more than that of the orbit. One pair of fleshy cirri exists on the snout, and a second pair at angles of the maxillæ. In the skeleton the maxilla is broad, with a thin anterior edge, and an external extremity inferiorly very concave. The lower jaw is also transverse, broad, flat above, rather concave below, and at its external superior margin also concave. Owing to the great width of the lower jaw a hollow exists under the chin, and here the suctorial disk is situated. The nostrils are nearer to the orbits than they are to the end of the snout, the posterior is round, the anterior tubular. Interorbital space nearly flat from side to side, and between it and the snout is a deep transverse furrow.

Teeth—The inferior pharyngeal teeth are sharp, curved, and in three rows, 2, 4, 5 | 5, 4, 2, the long plate above them is of an arrow-headed shape, directed posteriorly.

Fins.—The dorsal is situated rather nearer the snout than it is to the base of the caudal, and a little in advance of the ventrals, higher anteriorly than posteriorly, its base destitute of scales, and its first three rays flexible though undivided. Pectorals inserted sub-horizontally. Anal short, situated entirely in the posterior fourth of the body, its commencement being midway between the posterior extremity of the pectoral and the termination of the lower caudal lobe. Caudal large, with a broad base, emarginate: its base scaled.

Scales—Large.

Lateral line—Nearly straight from the upper margin of opercle to the centre of the caudal, and nearer to the back than it is to the abdominal surface.

Colours—Back deep olive, fading to dirty white along the abdomen, and a wide dull leaden blue stripe passing along the lateral line, and the four central caudal rays, where it is of a shot green. Cheeks and under surface of mouth pinkish or flesh coloured. Disk dull yellow, and a slight yellow tinge extends along the abdomen. Anal bright yellow, with minute black points between the rays: base of pectoral and ventral dull red, the remainder of the fins slate colour.

This fish is found in the rivers of the plains, but more abundantly, and up to eight inches in length, in the mountain streams. The *Rev. Henry Baker*, from whom I received my hill specimens, informs me that amongst the Europeans it goes by the name of "the hill trout," and that it takes a worm pretty freely.

Habitat—Rivers and mountain streams in Malabar.

Group Labeones, *Bleeker.*

Genus ROHITA, *Cuv. and Val.*

Rohitodes, *Bleeker.*

Branchiostegals, three: pseudobranchiæ. Body elliptical or moderately elongated. Mouth destitute of teeth: gape oval: lower jaw thin, and without a tubercle at the symphysis: postlabial sulcus simple. Lips crenated or fringed, those of the two jaws continuous, and without lateral lobes; the end of the lower jaw uncovered. Preorbital bone touches the margin of the orbit. Cirri four (*Rohita*, Cuv. & Val.), of which one pair are on the snout, the other on the maxilla: or only one pair present (*Rohitodes*, Bleeker), which are situated on the maxillæ. Pharyngeal teeth in three series. Dorsal fin moderate, or elongated, destitute of bony rays, and situated before the commencement of the ventral. Scales large or moderate.

Fig 1.

Fig 2.

F. Day, del. et sculp.

1. GARRA MALABARICA. 2. PUNTIUS PINNAURATUS.

ROHITA DUSSUMIERI.

ROHITA DUSSUMIERI, *Cuv. & Val.* xvi. p. 258, pl. 475.
CIRRHINUS DUSSUMIERI, *Jerdon*, Madras Journal, xv. p. 304.
TOOLEE, *Mal.*

B. iii. D. $\frac{3}{12\text{-}13}$. P. 17. V. 9. A. $\frac{3}{5}$. C. 19. L. l. 55. L. tr. $\frac{9}{7}$.

Length of head nearly $\frac{1}{7}$, of pectoral $\frac{1}{8}$, of caudal $\frac{1}{6}$, of base of dorsal nearly $\frac{1}{7}$, of base of anal $\frac{1}{20}$ of the total length. Height of head $\frac{1}{9}$, of body above $\frac{1}{5}$, of dorsal $\frac{1}{9}$, of ventral $\frac{1}{8}$, of anal $\frac{1}{10}$ of total length.

Eyes—Diameter $\frac{1}{4}$ of length of head, 1 diameter from end of snout, 2 diameters apart.

Body elongated, profile slightly rising from the snout to the dorsal fin, from whence it is nearly straight to the base of the caudal. The abdominal profile rather more convex than that of the back. Thickness of the body equals two-thirds of its height.

Mouth small, inferior, surrounded by fleshy lips, which as well as the mouth are covered with numerous pores, which extend posteriorly as far as orbits and under the nostrils. One pair of small fleshy cirri on either side of upper jaw. Some scattered mucous pores along the lower jaw, and on the horizontal limb of the preopercle. The lips fringed. Preorbital advanced to over the angle of the mouth. Suborbital ring narrow. Preopercle narrow, its angle rounded, and its horizontal limb nearly as long as its vertical one. Opercle large, its posterior margin rounded and ending in a soft flap; its inferior rather oblique, its superior horizontal. Sub- and interopercles narrow. Interorbital space smooth, and rather convex.

Fins—The pectoral fin arises in the lower third of the body, under the posterior border of the opercle: ventral slightly nearer to the base of the pectoral than to that of the anal, and opposite the third branched ray of the dorsal: anal arises below the thirty-first or thirty-second scale. Dorsal fin rather in advance of the ventral, long, highest in front, with a concave superior margin, and the last ray rather produced: first unbranched ray minute, the second fine, only half the length of the third, which has a soft extremity. The last dorsal and anal rays divided into two at their bases. Anal with the first hard ray minute, second thin, and the third with soft articulated extremity: anterior extremity of the fin twice the height of the posterior one: its margin straight. Caudal deeply forked, lobes rather expanded. Ventral fan-shaped. Anus a short distance in front of the anal fin.

Scales—Their longest diameter from above downwards, those on the abdomen smaller than those on the sides.

Lateral line—First curves slightly downwards; from about opposite the posterior end of the pectoral it generally passes straight to the centre of the caudal, but in some specimens is slightly undulating in this portion of its course.

Colours—Greyish, darkest above, becoming silvery beneath. Back olive grey. All the scales edged with a darker shade of grey, and many of them, especially those above the lateral line, have a golden spot in the centre of each. Fins dusky. There is a dull diffused dark spot on the lateral line, on the side of the tail, and in some specimens another on the tail.

Common in the Kurriavanoor river near Cochin. When attempts are made to capture these fish with nets, they take surprising leaps, sometimes even springing over the heads of the boatmen who are standing up at the time. Immediately on being captured, their necks are broken with a stick. They grow to about thirteen inches in length, are fair eating, and are greatly esteemed by the Natives.

Habitat—Rivers of Malabar.

Sub-Fam. BARBINI, *Bleeker.*

GROUP SYSTOMI, *Bleeker.*

GENUS PUNTIUS, *Ham. Buch.*

SYSTOMUS, *McClelland.*
BARBODES, *Bleeker.*
COPOËTA, *Cuv. & Val.*

Branchiostegals, three: pseudobranchiæ. Body oblong, sometimes compressed: abdomen more or less flat. Mouth destitute of teeth, it is of moderate size, and directed forwards: jaws slightly protrusible, the lower jaw the shortest; both are covered by the lips. Snout short. Preorbital pentagonal, not elongated, directed upwards, backwards, or downwards, but never directly anteriorly. Lips of the two jaws continuous, with the postlabial sulcus simple, and parallel with the margin of the jaws. Cirri four (*Barbodes*, Bleeker), one pair on snout, one on maxillæ: or two (*Capoëta*, Cuv. & Val.) on the supramaxillaries: or none (*Puntius*, Ham. Buch.). Pharyngeal teeth spoon-shaped summits 2,3,5 | 5,3,2: or 2,3,3 | 4,3,2; or with tubercular summits 1,3,4 | 4.3,1, or 2,3,4 | 4,3,2. Dorsal fin situated from before to hardly posterior to the commencement of the ventral, with a row of scales along its base: its first few rays are unbranched, and either osseous and serrated, or osseous and entire, or cartilaginous, or have the extremities of all prolonged into filaments. Anal short, with a scaly base. Caudal also with some scales over its base. Scales moderate, cycloid. Lateral line usually continuous, or it may abruptly cease as in the ***Puntius vittatus***, p. 215.

With four cirri (*Barbodes*, Bleeker.)

1. ***Unbranched dorsal rays osseous, and the last serrated posteriorly.***

PUNTIUS CHRYSOPOMA.

BARBUS CHRYSOPOMA, *Cuv. & Val.* xvi. p. 165, pl. 466.
BARBUS GIBBOSUS, *Cuv. & Val.* xv. p. 155.
SYSTOMUS CHRYSOPOMA, *Jerdon*, Madras Journal, xv. p. 314.
MUNDUTTEE, *Mal.*

B. iii. D. $\frac{4}{8}$. P. 15. V. 9. A. $\frac{3}{5}$. C. 19. L. l. 28. L. tr. $\frac{6}{4}$.

Length of head $\frac{1}{5}$, of pectoral $\frac{2}{13}$, of caudal $\frac{1}{5}$, of base of dorsal $\frac{1}{8}$, of base of anal $\frac{1}{11}$ of total length. Height of head $\frac{1}{6}$, of body $\frac{2}{7}$, of dorsal $\frac{1}{6}$, of ventral $\frac{1}{7}$, of anal $\frac{1}{9}$ of total length.

Eyes—Diameter in the immature $\frac{2}{7}$, in the adult $\frac{1}{4}$ of length of head, $1\frac{1}{4}$ diameters from end of snout, 2 diameters apart.

Body elongated, a considerable rise from snout to the occiput, from whence to the dorsal it is more gradual, and from that fin to the caudal the profile gradually sinks. Abdominal profile is as convex as that of the back.

Snout short, slightly protractile: the posterior extremity of the maxilla extends to beneath the anterior margin of the orbit. Preopercle, posterior limb vertical, its angle rounded, its lower limb horizontal. Opercle irregularly triangular, its posterior margin convex, its upper short and horizontal. Subopercle rather more than one third as high as long. Interopercle with a rather irregularly lower margin. Upper surface of head smooth, rather convex, and divided from the snout by a transverse and moderately deep groove. Nasal cirri equal to two-thirds the diameter of the orbit in length, and the maxillary cirri rather longer. Nostrils opposite the anterior superior angle of the orbit.

Fins—Pectoral situated in the lower fourth of body: dorsal arises midway between the snout and the base of the caudal: the ventral rather more anteriorly: the anal half way between the base of the ventral and the base of the caudal. Dorsal rather square, its upper margin slightly concave, and its two first undivided rays small, the third half the length of the fourth, which last is strong, bony, serrated posteriorly in its upper half, and ending in a soft point: the last branched ray is divided to its root. First three rays of anal undivided, the two first very thin, the third moderately strong; its last branched ray divided to its root. Caudal with a wide base, lobed in its posterior half.

Scales—Longest diameter vertical, with three or more striæ radiating from their anterior border towards their circumference.

Lateral line—Curves downwards to opposite the end of the pectoral, from whence it proceeds direct to the centre of the caudal.

Colours—Back greenish with silvery reflections, abdomen silvery. A dull diffused black mark on either side of the tail, which is often more visible in preserved than in fresh specimens. Cheeks golden. Ventral orange: the other fins grey, the dorsal and caudal margined with a darker colour, and the anal stained with orange. In immature specimens a dark line exists along each row of scales, but this becomes lost in the mature fish.

Very common in rivers, and also found in paddy fields and ponds, it is likewise kept in tanks in Hindu temples. During the monsoon time small ones are carried down to the mouths of the rivers on the western coast. It grows to upwards of two feet in length, and is good eating.

Habitat—Bombay and fresh waters of Malabar.

PUNTIUS PINNAURATUS. Plate XV. Fig. 2.

CYCLOCHEILICHTHYS PINNAURATUS, *Day*, Proc. Zool. Soc. 1865, p. 300.

B. iii. D. $\frac{3}{8}$. P. 17. V. 9. A. $\frac{2}{6}$. C. 21. L. l. 29. L. tr. $\frac{6}{5}$.

Length of head above $\frac{1}{4}$, of base of dorsal $\frac{1}{8}$, of base of anal $\frac{1}{11}$, of caudal $\frac{1}{4}$ of total length. Height of body $\frac{1}{3}$, of head $\frac{1}{6}$ of total length.

Eyes—Situated in the anterior half of the head, their upper margins do not reach the profile: diameter $\frac{1}{4}$ of length of head, 1 diameter from end of snout, upwards of 1 diameter apart.

Profile rises considerably to commencement of the dorsal fin, from whence it sinks more gradually to the caudal. Profile of abdomen not so convex as that of the back. Body strongly compressed.

Mouth directed forwards, the lower jaw covered by the upper when the two are closed. Preorbital triangular, apex directed above. Two pairs of cirri, those on snout equal two-thirds the length of the maxillary pair, which are nearly as long as the orbit. Nostrils situated nearer to the orbit than to the snout: the posterior patent, divided by a membraneous valve from the anterior, which is slightly tubular.

Fins—Dorsal commences midway between the snout and base of caudal, and is slightly in advance of the ventral: anal situated in the posterior fourth of the body: pectoral just reaches the ventral, which does not extend quite so far as the anal. Dorsal nearly triangular, its third undivided ray bony and serrated in its upper three-fourths: a row of scales along the base of the fin. Anal undivided rays weak, lower margin of the fin concave: a row of scales along its base. Caudal deeply lobed.

Scales—Each with from eight to ten radiating lines passing from the anterior margin, and diverging posteriorly.

Lateral line—In single distinct tubes in each scale: it first descends slightly for six scales, and opposite the centre of the opercle passes direct to the caudal.

Colours—Silvery, with a large diffused black spot on the lateral line, extending from the twenty-fourth to the twenty-eighth scale. A red spot on opercle. Dorsal and pectoral tinged with red, and minutely spotted with black, as are also the bases of the scales and the various pieces of the opercles. External half of ventral bright orange-scarlet; anal tipped with red: both minutely dotted with black. Caudal stained with black.

From a small pond in Cochin.

Habitat—Fresh waters of Malabar.

2. *Unbranched dorsal rays cartilaginous, and articulated in their whole extent.*

Puntius melanampyx. Plate XVI. Fig. 1.

Labeo melanampyx, *Day*, Proc. Zool. Soc. 1865, p. 298.

B. iii. D. $\frac{3}{9}$. P. 16. V. 9. A. $\frac{3}{6}$. C. 18. L. l. 20. L. tr. $\frac{4}{3}$.

Length of head $\frac{2}{9}$, of pectoral $\frac{1}{6}$, of base of dorsal $\frac{2}{13}$, of base of anal $\frac{1}{11}$, of caudal $\frac{2}{5}$ of total length. Height of head $\frac{1}{6}$, of body $\frac{1}{3}$, of dorsal $\frac{1}{6}$, of anal $\frac{1}{7}$ of total length.

Eyes—Diameter nearly $\frac{1}{3}$ length of head, upwards of 1 diameter from end of snout, and $1\frac{1}{2}$ apart.

Profile ascends to anterior margin of the dorsal, from whence to the caudal it gradually descends. Abdomen rather flat below, its profile not so convex as that of the back: sides compressed.

Mouth rather small, directed forwards and slightly downwards, upper jaw rather longer than the lower. Lips continuous from upper to lower jaw: lower lip with numerous fine pores, thickened below the symphysis. Preorbital rather triangular, with the base anterior. Snout bulging and laterally rather swollen, both it and the preorbital are covered by crenations: some widely scattered pores exist over the whole of the upper surface of the head. Nostrils nearer to the orbit than to the end of the snout, anterior tubular, and separated by a membraneous valve from the posterior which is oval and patent.

Teeth—Pharyngeal teeth in three rows, crooked and sharp, 4, 3, 2, | 2, 3, 4.

Fins—Dorsal arises midway between snout and base of caudal, it is slightly in advance of the origin of the ventral, which is sub-horizontal: the anal arises midway between the posterior extremity of the opercle and the termination of the caudal, and is entirely posterior to the whole of the dorsal. Caudal deeply lobed. Dorsal and anal fins with a row of scales at their bases. Pectoral reaches almost to the ventral, the tip of which last nearly touches the anal.

Scales—Large.

Lateral line—Slightly descends.

Colours—Reddish brown with three vertical black bands, one behind the eye, a second anterior to the base of the dorsal fin, which is wide at its origin but narrows close to the ventral: a third from the termination of the dorsal, crosses the lateral line, but does not reach the base of the anal: occasionally a fourth crosses the base of the caudal. Muzzle black. Fins dusky. Eyes reddish.

I am indebted to the *Rev. H. Baker, junior,* of Cottayam, for several specimens of this fish, which he captured in the river on the hills at Mundikyum, where it is common, and grows to three inches in length.

Habitat—Hill ranges of Travancore.

PLATE XVI.

Fig 1.

Fig 2.

F. Day, del, et sculp.

1. PUNTIUS MELANAMPYX. 2. PUNTIUS DENISONII

With 2 *cirri* (*Capoeta,* Cuv. & Val.)

1. *Unbranched dorsal rays osseous but entire.*

PUNTIUS PARRAH. Plate VII. Fig. 3.

? PUNTIUS AMPHIBIUS, *Jerdon*, Madras Journal, xv. p. 315 (not *Cuv. & Val.*)
PUNTIUS PARRAH, *Day*, Proc. Zool. Soc. 1865, p. 301.
PARRAH PERLEE, *Mal.*

B. iii. D. $\frac{3}{8}$. P. 15. V. 8. A. $\frac{2}{5}$. C. 19. L. l. 25. L. tr. $\frac{5}{4}$.

Length of head $\frac{1}{5}$, of base of dorsal $\frac{1}{6}$, of base of anal $\frac{1}{12}$, of pectoral $\frac{1}{7}$, of caudal $\frac{1}{5}$ of total length. Height of head $\frac{1}{6}$, of body $\frac{1}{4}$, of dorsal $\frac{1}{6}$, of anal $\frac{1}{7}$ of total length.

Eyes—Diameter nearly $\frac{1}{3}$ of length of head, almost $1\frac{1}{4}$ diameters apart, and 1 diameter from end of snout.

Profile curves gradually to the dorsal, descends along its base, and from its posterior extremity proceeds almost horizontally to the caudal. The height of the body is four-elevenths of its length, excluding the caudal fin.

One pair of thin cirri to maxillæ which are equal to two-thirds of the length of the orbit. Opercle, width four-sevenths of its height, subopercle two-fifths as high as long. Nostrils nearer to the orbit than to the end of the snout, the posterior patent, and divided by a valve from the anterior which is slightly tubular.

Fins—Dorsal commences midway between the snout and base of the caudal, and just over the ventral: its bony ray strong, smooth, and with a soft termination: its length equals the distance from the centre of orbit to the posterior extremity of opercle: the upper surface of fin rather concave, its two posterior rays elongated. The anal arises behind the posterior margin of the dorsal, midway between the orbit and the end of the caudal, its external margin concave. Caudal deeply lobed. The pectoral does not quite reach the ventral: nor the ventral the anal, by the width of two scales.

Scales—In regular horizontal rows, but in the one above the lateral line the fourth scale is rather large, and two rows commence behind it. Each scale has generally from three to four diverging lines, but in some there are more, especially along the abdominal surface.

Lateral line—Follows curve of the back in upper third of body.

Colours—Upper surface of back dark silvery green, divided from a silvery abdomen by a dark bluish line. Cheeks golden red. Pectoral, ventral and anal tinged with yellow. Dorsal and caudal dusky. A diffused black spot on the lateral line extending from the twentieth to twenty-second scale. Eyes golden.

Common in the rivers and inundated paddy fields of Malabar.

Habitat—Fresh waters of Malabar.

PUNTIUS PERLEE.

B. iii. D. $\frac{3}{8}$. P. 15. V. 10. A. $\frac{2}{5}$. C. 19. L. l. 24. L. tr. $\frac{5}{3}$.

Length of head $\frac{2}{9}$, of base of dorsal $\frac{1}{6}$, of base of anal $\frac{1}{10}$, of pectoral $\frac{1}{6}$, of caudal $\frac{1}{4}$ of the total length. Height of head $\frac{1}{5}$, of body $\frac{1}{3}$, of dorsal $\frac{1}{5}$, of anal $\frac{1}{6}$ of the total length.

Eyes—Diameter $\frac{1}{3}$ of length of head, $\frac{2}{3}$ of a diameter from end of snout, $1\frac{1}{3}$ diameters apart.

Body high and compressed, a considerable rise from the snout to the first dorsal, from whence it sinks to the base of the caudal. Abdominal profile not so convex as that of the back. The height of the body is one half its length, excluding the caudal fin.

Mouth rather oblique. Opercle nearly triangular, two-thirds as wide as high, upper margin rather concave. Subopercle half as high as long. Maxillary pair of cirri two-thirds of the length of the head.

Fins—The pectoral arises under the posterior third of the subopercle, and extends beyond the base of the ventral. Ventral with an enlarged scale at its base, and it reaches as far as the commencement of the base of the anal. The anal arises rather behind the origin of the last dorsal rays, its first unbranched ray is very short, its second one half shorter than the third, which equals the distance from the posterior nostril to the posterior extremity of opercle, and ends in a soft point: the last branched ray double and prolonged so as to reach the base of the caudal. Dorsal commences midway between snout and base of caudal, its first unbranched ray is minute, its second half the length of the third, which is strong, osseous, concave posteriorly, and ending superiorly in a soft prolongation: its last branched ray double, and reaches half way from its base towards th caudal fin. Caudal rather deeply lobed, with each of its extremities pointed.

Scales—High and narrow, the external portion one half higher than wide, with two or three badly marked radiating lines. A row exists along the base of the dorsal and anal fins. Opposite and above the sixth row of the lateral line a second row of scales commences.

Lateral line—Rather descends for five scales, then becomes slightly convex to the twenty-third scale, from whence it proceeds direct to the centre of the caudal.

Colours—Silvery green above, silvery white shot with gold below the lateral line. Cheeks golden. Fins yellowish. Dorsal and caudal minutely dotted with fine points, a few also are scattered on the scales. A badly marked black blotch exists on the lateral line from the twenty-second to the twenty-third scales inclusive.

Very common in all pieces of fresh water.

Habitat—Malabar.

3. *Unbranched dorsal rays cartilaginous, and articulated in their whole extent.*

Puntius Denisonii, Plate XVI. Fig. 2.

Labeo Denisonii, *Day*, Proc. Zool. Soc. 1865, p. 299.

B. iii. D. $\frac{2}{8}$. P. 15. V. 9. A. $\frac{2}{5}$ C. 19. L. l. 28. L. tr. $\frac{5}{3}$.

Length of head $\frac{1}{6}$, of pectoral $\frac{1}{7}$, of base of dorsal $\frac{1}{8}$, of base of anal $\frac{1}{12}$, of caudal $\frac{1}{5}$ of total length. Height of head $\frac{1}{10}$, of body $\frac{1}{5}$, of dorsal $\frac{1}{6}$, of anal $\frac{1}{10}$ of total length.

Eyes—Diameter about $\frac{1}{3}$ of length of head, rather more than 1 diameter apart, $1\frac{1}{5}$ diameters from end of snout.

Body elongated, compressed: profile from snout to dorsal slightly elevated, from whence to the caudal it gradually slopes.

Mouth small, directed forwards and slightly downwards, the upper jaw being the longest, and snout slightly prominent, with a small expansion laterally on either side, and pores on its apex: the lower jaw curves slightly upwards at its extremity, and has a small tubercle on the upper surface of the symphysis. Upper and lower lips continuous, edges entire, and a little thickened so as to form a small lobe below the symphysis of the lower jaw. Sulcus simple, not very deep. Preorbital irregularly triangular, longer than high, rounded anteriorly. Maxillary cirri one pair, fleshy, and one-third longer than the orbit. Nostrils nearer orbit than end of snout, the posterior closed by a membraneous valve, the margin of the anterior slightly elevated, so as to appear semi-tubular.

Teeth—In pharyngeals in three closely approximating rows, sharp, pointed, and slightly curved towards their extremities 4,3,2 | 2,3,4.

Fins—The commencement of the dorsal is the width of two scales nearer the snout than to the base of the caudal, and the fin is in advance of the ventral. Anal situated in the posterior quarter of the body, and entirely behind the termination of the dorsal. Dorsal highest in front, with a row of scales along its base. A large free scale at the base of the ventral, which fin is rounded. Anal highest anteriorly. Caudal deeply lobed.

Scales—Large.

Lateral line—Curved slightly in its anterior portion, then passing direct to the caudal.

Air bladder with a constriction, dividing one-third from the remaining two-thirds.

Colours—Silvery, with a line of black passing from the snout through the lower part of the eye to the centre of the base of the caudal fin: above it a wide line of bright scarlet, extending the same distance. Back glossy metallic blue; abdomen silvery white. Caudal with an oblique black band crossing the posterior third of each lobe. The other fins colourless.

I received several specimens of this very pretty fish from the *Rev. H. Baker*, jun. who obtained them in the stream at Mundikyum, in the hill ranges of Travancore, where it is not uncommon, and grows to about six inches in length. It is named after *H. E. Sir W. Denison, K.C.B.*, the Governor of Madras, who has devoted much attention to the natural productions of India.

Habitat—Hill ranges of Malabar.

PUNTIUS HAMILTONII.

? SYSTOMUS HAMILTONII, *Jerdon*, Madras Journal, xv. p. 316.
OOLEE PERLEE, *Mal.*

B. iii. D. $\frac{3}{8}$. P. 17. V. 9. A. $\frac{3}{5}$. C. 19. L. l. 24. L. tr. $\frac{5}{3}$.

Length of head $\frac{2}{11}$, of pectoral $\frac{1}{7}$, of caudal $\frac{2}{11}$, of base of dorsal $\frac{1}{8}$, of base of anal $\frac{1}{16}$ of total length. Height of head $\frac{1}{7}$, of body $\frac{1}{4}$, of dorsal $\frac{1}{7}$, of ventral $\frac{1}{7}$, of anal $\frac{1}{7}$ of the total length.

Eyes—Diameter $\frac{2}{5}$ of length of head, $\frac{3}{5}$ of a diameter from end of snout, 1 diameter apart.

Profile gradually ascends to the base of the dorsal fin, and sinks from thence to the caudal. The abdominal profile is about equally curved with that of the back.

Snout short: the posterior extremity of the maxilla extends as far as the anterior margin of the orbit. One pair of cirri on the maxilla, equal to about half the length of the orbit.

Fins—The pectoral commences under the posterior extremity of the subopercle, and opposite its lower third: the dorsal opposite the end of the pectoral: the anal below the fifteenth scale of the lateral line. Pectoral fin pointed. Dorsal spines thin and weak, articulated in their whole extent, the first very short, the second two-thirds the length of the third, which equals the first branched ray: upper margin of fin rather concave. Ventral, first ray undivided, a very small elongated scale at its base. Anal nearly square, its first unbranched ray very minute, in some specimens indeed, not to be discovered; the second and third very weak and thin. Caudal with a broad base, and rather deeply lobed.

Scales—With rarely more than two or three radiating lines on their exposed portions: the rows are not quite parallel, opposite and above the fifth scale of the lateral line a new one commences.

Lateral line—Slopes gradually down from the posterior superior margin of opercle to opposite the end of the pectoral, from whence it proceeds nearly direct to the centre of the caudal.

Colours—Back green, abdomen silvery, a slight golden tinge on the opercle, and a dark diffused spot on the lateral line from the twenty-first to the twenty-third scales. Dorsal stained rather dark along its upper margin. Pectoral, ventral and anal yellowish. Caudal dirty white. In the monsoon time a beautiful rosy streak extends from the eye to the centre of the caudal fin; the back is of a more olive green, and the fins redder.

When young the summit of the head is golden green, and a yellow streak runs from opposite the centre of the eye to the centre of the tail. When about two inches in length the black spot on the side of the tail commences to appear, and by degrees the golden streak along the side disappears.

Grows to five or six inches in length.

Habitat—Fresh waters of Southern India.

With no cirri (*Puntius,* Ham. Buch.)

1. *Unbranched dorsal rays osseous, the last serrated posteriorly.*

Puntius punctatus, Plate VII. f. 1.

Puntius punctatus, *Day*, Proc. Zool. Soc. 1865, p. 302.
Putter perlee, *Mal.*

B. iii. D. $\frac{3}{8}$. P. 15. V. 8. A. $\frac{2}{5}$. C. 18. L. l. 27. L. tr. $\frac{6}{4}$.

Length of head $\frac{1}{6}$, of pectoral $\frac{1}{6}$, of base of dorsal $\frac{1}{7}$, of base of anal $\frac{1}{10}$, of caudal $\frac{1}{6}$ of total length. Height of head $\frac{1}{6}$, of body $\frac{1}{3}$, of dorsal $\frac{1}{5}$ of total length.

Eyes—Large, close to profile, nearly $\frac{1}{2}$ the length of head, $\frac{1}{3}$ of a diameter from end of snout, nearly 1 diameter apart.

The posterior extremity of maxilla does not extend quite to the anterior margin of the orbit. Suborbital ring of bones very broad, almost entirely hiding the preopercle. Sub- and interopercles narrow.

Fins—Pectoral arises opposite the posterior inferior angle of the subopercle: the ventral, one scale beyond the extremity of the pectoral: anal just under the dorsal, opposite the fifteenth scale on the lateral line. Dorsal fin highest in front, superior border concave: its first unbranched ray very minute, second nearly half the height of the third, which is strong, broad, and serrated in the upper two-thirds of its posterior margin: a row of scales along its base. Pectoral pointed. Ventral with a large elongated scale at its base. Anal with its first unbranched ray very minute, often quite hidden. Caudal with a broad base, and moderately lobed.

Scales—With two or three radiating lines.

Lateral line—At first curves gradually downwards, and from opposite the base of the ventral passes direct to the caudal.

Colours—Olive green above, gradually fading into silvery on the abdomen. A black diffused spot on the twentieth and twenty-first scales of the lateral line. The anterior half of the fourth scale from the opercle in the row next the lateral line is of a deep black, as is also a portion of the scale above, and that beneath it. Fins yellowish, dorsal and anal tipped with orange. Dorsal spotted with black, in two longitudinal rows, with a third in the front part between the other two. The dark markings are much more visible in the months when the freshes are coming down.

Common; eaten by the Natives.

Habitat—Malabar.

2. *Unbranched dorsal rays osseous, but entire. Lateral line ceasing abruptly.*

PUNTIUS VITTATUS. Plate XIII. Fig. 1.

PUNTIUS VITTATUS, *Day*, Proc. Zool. Soc. 1865, p. 303.

B. iii. D. $\frac{2}{8}$. P. 12. V. 9. A. $\frac{2}{5}$. C. 20. L. l. 22. L. tr. $\frac{4}{3}$.

Length of head $\frac{2}{9}$, of pectoral $\frac{1}{6}$, of base of dorsal $\frac{1}{5}$, of base of anal $\frac{1}{11}$, of caudal $\frac{2}{7}$ of total length. Height of head $\frac{1}{4}$, of body $\frac{1}{3}$ of total length.

Eyes—Diameter $\frac{1}{2}$ the length of head, $\frac{2}{3}$ of a diameter from end of snout, 2 diameters apart.

Fins—Pectoral commences under the subopercle: ventral two scales beyond its termination: dorsal opposite the seventh scale of the lateral line: anal one scale beyond the end of the ventral. Pectoral pointed. Anal with the last ray divided into two. Caudal deeply lobed, each lobe pointed. Dorsal spines entire, in some specimens there is a very small one before the two others, but this is not always the case.

Scales—With four or more radiating lines.

Lateral line—Consists of a single tube in each scale: it passes for about five rows along the central line and there ceases.

Colours—Upper surface of body dusky green, abdomen silvery. Cheeks sometimes golden. There are four black spots in the adult, one just before the dorsal, one under its posterior margin, another at the base of the caudal, and the fourth at the base of the anal. The dorsal has a black streak down it, and a black tip, with orange markings. In the immature the colours vary. When the fish is about eight-tenths of an inch long, a vertical black stripe begins to show itself in the posterior third of the dorsal fin, the tip of which also becomes edged with black, and there is some irregular orange coloration about the fin. A black spot shows itself at the base of the caudal and anal fins; and in very young specimens the line of demarcation between the green of the back and the silver of the abdomen is very apparent, and seems as if a white line passed from the eye to the centre of the caudal.

Rarely grows to more than an inch and a half in length, and is the most common species found in the paddy fields. It is eaten by the slave castes.

Habitat—Malabar.

2. *Unbranched dorsal rays osseous, entire: the branched dorsal rays with filamentous prolongations.*

PUNTIUS FILAMENTOSUS.

LEUCISCUS FILAMENTOSUS, *Cuv. & Val.* xvii. p. 96, pl. 492.

LEUCISCUS MAHECOLA, *Cuv. & Val.* xvii. p. 305, pl. 502, (*young.*)

SYSTOMUS FILAMENTOSUS, ASSIMILIS, et MADERASPATENSIS, *Jerdon*, Madras Journal, xv. pp. 318, 319.

CURROAH, *Mal.*

B. iii. D. $\frac{3}{8}$. P. 17. V. 9. A. $\frac{2}{5}$. C. 15. L. l. 21. L. tr. $\frac{5}{4}$.

Length of head $\frac{1}{5}$, of pectoral $\frac{2}{13}$, of caudal $\frac{2}{9}$, of base of dorsal rather above $\frac{1}{7}$, of base of anal $\frac{1}{11}$ of total length. Height of head $\frac{2}{13}$, of body above $\frac{1}{3}$, of dorsal fin excluding its filamentous prolongation $\frac{1}{5}$, of dorsal including its filamentous prolongation $\frac{1}{4}$, of ventral $\frac{2}{13}$, of anal $\frac{1}{8}$ of total length.

Eyes—Circular, diameter $\frac{2}{7}$ of length of head, nearly 1 diameter from end of snout, $1\frac{1}{3}$ diameters apart.

Body rather elliptical, compressed, narrower posteriorly than anteriorly: profile rising from snout to the first dorsal from whence it sinks but more gradually to the caudal. Abdominal profile more convex than that of the back.

Mouth rather small, slightly oblique, the maxilla extends to beneath the anterior margin of the orbit. Opercle triangular, base in front, and posterior extremity rounded. Preopercle narrow, posterior margin slightly oblique, inferior nearly horizontal, angle rounded. Preorbital nearly square, extending forwards slightly over the maxilla, the anterior portion of the suborbital ring of bones narrowest, upper surface of head smooth, rather a notch between it and snout. Nostrils situated in front of the anterior superior angle of the orbit.

Teeth—Pharyngeal teeth curved, pointed, and in three rows, 5, 3, 2 | 2, 3, 5.

Fins—The pectoral arises in the lower fourth of the body, and under the posterior margin of the opercle: dorsal rather nearer snout than base of caudal: ventral under fourth dorsal ray: anal midway between base of pectoral and posterior extremity of lower lobe of the caudal. Dorsal with its first three rays unbranched, the first of which is very small, the second nearly half the length of the third, which ends in a soft point, and is often as long as the first branched ray: the whole of the branched rays end in filamentous prolongations, which are usually absent in the young (*Leuciscus Mahecola, C. & V.*). The third, fourth and fifth are mostly the longest, in certain seasons they appear to lose their prolongations, and generally one or more are deficient. The membrane between the rays only extends two-thirds of their height. Anal with external margins rather concave. Caudal with wide lobes.

Scales—Large, vertical diameter the longest, each with three or more lines radiating towards their circumference.

Lateral line—Concave, parallel with the abdomen to opposite the end of the dorsal, when it proceeds direct to the centre of caudal. A row of scales along the bases of dorsal and anal fins.

Colours—Silvery white with a greenish back, and a diffused black spot on the lateral line at the side of the tail; each scale is margined with a beautiful metallic green. Pectoral flesh-coloured: ventral colourless: anal margined with deep red: caudal red tipped with black, and having a white extremity.

Common in some tanks and also found in rivers. Is considered good eating by the Natives. Grows to eight inches in length.

Habitat—Fresh waters of Malabar and the Coromandel coast.

Group CATLÆ, *Bleeker.*

GENUS AMBLYPHARYNGODON, *Bleeker.*

BRACHYGRAMMA, *Day.*

Branchiostegals, three: pseudobranchiæ. Body elongated, sides compressed, abdomen rather flat beneath. Snout short, broad, depressed. Preorbital triangular, apex directed downwards. No cirri. Eyes of moderate size, with free circular lids. Mouth anterior, gape wide, cleft oblique and of moderate

PLATE XVII.

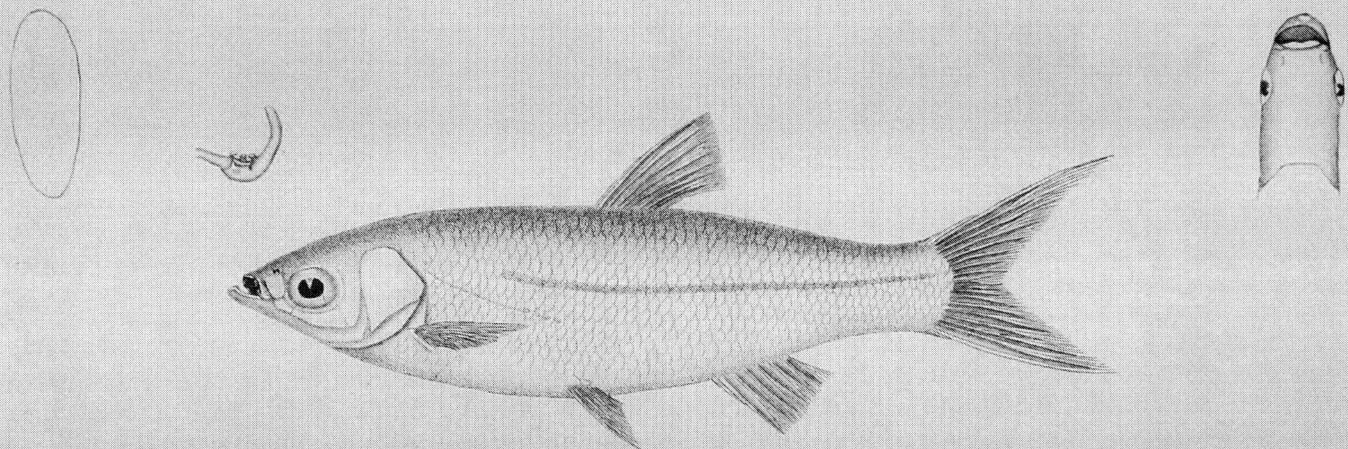

Fig 1.

Fig 2.

F. Day, del, et sculp.

AMBLYPHARYNGODON JERDONII. 2. PARADANIO AUROLINEATUS.

length: jaws completely covered by the lips: posterior labial sulcus simple on either side. Centre of upper jaw emarginate to receive a knob which exists at the symphysis of the lower jaw. Opercles smooth. Scales small and deciduous. Lateral line curves downwards and ceases abruptly opposite ventral fin. Dorsal fin short, its base without scales, it arises behind the commencement of the ventrals, but does not extend so far as to above the anal. Anal short, without bony rays, commencing behind the end of dorsal. Branchial aperture cleft to below the eyes. Pharyngeal teeth in three rows, large, molar like, with their free surfaces concave or spoon-shaped, 1, 2, 3 | 3, 2, 1.

AMBLYPHARYNGODON JERDONI. Plate XVII. Fig. 1.

BRACHYGRAMMA JERDONI, *Day*, Proc. Zool. Soc. 1865, p. 304.
WUMBOO. *Mal.*

B. iii. D. $\frac{2}{7}$. P. 15. V. 9. A. $\frac{3}{5}$. C. 19. L. l. 63. L. tr. $\frac{10}{6}$.

Length of head $\frac{1}{5}$, of pectoral $\frac{1}{7}$, of base of dorsal $\frac{1}{10}$, of base of anal $\frac{1}{10}$, of caudal $\frac{1}{5}$ of total length. Height of head $\frac{1}{6}$, of body $\frac{1}{4}$, of dorsal $\frac{1}{7}$, of anal $\frac{1}{9}$ of total length.

Eyes—The lower margins of the orbits are as close to the inferior, as their upper margins are to the superior profile of the head. Diameter $\frac{1}{5}$ of length of head, a little more than $\frac{1}{2}$ a diameter from end of snout, $1\frac{1}{2}$ diameters apart.

Profile rises gradually from the snout to the posterior end of the head, from whence there is a gradual decline to the caudal. The abdominal profile is rather more convex than that of the dorsal. Sides compressed, abdomen rather flat. Head compressed from side to side. Snout broad and depressed.

Mouth moderate in size and oblique, lower jaw the longest, armed with a hook at its symphysis, which is received into a corresponding emargination in the upper jaw. When the mouth is closed the upper surface of the lower jaw forms a portion of the superior profile of the head. Lips thin, covering both jaws. Muzzle apparently rather pointed when the jaws are closed. Intermaxillaries slightly protrusible. Preorbital triangular, apex below. Nostrils close to the anterior superior angle of the orbit, posterior broad and patent, divided by a valve from the anterior, the margins of which are raised. Opercle smooth and nearly triangular. Gill openings wide, and extending as far forwards as opposite the posterior margin of the orbits.

Fins—Dorsal arises rather nearer to the caudal than to the snout, is slightly behind the origin of the ventral, but does not extend as far backwards as to above the commencement of the anal, both are square: anal situated in the posterior third of the body, and arising midway between the orbit and the end of the inferior lobe of the caudal. Caudal deeply lobed.

Teeth—Pharyngeal short, wide and transversely oval: summits concave, both from side to side, and from before backwards, in fact similar to the concave surface of a spoon, 3, 2, 1 | 1, 2, 3.

Scales—Extremely deciduous, very small on the chest and as far as the ventral fins.

Lateral line—Formed of long single tubes in each scale. It only extends along fifteen rows, curving downwards, and then ceases.

Colours—Greenish above, silvery below. A bright silvery greenish yellow line separates the green of the back from the silvery sides and abdomen. Summit of head bright green. Inside of mouth and lips closely spotted with black. Fins colourless. Eyes white.

Is not uncommon in the rivers and ponds. I have named the species after Dr. Jerdon, who records two of this genus which he discovered in Southern India.

Habitat—Malabar.

GENUS BARILIUS, *Ham. Buch.*

OPSARION, *McClelland.*
PACHYSTOMUS, *Heckel.*
BENDILISIS et SHACRA, *Bleeker.*

Branchiostegals, three: pseudobranchiæ. Body oblong, moderately compressed. Snout short, compressed. Jaws covered by lips. Preorbital pentagonal or triangular, its apex directed upwards. Opening of mouth large: lower jaw with a knob at its extremity, received into an emargination in the end of the upper jaw. Cirri four (*Barilius*, Ham. Buch.) on the snout; or two (*Bendilisis*, Bleeker) on the maxillæ, or none (*Pachystomus*, Heckel). Eyes with free lids. Pharyngeal teeth in three rows, pointed and curved. Dorsal fin without scales at its base, and placed above or behind the commencement of the ventral. Anal with more rays than the dorsal. Scales large or of medium size. Lateral line strongly concave.

a. Without cirri (Pachystomus, Heckel).

BARILIUS BAKERI. Plate XVIII.

BARILIUS BAKERI, *Day*, Proc. Zool. Soc. 1865, p. 305.

B. iii. D. $\frac{3}{10}$. P. 15. V. 10. A. $\frac{3}{14}$. C. 17. L. l. 38. L. tr. $\frac{9}{2}$.

Length of head $\frac{1}{4}$, of pectoral $\frac{1}{6}$, of base of dorsal $\frac{1}{7}$, of base of anal $\frac{1}{6}$, of caudal $\frac{2}{9}$ of the total length. Height of head $\frac{1}{7}$, of body $\frac{2}{7}$, of dorsal $\frac{1}{6}$, of anal $\frac{1}{7}$ of total length.

Eyes—Diameter about $\frac{1}{4}$ of length of head, $1\frac{1}{4}$ diameters apart, 1 diameter from end of snout.

Profile more convex on the ventral than on the dorsal aspect.

Gape of mouth large, directed forwards, and compressed from side to side. Lower jaw slightly the longest, terminating in a knob, which is received into the apex of a triangle formed by the meeting of the intermaxillaries. Lips not fleshy; jaws entirely covered; some pores exist along the margin of the lower lip, on the snout, and on the anterior margin of the preorbital. Sulcus single, not deep: snout rather enlarged at its extremity, and divided by a small fissure from the margin of the preorbital, which is pentagonal, its inferior border being the longest. Nostrils rather closer to the orbit than to the end of the snout, divided from one another by a membraneous valve, the posterior broad and open, the anterior with raised margins. Upper surface of head rather convex from side to side.

Fins—Dorsal commences nearly midway between the snout and the base of the caudal, opposite the middle of the ventral, and extends backwards as far as opposite the fourth ray of the anal. Caudal deeply forked, the lower lobe the longest. Anterior margins of the dorsal and anal the highest, the former with a slightly convex, the latter with a concave margin. Base of dorsal scaleless, of anal scaled; two long free scales at the base of the ventral; some scales at the base of caudal.

Scales—Large and lineated.

Lateral line—In single tubes on each scale. It descends nearly as low as the abdominal profile, and is continued nearly parallel with it.

Teeth—Pharyngeal in three rows, curved, pointed, and slightly hooked at their extremities. They are arranged in the following order:—5,4,2 | 2,4,5.

Colours—Back bluish grey, fading to white on the abdomen. Some metallic silvery blue spots along the sides. Dorsal, anal, and pectoral fins margined with white; their bases dark grey. Caudal grey in the centre and whitish externally.

PLATE XVIII.

F. Day, del, et sculp.

BARILIUS BAKERI

I have named this fish after my excellent correspondent the ***Rev. H. Baker,*** jun. who obtained several specimens of it at Mundikyum, on the Travancore hills, where it grows to six inches in length.

The ***Opsarius Malabaricus,*** Jerdon, from North Malabar, appears to be allied to this species, but is much more beautiful in its coloration, and differs apparently in the number of rays, scales, and position of the fins.

Habitat—Hill ranges of Travancore, in South Malabar.

GROUP DANIONES.

GENUS PARADANIO.*

Branchiostegals, three. Body oblong, strongly compressed. Profile of back almost straight, that of the abdomen very convex. Lips thin. Mouth antero-superior, cleft moderately oblique: the superior jaws emarginate, the symphysis of the lower jaw hooked. Preorbital triangular, apex below. No cirri. Eyes with free lids. Pharyngeal teeth in three rows, pointed and curved. Dorsal fin without scales at its base; no hard rays to fin: it is situated behind the ventral, and its posterior portion is over the commencement of the anal. Anal elongated, with more rays than the dorsal. Scales of moderate size, or small. Lateral line strongly concave, situated near to the abdominal profile.

PARADANIO AUROLINEATUS, Plate XVII. f. 2.

PERILAMPUS AUROLINEATUS, *Day*, Proc. Zool. Soc. 1865, p. 306.

B. iii. D. $\frac{2}{12}$. P. 14. V. 7. A. $\frac{3}{15}$. C. 19. L. l. 34-40. L. tr. $\frac{7}{2}$.

Length of head $\frac{1}{5}$, of pectoral $\frac{1}{6}$, of base of dorsal $\frac{1}{6}$, of base of anal $\frac{1}{5}$, of caudal $\frac{1}{5}$ of the total length. Height of head $\frac{1}{6}$, of body $\frac{1}{3}$, of dorsal $\frac{1}{7}$, of anal $\frac{1}{7}$ of total length.

Eyes—Diameter $\frac{1}{3}$ length of head, $\frac{3}{4}$ of a diameter from end of snout, 1 diameter apart.

Profile slightly raised to base of dorsal, from whence it gradually sinks to the caudal; the inferior surface of the body much more convex than that of the back. The upper margin of the lower jaw when closed is flush with the upper surface of the head.

Mouth oblique. Lower jaw the longest; the extremity covered by a knob which is received into an emarginate space formed by the intermaxillaries. Lips thin, covering the jaws. Preorbital small, irregularly quadrilateral, the lower extremity the smallest, forming a sort of apex. Superior margin of orbit close to profile. Upper surface of head nearly flat. Opercles smooth.

Teeth—Pharyngeals curved and pointed: the external row much the largest—5,4,1 | 1,4,5.

Fins—Dorsal arises rather nearer to the snout than to the posterior extremity of the caudal, but is entirely situated in the last half of the body; anal arises opposite the dorsal. Caudal lobed. Pectoral just reaches the ventral, which does not extend to the anal. Anterior extremities of the dorsal and anal the highest. Margin of dorsal convex, of anal slightly concave.

---

* ***Dr. Bleeker*** having examined the species described in this work, considers that it might constitute a sub-genus of his ***Danio***, Ham. Buch. et ***Perilampus***, Bleeker, and suggests that it might be termed ***Paradanio***, which may be distinguished from the ***Danio*** by the absence of cirri, and by the inferior jaw having a more horizontal direction. As to my knowledge, this species is only one of a very large group in Southern India, I have placed it in a distinct genus, which would come next to Dr. Bleeker's ***Danio***.

Scales—With well-marked lines radiating from their anterior margins. The rows run obliquely towards the back.

Lateral line—Strongly concave, situated in the lower fifth of the body, and parallel with the abdomen.

Colours—Four horizontal yellow lines pass from the head to the tail, the highest and lowest of which are much less brilliant than the others: between these lines the colour is bright blue. Lower part of the abdomen silvery. A bright blue spot on the opercle. Fins finely dotted with black. A dark line runs along the centre of the caudal.

Common in the rivers of Malabar, and also found in most of the tanks of stagnant water. Is eaten by the Natives. Grows to three inches in length. It is closely allied to ***Perilampus Malabaricus,*** Jerdon (which I conclude belongs to this genus): but has one ray less in the dorsal and anal fins, and the coloration differs, as the ***Perilampus Malabaricus*** is said to have vertical streaks and spots of yellow, &c.

Habitat—Malabar.

GENUS RASBORA, *Bleeker.*

Branchiostegals, three: pseudobranchiæ. Body oblong or moderately elongated; abdomen rounded. Snout sharp, depressed: jaws covered by lips. Cleft of mouth oblique: tip of lower jaw hooked. Preorbital pentagonal. No cirri. Eyes with free lids. Pharyngeal teeth in three rows, hooked. Dorsal fin with scales at its base, situated behind the ventral. Anal short. Scales large or of moderate size. Lateral line strongly concave.

RASBORA MALABARICA.

LEUCISCUS MALABARICUS, *Jerdon*, Madras Journal, xv. p. 320.
KOKANUTCHEE, *Mal.*

B. iii. D. $\frac{2}{7}$. P. 15. V. 9. A. $\frac{3}{5}$. C. 19. L. l. 34. L. tr. $\frac{5}{3}$.

Length of head $\frac{1}{5}$, of base of dorsal $\frac{1}{13}$, of base of anal $\frac{1}{16}$, of caudal $\frac{1}{6}$ of the total length. Height of head $\frac{1}{8}$, of body $\frac{1}{5}$, of dorsal $\frac{1}{6}$ of the total length.

Eyes—Diameter above $\frac{1}{3}$ of length of head, 1 diameter from end of snout, upwards of 1 diameter apart.

Profile rises gradually to a little before the first dorsal, and then still more gently slopes to the root of the caudal. Abdominal surface about as convex as that of the back. Side compressed, and the head still more so.

Mouth oblique, and directed slightly upwards, with a short protuberance at the apex of the lower maxilla, which is received into a corresponding fissure in the intermaxillaries. Snout appears rather elevated. Preorbital irregularly quadrangular.

Fins—Pectoral situated under the margin of the posterior third of the subopercle. Ventral arises two scales beyond its extremity, and one scale in front of the dorsal: anal arises opposite the twenty-first scale of the lateral line The dorsal is highest in front. First unbranched ray rather more than half as long as the second, which is the highest: last ray not half as high as the anterior part of the fin. Anal with the first unbranched ray very short, the second nearly half as high as the third, the last being half as high as the front of the fin. Caudal cleft in its posterior two-thirds, the lobes pointed.

Scales—None on the bases of the fins.

Lateral line—Commences opposite the upper margin of the opercle, and curves downwards until it reaches the fifth scale, from whence it follows the curve of the abdomen to the lower half of the caudal.

Colours—Back greenish. A narrow streak of yellow passes from the eye to about the centre of the caudal fin, and beneath this there is a broad leaden-coloured line. The whole of the fish has a purplish reflection. Fins reddish orange. Caudal tipped with black.

Very common in the rivers, small streams, and tanks of Malabar. It takes a fly or bait readily.

Habitat—Malabar.

Fam. CYPRINODONTOÏDES, *Bleeker.*

Sub-Fam. APLOCHEILIFORMES, *Bleeker.*

GENUS PANCHAX, *Cuv. and Val.*

Branchiostegals, from five to six: pseudobranchiæ absent. Body elongated, sides compressed, upper surface of head and muzzle broad and depressed; jaws protractile. Maxilla thrown behind the descending branch of the intermaxillary, so that only the lower part contributes to form the angle of the mouth. Teeth in jaws in several rows, of which the external is the largest: a narrow band of minute teeth on the vomer. Dorsal fin short, a portion of it being placed opposite to the commencement of an elongated anal. Scales large or of moderate size, extended over the head.

PANCHAX LINEATUM.

PANCHAX LINEATUM, *Cuv. & Val.* xviii. p. 381, pl. 346.

APLOCHEILUS CHRYSOSTIGMUS, *McClelland*, J. A. S. xix. p. 301.

APLOCHEILUS VITTATUS, RUBROSTIGMA et AFFINIS, *Jerdon*, Madras Journal, xv. pp. 330, 331.

B. v-vi. D. 8-9. P. 15. V. 6. A. 15-17. C. 19. L. l. 34. L. tr. 9.

Length of head $\frac{1}{4}$, of pectoral $\frac{2}{11}$, of caudal nearly $\frac{1}{4}$, of base of dorsal $\frac{1}{13}$, of base of anal $\frac{2}{11}$ of total length. Height of head $\frac{1}{8}$, of body $\frac{2}{11}$, of dorsal $\frac{2}{13}$, of ventral $\frac{2}{11}$, of anal $\frac{1}{8}$ of total length.

Eyes—Oval, upper margins close to the profile. Horizontal diameter $\frac{1}{4}$, and vertical diameter $\frac{1}{5}$ of length of head, 2 diameters apart, $1\frac{1}{2}$ diameters from end of snout.

Body elongated, laterally compressed. Upper surface of head broadly depressed. Profile straight from the end of the upper jaw along the back, but that of the abdomen more curved.

Mouth large, broad anteriorly, its gape extending quite across the head. Snout semi-oval anteriorly, formed by the anterior margin of the intermaxillaries, which are large, semi-circular, flat above, very protractile, and slightly moveable up and down like lids. Jaws of equal length. No lips. Maxilla extending posteriorly to the anterior margin of the orbit. Lower jaw the widest, and rather depressed in front: a slight emargination at the symphysis. Upper surface of head flat. Preopercle with the posterior limb vertical, the angle produced and rounded: lower limb rather ascending. Opercle posteriorly rounded. Nostrils open laterally by a minute aperture in front of the margin of the orbit.

Teeth—In the upper jaw there is an external series of sharp curved teeth, with an internal and rather larger series. Between these there are several rows of villiform, the inner and outer of which are recurved, and rather the strongest. In the lower jaw are bands of villiform teeth. On the vomer there is a transverse narrow band rather produced anteriorly and in the centre, but parallel with the teeth in the upper jaw.

Fins—Pectoral arises a short distance behind the opercles: ventral opposite its posterior third: anal midway between the snout and the middle of the caudal fin. Dorsal situated in the posterior fifth of the body, its third ray the longest, its posterior margin rather concave. Caudal wedge-shaped, with the central rays the longest. Pectoral rounded. Ventral with the second ray elongated. Anal with the last rays slightly the longest. The length of the ventral and caudal fins varies greatly in different seasons of the year.

Scales—Cycloid, the longest diameter from above downwards. They extend over the opercles.

Colours—Vary according to the season of the year and the sex of the fish. Greenish with a gloss of purple on the abdomen. In the centre of each scale there is an emerald green spot, which in some lights looks golden. The under surface of the chest white, glossed with purple. A deep purple colour under the opercles and chin. Eyes of the same beautiful green as the spots. Eight or ten vertical black stripes—absent in some specimens—pass from the back to the abdomen. A silvery white spot at the summit of the occiput, and one at the anterior and another at the posterior margins of the base of the dorsal. Caudal margined with red, and spotted with green at its base, the tip being sometimes stained with black, and the membrane spotted with black, especially apparent in the immature. Anal and dorsal also tipped with red and dotted with black, almost forming bars. Anal also dotted all over, and with light yellow at its base in some of the larger specimens: in smaller ones the black lines of the body are extended on to the anal fin, and at the base of the pectoral there is a bright green spot. After death the silver spot disappears from the occiput.

Grows to four inches in length, and is exceedingly common in all the rivers, tanks, and paddy fields, and even extends its range into the backwaters within the influence of the tides. It may be easily recognized by the silvery spot on the summit of the head which all of them have when alive and in health. It is eaten by the Natives.

Habitat—Rivers, tanks, and paddy fields of Malabar.

Sub-order.—PHYSOSTOMI ABDOMINALES, *Müller*.

Fam. CLUPEOIDÆ, *Cuvier*.

Genus CHIROCENTRUS, *Cuvier*.

Branchiostegals, eight. Body much elongated and compressed, abdomen trenchant but not toothed. Eyes lateral. Cleft of mouth wide, lower jaw the longest. One dorsal, placed far backwards towards the caudal and opposite the anal. An elongated, triangular bony appendage in the axilla. Ventrals very small, placed anterior to the dorsal. Teeth in a single pointed row in the intermaxillaries and maxilla, those on either side of the symphysis being the largest: an oblique row of villiform teeth on the palatine bones, and a small group of velvety ones on the anterior pterygoid. A single row of long—but unequal sized—lance-shaped teeth on each branch of the lower jaw. A single row of minute and conical ones along the sides of the tongue, on the hyoid bone, and the margins of the branchial arches. Scales small and deciduous. Air vessel present. No pyloric appendages.

Chirocentrus dorab.

Clupea dorab, *Forsk.* 72, no. 108.
Wahlah, *Russell*, pl. 199.
Chirocentrus dorab, *Cuv. & Val.* xix. p. 150, pl. 565; *Cantor*, Catal. p. 277.

B. viii. D. 16-17. P. 14-15. V. 6-7. A. 33-34. C. 19.

Length of head above $\frac{1}{6}$, of pectoral $\frac{1}{8}$, of caudal nearly $\frac{1}{5}$, of base of dorsal $\frac{1}{14}$, of base of anal $\frac{2}{11}$ of total length. Height of head $\frac{1}{8}$, of body $\frac{1}{7}$, of dorsal $\frac{1}{18}$, of ventral about $\frac{1}{44}$, of anal $\frac{1}{18}$ of total length.

Eyes—Each having a strong adipose lid, with a vertical oval opening: horizontal diameter $\frac{1}{4}$, vertical diameter $\frac{2}{9}$ of length of head, $\frac{1}{2}$ of a horizontal diameter apart, $\frac{2}{3}$ of a diameter from end of snout.

Body elongated, strongly compressed, its upper profile almost horizontal as far as the base of the dorsal fin, from whence it slopes slightly downwards to the caudal: its abdominal profile is more convex than that of the back, and its margin is sharp and cutting.

Mouth anterior, upper jaw rather broad and obtuse, forming an arch, in its lower fourth it becomes much more oblique: lower jaw strongly compressed, considerably the longest, and when the mouth is closed its anterior margin forms a portion of the upper profile of the head. A supplementary bone from the preorbital extends to the maxilla, which has a second inferior to it. Preopercle, its posterior border thin and expanded, angle rounded, lower border horizontal. Opercle with its sides nearly straight, one-third higher than wide, its posterior border slightly convex. Sub- and interopercles small. Interorbital space broader posteriorly than anteriorly, and having a raised keel along its centre. Preorbital very wide and thin.

Teeth—One pair, long, sharp, straight, and approximating exist near the centre of the intermaxillaries, the remainder of which, and the whole extent of the maxilla armed with sharp straight teeth, of irregular lengths, and becoming smaller at the posterior extremity of the jaw. Each mandibula has a row of about twelve sharp laterally compressed teeth, of which the two first are the shortest, and those most anterior have an oblique anterior direction, whilst those posterior gradually become directed more and more backwards until the last form an acute angle with the jaw. Five or six large card-like teeth on the palatine bones, and a small oval group of smaller and velvety ones on the pterygoid.

Fins—Pectoral arises in the lower fourth of the body: the ventral midway between the gape of the mouth and the base of the caudal: the dorsal in the posterior third of the body: and the anal slightly in advance of it. The first ray of the pectoral strong and bony. Ventral small. Dorsal rather highest in front, and its upper margin concave. Anal of the same shape, the membrane between the rays of each deeply notched. Along the whole extent of the lower margin of the abdomen are short hair-like rays.

Scales—Small and deciduous.

Lateral line—Indistinctly marked, straight, situated in the upper third of the body.

Colours—Upper surface of head and back bluish green, sides and abdomen shining silvery, a line of yellow divides the colours of the back from the silvery sides. Cheeks golden. Fins transparent, pectoral with some minute fine black points. Iris silvery, upper margin deep green.

This fish is not uncommon in South Malabar, but much more abundant towards the north, where there are rocks. It is highly esteemed by the Natives when eaten fresh or salted, its taste varies with the season of the year in which it is captured. It grows to six feet in India, but specimens at New Guinea up to twelve feet are recorded.

Habitat—From the Red Sea, through the Seas of India, Malaysia, the Moluccas, to New Guinea and China, also the Eastern Coast of Africa and the Mauritius.

GENUS CHANOS, *Lacép.*

LUTODEIRA, *Rüppell.*

Branchiostegals, four. Body moderately elongated, abdomen rounded. Eyes lateral, with adipose lids. Cleft of mouth moderately deep. One dorsal with a row of scales along its base, ventral under centre of dorsal. Anal with a scaly base, and placed beyond posterior margin of dorsal. Pectoral and ventral enclosed by elongated scaly appendages. Caudal deeply cleft with two scaly semilunar laminæ, each fixed horizontally to the upper and lower of its short central rays. Teeth absent. Scales moderate or small. Air vessel with a constriction. Pyloric appendages numerous.

CHANOS PALA.

CYPRINUS (LEUCISCUS) PALA, *Cuvier*, Rég. anim. ii. p. 276.

CHANOS NUCHALIS, *Cuv. & Val.* xix. p. 197.

PALAH BONTAH, *Russell*, pl. 207.

CHANOS PALA, *Cantor*, Catal. p. 278.

BUTIRINUS MADERASPATENSIS, *Jerdon*, Madras Journ. xv. p. 344.

B. iv. D. 14-15. P. 17. V. 11. A. 9-11 C. 19. L. r. 75-77. L. tr. $\frac{12}{15}$.

Length of head $\frac{3}{16}$, of pectoral nearly $\frac{1}{9}$, of caudal $\frac{2}{11}$, of base of dorsal $\frac{1}{12}$, of base of anal $\frac{1}{23}$ of total length. Height of head $\frac{1}{6}$, of body $\frac{3}{16}$, of dorsal $\frac{1}{6}$, of ventral $\frac{1}{10}$, of anal $\frac{1}{18}$ of total length.

Eyes—Upper margins close to the profile. A thick adipose membrane exists over them, each having a central circular opening. Horizontal diameter $\frac{1}{9}$, vertical diameter $\frac{1}{4}$ of length of head, $\frac{1}{2}$ a horizontal diameter from end of snout, 1 horizontal diameter apart.

Body rather elongated, the profile slightly ascends to above the shoulder, from whence it proceeds nearly straight to the upper surface of the caudal. The slope of the lower is about the same as that of the upper surface of the head. The abdominal profile is more convex than that of the back.

Snout rather large. Upper jaw overhangs the lower. The posterior extremity of the maxilla extends to under the anterior margin of the orbit. The intermaxillaries form an acute angle, into which the triangular extremity of the lower jaw is received : the symphysis of the lower jaw has a tubercle which fits into a corresponding notch in the upper jaw. Opercle nearly twice as high as wide : posterior margin convex, and advances so far forward in its upper portion that it joins the anterior without leaving any appreciable superior margin.

Teeth—None.

Fins—Pectoral commences just posterior to the anterior superior angle of the opercle : dorsal midway between the snout and the base of the caudal : ventral under the seventh dorsal ray : anal midway between the base of the ventral, and the end of the scales on the base of the caudal. Dorsal fin highest in front, the first three rays undivided, the third the highest in the fin, and the last ray which is rather elongated, not quite half its height : the upper margin of the fin concave, and along its base are two rows of thirteen obliquely placed scales. Pectoral pointed, with an elongated scaly appendage at its base. Ventral triangular, with a long basal scale. Anal very small, first three rays undivided, fourth the longest, and more than twice the length of the last ; the lower margin of the fin concave, with two rows of scales along its base. Caudal deeply lobed, and its centre covered by two semi-lunar laminæ of scales.

Scales—Small, covering the body : a row along the base of the dorsal and anal fins, and covering the base of the caudal. There are some rows of enlarged scales over the nape.

Lateral line—Consists of a simple tube in each scale : at first it curves slightly downwards, and then passes nearly straight to opposite the end of the ventral, and from thence quite straight to the centre of the caudal.

Numerous cæcal appendages. "Air vessel very large, spindle-shaped, terminating behind "in an elongated point : the anterior margin is straight, with short pointed processes on each "side."—(*Cantor.*)

Colours—Summit of head and back of a brilliant glossy blue, fading into silvery on the abdomen : snout light brown. Dorsal and caudal rays greyish, which as well as the membranes are dotted with light brown : both these fins are margined with black. The caudal semi-lunar laminæ of scales pale slate colour, the pectorals and ventrals white, with the anterior halves of their external surfaces minutely dotted with dark brown, their elongated appendages bright silvery. The anal white, with the anterior half dotted with black. Iris silvery, orbital half pale brownish.

Usually captured at Cochin in the backwater during the S.W. monsoon. It grows to a large size and is excellent eating : it is termed the ***White mullet*** at Vizagapatam, but is inferior in flavour to the true mullet : it is also said to be called the ***Milk fish.***

Habitat—Seas, estuaries, tanks, and mouths of some rivers of India and Malaysia.

Genus DUSSUMIERIA, *Val.*

Branchiostegals, fifteen. Body rather long and compressed, the abdominal profile more curved than that of the back. Eyes, each with an adipose lid on either side. Cleft of mouth moderately wide. Upper jaw shorter than the lower. One moderately long dorsal, commencing about midway between snout and base of caudal. Ventral under centre of dorsal, anal behind it. Fine teeth in the jaws, on the tongue, the palatine and pterygoid bones: none on the vomer. Scales of moderate size, deciduous. Air vessel small.

Dussumieria acuta.

Dussumieria acuta, *Cuv. & Val.* xx. p. 467; pl. 606; *Cantor*, Catal. p. 286.
Koorie, *Mal.*

B. 15. D. 19-21. P. 14. V. 9. A. 14-17. C. 21.

Length of head $\frac{1}{5}$, of pectoral $\frac{1}{9}$, of caudal $\frac{1}{5}$, of base of dorsal $\frac{1}{9}$, of base of anal $\frac{1}{13}$ of total length. Height of head $\frac{1}{8}$, of body $\frac{1}{5}$, of dorsal $\frac{1}{10}$, of ventral $\frac{1}{12}$ of total length.

Eyes—Upper margins close to the profile, having narrow adipose lids on each side of the orbits. Diameter nearly $\frac{1}{3}$ of length of head, and almost 1 diameter from end of snout.

Body rather long and compressed, its thickness equals half its height. Upper line of profile nearly straight, the lower much more convex.

Mouth rather wide and slightly acute: lower jaw when closed a little the longest: the posterior extremity of the upper jaw reaches to below the anterior margin of the orbit. Opercle with the margins cut rather square, it is half as wide as high. Preopercle large, its angle rather produced. Subopercles small, a slightly elevated longitudinal crest from between the centre of the orbit to the snout. Abdominal edge smooth. Left branchiostegous membrane slightly overlaps the right.

Teeth—In jaws in a single row, which are fine and very deciduous. A band of the same description on the palate.

Fins—Dorsal arises midway between the anterior margin of the orbit and the base of the caudal: pectoral just under the opercle: ventral beneath the twelfth ray of the dorsal: anal about midway between the base of the ventral and the centre of the termination of the caudal. Dorsal with the first five rays single, the fifth and sixth the highest in the fin; superior margin rather concave. Pectoral rounded, and situated in the lower fourth of body. Ventral pointed. Caudal deeply lobed.

Scales—Small, and deciduous.

Colours—Of a beautiful green, shot with blue. Upper margin of the opercle and along the back of a light blue, below which is a bronzed line, and below that again a silvery one, shot with pink. Caudal beautifully shot with blue, green, and gold. Upper surface of head and eye emerald green. Pectoral, ventral, and anal white, except the first ray of the pectoral which has a little black on it. Dorsal yellowish green. End of snout greenish. Eyes white.

Very common and excellent eating. *Cantor* says this species has been preserved *à huile*. It is termed a *Sardine* by the inhabitants and residents in Malabar.

Habitat—Seas of India and Malaysia.

GENUS ELOPS, *Linn.*

Branchiostegals numerous and variable in their number, both in different specimens of the same species and on either side of the head of the same fish. Body elongated, back and abdomen rounded. Eyes with adipose membranes. Gape of mouth very large, intermaxillaries short. Maxillaries long and free, lower jaw the longest. One dorsal nearly medial: anal posterior to the last dorsal ray, ventral under dorsal. Pectoral and ventral with an elongated scaly appendage, last dorsal ray sometimes filamentous: rows of scales along the bases of dorsal and anal fins. Caudal forked, with a more or less elongated spine-like scale above and below its root. Fine velvety teeth in maxilla, mandibula, vomer, palatine, pterygoid, sphenoid, and hyoid bones. A single bony plate between the branches of the lower jaw under the branchiostegous membrane. Scales large or of moderate size. Air vessel large. Pyloric appendages numerous.

ELOPS MACHNATA.

ARGENTINA MACHNATA, *Forsk.* 68, No. 100.
ELOPS SAURUS, *Cuv. & Val.* xix. p. 365; *Cantor*, Catal. p. 287.
JINAGOW, *Russell*, pl. 179.

B. left xxxi., right xxx. to xxxix. D. 23. P. 17. V. 15. A. 17. C. 31. L. l. 109. L. tr. $\frac{12}{12}$.

Length of head $\frac{2}{5}$, of pectoral $\frac{1}{8}$, of caudal $\frac{1}{6}$, of base of dorsal $\frac{1}{7}$, of base of anal $\frac{1}{11}$ of total length. Height of head $\frac{1}{8}$, of body $\frac{1}{6}$, of dorsal $\frac{2}{13}$, of ventral $\frac{1}{9}$, of anal $\frac{1}{11}$ of total length.

Eyes—Oval: situated in the anterior half of the head, upper margins close to profile: each with a circular adipose covering, having a large round orifice corresponding to the pupil. Horizontal diameter $\frac{2}{9}$, and vertical diameter $\frac{1}{6}$ of length of head, rather above 1 horizontal diameter from end of snout, $\frac{4}{5}$ of a diameter apart anteriorly, but wider posteriorly.

Body elongated, rather compressed along its sides, upper and lower profiles almost straight.

Mouth large and wide, upper jaw forming the arc of a circle: lower jaw the longest, highest posteriorly, a little concave along its upper margin, and elevated at the symphysis: the posterior extremity of the upper jaw extends rather beyond the posterior margin of the orbit. Maxilla narrow, with a long supplementary bone posterior to it in its whole extent, and in the lower half there is another divided into two. Preopercle with the posterior margin rather produced at the angle, which is rounded: lower limb horizontal, and three-fourths the length of the vertical one. Interopercle almost hidden by the opercle. Opercle with its superior margin the shortest: the inferior oblique and nearly twice the length of the superior: posterior margin rounded. Subopercle broad, its depth rather more than half its length. Upper surface of the head with a broad longitudinal furrow, narrow in front and rugose on each side. Nostrils nearer the orbit than the snout. The left branchiostegous membrane overlaps the right, and contains one or two rays more, they vary according to *Cuv. & Val.* from twenty-nine to thirty-nine.

Teeth—In numerous villiform rows in both jaws, widest at the centre of the lowest: also on the vomer in two oval patches, joined together posteriorly by a thin wedge-shaped one: villiform teeth also on the palatine bones.

Fins—Pectoral in the lower fourth of the body, a short distance posterior to the opercle, and on a lower level: dorsal midway between the anterior margin of the orbit and the base of the caudal: ventral under the origin of the dorsal: anal midway between the origins of the ventral and caudal. Dorsal elevated in front, where it is more than four times as long as its posterior rays: upper margin concave; the first six rays are unbranched, the last are the longest. Pectoral, first ray strong and unbranched. Ventral with the two first rays bony, the second the longest in the fin, and twice the length of the last: a long elongated scale at its base. Anal with the first four rays bony and unbranched, the fourth the longest and three times the length of the last. Caudal deeply lobed, with scales along its centre.

Scales—The longest diameter from above downwards. The smallest are along the abdomen.

Lateral line—Consists of a central tube to each scale. It first makes a slight concavity, until it reaches a little above the centre of the body, and then passes direct to the caudal.

Colours—Summit of head silvery, upper surface of body dark bluish, fading into silvery white on the side, a golden tint about the head and jaws. Anal and caudal diaphanous, the other fins yellowish, dotted with black. Dorsal with the upper and lower margins blackish: eyes silvery.

Grows to two or three feet in length, and is eaten by Europeans, but not esteemed.

Habitat—Red Sea, Seas of India, Malaysia, China, and Japan: also the Mauritius and through the North and South Atlantic Oceans.

ELOPS APALIKE.

CLUPEA APALIKE, *Lacépède*, v. t. 13, f. 3.
KUNDINGA, *Russell*, pl. 203.
CYPRINODON CUNDINGA, *Ham. Buch.* pp. 254, 383.
MEGALOPS INDICUS, *Cuv. & Val.* xix. p. 388, p. 577.
ELOPS INDICUS, *Cuv. & Val.* xx. p. 472.
MEGALOPS FILAMENTOSUS, *Cuvier*, Règ. anim. ii. p. 324; *Jerdon*, Madras Journal, xv. p. 344.
ELOPS CUNDINGA, *Cantor*, Catal. p. 289.
CUNNAY, *Mal.*

B. Left xxv-xxvi, Right xxiv-xxv. D. 19-21. P. 15-16. V. 11. A. 24. C. 19. L. l. 39. L. tr. $\frac{6}{6}$.

Length of head $\frac{1}{5}$, of pectoral $\frac{2}{15}$, of caudal above $\frac{1}{5}$, of base of dorsal $\frac{1}{11}$, of base of anal $\frac{2}{15}$ of total length. Height of head $\frac{2}{15}$, of body $\frac{1}{5}$, of dorsal exclusive of filament $\frac{2}{13}$, of dorsal including filament above $\frac{1}{5}$, of ventral $\frac{1}{11}$ of total length.

Eyes—Upper margins close to the profile, situated in the anterior half of the head. Horizontal diameter $\frac{3}{10}$, vertical diameter $\frac{1}{4}$ of length of head, rather more than $\frac{1}{2}$ a diameter from end of snout, and rather more than $\frac{1}{2}$ a diameter apart. In the immature fish the proportionate size of the eyes is smaller.

General appearance somewhat resembling that of a large herring. Body elongated and compressed: head also compressed. Profile from snout to dorsal very slightly elevated, and from thence to the caudal a little depressed. There is rather a shallow concavity from the snout to opposite the posterior margin of the orbit. Lower profile more curved than the upper.

Mouth oblique, snout obtuse, anterior extremity of the lower jaw completing the anterior end of the upper profile. Intermaxillaries almost transverse, forming a broad space into which is received the end of the lower jaw: cleft of mouth about as deep as it is wide. No lips. The end of the maxillaries extend below the centre of the orbit in the adult, and to opposite the posterior margin in the immature. Maxilla very narrow, but posteriorly having two wide supplementary parallel bones, the internal appearing as if it were two. Upper jaw convex in front, concave posteriorly, with its extremity rounded. Lower jaw rather elevated opposite the symphysis, and its upper margin concave. When the mouth is closed the mandible is laterally concealed by the upper jaw. Preorbital narrow. Preopercle rather wide, lower limb almost horizontal. Opercle nearly semicircular posteriorly. Sub- and interopercles small. Upper surface of head nearly flat, with a central rather wide but very shallow depression, extending from opposite the preopercle to opposite the anterior margin of the orbit: for its anterior third it has a central longitudinal elevation. Nostrils, the anterior round, the posterior oval, situated midway between the eye and snout. The left branchiostegous membrane partially overlaps the right.

Teeth—Villiform in both jaws, in several wide bands in the mandibles: on the vomer there is a heart-shaped spot: also villiform ones on the palate, pterygoids, and sphenoids.

Fins—Pectorals in the lower fourth of the body, under the posterior border of the subopercle: dorsal midway between the snout and base of caudal: ventral under the origin of the dorsal, and the anal a short distance behind the posterior margin of the dorsal. Dorsal high in front, upper margin rather concave, last half of the posterior ray long, and reaching to opposite the end of the anal; the third ray the longest in front, the last ray but one equal to a little more than a third of its height. Pectoral pointed. Ventral with an elongated scale at its base. Anal with the fourth and fifth rays the longest; the fin is highest in front, and concave along the first part of its lower margin, then parallel with the abdomen, its last ray a little prolonged. Caudal deeply lobed, the lobes rather more expanded in the immature than in the adult fish.

Scales—Cycloid, longest diameter from above downwards, posterior fourth of exposed portions smooth, shining, and covered by membrane. No scales on the head. A few small ones over the base of the anal fin.

Lateral line—Is formed of a single tube in each scale, which branches off into six or eight smaller ones, and in the last half of the scale into from eight to twelve narrow channels, which proceed to its posterior margin. It first curves a little downwards; opposite the commencement of the dorsal it proceeds direct in the adult, but in the immature is slightly convex opposite the dorsal, from whence it proceeds straight to the caudal. Centre of the scales raised in the adult.

Colours—Summit of head dark olive, back bluish-green in the adult, lighter in the immature. Abdomen silvery, with bluish reflections. The margins of the scales of a brilliant silver, as is also the lateral line and the sides of the head. The centre of the jaws black. Dorsal and caudal greyish, minutely dotted with black, and the margins blackish, as is also the last elongated dorsal ray. Pectoral, ventral, and anal diaphanous, with some fine black dots, the last anal ray darkish. Eyes silvery, with the orbital margin of a darkish tint. The pupils oval, pointing downwards.

It is occasionally captured in the mouth of the river at Cochin, but much more commonly found in the tanks, and especially in the fort ditch. Amongst many specimens examined at Cochin, no difference existed in the number of scales in the adult and young fish, as noted by *Cantor* in the Straits, and the filamentous portion of the last dorsal was as long in the adult as in the young specimens, but the comparative size of the eye larger in the former than in the latter. Is considered good eating, but is bony. It makes tremendous springs out of the water. It is not river fish, but during the monsoon it is caught both there and in the sea.

Habitat—Fresh waters and estuaries of India, Ceylon, Malaysia, China, and Polynesia.

GENUS SARDINELLA, *Val.*

Branchiostegals, six. Body elongated and in most species the abdomen trenchant and toothed. Cleft of mouth small, upper jaw the shortest. One dorsal, medial: ventral opposite, and anal some distance posterior to the dorsal. Teeth on the palatine and pterygoid bones as well as on the tongue: none on the jaws or on the vomer. Scales large or of moderate size. Air vessel long.

SARDINELLA NEOHOWII.

SARDINELLA NEOHOWII, *Cuv. & Val.* xx. p. 274.
CHARLAY, *Mal.* Oil Sardine.

B. vi. D. 17. P. 17. V. 9. A. 16. C. 17. L. l. 45. L. tr. 13.

Length of head $\frac{1}{4}$, of pectoral $\frac{1}{7}$, of base of dorsal $\frac{1}{9}$, of base of anal $\frac{1}{9}$, of caudal $\frac{1}{6}$ of total length. Height of head $\frac{1}{6}$, of body $\frac{1}{5}$, of dorsal $\frac{1}{9}$ of the total length.

Eyes—Rather close to upper profile. Each have an anterior and posterior rather broad adipose membrane: diameter $\frac{1}{5}$ of length of head, 1 diameter apart, and a little more than 1 diameter from end of snout.

Body rather elongated, back broad, sides slightly compressed, abdominal surface rather rounded. Profile of back convex, the base of the dorsal being situated on the most superior part: abdominal profile not so convex as that of the back.

Mouth anterior, lower jaw the longest, the upper jaw slightly notched in its centre, and convex along its lower margin: lower jaw compressed and widest posteriorly. Maxilla widened by the addition of two supplementary bones, its posterior extremity extends to under the orbit. Opercle half as wide as high, its upper margin nearly straight, its posterior rather concave in its upper third, slightly convex in its lower third. Subopercle nearly square, one third as high as opercle. Preopercle wide, its posterior margin rather oblique, angle produced and rounded, lower limb horizontal. Interopercle large. Gill openings wide. Branchiostegous membrane partially uncovered.

Teeth—None apparent in the jaws, or on the vomer, but fine ones on the tongue, the palate, and the pterygoids.

Fins—Pectoral arises close to, and just beneath the posterior angle of the subopercle: the dorsal rather nearer to the snout than it does to the base of the caudal, the seventh ray being in about the centre of the body: ventral under the posterior third of the dorsal: and the anal in the posterior third of the body. First dorsal rays short, the third the highest, the upper margin of the fin concave, its last ray very short. Pectoral pointed. Ventral abdominal, and triangular, first ray undivided. Anal highest anteriorly, its lower margin concave. Caudal lobed in its posterior half, its base wide.

Scales—Longest diameter vertical: none on the head.

Colours—Green with golden reflections, abdomen silvery shot with purple. Head of the same colour as the body with a large greenish gold spot on the upper margin of the opercle and preopercle. Dorsal sea green. Caudal stained with green. The other fins transparent.

Arrives in some years in enormous numbers, and from it fish oil is prepared, when ***Dussumier*** was in Malabar, probably about 1827, he observed that those not eaten were used for manuring the fields as they were too fat to salt well; at the present time, mostly from this species, an average of upwards of seven thousand pounds worth of fish oil is annually exported from Malabar. But the oil sardine is very capricious as to its arrival and departure, thus in 1855-56 from the port of

Cochin only 45 cwt. of fish oil were exported, the next year merely 181 cwt., but in 1857-58, 68,499 cwt., which augmented in the succeeding year to 102,924 cwt., and the year after to 133,143 cwt. Again it gradually fell off until in 1862-63, as little as 115 cwt. were exported, but the shoals suddenly returned and in 1863-64, the exports rose to the enormous quantity of 148,206 cwt. The fish is excellent eating, but too fat to salt well. Its general length is from six to seven inches.

Habitat—Seas of Malabar and Ceylon.

Genus PELLONA, *Valen.*

Platygaster, *Swainson.*

Branchiostegals, six. Body rather elongated and compressed, abdomen strongly toothed. Mouth of moderate size. Upper jaw emarginate in the majority of the species, and shorter than the lower. Dorsal fin medial, ventral inserted before the dorsal, anal elongated. Teeth on jaws, palatine and pterygoid bones also on the tongue, but none on the vomer. Scales large or of moderate size. Air vessel present, communicating with the œsophagus by a small duct inserted at the extremity of the stomach.

* Pellona Dussumieri.

Pellona Dussumieri, *Cuv. & Val.* xx. p. 316, pl. 596.

B. vi. D. 18. P. 16. V. 6. A. 44-54. C. 21.

Length of head nearly $\frac{1}{5}$ of the total length. Height of the body $\frac{1}{4}$ of the total length.

Eyes—Diameter $\frac{1}{3}$ of length of head.

Teeth—Those on the maxilla almost horizontal behind the bone on which they are inserted.

Body oblong, the lower profile more convex than that of the back.

Lower jaw considerably advanced before the upper. The opercle has some striæ upon it, and the preopercle some veins.

Fins—Dorsal high in front: its last rays very low, and its border sloping very obliquely; it is entirely scaled, and the base of the rays is in a groove formed by rows of scales on either side larger than those of the back. The pectoral has a long scale at its axil, its first ray is strong, and its extremity rounded. The ventral small, and arises near the end of the pectoral, on the chest, and in advance of the dorsal: no long scale at its base. Anal long and very low, the number of its rays varies.

Scales—Large and smooth, those on the abdominal keel similar to those of the other species of this genus.

Colours—Glittering with a beautiful silvery lustre: back fawn colour with a green reflection. The fins bordered with black.

Grows to one foot in length.

Habitat—Malabar.

Genus PRISTIGASTER, *Cuvier*.

Branchiostegals, six. Body rather elongated and compressed. Abdomen strongly toothed, mouth of moderate size, upper jaw shorter than the lower. Dorsal fin medial and very low: ventrals absent: anal elongated. Teeth on jaws, palatine and pterygoid bones, also on the tongue, but none on the vomer. Scales large or of moderate size. Air vessel either large and forked, with the horns prolonged on each side of the vertebræ into the coccygeal muscles, or else simple and oval. Pyloric appendages numerous.

Pristigaster tartoore.

Tartoore, *Russell*, pl. 193.

Pristigaster tartoore, *Cuv. & Val.* xx. p. 328.

B. vi. D. 13-17. P. 13-15. A. $\frac{1}{57\text{-}60}$. C. 21. L. l. 50. Spines 28.

Length of head above $\frac{1}{5}$, of pectoral $\frac{1}{5}$, of caudal $\frac{1}{6}$, of base of dorsal $\frac{1}{14}$, of base of anal $\frac{1}{2}$ of total length. Height of head $\frac{1}{5}$, of body $\frac{1}{3}$ of the total length.

Eyes—With free orbital margins, diameter above $\frac{1}{3}$ of the length of head, $\frac{2}{3}$ of a diameter from end of snout, $\frac{1}{3}$ of a diameter apart.

Body strongly compressed, its thickness being hardly equal to one fourth of its height. Superior profile rising as far as occiput, from whence it forms a very long and low curve as far as the caudal, whilst the extremity of the lower jaw forms a portion of the upper profile. Abdominal profile nearly straight.

Mouth directed slightly upwards and forwards, the lower jaw the longest, the symphysis being extended beyond the portion forming the mouth, the upper jaw very short, the preorbital long and extended over the posterior portion of the maxilla when the mouth is closed. The maxilla wide, first directed downwards and slightly forwards, but opposite the angle of the mouth it expands into a wide oval plate directed backwards and extending as far as the anterior third of the orbit. Opercle triangular, ending in a soft point. A long triangular groove exists on the head, its apex being in front and its base at the occipital process, it has a small spine in the centre of its posterior margin, and one on either side.

Teeth—A few fine distant teeth in the intermaxillaries and the central third of the lower jaw, none in the upper jaw where it forms a portion of the mouth, but the external edge of its lower limb is finely denticulated. A band of villiform teeth along the palatine bones, none on the vomer. Villiform teeth also on the tongue and pterygoids.

Fins—Pectoral commences under the posterior margin of the end of the opercle; dorsal nearer the tail than the snout: anal opposite the end of the pectoral: from the throat to the commencement of the anal fin there are twenty-eight sharp spines along the lower line of the profile, which increase in length and strength posteriorly. Dorsal small and low. Pectoral pointed. Anal low.

Scales—Smooth without striæ.

Lateral line—In single tubes in each scale, dividing and sub-dividing posteriorly. It ascends from the posterior margin of the opercle and is lost below the posterior end of the dorsal fin. A second lateral line passing direct to the centre of the caudal is just apparent.

Colours—Superiorly yellowish-white shot with silver, becoming silvery beneath. Fins yellowish, caudal minutely dotted with black points, also some black dots on snout, upper surface of the head and along the upper margins of the opercles, which are silvery.

Not common in Malabar. Grows to nine inches in length and is good eating.

Habitat—Seas of India.

GENUS SPRATELLA, *Val.*

Branchiostegals, five or six. Body moderately elongated, and compressed: abdomen trenchant and serrated. Upper jaw shorter than the lower. One dorsal, medial: ventral under dorsal: anal moderately elongated and posterior to the dorsal. Teeth on the palatine bones and on the tongue, none on the jaws or vomer.

SPRATELLA FIMBRIATA.

SPRATELLA FIMBRIATA, *Cuv. & Val.* xx. p. 359, pl. 600.
CUTTAY CHARLAY, *Mal.*

B. v. D. 19-20. P. 17. V. 8. A. 20 C. 19-20. L. l. 46. L. tr. 11.

Length of head $\frac{1}{5}$, of pectoral $\frac{1}{6}$, of caudal $\frac{2}{9}$, of base of dorsal $\frac{1}{7}$, of base of anal $\frac{1}{8}$ of total length. Height of head $\frac{1}{6}$, of body $\frac{1}{3}$, of dorsal $\frac{2}{13}$, of anal $\frac{1}{19}$, of ventral $\frac{1}{15}$ of total length.

Eyes—With wide adipose lids, having a circular orifice in the centre of each, diameter $\frac{2}{7}$ of length of head, $\frac{3}{4}$ of a diameter from end of snout, and 1 diameter apart.

Body elliptical, highest opposite the front of the dorsal fin. Sides rather compressed, abdominal line ending in a sharp toothed keel. Profile from snout to dorsal gradually rising, from the posterior end of the dorsal sinking as gradually to the caudal. The lower profile slightly convex.

Mouth small, half wider than deep. Lower jaw the longest, with a tubercle at the symphysis. Posterior extremity of the upper jaw reaches to opposite the centre of the orbit. The nearest supplementary bone to the maxilla thick and rounded above, flattened expanded and sulcated inferiorly: posterior bone narrow, and with a circular expansion inferiorly. Opercle two and a quarter times as high as wide, its superior and inferior margins oblique, its anterior and posterior ones straight, (in immature specimens there is a slight bulging at the centre of the posterior margin) some oblique badly marked veinings on the opercle. Subopercle trapezoid, half longer than it is high. Preopercle large, with the posterior border vertical and its angle rounded. Subopercle small. Branchiostegous membrane wide. Interorbital space with a V-shaped elevation in its centre, apex in front, and its base emarginate behind. Nostrils oval, large, and nearer to the snout than to the anterior margin of the orbit. Abdomen sharp, keeled, and its margin denticulated.

Teeth—Very small in the lower jaw, and deciduous. There are some minute ones on the palate, and also a small longitudinal band in the centre of the tongue.

Fins—The distance from the snout to the anterior extremity of the dorsal fin, is equal to the distance from the base of the caudal to the posterior extremity of the same fin: pectoral situated just beneath the posterior inferior angle of the subopercle: ventral under the centre of the dorsal: anal midway between the commencement of the ventral and the base of the caudal. Dorsal highest in front, first five rays undivided, the fifth the highest, the last rays slightly prolonged: upper margin concave; at the base of the fin there is a double row of scales, forming a groove, which at its posterior end almost conceals the whole of the last two rays. Pectoral pointed. Ventral triangular, with an elongated scale at its base. Anal with the first three rays undivided, the fin parallel with the abdominal surface. Caudal deeply lobed, the longest ray equal to the length of the head, or even more.

Scales—Vertical diameter the longest.

Colours—Upper surface of head and back greenish, abdomen silvery shot with green and gold. Four or five badly marked horizontal lines pass along the centre of each scale. Opercles and the lower surface of the head beautifully shot with golden and green. Dorsal, pectoral, ventral, and anal colourless. Caudal shot with blue, and having a darkish margin.

Very much esteemed for eating by the Natives, and also extensively salted. It is not a good species for the manufacture of oil, as it contains but little, which is probably the reason why it is salted in such quantities. It is very abundant, and commonly known as the *Sardine,* but is not the species used for the manufacture of oil, which is the *Sardinella Neohowii* of *Cuv. & Val.* It grows to about six inches in length.

Habitat—Malabar.

GENUS MELETTA, *Val.*

Branchiostegals, from five to seven. Body elongated and compressed, abdomen trenchant and serrated. Cleft of mouth moderate. Upper jaw the shortest. One dorsal medial, ventral beneath the dorsal, anal moderately elongated and behind the dorsal. Teeth none on the jaws, vomer, or palatine bones, but a small rough band on the tongue. Air vessel large and cylindrical.

* MELETTA LILE.

MELETTA LILE, *Cuv. & Val.* xx. p. 378.

B. v. D. 14. P. 12. V. 7. A. 17. C. 21. L. l. 40.

Length of head $\frac{2}{11}$ of that of the body. Height of body equal to $\frac{3}{11}$ of the total length.

Profile of back almost straight, that of the abdomen very convex, and its surface trenchant. Its thickness one-fourth of its height.

Mouth small; the lower jaw slightly longer than the upper.

Teeth—In upper jaw absent, very small ones present (?) in lower jaw. A longitudinal band on the tongue.

Fins—Ventrals small and inserted under the first ray of the dorsal, which as well as the caudal is scaly; the last of which fins is forked.

Colours—Transparent white: lateral line opaque and marked by a silver band, softened with nacreous rose colour. Fins transparent with the exception of the caudal, which has a black border.

Grows to four or five inches in length, and said to be very common in Malabar, where it is termed *cooba.*

Habitat—Seas of India.

GENUS ALAUSA, *Val.*

Branchiostegals, from five to eight. Body moderately elongated and compressed, abdomen trenchant and serrated. Eye with broad adipose lids on either side. Upper jaw shorter than the lower. Dorsal medial, ventral below it: anal elongated, and posterior to dorsal. No teeth in any of the bones of the mouth or on the tongue, except occasionally small deciduous ones on the jaws. Air vessel large, pointed at both ends and simple. Pyloric appendages numerous.

* Alausa palasah.

Palasah, *Russell*, pl. 198.

Clupanodon ilisha, *Ham. Buch.* pp. 243, 382, pl. 19, f. 73 (*young*).

Alausa palasah, *Cuv. & Val.* xx. p. 432; *Jerdon*, Madras Journal xv. p. 345; *Cantor*, Catal. p. 300.

Sable fish.

B. vi. D. 19. P. 14-16. V. 8. A. 19. C. 19. L. l. 47-49. L. tr. 19.

Body oblong, the abdominal edge toothed.

Length of head $\frac{3}{13}$ of the total length. Height of body $\frac{4}{13}$ of the total length.

Eyes—With thick adipose lids, upper margins near the profile.

Snout slightly pointed: upper jaw strongly emarginate, mouth small.

Teeth—Absent.

Fins—Pectoral pointed. Dorsal nearly central, cut square. Caudal scaly and deeply forked.

Scales—Closely set. None on the head.

Colours—Greenish above, silvery beneath. Eyes silvery.

It is captured both in the sea and in the fresh water. It is said by ***Dr. Jerdon*** to ascend the Cavery during the freshes for the purpose of spawning, and is taken for the sake of its roe, which is highly esteemed. ***Cantor*** observes upon its affinity to the ***Alausa toli,*** C. & V., or ***shad,*** from which the best fish roes are prepared, and the fishing of which is stated to form a distinct and important branch of trade in the Indian Archipelago.

It is good eating, but rather oily: growing to sixteen inches in length. It is said to ascend the Ganges in August.

Habitat—Seas and rivers near the coasts of India and Malaysia.

Alausa melanura.

Alausa melanura, *Cuv. & Val.* xx. p. 441.

B. vi. D. 16-18. P. 14. V. 8. A. 17-18. C. 21. L. l. 39. L. tr. 9.

Length of head $\frac{1}{5}$, of pectoral $\frac{1}{6}$, of caudal $\frac{1}{6}$, of base of dorsal $\frac{1}{9}$, of base of anal $\frac{1}{7}$ of the total length. Height of head $\frac{1}{6}$, of body $\frac{1}{3}$, of dorsal $\frac{1}{7}$ of the total length.

Eyes—Diameter $\frac{1}{3}$ of length of head, $\frac{3}{4}$ of a diameter from end of snout, 1 diameter apart.

Body compressed, abdominal profile more convex that that of the back.

Mouth small, anterior: maxilla broad, and extending to beneath the centre of the orbit. Opercle above twice as high as wide: subopercle almost triangular, its posterior and inferior margins forming a curve. Interopercle broad. Abdominal margin sharp, keeled, and having twenty-seven imbricated spinous scales along its edge.

Teeth—Not apparent.

Fins—Pectoral arises close to and beneath the lower angle of the subopercle: dorsal rather nearer the snout than it is to the base of the caudal: ventral under the origin of the dorsal: anal commences midway between the origin of the ventral and the base of the caudal. Pectoral pointed. Dorsal highest in front, its first three rays unbranched, the fourth the longest. A row of scales exists along its base, that of the anal, and of the caudal, which last fin is deeply lobed.

Scales—Vertical diameter about three times as long as their horizontal.

Lateral line—Not apparent.

Colours—A tinge of green along the back; silvery tinged with purple on the abdomen. Opercle bluish. A black mark on the occiput, and a line of fine black dots along the base of the dorsal. Posterior extremity of caudal lobes darkish, and when alive shot with blue.

Grows to six inches in length, and is esteemed for eating.

Habitat—Seas of Malabar, Malaysia, New Guinea, and Bourbon.

Alausa scombrina.

Alausa scombrina, *Cuv. & Val.* xxi. p. 442.

B. vi. D. 14-15. P. 15. V. 9. A. 14-15. C. 21. L. l. 45-50.

Length of head above $\frac{1}{4}$, of pectoral $\frac{1}{6}$, of base of dorsal $\frac{2}{17}$, of base of anal $\frac{1}{6}$, of caudal $\frac{1}{6}$ of the total length. Height of head $\frac{1}{6}$, of body $\frac{1}{5}$, of dorsal $\frac{1}{6}$, of ventral $\frac{1}{8}$, of anal $\frac{1}{12}$ of the total length.

Eyes—Each with an adipose lid on either side, and their upper margins rather close to the profile: diameter $\frac{1}{3}$ of length of head, $\frac{2}{3}$ of a diameter from end of snout, $\frac{1}{2}$ a diameter apart.

Body subcylindrical, its thickness equal to half its height. The abdominal profile slightly more convex than that of its back.

Lower jaw the longest; the posterior extremity of the maxilla extends to beneath the anterior third of the orbit. Opercular pieces large and smooth.

Teeth—In a fine single row in either jaw, and extending along the margin of the maxilla. Apparently none on the vomer, palatine bones, or tongue.

Fins—The anterior extremity of the dorsal is situated midway between the snout and the base of the caudal, and slightly behind the posterior extremity of the pectoral. The ventral arises beneath the third dorsal ray: the anal midway between ventral and base of caudal. Dorsal highest anteriorly, and rather pointed. Caudal deeply lobed.

Scales—Of moderate size.

Colours—Silvery, with a slight tinge of green along the back.

Grows to eight inches in length and is good eating. It abounds in the rivers, and even in the paddy fields and ditches at certain seasons.

Habitat—Seas, estuaries, and even fresh waters of Malabar and the Seychelles.

Genus Engraulis, *Cuvier*.

Setipinna, *Swainson*.
Thrissa, *Rafin*.

Branchiostegals, from nine to fourteen, but varying in number not only in different specimens of the same species but on either side of the head in the same individual. Body moderately elongated, rounded or compressed: abdomen trenchant, toothed, serrated, or smooth. Eyes lateral with adipose lids. Snout projecting, pointed, the nasal bone advanced in front of the jaws: intermaxillaries soldered to the maxillaries, and hidden beneath the muzzle. Mouth cleft to far behind the eyes, upper jaw the longest, in some the maxillaries are greatly elongated (*Thrissa*, Rafin). Dorsal medial: ventral small, in front of to beneath the dorsal. Anal behind the dorsal, moderately elongated or very long, extending to under or from even anterior to the dorsal (*Telara*), the pectoral occasionally has its anterior ray elongated and filamentous (*Setipinna*, Swainson). Caudal forked. Teeth on upper and lower maxillaries, a few on the anterior part of the vomer, palatine and pterygoid bones narrow and bristling with minute teeth, or rough. Gill openings very large. Scales moderate or small. Air vessel present. Pyloric appendages numerous.

ENGRAULIS BROWNII.

ATHERINA BROWNII, *Linn.* Syst. 1397.
NATTOO, *Russell*, pl. 187.
ENGRAULIS FASCIATA, *Cuv. & Val.* xxi. p. 43.
ENGRAULIS BROWNII, *Cuv. & Val.* xxi. p. 41; *Cantor*, Catal. p. 303.

B. xi. D. 14-16. P. 15-16. V. 7. A. 20-21. C. 19. L. l. 35-38. L. tr. 7.

Length of head nearly $\frac{1}{5}$, of pectoral $\frac{1}{9}$, of caudal $\frac{1}{6}$, of base of dorsal $\frac{1}{8}$, of base of anal $\frac{1}{7}$ of total length. Height of head $\frac{1}{8}$, of body $\frac{1}{6}$, of dorsal $\frac{1}{9}$, of ventral $\frac{1}{13}$, of anal $\frac{1}{10}$ of total length.

Eyes—Upper margins near the superior profile, and with wide adipose lids. Diameter $\frac{2}{7}$ of length of head, $\frac{2}{3}$ of a diameter from end of snout, nearly 1 diameter apart.

Thickness of body equals two-thirds of its height: head compressed. The abdominal profile is more rounded than trenchant, and the teething more like hairs than spines.

Snout obtuse, overhanging the mouth which is deeply cleft. Posterior extremity of the maxilla extends to a short distance before the root of the pectoral. Lower jaw the shortest and compressed.

Teeth—In fine rows on the maxilla, increasing in strength posteriorly: a fine band of inwardly curved ones in the lower jaw, and also a few villiform ones on the vomer and palate.

Fins—Dorsal commences rather nearer the base of the caudal than the anterior extremity of the snout: ventral between it and the posterior extremity of the pectoral: and the anal under the last fourth of the dorsal. Caudal deeply lobed. Dorsal triangular.

Scales—Large and deciduous, their horizontal diameter half their vertical. An elongated scale exists at the base of the pectoral fin.

Lateral line—Straight on the anterior twelve scales, in the form of a central tube, beyond which it becomes indistinct.

Colours—Greenish silvery above, opercles shining silvery shot with gold. A large black spot on the posterior half of the occiput. A broad silvery band passes from the centre of the posterior margin of the opercle to the centre of the caudal. Abdomen light buff colour. Fins yellowish, with minute black dots. Eyes silvery, orbital margin dark.

Grows to eight inches in length, and is much esteemed for eating. It is known as ***Whitebait*** amongst Europeans, and is captured in Malabar in great numbers. In the Straits ***Cantor*** states that large quantities of them are preserved for exportation to China and India, as well as for home consumption, forming a delicious condiment known under the designation of "***Red-fish.***" The following is the mode of preparation:—" After the heads have been removed, the fishes, (those of middling size are preferred), are cleansed, salted, (in the proportion of one to eight parts of fish) and deposited in flat glazed earthen vessels. In the latter they are for three days submitted to pressure, by means of stones placed on thin boards or dried plantain leaves. The fishes are next freed from salt, and saturated with vinegar and cocoa-palm toddy, after which are added powdered ginger and black pepper (the latter mostly entire), and some brandy and powdered 'Red rice.'

After having been kept for three days a little more vinegar is added before placing the fishes in well closed jars or bottles. They should be kept four or five months before being used."—*Cantor*, p. 305. "*Red rice* is a variety of *Oryza sativa* called *glutinosa* steeped in an infusion of cochineal."

Habitat—Seas of India, Malaysia, China, Australia, New Zealand, and the Mauritius. Also through the North and South Atlantic oceans.

2. *Maxillæ greatly elongated.*

ENGRAULIS AURATUS, Pl. xix. f. 2.

ENGRAULIS AURATUS, *Day*, Proc. Zool. Soc. 1865, p. 312.

B. x. D. $\frac{1}{14}$. P. 12. V. 7. A. 34. C. 19. L. l. 40. L. tr. 9.

Length of head nearly $\frac{1}{7}$, of pectoral $\frac{1}{7}$, of base of dorsal $\frac{1}{9}$, of base of anal $\frac{1}{4}$, of caudal $\frac{1}{7}$ of the total length. Height of head $\frac{1}{6}$, of body $\frac{1}{4}$, of dorsal $\frac{1}{7}$, of anal $\frac{1}{9}$ of the total length.

Eyes—Oval, with their anterior and posterior thirds covered by adipose lids: diameter $\frac{1}{3}$ of length of head, $\frac{1}{2}$ a diameter from end of snout, 1 diameter apart.

Profile scarcely ascends from the snout to the dorsal fin, or descends much from thence to the caudal, the abdominal surface is very much more convex. Sides compressed.

Snout short; gape of mouth extending to below the posterior margin of the orbit. Maxilla greatly elongated, reaching to opposite the last fourth of the pectoral, and equal to nearly a third of the total length of the fish. A raised crest extends from the snout along the whole central line of the head. Opercle narrow and octagonal, posterior margin having its central three-fifths straight, directed a little obliquely backwards, and forming an obtuse angle at its upper and lower fifths; superior and inferior margins straight but very short. Preopercle with its posterior margin nearly vertical. Branchiostegous opening very wide, extending nearly to the lower margin of the symphysis.

Teeth—A series of fine villiform teeth in the lower jaw, also along the whole extent of the elongated maxilla: only a few in the external half of each intermaxillary, and a few also on the vomer. A long double line of fine teeth on the palatine bones, with a large oval toothed space on the pterygoids.

Fins—Dorsal commences midway between the snout and the base of the caudal fin; anal midway between the anterior surface of the chest and the commencement of caudal: pectoral arises below the posterior margin of the opercle, and reaches to the ventral. Dorsal triangular, with a small spine a short distance before its first ray. Pectoral falciform. Anal with the anterior portion the highest. Caudal lobed, lobes of equal length.

Scales—About thirteen sharp compressed scales along abdominal margin of the body anterior to the commencement of the ventral fins, and seven between their termination and the origin of the anal.

Colours—The upper surface of the body of a brilliant coppery tinge, closely dotted with black, but becoming of a pure white on the sides. A large black spot on the shoulder. Dorsal with minute black dots, more especially at its upper margin, otherwise it is colourless, as are also the pectoral, anal, and ventral fins. Caudal light straw-coloured, with a darkish tip. Eyes tinged with brown superiorly, and yellow inferiorly.

Common during the S.W. monsoon, and considered good eating.

Habitat—Cochin on the Malabar Coast.

PLATE XIX.

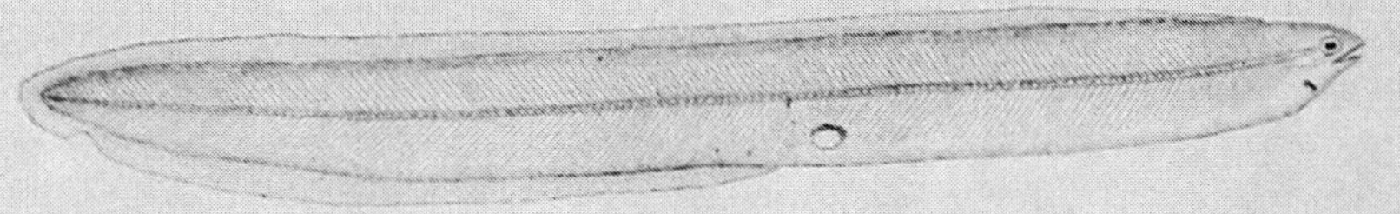

Fig 1.

Fig 2.

F. Day, del, et sculp.

1. LEPTOCEPHALUS MALABARICUS. 2. ENGRAULIS AURATUS.

* ENGRAULIS HAMILTONII.

ENGRAULIS HAMILTONII, *Gray*, Ill. I. Z., pl. 92, f. 3; *Cuv. & Val.* xxi. p. 66.
POORAWAH, *Russell*, pl. 189.

B. xii. D. $\frac{1}{13}$. P. 14. V. 7. A. 35-37. C. 18.

Body oblong and compressed.

Head thick, long: the posterior extremity of the maxilla passes the base of the pectoral fin.

Fins—Anal situated in the last half of the body and completely posterior to the dorsal fin.

Teeth—In both jaws, palate, and tongue.

Colours—Back plumbaceous, the rest of the body yellowish silvery. The dorsal, pectoral, ventral, and caudal yellowish, the last bordered with black. Anal bluish.

Grows to nine inches in length.

Habitat—Seas of India.

ENGRAULIS MALABARICUS.

CLUPEA MALABARICA, *Bloch*, pl. 432.
ENGRAULIS MALABARICUS, *Cuv. & Val.* xxi. p. 63.
MONANGOO, *Mal.*

B. xii. D. 13. P. 14. V. 7. A. 40. C. 19. L. l. 42. L. tr. 11.

Length of head $\frac{2}{11}$, of pectoral $\frac{1}{6}$, of caudal $\frac{1}{6}$, of base of dorsal $\frac{1}{11}$, of anal nearly $\frac{1}{4}$ total length. Height of head $\frac{1}{6}$, of body nearly $\frac{1}{4}$, of dorsal $\frac{1}{7}$, of ventral $\frac{1}{16}$, of anal $\frac{1}{10}$ of total length.

Eyes—With adipose lids each having a vertical elliptical orifice. Diameter $\frac{1}{4}$ of length of head, $\frac{2}{3}$ of a diameter from end of snout, $1\frac{1}{4}$ diameters apart.

Body rather short, and strongly compressed. Profile from snout to caudal nearly straight; from anterior extremity of the mandibulæ to the end of the anal fin it is strongly curved.

Mouth wide and compressed. Upper jaw the longest. The posterior extremity of the maxilla reaches nearly to the posterior extremity of the subopercles: it has a supplementary bone posteriorly in the first three-fourths of its course, opposite the inferior extremity of which there is another bone irregularly elliptical at its extremity and quite fine at its upper end. Lower jaw with an elevation at the symphysis, and the openings of three large glands along its outer margin. Snout large, overhanging the upper jaw. A longitudinal sharp ridge along the centre of the interorbital space. Nostrils large, and oval, surrounded by a raised bony arch. Opercle three times as high as wide. Subopercle small and triangular, with its apex behind and below.

Teeth—In single rows in the whole extent of the maxilla, and also on the mandibulæ: a very small patch of sharp teeth on the anterior part of the vomer, and some fine deciduous ones on the palatine bones.

Fins—Pectoral commences under the posterior superior angle of the subopercle: dorsal midway between the snout and the base of the caudal: ventral at the posterior extremity of the pectoral: anal under the posterior extremity of the dorsal. Dorsal with a minute spine situated a short distance before it, and partially concealed by the scales: the first three rays of the fin undivided, the third the longest, and four times more so than the last: the upper margin nearly straight: a groove of scales along its base. Pectoral pointed, with an elongated scale at its base.

Ventral very small and triangular, with an elongated scale at its base. Anal highest in front, its three first rays undivided, the fourth the highest, from whence they decrease, forming a concave edge in the anterior half of the upper margin, but the last half is parallel to the back, a scaly groove is present along its base, and highest opposite about the eighth ray. Caudal deeply lobed.

Scales—Vertical diameter the longest, very deciduous. Abdominal keel sharp, with about twenty-seven spines along its extent: the largest being between the ventral and anal fins.

Colours—Greenish on the back shot with purplish, which towards the abdomen becomes silvery white. The centre of each scale is rather the darkest, forming longitudinal lines which are most apparent in the upper half of the body. A series of wide, deep, black bands commence from behind the upper half of the opercle, and proceed backwards, dividing and subdividing, and covering a space about as wide as the orbit: these bands under a magnifying glass are seen to consist of raised, round, black spots. Upper surface of the head greenish. Posterior margin of the orbit, and the upper portions of the opercle and preopercle greenish golden. Iris yellowish. Posterior half of the dorsal and its anterior margin stained with black. Pectoral, ventral, and anal fins yellowish. Caudal stained with black at its posterior third. In the young the fins are darker than in the adult.

Grows to about nine inches in length. It is common in Malabar, and is even captured in the estuaries. Eaten by the Natives, but is bony, and not esteemed by Europeans.

Habitat—Seas of India.

b. Superior pectoral ray elongated and filamentous.

* Engraulis taty.

Engraulis taty, *Cuv. & Val.* xxi. p. 60; *Cantor*, Catal. p. 306.

B. xiii. D. $\frac{1}{14}$. P. 16. V. 7. A. 52-56. C. 19.

Length of head $\frac{3}{20}$, of base of anal $\frac{3}{8}$, of first pectoral ray $\frac{5}{9}$, of second pectoral ray $\frac{2}{7}$ of the total length. Height of head $\frac{3}{13}$ of the total length.

Eyes—Horizontal diameter $\frac{1}{4}$ of the length of head; distance across the forehead $1\frac{1}{2}$ diameters.

Mouth cleft far beyond the eyes, muzzle pointed and projecting.

Teeth—A few fine villiform ones on the vomer: numerous, and of the same description on the palatine and pterygoid bones.

Fins—Dorsal commences rather nearer to the snout than it does to the root of the caudal: the anal commences opposite the centre of the dorsal. The ventral midway between the base of the pectoral and the fifth anal ray. Upper lobe of caudal truncated.

Scales—Very deciduous and striated. Some exist on the base of anal and dorsal fins.

Colours—Upper surface of head and back green, or greenish slate colour, sparingly dotted with black: sides above the lateral line pale silvery green; the abdomen, cheeks, and opercles silvery; dorsal, caudal, and anal yellow; ventrals and pectorals transparent; in some the posterior margin of the caudal is blackish. Iris silvery, orbital half bluish black.—*(Cantor.)*

Good eating either fresh or dried: grows to six inches in length.

Habitat—Seas of India and Malaysia.

Genus COILIA, *Gray*.

Trichosoma et trichosomus, *Swainson*.
Chætomus, *McClelland*.

Branchiostegals, about ten. Body elongated, compressed, and tapering to a pointed tail: abdomen trenchant and toothed. Snout projecting, pointed: the nasal bones advanced in front of the jaws: intermaxillaries soldered to the maxillaries, and hidden beneath the muzzle. Mouth cleft to far behind the eyes, the upper jaw the longest. Dorsal placed in the anterior part of the back: anal elongated, low, joining the caudal (in one species the tail is shortened and the caudal widened and rounded). Above the pectoral fin are two groups of filaments parting from a common base. Teeth on upper and lower maxillaries, a few on the anterior part of the vomer; palatine and pterygoid bones narrow, bristling with minute teeth or rough; anterior pharyngeals distinctly but minutely toothed. Scales moderate or small. Air vessel present. Pyloric appendages numerous.

Coilia Reynaldi.

Coilia Reynaldi, *Cuv. & Val.* xxi. p. 81; *Cantor*, Catal. p. 310.

B. x. D. $\frac{1}{14\text{-}15}$. P. $\frac{iv}{11\text{-}15}$. V. 15. A. 104-107. C. 11-15.

Length of head $\frac{2}{13}$, of base of dorsal $\frac{1}{16}$ of total length. Height of head $\frac{1}{8}$, of body $\frac{2}{13}$, of dorsal $\frac{1}{8}$, of anal about $\frac{1}{40}$ of total length.

Eyes—Diameter $\frac{1}{4}$ of length of head, 1 diameter from end of snout, $1\frac{1}{4}$ diameters apart.

Body highest opposite the dorsal fin, long and tapering posteriorly to a point, also becoming much smaller towards the head. Profile rises considerably to the dorsal, from whence it proceeds straight to the caudal. Lower profile about equally curved with the upper. Body strongly compressed, its sides being quite flat.

Mouth wide and cleft oblique, posterior extremity of the maxilla extending nearly to the end of the opercles, close to the origin of the pectoral fin. Snout overhanging the upper jaw, which also is longer than the mandibulæ. Opercle rounded posteriorly. Gill openings wide.

Teeth—Fine in both jaws, and very minute along the whole anterior margin of the maxilla.

Fins—Pectoral arises close to the posterior margin of the opercles in the lower fifth of the body: the dorsal commences in the first fourth: the ventral beneath it: the anal under and slightly beyond the posterior margin of the dorsal. Dorsal with a short spine a very little distance anterior to the fin: the anterior margin is the highest, the third ray being the longest, from whence they gradually decrease to the last. Pectoral pointed, with the upper four rays prolonged to nearly the middle of the body. Anal continuous with the caudal, and parallel to the abdominal profile.

Scales—Deciduous; twelve sharp spines exist along the abdominal keel.

Lateral line—Straight, passing from the upper part of the opercle to the centre of the caudal fin.

Colours—Silvery white with pinkish reflections: a line of white dots passes along the lower surface of the abdomen, and another commences opposite the centre of the opercle and is continued backwards towards the centre of the caudal. End of the caudal stained blackish. A slight greyish streak runs down the centre of the back. Opercles of a bright silvery tint.

Not rare in Malabar; generally found during the south-west monsoon. It grows to four inches in length.

Habitat—Seas and estuaries of Malabar, Burmah, and Malaysia.

* Coilia Dussumieri.

Coilia Dussumieri, *Cuv. & Val.* xxi. p. 81, pl. 610.

D. 14. P. $\frac{vi}{10}$. V. 7. A. 80. C. 11. L. l. 60.

Distinguishable from the *C. Reynaldi* by the size of the pectoral, the free rays of which are rather shorter: and the dorsal is not quite so pointed.

Teeth—Fine and similar to the *C. Reynaldi.*

Colours—Body of a brilliant golden, having two or three irregular rows of nacreous spots along its inferior half.

Grows to six inches in length, and is considered good eating at Bombay, where it is common and abundant throughout the whole year.

Habitat—Seas and estuaries of India.

Genus CHATOESSUS, *Cuvier.*

Branchiostegals, about six. Body short, deep, oval, and moderately compressed: abdomen trenchant and denticulated. Eyes with lateral adipose lids. Muzzle projecting, intermaxillary small, attached to the extremity of the snout, and with what looks like a fibrous lip stretched from its extremity and continuing it to the upper end of the maxilla, which bone is placed behind it, and articulates with the tuberosity of the nasal. There is an emargination at the end of the upper jaw and a corresponding tubercle on the lower. A single dorsal, medial, with the last ray prolonged in some species. Ventral in front of or under dorsal. Anal elongated and behind the dorsal. Caudal forked. No teeth. The superior combs of the first branchial arches unite with those of the opposite side, forming a pennated point under the palate. Air vessel large, rounded anteriorly, and pointed posteriorly. Pyloric appendages numerous.

Chatoessus chacunda.

Clupanodon chacunda, *Ham. Buch.* pp. 246, 383.

Chatoessus chacunda, *Cuv. & Val.* xxi. p. 111; *Cantor.* Catal. p. 311.

B. vi. D. 19-20. P. 17. V. 8. A. 20. C. 19. L. l. 45. L. tr. 11-13.

Length of head $\frac{2}{11}$, of pectoral $\frac{2}{15}$, of caudal $\frac{1}{5}$, of base of dorsal $\frac{2}{17}$, of base of anal $\frac{2}{15}$ of total length. Height of head $\frac{1}{7}$, of body $\frac{1}{5}$, of dorsal $\frac{2}{17}$, of ventral $\frac{1}{12}$, of anal about $\frac{1}{40}$ of the total length.

Eyes—Covered on their anterior and posterior thirds by adipose lids, having vertical elliptical openings: diameter $\frac{1}{3}$ of the length of head, $\frac{5}{7}$ of a diameter from end of snout, 1 diameter apart.

Body rather oval: abdominal profile sharp and keeled.

Lower jaw the longest, the superior slightly emarginate at the symphysis, receiving the upper portion of the lower jaw: cleft of mouth narrow: maxilla extends posteriorly to opposite the anterior third of the orbit, and has supplementary bones posterior to it. Opercle placed rather obliquely, twice and a fourth as high as broad: exposed portion of the subopercle wider than high. Preopercle of moderate width, angle rounded, lower limb horizontal. Interorbital space smooth, rather elevated longitudinally along the central line: some raised ridges bound the posterior portion of a triangular depression on the summit of the head, passing from the posterior superior margin of the orbit obliquely backwards towards the central line. Preorbital long, wide, very apparent, from there being some dark lines on it. Nostrils round and near the snout.

Teeth—A minute row in the anterior portion of the lower jaw.

Fins—Pectoral arises close under the posterior third of the subopercle: dorsal opposite its extremity, midway between the snout and the base of the caudal; ventral opposite the fifth dorsal ray: anal midway between the base of the ventral and that of the caudal. Pectoral pointed. Ventral with an elongated scale at its base, the first ray very broad and undivided. Dorsal, first three rays undivided, a broad row of scales runs along the base of the fin, completely covering the last six rays, the fin is highest in front, and slopes posteriorly, its summit being concave. Anal almost hidden by a row of scales. Caudal deeply lobed and scaled over its base.

Scales—Ctenoid, large and adherent. There are twenty-eight spines along the abdominal profile.

Lateral line—Not apparent.

Colours—Back bluish or greenish-silvery, with three or four darker longitudinal lines along the centre of the upper rows of scales. Sides silvery, glossed with gold. Snout and upper end of the mandibulæ black. Some fine black dots on the upper portion of the opercle which are more numerous on the shoulder, where they form a black mark. Pectoral, ventral, and anal yellowish, a few black dots along the first ray of the pectoral. Dorsal yellowish, with the anterior portion of the base of the first three rays black, and the upper part of the fin minutely dotted with black. Caudal darkest at its extremity, and shot with blue.

Grows to eight inches in length, and is esteemed for eating by the Natives, but not by Europeans as it is bony and dry.

Habitat—Seas and estuaries of India, Malaysia, and the Moluccas.

Chatoessus altus.

Chatoessus altus, *Gray*, Ill. Ind. Zool. pl. 91, f. 2.
? Kome, *Russell*, pl. 196.
Pedda Kome, *Russell*, pl. 197.
Noonah, *Mal.*

B. vi. D. 18-19. P. 15. V. 9. A. 23-25. C. 19. L. l. 48. L. tr. 18.

Length of head $\frac{1}{5}$, of pectoral $\frac{2}{11}$, of caudal $\frac{2}{11}$, of base of dorsal $\frac{2}{15}$, of base of anal $\frac{2}{11}$ of total length. Height of head $\frac{2}{11}$, of body $\frac{1}{3}$, of dorsal filament $\frac{1}{5}$, of anal $\frac{1}{15}$, of ventral $\frac{1}{9}$ of total length.

Eyes—With broad adipose membranes, having vertical elliptical openings. Diameter $\frac{1}{3}$ of length of head, $\frac{2}{5}$ of a diameter from the end of snout, 1 diameter apart.

Body elliptical, but tapering off more towards the caudal than towards the head. Upper and lower profiles about equally curved, profile to anterior margin of the anal sharp and keeled with a row of twenty-eight sharp pointed scales along its edge.

Mouth a third longer than it is broad, overhung by the snout: upper jaw the longest, and the intermaxillaries triangular and broad, forming three-fourths of the upper lip, extending posteriorly to below the anterior margin of the orbit. Maxilla extends to beneath the anterior third of the orbit. Mandibula wedge-shaped anteriorly. Opercle rather narrow, twice as high as wide, the posterior margin rather convex, and the anterior slightly more so. Preopercle broad, with rounded angles. Sub- and interopercles of moderate size. The uncovered branchiostegous membrane is broad. Nostrils rather wide apart, the posterior oval and the anterior round, both opposite the anterior superior margin of the orbit. Summit of head lanceolate, and moderately flat, broadest opposite the centre of the orbits. A small lanceolate longitudinal furrow passes from opposite the centre of the orbit to the snout; posteriorly it has an elevated ridge.

Teeth—None.

Fins—Pectoral arises close under the posterior margin of the subopercle, and extends to the ventral, which commences opposite the fourth ray of the dorsal: anal arises on the posterior third from the snout to the base of the caudal. Dorsal with its first three rays unbranched, the third the highest, upper margin of the fin concave, the last ray with its posterior half prolonged as far as the base of the caudal. Pectoral pointed. Ventral small, with a long scale at its base. Anal with the first two rays unbranched, the second the longest, the fin rather concave. Caudal wide, and deeply forked.

Scales—High and narrow. None on the head.

Colours—Back greyish-green, with the centre of each scale in the first seven rows the darkest, thus forming horizontal lines, the lower of which do not extend to the caudal. Abdomen whitish, shot with gold. A bluish spot at the posterior portion of the upper half of the opercle. Preopercle of a brilliant golden tint. Dorsal greenish-yellow, with the posterior margin stained blackish. Pectoral, ventral, anal, and caudal yellowish, the last with a darkish extremity.

Common, good eating, but rather bony.

Habitat—Seas of India and China.

Sub-Ord. PHYSOSTOMI APODES.

Fam. MURÆNIDÆ.

Sub-Fam. ANGUILLOIDEI, *Bleeker*.

Genus MURÆNA, *Bleeker*.

Enchelyopus, *Ag.*
Anguilla, *Thunb.*

Branchiostegals from ten to thirteen, thin and flexible. Body cylindrical. Snout, not prominent before the lower jaw. Dorsal, caudal, and anal fins continuous, well developed. Many rows of sub-equal small teeth, on the palatines, inframaxillaries, nasal, vomer, and pharyngeals. Scales small, almost hidden in the skin. Branchial aperture situated on either side before the base of either pectoral fin.

Muræna maculata.

Muræna maculata, *Ham. Buch.* pp. 23, 364; *Bleeker*, Atl. Ich. iv. p. 9, t. 145, f. 2.
Muræna Bengaliensis, *Gray*, Ill. I. Z. i. t. f. 5.
Anguilla Elphinstonii, *Sykes*, Trans. Zool. Soc. ii. p. 377, t. 67, f. 3.
Anguilla variegata, *McClelland*, Cal. J. N. H. v. p. 179, t. 9, f. 7.
Anguilla marmorata, *Kaup*. Catal. Brit. Mus. p. 43, f. 32.
Anguilla Dussumieri, *Kaup*. Catal. Brit Mus. p. 51, f. 43.
Anguilla Malabarica, *Kaup*. Catal. Brit. Mus. p. 52, f. 47.

B. xi. D. 240-260. C. 12. A. 220-230. P. 22-24.

Length of head $\frac{1}{9}$, of pectoral $\frac{1}{27}$, of base of dorsal $\frac{5}{9}$, of base of anal nearly $\frac{5}{9}$ of the total length. Height of head $\frac{1}{18}$, of body $\frac{1}{18}$, of dorsal about $\frac{1}{36}$, of anal about $\frac{1}{36}$ of the total length.

Eyes—Diameter $\frac{1}{9}$ to $\frac{1}{13}$ in the length of the head, 2 to 3 diameters apart.

Body anteriorly cylindrical, posteriorly compressed, head depressed.

Opening of mouth extends to opposite or even behind the posterior border of the orbit: the upper jaw rather the shortest. Posterior opening of nostrils high, and close to the anterior margin of the eye; the anterior nostril tubular, and near to the antero-lateral margin of the snout. A row of pores exists along either mandible on its lower surface. Branchial aperture oval, and situated just in front of the pectoral fin.

Teeth—In lower jaw in several rows anteriorly, decreasing in number posteriorly. On the vomer in a crowded semi-oval spot, becoming pointed behind, but in front its sides almost touch the palatine bands, which are of the same shape. Pharyngeal teeth on two oval patches above, and below on two elongated triangles.

Fins—The pectoral rounded. The dorsal commences the length of the head below the origin of the anal: or slightly before it, *Muræna* (*anguilla*) *Malabarica*, Kaup: or over it, *Muræna* (*anguilla*) *Dussumieri*, Kaup. Caudal rounded.

Scales—Small, but visible.

Lateral line—Marked by distant pores in its first three quarters, posterior to which tubes are better developed.

Colours—Brownish green above, fading to dirty white on the abdomen. The whole of the upper part of the body appears as if it were covered by bamboo matting.

Common, and excellent eating. It grows to four feet in length. Its comparative thickness varies greatly in different places, and according to the seasons of the year.

Habitat—Fresh waters and estuaries of India, Malaysia, and the Society Islands.

Sub-Fam. CONGROIDEI, *Bleeker*.

Group CONGRIFORMES, *Bleeker*.

Sub-Group MURÆNESOCES, *Bleeker*.

Genus MURÆNESOX, *McClelland*.

Branchiostegals, from fifteen to twenty-two. Body moderately elongated: tail more than twice as long as the body. Mouth cleft far behind the eyes; snout thin and elevated: maxilla elongated: the anterior nostril perforating above the margin of the upper lip before the middle of the eyes, the posterior open and thrown far behind the apex of the snout. Vertical fins well developed; the dorsal commencing above or before the branchial aperture: the dorsal, caudal, and anal continuous. Pectoral present. Teeth, those of the palatines in from one to three rows: the nasal and mandibular elongated anteriorly and subulate: vomerine teeth in three series, the central row elongated and compressed. Scales absent. Branchial aperture semicircular on either side of body, and not confluent with one another. Heart near the branchiæ. Anus a long distance posterior to the branchial aperture.

MURÆNESOX TELABON.

TALA BON, *Russell*, pl. 38.
CONGER TELABON, *Cuvier*, Règ. an. p. 350.
MURÆNESOX LANCEOLATA, *McClelland*, Cal. J. N. H. iv. p. 409, et v. pp. 181, 210.
MURÆNESOX EXODON, *McClelland*, Cal. J. N. H. iv. p. 409.
MURÆNESOX SERRADENTATA, *McClelland*, ibid.
MURÆNESOX EXODENTATA, *McClelland*, Cal. J. N. H. v. pp. 180, 210, pl. 8, f. 4.
CONGER TELABON, *Cantor*, Catal. p. 312.
MURÆNESOX PRISTIS, *Kaup*, Catal. Brit. Mus. p. 116.
MURÆNESOX TELABON, *Bleeker*, Atl. Ich. iv. p. 22, pl. 152, f. 2.

B. xv-xxii. D. 238-287. C. 9-11. A. 151-213. P. 15-16.

The comparative proportions vary considerably with age, season, and the health of the fish.

Length of head about $\frac{1}{6}$ to $\frac{1}{7}$, of pectoral $\frac{1}{19}$ of the total length. Height of head about $\frac{2}{3}$ of that of the body. Height of body from about $\frac{1}{16}$ to $\frac{1}{20}$ of the total length. Height of dorsal fin about $\frac{1}{3}$ of height of body.

Eyes—Diameter from $\frac{1}{7}$ to $\frac{1}{9}$ in the length of the head, 1 diameter apart, 3 diameters from end of snout.

Body much elongated and strongly compressed, especially towards the tail. Head elongated and conical.

Snout very acute: upper jaw slightly the longest, the lower laterally compressed, but both of about equal width, with their anterior extremities rather expanded, causing the muzzle to be somewhat rounded. Mouth widely cleft, the anterior margin of the orbit being about midway between the snout and the cleft of the mouth. The anterior nasal orifice sub-tubular, and placed just above the lip at the termination of the groove, the posterior oblong and situated before the middle of the orbit. Gill openings small. A transverse series of pores exist across the crown of the head.

Teeth—In lower jaw in several rows internally, and a strong external row directed outwards, separated from the internal series by an edentulous interspace: round the anterior margin of the jaw a row of conical teeth, and an internal somewhat large row of ten or twelve. Palatine teeth anteriorly in one row, posteriorly in many: the vomer with a central row of large lanceolate ones, with a small interspace between each, and having a small row on either side. Nasal teeth in a single central series, whilst round the anterior extremity of the snout two rows exist, the same as in the mandibulæ.

Fins—Dorsal commences a short distance before the base of the pectoral: the anal under about the fifty-fifth dorsal ray, just posterior to the anus. Each fin ray arises by two distinct roots, and the separate portions, though closely approximating continue distinct.

Lateral line—Gradually descends from the upper third of the body to the central line, which it reaches in the anterior fourth of the total length. It consists of tubes sending two branches downwards, between which is a pore.

Colours—Upper surface of head and back olive, becoming brown posteriorly. Abdomen dirty white, becoming silvery inferiorly. The throat, cheeks, and gill-covers shot with golden green. Eye silvery, with a purplish tinge along its upper half. Dorsal, caudal, and anal dirty white, margined with deep black. Pectorals dirty yellow.

It grows to eight feet in length, and is generally considered good eating. *Bleeker* observes that it is coarse in the Straits. Wounds from its teeth are much dreaded.

Habitat—Seas and estuaries of India and Malaysia.

Sub-Fam. OPHISUROIDEI, *Bleeker*.

Group OPHISURI, *Bleeker*.

Genus OPHICHTHYS, *Ahl.*

MURÆNOPSIS, *Les.*

PŒCILOCEPHALUS, *Lp.*

CENTRUROPHIS, MICRODONOPHIS, CÆCILOPHIS, HERPETOICHTHYS, ELAPSOPIS, ECHIOPSIS, SCYTALOPHIS, LEPTORHINOPHIS, et CRYPTOPTERUS, *Kaup.*

Branchiostegals, from seventeen to thirty-five. Body eel-like or vermiform, greatly elongated, its height from one-twentieth to one-fortieth in its length. Cleft of mouth moderate or large. Lips not fringed; posterior nostril perforating the upper lip on its internal or lower aspect. Teeth very or moderately acute, situated in from one to three rows on the palatines and mandibulæ, and in from one to four rows on the vomer. Dorsal, pectoral, and anal fins well developed; no fin at end of tail: the dorsal commences above or behind the branchial aperture, which is single, semi-lunar, and on each side. Heart near to the branchial aperture. No scales.

* OPHICHTHYS ORNATISSIMUS.

HERPETOICHTHYS ORNATISSIMUS, *Kaup*, Catal. Brit. Mus. p. 7, fig. 5.

Total length 20·88 in. Length of tail, 9·46 in. Length from the tip of the snout to the gill openings, 2·56 in. Length of the pectoral 0·63 in.

Head depressed, so that the eyes which are near to the end of the snout are closer to the upper surface than they are distant from each other laterally. Snout short: jaws of nearly equal length. Anterior tubular nostril at the extremity of the snout and the hinder one at the commencement of the outer row of the palatine teeth: between the two on the border of the upper lip there is a small cutaneous tag. Gullet wide.

Teeth—Nasal six: three of them on the mesial line and the foremost, two of them standing nearly abreast. Vomerine teeth nine, standing irregularly to the right and left. Exterior palatine teeth sixteen, inner row twenty. Mandibular teeth twenty-four.

Fins.—Pectoral with twenty-four rays. The dorsal fin begins 0·59 in. behind the tip of the pectoral, and is not much developed.

Colours—Irregular dark spots on the head. On the occiput a transverse line of white spots, and two longitudinal ones: while between the eyes there are curved whitish lines. Along the lateral line there are sixteen or seventeen large round black spots, which are parted by another band of spots of different sizes. Dorsal fin with black marginal spots and stripes.—(*Kaup.*)

This specimen is said to have been brought from Malabar by *Dussumier*.

Habitat—Malabar.

GENUS PISOODONOPHIS, *Kaup*.

Branchiostegals from twenty-one to thirty-one. Body eel-like or vermiform, greatly elongated, its height from one twenty-second to one forty-sixth in its length. Caudal portion not much longer than the trunk. Head acutely convex, cleft of mouth moderate. Lips not fringed. Posterior nostril perforating the upper lip on its internal or lower aspect. Teeth obtuse and granular, in many rows on the nasal, palatine, vomer, and mandibular bones. Dorsal, anal, and pectoral fins present, none at the end of tail. Dorsal commences behind the branchial aperture, which is single, semi-lunar, and on either side. Pectoral well developed.

PISOODONOPHIS BORO.

OPHISURUS BORO, *Ham. Buch.* pp. 20, 363; *Gray*, Ill. I. Z. i. pl. 95, f. 1; *McClelland*, Cal. J. N. H. v. pp. 185, 211.

OPHISURUS HARANCHA, *Ham. Buch.* pp. 21, 363; *Gray*, Ill. I. Z. i. pl. 95, f. 2; *McClelland*, Cal. J. N. H. v. p. 211, pl. 12, f. 4.

OPHISURUS CAUDATUS, *McClelland*, Cal. J. N. H. v. p. 185, pl. 12, f. 3.

OPHISURUS BORO, *Cantor*, Catal. p. 322, pl. 5, f. 2 (teeth).

PISOODONOPHIS BORO, *Kaup*, Catal. Brit. Mus. p. 17; *Bleeker*, Atl. Ich. iv. p. 62, t. 164, f. 3.

B. xxix-xxxi. D. 315-402. P. 12-13. A. 205-270.

Length of head $\frac{2}{19}$ to $\frac{1}{15}$ in the total length, and $\frac{1}{4}$ of the distance between the snout and the anus. Height of body $\frac{1}{32}$ to $\frac{1}{36}$ of the total length.

Eyes—Diameter $\frac{1}{12}$ to $\frac{1}{17}$ in the length of the head, 2 to $2\frac{1}{2}$ diameters from end of snout, 2 diameters apart.

Body cylindrical and much elongated, compressed and tapering in its posterior sixth or seventh.

Snout longer than wide at its base, its apex rather fleshy, and one diameter of the eye longer than the lower jaw: the distance from the snout to the angle of the mouth equals two-sevenths of the length of the head: the cleft extends behind the eye. The anterior nasal aperture opens close to the symphysis in a tube rather shorter than the diameter of the orbit: the posterior aperture perforates the lower surface of the lip. From between the orbits on either side is a line of fine pores extending to the muzzle, whilst there are three behind the eyes, and other rows along the jaws and behind the occiput.

Teeth—The nasal teeth cover a small oblong space, they consist of three or four rows, are from sixteen to eighteen in number, of rather irregular sizes, and have globular crowns: the vomerine teeth are placed on an elongated oval patch which extends further posteriorly than do the palatines: the palatine patch is longest in front and extends close to the nasal teeth, their crowns are rounded; the mandibular teeth are placed in a band broadest in front, and there is a small edentulous interspace on the symphysis between those of either side, the anterior ones are the longest, and larger than the corresponding ones in the palatines.

Fins—The dorsal commences a short distance behind the apex of the pectoral, and half the length of the head or even more behind the branchial aperture. Pectoral rounded, and from one-fourth to one-fifth of the length of the head. Dorsal rays one-third of the height of the body, there is a groove along the base of the fin. Anal rays about the same length as those of the dorsal, a groove also along its base.

Lateral line—At first in the upper third of the body, it reaches the centre opposite the anus and is thus continued to the caudal: it consists of minute pores.

Colours—Superiorly olive green, becoming white along the abdomen. Dorsal greenish with a black margin: anal whitish with a dark margin: pectoral yellowish.

Not rare in the backwater: is eaten by the Natives.

Habitat—Seas and estuaries of India, and Malaysia.

Sub-Fam. GYMNOTHORACOIDEI, *Bleeker.*

Group MURÆNOPHIDES, *Bleeker.*

GENUS GYMNOTHORAX, *Bloch.*

MURÆNOPHIS, *Lacép.*

MURÆNA, *Cuvier.*

SIDERA, ENCHELYNASSA, EURYMYCTERA, ENCHELYCORE, LIMAMURÆNA, THYRSOIDEA, (pt.), POLYURANODON, et TÆNIOPHIS, *Kaup.*

THÆRODONTIS, STROPHIDON (pt.), et LYCODONTIS, *McClelland.*

Body eel-like compressed, its height less than one-thirtieth of its length: the tail and the body of nearly equal lengths. Cleft of mouth large, and extending behind the orbits, jaws of nearly equal length: the posterior nostril situated above the margin of the orbit. Teeth sharp, conical, or compressed, in from one to four rows, those in palatines and mandibulæ always pointed and sharp. Pectoral fin absent: a fin at the extremity of the tail. The dorsal commences before or above the branchial apertures. Lateral line absent, or marked by minute pores. Heart situated near to the branchial apertures which are single, linear, and in about the mid-height of the body. Scales absent.

GYMNOTHORAX TILE.

MURÆNOPHIS TILE, *Ham. Buch.* pp. 18, 363.

LYCODONTIS PUNCTATA, *McClelland*, Cal. J. N. H. v. p. 187.

STROPHIDON PUNCTATA, *McClelland*, Cal. J. N. H. v. p. 203, t. 7, f. 3.

STROPHIDON MACULATA, *McClelland*, Cal. J. N. H. v. p. 203, t. 8, f. 1.

LYCODONTIS LITERATA, *McClelland*, Cal. J. N. H. v. p. 215, t. 7, f. 2.

MURÆNA TILE, *Cantor*, Catal. p. 331.

THYRSOIDEA TILE, *Kaup*, Catal. Brit. Mus. p. 93, f. 66.

GYMNOTHORAX TILE, *Bleeker*, Atl. Ich. iv. p. 97, t. 178, f. 1.

D. 312-325. C. 10. A. 154-172.

Length of head about $\frac{1}{8}$ of total length. Height of head $\frac{1}{25}$, of body $\frac{1}{16}$-$\frac{1}{24}$, of dorsal about $\frac{1}{10}$, of anal about $\frac{1}{80}$ of total length.

Eyes—Diameter from $\frac{1}{12}$ to $\frac{1}{14}$ of length of head, 2 diameters from end of snout.

Body elongated and compressed.

Opening of mouth horizontal. Eyes above the middle of the cleft. Snout rather longer than the lower jaw: upper profile of snout horizontal, with a concavity over the eye, and a sudden rise on the back of the head and nape. Nostrils, the anterior tubular, the posterior not so. There are some well marked open pores along the jaws.

Teeth—In the palate conical and acute, anteriorly in two but posteriorly in a single row, those in the outer row the shortest, and fourteen or fifteen in number: the inner row of five or seven. Nasal teeth, a mesial row of three large ones: those on the vomer in a single row, sometimes forming two, and from twelve to twenty-four in number. In the lower jaw there are twenty-four conical teeth, which towards the symphysis form two rows, but laterally only one.

Fins—Dorsal arises slightly before the branchial aperture. The anal commences about the centre of the body, and is lower than the dorsal.

Lateral line—Little apparent.

Colours—Ground colour yellowish olive, forming reticulations between numerous black spots and blotches, which are distributed over the whole of the head and body.

Grows to two feet in length, and is very common in Malabar.

Habitat—Fresh waters and estuaries of India and Malaysia.

* GYMNOTHORAX FAVAGINEA.

MURÆNA FAVAGINEA, *Cuvier*, Règ. An.; *Kaup*, Catal. Brit. Mus. p. 68, f. 53.
GYMNOTHORAX FAVIGINEA, *Bloch. Schn.* 525, t. 105.
THÆRODONTIS RETICULATUS, *McClelland*, Cal. J. N. H. July, 1854.

"Total length 28·26 in. Length of tail, 14·18 in. To the gill opening, 3·78 in. Length of jaws, 1·69 in."

Teeth—"Nasal teeth twelve: on the mesial line three: palatines three: vomerines eleven or twelve: mandibulars eighteen, of which the foremost five are the longest. Between the second and third foreones there is a little toothlet which is easily overlooked. . . . . In a specimen from Malabar, I could perceive only a single row of ten or twelve teeth in the middle of the vomer. Another, a stuffed one sent from Pondicherry, by *Leschenault*, shows two distinct rows, which towards the gullet, run into one series. I consider two rows of vomerines to be the normal number."—*Kaup.*

Colours—Every part of the body and head marked with black pentagonal spots separated by narrow white lines.

Habitat—Seas and estuaries of India.

Fam. SYNBRANCHIDÆ.

Sub-Fam. SYNBRANCHOIDEI, *Bleeker*.

Group SYNBRANCHINI, *Bleeker*.

GENUS SYNBRANCHUS, *Bloch*.

UNIBRANCHAPERTURA, *Lacép.*
UNIPERTURA, *Kaup.*
OPHISTERNON, *McClelland.*
TETRABRANCHUS, *Bleeker.*

Branchiostegals, apparently four. Body much elongated. Eyes covered with skin. Nostrils double. The dental border of the upper jaw is formed by the intermaxillaries and not by the palatine bones, it is protrusible and overlapped superiorly in almost its entire length by a very thin maxilla. Teeth in intermaxillaries, mandibulæ, and palatine bones in several rows. Pectoral fins absent. Vertical fins adipose and rudimentary. No accessory respiratory sac. The external branchial aperture single, transverse, and situated on the lower aspect of the body; the cavity not divided internally. No scales. The circulation approaches to that of the reptiles, the branchial artery ramifying not only in the respiratory organs but also on the head and in the brain.

Synbranchus Bengaliensis.

Ophisternon Bengaliensis, *McClelland*, Cal. J. N. H. v. pp. 197, 220, t. 2, f. 1, 2; *Kaup*. Catal. Brit. Mus. p. 121, f. 76.
Synbranchus immaculatus, *Cantor*, Catal. p. 337.
Synbranchus Bengaliensis, *Bleeker*, Atl. Ich. iv. p. 119, t. 192, f. 1.

Length of head $\frac{1}{10}$ to $\frac{1}{12}$ in length of body.

Eyes—Diameter about $\frac{1}{20}$ of length of head.

Body much elongated, cylindrical anteriorly, compressed posteriorly. The girth of the body is equal to about three times its height. The skin thin.

Snout acute, anteriorly rounded, lips fleshy, the upper jaw rather the longest: cleft of mouth extending to some distance behind the orbits. Nostrils placed between the orbits near to their anterior superior margins.

Teeth—Intermaxillary teeth conical, and do not meet at the symphysis, those on either side terminating in a triangular patch with a narrow edentulous interspace; those in the lower jaw are rather larger, and there is a narrow edentulous interspace between those of each side, laterally they are in a single row. Palatine teeth in a single row.

Fins—The dorsal commences before the anal, which is situated in the last fourth or fifth of the total length: the caudal is hardly conspicuous: all the fins are low.

Lateral line—Conspicuous.

Colours—Of a dull dirty brownish red in the estuaries of Malabar, lightest on the abdomen. In clearer water it is greenish or blackish green, the abdomen being the lightest.

Grows to several feet in length, and is not rare in the backwaters and estuaries of Malabar. It also may be captured in the fresh water. It appears to be more common in Bengal.

Habitat—Estuaries and fresh waters within the influence of the tides along the coasts of India and Malaysia.

Fam. LEPTOCEPHALIDÆ.

Genus LEPTOCEPHALUS, *Linn.*

Body soft, elongated, compressed, diaphanous, and scaleless. Vertebral column rudimentary and cartilaginous. Intestinal canal straight and tubular. Teeth present or absent. Vertical fins rudimentary. Pectoral present or absent.

LEPTOCEPHALUS MALABARICUS. Plate XIX. Fig. 1.

LEPTOCEPHALUS MALABARICUS, *Day*, Proc. Zool. Soc. 1865, p. 308.

Length of specimen $3\frac{5}{10}$ inches. Lateral muscles about 212.

Length of head $\frac{1}{14}$ of total length. Height of head about $\frac{1}{35}$, of body $\frac{1}{12}$, of dorsal fin about $\frac{1}{35}$, of anal about $\frac{1}{35}$ of total length.

Eyes—In the centre of the height of the head: diameter $\frac{1}{5}$ of length of head, 1 diameter from end of snout.

Profile from snout nearly horizontal to the upper margin of the occiput, from whence it is slightly raised. Body very compressed.

Mouth cleft to beyond the posterior margin of the orbit: snout produced overlapping the lower lip.

Probably due to accident, a circular hole exceeding the diameter of the eye, exists at the posterior extremity of the anterior two-fifths of the body, midway below the vertebral column and the ventral surface: also a notch near the under surface of the caudal.

Fins—Destitute of rays. The dorsal commences a short distance behind the head, and is continuous with the caudal and anal. Anal occupies the posterior half of the body. Pectoral absent. Caudal short.

Colours—Body whitish. Eye golden, its lower surface orange. A line of yellow spotted with green proceeds backwards from the eye, a second from the mouth, which last also traverses the lower lip.

This little fish was brought alive, and remained about two hours swimming about in a globe of water.

* LEPTOCEPHALUS ACUTICAUDATUS.

LEPTOCEPHALUS ACUTICAUDATUS, *Kaup*, Catal. Brit. Mus. p. 151, f. 16.

Head moderately blunt. Ring-like dots on the anterior part of the ventral border.

Teeth—Absent.

Fins—Caudal and pectoral pointed. The dorsal fin, destitute of visible rays, begins near the head.

Colours—The pigmentary rings on the fore part of the ventral rim pass into black points, which probably extend to the tip of the tail.

This specimen was brought from Malabar by *Dussumier*.

Habitat—Malabar.

* LEPTOCEPHALUS DUSSUMIERI.

LEPTOCEPHALUS DUSSUMIERI, *Kaup*, Catal. Brit. Mus. p. 151, f. 17.

"*Diag.* A very small head, no teeth, and a pointed tail destitute of a caudal fin. No dots either on the lateral line or along the edge of the belly.

Descr. Three examples exist in the Paris Museum, one of which is dried up to the thinness of paper; and a small one was sent from Malabar by *Dussumier*. It is a moderately elongated species, whose transverse muscular furrows are very fine, and not near each other. The pectorals are wanting. In none of the fins could I discover rays."—*Kaup*.

ORDER.—PLECTOGNATHI.

SUB-ORDER.—OSTRACIONIDÆ.

Fam. OSTRACIONOIDEI, *Bleeker*.

GENUS OSTRACION, *Linn.*

LÆTOPHRYS, et TETROSOMUS, *Swainson*.
ACANTHOSTRACION, *Bleeker*.

Branchiostegals, six. Body shortened and angular, invested by a solid covering composed of fibro-osseous angular plates placed in juxtaposition, leaving holes for the mouth, eyes, gill-openings, dorsal, anal, and caudal fins. Each jaw with from ten to twelve conical teeth; the maxillæ and intermaxillæ are intimately soldered together. Dorsal fin single, short, or absent. Ventrals none.

The genus is divisible into four subgenera, 1. *Ostracion*, in which the species are destitute of spines: 2. *Lætophrys*, with the sides of the ventral keel posteriorly armed with spines: 3. *Tetrosomus*, preorbital spine directed upwards, and ventral keel spinate, or armed posteriorly by a strong spine; in some the posterior superior extremity of the carapace transformed into a strong spine: 4. *Acanthostracion*, preorbital spines directed forwards. Ventral keel posteriorly armed with a strong spine: in some the dorsal keel is also armed with a strong spine, in others the spines (except the anal) are absent.

OSTRACION NASUS.

OSTRACION NASUS, *Bloch*, t. 138; *Bleeker*, Atl. Ich. v. p. 36, t. 202, f. 5.
OSTRACIUM TESSERULA, *Cantor*, Catal. p. 367, pl. viii. f. 2, 3, (*immature*.)

B. vi. D. 9. P. 10. A. 9. C. 8. L. l. 12. L. tr. 5.

Length of head $\frac{2}{7}$, of pectoral $\frac{1}{7}$, of caudal $\frac{2}{7}$ of the total length. Height of head $\frac{1}{3}$, of body above $\frac{1}{3}$, of dorsal $\frac{1}{8}$, of anal $\frac{1}{8}$ of the total length.

Eyes—Not far from profile: diameter $\frac{1}{3}$ of the length of the head, 1 diameter from end of snout.

Body tetragonal, the back elongated, forming rather a long oval, and slightly convex, owing to its having a raised longitudinal crest, which is most prominent near to the base of the dorsal fin. The transverse diameter across the back is rather more than the height of the body, the abdominal surface is slightly broader. The vertical diameter of the sides is concave, much more so in the very young, as eight-tenths of an inch in length, than in another twice that length; also there is a concave groove along either side of the mesial crest of the body between it and the superior lateral ridge.

Teeth—In the Cochin specimens only eight in each jaw; sharp, rather distant, red and gleaming: some are probably absent, as there should be twelve in the upper and ten in the lower jaw.

Lips fleshy.

Fins—The dorsal is situated in the posterior sixth of the back, the anal rather behind it. Caudal rather broad and rounded at its extremity. Pectoral broad and fan-shaped. All the rays are unbranched.

Plates—Consist of hexagonal pieces with ctenoid margins, from the centre of each hexagon six raised lines radiate towards its margins.

Colours—Bright orange with numerous black spots along the sides, which are not situated in the centre of the plates; some black spots also exist over the caudal and on the base of the pectoral, the fins are yellowish, the abdominal surface of a whitish yellow. Pupil golden.

Of the only two specimens taken in Cochin, the largest was not two inches in length. *Dr. Bleeker* has fully described the *Ostracion tesserula,* and identified it as the young of the *O. nasus,* Bloch.

Habitat—Seas of Malabar, Malaysia, and New Guinea.

Ostracion tetragonus.

Ostracion tetragonus, *Linn,* Mus. ad Frider, p. 59, Atl. tab. 201, 203; *Bleeker,* Atl. Ich. v. p. 39, pl. 201, f. 2.
? Ostracium nasus, *Cantor,* Catal. p. 369.

B. vi. D. 9. P. 10. A. 9. C. 8. L. l. 12. L. tr. 7.

Length of head $\frac{1}{5}$, of pectoral $\frac{1}{7}$, of caudal $\frac{1}{5}$, of base of dorsal $\frac{1}{17}$, of base of anal $\frac{1}{17}$ of the total length. Height of head $\frac{1}{5}$, of body $\frac{1}{4}$, of dorsal $\frac{1}{5}$, of anal $\frac{1}{6}$ of the total length.

Eyes—Close to profile, diameter $\frac{2}{5}$ of length of head, 2 diameters apart anteriorly, nearly 3 posteriorly, $1\frac{3}{4}$ diameters from end of snout.

Body nearly quadrangular, profile from snout to forehead slightly convex, of back straight or a little convex, back elongated, forming rather a long oval, and slightly convex owing to its being a little highest along the mesial line. Hardly any nasal protuberance in a specimen $5\frac{1}{10}$ inches in length. The height of the body is equal to the transverse width of the back, but the breadth of the abdomen is slightly more. The vertical diameter of the sides is rather concave. Interorbital space slightly concave.

Lips fleshy. Nostrils close to anterior superior margin of orbit.

Teeth—Nine to eleven, the six central ones being slightly the largest, but becoming blunted with age.

Fins—The dorsal commences in the posterior fifth of the back opposite to the anus, but rather before the anal fin, which last arises opposite its last ray. Caudal broad and triangular. Pectoral broad and rather pointed.

Plates—Consist of pentagonal, hexagonal, or heptagonal plates with finely serrated or ctenoid margins, and covered with small bony tubercles arranged parallel to their margins. There are five and two half-rows vertically on the sides.

Colours—Greenish or yellowish olive, with one—rarely more—large dark spot generally in the centre of each plate along the sides, on the back each has a white centre: about the snout they are black and more numerous: the abdomen of a light colour. Fins transparent, with a round brown mark on the base of the dorsal, and a few scattered spots or blotches over the caudal. Eyes greenish yellow.

This specimen was slightly above five inches in length, but it grows to more than a foot.

Habitat—Red Sea, Seas of India, and Malaysia to Japan.

SUB-ORDER GYMNODONTIDÆ.

Fam. TETRAODONTOIDEI, *Bleeker*.

Sub-Fam. TETRAODONTIFORMES, *Bleeker*.

Group TETRAODONTINI, *Bleeker*.

GENUS TETRAODON, *Linn.*

LAGOCEPHALUS, *Swainson.*

PHYSOGASTER, GASTROPHYSUS, et CHEILICHTHYS, *Müll.*

STENOMETOPUS, PROMECOCEPHALUS, AMBLYRHYNCHOTUS, GENEION, CATAPHORHYNCHUS, et BATRACHOPS, *Bib.*

ANCHISOMUS, pt. *Kaup.*

BRACHYCEPHALUS, et APSICEPHALUS, pt. *Holl.*

URANOSTOMA, et PLEURANACANTHUS, *Mus. Par.*

Branchiostegals, from four to six. Body oblong, not keeled. The maxillæ and intermaxillaries soldered together, and appearing like a parrot's bill invested with dentary enamel, trenchant, and divided or continuous in the mesial line. Nostrils in the shape of small foraminæ, perforating either side of a more or less elevated papilla. Body partially spined or altogether smooth. Dorsal and anal fins short. Branchial orifice consisting of a slender slit. Vertebral column with never more than thirty vertebræ, of which ten or less belong to the trunk.

TETRAODON LUNARIS.

TETRAODON LUNARIS, *Cuvier*, Règ. An. Ed. 1, ii. p. 148; *Cantor*, Catal. p. 378; *Bleeker*, Atl. Ich. v. p. pl. 205, f. 2.

KAPPA KOORAWAH, *Russell*, pl. 30.

TETRODON TEPA, *Ham. Buch.* pp. 10, 362.

TETRODON LEIOPLEURA, *Gray*, Ill. I. Z. i. pl. 87, f. 2, (*young.*)

B. v. D. 12-14. P. 16-19. A. 11-12 C. 8-11.

Length of head $\frac{1}{3}$, of pectoral $\frac{1}{8}$, of caudal $\frac{1}{7}$, of base of dorsal $\frac{1}{16}$, of base of anal $\frac{1}{16}$ of total length. Height of head $\frac{1}{5}$, of body $\frac{1}{4}$, of dorsal $\frac{1}{8}$, of anal $\frac{1}{8}$ of the total length.

Eyes—Close to profile, diameter $\frac{3}{10}$ of length of head, $1\frac{3}{4}$ diameters from end of snout, and $1\frac{1}{2}$ diameters apart.

The body tapers off considerably towards the tail, and the width of the orbits is equal to two-thirds of its height when uninflated.

Nasal papilla oval, perforated on either side by an opening of the nostril; it is situated midway between the orbit and muzzle.

Fins—Dorsal situated rather behind the posterior third of the body, its first ray unbranched: it is elevated in front and pointed: anal of the same shape, its first ray undivided: pectoral rounded: caudal with its posterior margin rather crescent-shaped, its external longest ray unbranched.

Spines—Short and crowded over the chest, and summit of the head.

Lateral line—Commences in the form of an irregular circle, surrounding the eye, and when it arrives opposite the centre of the posterior margin of the orbit, it gives off a branch to join the opposite portion, it then describes a gentle curve towards the end of the dorsal and anal fins from whence it proceeds direct to the centre of the caudal: a second lateral line goes from the centre of the mouth along the abdominal surface to beyond the anal fin, it runs parallel with the superior one.

Colours—Upper surface of head and back greenish olive; sides and abdomen of a satin-white, having a line of gold colour passing from the orbit to the centre of the caudal. Fins yellow: posterior margin of caudal black. Iris golden, dark towards the orbit.

Grows to a foot in length.

Habitat—Seas and estuaries of Red Sea, India, Malaysia and Japan.

Genus CRAYRACION, *Klein.*

Cirrhostomus, *Swain.*
Arothron, *Müll.*
Epipedorhynchus, dichotomycterus, et dilobomycterus, *Bib.*
Brachycephalus et apsicephalus, pt. *Holl.*

Differs from the Genus *Tetraodon*, by the nostrils on each side being provided with a broad, single, or double, imperforate tentacle, in some bifid only at its extremity. Body entirely or only superiorly and inferiorly spined. Dorsal and anal fin short.

Crayracion fluviatilis.

Tetrodon fluviatilis, *Ham. Buch.* pp. 6, 361, pl. 30, f. 1.
? Tetraodon simulans, *Cantor*, Catal. p. 374.
Crayracion fluviatilis, *Bleeker*, Atl. Ich. v. p.   t. 205, f. 4.

B. v. D. 12-14. P. 21. A. 10-12. C. 8-12.

Length of head $\frac{1}{4}$, of pectoral $\frac{1}{9}$, of caudal $\frac{1}{5}$, of base of dorsal $\frac{1}{11}$, of base of anal $\frac{1}{16}$ of total length. Height of head $\frac{1}{5}$, of body uninflated $\frac{1}{3}$, of dorsal $\frac{1}{8}$, of anal $\frac{1}{8}$ of total length.

Eyes—Protrude considerably: diameter nearly $\frac{1}{4}$ of length of head, $1\frac{1}{4}$ diameters from end of snout, 3 diameters apart anteriorly, but nearly 4 posteriorly.

Abdominal profile, when the fish is not inflated, is scarcely more convex than that of the back. The width of the head at its widest part equals two-thirds of the height of the uninflated body, but the thickness decreases as the tail is approached.

Upper jaw slightly the longest, lips fleshy: two tentacles arise one from the base of each nostril, which are situated rather in front of the orbits. The anterior is single, the posterior double.

Teeth—Generic.

Fins—Pectoral with a broad rounded base: dorsal arises over the anal in the posterior fourth of the body, its first three rays are unbranched: anal has its first two rays unbranched: caudal rays coarse, and mostly crooked.

Spines extend from below the posterior third of the orbit round the chest, and superiorly as far as to above the posterior third of the orbit, whilst they are continued along the back to nearly the base of the dorsal fin, and along the sides to midway between the end of the pectoral and the base of the dorsal: the spinous portion ends in a curved line from nearly the anterior margin of the dorsal to the anterior margin of the anal fin. The spines are coarse, those most posterior being more widely separated than the anterior ones: their divided roots are very apparent.

Lateral line—None visible.

Colours—Greenish-grey above, white beneath; two undulating narrow bright green or yellow bands pass from one eye to the other, and several more irregularly across the back; the sides are covered with round, oval, or irregularly-shaped blotches, surrounded by yellow or green bands, which become whiter and broader towards the abdomen. Fins yellowish. Eyes hazel or yellow. The coloration varies exceedingly, according to the pieces of water which the fish inhabits.

Grows to six inches in length.

Habitat—Seas, estuaries, and salt marshes of India and Malaysia.

CRAYRACION TESTUDINEUS.

TETRAODON TESTUDINEUS, *Linn.* Syst. 1444; *Cantor*, Catal. p. 376; *Bleeker*, Atl. Ich. v. p. pl. 212, f. 3.

PAATTHA, *Mal.*

B. v. D. 10. P. 17. A. 10. C. 10.

Length of head $\frac{1}{4}$, of pectoral $\frac{1}{7}$, of base of dorsal $\frac{1}{27}$, of base of anal $\frac{1}{27}$, of caudal $\frac{1}{4}$ of the total length. Height of dorsal $\frac{1}{8}$, of anal nearly $\frac{1}{8}$ of the total length.

Eyes—Border on the profile, and are rather nearer to the snout than to the gill openings. Diameter $\frac{1}{6}$ of length of head, 3 diameters apart, 2 diameters from end of snout.

Nostrils are situated slightly behind and above the anterior margin of the orbit: the apertures are small, and the tentacle bifurcated.

Fins—Dorsal commences in the posterior fourth of the body, its first ray is unbranched. Anal arises below the termination of the dorsal. The pectoral is broad: the dorsal, caudal and anal are rounded.

Spines—From the interorbital space to the caudal fin the fish is entirely covered by spines, which are much longer, finer, and more crowded on the abdominal surface than on the back and sides. A fine line of spines also passes from the anterior superior angle of the eye, around the nostrils, to the mesial line of the head where it joins a similar line from the opposite side, the two conjoined are continued backwards to the centre of the interorbital space. There are no spines on either jaws or at the axils of the pectorals.

Colours—Upper surface of body deep grey, under surface dirty white, with nine longitudinal stripes of black, which pass in a concave direction under the eye, round the mouth, and round the pectoral fin. The back is marked with darker blotches anteriorly, and is chequered with black in its posterior half and in that of the body: these blotches consist of black bands, surrounding circular patches of white or light grey. Caudal fin chequered with black, which is the predominant colour, but it also has round marks as on the body. Dorsal, anal, and pectoral dirty white. Eye dirty yellow.

In a specimen not two inches in length the spines exist all over the body, as in the adult, but the horizontal lines along the abdomen are absent, and the back and sides alone show the coloration of the mature.

Not common in Malabar. Captured to seven and a half inches in length. The Natives occasionally eat them, but as they frequently cause indigestion and irritation of the intestines, they are generally avoided as food. The Native doctors prescribe them in cases of phthisis.

Habitat—Seas and estuaries of Malabar, Malaysia, China, and Japan.

Crayracion Cochinensis. Plate XX. f. 2.

Crayracion Cochinensis, *Day*, Proc. Zool. Soc. 1865, p. 314.

B. v. D. 9. P. 18. A. 10. C. 11.

Length of head nearly $\frac{1}{4}$, of pectoral $\frac{1}{11}$, of base of dorsal $\frac{1}{8}$, of base of anal $\frac{1}{9}$, of caudal $\frac{1}{5}$ of total length.

Eyes—Diameter $\frac{1}{5}$ of length of head, $2\frac{1}{3}$ diameters apart posteriorly, $1\frac{3}{4}$ anteriorly, 2 diameters from end of snout.

Fins—Dorsal arises at the commencement of the posterior third of the back, and at a distance equal to its base in front of the anterior margin of the anal. All the fins are rounded. The first ray of the anal, and three first of the dorsal are undivided.

Spines—Single, sharp, closely set, commencing from the interorbital space, and behind the upper and lower jaws, and continued on the back as far as the anus. Anteriorly from the interorbital space they are continued in rather a fine band, surrounding the nostrils, posteriorly in a crescentic form. There are none on the space around the pectoral fin anteriorly. Nostrils provided with a broad, imperforate, bifurcated tentacle, and placed above and slightly behind the anterior margin of the orbit.

Colours—Olive green on the back, becoming lighter on the sides, and dirty white on the abdomen. A large spot of pure white—longer than the diameter of the eye—exists over each orbit. Dorsal, caudal, and anal fins of a yellowish green, stained with a darker shade at their extremities. Pectoral brownish olive.

Rare. A single specimen was captured in June, 1863, five and a half inches in length.

Habitat—Cochin on the Malabar coast.

Genus LEIODON, *Swains.*

Leiosomus, *Swains.*
Chelonodon, *Müll.*
Aphanacanthus, tetrodon, et monotretus, *Bib.*

Differs from the *Tetraodon* and *Crayracion*, in that the nostrils are situated on either side in a wide imperforate pit having raised edges. Body above and below spinate or smooth. Lateral line simple. Dorsal and anal fins short.

Leiodon viridipunctatus. Plate XX. f. 2.

Leiodon viridipunctatus, *Day*, Proc. Zool. Society, 1865, p. 315.

B. v. D. 12. P. 18. A. 11. C. 10.

Length of head $\frac{1}{4}$, of pectoral $\frac{1}{8}$, of base of dorsal $\frac{1}{12}$, of base of anal $\frac{1}{20}$, of caudal $\frac{1}{5}$ of the total length.

PLATE XX.

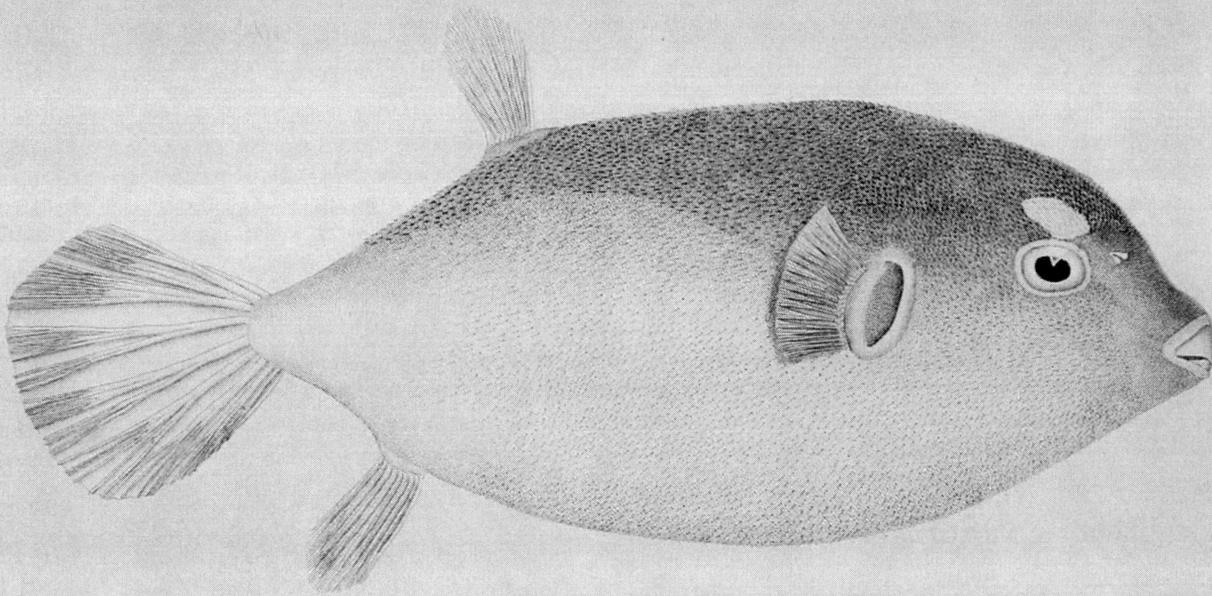

Fig 1.

Fig 2.

F. Day, del. et sculp.

1. CRAYRACION COCHINENSIS 2. LEIODON VIRIDIPUNCTATUS

Eyes—Rather nearer the gill openings than the muzzle. Diameter $\frac{1}{5}$ of length of head, 2 diameters apart in front, but further behind.

Nostrils broad and open, situated above, and slightly behind the anterior margin of the orbit.

Fins—Dorsal arises at commencement of the last fourth of the body, and its posterior margin is above the first ray of the anal. All the fins are rounded. First three dorsal and two anal rays are undivided.

Spines—Short, some distance asunder, and commencing from the occiput, pass along the back two-thirds of the distance towards the commencement of the dorsal fin: inferiorly the spines begin from below the orbit, surround the lower and posterior margins of the pectoral fin, and are continued as far as the anus; at first they are directed backwards, but from the posterior margin of the pectoral they are turned downwards.

Lateral line—Curves upwards from above the pectoral fin, and is continued to the centre of the caudal. It is very indistinct.

Colours—Back light green; abdomen silvery white. Back and sides covered with emerald-green spots, a bar of the same colour passes across the vertex from one eye to the other, and also goes backwards in the mesial line towards a second irregular band of the same colour, which passes across the back more posteriorly. Eye brown, with a golden rim surrounding the iris. Caudal and anal tipped with black. Dorsal yellowish. Four black spots under the throat.

Rare, grows to six inches in length.

Habitat—Cochin on the Malabar Coast.

Family BALISTISIDÆ.

Genus ALUTARIUS, *Cuvier.*

Body elongated, compressed, and covered with fine, closely set granules, scarcely visible to the naked eye. Pelvis entirely hidden beneath the skin. Two dorsal fins, the anterior having its first spine elongated, moderately stout, and capable of being laid flat in a groove posterior to it.

Alutarius lævis.

Balistes lævis, *Bloch*, t. 414.
Alutarius lævis, *Cantor*, Catal. p. 355.
Mullah purroah, *Mal.*

B. vi. D. 2 | 46. P. 15. A. 49. C. 12.

Length of head $\frac{2}{7}$, of pectoral $\frac{1}{14}$, of caudal $\frac{2}{7}$, of base of first dorsal about $\frac{1}{60}$, of base of second dorsal $\frac{1}{3}$, of base of anal $\frac{1}{4}$ of total length. Height of head $\frac{1}{5}$, of body rather above $\frac{1}{5}$, of first dorsal $\frac{1}{9}$, of second dorsal about $\frac{1}{30}$, of anal about $\frac{1}{30}$ of total length.

Eyes—Oval, situated close to the profile, behind the posterior extremity of the opercles, and under the first dorsal fin: horizontal diameter $\frac{1}{5}$, vertical diameter $\frac{1}{8}$ of length of head, $3\frac{1}{2}$ diameters from end of snout, nearly 1 diameter apart.

Body elongated and compressed, terminating in a point at the snout, but broad at the base of caudal fin. Profile rises to the first dorsal, from whence it sinks slightly to the caudal.

Mouth anterior, lower jaw longest, cut obliquely, its posterior end being the highest, and its extremity forming more than half a circle. Lips thin. Nostrils situated in front of the eyes, approximating, rather tubular, the anterior largest and furnished with a valve. Gill openings small, linear, oblique, their upper ends opposite the posterior margin of the orbit, and their length one-third more than that of the orbit.

Teeth—About eight pointed and cutting, the largest being in the centre.

Fins—First dorsal arises over the centre of the orbit and base of pectoral: the second dorsal and anal opposite one another, or the last rather the most anterior, they are situated in the posterior half of the body. First dorsal consists of one long and thin spine, which can be laid flat, and a smaller one posterior to it, a groove equal to half its length exists along the back behind its base. Second dorsal consists of unbranched rays of about equal height. Pectoral pointed. Anal the same as the second dorsal. Caudal large, rounded with coarse branched rays. The finless portion of the tail between the end of the vertical fins and the base of the caudal, equals one and a half transverse diameters of the orbit.

Skin—Body covered with minute closely placed granules—in some places becoming hair-like and rough: the dorsal spine also rough.

Colours—Yellowish, with small spots all over the head and body. Some fine blue lines round the eyes and encircling the mouth. Large blue spots and blotches in four or five irregular rows over the whole surface of the body. Dorsal and anal pinkish: caudal tipped with the same colour, otherwise of a dark brown very indistinctly barred.

Grows to about ten inches in length.

Habitat—Seas of Malabar, Malaysia, China, Canary Islands and Caribbean Sea.

Genus TRIACANTHUS, *Cuvier*.

Body moderately compressed: skin covered with minute closely set scales. Two dorsal fins, the anterior dorsal having its first spine elongated and stout: and a strong spine representing the ventral fin, which is moveable and articulated to a pelvis which is not prominent. All these spines can be laid flat in grooves posterior to them. Caudal fin moderately long.

Triacanthus biaculeatus.

Balistes biaculeatus, *Bloch*, t. 148, f. 2; *Bennett*, pl. 15.
Bowree or Abatoo, *Russell*, pl. 21.
Triacanthus biaculeatus, *Cantor*, Catal. p. 360.

B. vi. D. 5 | 24-25. P. 14. V. 1. A. 19-20. C. 14.

Length of head $\frac{1}{4}$, of pectoral $\frac{1}{12}$, of caudal $\frac{1}{5}$, of base of first dorsal $\frac{1}{10}$, of base of second dorsal $\frac{2}{9}$, of base of anal $\frac{1}{7}$ of the total length. Height of head $\frac{1}{4}$, of body $\frac{1}{3}$, of first dorsal $\frac{1}{5}$, of second dorsal $\frac{1}{12}$, of ventral $\frac{1}{7}$, of anal $\frac{1}{12}$ of the total length.

Eyes—Oval and close to profile: horizontal diameter $\frac{1}{3}$, vertical diameter $\frac{1}{5}$ of length of head, 2 horizontal diameters from end of snout, 1 diameter apart.

Body elliptical, decreasing in size towards the caudal fin: a considerable rise from snout to first dorsal, and rather a protrusion opposite the orbits, its highest portion being between the first dorsal and ventral fins.

Head broad, pyramidal, becoming narrower towards an elongated muzzle, lips fleshy and surrounding a small mouth: a furrow extends from the orbit to the snout. Preopercle oblique. Intermaxillaries raised, prominent, and slightly triangular. Summit of head flattened, and having a central longitudinal keel passing upwards towards the first dorsal spine. Apertures of nostrils approximating, oval, and close to the anterior superior angle of the orbit, the posterior the largest and the most superior.

Teeth—An external series of ten trenchant teeth, the central ones the longest; in the upper jaw there are four tubercular teeth posterior to the anterior ten, the central pair of which are the longest. Tongue fleshy, small, without teeth.

Fins—Dorsal, pectoral, and ventral arise on a line, of which the first dorsal is slightly in advance; the second dorsal arises the width of the base of the first dorsal posterior to it; the anal arises under the centre of the second dorsal. The first dorsal consists of one strong, long, triangular, roughened and moveable spine, which can be laid flat on the back; the spines behind it are short, the first one-fourth the length of the spine, from whence they rapidly decrease. The second dorsal low, its upper margin parallel with the back, from its fourth to its sixth rays rather the highest: the space between the end of the fin and the commencement of the caudal equals the length of the base of the anal. Anal highest anteriorly, its lower margin concave, its third ray slightly the longest. Ventral formed of one strong spine, slightly shorter than that of the first dorsal, but of the same description; it can be raised at an acute angle to the body, or be received into a groove along the side of the abdomen. Caudal with deep lobes, each of which are rounded. Pectoral short, and rounded.

Scales—Small minute granules, which are covered with a mucous secretion: they are largest on the back, chest, and over the spine of the first dorsal and each of the ventral fins: on these last they gradually decrease in size towards their summits.

Lateral line—Forms a curve to opposite the centre of the second dorsal, from whence it proceeds direct to the centre of the caudal: at its origin another line arises which in front of the dorsal spine joins one from the opposite side. Another passes along the supraorbital margin to the front of the nostrils and along the muzzle; and a third along the inferior margin of the orbit, passing obliquely over which, and behind the mouth, it ascends to join a similar branch from the opposite side: a fourth branch passes a little in front of the gill openings, beneath which it forms a short arch backwards, and then proceeds obliquely downwards to the centre of the ventral groove.

Colours—Back greyish shot with golden: abdomen of burnished silver. The lower half of the dorsal spine black, as is also the membrane between it and the second and third spines, the outer edges of which are white. Fins greyish, dashed with yellow. Caudal tipped with yellow. Pectoral yellow. Eyes golden.

Gill openings small, linear, slightly oblique, and situated just in front of the pectoral fins, their length hardly exceeding that of the orbits.

Body rough to the touch, owing to which circumstance it has been named the "File fish."

Grows to nine inches and a half in length. Is not eaten.

Habitat—Seas of India, Malaysia, China, and extending to Australia.

ORDER.—LOPHOBRANCHII.

Fam. SYNGNATHIDÆ, *Kaup.*

Group HIPPOCAMPINÆ, *Bon.*

GENUS HIPPOCAMPUS, *Cuvier.*

Body heptagonal, laterally compressed: snout moderately elongated: mouth anterior: breast developed, it and the abdomen with acute ridges, the quadrangular tail exceeding the length of the body. The lateral line connected with the inferior caudal ridge: the superior caudal ridge reaching as far as the middle of the dorsal fin. The posterior portion of the head more or less elevated, with an occipital bone bearing a coronet, which is surmounted by spines and knobs: orbit also spiny. Breast-ring with two or three spines; body having from ten to thirteen rings, all of which are spiny: the acuteness of the spines and knobs decreases with age. Tail prehensile at the extremity, and destitute of any fin. Dorsal fin usually rests upon three rings, but it may on any number up to six, of which two only form part of the tail; the anal fin often hidden in the pouch of the males, which is formed of thick skin, and only opens at its commencement. Gill openings small, very narrow, circular, and placed high up at the extremity of the opercle, close to the occiput.

HIPPOCAMPUS COMES.

HIPPOCAMPUS COMES, *Cantor*, Catal. p. 389, pl. xi. f. 2 (*young*); *Kaup*, Catal. Brit. Mus. Lophobranchiate fish, p. 10.
COODRA MEEN, *Mal.*

D. 16. P. 17. A. 4. Rings of body 11, of tail 33.

Length of head $\frac{2}{11}$ of total length.

Eyes—Diameter equals $\frac{2}{11}$ of total length of head, the anterior margins of the orbits situated midway between the end of the snout and the posterior extremity of the opercle.

Mouth anterior, small, triangular: the upper surface of the snout with a raised mesial longitudinal ridge. Opercle with raised ridges passing downwards and outwards.

There are great diversities in the modes in which the spines are placed in this species, and amongst several from Cochin none are exactly similar. In the immature the nasal spine is present, but absent in the mature. There are two sharp spines on the posterior superior angle of the orbit directed backwards and outwards: a smaller one rather above the centre of the posterior margin of the orbit: a longer and stronger one just above the superior margin of the opercle, and another on a line between it and the first spine. There is a sharp spine on the lower profile beneath the centre of the orbit, and a blunt one between it and the orbit: also a sharp spine on either edge of the throat corresponding to the anterior extremities of two antero-lateral ridges; whilst another exists on a line close to the inferior edge of the base of the pectoral fin. The coronet is moderately elevated, with from four to six blunt points surrounding its superior margin, the ridge descending from it in the mesial line is also spined.

Body heptagonal, one surface being posterior, two anterior, and two on either side: most of the angles formed by the meetings of the sides are spined. On the first five rings of the anterior ridge are no spines: then they become moderately developed, and above the ring on which the anal is situated they are sharp. On the antero-lateral ridges there are no spines for the first two or three rings, then they become well developed. The lateral ridges are moderately spined in their whole extent, except on the ring opposite to the last antero-lateral one. The postero-lateral ridges have rather prominent spines at their upper rings, but they are not constant, neither are the number of body rings, which vary one or two, more or less. The caudal is quadrangular, angles rather thickened, scarcely spined. The anterior ridge of the body and the two antero-lateral ones coalesce at the anal fin. The postero-lateral ones commence separately from the occipital crest: passing outwards they form with the first ring an acute angle, and are continued downwards on either side of the back for eight more rings, when they bulge outwards for three more, and on this portion the dorsal fin is placed. All the sides and back of the body are slightly concave.

Colours—Brownish, opercles slightly bluish, fins transparent. Iris white, with some brown lines radiating from the pupil.

Not very common in Malabar, except in rocky situations. Grows to eleven or twelve inches in length; is commonly known as the "Horse fish."

Habitat—Seas of India, Malaysia, China, and Australia.

Sub-Fam. SYNGNATHIDÆ, *Kaup.*

Group SYNGNATHINA, *Kaup.*

Genus ICHTHYOCAMPUS, *Kaup.*

Body heptagonal: dorsal surface slightly or very concave, caudal nearly as wide as body. Head short, with a shorter compressed sharp-ridged snout. Opercle round, swollen, higher than wide. Fins four or five. The supero-lateral ridge of the back is continuous with that of the caudal region. The anus is situated under the commencement of the dorsal fin. Males furnished with a caudal egg pouch, which is open throughout.

Ichthyocampus Ponticerianus.

Typhlus Ponticerianus, *Bibron*, Mus. Paris.

Ichthyocampus Ponticerianus, *Kaup*, Catal. Brit. Mus. p. 31.

D. 24. P. 16-17. A. 2. C. 8. Body rings, 15. Caudal rings, 38 to 40.

Length of head including snout $\frac{1}{8}$ of the total length: from the anterior margin of the orbit to the end of the snout is very slightly longer than the distance from the anterior margin of the orbit to the posterior extremity of the opercle. The length of the body is scarcely $\frac{1}{4}$ of the total length, and not half so long as the caudal portion.

Eyes—Round, diameter $\frac{1}{6}$ of length of head, nearly 3 diameters from end of snout, $\frac{1}{3}$ of a diameter apart anteriorly, but more so posteriorly.

The supero-lateral ridge of the back is continuous with that of the caudal portion: the infero-lateral ridge of the body is continuous with the same on the caudal: the inferior margin of the body has a very moderately prominent ridge. The lateral line curves downwards in the last part of its course, and then passes horizontally along the first caudal ring.

Body moderately elongated, heptagonal, back nearly flat, the caudal portion being about two and a third times longer than the body, which is slightly higher than it is wide.

Snout very slightly elevated in its anterior third: interorbital space widest posteriorly, with a sharp low mesial longitudinal ridge passing from between the centre of the orbits along the first fourth of the snout: the orbit with a blunt elevation in the middle of its anterior margin. A very prominent sharp horizontal crest across the opercle.

Fins—The dorsal is situated on the third to the eighth caudal rings (from the second to the seventh, according to *Dr. Kaup*): pectoral short, but with a broad base: anal rays minute: caudal rounded at its extremity, and its length equals twice that of the orbit.

Rings—With smooth edges, the divisions between each being distinct.

Colours—Deep brown, with one—occasionally two—milk-white spots in the centre of each body ring along the infero-lateral ridge: the lower surface of the snout dotted with black spots. Dorsal fin yellow, pectoral and caudal leaden colour. Eye greenish blue.

This resembles the *Syngnathus argyrostictus*, but is easily recognised from it, because its supero-lateral ridges are continuous, its chest is not so acutely keeled, and it has a row of milk-white spots along the infero-lateral ridge of the body.

Common in Malabar, where it grows to about five inches in length.

Habitat—Seas and estuaries of India and Malaysia.

Genus SYNGNATHUS, *Linn.*

Body heptagonal, dorsal surface flat or slightly concave, never much compressed or arched. No spines on snout. Fins four or five; the dorsal stands on a level with the back, its base not being elevated. The number of body rings never amounts to twenty-seven. The supero-lateral ridge of the back is never continuous with that of the tail. Males furnished with a caudal egg pouch, which is open throughout.

Syngnathus argyrostictus.

Syngnathus argyrostictus, *Kuhl & v. Hass.*; *Kaup*, Catal. Brit. Mus. p. 33.
Syngnathus spicifer, *Rüppell*, Neue Wirbelth.

D. 25-27. P. 16. A. 2. C. 8. Body rings, 15 to 16. Caudal rings, 40 to 41.

Length of head, including snout, $\frac{1}{11}$ of the total length: from the anterior margin of the orbit to the end of the snout, equals the distance from the anterior margin of the orbit to the posterior extremity of the opercle. The length of the body is $\frac{1}{4}$ of the total length, and not $\frac{1}{2}$ as long as the caudal portion.

Eyes—Rather oval, nearly $\frac{1}{4}$ of the total length of the head, nearly 2 diameters from end of snout, $\frac{3}{4}$ of a diameter apart.

The supero-lateral ridge of the back extends to the fourth caudal ring but is not continuous with the supero-lateral ridge of the caudal which ends opposite to the anterior extremity of the root of the dorsal fin. The infero-lateral ridge of the body is continuous with that of the tail. The inferior margin of the body has a very acute and prominent ridge. The lateral line arches downwards in the last two rings of its course and ends at the inferior margin of the first caudal ring.

Body moderately elongated, heptagonal, the caudal portion above twice the length of that of the body: the height of which is equal to about twice its width.

Snout elevated in its anterior half, interorbital space widest posteriorly, having a lateral ridge on either side, whilst opposite the anterior margin of the orbit it ends in a sharp mesial longitudinal crest which is continued half way along the snout. Opercle with a prominent horizontal raised ridge along its centre.

Fins—The dorsal is situated on the first five rings of the caudal: the anal rays are minute and sometimes imperceptible.

Rings—With smooth edges, the division between each being but little apparent.

Colours—Generally light brownish, with a dark brown streak extending from the orbit to the angle of the mouth, and a second from the posterior angle of the eye over the opercle: a few black spots on the under surface of lower jaw; body inferiorly with fine brown bars. Dorsal fin barred with brown spots. Caudal blackish, with a light brown base.

By no means rare in Malabar, and ascends rivers high above the influence of the tides. Grows to about five inches in length.

Habitat—Red Sea, Seas, estuaries, and freshwaters of India, and Malaysia.

Group **NEROPHINÆ**, *Kaup*.

Genus MICROPHIS, *Kaup*.

Body heptagonal, composed of rough rings, and continued of equal thickness up to the commencement of the tail. The eggs uncovered by membrane are distributed in rows along the breast and abdomen of the males. Fins five.

Microphis Bleekeri.

D. 41-45. P. 21. A. 2. C. 9. Body rings 21. Caudal rings 22.

Length of head a little above $\frac{1}{5}$, of snout to anterior margin of the orbit rather above $\frac{1}{8}$ of the total length. Length of body from base of pectoral to the anal ring more than half the length of the snout longer than the caudal portion. Height of body equal to its depth.

Eyes—Slightly oval, diameter $\frac{2}{13}$ of the total length of the head, $\frac{1}{2}$ a diameter apart anteriorly, rather more posteriorly.

The lateral ridge of the back is continuous with the supero-lateral caudal ridge which it joins a little behind the posterior extremity of the dorsal fin: but the supero-lateral caudal ridge anterior to this junction bulges outwards and proceeds forwards in a curved line as far as the anterior margin of the anal ring midway between the lateral ridge of the back and the lateral line. The lateral line posteriorly arches downwards and reaches the infero-lateral caudal ridge at the base of the ring behind the anal one. The infero-lateral ridge of the body is expanded into a sharp flattened ridge which ceases at the posterior margin of the ring behind the anal one.

Body moderately elongated, heptagonal, and longer than the tail, the back a little arched, the thickness as far as the commencement of the caudal about the same, the height the same as the width, the lower surface with expanded sides (in the males) to protect the ova: flattened in the female.

Snout compressed, curving slightly upwards at its extremity with two moderately raised lateral ridges along either side above, and the same below. No spines. Upper surface of orbit

2 M

close to the profile. Opercle with a well marked horizontal ridge along its centre, having five more ridges proceeding below it to the posterior and inferior margins: rather a prominent but irregular ridge above the opercle (smallest in the female) which ends opposite its posterior superior angle in a wide smooth furrow directed upwards and slightly backwards. A lanceolate keeled ridge, rounded anteriorly, and directed forward exists in the occipital region.

Fins—The dorsal fin is placed upon nine rings the first of which is the anal ring. The pectoral wide and short. The caudal lanceolate and equal in length to half that of the snout.

Rings—Each very distinctly separated from the next, and ending in a moderately sharp spine posteriorly, causing the surface to feel quite rough to the finger passed from behind forward. In the female there are sometimes two spines to the end of each ring, and they are much sharper and longer than in the male.

Colours—A bright red line at the gills, and along the lateral line, otherwise of a light brown with a dark line proceeding forward from the eye, and the snout barred with brown. Fins light brown.

Not rare in the river at Cochin. This specimen, a male, was nearly eight inches in length.

I conclude this is the species referred to by *Dr. Kaup,* as having been published by *Dr. Bleeker* as the *Syngnathus cunculus,* but as he gives no reference I have been unable to ascertain the fact.

Habitat—Seas and estuaries of Malabar and (?) Malaysia.

* Microphis cunculus.

Syngnathus cunculus, *Ham. Buch.* pp. 12, 362.
Microphis cunculus, *Kaup,* Catal. Brit. Mus. p. 64.

D. about 50. P. 16. A. 2. C. 8-9. Body rings 17-18. Caudal rings 25-27.

Length of head $\frac{1}{10}$, of body $\frac{2}{5}$, of tail $\frac{1}{2}$, of caudal fin $\frac{1}{19}$ of the total length.

"A prominent line divides the silvery gill-cover into two similar parts. The lateral line unites in an arch with the under border of the first caudal ring. Ten rings: three of them belonging to the body sustain the dorsal fin, before which there are 14 rings, and up to the anal ring there are 17."—*Kaup.*

Colours—"Green above, and white beneath, with a gloss of silver on the sides. On the back several dusky lines intersect each other and form a net-work. On each side is a longitudinal stripe formed of numerous dots. The eyes are silvery."—*Hamilton Buchanan.*

Habitat—Seas and estuaries of India.

SUB-CLASS.—SELACHII.

ORDER.—PLAGIOSTOMI.

SUB-ORDER.—SQUALI.

Fam. SCYLLIÆ.

GENUS CHILOSCYLLIUM, *Müll. & Henle.*

Snout blunt: nostrils cleft up to the mouth: nasal valves separated, each with a filament: a hem-like valve on the outer side of each nostril which is continued to the upper corner of the mouth: under lip broad, skinny, and separated from the throat by a transverse furrow. Mouth slightly arched. Spiracles behind and beneath the orbits, with a projecting tubercle at their posterior margins: fourth and fifth gill openings approximating. Teeth pointed with one or two or even four smaller points on either side. The anterior dorsal fin behind the ventral, but both dorsals before the anal: pectorals and ventrals rounded, as are also the anal and caudal: the anal without an anterior angle and arched downwards, terminating posteriorly in a point: lower margin of caudal convex.

CHILOSCYLLIUM PLAGIOSUM.

SCYLLIUM PLAGIOSUM, *Bennett*, Life of Raffles, p. 693, (*young.*)
BOKEE SORRAH, *Russell*, pl. xvi. (*young.*)
RA SORRAH, *Russell*, pl. x. (*adult.*)
SCYLLIUM ORNATUM, *Gray*, Ill. I. Z. i. pl. 98, f. 2, (*young.*)
CHILOSCYLLIUM PLAGIOSUM, *Cantor*, Catal. p. 392; *Duméril*, Suite de Buffon, Ichthyologie générale, i. p. 328.
ETTEE, *Mal.*

Snout rounded, mouth slightly arched, under lip skinny, broad, and divided from the throat by a transverse fissure. Nostrils with separated nasal valves, each having a projecting tubercle at their posterior margins.

Teeth—Pointed, with one or two toothlets on either side.

Fins—All more or less rounded. The pectoral commences under the second spiracle, and its posterior margin is midway between the orbit and the ventral fins, its base equals the distance between the first and last spiracle. The base of the ventral is about as broad as that of the pectoral, and the length of its anterior margin is equal to that of its base, but its posterior margin is half shorter. The anterior dorsal commences opposite the last third of the ventral, its front edge is rather longer than its base, and twice as long as its posterior border. The second dorsal commences midway between the last spiracle and the termination of the caudal, its anterior border is longer than its base. The anal is as far from the anterior margin of the second dorsal as that fin is from the posterior margin of the first dorsal, it is low, rounded behind, and scarcely so high as the body above it. Caudal commences superiorly opposite the first third of the anal, it is very low, its posterior extremity is inferiorly rounded, and it extends as far as the anal fin.

Scales and ridges—The former are minute in the young, but in the adult they are moderately wide, lanceolate, and keeled: along the centre of the back is a raised ridge extending from the head as far as the second dorsal fin, along it the scales are larger than those on the sides: laterally a second ridge is apparent in the upper third of the body, opposite the anterior dorsal it passes as far backwards as the posterior extremity of the anal where it bends down close to the abdominal line: a third badly marked ridge extends from the pectoral to the ventral and along the edge of the abdomen as far as the anal fin, separating the side from the abdomen.

Colours—In the immature. Ground colour buff with a tinge of red and there are about ten vertical wide dark bands, from opposite the pectoral to the end of the caudal fin: they are much wider than the ground colour: one passes across the back of the head, another over the snout. The pectoral and ventral are black, with a white edge: the central portions of the two dorsals are also black and their edges whitish. Sometimes between the bands there are intermediate spots; or the ground colour may be the darkest: or all the fins may be adorned with black rings each having a black central spot.

As the age of the fish increases the darker markings become obsolete.

In the adult (my specimen is twenty-one inches in length) the upper surface of the back is of an uniform grey, the abdominal surface whitish, stained with a dull red. Fins greyish, the vertical ones having a reddish tinge, except the edges of the dorsals which are almost white.

Common in Malabar, especially the immature. The flesh is considered nourishing, the livers good for medicinal oils, and the skins for polishing wood.

Habitat—Seas of India, Malaysia, China, and Japan.

Fam. CARCHARIÆ, *Müll. and Henle.*

Genus SCOLIODON, *Müll. and Henle.*

Snout flattened, more or less rounded, and moderately long. Nostrils central between the mouth and the point of the snout, or nearer the mouth at the lateral margins of the snout. Labial cartilage minute or absent. Spiracles none. Nictitating membrane distinct. Teeth of upper and lower jaws similar, except an extra trenchant central one in the former, with its point directed outwards, but it is not denticulated; the outer part of the base forms a blunt ledge, in which an indentation may be absent or present. Posterior dorsal fin either immediately opposite the anal or above its posterior extremity. A distinct caudal groove above and below. Scales small, and three-keeled. Oviduct of embryo flocculent.

Scoliodon acutus.

Carcharias acutus, *Rüppell*, Chond. v. t. 18, f. 4.

Scoliodon acutus, *Cantor*, Catal. p. 399; *Gray*, Catal. Brit. Mus. p. 41; *Duméril*, Ich. gén. i. p. 345.

Snout flattened, pointed: the distance from the nostril to the extremity of the snout, equals two-thirds of that which separates the angles of the mouth, the breadth and width of which are equal. Labial cartilage, if present, very minute. The fifth gill opening is situated above the commencement of the pectoral fin. There is a distinct caudal groove both above and below.

Teeth—Those in both jaws similar, but an odd central one exists in the upper, which is trenchant, smooth, and directed outwards, while in the immature it is considerably smaller than the others.

Fins—The anterior dorsal is situated nearer to the pectoral than to the ventral fin, its posterior border is emarginate, and its upper and posterior angle forms an elongated point: the posterior dorsal commences opposite the last half of the base of the anal, which is two-thirds as long as that of the second dorsal. The interval between the caudal and anal is double the length of the base of the latter. Caudal low, its superior lobe cut very obliquely at its free extremity, which is slender.

Scales—Minute, rounded, and with five, four, or three keels.

Colours—Grey above; white beneath.

Habitat—Red Sea, Seas of India, Malaysia, China.

Genus PRIONODON, *Müll. and Henle.*

Prionace, *Cantor.*

Differs from the *Genus Scoliodon* by the teeth of either the upper or of both jaws being finely denticulated on either side, oblique or straight, trigonal, or with a broad base and small apex. There is almost invariably an extra central tooth in the upper jaw. Oviduct of embryo smooth.

Prionodon melanopterus.

Carcharias melanopterus, *Quoy & Gaim.* Freycin. Voy. p. 194, pl. 43, f. 1, 2.
Prionace melanopterus, *Cantor*, Catal. p. 400.
Prionodon melanopterus, *Gray*, Catal. Brit. Mus. p. 46; *Duméril*, Ich. gén. i. p. 365.

Snout short, rounded, in some almost pointed. The space between the eyes longer than that anterior to them. Nostrils nearer the centre of the margin of the snout than they are to the anterior border of the mouth. The fourth and fifth branchial apertures situated above the pectoral fin.

Teeth—Trigonal, and situated either obliquely or straight; those in the lower jaw the smallest and narrowest: the teeth in both jaws denticulated on either side in the adult, but in the immature only those of the upper jaw. There is generally an odd central tooth in the upper jaw.

Fins—Anterior dorsal situated nearer to the pectoral than to the ventral, it commences slightly behind the termination of the pectoral, and is much higher than the posterior dorsal, which is slightly in advance of the anal, and extends to opposite its posterior third. Pectoral emarginate. Ventral begins in the last third of the distance between the commencement of the pectoral and of the anal. Caudal nearly one-fourth of the total length, the angle of its lower lobe slightly rounded.

The male appendages are shorter than the internal margin of the ventral fin.

Scales—Minute, with from three to seven keels.

Colours—Bluish grey, fading to whitish beneath. Iris grey, stained darker at its superior portion.

Habitat—Red Sea, Seas of India, Malaysia, the Moluccas, New Guinea, China, Australia, and the Cape of Good Hope.

* Prionodon lamia.

Carcharias lamia, *Müll. & Henle*, Plag. 37, pl. 12.
Carcharinus lamia, *Gray*, Catal. Brit. Mus. p. 44.
Prionodon lamia, *Duméril*, Ich. gen. i. p. 356.

Snout short and rounded: nostrils situated at about equal distance from its terminal extremity and the anterior border of the mouth.

Teeth—In upper jaw triangular, with their internal border a little convex, and the external slightly concave: they and the inferior are denticulated, the latter are straight, narrower, and in the form of a triangle, supported upon an enlarged base: a small central tooth in each jaw denticulated above and smooth below.

Fins—Anterior dorsal commences immediately behind the base of the pectoral; it is a little higher than its base is long: upper margin convex, superior angle rounded, and its posterior border almost straight, with a pointed angle. Posterior dorsal much smaller than the anterior. Pectorals about half as wide as long. The upper caudal lobe equal to about one-fourth of the total length, and double that of the inferior lobe.

Colours—Grey above, whitish beneath, or with the tips of the fins with dark spots: or a white spot at the extremity of the pectoral, the upper angle of the first dorsal, and the end of the two lobes of the caudal, with a black spot on the superior angle of the posterior dorsal and of the anal.

This species was brought from Malabar by *Dussumier*.

Habitat—Seas of India, China, Australia, Cape of Good Hope, and the Mediterranean.

Fam. CESTRACIONTES, *Duméril.*

Genus CESTRACION, *Klein.*

Zygæna, *Cuvier.*
Cestrorhinus, *Blainv.*

The anterior part of the head is broad, flattened, and laterally elongated, with the eyes situated at its lateral extremities, and the nostrils on its fore-border. The nasal valve is a small triangular lobe situated at the anterior margin of the nostril. Labial cartilages small or absent. Teeth in both jaws similar, resembling outwardly pointing flattened pyramids, and are either trenchant, denticulated, or with a ledge at the outer side of the base: there is a central tooth in each jaw. The anterior dorsal is nearer to the pectoral than it is to the ventral: the posterior dorsal is smaller than the anterior, and situated opposite to or rather behind the commencement of the anal: the incision of the caudal fin distinct. Oviduct of embryo flocculent, and the ovary unconnected to the walls of the uterus.

Cestracion zygæna.

Squalus zygæna, *Linn*, Sys. 1494.
Koma sorra, *Russell*, pl. 12, (*young*).
Sphyrna zygæna, *Cantor*, Catal. p. 401.

SPHYRNIAS ZYGÆNA, *Gray*, Catal. Brit. Mus. p. 48.
CESTRACION ZYGÆNA, *Duméril*, Ich. gén. i. p. 382.
HAMMER-HEADED SHARK.

The anterior portion of the head is broad, flattened, and laterally elongated, with eyes on its external margins, and nostrils situated anteriorly: its length from the angle of the mouth is about one-third its breadth: its posterior margin is placed at acute angles with the body: its mouth small and on the inferior surface. Nostrils patent, near the external portion of the anterior aspect of the head, with a triangular lobe at their internal margins forming a valve, from which extends a fissure along their external third.

Teeth—Pyramidal, all trenchant with smooth edges, those in the upper jaw somewhat the broadest: there is a middle elongated tooth in either jaw.

Fins—The anterior dorsal commences opposite the termination of the pectoral, its anterior margin one third longer than its base. The second dorsal smaller, it commences opposite the anterior margin of the anal, but terminates before the latter in an elongated point. Ventrals situated midway between the base of the pectoral and the base of the caudal.

Scales—Minute, with several ridges.

Colours—Body and fins of a dull slate-grey: under surface white: iris golden.

Its flesh is considered very nourishing, and is extensively salted: its fins are dried: whilst a medicinal oil is extracted from its liver, which is believed by the Natives to be a good remedy for "night blindness" (nyctalopia). It grows to eleven feet or more in length, and is much dreaded.

Habitat—Tropical and temperate seas of both hemispheres.

* CESTRACION LEEUWENII.

ZYGÆNA LEEUWENII, *Griffith*, Cuv. Animal Kingdom, p. 640, pl. 50.
CESTRACION LEEUWENII, *Duméril*, Ich. gén. i. p. 383.

Head shaped as in the *C. zygæna,* its width as compared to its length and to that of the tail has the same proportions as in the last species.

Fins—The same as in the last species, but the lower lobe of the caudal, instead of being directed very obliquely from above downwards, and from before backwards, and forming with the horizontal portion of the fin a sort of fork, follows a slightly oblique direction, from which it results that its posterior border approaches to the vertical and reunites almost at a right angle with the upper lobe.

Habitat—Red Sea, Seas of Malabar, Australia, and New Zealand; also of Senegal, Algeria, and the Brazils.

SUB-ORDER.—RAJÆ.

Fam. SQUATINORAIJOIDÆ.

SQUATINORAIES, *Duméril.*
GALEOBATIDES, *Duméril.*

Group PRISTISIDÆ.

Genus PRISTIS, *Latham.*

Pristibatis, *Blainville.*

Snout prolonged, flattened, and laterally armed with numerous flattened, trenchant teeth, which are directed almost directly outwards, commencing from in front of the nostril and continued almost to its termination. Nostrils some distance anterior to the mouth, each with a narrow, long, triangular valve at its upper margin, and a hem-like one at its lower. Mouth straight and transverse, having a membraneous transverse valve with a straight lower margin behind the teeth in the upper jaw. Spiracles large, separated by a broad bridge from the eyes. Upper eyelid without a projection. Teeth flattened like paving stones. Anterior dorsal partly above the ventral, the two dorsals of equal size. Caudal short, with or without a lower lobe.

Pristis semisagittatus.

Squalus semisagittatus, *Shaw*, Zool. v. pt. II. p. 361; *Cantor*, Catal. p. 407; *Duméril*, Ich. gén. i. p. 477.
Yahla, *Russell*, pl. 13.

Snout extended anteriorly into a flattened bone, armed with laterally compressed teeth directed outwards, and varying from twenty-four to thirty-five on a side, whilst there are six or seven more on one side (generally the right) than on the other. In the immature the teeth are only situated in the last three-fourths of the snout, whilst in the fœtus they are not apparent. The first six pairs of the anterior teeth in the adult are opposite, their front edge rather convex, their posterior barbed at their inferior third.

Mouth transverse with a transversal membraneous valve (fringed in the young) behind the teeth in the upper jaw, and with a deep notch near the symphysis. No cartilages exist at the angle of the mouth. The upper eyelid has no projection. The pupil is transverse, with one semicircular flap above and another below; these flaps are easily raised, depressed, or expanded, apparently at the pleasure of the fish, or perhaps according to the stimulus of light received, which they can partially or entirely exclude: lens very soft. Spiracles large, posterior to the eyes, from which they are separated by a broad ridge. Anterior branchial aperture placed just below the origin of the pectoral. Nostrils situated about their transverse length from the mouth, each has a long triangular narrow valve in its upper, and a hem-like one at its lower margin: they are three-fourths of their length apart posteriorly, and one and a half times anteriorly, whilst externally they are close to the margin of the snout.

Teeth—Flattened like paving stones.

Fins—The first dorsal commences opposite the posterior end of the ventral: the second dorsal midway between the posterior extremity of the first dorsal and the base of the caudal. The two dorsals are of equal size, their anterior extremities one-third longer than their posterior ones, their upper margins concave, and their posterior rather produced. Posterior margin of the caudal deeply excavated so as to form two lobes. The external margin of the pectoral concave, its posterior margin rather more than one-third the length of its anterior.

There is a sharp ridge or keel laterally along the tail between the sides and the abdominal surfaces. The male appendages are joined by their anterior two-thirds to the inner margins of the ventrals.

Scales—Minute, of irregular sizes, and situated over the whole of the surface except the summit of the male appendages and the teeth of the saw. They are rather the largest and roughest on the back.

Colours—Greyish yellow above, whitish beneath. Iris golden with a black edge.

Grows to seven feet and upwards in length. The flesh is as much esteemed as that of the sharks. The fins are prepared and sent to China: oil is extracted from the livers, whilst the skins are useful for sword belts or for smoothing down wood.

Habitat—Seas of India and Malaysia.

Group RHAMPHOBATIDES.

Genus RHYNCOBATUS, *Müll. & Henle.*

Snout elongated, acute, with a central, longitudinal, tapering keel, the interval between which and the inner margin of the pectoral is membraneous: undulations of snout are shallow, especially the lateral ones. Superior and inferior nasal valves extend only half way to the inner angle of the nostril, whilst external to the nostril at its upper and outer part is a narrow hem. Spiracles close behind the eyes. The upper eyelid with a simple projection. Teeth broader than long, with a transverse ridge. An arched row of pores extends across the abdominal surface of the scapular region.

Rhyncobatus Djeddensis.

Raja Djiddensis, *Forsk.* 18.
Walawah tenkee, *Russell*, pl. x. (*young.*)
Rhyncobatus Djeddensis, *Cantor*, Catal. p. 412.
Rhyncobatus lævis, *Gray*, Catal. Brit. Mus. p. 92; *Duméril*, Ich. gén. i. p. 483.

Snout elongated, with a tapering keel along its centre. From its anterior extremity to its mouth, equals about one-sixth of its entire length. The distance from the nostrils to the lateral margin is about one-third of their length, whilst their distance apart posteriorly nearly equals their total length, anteriorly they are rather more than twice as far asunder. Eyes large, upper lid with a simple projection. Spiracle close behind the orbit. There is a narrow membraneous hem to the upper margin of the nostril: the superior and inferior nasal valves do not extend so far as the inner margin of the nostrils. Mouth transverse, situated midway between the anterior extremity of the snout and the posterior margin of the pectoral fin, it is about half the width of the head. A transverse arched row of pores exists on the abdominal side of the scapular region.

Teeth—Broader than long with transverse ridges.

Fins—First dorsal commences opposite the centre of the base of the ventral, the length of their bases are about equal, and half the anterior height of the anterior margin of the first dorsal. The second dorsal is half nearer to the base of the caudal than to the posterior extremity of the first dorsal, it is smaller than the latter fin, but its shape is the same. Pectoral irregularly triangular, its posterior free margin being only one-third as long as its anterior edge. Upper margin of caudal convex, lower concave: superior lobe slightly the largest.

Scales—Minute, of irregular shapes and sizes, keeled: a number of sharp curved spines directed backwards in rows exist in various parts of the body. A supraorbital row of them extends from the anterior margin of the orbit round its upper edge to above the spiracle: a second extends from a central point between the termination of the last two and proceeds along the back to the base of the first dorsal, the spines on it being much further apart than in the other lines: from slightly behind the commencement of the dorsal line of spines is a short diverging row on either side; also a row on the shoulder: and two or three spines on the scapular.

The lateral keel commences a little above the termination of the ventrals.

Colours—The immature are dull grey above, whitish—sometimes tinged reddish—beneath, with a dark or black band on the upper eyelid and a dark spot on either side of the snout. Also there is usually, but not invariably, a black spot at the root of the pectoral. The body is spotted with whitish, or light grey. Iris golden: pupils transverse. The adult is of a dull grey above and lighter on the abdomen.

Its flesh is considered nourishing whether eaten salted or fresh, and oil from its liver is much esteemed. It grows to five feet in length.

Habitat—Red Sea, Seas of India and Malaysia.

Group RHINOBATIDES.

Genus RHINOBATUS, *Bl. Schn.*

Snout more or less acute: the skull prolonged anteriorly into a keel, the interval between which and the inner margin of the pectoral fin is membraneous. The upper nasal valve is longer and more slender than the inner, which is shorter and broader: the outer lappet, which is nearly in the middle of the upper edge of the nostril, is slender, but extends in the form of a rounded point to the under margin of the nostril, and is not sharply divided from the inner valve, which extends more or less widely inwards. Spiracles and eyes approximating, both surrounded by a thick wall of skin: the upper eyelid has a central projection. The fore-lateral edge of the disk is twice gently incurved.

* Rhinobatus obtusus.

Rhinobatus obtusus, *Müll. & Henle*, Plag. 122; *Gray*, Catal. Brit. Mus. p. 97; *Blyth*, Journ. Asiatic Soc. xxix. p. 37; *Duméril*, Ich. gén. i. p. 493.

The disk is from $\frac{1}{5}$ to $\frac{1}{6}$ longer than wide, and is rather more than $\frac{1}{3}$ of the total length.

Snout short, blunt, and rounded; its length—from the middle of a line passing before the nostrils, from one external angle to the other—is equal to the space which this line measures. From the anterior margin of the eyes it is two and a half times longer than is the interorbital space. Keel on the snout (seen from above) is three times longer than wide at its base; it is narrowed in its central portion, and has a well marked groove behind, scarcely perceptible in its middle, but reappearing towards its anterior extremity. The distance between the nostrils is less than that which separates them from the border of the disk, but similar to the width of their opening. A prolongation or rather strong fold of skin exists at the posterior part of the air-hole.

Scales—Are in the form of an ace of spades, with a very dull point directed backwards; many are covered with an enamel-like substance, which causes its lateral grooves to appear dotted with white, more especially in the immature: there are traces of tubercles in the mesial line only, before the eyes, at the posterior border of the air-holes and on a level with the scapular constriction; they are always blunt, excepting in the immature, when they are spinous.

Colours—Brown inclining to reddish-violet along the border of the disk and the region of the snout.

Habitat—Seas of India, and of the Cape of Good Hope.

* Rhinobatus granulatus.

? Rhinobatus rhinobatus, *Bl. Schn.* p. 353.

Rhinobatus granulatus, *Cuvier*, Règ. An. 2nd Ed. t. ii. p. 396; *Gray*, Catal. Brit. Mus. p. 95; *Blyth*, Journ. Asiatic Soc. 1860, xxix. p. 36.

Disk equal to about $\frac{1}{3}$ of the total length: its width is $\frac{2}{3}$ of the length.

Snout much elongated: its length is double as long as the distance between the external angles of the nostrils, and five times or more of that between the superciliary ridges. Keel on snout visible in the immature, but absent or only present at its base in the mature. Openings of the nostrils equal to the space between them, or a little shorter, and nearly double the interval which separates their external margins from the edge of the disk. There are two cutaneous prolongations at the posterior border of the air-holes.

Scales—Very small in the lateral regions, and scarcely elevated: they become more numerous and larger on the keel of the snout, between the eyes, on the anterior borders of the vertical fins, and in the mesial region where they occupy a considerable space: at these various places they become granulations more or less obtuse, the largest of which constitute tubercles. They are more developed in the immature.

Colours—Greenish grey.

Habitat—Seas and estuaries of India.

Fam. RALÆ.

Raies, *Duméril.*

Group.—TORPEDINES.

Sub-Group.—With two dorsal fins.

Genus NARCINE, *Henle.*

Disk orbicular, elliptical, or angular, anteriorly rounded and provided with a broad keel. Mouth small, protractile, surrounded by a circular fold of skin which terminates superiorly in the frænulum of the nasal valve. Nasal valve straight, having a central projection, and occasionally being slightly produced laterally, so that it appears trifid. A labial cartilage above and below. Lips not fixed to the jaws, but moveable: a membraneous valve behind the upper jaw. Spiracles immediately behind the eyes: their margins smooth. Teeth in quincuncial order, with a central point: they project beyond the margins of the jaws in the form of an elliptical plate. Tail equal to or longer than the disk. Two dorsal fins, the anterior behind the ventral and generally smaller than the posterior.

* Narcine Indica.

Narcine Indica, *Müll. & Henle*, 35, t. ii. f. 2; *Cantor*, Catal. p. 417; *Gray*, Catal. Brit. Mus. p. 102; *Duméril*, Ich. gén. i. p. 517.

Disk pentagonal, slightly broader than long, rounded anteriorly and provided with a broad keel. Mouth small, protractile, surrounded by a circular fold of skin: a labial cartilage above and beneath: lips moveable, not fixed to the jaws. Nasal valve straight, with a central projection. Eyes much smaller than the air-holes. Spiracles immediately behind the eyes, their margins smooth.

Teeth—In quincunx with a point in the middle: they project beyond the margin of the jaw like an elliptical plate.

Fins—The anterior dorsal commences behind the ventrals, and is smaller than the posterior, its base equals half the length of its anterior margin: in the young its apex forms an acute angle, but in the adult becomes rounded. The distance between the two dorsals equals that between the posterior dorsal and the caudal. The size and shape of the two dorsals is similar. Ventrals triangular. The tail is slightly longer than the body, except in the very young, when it is shorter.

The male appendages project but slightly beyond the inner margins of the ventral fin.

Colours—Body and fins above reddish brown, with numerous irregularly sized chocolate coloured spots: lower surface white. Pupil triangular, apex below. Iris golden. In the immature the spots have a white margin.

This fish—my specimens of which have been mislaid—is rare along the coast of Malabar, except where there are rocks: to the south it is very abundant. It grows to eighteen inches in length. "Out of the water they may be handled with impunity."—*Cantor*.

Habitat—Seas of Malabar and Malaysia.

Sub-Group.—With one dorsal fin.

Genus ASTRAPE, *Müll. & Henle*.

Generally similar to the *Genus Narcine*. Snout short and without a keel. Frænulum of the nasal valve with a cylindrical cartilage. Teeth pointed, each having a tetragonal base, and projecting slightly beyond the margin of the jaw. A membraneous valve in both jaws. Eyes and spiracles approximating, the latter smooth. Dorsal fin single, both it and the caudal rounded.

Astrape dipterygia.

Rajah dipterygia, *Bl. Schn.* 359.

Astrape dipterygia, *Cantor*, Catal. p. 419; *Gray*, Catal. Brit. Mus. p. 103; *Duméril*, Ich. gén. i. p. 523.

Disk rounded, as wide as long, covering the anterior margins of the ventrals. Snout short without any keel. A membraneous valve to both jaws. Spiracles smooth, close to and much larger than the eyes. A cylindrical cartilage to the bridle of the nasal flap.

Teeth—Pointed, with tetragonal bases; they slightly project beyond the margin of the jaws.

Fins—Ventrals tetragonal, with the angles acute in the young, rounded in the adult. Caudal rounded.

Colours—Dull reddish-olive above, whitish beneath: a large whitish spot at the posterior margin of the disk, another above the termination of the ventrals, and a third on either side of the root of the caudal. Anterior half of ventrals whitish. Dorsal and caudal darkish above, light beneath. Iris golden.

Rather rare in Malabar, grows to nine inches or more in length.

Habitat—Seas of India and Malaysia.

Group TRYGONES.

GENUS TRYGON, (*Adanson,*) *Müll. & Henle.*

TRIGONOBATUS, *Blainv.*
DASYBATUS, *Rafin.*
PASTINACÆ, *Duméril.*

Disk oval or rhomboidal. Tail of equal length to, or longer than the body, without a hem (*Himantura*), or with one not extending to its apex. Mouth slightly arched. Teeth with a central point or transverse tubercle, which in some is rough, and with a more or less distinct transverse furrow in front and behind, that of the lateral teeth being most distinct: the whole surface is more or less wrinkled: membraneous valve of the upper jaw with a straight deeply fringed margin, a second behind it which is deeply notched. In the lower jaw several papillæ behind the teeth.

Tail without fin.

TRYGON UARNAK.

RAJAH UARNAK, *Forsk.* p. 18, no. 16, b.
TRYGON RUSSELLII, *Gray*, Ill. I. Z. ii. pl. 100.
TRYGON VARIEGATUS, *McClelland*, Cal. J. N. H. i. p. 60, pl. 2, f. 2.
TRYGON UARNAK, *Cantor*, Catal. p. 423; *Blyth*, Cartilaginous Fishes of lower Bengal, Journal Asiatic Society, xxx. p. 44, no. 23; *Duméril*, Ich. gén. i. p. 585.

Disk slightly broader than long, snout triangular, pointed, and very prominent in the young, but in the adult its length from between the centre of the nostrils exceeds by one-third the breadth of that interval.

Mouth slightly arched: membraneous valve of the upper jaw having a straight deeply fringed margin, the posterior valve deeply notched. In the immature the eyes are prominent, not so in the adult, in which last they do not project beyond the level of the spiracles.

Teeth—With a central point or transverse tubercle, having a shallow groove before and behind: there are several papillæ in the mandibulæ behind the teeth.

Fins—Caudal about four times as long as the body, compressed laterally, and widest in front of its serrated spine, which is situated about the end of the first eighth of the tail: beyond this spine the tail tapers off to a very fine extremity, it has a narrow skinny margin which commences from opposite its spine but does not extend so far as to the extremity of the caudal.

Scales—In the very young—with a disk of six inches across—there are two or three rows of widely separated oval scales on either side of the head, internal to the eyes, and meeting on the occiput, from thence towards the scapular is a single row of larger and more widely separated ones. In the centre of the back three large closely approximating scales, the centre one heart-shaped, the anterior round, and the posterior almost heart-shaped. In some specimens of a large size, there are also numerous distant thorns on the tail which disappear with age.

In specimens with a disk of three feet across, the head, back, and sides are covered with smooth, roundish scales, with smaller ones intermediate.

Colours—Vary according to age: up to the period when the breadth of the disk is about nine inches, the body is of a yellowish brown darkest along the back, and the abdomen white: a short distance beyond the commencement of the tail it is irregularly annulated with alternate narrow light brown, and broad or narrow dark brown rings.

As its age increases black spots commonly appear on the body, and when it has attained the width of three feet across its disk it is light brown or greyish olive, covered with lighter and in some almost white spots, whilst the anterior extremity of the tail also shows the remains of the rings.

The adult is uniformly brownish or greenish olive. Iris golden.

Grows to a very large size: the immature are frequently captured in the backwaters, and wounds from their caudal spines are much dreaded. In one instance an old man was admitted the Civil Hospital in Cochin for mortification of the arm, due to a wound inflicted by one of these fish, which he attempted to drag out of the sea into a boat: it wound its tail round his arm, and dragged its spine through the muscles down nearly to the bone.

Habitat—Red Sea, Seas and estuaries of India, Malaysia, China, and the Cape of Good Hope.

Genus PTEROPLATEA, *Müll. & Henle.*

Dasyatis, *Rafin.*

Disk is almost or more than twice as broad as long. Tail short, generally shorter than the body, and either with low fins or naked. Mouth slightly arched. The teeth do not extend so far as the angle of the mouth; they have from one to three points. The upper membraneous valve of the jaw is indistinct, and without a fringe. There are no papillæ in the lower jaw. The skin is smooth or covered with tubercles. Often a slight papilla at the posterior border of the spiracles.

Pteroplatea micrura.

Rajah micrura, *Bl. Schn.* p. 360.

Tenkee kunsul, *Russell*, pl. 6.

Pteroplatea micrura, *Cantor*, Catal. p. 427; *Duméril*, Ich. gén. p. 613.

Dasyatis micrura, *Gray*, Catal. Brit. Mus. p. 122.

The length of the disk in the adult is three-fourths of its width, but in the immature it is less than half.

Snout moderately prominent, more so in the immature. Mouth rather arched. The distance between the inner angles of the nostrils equals about half their longest diameter, but that between their external angles is double what obtains from the centre to the point of the snout in the adult. A depression exists in the upper jaw, external to the teeth, and a corresponding elevation in the lower jaw. No denticle on the margin of the spiracles.

Teeth—Tricuspidate, their central elevations being longer than their lateral ones, which are horizontal. In both jaws the teeth are confined to the central third.

Fins—The anterior margin of the pectoral rather convex, and slightly exceeding in length that of its posterior, which is slightly concave, its external angle conical, its internal moderately rounded. Ventrals elongated, tetragonal, with their posterior angles rounded. Caudal shorter than the body in the immature, but rather longer in the adult, its spine slender and situated on its anterior fifth.

Colours—In the immature superiorly reddish brown, with numerous indistinct dark dots and light spots: underneath dirty white. In the adult bluish brown above, dirty white underneath; tail annulated with dark brown and pinkish-white rings, in the centre of each of which last on the upper surface is usually a round dark spot.

Eaten by the Natives of Malabar, where however it is not common. It grows to as large as four feet across the disk.

Habitat—Red Sea, Seas of India, Malaysia, and China.

GENUS HYPOLOPHUS, *Müll. & Henle.*

Form of the body the same as in the *Trygons*, but considerable difference in the mouth. Tail with a fin which does not reach to its apex: upper fin absent. The centre of the lower jaw is pointed and projecting, and on each side has a cavity directed forwards: the margin of the upper jaw is excavated in the centre for the purpose of receiving the point of the lower jaw, and also bulges on the sides. Teeth like paving stones, hexagonal, broader than long: in the upper jaw the central ones are small, those at the sides larger; in the lower jaw they are of nearly equal size, but the external ones are the smallest.

HYPOLOPHUS SEPHEN.

RAJA SEPHEN, *Forsk.* 17, no. 16.
WOLGA TENKEE, *Russell*, pl. 3.
HYPOLOPHUS SEPHEN, *Cantor*, Catal. p. 429; *Gray*, Catal. Brit. Mus. p. 123; *Blyth*, Journ. Asiatic Soc. xxix. p. 37, no. 14; *Duméril*, Ich. gén. i. p. 616.

Disk rhombic, angles rounded, the snout more pointed in the young than in the adult. The distance from the snout to the mouth is two-sevenths of the length between the snout and the anus. The distance between the nostrils equals half their distance from the snout. Under jaw pointed in its centre, and on either side of its extremity is an elliptical cavity: the margin of the upper jaw is excavated in its centre to receive the point of the lower jaw, whilst externally it is very convex. Pupils of eyes transversely oval.

Teeth—Like a pavement, hexagonal, broader than long: in the centre of the upper jaw they are small, but larger at its sides. In the lower jaw those in the centre of equal size to the teeth in the upper, but smaller externally.

Fins—The external angles of the ventrals are acute, the internal obtuse. Tail three or four times the length of the body, with a broad serrated spine varying from one-fifth to one-eighth of its length, and situated slightly behind its anterior third: the membraneous fin is high, and begins beneath the base of the spine and is continued beyond the middle third of its lower margin.

Scales—Upper surface of the head and body covered by thick concave or flat headed, several sided scales, the slightly raised edges of which are rough. In the scapular region and central line of the back are two in the young and three in the adult, of large, smooth, approximating scales, the middle and largest of which is usually oval, the second in size posterior and heart-shaped, the anterior or smallest round or heart-shaped.

Colours—The upper surface of the immature is reddish brown, but in the adult lead-coloured, becoming black in the posterior two-thirds of the tail.

This fish grows to a large size, when it is coarse eating. It is most common during the S.W. monsoon. From the skin of its back some of the true "Shagreen" of commerce is prepared. Wounds inflicted by the spine of its tail are considered dangerous.

Habitat—Seas of India and Malaysia.

Group MYLIOBATIDES, *Duméril.*

GENUS ÆTOBATIS, (*Blainville*), *Müll. & Henle.*

Snout pointed, composed by the united anterior pectoral rays. Nasal valves united with a straight margin. Mouth transverse. Both jaws with a straight margin. Teeth hexagonal, in the centre a series of broader ones, posteriorly increasing in breadth; on either side smaller tetragonal plates resembling paving stones, and fitting into the zig-zags of the central teeth; those in the upper jaw longitudinally and transversely convex: those of the lower flat or very slightly concave: the teeth of neither jaw occupy the entire breadth.

ÆTOBATIS NARINARI.

RAJAH NARINARI, *Bl. Schn.* 361.
EEL-TENKEE, *Russell*, pl. 8.
MYLIOBATIS MACROPTERA, *McClelland*, Cal. J. N. H. i. p. 60, f. 1, a. b.
STOASODON NARINARI, *Cantor*, Catal. p. 434.
ÆTOBATIS NARINARI, *Gray*, Catal. Brit. Mus. p. 130; *Duméril*, Ich. gén. i. p. 641.
THERRUNDEE, *Mal.*

The comparative sizes vary greatly with age. The distance from the mouth to the anus equals about half the width of the disk. The snout is conical, slightly broader at its base than it is long: the lower jaw is acute and longer than the upper which has a straight margin. The nasal valve is half the length of the snout, with a broad and conical lobule having a fringed edge near to its external margin.

Teeth—The dental plates of both jaws do not extend the whole distance across: they form a series which are slightly arched in the upper jaw and have vertical denticulations. Those in the lower jaw are two-thirds the breadth of those in the upper but more convex, forming the centre of an obtuse angle and parallel to the margin of the jaw.

Fins—The dorsal commences opposite the end of the ventral, but does not extend so far as to opposite its apex. Ventral about three times as long as broad. Tail three or four times as long as the body, triangular in shape as far as the spine,' which is serrated and situated just behind the termination of the dorsal: beyond the spine the tail is compressed; in this, as well as in some other species, there is occasionally a second spine on the caudal fin a little behind the root of the first.

Scales—None.

Colours—Greyish olive, sometimes greenish above, covered from beyond the occiput with numerous dirty white spots edged with black: abdominal surface white: tail black. Iris golden green, teeth greenish yellow.

In the immature the back is of a deep leaden colour, and the spots hardly apparent.

Eaten by the Natives. Is captured to upwards of six feet in width, and its flesh is salted.

Habitat—Red Sea, Seas and estuaries of India and Malaysia.

INDEX.

2 o 2

FINIS.

G. NORMAN, PRINTER, MAIDEN LANE, COVENT GARDEN.